Modern
REAL ESTATE
Practice

EIGHTEENTH EDITION

Fillmore W. Galaty

Wellington J. Allaway

Robert C. Kyle

Dearborn™
Real Estate Education

President: Dr. Andrew Temte
Chief Learning Officer: Dr. Tim Smaby
Vice President, Real Estate Education: Asha Alsobrooks
Development Editor: Trude Irons

MODERN REAL ESTATE PRACTICE 18TH EDITION
© 2010 by Kaplan, Inc.
Published by DF Institute, Inc., d/b/a Kaplan Real Estate Education
332 Front St. S., Suite 501
La Crosse, WI 54601
www.dearbornRE.com

Printed in the United States of America
Eighth revision, June 2013
ISBN: 1-4277-8790-5
PPN: 1510-0118

Contents

PART II PRACTICE

Preface

Since it first appeared in 1959, *Modern Real Estate Practice* has set the industry standard for real estate education. This book has helped provide well over three million readers with a critical edge as they enter the world of real estate. Whether you are preparing for a state licensing examination, fulfilling a college or university requirement, looking for specific guidance about buying a home or an investment property, or simply expanding your understanding of this fascinating field, you can rely on *Modern Real Estate Practice*, the recognized authority for accurate and comprehensive information in a user-friendly format.

Just as today's real estate market is challenging and complex, today's real estate students are increasingly sophisticated and demand a high level of expertise and efficiency. This 18th edition of *Modern Real Estate Practice* meets those expectations. In response to expanding state licensing requirements and the growing body of laws that govern the practice of real estate, this edition contains revisions and new features designed to make it an even more effective tool, no matter what your goal.

■ SPECIAL FEATURES

Web Site The 18th edition of *Modern Real Estate Practice* has a Web site dedicated exclusively to this text and all of its ancillary products. At *www.modernrealestatepractice.com/18e*, both students and instructors will have access to a robust assortment of study and teaching tools, including a student Test-Builder, an instructor Test-Builder, and Instructor Resource materials.

To access the student Test-Builder—which allows students to mix and match the hundreds of questions in the *Modern Real Estate Practice* text into their own customized quizzes and exams—please go to *www.modernrealestate practice.com/18e* and enter your personal Student Access Code: 80518.

We have developed a suite of products that align with *Modern Real Estate Practice*, including a study guide, flash cards, and audio CDs. For additional information, please visit *www.modernrealestatepractice.com/18e*.

Media Now available exclusively online, the *Modern Real Estate Practice* Test-Builders allow students and instructors to mix and match the hundreds of questions in *Modern Real Estate Practice* into their own custom quizzes. The Test-Builders track performance on each self-built test and provide helpful rationales explaining the why behind the answers.

Quick Math Reference Inside the front and back covers of the book, we've provided a great time-saving reference tool: the most frequently used real estate math equations.

Key Point Reviews   Chapter summaries are organized into key point, bulleted reviews providing students with a quick review tool of the most essential content covered in each chapter.

Glossary with Page References   This glossary features not only the definitions of the terms but also page references that allow readers to find where the terms are first addressed in the text.

Updated and Revised Chapter Review and Sample Examination Questions   These questions have been thoroughly reviewed by a testing expert with experience in actual real estate licensing exam design. Questions have been revised and replaced, where necessary, with more demanding fact-pattern problems that encourage students to not just memorize but to understand and apply information, which are important test-taking and exam-preparation skills. The questions have been carefully designed to follow the style and content of the most widely used testing services and to demonstrate the types of questions that students will likely encounter on their state licensing exams. The answer key includes specific page references to the text.

New Links   New and updated "Related Web Sites" direct students to federal and industry resources, as well as their state's real estate regulatory agencies, where they can often find state statutes, real estate regulations, and other useful information online.

While we've provided the most current and accurate site addresses at the time of printing, please note that Web site addresses change frequently.

This edition of *Modern Real Estate Practice* retains the successful features developed for previous editions, including the following:

- *Modern Real Estate Practice* connects you to the Internet with *related Web sites*—a list of relevant Web sites provided at the end of each chapter that point to the Web addresses of relevant government and professional association Internet sites, essentially bringing a whole world of information to you!
- *Key terms* appear at the beginning of each chapter. This feature not only lets you know what important vocabulary words you should look for as you read but helps you to study and review as well.
- *Chapter review and sample examination questions* reemphasize essential material.
- *Margin notes* help direct readers' attention to important vocabulary terms, concepts, and study tips. The margin notes help readers move more easily through the text, locate issues for review, and serve as memory prompts for more efficient and effective studying.

One thing, however, has stayed the same: the fundamental goal of *Modern Real Estate Practice*, 18th edition, is to help students understand the dynamics of the real estate industry, providing the critical information you need to pass the licensing examination, buy or sell property, or establish a real estate career.

■ A FINAL NOTE

With the publication of *Modern Real Estate Practice*, 18th edition, we think it is fair to consider the book as a classic. For over two generations, this book has provided readers accurate and comprehensive real estate information. Over 50,000 copies continue to be sold every year.

Looking back over this half-century journey, we asked the question, "What could we do to make a great book even better?" We brought the question to the users of the book, soliciting feedback from instructors, students, and highly qualified individuals involved in the field of real estate.

A common refrain was brought to our attention. Though readers found the book to be a quality source of information, they felt the content went into more depth than needed for an introductory real estate book.

With this edition, we aimed for clear, concise content that would flow with the collective voice of the original authors. You will find the book selectively edited, with a balance between emphasizing teaching points and the thoroughness needed to round out a quality education.

We believe we've succeeded, but the only way we can be sure is if you tell us. Please let us know what you thought of this edition at *contentinquiries@dearborn .com.*

Thank you for your help and for joining the ranks of successful *Modern Real Estate Practice* users.

—The Publisher

Acknowledgments

Like a real estate transaction, this book is the product of teamwork and cooperation among professionals. We would like to express our gratitude and appreciation to the instructors and other real estate professionals whose invaluable suggestions and advice help *Modern Real Estate Practice* remain the industry's leading real estate principles text. Whether they responded to instructor surveys, provided reviews and suggestions for improving the previous edition, or reviewed the manuscript for this edition, the participation of these professionals—and their willingness to share their expertise—is greatly appreciated.

■ REVIEWERS—18TH EDITION

Doris Barrell, DSB Seminars
Chuck Byers, Professional Marketing Concepts
Stephen Etzel, Kaplan Professional Schools, Texas
Ignacio Gonzales, Mendocino Community College, Ukiah, California
Randall S. Guttery, PhD, CLU, CLFC, Associate Dean and Professor of Finance and Real Estate, University of North Texas
George W. Lawrence, Master Instructor Faculty, California Association of REALTORS®
John D. Mathis III, Kaplan Real Estate Education
Katherine Pancak, University of Connecticut
Marie S. Spodek, DREI, Professional Real Estate Services
Sherry Steele, Kaplan Professional Schools, Colorado
Dennis Tosh, FNC, Inc.

Each new edition of *Modern Real Estate Practice* builds on earlier editions. We gratefully acknowledge the many real estate professionals and others who have contributed to prior editions of this book.

Robert H. Allen, National Real Estate Institute
Penny Alston, Wardley Real Estate School
Jean Anglin, Chattanooga State Community College
Jim Anselmi, Academy Real Estate School
Christopher O. Ashe, Learning Unlimited
Donald R. Bates, Mountain Empire Community College
Thomas E. Battle, Center for Real Estate Education and Research
E. E. Bayliss III, Ford Fairfax Community College
Tom Bowen, Professional School of Real Estate
Paul Boyter, CRS, GRI, McColly School of Real Estate
Dianna Brouthers, Homefinders of America
Thomas Bull, McColly School of Real Estate
Virgil V. Bullis, Sr., Delaware Tech

Leona Busby, Long & Foster Institute of Real Estate
Marie Callas, Iowa Association of REALTORS®
Alice W. Cater, Lamar University Institute of Technology
Peter J. Certo, Gabelli School of Business
Charles Civer, Scottsdale Community College
Richard J. Clemmer, D&D School of Real Estate
Ginny Commins, Windermere Education
Kay Knox Crawford, Continual Learning Institute
David Dean, Litchfield County Real Estate School
Gregory Dunn, U.S. Books, Inc.
John Eaton, Ocean School of Real Estate
Dr. Kenneth W. Edwards, GRI, Linn-Benton Community College
William B. Frost, Weichert Real Estate School
Katherine J. Gandy, Spokane Falls Community College and American Business
    and Professions Institute
Richard Garnitz, Kelley Academy of Real Estate
Michael Craig Glazer, Ivy Tech State College
Helen L. Grant, Moseley-Flint Schools of Real Estate, Inc.
Edward A. Guinane, Real Estate School of Siouxland
Terry Hastings, Ridgefield Adult Education
Terry Hayes, Real Estate Brokerage Education
Arthur W. Heinbuch, Allied Institutes of Real Estate
Ray Henry, Arizona Institute of Real Estate
Mary Hibbler-Kee, Bess Technical College/UAB Options
Russell S. Hicks, The Real Estate School
Carl R. Hurst, Hurst Education Center
Diana T. Jacob-Rouhoff, Northwestern State University of Louisiana and
    Lincoln Graduate Center
F. Jeffrey Keil, J. Sargeant Reynolds Community College
John H. Kilroy, Jefferson County Board of Education
Rick Knowles, Capital Real Estate Training
Dr. Corbet J. Lamkin, Southern Arkansas University
Allen Lamont, Lamont School of Real Estate
Craig Larabee, Larabee School of Real Estate
Jerome D. Levine, Tunxis Community-Technical College
Richard S. Linkemer, American School of Real Estate, Ltd.
Joyce Magee, Genesee Community College
Denise M. Mancini, J.W. Riker
Charline Mason, Charline Mason Seminars Unlimited
Peggy Ann McConnochie, Alaska Coastal Homes, Inc.
Paul McLaughlin, Esquire
Thomas L. Meyer, Cape Girardeau School of Real Estate
Coad Miller, Central Nebraska Community College
J. Leo Milotte, CRB, CRS, GRI, Milotte Associates Real Estate School
John R. Morgan, Morgan Testing Services
Monte Needler, Ivy Tech State College
Edward Neeley, Russell & Jeffcoat Real Estate Institute of Training & Education
Robert Neuwoehner, Heartland School of Real Estate
Jessie L. Newman, Grempler Real Estate Institute
Judith A. Nolde, JD, Content Consultant

Mary M. Otis, Northern Virginia Association of REALTORS®
Andrew G. Pappas, Capital Community Technical College/Manchester
    Community Technical College
Joyce D. Remsburg, Trident Technical College
Walter L. Rice, Quality Workshops
John D. Rinehart, CRB, CRS, GRI, The Real Estate Institute of York County, Inc.
Robbie Robison, Allegany College
Kathy Roosa, Kathy Roosa School of Real Estate
Jay Rose, Esq., Tucker School of Real Estate
Phyllis Rudnick, CRS, GRI, Annex Real Estate School
Susann Shadley, Eastern Idaho Technical College
Don Shrum, The Real Estate School, Houston
Bill Standiford, Ed Smith School of Real Estate
Allan R. Stevenson, GRI, CRB, Frostburg State University
Rita Stuckart, Jack White Real Estate School
Wayne A. Tarter, Greenville Tech
Ruth A. Vella, Omega Real Estate School
Howard E. Walker, Nashville School of Real Estate
Darline C. Waring, Charleston Trident Association of REALTORS®
Cynthia L. Weber, ABC Real Estate School
Donald Dwight Wells, Troy State University
Brenda S. White, Brenda White School of Real Estate
John P. Wiedemer, Houston Community College
Don W. Williams, Alabama Courses in Real Estate—ACRE
Martha R. Williams, JD, Real Estate Author/Consultant
Judith B. Wolk, Charleston Trident Association of REALTORS®
Jerry L. Wooten, Tucker School of Real Estate
John Wright, Iowa Real Estate School of Cedar Rapids

PART

I

PRINCIPLES

Introduction to the Real Estate Business

■ **LEARNING OBJECTIVES** *When you have finished reading this chapter, you should be able to*

- **identify** the various careers available in real estate and the professional organizations that support them;

- **describe** the six categories of real property;

- **explain** the operation of supply and demand in the real estate market;

- **distinguish** the economic, political, and social factors that influence supply and demand; and

- **define** the following *key terms:*

broker	market	supply and demand
licensee	salesperson	

■ THE REAL ESTATE BUSINESS

Real estate transactions are taking place all around you, all the time. When a commercial leasing company rents space in a mall or the owner of a building rents an apartment to a retired couple, it's a real estate transaction. Most common of all, when an American family sells its old home and buys a new one, the family takes part in the real estate industry. Consumers of real estate services include buyers and sellers of homes, tenants and landlords, investors, and developers. Nearly everyone, at some time, is involved in a real estate transaction.

All this adds up to big business—complex transactions that involve trillions of dollars every year in the United States alone. The services of millions of highly trained individuals are required: attorneys, bankers, trust company representatives, abstract and title insurance company agents, architects, surveyors, accountants, tax experts, and many others, in addition to buyers and sellers. All these people depend on the skills and knowledge of licensed real estate professionals.

■ REAL ESTATE: A BUSINESS OF MANY SPECIALIZATIONS

Despite the size and complexity of the real estate business, many people think of it as being made up of real estate brokers and real estate salespeople only. Actually, the real estate industry is much broader than that. Appraisal, property management, financing, subdivision and development, counseling, and education are all separate businesses within the real estate field. To succeed in a complex industry, every real estate professional must have a basic knowledge of these specialized areas.

Brokerage   Brokerage is the business of bringing people together in a real estate transaction. A real estate **broker** acts as a point of contact between two or more people in negotiating the sale, purchase, or rental of property. A broker is defined as a person or company licensed to buy, sell, exchange, or lease real property for others and to charge a fee for these services. A real estate **salesperson** is a **licensee** employed by or associated with the broker. The real estate salesperson conducts brokerage activities on behalf of or for the broker. (See Chapter 5.)

Licensee   A licensee refers to a person who has satisfied the requirements set forth by a licensing agency or state legislation. The requirements include course hours or work experience and passing a state-mandated real estate exam.

Appraisal   Appraisal is the process of estimating a property's market value, based on established methods and the appraiser's professional judgment. Although brokers may have some understanding of the valuation process, lenders generally require a professional appraisal. Appraisers must have detailed knowledge of the methods of valuation. In many states, appraisers must be licensed or certified to carry out local transactions. Appraisers must also be licensed or certified for many federally related transactions. (See Chapter 18.)

Property management A property manager is a person or company hired to maintain and manage property on behalf of its owner. By hiring a property manager, the owner is relieved of such day-to-day management tasks as finding new tenants, collecting rents, altering or constructing new space for tenants, ordering repairs, and generally maintaining the property. The scope of the manager's work depends on the terms of the individual employment contract, known as a management agreement. Whatever tasks are specified, the basic responsibility of the property manager is to protect the owner's investment and maximize the return on that investment. (See Chapter 17.)

Financing Financing is the business of providing the funds that make real estate transactions possible. Most transactions are financed by means of mortgage loans or trust deed loans secured by the property. Individuals involved in financing real estate may work in commercial banks, savings associations, and mortgage banking and mortgage brokerage companies. (See Chapters 14 and 15.)

Subdivision and development Subdivision is the dividing of a single property into smaller parcels. Development involves the construction of improvements on the land. These improvements may be either on-site or off-site. Off-site improvements, such as water lines and storm sewers, are made on public lands to serve the new development. On-site improvements, such as new homes or swimming pools, are made on individual parcels. While subdivision and development normally are related, they are independent processes that can occur separately. (See Chapter 19.)

Home inspection Home inspection is a profession that allows practitioners the chance to combine their interest in real estate with their professional skills and training in the construction trades or in engineering. Professional home inspectors conduct a thorough visual survey of a property's structure, systems, and site conditions and prepare an analytical report that is valuable to both purchasers and homeowners. Increasingly, wary consumers are relying on the inspector's report to help them make purchase decisions. Frequently, a real estate sales contract will be contingent upon the inspector's report. (See Chapter 21.)

Counseling Counseling involves providing clients with competent independent advice based on sound professional judgment. A real estate counselor helps clients choose among the various alternatives involved in purchasing, using, or investing in property. A counselor's role is to furnish clients with the information needed to make informed decisions. Professional real estate counselors must have a high degree of industry expertise.

Education Real estate education is available to both practitioners and consumers. Colleges and universities, private schools, and trade organizations all conduct real estate courses and seminars, from the principles of a prelicensing program to the technical aspects of tax and exchange law. State licensing laws establish the minimum educational requirements for obtaining—and keeping—a real estate license. Continuing education helps ensure that licensees keep their skills and knowledge current.

Other areas Many other real estate career options are available. Practitioners will find that real estate specialists are needed in a variety of business settings. Lawyers who specialize in real estate are always in demand. Large corporations with extensive land holdings often have their own real estate and property tax departments. Local governments must staff both zoning boards and assessment offices.

■ PROFESSIONAL ORGANIZATIONS

Many trade organizations serve the real estate business. The largest is the National Association of REALTORS® (NAR), whose Web site is *www.realtor.org*. The NAR is composed of state, regional, and local associations. The NAR also sponsors various affiliated organizations that offer professional designations to brokers, salespersons, appraisers, and others who complete required courses in areas of special interest. Members subscribe to a Code of Ethics and, if eligible, are entitled to be known as REALTORS® or REALTOR-ASSOCIATES®.

The NAR has the following affiliated institutes, societies, and councils:

- Counselors of Real Estate (CRE)
- Commercial Investment Real Estate Institute (CIREI)
- Institute of Real Estate Management (IREM)
- REALTORS® Land Institute (RLI)
- REALTORS® National Marketing Institute (RNMI)
- Certified Real Estate Brokerage Manager (CRB)
- Certified Residential Specialist (CRS)
- Graduate, Real Estate Institute (GRI)
- Council of Residential Specialists (CRS)
- Society of Industrial and Office REALTORS® (SIOR)
- Women's Council of REALTORS® (WCR)

The National Association of Real Estate Brokers (NAREB), whose members are known as *Realtists*, also adheres to a Code of Ethics. The NAREB arose out of the early days of the civil rights movement as an association of racial minority real estate brokers in response to the conditions and abuses that eventually gave rise to fair housing laws. Today, the NAREB remains dedicated to equal housing opportunity.

Other professional associations include the following:

- American Society of Appraisers (ASA)
- National Association of Independent Fee Appraisers (NAIFA)
- Real Estate Educators Association (REEA)
- Real Estate Buyer's Agent Council (REBAC)
- National Association of Exclusive Buyer's Agents (NAEBA)
- Building Owners and Managers Association (BOMA)
- Certified Commercial Investment Managers (CCIM)
- American Society of Home Inspectors® (ASHI)

Members are expected to comply with the Standards of Practice and Code of Conduct as set forth by each organization.

■ TYPES OF REAL PROPERTY

Just as there are areas of specialization within the real estate industry, there are different types of property in which to specialize. Real estate can be classified as

Six Categories of Real Property
■ Residential
■ Commercial
■ Mixed-use
■ Industrial
■ Agricultural
■ Special-purpose

- *residential*—all property used for single-family or multifamily housing, whether in urban, suburban, or rural areas;
- *commercial*—business property, including office space, shopping centers, stores, theaters, hotels, and parking facilities;
- *mixed-use*—property that allows for two uses, commercial and residential, in the same building;
- *industrial*—warehouses, factories, land in industrial districts, and power plants;
- *agricultural*—farms, timberland, ranches, and orchards; or
- *special-purpose*—churches, schools, cemeteries, and government-held lands.

The market for each of these types of real property can be divided into three main functions: buying, selling, and leasing.

IN PRACTICE Although it is possible for a single real estate firm or an individual real estate professional to perform all the services and handle all classes of property discussed in this chapter (unless restricted by a state's license law), this is rarely done. General services may be available in small towns, but most firms and professionals specialize to some degree.

■ THE REAL ESTATE MARKET

A **market** is a place where goods can be bought and sold. A market may be a specific place, such as the village square. It also may be a vast, complex, worldwide economic system for moving goods and services around the globe. In either case, the function of a market is to provide a setting in which supply and demand can establish market value, making it advantageous for buyers and sellers to trade.

Supply and Demand

Prices for goods and services in the market are established by the operation of **supply and demand**. Essentially, when supply increases and demand remains stable, prices go down; when demand increases and supply remains stable, prices go up. Greater supply means producers need to attract more buyers, so they lower prices. Greater demand means producers can raise their prices because buyers compete for the product.

When supply increases and demand remains stable, prices go down.

When demand increases and supply remains stable, prices go up.

■ **FOR EXAMPLE** Here's how one broker describes market forces: "In my 17 years in real estate, I've seen supply and demand in action many times. When a carmaker relocated its factory to my region a few years back, hundreds of people wanted to buy the few higher-bracket houses for sale at the time. Those sellers were able to ask ridiculously high prices for their properties, and two houses actually sold for more than the asking prices! On the other hand, when the naval base closed and 2,000 civilian jobs were transferred to other parts of the country, it seemed like every other house in town was for sale. We were practically giving houses away to the few people who were buying."

Supply and demand in the real estate market   Two characteristics of real estate govern the way the market reacts to the pressures of supply and demand: uniqueness and immobility. (See Chapter 2.) *Uniqueness* means that, no matter how identical they may appear, no two parcels of real estate are ever exactly alike; each occupies its own unique geographic location. *Immobility* refers to the fact that property cannot be relocated to satisfy demand where supply is low. Nor can buyers always relocate to areas with greater supply. For these reasons, real estate markets are local markets. Each geographic area has different types of real estate and different conditions that drive prices. In these small, well-defined areas, real estate offices can keep track of both what types of property are in demand and what parcels are available.

> Uniqueness and immobility are the two characteristics of land that have the most impact on market value.

IN PRACTICE   Technological advances and market changes have widened the real estate professional's local market. No longer limited to a single small area, real estate brokers and real estate salespeople must track trends and conditions in a variety of different and sometimes distant local markets. Technological devices—computers, the Internet, cellular phones, e-fax, fax machines, global positioning systems, and an ever-expanding gallery of other tools—help real estate practitioners stay on top of their wide-ranging markets.

Because of real estate's uniqueness and immobility, the market generally adjusts slowly to the forces of supply and demand. Though a home offered for sale can be withdrawn in response to low demand and high supply, it is much more likely that oversupply will result in lower prices. When supply is low, on the other hand, a high demand may not be met immediately because development and construction are lengthy processes. As a result, development tends to occur in uneven spurts of activity.

Even when supply and demand can be forecast with some accuracy, natural disasters such as hurricanes and earthquakes can disrupt market trends. Similarly, sudden changes in financial markets or local events such as plant relocations or environmental factors can dramatically disrupt a seemingly stable market.

Factors Affecting Supply

Factors that tend to affect the supply side of the real estate market's supply and demand balance include labor force availability, construction and material costs, and governmental controls and financial policies.

Labor force, construction, and material costs   A shortage of skilled labor or building materials or an increase in the cost of materials can decrease the amount of new construction. High transfer costs, such as taxes, and construction permit fees can also discourage development. Increased construction costs may be passed along to buyers and tenants in the form of higher prices and increased rents that can further slow the market.

Governmental controls and financial policies The government's monetary policy can have a substantial impact on the real estate market. The Federal Reserve Board (the Fed) establishes a discount rate of interest for the money it lends to commercial banks. That discount rate has direct impact on the interest rates the banks charge to borrowers, which in turn plays a significant part in people's ability to buy homes. The Federal Housing Administration (FHA) and the Government National Mortgage Association (Ginnie Mae) can also affect the amount of money available to lenders for mortgage loans.

In 2008, America's greatest challenge became the uncertainty of the financial institutions. Until then, the Federal National Mortgage Association (Fannie Mae) and the Federal Home Loan Mortgage Corporation (Freddie Mac), which were private companies under congressional charter, had been the driving force of monies to provide loans to low-, moderate-, and middle-income families. Failed judgments in buying mortgages on the secondary market and irregular accounting practices contributed to the unpredictable and chaotic real estate market in 2009. This resulted in the federal government taking over Freddie Mac and Fannie Mae by placing them into conservatorship.

Virtually any government action has some effect on the real estate market. For instance, federal environmental regulations may increase or decrease the supply and value of land in a local market. Real estate taxation is one of the primary sources of revenue for local governments. Policies on taxation of real estate can have either positive or negative effects. High taxes may deter investors. On the other hand, tax incentives can attract new businesses and industries. And, of course, along with these enterprises come increased employment and expanded residential real estate markets.

Local governments also influence supply. Land-use controls, building codes, and zoning ordinances help shape the character of a community and control the use of land. Careful planning helps stabilize and even increase real estate values.

Factors Affecting Demand

Factors that tend to affect the demand side of the real estate market include population, demographics, and employment and wage levels.

Population Because shelter is a basic human need, the demand for housing grows with the population. Although the total population of the country continues to rise, the demand for real estate increases faster in some areas than in others. In some locations, growth has ceased altogether or the population has declined. This may be due to economic changes (such as plant closings), social concerns (such as the quality of schools or a desire for more open space), or population changes (such as population shifts from colder to warmer climates). The result can be a drop in demand for real estate in one area, matched by an increased demand elsewhere.

Demographics *Demographics* is the study and description of a population. The population of a community is a major factor in determining the quantity and type of housing in that community. Family size, the ratio of adults to children, the

---

Factors affecting real estate supply are

- labor force availability,
- construction and material costs,
- government controls, and
- financial policies.

Factors affecting real estate demand are

- population,
- demographics, and
- employment and wage levels.

ages of children, the number of retirees, family income, lifestyle, and the growing number of single-parent and empty-nester households are all demographic factors that contribute to the amount and type of housing needed.

IN PRACTICE   *Niche marketing* is the phrase used to refer to the targeted marketing of specific demographic populations. For example, as baby boomers age and look for retirement housing, their need or demand is considered a niche market.

Employment and wage levels   Decisions about whether to buy or rent and how much to spend on housing are closely related to income. When job opportunities are scarce or wage levels low, demand for real estate usually drops. The market might, in fact, be affected drastically by a single major employer moving in or shutting down. Licensees must be aware of the business plans of local employers.

As we've seen, the real estate market depends on a variety of economic forces, such as interest rates and employment levels. To be successful, licensees must follow economic trends and anticipate where those trends will lead. How people use their income depends on consumer confidence. Consumer confidence is based not only on perceived job security but also on the availability of credit and the impact of inflation. General trends in the economy, such as the availability of mortgage money and the rate of inflation, will influence people's decisions as to how to spend their income.

■ KEY POINT REVIEW

Real estate brokerage is the business of bringing people together in a real estate transaction conducted by

- a **real estate broker** who is a person or company licensed to buy, sell, exchange, or lease real property for others for compensation and who may
  — be the agent of buyer, seller, or both, and
  — not be the agent of any party to the transaction, or
- a **real estate salesperson** who conducts brokerage activities on behalf of the broker.

Appraisal is the process of estimating a property's value (typically, market value) that is based on established methods and an appraiser's professional judgment and is regulated by the following:

- Licensing or certification is required for many **federally related transactions**.
- Many states require licensing or certification for local transactions.

Property management is conducted by a **property manager**, a person or company hired to maintain and manage property on behalf of its owner whose

- scope of work depends on a **management agreement**, and
- basic responsibility is to protect owner's investment while maximizing the owner's financial return.

Financing is the business of providing the funds that make real estate transactions possible through

- mortgage or deed of trust loans secured by the property, and
- commercial banks, savings associations, mortgage bankers, and mortgage brokerage companies.

Subdivision and development involve splitting a single property into smaller parcels (subdividing) and constructing improvements on the land (development).

Home inspection is a growing area of interest to both purchasers and homeowners, but note the following:

- A state **license** may be required of a home inspector.
- An **inspection report** will show results of a thorough visual survey of a property.

Real estate counseling involves independent advice based on sound professional judgment.

Types of real property include the following:

- **Residential**—single-family and multifamily
- **Commercial**—office space, shopping centers, stores, theaters, hotels, parking facilities
- **Mixed-use**—commercial and residential uses in the same building
- **Industrial**—warehouses, factories, land in industrial districts, power plants
- **Agricultural**—farms, timberland, ranches, orchards
- **Special-purpose**—schools, places of worship, cemeteries, government-held property

The **real estate market** reflects principles of **supply and demand**, influenced by the **uniqueness** and **immobility** of parcels of real estate so that

- when the **supply increases** and demand remains stable, **prices go down**; and
- when **demand increases** and supply remains stable, **prices go up**.

The factors affecting the **supply** of real estate include the following:

- **Labor force** availability
- Construction and material costs
- **Government controls**—environmental restrictions, land use, building codes, zoning
- **Government financial policies** that impact interest rates and the money supply

The factors affecting the **demand** for real estate include the following:

- **Population**—some areas grow faster than others; some decline
- **Demographics**—family size, lifestyles, niche marketing
- **Employment and wage levels**—influence housing affordability

■ RELATED WEB SITES

American Society of Home Inspectors: *www.ashi.org*
Appraisal Institute: *www.appraisalinstitute.org*
Building Owners and Managers Association International: *www.boma.org*
Commercial Investment Real Estate Institute: *www.ccim.com*
Counselors of Real Estate: *www.cre.org*
Fannie Mae: *www.fanniemae.com*
Federal Reserve Board: *www.federalreserve.gov*
Freddie Mac: *www.freddiemac.com*
Ginnie Mae: *www.ginniemae.gov*
Institute of Real Estate Management: *www.irem.org*
National Association of Exclusive Buyer Agents: *www.naeba.org*
National Association of Independent Fee Appraisers: *www.naifa.com*
National Association of Real Estate Brokers: *www.nareb.com*
National Association of REALTORS®:   *www.realtor.org*
Real Estate Buyer's Agent Council: *www.rebac.net*
Real Estate Educators Association: *www.reea.org*
U.S. Department of Housing and Urban Development: *www.hud.gov*

CHAPTER 1 QUIZ

1. A professional estimate of a property's market value, based on established methods and using trained judgment, is performed by a
   a. real estate broker.
   b. real estate appraiser.
   c. real estate counselor.
   d. home inspector.

2. In general, when the supply of a certain commodity increases,
   a. price tends to rise.
   b. price tends to drop.
   c. demand for it tends to rise.
   d. demand for it tends to drop.

3. Which factor primarily affects supply in the real estate market?
   a. Population
   b. Demographics
   c. Employment
   d. Governmental financial policies

4. Which factor is MOST likely to influence demand for real estate?
   a. Number of real estate brokers in the area
   b. Number of full-time real estate salespeople in the area
   c. Wage levels and employment opportunities
   d. Price of new homes being built in the area

5. Property management, appraisal, financing, and development are all examples of
   a. factors affecting demand.
   b. specializations within the real estate industry.
   c. non–real estate professions.
   d. activities requiring broker management and supervision.

6. A REALTOR® is BEST described as an individual who is
   a. a specially licensed real estate professional who acts as a point of contact between two or more people in negotiating the sale, purchase, or rental of property.
   b. any real estate broker or salesperson who assists buyers, sellers, landlords, or tenants in any real estate transaction.
   c. a member of the National Association of Real Estate Brokers who specializes in residential properties.
   d. a member of the National Association of REALTORS®.

7. A major manufacturer of automobiles announces that it will relocate one of its factories, along with 2,000 employees, to a small town. What effect will this announcement MOST likely have on the small town's housing market?
   a. Houses will likely become less expensive as a result of the announcement.
   b. Houses will likely become more expensive as a result of the announcement.
   c. Because the announcement involves an issue of demographics, not of supply and demand, housing prices will stay the same.
   d. The announcement involves an industrial property; residential housing will not be affected.

8. A licensee who has several years of experience in the industry decided to retire from actively marketing properties. Now this licensee helps clients choose among the various alternatives involved in purchasing, using, or investing in property. What is this licensee's profession?
   a. Real estate counselor
   b. Real estate appraiser
   c. Real estate educator
   d. REALTOR®

9. The words *broker* and REALTOR® are
   a. interchangeable.
   b. different categories of membership in the National Association of REALTORS®.
   c. different titles offered by separate professional organizations.
   d. unrelated; a broker is a real estate licensee, and a REALTOR® is a member of the National Association of REALTORS®.

10. Schools would be considered part of which real estate classification?
    a. Special-purpose
    b. Industrial
    c. Commercial
    d. Government-held

11. When demand for a commodity decreases and supply remains the same,
    a. price tends to rise.
    b. price tends to fall.
    c. price is not affected.
    d. the market becomes stagnant.

12. A licensed real estate professional acting as a point of contact between two or more people in negotiating the sale, rental, or purchase of a property is known as a(n)
    a. sales affiliate.
    b. broker.
    c. property manager.
    d. appraiser.

13. All of the following would affect supply *EXCEPT*
    a. population.
    b. construction costs.
    c. governmental controls.
    d. the labor force.

14. All of the following are categories of the uses of real property *EXCEPT*
    a. residential.
    b. developmental.
    c. agricultural.
    d. industrial.

15. All of the following would affect demand *EXCEPT*
    a. population.
    b. demographics.
    c. wage levels.
    d. fiscal policy.

16. All of the following affect how quickly the forces of supply and demand work *EXCEPT*
    a. degree of standardization of the product.
    b. mobility of the product.
    c. degree of standardization of the product's price.
    d. mobility of the parties to the transaction.

17. A real estate professional who performs a visual survey of a property's structure and systems and prepares an analytical report for a purchaser or an owner is acting as a(n)
    a. educator.
    b. appraiser.
    c. property manager.
    d. home inspector.

18. When the supply of a commodity decreases while demand remains the same,
    a. price tends to rise.
    b. price tends to drop.
    c. price tends to not be affected.
    d. price tends to go in the direction of supply.

19. When responsible for maintaining a client's property and maximizing the return on the client's investment, a broker is serving as a(n)
    a. rental agent.
    b. building maintenance specialist.
    c. property manager.
    d. investment counselor.

20. Detailed information about the age, education, behavior, and other characteristics of members of a population group is called
    a. population analysis.
    b. demographics.
    c. family lifestyles.
    d. household data.

CHAPTER 2

Real Property and the Law

■ **LEARNING OBJECTIVES**   *When you have finished reading this chapter, you should be able to*

■ **identify** the rights that convey with ownership of real property and the characteristics of real estate;

■ **describe** the difference between real and personal property;

■ **explain** the types of laws that affect real estate;

■ **distinguish** between the concepts of land, real estate, and real property; and

■ **define** the following *key terms:*

accession	fixture	real property
air rights	improvement	severance
annexation	land	situs
appurtenance	manufactured housing	subsurface rights
area preference	nonhomogeneity	surface rights
bundle of legal rights	personal property	trade fixture
chattel	real estate	water rights
emblements		

■ REAL PROPERTY AND THE LAW

Real estate is a market like any other one. Real property is a product, and the licensee is the salesperson. As any successful salesperson will tell you, product knowledge is the key to success. You need to know enough about your product to be able to educate and guide your clients and customers, whether they are buyers, sellers, renters, or investors. Also, you are dealing with a product that involves very specific and often very complicated legal issues. This chapter will help you understand the fundamental principles of the product that you will be handling for the rest of your career.

■ LAND, REAL ESTATE, AND REAL PROPERTY

The words *land*, *real estate*, and *real property* are often used interchangeably. To most people, they mean the same thing. Strictly speaking, however, the terms refer to different aspects of ownership interests in land. To fully understand the nature of real estate and the laws that affect it, real estate licensees must be aware of the subtle yet important differences in meaning of these words.

Land

Land is defined as the earth's surface extending downward to the center of the earth and upward to infinity, including permanent natural objects, such as trees, and water. (See Figure 2.1.)

FIGURE 2.1

Land, Real Estate, and Real Property

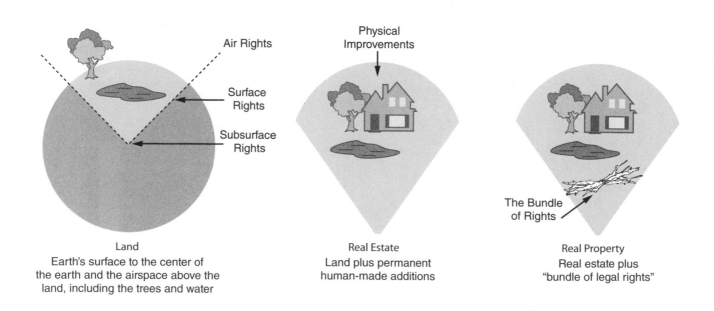

Land
Earth's surface to the center of
the earth and the airspace above the
land, including the trees and water

Air Rights

Surface Rights

Subsurface Rights

Physical Improvements

Real Estate
Land plus permanent
human-made additions

The Bundle of Rights

Real Property
Real estate plus
"bundle of legal rights"

Land includes not only the surface of the earth but also the underlying soil. It refers to things that are *naturally* attached to the land, such as boulders and plants. It includes the minerals and substances that lie far below the earth's surface. Land even includes the air above the earth, all the way into space. These are known respectively as the *subsurface* and the *airspace*. Most of the surface of the earth, of course, is not land at all, but water. Special state and local laws govern the ownership of the wetter parts of the earth, including lakes and rivers. (See Chapter 7.)

Real Estate

Real estate is defined as land at, above, and below the earth's surface, plus all things permanently attached to it, whether natural or artificial. (See Figure 2.1.)

The term real estate, or realty, is similar to the term land but includes not only the natural components of the land but also all permanent man-made improvements on and to the land. An **improvement** is any artificial thing attached to the land, such as a building or a fence as well as infrastructures, such as sewers.

Real Property

The term *real property* is the broadest of all. It includes both land and real estate. **Real property** is defined as the interests, benefits, and rights that are automatically included in the ownership of land and real estate. (See Figure 2.1.)

Real property includes the earth's surface, subsurface, and airspace, including all things permanently attached to it by nature or people, and the legal rights innate to the ownership of a parcel of real estate.

Traditionally, ownership rights of real property are described as a **bundle of legal rights**. These rights include the

- right of *possession*,
- right to *control* the property within the framework of the law,
- right of *enjoyment* (to use the property in any legal manner),
- right of *exclusion* (to keep others from entering or using the property), and
- right of *disposition* (to sell, will, transfer, or otherwise dispose of or encumber the property).

The concept of a bundle of rights comes from old English law. In the Middle Ages, a seller transferred property by giving the purchaser a handful of earth or a bundle of bound sticks from a tree on the property. After accepting the bundle, the purchaser became the owner of the tree from which the sticks came and the land to which the tree was attached. Because the rights of ownership (like the sticks) can be separated and individually transferred, the sticks became symbolic of those rights. (See Figure 2.2.)

The word *title*, as it relates to real property, has two meanings: (1) the right to or ownership of the land, including the owner's bundle of legal rights; and (2) evidence of that ownership by a deed. Title refers to *ownership* of real property, not to a printed document. The document by which the owner transfers title to the real property is the deed.

FIGURE 2.2

**The Bundle of
Legal Rights**

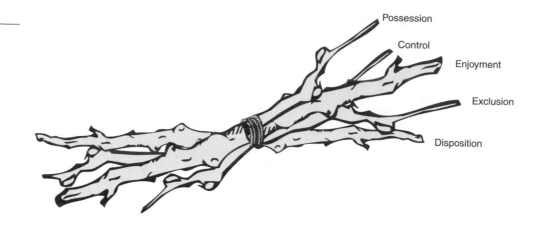

Real property is often coupled with the word *appurtenance*. An **appurtenance** (runs with the land) is a right or privilege associated with the property, although not necessarily a part of it. Typical appurtenances include parking spaces in multiunit buildings, easements, water rights, and other improvements. An appurtenance is connected to the property, and ownership of the appurtenance normally transfers to the new owner when the property is sold.

IN PRACTICE   When people talk about buying or selling homes, office buildings, and land, they usually call these things real estate. For all practical purposes, the term *real estate* is synonymous with *real property* as defined here. Thus, in everyday usage, *real estate* includes the legal rights of ownership specified in the definition of real property. Sometimes people use the term realty instead.

Subsurface, air, and water rights   **Surface rights** refer to the use of the surface of the earth. **Subsurface rights** are the rights to the natural resources below the earth's surface. An owner may transfer surface rights without transferring subsurface rights.

■ **FOR EXAMPLE**   A landowner sells the rights to any oil and gas found beneath the owned farm to an oil company. Later, the same landowner sells the remaining interests (the surface, air, and limited subsurface rights) to a buyer, reserving the rights to any coal that may be found and pasture in the land. This buyer sells the remaining land to yet another buyer but retains the farmhouse, stable, and pasture. After these sales, four parties have ownership interests in the same real estate: (1) the original landowner owns all the coal; (2) the oil company owns all the oil and gas; (3) the first buyer owns the farmhouse, stable, and pasture; and (4) the second buyer owns the rights to the remaining real estate. (See Figure 2.3.)

Air rights, the rights to use the space above the earth, may be sold or leased independently, provided the rights have not been preempted by law. Air rights can be an important part of real estate, particularly in large cities, where air rights over railroads must be purchased or leased to construct office buildings, such as the MetLife Building in New York City and the Prudential Building in Chicago. To construct such a building, the developer must purchase not only the air rights but also numerous small portions of the land's surface for the building's foundation supports.

F I G U R E   2.3

Surface and Subsurface Rights

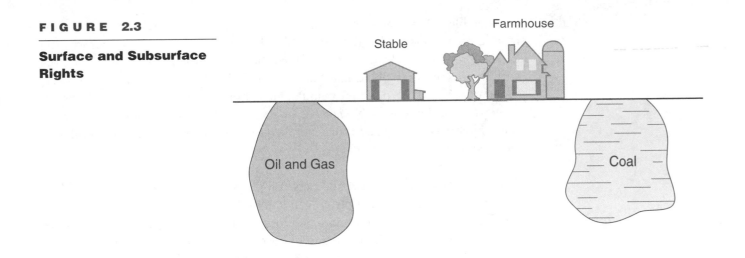

Before air travel was common, a property's air rights were considered to be unlimited, extending upward into the farthest reaches of outer space. However, now that air travel is common, the courts and the U.S. Congress have put limits on air rights. Today, the courts permit reasonable interference with these rights, such as that necessary for aircraft (and presumably spacecraft), as long as the owner's right to use and occupy the land is not unduly lessened. Government and airport authorities often purchase adjacent air rights to provide approach patterns for air traffic.

With the continuing development of solar power, air rights—and, more specifically, light or solar rights—are being closely examined by the courts. A new tall building that blocks sunlight from a smaller existing building may be held to be interfering with the smaller building's right to sunlight, particularly if systems in the smaller building are solar powered. Air and solar rights are regulated by state and local laws and ordinances.

Water rights are special common-law rights held by owners of land adjacent to rivers, lakes, or oceans and are restrictions on the rights of land ownership. Water rights are particularly important rights in drier western states, where water is a scarce and valuable public commodity. (See Chapter 7.)

■ REAL PROPERTY VERSUS PERSONAL PROPERTY

Property may be classified as either real or personal. **Personal property**, sometimes called personalty, is all the property that can be owned and that does not fit the definition of real property. An important distinction between the two is that personal property is movable. Items of personal property, also referred to as **chattels,** include such tangibles as chairs, tables, clothing, money, bonds, and bank accounts.

Manufactured Housing

Manufactured housing is defined as dwellings that are not constructed at the site but are built off-site and trucked to a building lot where they are installed

chattels
—personal
property

or assembled. Manufactured housing includes modular, panelized, precut, and mobile homes. Generally, the term *mobile homes* is used to refer to factory-built housing constructed before 1976. Use of the term *mobile homes* was phased out with the passage of the National Manufactured Housing Construction and Safety Standards Act of 1976, when manufactured homes became federally regulated. Nevertheless, the term *mobile home* is still commonly used among licensees. Most states have agencies that administer and enforce the federal regulations for manufactured housing.

The distinction between real and personal property is not always obvious. Manufactured housing, for example, is generally considered personal property, even though its mobility may be limited to a single trip to a park or development to be hooked up to utilities. Manufactured housing may, however, be considered real property if it becomes permanently affixed to the land. The distinction is generally one of state law. Real estate licensees should be familiar with local laws before attempting to sell manufactured housing.

Plants

The legal term for plants that do not require annual cultivation (such as trees and shrubbery) is *fructus naturales* (fruits of nature); plant or crops that require annual cultivation are legally known as **emblements** or *fructus industriales* (fruits of industry).

Trees and crops generally fall into one of two classes: (1) Trees, perennial shrubbery, and grasses that do not require annual cultivation are known as *fructus naturales*. These items are considered real estate. (2) Annually cultivated crops such as fruit, vegetables, and grain are known as **emblements**, or *fructus industriales*, and are generally considered personal property. For example, a farmer who sells his farm won't have to dig up growing corn plants and haul them away unless the sales contract says so. The young corn remains on the land. The farmer may come back and harvest the corn when it's ready. The former owner or tenant is entitled to harvest the crops that result from his labor. Perennial crops, such as orchards or vineyards, are not personal property and so transfer with the land.

An item of real property can become personal property by **severance**, or separating from the land. For example, a growing tree is real estate until the owner cuts it down, literally severing it from the property. Similarly, an apple becomes personal property once it is picked from a tree.

It is also possible to change personal property into real property through the process known as **annexation**. For example, if a landowner buys cement, stones, and sand and mixes them into concrete to construct a sidewalk across the land, the landowner has converted personal property (cement, stones, and sand) into real property (a sidewalk).

Real estate licensees need to know whether property is real or personal. An important distinction arises, for instance, when the property is transferred from one owner to another. Real property is conveyed by deed, while personal property is conveyed by a bill of sale or receipt. (See Chapter 12.)

Classifications of Fixtures

In considering the differences between real and personal property, it is necessary to distinguish between a fixture and personal property.

Fixtures   A fixture is personal property that has been so affixed to land or a building that, by law, it becomes part of the real property. Examples of fixtures are heating systems, elevator equipment in high-rise buildings, radiators, kitchen cabinets, light fixtures, and plumbing. Almost any item that has been added as a permanent part of a building is considered a fixture.

During the course of time, the same materials may be both real and personal property, depending on their use and location.

Legal tests of a fixture   The overall test used to determine whether an item is a fixture (real property) or personal property is a question of *intent*. (See Figure 2.4.) Did the person who installed the item intend it to remain permanently on the property or to be removable in the future? In determining intent, courts use the following three basic tests:

- *Method of annexation*: How *permanent* is the method of attachment? Can the item be removed without causing damage to the surrounding property?
- *Adaptation to real estate*: Is the item being *used* as real property or personal property? For example, a refrigerator is usually considered personal property. However, if a refrigerator has been adapted to match the kitchen cabinetry, it becomes a fixture.
- *Agreement*: Have the parties *agreed* on whether the item is real or personal property in an offer to purchase?

Although these tests may seem simple, court decisions have been complex and inconsistent. Property that appears to be permanently affixed has sometimes been ruled to be personal property, while property that seems removable has been ruled a fixture. It is important that an owner clarify *what* is to be sold with the real estate at the very beginning of the sales process.

IN PRACTICE   At the time a property is listed, the seller and the listing agent should discuss which items to include in the sale. The written sales contract between the buyer and the seller should specifically list all articles that are being included in the sale, particularly if any doubt exists as to whether they are personal property or fixtures (for instance, built-in bookcases, chandeliers, ceiling fans, or exotic shrubbery). This specificity will avoid a misunderstanding between the parties that might result in the collapse of the transaction and expensive lawsuits. The most commonly disputed items between buyers and sellers are draperies, light fixtures, and appliances.

Trade fixtures   A special category of fixtures includes property used in the course of business. An article owned by a tenant and attached to a rented space

FIGURE 2.4

Legal Tests of a Fixture

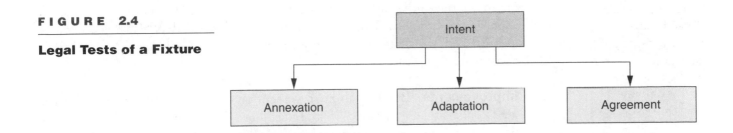

or building or used in conducting a business is a **trade fixture**, or a chattel fixture. Some examples of trade fixtures are bowling alleys, store shelves, and barroom and restaurant equipment. Agricultural fixtures, such as chicken coops and tool sheds, are also included in this category. Trade fixtures must be removed on or before the last day the property is rented. The tenant is responsible for any damage caused by the removal of a fixture. Trade fixtures that are not removed become the real property of the landlord. Acquiring the property in this way is known as **accession** (this is related to the legal principle of constructive annexation).

■ **FOR EXAMPLE** A pizza parlor leases space in a small shopping center. The restaurateur bolted a large iron oven to the floor of the unit. When the pizza parlor goes out of business or relocates, the restaurateur will be able to remove the pizza oven if the bolt holes in the floor can be repaired. The oven is a trade fixture. On the other hand, if the pizza oven was brought into the restaurant in pieces, welded together, and set in concrete, the restaurateur might not be able to remove it without causing structural damage. In that case, the oven might become a fixture.

Trade fixtures differ from other fixtures in the following ways:

■ Fixtures belong to the owner of the real estate, but trade fixtures are usually owned and installed by a tenant for the tenant's use.
■ Fixtures are considered a permanent part of a building, but trade fixtures are removable. Trade fixtures may be attached to a building so they appear to be fixtures.

Legally, fixtures are real property, so they are included in any sale or mortgage. Trade fixtures, however, are considered personal property and are not included in the sale or mortgage of real estate, except by special agreement.

■ CHARACTERISTICS OF REAL PROPERTY

Real property possesses seven basic characteristics that define its nature and affect its use. These characteristics fall into two broad categories—*economic* and *physical*.

Economic Characteristics

The four economic characteristics of land that affect its value as a product in the marketplace are scarcity, improvements, permanence of investment, and area preference.

Four Economic Characteristics of Real Estate

■ Scarcity
■ Improvements
■ Permanence of investment
■ Location or area preference

Scarcity We usually do not consider land a rare commodity, but only about a quarter of the earth's surface is dry land; the rest is water. The total supply of land, then, is not limitless. While a considerable amount of land remains unused or uninhabited, the supply in a given location or of a particular quality is generally considered to be finite.

Improvements Building an improvement on one parcel of land can affect the land's value and use as well as that of neighboring tracts and whole communities. For example, constructing a new shopping center or selecting a site for a nuclear power plant or toxic waste dump can dramatically change the value of land in a large area.

Permanence of investment   The capital and labor used to build an improvement represent a large fixed investment. Although even a well-built structure can be razed to make way for a newer building, improvements such as drainage, electricity, water, and sewerage remain. The return on such investments tends to be long term and relatively stable.

Area preference   **Area preference**, or **situs** ("to place"), is commonly referred to as "location, location, location." This economic characteristic refers not only to geography but also to people's preference for a specific area. Area preference is based on several factors, such as convenience, reputation, and history. It is the unique quality of these preferences that results in the different price points for similar properties. Location is often considered the single most important economic characteristic of land.

■ **FOR EXAMPLE**   A river runs through a town, dividing it more or less in half. Houses on the north side of the river sell for an average of $170,000. On the south side of the river, identical houses sell for more than $200,000. The only difference is that homebuyers think that the area south of the river is a better neighborhood, even though no obvious difference exists between the two equally pleasant sides of town.

Physical Characteristics

Land has three physical characteristics: immobility, indestructibility, and uniqueness.

Immobility   It is true that some of the substances of land are removable and that topography can be changed, but the geographic location of any given parcel of land can never be changed. It is fixed, immobile.

Indestructibility   Land is also indestructible. This permanence of land, coupled with the long-term nature of improvements, tends to stabilize investments in real property.

Three Physical Characteristics of Real Estate
- Immobility
- Indestructibility
- Uniqueness

The fact that land is indestructible does not, however, change the fact that the improvements on land depreciate and can become obsolete, which may dramatically reduce the land's value. This gradual depreciation should not be confused with the knowledge that the economic desirability of a given location can change.

Uniqueness   Uniqueness, or **nonhomogeneity**, is the concept that no two parcels of property are exactly the same or in the same location. The characteristics of each property, no matter how small, differ from those of every other. An individual parcel has no substitute because each is unique.

■ LAWS AFFECTING REAL ESTATE

The unique nature of real estate has given rise to an equally unique set of laws and rights. Even the simplest real estate transaction involves a body of complex laws. Real estate licensees must have a clear and accurate understanding of the laws that affect real estate.

The specific areas of law that are important to the real estate licensee include the *law of contracts*, the *general property law*, the *law of agency*, and specific state *real estate license law*. Federal regulations, such as environmental laws, as well as federal, state, and local tax laws, also play an important role in real estate transactions. State and local land-use and zoning laws have a significant effect on the practice of real estate, too.

Laws Affecting Real Estate

- Contract law
- General property law
- Agency law
- Real estate license law
- Federal regulations
- Federal, state, and local tax laws
- Zoning and land-use laws
- Federal, state, and local environmental regulations

A real estate licensee can't be an expert in all areas of real estate law. However, licensees should know and understand some basic principles. Perhaps most important is the ability to recognize problems that should be referred to a competent attorney. Only attorneys are trained and licensed to prepare documents defining or transferring rights in property and to give advice on matters of law. *Under no circumstances may real estate brokers or real estate salespeople act as attorneys unless they are also licensed attorneys representing clients in that capacity.*

Real estate license laws   Because real estate brokers and real estate salespeople are involved with other people's real estate and money, the need for regulation of their activities has long been recognized. The purpose of real estate license laws is to protect the public from fraud, dishonesty, and incompetence in real estate transactions. All 50 states, the District of Columbia, and all Canadian provinces have passed laws that require real estate brokers and real estate salespeople to be licensed. Although state license laws are similar in many respects, they differ in some details, such as the amount and type of prelicensing education required.

■ KEY POINT REVIEW

Land

- is the earth's **surface**, where **water rights** are held by owners of land adjacent to rivers, lakes, or oceans;
- extends downward to the center of the earth, where **subsurface rights** include **mineral rights** and other natural resources that can be transferred separately from surface rights;
- stretches upward to infinity, where **air rights** can be sold separately from surface rights with some limitations to enable air travel; and
- includes things **naturally attached** (*fructus naturales*) to the land, such as trees and crops that do not need cultivation and perennial crops, orchards, and vineyards.

Real estate includes

- land at, above, and below the earth's surface, plus
- all things **permanently attached** to the land, both natural and man-made.

Real property includes

- interests,
- benefits, and
- rights that are automatically included in the ownership of land and real estate.

Bundle of legal rights includes the

- right of **possession,**
- right to **control** the property,
- right of **enjoyment,**
- right of **exclusion,** and
- right of **disposition.**

Title is the

- **right to ownership** of the land,
- **bundle of legal rights,** and
- **evidence of ownership** provided by a written document, a **deed,** by which title is transferred.

Appurtenance is a right or privilege associated with real property in some way, such as a parking space in a multiunit building, an easement, or water rights, and is normally conveyed to the new owner when the property is sold.

Personal property (chattel) includes

- movable items, such as a chair or a sofa;
- **emblements** (*fructus industriales*), annual plantings or crops of grains, vegetables, and fruit;
- items of real property that can become personal property by **severance;**
- items of personal property that can become real property by **attachment** (construction materials); and
- **manufactured homes** that can be personal property unless **permanently affixed** to land.

A **fixture** is personal property that has been affixed to the land or to a building so that by law it becomes part of the real property.

Legal tests for a fixture include the following:

- **Method of annexation**—not easily removable
- **Adaptation to real estate**—ordinarily considered a permanent addition
- **Agreement of the parties**—stated as part of real estate in the offer to purchase

Trade fixtures include property attached to the structure but used in the course of business such as

- **personal property,** if removed by tenant and the premises are returned to original condition before the lease expires; and
- real property if left behind by tenant. The landlord can acquire this type of property by **accession.**

The **characteristics of real estate** include the following:

■ Economic
  — Scarcity
  — Improvements
  — Permanence of investment
  — **Location** (most important)

■ Physical
  — Immobility
  — Indestructibility
  — **Nonhomogeneity**, or uniqueness

Laws that affect real estate include

■ contracts, property, agency, and real estate licensing, where all states require real estate brokers and salespeople to be licensed with requirements differing from state to state;
■ state and local land-use and zoning laws; and
■ federal and state environmental regulations and tax laws.

■ RELATED WEB SITES

Manufactured Housing Institute: *www.manufacturedhousing.org*
Alabama Real Estate Commission: *www.arec.alabama.gov*
Alaska Real Estate Commission: *www.commerce.state.ak.us/occ/prec.htm*
Arizona Department of Real Estate: *www.re.state.az.us*
Arkansas Real Estate Commission: *www.state.ar.us/arec/frmain.htm*
California Department of Real Estate: *www.dre.ca.gov*
Colorado Department of Regulatory Agencies, Division of Real Estate:
      www.dora.state.co.us/Real-Estate/
Connecticut Department of Consumer Protection: *www.state.ct.us/dcp/*
District of Columbia Real Estate Commission: *http://app.dcra.dc.gov*
Florida Department of Business and Professional Regulation:
      www.myfloridalicense.com/dbpr/
Georgia Real Estate Commission: *www.grec.state.ga.us*
Hawaii Department of Commerce and Consumer Affairs, Real Estate
      Branch: *www.hawaii.gov/dcca/real/*
Idaho Real Estate Commission: *www.idahorealestatecommission.com*
Illinois Division of Professional Regulation:
      www.idfpr.com/DPR/RE/realmain.asp
Indiana Professional Licensing Agency: *www.ai.org/pla/real.htm*
Iowa Real Estate Commission:
      www.state.ia.us/government/com/prof/sales/home.htm
Kansas Real Estate Commission: *www.accesskansas.org/krec*
Kentucky Real Estate Commission: *www.krec.ky.gov*
Louisiana Real Estate Commission: *www.lrec.state.la.us*
Maine Real Estate Commission:
      www.maine.gov/pfr/professionallicensing/professions/real_estate/
Maryland Real Estate Commission: *www.dllr.state.md.us/license/mrec/*
Massachusetts Division of Registration: *www.state.ma.us/reg/*

Michigan Department of Energy, Labor, and Economic Growth:
    www.michigan.gov/dleg/
Minnesota Department of Commerce: *www.commerce.state.mn.us*
Mississippi Real Estate Commission: *www.mrec.state.ms.us*
Missouri Real Estate Commission: *www.pr.mo.gov/realestate.asp*
Montana Department of Commerce: *www.commerce.mt.gov/*
Nebraska Real Estate Commission: *www.nrec.state.ne.us/*
Nevada Real Estate Division: *www.red.state.nv.us*
New Hampshire Real Estate Commission: *www.nh.gov/nhrec/*
New Jersey Real Estate Commission: *www.state.nj.us/dobi/division_rec/*
New Mexico Real Estate Commission:
    www.rld.state.nm.us/realestatecommission/
New York Department of State, Division of Licensing Services:
    www.dos.state.ny.us/lcns/
North Carolina Real Estate Commission: *www.ncrec.state.nc.us*
Ohio Division of Real Estate and Professional Licensing:
    www.com.state.oh.us/real/
Oregon Real Estate Agency: *www.rea.state.or.us*
Pennsylvania Real Estate Commission: *www.dos.state.pa.us/bpoa*
Rhode Island Department of Business Regulation: Real Estate:
    www.dbr.state.ri.us/divisions/commlicensing/realestate.php
South Carolina Real Estate Commission: *www.llr.state.sc.us/pol/rec/*
South Dakota Real Estate Commission: *www.state.sd.us/sdrec/*
Tennessee Real Estate Commission: *www.state.tn.us/commerce/boards/trec/*
Texas Real Estate Commission: *www.trec.state.tx.us*
Utah Division of Real Estate: *www.realestate.utah.gov*
Vermont Real Estate Commission: *www.vtprofessionals.org/opr1/real_estate*
Virginia Department of Professional and Occupational Regulation:
    www.dpor.virginia.gov/dporweb/
Washington State Department of Licensing, Real Estate:
    www.dol.wa.gov/business/realestate/
West Virginia Real Estate Commission: *www.wvrec.org*
Wisconsin Department of Regulation and Licensing: *www.drl.wi.gov*
Wyoming Real Estate Commission: *http://realestate.state.wy.us*

CHAPTER 2 QUIZ

1. Real estate generally includes all the following *EXCEPT*
   a. trees.
   b. air rights.
   c. annual crops.
   d. mineral rights.

2. A woman rents space in a commercial building where she operates a bookstore. In the bookstore, she has installed large reading tables fastened to the walls and bookshelves that create aisles from the front of the store to the back. These shelves are bolted to both the ceiling and the floor. Which of the following *BEST* characterizes the contents of the bookstore?
   a. The shelves and tables are trade fixtures and will transfer when the property owner sells the building.
   b. The shelves and tables are trade fixtures and may properly be removed by the woman before her lease expires, and the tenant would be responsible to the landlord for any damage that their removal caused to the premises.
   c. Because the woman is a tenant, the shelves and tables are fixtures and may not be removed except with the building owner's permission.
   d. Because the shelves and tables are attached to the building, they are treated the same as other fixtures.

3. The term *nonhomogeneity* refers to
   a. scarcity.
   b. immobility.
   c. uniqueness.
   d. indestructibility.

4. Another term for *personal property* is
   a. realty.
   b. fixtures.
   c. chattels.
   d. *fructus naturales*.

5. When an owner of real estate sells the property to someone else, which of the "sticks" in the bundle of legal rights is the owner as seller using?
   a. Exclusion
   b. Legal enjoyment
   c. Control
   d. Disposition

6. A man inherited a piece of vacant property from his uncle. First, he removed all the topsoil, which he sold to a landscaping company. He then removed a thick layer of limestone and sold it to a construction company. Finally, he dug 40 feet into the bedrock and sold it for gravel. When the man died, he left the property to his daughter. Which of the following statements is *TRUE*?
   a. The daughter inherits nothing because the property no longer exists.
   b. The daughter inherits a large hole in the ground because the property goes down to the center of the earth.
   c. The daughter owns the gravel, limestone, and topsoil, no matter where it is.
   d. The man's estate must restore the property to its original condition.

7. The buyer and the seller of a home are debating whether a certain item is real or personal property. The buyer says it is real property and should convey with the house; the seller says it is personal property and would not convey without a separate bill of sale. In determining whether an item is real or personal property, a court would *NOT* consider which of the following?
   a. The cost of the item when it was purchased
   b. Whether its removal would cause severe damage to the real estate
   c. Whether the item is clearly adapted to the real estate
   d. Any relevant agreement of the parties in their contract of sale

8. Which of the following is a physical characteristic of land?
   a. Indestructibility
   b. Improvements
   c. Area preference
   d. Scarcity

9. Which of the following describes the act by which real property can be converted into personal property?
   a. Severance
   b. Accession
   c. Conversion
   d. Attachment

10. While moving into a newly purchased home, the buyer discovered that the seller had taken the ceiling fan that hung over the dining room table. The seller had not indicated that the ceiling fan would be removed, and the contract did not address this issue. Which statement is *TRUE?*
    a. Ceiling fans are normally considered to be real estate.
    b. The ceiling fan belongs to the seller.
    c. Ceiling fans are considered trade fixtures.
    d. Ceiling fans are considered personal property.

11. A buyer purchased a parcel of land and immediately sold the mineral rights to an oil company. The buyer gave up which of the following?
    a. Air rights
    b. Surface rights
    c. Subsurface rights
    d. Occupancy rights

12. A homeowner is building a new enclosed front porch on his home. A truckload of lumber that the homeowner purchased has been left in the driveway for use in building the porch. At this point, the lumber is considered to be
    a. real property because it will be permanently affixed to the existing structure.
    b. personal property.
    c. a chattel that is real property.
    d. a trade or chattel fixture.

13. Method of annexation, adaptation to real estate, and agreement between the parties are the legal tests for determining whether an item is
    a. a trade fixture or personal property.
    b. real property or real estate.
    c. a fixture or personal property.
    d. an improvement.

14. Parking spaces in multiunit buildings, water rights, and similar things of value are classified as
    a. covenants.
    b. emblements.
    c. chattels.
    d. appurtenances.

15. A paint company purchases 100 acres of scenic forest land and builds several tin shacks there to store used turpentine, varnish, and similar chemical waste. Based on these facts alone, which statement is *TRUE?*
    a. The company's action constitutes improvement of the property.
    b. The chemicals are considered appurtenances.
    c. If the company is in the business of storing toxic substances, the tin shacks are considered trade fixtures.
    d. Altering the property in order to store waste is not included in the bundle of legal rights.

16. The phrase *bundle of legal rights* is properly included in
    a. the definition of real property.
    b. a legal description.
    c. real estate transactions.
    d. leases for less than one year.

17. All of the following are included in the right to control one's property *EXCEPT* the right to
    a. sell the property to a neighbor.
    b. exclude utility meter readers.
    c. erect No Trespassing signs.
    d. enjoy profits from its ownership.

18. According to law, a trade fixture is usually treated as
    a. a fixture.
    b. an easement.
    c. personalty.
    d. a license.

19. A buyer is interested in a house that fits most of her needs, but it is located in a busy area where she is not sure she wants to live. Her concern about the property's location is called
    a. physical deterioration.
    b. area preference.
    c. permanence of investment.
    d. immobility.

20. Which of the following is considered personal property?
    a. Wood-burning fireplace
    b. Awnings
    c. Bathtub
    d. Patio furniture

CHAPTER 3

Concepts of Home Ownership

■ **LEARNING OBJECTIVES** *When you have finished reading this chapter, you should be able to*

- ■ **identify** the various types of housing choices available to homebuyers;
- ■ **describe** the issues involved in making a home ownership decision;
- ■ **explain** the tax benefits of home ownership;
- ■ **distinguish** the various types of homeowners' insurance policy coverage; and
- ■ **define** the following *key terms*:

coinsurance clause	liability coverage	replacement cost
homeowners' insurance policy	PITI (principal, interest, taxes, and insurance)	

■ HOME OWNERSHIP CONCEPTS

In the past, most homes were single-family dwellings bought by married couples with small children. Today, social, demographic, and economic changes have altered the residential real estate market considerably. Many real estate buyers today are single men and women, childless professional couples, unmarried couples, and domestic partners. An aging baby boom generation has given rise to empty nesters—couples whose children have moved away from home. Still other buyers may be friends or relatives who plan to co-own a home in the same way they might share an apartment lease. Today's homebuyers come from all economic classes, from all ethnic backgrounds, and from all over the world.

There are nearly as many different kinds of home ownership as there are people who own homes. As the real estate market changes and evolves, the successful real estate agent will understand the various (and sometimes conflicting) motivations that move people to buy property and the options and opportunities that are broadening their range of choices.

■ HOME OWNERSHIP

People buy their own homes for psychological as well as financial reasons. To many people, home ownership is a sign of financial stability. A home is an investment that can appreciate in value and provide federal income tax deductions. Home ownership also offers benefits that may be less tangible but are no less valuable, such as pride, security, and a sense of belonging to a community.

Types of Housing

As U.S. society evolves, the needs of its homebuyers become more specialized. Some housing types are not only innovative uses of real estate, but they also incorporate a variety of ownership concepts. These different forms of housing respond to the demands of a diverse marketplace.

Apartment complexes are groups of apartment buildings with a varying number of units in each building. The buildings may be low-rise or high-rise, and the complexes may include parking, security, clubhouses, swimming pools, tennis courts, and even golf courses.

Condo = conventional ownership; deed
Co-op = proprietary lease

The *condominium* is a popular form of residential ownership, particularly for people who want the security of owning property without the care and maintenance that a house demands. It is also a popular ownership option in areas where property values make single-unit ownership inaccessible for many people. Condominium owners own their units individually and share ownership of common facilities (called *common elements*), such as halls, elevators, swimming pools, clubhouses, tennis courts, and surrounding grounds. Management and maintenance of building exteriors and common facilities are provided by the governing association and outside contractors, with expenses paid out of monthly assessments charged to owners. While condos are often apartment-style homes, this ownership form includes single-family and even commercial properties. (See Chapter 8.)

A *cooperative* also has units that share common walls and facilities within a larger building. The owners, however, do not actually *own* the units. Instead, a corporation holds title to the real estate itself. The unit owners actually purchase shares of stock in the corporation, not their individual units. Owners receive *proprietary leases and a share of stock*. Like condominium unit owners, cooperative unit owners pay their share of the building's expenses. (See Chapter 8.)

Planned unit developments (PUDs), sometimes called *master-planned communities*, merge such diverse land uses as housing, recreation, and commercial units into one self-contained development. PUDs are planned under special zoning ordinances. These ordinances permit maximum use of open space by reducing lot sizes and street areas. Owners do not have direct ownership interest in the common areas. A community association is formed to maintain these areas, with fees collected from the owners. A PUD may be a small development of just a few homes or an entire planned city.

Retirement communities, many of them in temperate climates, are often structured as PUDs. They may provide shopping, recreational opportunities, and health care facilities in addition to residential units. Security and convenience are major advantages offered by retirement communities to older homeowners.

High-rise developments, sometimes called *mixed-use developments* (MUDs), combine office space, stores, theaters, and apartment units into a single vertical community. MUDs usually are self-contained and offer laundry facilities, restaurants, food stores, valet shops, beauty parlors, barbershops, swimming pools, and other attractive and convenient features.

Converted-use properties are factories, warehouses, office buildings, hotels, schools, barns, churches, and other structures that have been converted to residential use. Developers often find renovation of such properties more aesthetically and economically appealing than demolishing a perfectly sound structure to build something new. An abandoned warehouse may be transformed into luxury loft condominium units; a closed hotel may reopen as an apartment building; and an old factory may be recycled into a profitable shopping mall.

Manufactured housing (also known as a *mobile home*) was once considered a temporary residence. Today mobile homes are permanent principal residences or stationary vacation homes. Relatively low cost, coupled with the increased living space available in the newer models, makes such homes an attractive option for many people. Increased sales have resulted in growing numbers of *housing parks* in some communities. These parks offer complete residential environments with permanent community facilities as well as semi-permanent foundations and hookups for gas, water, and electricity.

Modular homes (also referred to as *prefabricated homes*) are also gaining popularity as the price rises for newly constructed "stick-built" homes (i.e., homes built on the construction site). Each room in a modular home is preassembled at a factory, driven to the building site on a truck, and then lowered onto its foundation by a crane. Later, workers finish the structure and connect plumbing and wiring. Entire developments can be built at a fraction of the time and cost of conventional stick-built construction.

Time-shares allow multiple purchasers to share ownership of a single property, usually a vacation home or resort property. Each owner is entitled to use the property for a certain period each year, usually a specific week or month. In addition to their share of the purchase price, owners pay an annual maintenance fee.

■ HOUSING AFFORDABILITY

Congress, state legislatures, and local governments work diligently to increase the affordability of housing. Because more homeowners mean more business opportunities, real estate and related industry groups have a vital interest in ensuring affordable housing for all segments of the population. In recent years, creative financing, low-interest loans, and interest-only loans helped make housing costs more manageable. As a result, according to the U.S. Bureau of the Census, by the end of 2008, 67.5 percent of households were homeowners. By 2010, real estate prices had fallen and unemployment had risen, making it more difficult for buyers to save the down payment and closing costs needed to secure a mortgage loan.

Certainly, not everyone wants to or should own a home. Home ownership involves substantial commitment and responsibility. People whose work requires frequent moves or whose financial position is uncertain particularly benefit from renting. Renting also provides more leisure time by freeing tenants from management and maintenance.

Those who choose home ownership over renting must evaluate many factors before they decide to purchase property. And the purchasing decision must be weighed carefully in light of each individual's financial circumstances.

The decision to buy or to rent property involves considering

■ how long a person wants to live in a particular area,
■ a person's financial situation,
■ housing affordability,
■ current mortgage interest rates,
■ tax consequences of owning versus renting property, and
■ what might happen to home prices and tax laws in the future.

Mortgage Terms

Mortgage terms and payment plans are two of the biggest factors when deciding whether to own or rent a home. Although many loan programs of the past are either not offered or offered only to highly qualified borrowers, liberalized mortgages are still available to those who qualify. For example, the Federal Housing Administration (FHA) and the Department of Veterans Affairs (VA) have programs with low down payments and lower credit score requirements.

Ownership Expenses and Ability to Pay

Home ownership involves many expenses, including utilities, such as electricity, natural gas, and water, trash removal, sewer charges, and maintenance and repairs. Owners also must pay real estate taxes, buy property insurance, and repay the mortgage loan with interest. This is what lenders refer to as **PITI (principal, interest, taxes, and insurance)**; those expenses that comprise a monthly payment.

To determine whether a prospective buyer can afford a certain purchase, most lenders use automated underwriting and credit scoring. In the past, the formula for homebuyers who were able to provide at least 10 percent of the purchase price as a down payment was that the monthly cost of buying and maintaining a home—mortgage payments, both principal and interest, plus taxes and insurance impounds—could not exceed 28 percent of gross (i.e., pretax monthly income). The payments on all debts—normally including long-term debt such as car payments, student loans, or other mortgages—could not exceed 36 percent of monthly income. Expenses such as insurance premiums, utilities, and routine medical care were not included in the 36 percent figure but were considered to be covered by the remaining 64 percent of the buyer's monthly income. These formulas may vary, however, depending on the type of loan program and the borrower's earnings, credit history, number of dependents, and other factors. But today, credit scores play a key role when lending institutions decide whether to lend money. (Note that these financial qualification ratios are true for most Fannie Mae and Freddie Mac conforming mortgages, but loans with more liberal ratios are available.)

■ **FOR EXAMPLE** Prospective homebuyers want to know how much house they can afford to buy. The buyers have a gross monthly income of $5,000. The buyers' allowable housing expense may be calculated as follows:

$5,000 gross monthly income × 28% = $1,400 total housing expense allowed
$5,000 gross monthly income × 36% = $1,800 total housing and other debt expense allowed

These formulas allow for other debts of 8 percent of gross monthly income—the difference between the 36 percent and 28 percent figures. If actual debts exceed the amount allowed and the borrowers are unable to reduce them, the monthly payment must be lowered proportionately because the debts and housing payment combined cannot exceed 36 percent of gross monthly income. However, lower debts would not result in a higher allowable housing payment; rather, it would be considered a factor for approval.

Investment Considerations

Purchasing a home offers several financial advantages to a buyer. First, if the property's value increases, a sale might bring in more money than the owner paid—a long-term gain. Second, as the total mortgage debt is reduced through monthly payments, the owner's actual ownership interest in the property increases. A tenant accumulates a good credit rating by paying rent on time; a homeowner's mortgage payments build personal net worth. The third financial advantage of home ownership is the tax deduction available to homeowners but not to renters.

Tax Benefits

To encourage home ownership, the federal government allows homeowners certain income tax advantages. Homeowners may deduct from their income some or all of the mortgage interest paid, as well as real estate taxes and certain other

---

Memory Tip

The basic costs of owning a home—mortgage **P**rincipal, **I**nterest, **T**axes, and **I**nsurance can be remembered by the acronym **PITI**.

expenses. Tax considerations may be an important part of any decision to purchase a home.

In the late 1990s, the federal government enacted several federal tax reforms that significantly changed the importance of tax considerations for most homesellers. For instance, $500,000 is now excluded from capital gains tax for profits on the sale of a principal residence by married taxpayers who file jointly. Taxpayers who file singly are entitled to a $250,000 exclusion. The exemption may be used repeatedly, as long as the homeowners have both owned and occupied the property as their residence for at least two of the past five years.

First-time homebuyers may make penalty-free withdrawals from their tax-deferred individual retirement accounts (IRAs) for down payments on their homes. However, these withdrawals are still subject to income tax. The limit on such withdrawals is $10,000 and must be spent entirely within 120 days on a down payment to avoid any penalty.

In short, the changes in tax laws have generally benefited home ownership, which is good news for homeowners and real estate licensees.

Tax deductions   Homeowners may deduct from their gross income

■ mortgage *interest* payments on first and second homes (for mortgage balances below $1 million, or $500,000 if married filing separately),
■ real estate taxes (but *not* interest paid on overdue taxes),
■ certain loan origination fees,
■ loan discount points (whether paid by the buyer or the seller), and
■ loan prepayment penalties.

IN PRACTICE   Note that appraisal fees, notary fees, preparation costs, mortgage insurance premiums, and VA funding fees are not interest but are part of the cost of acquiring a home. When the home is sold at a later date, these charges can be figured into the cost *basis*. Points are deductible in the year of a house purchase if certain criteria are met. Points are deducted over the life of the loan for a refinance. Note that real estate licensees should not provide tax advice and that homeowners should consult with accountants or attorneys about home ownership tax deductions. The rules are complicated and constantly changing.

■ HOMEOWNERS' INSURANCE

A home is usually the biggest purchase many people ever make. Most homeowners see the importance of protecting their investment by insuring it. Lenders usually require that a homeowner obtain insurance when the loan is secured by the property. While owners can purchase individual policies that insure against destruction of property by fire or windstorm, injury to others, and theft of personal property, most buy a combined **homeowners' insurance policy** to cover all these risks.

Coverage and Claims

The most common homeowners' policy is called a *basic form*. The basic form provides property coverage against

- fire and lightning,
- glass breakage,
- windstorm and hail,
- explosion,
- riot and civil commotion,
- damage by aircraft,
- damage from vehicles,
- damage from smoke,
- vandalism and malicious mischief,
- theft, and
- loss of property removed from the premises when it is endangered by fire or other perils.

A *broad-form* policy is also available. Broad-form homeowners' insurance covers

- falling objects;
- damage due to the weight of ice, snow, or sleet;
- collapse of all or part of the building;
- bursting, cracking, burning, or bulging of a steam or water heating system or of appliances used to heat water;
- accidental discharge, leakage, or overflow of water or steam from within a plumbing, heating, or air-conditioning system;
- freezing of plumbing, heating, and air-conditioning systems and domestic appliances; and
- damage to electrical appliances, devices, fixtures, and wiring from short circuits or other accidentally generated currents.

Further insurance is available from policies that cover almost all possible perils. Special apartment and condominium policies generally provide fire and windstorm, theft, and public **liability coverage** for injuries or losses sustained within the unit. However, they usually do not cover losses or damages to the structure. The basic structure is insured by either the landlord or the condominium owners' association.

Most homeowners' insurance policies contain a **coinsurance clause**. This provision usually requires that the owner maintain insurance equal to a specified percentage (usually 80 percent) of the **replacement cost** of the dwelling (not including the price of the land). An owner who has this type of policy may make a claim for the full cost of the repair or replacement of the damaged property without deduction for depreciation or annual wear and tear.

■ **FOR EXAMPLE** A homeowners' insurance policy is for 80 percent of the replacement cost of the home, or $80,000. The home is valued at $100,000, and the land is valued at $40,000. The homeowner sustains $30,000 in fire damage to the house. The homeowner can make a claim for the full cost of the repair or replacement of the damaged property without a deduction for depreciation. However, if the owner has insurance of only $70,000, the claim will be handled in one of two ways. The owner will receive either actual cash value (replacement cost of $30,000 less depreciation cost of say $3,000, or $27,000), or the claim will be prorated by dividing the percentage of replacement cost actually covered (0.70) by the policy minimum coverage requirement (0.80). So, 0.70 divided by 0.80 equals 0.875, and $30,000 multiplied by 0.875 equals $26,250.

Comprehensive Loss Underwriting Exchange

Comprehensive Loss Underwriting Exchange (CLUE) is a database of consumer claims history that enables insurance companies to access prior claims information in the underwriting and rating process. The database contains up to five years of personal property claims history. The reports include policy information such as name, date of birth, policy number, and claim information date (date and type of loss, amounts paid, and description of property covered).

IN PRACTICE   Water-related problems have emerged in some properties over time. In particular, significant problems can occur with synthetic stucco exterior finishes and mold. The exterior insulating finishing system (EIFS) is a highly effective moisture barrier that also tends to seal in moisture—trapping water in the home's walls and resulting in massive wood rot. Frequently, the effects of the rotting cannot be seen until the damage is extensive and sometimes irreparable. Homeowners who suspect that EIFS was used on their home and is causing damage should have the property inspected. Some insurance companies refuse to cover homes with EIFS exteriors, and class action lawsuits have been brought against builders by distressed homeowners.

■ FEDERAL FLOOD INSURANCE PROGRAM

The National Flood Insurance Act of 1968 was enacted by Congress to help owners of property in flood-prone areas by subsidizing flood insurance and by taking land-use and land-control measures to improve future management for floodplain areas. The Federal Emergency Management Agency (FEMA) administers the flood program. The Army Corps of Engineers has prepared maps that identify specific flood-prone areas throughout the country. To finance property with federal or federally related mortgage loans, owners in flood-prone areas must obtain flood insurance.

In designated areas, flood insurance is required on all types of buildings—residential, commercial, industrial, and agricultural—for either the value of the property or the amount of the mortgage loan, subject to the maximum limits available. Policies are written annually and can be purchased from any licensed property insurance broker, the National Flood Insurance Program (NFIP), or the designated servicing companies in each state. However, a borrower who can produce a survey showing that the lowest part of the building is located above the 100-year flood mark may be exempted from the flood insurance requirement, even if the property is in a flood-prone area.

Flood Insurance: What's Covered and What's Not

FEMA defines a flood as "a general and temporary condition of partial or complete inundation of two or more acres of normally dry land or two or more properties from

■ an overflow of inland or tidal waves;
■ an unusual and rapid accumulation or runoff of surface waters;
■ mudflows or mudslides on the surface of normally dry land; or
■ the collapse of land along the shore of a body of water (under certain conditions)."

The physical damage to a building or personal property "directly" caused by a flood is covered by flood insurance policies. For example, damage from sewer backups is covered if it results directly from flooding. Flood policies exclude coverage for losses such as swimming pools, cars, money, animals, groundcover, or underground systems.

Policies are of two types: replacement cost value (RCV) or actual cost value (ACV). Deductibles and premiums vary accordingly.

IN PRACTICE   Massive losses in the NFIP due to the Mississippi floods in 1993 caused Congress to pass laws that greatly increase the number of properties that are required to be covered by the NFIP. This requirement results not only in higher expenses for the buyer but also negatively affects property values. Agents should pay attention to what property is in a flood zone and communicate that to potential buyers.

■ KEY POINT REVIEW

Types of housing include the following:

■ Single-family homes
■ Apartment complexes
■ Condominiums
■ Cooperatives
■ Planned unit developments (PUDs)
■ Mixed-use developments (MUDs)
■ Modular homes (prefabricated homes)
■ Manufactured housing (mobile homes)
■ Time-shares

Housing affordability has been aided by creative financing, low interest loans, adjustable-rate loans, interest-only loans, and low-down-payment loans sponsored by the **Federal Housing Administration (FHA)** and the **Department of Veterans Affairs (VA)**.

The decision to rent or buy is influenced by the following:

- Length of time the individual will reside in the area
- Individual's financial situation
- Housing **affordability**
- Current **mortgage interest rates**
- **Tax consequences** of owning versus renting property
- What may happen to home prices and tax laws in the future

PITI is an acronym for the following:

- **P**rincipal
- **I**nterest
- **T**axes
- **I**nsurance

Investment considerations include the following:

- **Appreciation** in the value of the property
- **Equity increase** with an **amortized** loan as the principal is paid
- **Tax deductions**
- **Capital gains taxation exclusion** of $250,000 or $500,000 profit on sale of principal residence, if owned and occupied at least two of the past five years
- Penalty-free withdrawals from an **individual retirement account (IRA)** for a down payment on a home within certain limits

A **homeowners' insurance policy** usually covers the following:

- Fire and lightning, windstorm and hail, and glass breakage
- Explosion, riot, and civil commotion
- Damage by aircraft, vehicles, and smoke
- Vandalism, malicious mischief, and theft
- Loss of property removed from the premises when it is endangered by fire or other perils

The **homeowners' insurance broad-form policy** covers

- falling objects and damage due to weight of ice, snow, or sleet;
- collapse of all or part of the building;
- bursting, cracking, burning, or bulging of steam or water heating system or appliances used to heat water;
- accidental discharge, leakage, or overflow of water or steam from within a plumbing, heating, or air-conditioning system;
- freezing of plumbing, heating, and air-conditioning systems and domestic appliances; and
- damage to electrical appliances, devices, fixtures, and wiring from short circuits or other accidentally generated currents.

A **coinsurance clause**

- requires the homeowner to maintain insurance equal to at least 80 percent of replacement cost of the dwelling for full replacement on loss; or
- if not, the loss will be settled for **actual cash value** or a **prorated amount**.

Comprehensive Loss Underwriting Exchange (CLUE) is a database of consumer insurance claim history.

The **National Flood Insurance Act of 1968**

■ subsidizes flood insurance, and
■ is administered by the **Federal Emergency Management Agency (FEMA)**.

■ RELATED WEB SITES

Federal Emergency Management Agency: *www.fema.gov*
U.S Department of Housing and Urban Development: *www.hud.gov*
U.S. Department of Veterans Affairs: *www.va.gov*

CHAPTER 3 QUIZ

1. Which of the following is *NOT* a cost or expense of owning a home?

   a. Interest paid on borrowed capital
   b. Homeowners' insurance
   c. Maintenance and repairs
   d. Taxes on personal property

2. Homeowners may deduct all of the following expenses when preparing their income tax return *EXCEPT*

   a. real estate taxes.
   b. mortgage interest on a first home.
   c. mortgage interest on a second home.
   d. mortgage interest on a third home.

3. A building that is remodeled into residential units and is no longer used for the purpose for which it was originally built is an example of a(n)

   a. converted-use property.
   b. urban homesteading.
   c. planned unit development.
   d. modular home.

4. A high-rise development that includes office space, stores, theaters, and apartment units is an example of which of the following?

   a. Planned unit development
   b. Mixed-use development
   c. Proprietary lease properties
   d. Special cluster zoning

5. Each room of a house was preassembled at a factory, driven to the building site on a truck, and then lowered onto its foundation by a crane. Later, workers finished the structure and connected plumbing and wiring before the owners moved in. Which term *BEST* describes this type of home?

   a. Mobile
   b. Modular
   c. Manufactured
   d. Converted

6. Five years ago, a woman bought a home for $250,000. Home values in her area have improved, and the current market value of her house has increased by 15 percent. If she has $95,875 left to pay on her mortgage loan, what is her current equity in her home?

   a. $138,712
   b. $154,125
   c. $191,625
   d. $250,000

7. For which of the following risks would a homeowner have to purchase a special policy in addition to a typical basic or broad-form homeowners' insurance policy?

   a. The cost of medical expenses for a person injured in the policyholder's home
   b. Theft
   c. Vandalism
   d. Flood damage

8. A man wants to buy his first home but doesn't know how much he can afford to pay. He has a gross monthly income of $3,000. According to the traditional lender's rule of thumb formula, what is the total housing expense (principal, interest, taxes, and insurance) he can bear?

   a. $1,080
   b. $840
   c. $648
   d. $1,152

9. A married couple bought their house ten years ago for $150,000. Last week, they sold their home for $225,500. Based on these facts, how much capital gains tax will the couple have to pay this year?

   a. None
   b. $7,550
   c. $11,325
   d. $75,500

10. Which of the following *BEST* expresses the concept of equity?

    a. Current market value minus capital gain
    b. Current market value minus property debt
    c. Current market value minus cost of land
    d. Replacement cost minus depreciation

11. A couple bought a house in 1968 (when they were 21 years old) for $25,000 and have lived in it ever since. Today, the neighborhood is very fashionable, and the house sells for $450,000. How much of the gain is taxable on the couple's joint return this year?
    a. $25,000
    b. All
    c. None
    d. $637,000

12. A married couple files a joint income tax return and has lived in their home for 20 years. A single homeowner has lived in a home for five years. A father and daughter bought their home together last year. Based on these facts, which statement is TRUE if all three homes are sold today?
    a. All of these homeowners qualify for a $500,000 exclusion from capital gains taxation on the transactions.
    b. A $500,000 exclusion applies to the couple as well as to the father and daughter; a $250,000 exclusion applies to the single homeowner.
    c. A $500,000 exclusion applies to the married couple; a $250,000 exclusion applies to the single homeowner; and no exclusion applies to the father and daughter.
    d. Only the married couple qualifies for any exclusion from capital gains taxation.

13. Theft, smoke damage, and damage from fire are covered under which type of homeowners' insurance policy?
    a. Basic form
    b. Broad form
    c. Coinsurance
    d. National Flood Insurance Program policies

14. A community that merges housing, recreation, and commercial units into one self-contained development is called a
    a. MUD.
    b. PUD.
    c. cooperative.
    d. condominium.

15. All of the following damages would be covered by a basic-form homeowners' insurance policy, EXCEPT
    a. glass breakage.
    b. riot.
    c. frozen pipes.
    d. vandalism.

16. Efforts to increase home ownership include all the following EXCEPT
    a. requiring lower down payments.
    b. offering adjustable-rate mortgages.
    c. penalizing first-time homebuyers for using funds from IRAs.
    d. lowering closing costs for first-time homebuyers.

17. The real cost of owning a home includes certain costs/expenses that many people overlook. Which of the following is NOT such a cost/expense of home ownership?
    a. Income lost on cash invested in the home
    b. Interest paid on borrowed capital
    c. Maintenance and repair expenses
    d. Personal property taxes

18. Damage from which of the following is NOT covered in a basic homeowners' policy?
    a. Fire and lightning
    b. Explosion
    c. Windstorm and hail
    d. Flood

19. Most homeowners' insurance policies contain which clause?
    a. Property improvement clause
    b. Coinsurance clause
    c. Co-ownership clause
    d. Property devaluation clause

20. That portion of the value of an owners' property that exceeds the amount of their mortgage debt is called
    a. equality.
    b. escrow.
    c. surplus.
    d. equity.

CHAPTER 4

Agency

When you have finished reading this chapter, you should be able to

- **identify** the various types of agency relationships common in the real estate profession and the characteristics of each;

- **describe** the fiduciary duties involved in an agency relationship;

- **explain** the process by which agency is created and terminated and the role of disclosure in agency relationships;

- **distinguish** the duties owed by an agent to clients from those owed to customers; and

- **define** the following *key terms*:

agency	express agreement	listing agreement
agent	fiduciary	negligent
buyer's agent	fiduciary relationship	misrepresentation
client	fraud	nonagent
customer	general agent	principal
designated agent	implied agency	puffing
designated agency	implied agreement	special agent
dual agency	latent defect	universal agent
express agency	law of agency	

■ INTRODUCTION TO REAL ESTATE AGENCY

The relationship between a real estate licensee and the parties involved in a real estate transaction is not a simple one. In addition to the parties' assumptions and expectations, the licensee is subject to a wide range of legal and ethical requirements designed to protect the seller, the buyer, and the transaction itself. **Agency** is the word used to describe this special relationship. Agency is governed by two kinds of law: *common law*, the rules of a society established by tradition and court decisions; and *statutory law*, the laws, rules, and regulations enacted by legislatures and other governing bodies.

History of Agency

The fundamentals of agency law have remained largely unchanged for hundreds of years. However, the application of law has changed dramatically, particularly in residential transactions, especially in recent years. As states enact laws that define and govern the broker-client relationship, brokers are reevaluating their services. They must determine whether they will represent the seller, the buyer, or both (if that is permitted by state law) in a transaction. Where state laws permit, an increasing number of brokers are choosing to represent buyers exclusively. They also must decide how they will cooperate with other brokers, depending on which party the broker represents.

Even as the laws change, the underlying assumptions that govern the agency relationship remain intact. The principal-agent relationship evolved from the master-servant relationship in English common law. The loyalty replaced the servant's personal interests as well as any loyalty the servant might owe to others. In today's agency relationship, the agent owes the principal similar loyalty. Just as masters used the services of servants to accomplish what they could not or did not want to do for themselves, principals use the services of agents.

■ LAW OF AGENCY

The **law of agency** defines the rights and duties of the parties in a real estate transaction—the principal, the agent, and the customer. In real estate transactions, contract law and real estate licensing laws—in addition to the law of agency—interpret the relationship between licensees and their clients. The law of agency is a common-law concept (law from the judgments and decrees of courts as opposed to the legislature); it is being widely replaced by state statute.

Definitions

Legally, *agency* refers to a strict, defined legal relationship. In the case of real estate, the relationship is between buyers and sellers or between landlords and tenants. In the law of agency, the body of law that governs these relationships, the following terms have specific definitions:

■ **Agent**—the individual who is authorized and consents to represent the interests of another person. In the real estate business, a firm's broker is the agent and shares this responsibility with the licensees who work for the firm.

An **agent** is a person authorized to act on behalf of the client.

- **Principal**—the individual who hires the agent and delegates to that agent the responsibility of representing the principal's interests. In the real estate business, the principal is the buyer or seller or the landlord or tenant.
- **Agency**—the fiduciary relationship between the principal and the agent wherein the agent is authorized to represent the principal in a certain transaction
- **Fiduciary**—the relationship in which the agent is held in a position of special trust and confidence by the principal
- **Client**—the principal
- **Customer**—the third party or nonrepresented consumer for whom some level of service is provided and who is entitled to fairness and honesty
- **Nonagent**—(also referred to as a *facilitator*, *intermediary*, *transactional broker*, *transactional coordinator*, or *contract broker*) a middleman between a buyer and a seller (or a landlord and a tenant), who assists one or both parties with the transaction without representing either party's interests. Nonagents are often subject to specific statutory responsibilities. Licensees may be known as *nonagents* with a customer relationship.

IN PRACTICE   The general discussion in this chapter is limited to the concepts and principles that govern traditional common-law agency relationships. In many states, agency reform legislation that includes language superseding the common law of agency has been passed, drafted, or is under consideration.

It should be noted, however, that many agency statutes make the common-law duties a matter of statutory law rather than (or in addition to) creating totally new legal relationships. While this chapter provides an overview of current agency legislation, a licensee should be familiar with the specific terms of any agency statute adopted by the relevant state legislature.

There is a distinction between the level of services that an agent provides to a *client* and those services that the agent provides to a *customer*. The *client* is the principal to whom the agent gives advice and counsel. The agent is entrusted with certain *confidential information* and has *fiduciary responsibilities* (discussed in greater detail later in this chapter) to the principal. In contrast, the *customer* is entitled to factual information and fair and honest dealings as a consumer but does not receive advice and counsel or confidential information about the principal. Any third party is a customer. The agent works *for* the principal and *with* the customer. Essentially, the agent supports and defends the principal's interests, not the customer's.

The relationship between the principal and agent must be *consensual*—that is, the principal *delegates* authority, and the agent *consents* to act. The parties must agree to form the relationship.

Just as the agent owes certain duties to the principal, the principal has responsibilities toward the agent. The principal's primary duties are to comply with the agency agreement and cooperate with the agent—that is, the principal must not hinder the agent and must deal with the agent in good faith. The principal also must compensate the agent according to the terms of the agency agreement.

■ CREATION OF AGENCY

An agency relationship may be created with a formal agreement between the parties, an **express agency**, or it may result from the parties' behavior, an **implied agency**.

Express agency   The principal and agent may enter into a contract, or an **express agreement**, in which the parties formally express their intention to establish an agency and state its terms and conditions. The agreement may be either oral or written. An agency relationship between a seller and a broker is generally created by a written employment contract, commonly referred to as a **listing agreement**, which authorizes the broker to find a buyer or a tenant for the owner's property. Although a written listing agreement is usually preferred, some states consider an oral agreement binding. An express agency relationship between a buyer and a broker is created by a buyer agency agreement. Similar to a listing agreement, it stipulates the activities and responsibilities the buyer expects from the broker in finding the appropriate property for purchase or rent.

Implied agency   An agency may also be created by **implied agreement**. This occurs when the actions of the parties indicate that they have mutually consented to an agency. A licensee acts on behalf of another party as that party's agent. Even though the licensee may not have consciously planned to create an agency relationship; nonetheless, the parties can create one *unintentionally, inadvertently,* or *accidentally* by their actions.

■ **FOR EXAMPLE**   Prospective buyers enter a real estate office asking to see a property listed with another brokerage. A real estate salesperson immediately calls the sellers' agent and makes an appointment to show the property. Without having the customers sign a written agency agreement, the salesperson drives them to the house. Through the actions of the salesperson, the customers think they are being represented.

Even though licensees may be required to disclose their agency status, consumers often find it difficult to understand the complexities of the law of agency. Buyers can easily assume that when they contact a real estate salesperson in order to be shown a property, the real estate salesperson becomes their agent, even though, under a listing contract, the real estate salesperson may legally represent the seller. An implied agency with the buyer can result if the words and conduct of the salesperson do not dispel this assumption. Otherwise, one agency relationship is created in conflict with another. Note that some state laws prohibit the creation of agency by implied actions or conduct.

Compensation   *The source of compensation does not determine agency.* An agent does not necessarily represent the person who pays the agent's commission. In fact, agency can exist even if no fee is involved (called a *gratuitous agency*). For instance, a seller might agree to pay a commission to the buyer's agent, even though the agent is representing the buyer. The written agency agreement should state how the agent is being compensated and explain all the alternatives available.

Fiduciary Responsibilities

The agency agreement usually authorizes the broker to act on the principal's behalf. The agent's **fiduciary relationship** of trust and confidence means that the real estate broker owes the principal certain duties. These duties are not simply moral or ethical, they are the law—the common law of agency or the statutory law governing real estate transactions. Under the common law of agency, an agent owes the principal the six duties of *care, obedience, loyalty, disclosure, accounting,* and *confidentiality.* Table 4.1 illustrates the agent's obligations to the buyer.

TABLE 4.1

Obligations to Buyer

Seller's Agent (buyer is customer)	Buyer's Agent (buyer is client or principal)
Responsibilities	
Be honest with buyer but responsible to seller, including duty of skill and care to promote and safeguard seller's best interests	Be fair with seller but responsible to buyer, including duty of skill and care to promote and safeguard buyer's best interests
Earnest Money Deposit	
Collect amount sufficient to protect seller	Suggest substantial deposit indicating sincerity in offer; put money in interest-bearing account if required by state law; suggest that forfeiture of earnest money be sole remedy if buyer defaults
Seller Financing	
Can discuss but should not encourage financing terms and contract provisions unfavorable to seller, such as (1) no due-on-sale clause, (2) no deficiency judgment (nonrecourse), (3) unsecured note. If a corporate buyer, suggest seller require personal guaranty	Suggest terms in best interests of buyer, such as low down payment, deferred interest, long maturity dates, no due-on-sale clause, long grace period, nonrecourse
Property Condition	
Require seller to fill out all disclosure forms	Require that seller sign property condition statement and confirm representations of condition; require soil and termite inspections, if appropriate; look for negative features and use them to negotiate better price and terms
Documents	
Give buyer a copy of important documents, such as mortgage to be assumed, declaration of restrictions, title report, condominium bylaws, house rules	Research and explain significant portions of important documents affecting transaction, such as prepayment penalties, subordination, right of first refusal; refer buyer to expert advisers when appropriate
Negotiation	
Use negotiating strategy and bargaining talents in seller's best interests	Use negotiating strategy and bargaining talents in buyer's best interests
Showing	
Show buyer properties in which broker's commission is protected, such as in-house or MLS-listed properties. Pick best times to show properties. Emphasize attributes and amenities	Search for best properties for buyer to inspect, widening marketplace to for-sale-by-owner properties, lender-owned (REO) properties, probate sales, unlisted properties. View properties at different times to find negative features, such as evening noise, afternoon sun, traffic congestion

TABLE   4.1

Obligations to Buyer (Continued)

Seller's Agent (buyer is customer)	Buyer's Agent (buyer is client or principal)
Property Goals	
Be more concerned with sale of seller's property that fits buyer's stated objectives	Counsel buyer as to developing accurate objectives; may find that buyer who wants apartment building might be better off with duplex at half the price or that buyer looking for vacant lot would benefit more from investment in improved property
Offers	
Transmit all offers to seller. Consult with seller about possible action steps (e.g., accept offer, counteroffer, reject offer)	Help buyer prepare strongest offer
Possession Dates	
Consider best date for seller in terms of moving out, notice to existing tenants, impact on insurance, risk of loss provision	Consider best date for buyer in terms of moving in, storage, favorable risk of loss provision if fire destroys property before closing
Default	
Discuss remedies upon default by either party. Point out to seller any attempt by buyer to limit liability (nonrecourse, deposit money is sole liquidated damages)	Suggest seller's remedy be limited to retention of deposit money; consider having seller pay buyer's expenses and cancellation charges if seller defaults
Efficiency	
As listing broker, expend much time and effort in helping seller sell property	Broker's role is to assist buyer in locating and acquiring best property, not to sell buyer a particular property
Negotiation	
Use negotiating strategy and bargaining talents in seller's best interests	Use negotiating strategy and bargaining talents in buyer's best interests
Appraisal	
Unless asked, no duty to disclose low appraisal or fact broker sold similar unit yesterday for $10,000 less	Suggest independent appraisal be used to negotiate lower price offer; review seller's comparables from buyer's perspective

Care Agents must exercise a reasonable degree of care while transacting the business entrusted to them by principals. Principals expect the agent's skill and expertise in real estate matters to be superior to that of the average person. The most fundamental way in which the agent exercises care is to use that skill and knowledge on the principal's behalf. The agent should know all facts pertinent to the principal's affairs, such as the physical characteristics of the property being transferred and the type of financing being used.

If the agent represents the seller, care and skill include helping the seller arrive at an appropriate and realistic listing price, discovering and disclosing facts that affect the seller, and properly presenting the contracts that the seller signs. It also means making reasonable efforts to market the property, such as advertising and holding open houses, and helping the seller evaluate the terms and conditions of offers to purchase.

An agent who represents the buyer is expected to help the buyer locate suitable property and evaluate property values, neighborhood and property conditions, financing alternatives, and offers and counteroffers with the buyer's interest in mind.

An agent who does not make a reasonable effort to properly represent the interests of the principal may be found negligent by a court of law. The agent is liable to the principal for any loss resulting from the agent's negligence or carelessness.

IN PRACTICE   Because real estate licensees have, under the law, enormous exposure to liability, some licensees purchase what is known as *errors and omissions* (E&O) *insurance.* Similar to malpractice insurance in the medical and legal fields, E&O policies cover liability for errors and negligence in the listing and selling activities of a real estate licensee. Individual salespersons might also be insured. Licensing laws in several states now require E&O insurance for brokers and, in some cases, for individual salespersons as well. However, no insurance policy will protect a licensee from a lawsuit or prosecution arising from criminal acts. Insurance companies normally exclude coverage for violation of civil rights and antitrust laws as well.

Obedience   The fiduciary relationship obligates the agent to act in good faith at all times, obeying the principal's legal instructions in accordance with the contract.

However, that obedience is not absolute. The agent may not obey instructions that are unlawful or unethical. On the other hand, an agent who exceeds the authority assigned in the contract will be liable for any losses that the principal suffers as a result.

Loyalty   The duty of loyalty requires that the agent place the principal's interests above those of all others, including the agent's own self-interest. The agent must be particularly sensitive to any possible conflicts of interest. Because the agent may not act out of self-interest, the negotiation of a sales contract must be conducted without regard to how much the agent will earn in commission. All states forbid agents to buy property listed with them for their own accounts or for accounts in which they have a personal interest without first disclosing that interest and receiving the principal's consent. Neither real estate brokers nor real estate salespeople may sell property in which they have a personal interest without informing the purchaser of that interest.

Disclosure   It is the agent's duty to keep the principal informed of all facts or information that might affect a transaction. Duty of disclosure includes relevant information or *material facts* that the agent *knows* or *should have known.*

The real estate agent is obligated to discover facts that a reasonable person would feel are important in choosing a course of action, regardless of whether those facts are favorable or unfavorable to the principal's position. The agent may be held liable for damages for failing to disclose such information; for example,

- once an offer is accepted, further offers unless instructed in writing not to;
- all offers, unless directed by the seller to not present an offer after one has been accepted;

Memory Tip

The six common-law fiduciary duties:
Care
Obedience
Loyalty
Disclosure
Accounting
Confidentiality

- the identity of the prospective purchasers, which may include any relationships they might have with the agent or the agent has to them (such as when the licensee or a relative is a purchaser);
- the purchaser's ability to complete the sale or offer a higher price;
- any interest the agent has in the buyer (such as the broker's agreement to manage the property after it is purchased);
- the buyer's intention to resell the property for a profit; and
- an incorrect market value of the property.

A seller's real estate agent is also expected (and required under many states' laws) to disclose information about known material defects in the property to prospective buyers. While this seems a violation of the agent's duty of total allegiance to the seller, this requirement falls under the broader duty to serve the general public and is in the agent's long-term best interest.

In turn, the buyer's agent must disclose deficiencies of a property and the sales contract provisions and financing that may affect the buyer's decision to purchase. The buyer's agent would suggest the lowest price the buyer should pay based on comparable values, regardless of the listing price. The agent would also disclose how long a property has been listed or why the owner is selling, because such information would affect the buyer's ability to negotiate the lowest purchase price. If the agent represents the seller, of course, disclosure of any of this information would violate the agent's fiduciary duty to the seller.

IN PRACTICE Selling a property "as is" does not negate provisions already in the contract. If sellers truly mean "as is," they amend any printed provisions existing in the contract that relate to the condition of systems and appliances.

Accounting The agent must be able to report the status of all funds received from or on behalf of the principal. Most state laws require that a real estate licensee give accurate copies of all documents to all parties affected by them and keep copies on file for a specified period. Most license laws also require monies to be deposited immediately, or within a statutory time frame. Commingling client monies with personal or general business funds is strictly illegal. *Conversion* is the illegal use of such entrusted money.

Confidentiality Confidentiality is a key element of fiduciary duties. An agent may not disclose the principal's financial condition. If the principal is the seller, the agent may not reveal such things as willingness to accept less than the listing price or urgency to sell, unless the principal has authorized the disclosure. If the principal is the buyer, the agent may not disclose that the buyer is willing to pay a higher price, is under a tight moving schedule, or other facts that might affect the principal's bargaining position. Confidentiality can change when the business relationship changes, such as when a seller's agent becomes a disclosed dual agent, because the broker is now also representing the buyer.

Under the laws of most states, the agent must disclose material facts about the condition of the property itself. Some states, however, permit a seller disclaimer—essentially a statement that the property is sold as is, with no promises regarding its quality. Note, however, that even with this disclaimer, sellers are still required to disclose known problems with the property if they affect the health and well-being of the occupants.

It is important to remember that anything a real estate agent learns about a client must remain confidential forever. In most states, confidentiality terminates upon completion, expiration, or termination of the agency relationship. Check your state's laws for guidance in dealing with confidentiality issues.

Termination of Agency

An agency may be terminated for any of the following reasons:

- *Completion, performance, or fulfillment* of the purpose for which the agency was created
- *Death or incapacity* of either party
- *Destruction or condemnation* of the property
- *Expiration* of the terms of the agency
- *Mutual agreement* by all parties to cancel the contract
- *Breach* by one of the parties
- By *operation of law*, as in bankruptcy of the principal (bankruptcy terminates the agency contract and title to the property transfers to a court-appointed receiver)

■ TYPES OF AGENCY RELATIONSHIPS

An agent's empowerment to represent the principal depends solely on the authorization to do so.

A **universal agent** is a person empowered to do *anything* the principal could do personally. The universal agent's authority to act on behalf of the principal is virtually unlimited. A real estate licensee typically does not have this scope of authority in a real estate transaction.

A **general agent** may represent the principal in a broad range of matters related to a *particular business or activity*. The general agent may, for example, bind the principal to any contract within the scope of the agent's authority. A property manager is typically a general agent for the owner. Most real estate salespeople are general agents of their broker.

A **general agent** represents the principal *generally*; a **special agent** represents the principal only for *special occasions*, such as the sale of a house.

A **special agent**, or *limited agent*, is authorized to represent the principal in *one specific act or business transaction only*. A real estate broker is usually a special agent. If hired by a seller, the broker is limited to finding a ready, willing, and able buyer for the property. A special agent for a buyer would have the limited responsibility of finding a property that fits the buyer's criteria. As a special agent, the real estate broker may not bind the principal to any contract.

■ **FOR EXAMPLE**   You are very busy with an important project, so you give your colleague $5 and ask him to buy your lunch. Your colleague is your *general agent.* You have limited your colleague's scope of activity to a particular business (buying your lunch) and established the amount that may be spent (up to $5). Still, your colleague has broad discretion in selecting what you will eat and where to buy it. However, if you had told your colleague, "Please buy me a chef's salad at the corner café," you would have further limited his authority to a very specific task. Your colleague, therefore, would have been your *special agent.*

Finally, a **designated agent,** or designated representative, is a person authorized by the real estate broker to act as the agent of a specific principal. A designated agent is the only agent in the company who has a fiduciary responsibility toward the principal. When one licensee in the company is a designated agent, the others are free to act as agents for the other party in a transaction. Therefore, two licensees from the same real estate company might end up representing opposite sides in a property sale. The real estate broker is often put in the position of being a dual agent in designated agency situations. Disclosure of such status is required. The availability of designated agency varies from state to state.

Single Agency

In single agency, the agent represents only one party in any single transaction. The real estate agent must provide either fiduciary or statutory duties exclusively to one principal within the transaction (who may be *either* the buyer or the seller or the landlord or the tenant). The customer is the party not represented by the agent. (See Figure 4.1.)

While a single agency broker may represent both sellers and buyers, that broker cannot represent both the buyer and the seller in the same transaction and remain a single agent. This avoids conflicts and results in client-based service and loyalty to only one principal. On the other hand, it traditionally rules out the sale of in-house listings to prospective buyers.

Seller Representation

If a seller enters a listing agreement with a broker to market the seller's real estate, the broker becomes an *agent* of the seller; the seller is the *principal*, the broker's *client*. The broker is obligated to deal fairly with all parties in the transaction and within the licensing law. The broker is strictly accountable to the principal. The listing contract usually authorizes the broker to use licensees employed by the broker, as well as the services of other cooperating brokers in marketing the seller's real estate.

FIGURE 4.1

Single Agency

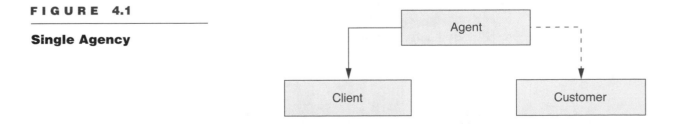

The relationship of a salesperson or an associate broker to an employing broker is also an agency. These licensees are thus agents of the broker and owe the same fiduciary duties as the broker to the principal.

Buyer Representation

A buyer who contracts with a broker to locate property and represent the buyer's interests in a transaction is the *principal*—the broker's client. The broker, as *agent*, is strictly accountable to the buyer.

In the past, it was simple: real estate brokers always represented sellers, and buyers were expected to look out for themselves. Today most residential brokers and salespeople are discovering the opportunities of buyer representation, or of being a **buyer's agent**. Real estate commissions or boards across the country have developed rules and procedures to regulate such buyer's agents. Local real estate associations have developed agency representation forms and other materials for buyer's agents to use. Professional organizations offer assistance, certification, training, and networking opportunities.

A buyer agency relationship is established in the same way as any other agency relationship: by contract or agreement. The buyer's agent may receive a flat fee or a share of the commission or both, depending on the terms of the agency agreement. (See Chapter 6.)

Owner as Principal

An owner may employ a broker to market, lease, maintain, or manage the owner's property. Such an arrangement is known as *property management*. The broker is made the agent of the property owner through a property management agreement. As in any other agency relationship, the broker has a fiduciary or statutory responsibility to the client-owner. Sometimes, an owner may employ a broker for the sole purpose of marketing the property to prospective tenants. In this case, the broker's responsibility is limited to finding suitable tenants for the owner's property. (See Chapter 17.)

Dual Agency

In **dual agency**, the agent represents two principals in the same transaction. Dual agency requires equal loyalty to two different principals at the same time. Because agency originates with the broker, dual agency arises when the broker is the agent of the buyer *and the seller*. The salespeople, as agents of the broker, have fiduciary or statutory responsibilities to the same principals as well. The challenge is to fulfill the fiduciary or statutory obligations to one principal without compromising the interests of the other, especially when the parties' interests may be not only separate but also opposite. While practical methods of ensuring fairness and equal representation may exist, it should be noted that a dual agent can never fully represent either party's interests. (See Figure 4.2.)

Dual Agency

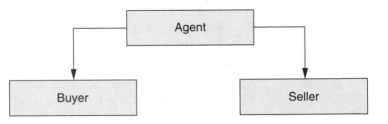

Because of the risks inherent in dual agency—ranging from conflicts of interest to outright abuse of trust—the practice is illegal in some states. In those states where dual agency is permitted, all parties must consent to the arrangement, preferably in writing.

■ **FOR EXAMPLE**   A real estate broker is the agent for the owner of a large mansion. A prospective buyer comes into the broker's office and asks her to represent him in a search for a modest home. After several weeks of activity, including two offers unsuccessfully negotiated by the broker, the prospective buyer spots the For Sale sign in front of the mansion. He tells the broker that he wants to make an offer and asks for the broker's advice on a likely price range. The broker is now in the difficult position of being a dual agent. She represents the seller, who naturally is interested in receiving the highest possible price, and the buyer, who is interested in making a successful low offer.

Disclosed dual agency   Although the possibility of conflict of interest still exists, disclosure is intended to minimize the risk *for the broker*. The disclosure alerts the principals that they might have to assume greater responsibility for protecting their interests than they would if they had independent representation. Because the duties of disclosure and confidentiality are limited by mutual agreement, they must be carefully explained to the parties in order to establish *informed consent*.

Designated agency is a process that accommodates an *in-house* sale in which two different agents are involved. The broker designates one agent to represent the seller and one agent to represent the buyer. Designated agency is currently legal in several states. However, designated agency does not apply to a single agent who represents both parties at the same time in the same transaction.

Undisclosed dual agency   A broker may not intend to create a dual agency. It might occur *unintentionally* or *inadvertently*. Sometimes the cause is carelessness. At other times, a salesperson does not fully understand the fiduciary responsibilities. Some salespeople lose sight of other responsibilities when they focus intensely on bringing buyers and sellers together. For instance, a salesperson representing the seller might suggest to a buyer that the seller will accept less than the listing price. Or that same salesperson might promise to persuade the seller to accept an offer that is in the buyer's best interests. Giving a buyer any specific advice on how much to offer can lead the buyer to believe that the salesperson represents the buyer's interests and is acting as the buyer's advocate.

Any of these actions can create an *implied* agency with the buyer and violate the duties of loyalty and confidentiality to the principal-seller. Because neither party has been informed of the situation and given the opportunity to seek separate representation, the interests of both are jeopardized. This undisclosed dual agency violates licensing laws. It can result in the rescission of the sales contract, forfeiture of a commission, a lawsuit for damages, and possible license problems.

■ **FOR EXAMPLE**   Using the previous large-mansion example, if the broker doesn't tell the prospective buyer that he represents the seller of the property, he will be an undisclosed dual agent. The broker has two options. First, knowing the prospective buyer's comfortable financial situation and intense desire for the property, he might choose not to tell the buyer about the dual agency situation. Instead, he could tell her that the mansion's owner will accept nothing less than the full asking price. While this will ensure that the broker receives the maximum possible commission, it will also subject him to severe penalties for violating the state's licensing laws. Alternatively, he can disclose his relationship with the seller and work out a dual agency agreement with both parties in which he legally represents both parties' interests.

A more common example of dual agency occurs when a broker, who employs two salespeople, has the first salesperson act as the listing salesperson for the mansion. The second salesperson meets and begins representing the buyer. Because both salespeople are associated with the broker's real estate brokerage, the broker might be construed as a dual agent and will have to enter into a disclosed dual agency agreement with the parties.

Disclosure of Agency

Real estate licensees are required to disclose the parties they represent. Understanding the scope of the service a party can expect from the agent allows consumers to make an informed decision about whether to seek their own representation.

Mandatory agency disclosure laws now exist in every state. These laws stipulate when, how, and to whom disclosures must be made. They may, for instance, dictate that a particular type of written form be used. The laws might state what information a real estate licensee must provide to gain informed consent where disclosed dual agency is permitted. The laws might require that all agency alternatives be explained, including the brokerage firm's policies regarding the firm's services. Frequently, printed brochures outlining agency alternatives are available to a firm's clients and customers.

Whether or not the law requires it, licensees should explain to both buyers and sellers what agency alternatives exist. Good business practice is to make the disclosure of agency before any confidential information is disclosed about an individual's motivation or financial situation. (See Figure 4.3.)

Nonagency

A nonagent (also referred to as a *transactional broker, facilitator, coordinator, or contract broker*) is not an agent of either party. A nonagent's job is simply to help both the buyer and the seller with the necessary paperwork and formalities involved in transferring ownership of real property. The buyer and the seller negotiate the sale without representation.

FIGURE 4.3

Agency Disclosure Form

NOTICE OF AGENCY RELATIONSHIP

When working with a real estate agent in buying or selling real estate West Virginia Law requires that you be informed of whom the agent is representing in the transaction.

The agent may represent the seller, the buyer, or both. The party represented by the agent is known as the agent's principal and as such, the agent owes the principal the duty of utmost care, integrity, honesty and loyalty.

Regardless of whom they represent, the agent has the following duties to <u>both</u> the buyer and the seller in any transaction:

  * Diligent exercise of reasonable skill and care in the performance of the agent's duties.
  * A duty of honest and fair dealing and good faith.
  * Must offer all property without regard to race, color, religion, sex, ancestry, physical or mental handicap, national origin or familial status.
  * Must promptly present all written offers to the owner.
  * Provide a true legible copy of every contract to each person signing the contract.

The agent is not obligated to reveal to either party any confidential information obtained from the other party which does not involve the affirmative duties set forth above.

Should you desire to have a real estate agent represent you as your agent, you should enter into a written contract that clearly establishes the obligations of both parties. If you have any questions about the roles and responsibilities of a real estate agent, they can provide information upon your request.

In compliance with the West Virginia Real Estate License Act, all parties are hereby notified that:

(printed name of agent) _____ , affiliated with

(firm name)_____ , is acting as agent of:

  _____The Seller, as listing agent or subagent. _____ The Buyer, as the buyer's agent.
  _____ Both the Seller and Buyer, with the full knowledge and consent of both parties.

CERTIFICATION

By signing below, the parties certify that they have read and understand the information contained in this disclosure and have been provided with signed copies prior to signing any contract.

_____	_____	_____	_____
Seller	Date	Buyer	Date
_____	_____	_____	_____
Seller	Date	Buyer	Date
_____	_____	_____	_____
Seller	Date	Buyer	Date

I hereby certify that I have provided the above named individuals with a copy of this form prior to signing any contract.

Agent's Signature _____

Date _____

WV Real Estate Commission
300 Capitol Street, Suite 400
Charleston, WV 25301
304.558.3555
<www.wvrec.org>

This form has been promulgated by the WVREC for required use by all West Virginia real estate licensees.

EQUAL HOUSING
OPPORTUNITY

Revised - 03/12/09

Source: Northern Virginia Association of REALTORS®.

The nonagent is expected to treat all parties honestly and competently, to locate qualified buyers or suitable properties, to help the parties arrive at mutually acceptable terms, and to assist in the closing of the transaction. Nonagents are equally responsible to both parties and must disclose known defects in a property. However, they may not negotiate on behalf of either the buyer or the seller, and they must not disclose confidential information to either party.

Agency Statutes

A rapidly growing number of state legislatures are enacting agency reform legislation. Such reform laws are either in place or under consideration in most states. While each state's agency statute is different, many still incorporate the common-law fiduciary principles. For instance, most statutes contain language requiring agents to

- exercise reasonable *care* and skill in performing their duties,
- *obey* the client's specific directions,
- *account* for all money and property received,
- promote the client's best interests at all times (i.e., *loyalty*),
- *disclose* material facts concerning the transaction,
- perform according to the terms of the brokerage agreement,
- keep confidential all confidential information received from the client, and
- generally comply with the terms of the statute.

If a state's agency law does not specifically replace the common law of agency, a licensee will be subject to the requirements of both the statute and common law.

■ CUSTOMER-LEVEL SERVICES

Even though an agent's primary responsibility is to the principal, the agent also has duties to third parties. Any time a licensee works with a third party, or **customer,** the licensee is responsible for adhering to state and federal consumer protection laws, as well as the ethical requirements imposed by professional associations and state regulators. In addition, the licensee's duties to the customer include

An agent owes a **customer** the duties of *reasonable care and skill, honest and fair dealing,* and *disclosure of known facts* about the property.

- reasonable care and skill in performance,
- honest and fair dealing, and
- disclosure of all facts that the licensee knows or should reasonably be expected to know that materially affect the value or desirability of the property.

As part of the recent trend for more consumer protection for purchasers, many states have enacted statutes requiring the disclosure of known adverse property conditions to prospective buyers. Generally, these apply to sellers of residential properties, often for those of one to four dwelling units. Prepurchase structural inspections, termite infestation reports, or other protective documentation may also be used. The actual disclosures that sellers are required to make vary according to each state's law.

Environmental Hazards

Disclosure of environmental health hazards, which can render properties unusable for the buyer's intended purpose, may be required. For instance, federal law requires the disclosure of lead-based paint hazards. Frequently, the buyer or the buyer's mortgage lender requests inspections or tests to determine the presence or level of risk.

IN PRACTICE Licensees are encouraged to obtain advice from state and local authorities responsible for environmental regulation whenever the following conditions might be present: toxic-waste dumping; underground storage tanks; contaminated soil or water; nearby chemical or nuclear facilities; and health hazards such as radon, asbestos, and lead paint.

Opinion Versus Fact

Real estate brokers and salespeople must always be careful about the statements they make. They must be sure that the consumer understands whether the statement is an opinion or a fact. Statements of opinion are permissible if there is no intention to deceive.

Statements of fact, however, must be accurate. Exaggeration of a property's benefits is called **puffing**. While puffing is legal, real estate licensees must ensure that none of their statements can be interpreted as fraudulent. **Fraud** is the intentional misrepresentation of a material fact in such a way as to harm or take advantage of another person. That includes not only making false statements about a property but also intentionally concealing or failing to disclose important facts.

The misrepresentation or omission does not have to be intentional to result in broker liability. A **negligent misrepresentation** occurs when the broker *should have known* that a statement about a material fact was false. A broker's lack of awareness of an issue is no excuse. If the buyer relies on the broker's statement, the broker is liable for any damages that result. Similarly, a broker who accidentally fails to perform some act—for instance, forgetting to deliver a counteroffer—may be liable for damages that result from such a negligent omission.

■ **FOR EXAMPLE** While showing a potential buyer an average-looking house, the broker described even its plainest features as "charming" and "beautiful." Because the statements were obviously the broker's personal opinions designed to encourage a positive feeling about the property (or puff it up), the truth or falsity of the statements is not an issue.

A broker was asked by a potential buyer if a particular neighborhood was safe. The broker knew that the area was experiencing a skyrocketing rate of violent crime but assured the buyer that no problem existed. The broker also neglected to inform the buyer that the lot next to the house the buyer was considering had been sold to a waste disposal company for use as a toxic dump. Both might be examples of fraudulent misrepresentation.

Property Conditions

The seller has a duty to discover and disclose any known defects that threaten structural soundness or personal safety. A **latent defect** is a hidden structural defect that would not be discovered by ordinary inspection. Buyers may cancel the sales contract or receive damages when a seller fails to reveal known latent defects. The courts also have decided in favor of the buyer when the seller neglected to reveal violations of zoning or building codes. Increasingly, however, there is a growing trend of not only the right but the responsibility of the buyer to discover any material problems with the property. In addition to the seller's duty to disclose latent defects, in some states, the agent has an independent duty to conduct a reasonably competent and diligent inspection of the property. It is the licensee's duty to discover any material facts that may affect the property's value or desirability, whether or not they are known to or disclosed by the seller. Any such material facts discovered by the licensee must be disclosed to prospective buyers. If the licensee should have known about a substantial defect that is detected later by the buyer, the agent may be liable to the buyer for any damages resulting from that defect.

■ **FOR EXAMPLE**   A broker knew that a house had been built on a landfill. A few days after the house was listed, one of the broker's salespeople noticed that the living room floor was uneven and sagging in places. In some states, both the broker and the salesperson have a duty to conduct further investigations into the structural soundness of the property. In other states, no such duty exists, but the broker and the salesperson would have the duty of discussing the issue with the seller and advising the buyer to have an inspection performed. They cannot simply ignore the problem or place throw rugs over particularly bad spots and hope buyers won't look underneath. If the seller refuses to disclose the problem, then the broker should refuse the listing.

Stigmatized Properties

Stigmatized properties are those that society has found undesirable because of events that occurred there or because a known sex offender lives in the area. For example, Megan's Law requires all states to release information to the public about known convicted sex offenders. The federal law does not mandate active notification, but most state laws do.

A common stigma is a criminal event, such as a homicide, illegal drug manufacturing, gang-related activity, or a suicide. Properties have even been stigmatized by rumors that they are haunted. Because of the potential liability to a licensee for inadequately researching and disclosing material facts concerning a property's condition, licensees should seek legal counsel when dealing with a stigmatized property.

Some states have laws regarding the disclosure of information about such properties, designed to protect sellers and local property values against a baseless psychological reaction. In other states, the licensee's responsibility may be difficult to define because the issue is not a physical defect but merely a perception that a property is undesirable. The stigmatized property issue can be even more complicated: In some cultures, a house in which someone has died is considered uninhabitable. While licensees must not discriminate based on nationality, culture, or religious beliefs, state laws on stigmatized properties may put the agent in an awkward position. That's why getting competent legal counsel is important.

IN PRACTICE A disclosure that a property's previous owner or occupant died of AIDS or was HIV positive constitutes illegal discrimination against the handicapped under the federal Fair Housing Act. (See Chapter 20.)

■ KEY POINT REVIEW

An **agent** is hired by principals to act on their behalf.

Agency is the fiduciary relationship in which the agent is held in a position of special trust and confidence by the principal.

A **client** is the principal.

A **customer** is the nonrepresented party for whom some level of service is provided and who is entitled to fairness and honesty.

A **nonagent** (also known as a **facilitator, intermediary, transactional broker, transactional coordinator,** or **contract broker**) assists one or both parties with the transaction without representing either party's interests and often is subject to specific statutory responsibilities.

Real estate agency relationships are governed by **common law**, which is established by tradition and court decisions, and **statutory law**, which is passed by state legislatures and other governing bodies.

Disclosure by real estate brokers of agency relationship is required in every state.

Agency relationships encompass the following:

- **Express agency** is based on a formal agreement between the parties.
- **Implied agency** results from the behavior of the parties.
- The **compensation** source does not determine agency because
    — the agent may be compensated by someone other than agent's client, and
    — agency can exist even if no compensation is involved—**gratuitous agency.**

An agent has a **fiduciary relationship** of trust and confidence with the principal. The six common-law fiduciary duties can be remembered as **COLD AC**, which is an acronym for the following:

1. **C**are—An agent must exercise a reasonable degree of care.
2. **O**bedience—An agent must act in good faith at all times, with obedience toward the principal's instructions.
3. **L**oyalty—An agent must place the principal's interests above those of all others, including the agent's own interests.

4. <u>D</u>isclosure—An agent is duty-bound to inform the principal of certain relevant facts concerning the transaction, particularly those mandated by state law.
5. <u>A</u>ccounting—An agent must be able to report the status of all funds received from or on behalf of the principal.
6. <u>C</u>onfidentiality—An agent owes the principal confidentiality in carrying out agency obligations.

Termination of agency may be accomplished by the

- completion, performance, or fulfillment of purpose of agency;
- destruction or condemnation of the property;
- expiration of the terms of the agency;
- mutual agreement of all parties to the contract;
- breach by one of the parties, who may be liable for damages; and
- operation of law, as in the bankruptcy of the principal.

Agency coupled with an interest cannot be revoked by the principal or terminated upon the principal's death.

A **universal agent** is empowered to do anything the principal could do personally.

A **general agent** represents the principal in a broad range of matters.

A **special agent** (or **limited agent**) represents the principal in one specific act or business transaction only, under detailed instruction.

A **designated agent** (or **designated representative**) is authorized by the broker to act as the agent of a specific principal.

A **single agency** is one in which an agent represents only one party in a transaction.

A **dual agency** (or **limited agency**) is one in which an agent represents two principals in the same transaction.

A **buyer's broker** represents a buyer as an agent to find property that meets the buyer's specifications, as set out in the **buyer-broker agreement**.

Statements to clients and customers should be clearly identified as **opinion** or **fact**. Note the following distinctions:

- **Puffing** is legal exaggeration of a property's benefits.
- **Fraud** is the intentional misrepresentation of a material fact to harm or take advantage of another person.
- **Negligent misrepresentation** occurs when a broker **should have known** that a statement about a material fact was false.

A **seller** has the duty to discover and disclose any known **latent** (i.e., hidden) **defects** that threaten a building's structural soundness or an occupant's personal safety. For some agents, the following is important to remember:

■ In some states, an agent has an independent duty to conduct a **reasonably competent and diligent inspection** of the property and to disclose defects to prospective buyers.

Stigmatized properties may require an agent to consult an attorney.

■ RELATED WEB SITE

National Association of REALTORS®:   *www.realtor.org*

CHAPTER 4 QUIZ

1. In a real estate transaction, the term *fiduciary* typically refers to the
   a. sale of real property.
   b. person who gives someone else the legal power to act on his or her behalf.
   c. person who has legal power to act on behalf of another.
   d. agent's relationship to the principal.

2. The relationship between broker and seller is generally what type of agency?
   a. Special
   b. General
   c. Implied
   d. Universal

3. Which statement is *TRUE* of a real estate broker acting as the agent of the seller?
   a. The broker is obligated to render loyalty to the seller.
   b. The broker can disclose confidential information about the seller to a buyer if it increases the likelihood of a sale.
   c. The broker can agree to a change in price without the seller's approval.
   d. The broker can accept a commission from the buyer without the seller's approval.

4. A real estate broker lists a woman's home for $189,500. Later that same day, a man comes into the broker's office and asks for general information about homes for sale in the $130,000 to $140,000 price range but refuses representation by the broker's company at this time. Based on these facts, which statement is *TRUE*?
   a. Both the woman and the man are the broker's customers.
   b. The woman is the broker's client; the man is a customer.
   c. The broker owes fiduciary duties to both the woman and the man.
   d. If the man later asks for buyer representation by the broker's firm, he cannot have it because of the firm's earlier agreement with the woman.

5. In a dual agency situation, a broker may represent both the seller and the buyer if
   a. the broker informs either the buyer or the seller of this fact.
   b. the buyer and the seller are related by blood or marriage.
   c. both parties give their informed consent, usually in writing, to the dual agency.
   d. both parties are represented by attorneys.

6. Which event will terminate an agency in a broker-seller relationship?
   a. The broker discovers that the market value of the property is such that an adequate commission will not be earned.
   b. The owner declares personal bankruptcy.
   c. The owner abandons the property.
   d. The broker appoints other brokers to help sell the property.

7. Designated agency is MOST likely to occur when
   a. there is a client-buyer and a customer-seller.
   b. the seller and the buyer are represented by different companies.
   c. both the buyer and the seller are customers.
   d. the buyer and the seller are represented by the same company.

8. A real estate broker hired by an owner to sell a parcel of real estate must comply with
   a. the common law of agency, even if a state agency statute exists.
   b. dual agency requirements.
   c. the concept of caveat emptor.
   d. all lawful instructions of the owner.

9. A licensee is hired as a buyer's agent by a first-time buyer to help the buyer purchase a home. The buyer confides that being approved for a mortgage loan may be complicated by the fact that the buyer filed for bankruptcy two years ago. The buyer would like to find a seller who will accept an installment sale. In this situation, a correct statement about the licensee's responsibility regarding this information during the presentation of an offer to purchase a property is that the licensee is

   a. required to disclose it under the Fair Credit Registry Act.
   b. required to disclose it because it is a material fact—information important to the seller's evaluation of the offer.
   c. not required to disclose it because the seller might reject the offer.
   d. not required to disclose it because the licensee has no agency relationship with the seller.

10. A licensee lists a residence. For various reasons, the owner must sell the house quickly and confides to the licensee that a lower price would probably be acceptable, although the asking price is reasonable. To expedite the sale, the licensee tells a prospective purchaser that the seller will accept up to $5,000 less than the asking price for the property. Based on these facts, which statement is *TRUE*?

   a. The licensee has not violated any agency responsibilities to the seller.
   b. The licensee should have disclosed this information, regardless of its accuracy.
   c. The disclosure was improper—and possibly illegal—regardless of the licensee's motive.
   d. The relationship between the licensee and the seller ends automatically if the purchaser submits an offer.

11. A buyer who is a client of the broker wants to purchase a house that the broker has listed for sale. Which statement is *TRUE*?

   a. The broker may proceed to write an offer on the property and submit it.
   b. The broker should refer the buyer to another broker to negotiate the sale.
   c. The seller and the buyer must be informed of the situation and agree, usually in writing, to the broker's representing both of them.
   d. The buyer should not have been shown a house listed by the broker.

12. What does the phrase *the law of agency is a common-law doctrine* mean?

   a. It is a legal doctrine that is not unusual.
   b. It is one of the rules of society enacted by legislatures and other governing bodies.
   c. It is part of a body of law established by tradition and court decisions.
   d. It may not be superseded by statutory law.

13. A broker helps a buyer and a seller with paperwork but does not represent either party. This is

   a. dual agency.
   b. prohibited in all states because a broker must always represent one party.
   c. transactional brokerage.
   d. designated agency.

14. A real estate licensee was representing a buyer. At their first meeting, the buyer revealed plans to operate a dog-grooming business out of the purchased house. The licensee did not check the local zoning ordinances to determine in which parts of town such a business could be conducted. Which common-law duty did the licensee violate?

   a. Care
   b. Obedience
   c. Loyalty
   d. Disclosure

15. A broker tells a prospective buyer, "This property has the most beautiful river view." In fact, the view includes the river and the back of a shopping center. Which statement is *TRUE*?

    a. The broker has committed fraud.
    b. The broker is guilty of negligent misrepresentation.
    c. The broker is guilty of intentional misrepresentation.
    d. The broker is merely puffing.

16. A real estate broker's responsibility to keep the principal informed of all the facts that could affect a transaction is the duty of

    a. care.
    b. disclosure.
    c. obedience.
    d. accounting.

17. Which of the following would be considered dual agency?

    a. A broker acting for both the buyer and the seller in the same transaction
    b. Two brokerage companies cooperating with each other
    c. A broker representing more than one principal
    d. A broker listing and then selling the same property

18. The relationship of broker to client is that of a(n)

    a. trustee.
    b. subagent.
    c. fiduciary.
    d. attorney-in-fact.

19. A real estate broker acting as the agent of the seller

    a. must promote and safeguard the seller's best interests.
    b. can disclose the seller's minimum price.
    c. should present to the seller only the highest offer for the property.
    d. can accept an offer on behalf of the seller.

20. A broker is permitted to represent both the seller and the buyer in the same transaction when

    a. the principals are not aware of such action.
    b. the broker is a subagent rather than the agent of the seller.
    c. commissions are collected from both parties.
    d. both parties have been informed and agree to the dual representation.

CHAPTER 5

Real Estate Brokerage

LEARNING OBJECTIVES   *When you have finished reading this chapter, you should be able to*

- **identify** the roles of technology, personnel, and license laws in the operation of a real estate business;

- **describe** the various types of antitrust violations common in the real estate industry and the penalties involved with each;

- **explain** how a broker's compensation is usually determined;

- **distinguish** employees from independent contractors and explain why the distinction is important; and

- **define** the following *key terms*:

antitrust laws
brokerage
commission
disclaimers
electronic contracting
Electronic Signatures in Global and National Commerce Act (E-Sign)

employee
independent contractor
Internet advertising
Internet Listing Display Policy
minimum level of services
National Do Not Call Registry

procuring cause
ready, willing, and able buyer
Uniform Electronic Transactions Act (UETA)

REAL ESTATE BROKERAGE

Real estate is an industry driven by small businesses. Most brokerages are not giant national companies, and even those that are members of large franchises are still small businesses at heart, run locally to serve what is essentially a local market. Like any small business, there are advantages. To be successful, a real estate licensee has to know the product—real estate—but also how to run a business. Economics are part of running any operation, as are personnel decisions, such as how many people to hire and in what capacity. What positions are needed? How do you find to right people to fill those jobs? Who's your competition? The answers to these questions are not easy ones, but a successful real estate licensee needs to think like a businessperson.

THE HISTORY OF BROKERAGE

The nature of real estate brokerage services, particularly those provided in residential sales transactions, has changed significantly in recent years. In the 1950s, real estate brokerage firms were primarily one-office, minimally staffed, family-run operations. The real estate broker listed an owner's property for sale and found a buyer without assistance from other brokerage companies. The sale was negotiated and closed. It was relatively clear that the real estate broker represented the seller's interests. The common-law doctrine of *caveat emptor* ("let the buyer beware") was the rule; buyers were pretty much on their own.

In the 1960s, the way that buyers and sellers were brought together in real estate transactions began to change. Brokers started to share information about properties they listed, resulting in two brokers cooperating to sell a property. The brokers formalized this exchange of information by creating multiple listing services (MLSs). The MLS expedited sales by increasing a single property's exposure to more potential buyers. Because it generated more sales, the MLS quickly became a widely used industry service. But one thing remained the same: both brokers still represented the seller's interest.

While sellers benefited from this arrangement, buyers came to question whether their interests were being protected. They began to demand not only accurate, factual information but also objective advice, particularly in the face of increasingly complex real estate transactions. Buyers view the real estate licensee as the expert on whom they can rely for guidance. In short, buyers now seek not only protection but representation as well. Most states recognize buyer agency today, and a large percentage of sales contracts are written by buyer's agents.

REAL ESTATE LICENSE LAWS

All 50 states, the District of Columbia, and all Canadian provinces license and regulate the activities of real estate brokers and licensees. While the laws share a common purpose, the details vary from state to state. Uniform policies and standards for administering and enforcing state license laws are promoted by ARELLO, the Association of Real Estate License Law Officials.

Purpose of License Laws

Real estate license laws protect the public by ensuring a standard of competence and professionalism in the real estate industry. The laws achieve this goal by

- establishing basic requirements for obtaining a real estate license and, in many cases, requiring continuing education to keep a license;
- defining which activities require licensing;
- describing the acceptable standards of conduct and practice for licensees; and
- enforcing those standards through a disciplinary system.

The purpose of these laws is not merely to regulate the real estate industry. Their main objective is to make sure that the rights of purchasers, sellers, tenants, and owners are protected from unscrupulous or negligent practices. The laws are not intended to prevent licensees from conducting their businesses successfully or to interfere in legitimate transactions. Laws cannot create an ethical or a moral marketplace. But by establishing minimum levels of education and standards of behavior, laws can make the marketplace more honest.

Each state has a licensing authority—a commission, a department, a division, a board, or an agency—for real estate brokers and salespeople. This authority has the power to issue licenses, make real estate information available to licensees and the public, and enforce the statutory real estate law.

Each licensing authority has also adopted a set of administrative rules and regulations that further define the statutory law. The rules and regulations provide for administering the law and set operating guidelines for licensees. The rules and regulations have the same force and effect as statutory law. Both the law and the rules are usually enforced through fines and the denial, suspension, or revocation of licenses. Civil and criminal court actions can be brought against violators in some serious cases.

IN PRACTICE   Each state's real estate license laws and the rules and regulations of its real estate commission or board establish the framework for all of a licensee's activities. *It is vital that licensees have a clear and comprehensive understanding of their state's laws and regulations, not only for purposes of the licensing examination but also to ensure that the licensee's practice of real estate is both legal and successful.* This is the case for licensees who hold licenses as a result of reciprocity and who were granted a license in another state without being required to take special courses or examinations.

■ REAL ESTATE BROKERAGE

Brokerage is simply the business of bringing parties together. A *real estate broker* is defined as a person licensed to buy, sell, exchange, or lease real property for others and to charge a fee for these services.

A brokerage business may take many forms. It may be a sole proprietorship (a single-owner company), a corporation, or a partnership with another real estate broker. The office may be independent or part of a regional or national franchise.

The business may consist of a single office or multiple branches. Brokers' offices may be located in highrises, suburban shopping centers, or their homes. A typical real estate brokerage may specialize in one kind of transaction or service, or it may offer a variety of services.

No matter what form it takes, a real estate brokerage has the same demands, expenses, and rewards as any other small business. The real estate industry, after all, is made up of thousands of small businesses operating in defined local markets. A real estate broker faces the same challenges as an entrepreneur in any other industry. In addition to mastering the complexities of real estate transactions, the real estate broker must be able to handle the day-to-day details of running a business and to set effective policies for every aspect of the brokerage operation: maintaining space and equipment, hiring employees and real estate salespeople, determining compensation, directing staff and sales activities, and implementing procedures to follow in carrying out agency duties. Each state's real estate license laws and regulations establish the business activities and methods of doing business that are permitted.

IN PRACTICE   A broker should advise parties to secure legal counsel to protect their interests. Although real estate brokers and salespeople may bring buyers and sellers together, and in most states may fill in preprinted blank purchase agreement forms, only an attorney may offer legal advice or prepare legal documents. *Licensees who are not attorneys are prohibited from practicing law.*

Broker-Salesperson Relationship

Although brokerage firms vary widely in size, few brokers today perform their duties without the assistance of salespeople. Consequently, much of the business's success hinges on the broker-salesperson relationship.

A *real estate salesperson* is any person licensed to perform real estate activities on behalf of a licensed real estate broker. The broker is fully responsible for the actions performed in the course of the real estate business by all persons licensed under the broker. In turn, all of a salesperson's activities must be performed in the name of the supervising broker. The salesperson can carry out *only* those responsibilities assigned by the employing broker and can receive compensation *only* from that broker. As a general agent of the broker, the salesperson has no authority to make contracts with or receive compensation from any other party. The broker is liable for the acts of the salesperson within the scope of the employment agreement.

IN PRACTICE   The salesperson must always be supervised by a broker. The broker cannot delegate office supervision of salespeople to an unlicensed broker.

Real Estate Assistants

A real estate assistant (also known as a personal assistant or professional assistant) is a combination office manager, marketer, organizer, and facilitator who has a fundamental understanding of the real estate industry. An assistant may or may not have a real estate license, depending on state law. The extent to which the assistant can help the real estate broker or real estate salesperson with transactions is often determined by licensing laws. An assistant may perform duties that include clerical tasks, office management, telemarketing, market strategy development, and direct contact with consumers. A licensed assistant can set up and host open houses and assist in all aspects of a real estate transaction.

Broker's Compensation

The broker's compensation is specified in the contract with the principal. Real estate license laws may stipulate that a written agreement must establish the compensation to be paid. Compensation can be in the form of a **commission** or broker's fee (computed as a percentage of the total sales price), a flat fee, or an hourly rate. The amount of a broker's commission is negotiable in every case. Even subtle attempts to impose uniform commission rates are clearly a violation of state and federal antitrust laws. A broker may set the minimum rate acceptable for that broker's firm. The important point is for broker and client to agree on a rate before the agency relationship is established.

A commission is usually considered earned when the work for which the real estate broker was hired has been accomplished. Most sales commissions are payable when the sale is consummated by *delivery of the seller's deed*. This provision is generally included in the listing agreement. When the sales or listing agreement specifies no time for the payment of the broker's commission, the commission is usually earned when

- a completed sales contract has been executed by a ready, willing, and able buyer;
- the contract has been accepted and executed by the seller; and
- copies of the contract are in possession of all parties.

To be entitled to a sales commission, an individual must be

- a licensed real estate broker,
- the procuring cause of the sale, and
- employed by the buyer or the seller under a valid contract.

> To be a **procuring cause**, the broker must have started a chain of events that resulted in a sale.

To be considered the **procuring cause** of a sale, the broker must have started or caused a chain of events that resulted in the sale. For example, activities such as conducting open houses, placing advertisements in the newspaper, and showing the house to the buyer are considered procuring cause. A broker who causes or completes such an action without a contract or without having been promised payment is a *volunteer* and may not legally claim compensation.

> A **ready, willing, and able buyer** is one prepared to buy on the seller's terms and ready to complete the transaction.

Once a seller accepts an offer from a ready, willing, and able buyer, the real estate broker is entitled to a commission. A **ready, willing, and able buyer** is one who is *prepared to buy on the seller's terms and ready to take positive steps toward consummation of the transaction*. Courts may prevent the real estate broker from receiving a commission if the real estate broker knew the buyer was unable to perform. If the transaction is not consummated, the real estate broker may still be entitled to a commission if the seller

- had a change of mind and refused to sell,
- has a spouse who refused to sign the deed,
- had a title with uncorrected defects,

- committed fraud with respect to the transaction,
- was unable to deliver possession within a reasonable time,
- insisted on terms not in the listing (e.g., the right to restrict the use of the property), or
- had a mutual agreement with the buyer to cancel the transaction.

Real Estate Salesperson's Compensation

The amount of compensation a salesperson receives is set by mutual agreement between the broker and the salesperson. A broker may agree to pay a fixed salary or a share of the commissions from transactions originated by a salesperson. In some cases, a salesperson may draw from an account against earned shares of commissions. Some brokers require salespersons to pay all or part of the expenses of advertising listed properties.

Some firms have adopted a 100 percent commission plan in which salespeople pay a monthly service charge to their brokers to cover the costs of office space, telephones, and supervision in return for keeping 100 percent of the commissions from the sales they negotiate. Salespeople on a 100 percent commission plan pay all of their related business expenses.

Other companies have *graduated commission splits* based on a salesperson's achieving specified production goals. For instance, a broker might agree to split commissions 50/50 up to a $25,000 salesperson's share, 60/40 for shares from $25,000 to $30,000, and so on. Commission splits as generous as 80/20 or 90/10 are possible, particularly for high producers.

No matter how the salesperson's compensation is structured, only the employing real estate broker can pay it. In cooperating transactions, the commission must first be received by the employing broker and is then paid to the salesperson, unless otherwise permitted by license laws.

Fee for Services

The Internet has revolutionized the real estate profession in many ways. One of the more notable impacts of the Internet is that it has allowed buyers and sellers to have tremendous access to information about real estate, housing, financing, and law. The Internet has caused a radical shift in that the average consumer is now much more knowledgeable about real estate matters. With knowledge and information, a consumer is more innovative and independent. The advent of the Internet has also meant that the consumer is privy to information immediately. Consumers now want instant access to real estate information.

MATH CONCEPTS

SHARING COMMISSIONS

A commission might be shared by many people: the listing broker, the listing salesperson, the buyer's broker, and the buyer's salesperson. A diagram may help you determine which licensee is entitled to receive what amount of the total commission. For example, a salesperson, while working for the broker, took a listing on a $189,000 house at a 6 percent commission rate. A second salesperson, while working for a different broker, found the buyer for the property. If the property sold for the listed price, the listing broker and the buyer's broker shared the commission equally, and the buyer's broker kept 45 percent of the commission received, how much did the buyer's salesperson receive? (If the broker retained 45 percent of the total commission received, the broker's salesperson would receive the balance: 100% − 45% = 55%.)

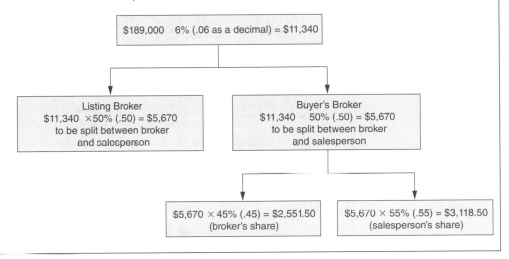

Successful real estate licensees will understand and encourage consumers' innovation. In the process, it is critical for real estate licensees to identify what services they can provide and underscore the value of those services. While emphasizing the services that a licensee provides, it may be important for licensees to think of themselves as *consultants*. Although consumers are more independent, real estate expertise is almost always needed.

It may be important for licensees to be more flexible and open to seeing their occupation as a bundle of services that can be unbundled.

Unbundling services means offering services in a piecemeal fashion. For example, a consultant may want to offer a seller the following services:

- Helping the seller prepare the property for sale
- Performing a competitive market analysis (CMA) and pricing the property
- Assisting with marketing the property using the MLS and any Web sites
- Locating and screening a buyer
- Drafting a purchase sales agreement and helping with negotiations
- Assisting with the closing transaction

Other services are directed toward buyers. For example, a consultant may offer a buyer the following services:

- Consulting on renting versus owning
- Helping a buyer with a mortgage preapproval
- Consulting on a buyer's desired location
- Visiting properties with a buyer and checking property information
- Drafting a purchase sales agreement and helping with negotiations
- Assisting with the closing transaction

While real estate licensees want to encourage consumers to use all their services (full service) for a commission rate, when it becomes apparent that a consumer wants help with one or several services only, then it would be helpful for the real estate licensee to have in mind the best compensation model. Many real estate licensees use either an hourly rate or a flat fee for particular services.

Real estate licensees may also want to develop their own lists of services for sellers and buyers and also a specific list of services to help people who decide to sell their own home, known as for sale by owners (FSBOs).

Communicating with consumers and identifying their real estate needs are key. Licensees provide an array of valuable services that consumers can pick and choose from. Knowledgeable and independent consumers can seem threatening to a licensee; however, the licensee has the opportunity to emphasize the value and variety of real estate services offered, for varying fees. Remember that it is ultimately the broker who decides whether an unbundling of services is good for the company.

■ **FOR EXAMPLE** A buyer wants to buy a house without contracting with a licensee but needs help writing an offer. The buyer asks a broker friend to write an offer to purchase. The broker consults with the buyer, writes the offer to purchase, and charges the buyer a set fee for the service.

Minimum Level of Services

Problems have emerged with the growing number of brokerages offering limited-service listing agreements. These agreements stipulate that a listing real estate broker offer no services other than that of listing a property in the MLS. When sellers enter into this kind of agreement, they are essentially representing themselves. However, when questions emerge involving the transaction, sellers sometimes turn to the buyer's representative for answers that put the real estate licensee in an unethical situation. Seller questions and real estate licensee answers of this type of agreement might lead to a claim of dual agency.

In response to this problem, some states have enacted legislation defining an exclusive brokerage agreement. Other states have proposed regulations that define the **minimum level of services** a consumer should expect from a real estate licensee. For example, one state now requires all exclusive brokerage agreements to specify that the broker—through one or more sponsored licensees—must provide, at a minimum, the following:

- Accept delivery of and present offers and counteroffers to the client
- Assist the client in developing, negotiating, and presenting offers and counteroffers
- Answer the client's questions about offers, counteroffers, and contingencies

Independent contractor versus employee   The employment agreement between a broker and a salesperson should define the nature, obligations, and responsibilities of the relationship. Essentially, the real estate salesperson may be either an *employee* or an *independent contractor*. State license laws generally treat the real estate salesperson as the employee of the affiliate broker, regardless of whether the real estate salesperson is considered an employee or an independent contractor for income tax purposes. Whether a real estate salesperson is treated as an employee or an independent contractor affects the structure of the real estate salesperson's responsibilities and the real estate broker's legal obligation to pay and withhold taxes from the salesperson's earnings.

A real estate broker can exercise certain controls over salespeople who are employees. The real estate broker may require an **employee** to follow rules such as those governing working hours, office routine, attendance at sales meetings, assignment of sales quotas, and adherence to dress codes. As an employer, a broker is required by the federal government to withhold Social Security taxes and income taxes from wages paid to employees. The broker is also required to pay unemployment compensation taxes on wages paid to one or more employees, as defined by state and federal laws. In addition, employees might receive benefits such as health insurance, profit-sharing plans, and workers' compensation.

A broker's relationship with a salesperson who is an **independent contractor** is completely different. As the name implies, an independent contractor operates more independently than an employee, and a broker may not exercise the same degree of control over an independent salesperson's activities. Although the broker may control *what* the independent contractor does, the broker cannot dictate how to do it. The broker cannot *require* the independent contractor to keep specific office hours or attend sales meetings. Independent contractors are responsible for paying their own income and Social Security taxes and receive nothing from brokers that could be construed as an employee benefit, such as health insurance or paid vacation time. As a rule, independent contractors use their own materials and equipment.

The Internal Revenue Service (IRS) often investigates the independent contractor-employee situation in real estate offices. Under the *qualified real estate agent* category in the Internal Revenue Code, the following three requirements are needed to establish an independent contractor status:

- The individual must have a current real estate license.
- The licensee must have a written contract with the broker that specifies that the licensee will not be treated as an employee for federal tax purposes.
- At least 90 percent of the individual's income as a licensee must be based on sales production and not on the number of hours worked.

■ ANTITRUST LAWS

The real estate industry is subject to **antitrust laws**. At the federal level, the Sherman Antitrust Act provides specific penalties for a number of illegal business activities. Each state has its own antitrust laws as well. These laws prohibit monopolies and any contracts, combinations, and conspiracies that unreasonably restrain trade—that is, behaviors that interfere with the free flow of goods and services in a competitive marketplace. The most common antitrust violations are price-fixing, group boycotting, allocation of customers or markets, and tie-in agreements.

Price-Fixing

Price-fixing is the practice of setting prices for products or services rather than letting competition in the open market establish those prices. In real estate, price-fixing occurs when competing brokers agree to set sales commissions, fees, or management rates. *Price-fixing is illegal.* Real estate brokers must independently determine commission rates or fees for their own firms only. These decisions must be based on a broker's business judgment and revenue requirements without input from other brokers.

Antitrust violations include

■ price-fixing,
■ group boycotting,
■ allocation of customers,
■ allocation of markets, and
■ tie-in agreements.

Multiple-listing organizations, boards of REALTORS®, and other professional organizations may not set fees or commission splits. Nor can they deny membership to brokers based on the fees that real estate brokers charge.

The challenge for real estate brokers and salespeople is to avoid even the impression of price-fixing. Hinting to prospective clients that there is a "going rate" of commission or a "normal" fee implies that rates are, in fact, standardized. The broker must make it clear to clients that the rate stated is only what that broker's firm charges.

Group Boycotting

Group boycotting occurs when two or more businesses conspire against another business or agree to withhold their patronage to reduce competition. Group boycotting is illegal under the antitrust laws.

Allocation of Customers or Markets

Allocation of customers or markets involves an agreement between real estate brokers to divide their markets and refrain from competing for each other's business. Allocations may be made on a geographic basis, with real estate brokers agreeing to specific territories within which they will operate exclusively. The division may also occur by markets, such as by price range or category of housing. These agreements result in reduced competition.

Tie-in Agreements

Finally, *tie-in agreements* (also known as *tying agreements*) are agreements to sell one product only if the buyer purchases another product as well. The sale of the first (desired) product is *tied* to the purchase of a second (less desirable) product.

Penalties

The penalties for violating antitrust laws are severe. For instance, under the federal Sherman Antitrust Act, people who fix prices or allocate markets may be subject to a maximum $1 million fine and ten years in prison. For corporations, the penalty may be as high as $100 million. An individual who has suffered a loss because of an antitrust activity may sue for threefold the damages sustained. This is known as treble-damages. In addition, the injured party may recover the cost of the suit, which includes reasonable attorney fees.

Legal Consideration and Technology

The Internet has brought tremendous change to the real estate industry. Real estate practitioners and consumers rely heavily on the Internet for a variety of services. The Internet is a powerful tool for consumers in finding information about properties, relocation services, and particular communities. Often, real estate Web site information is updated daily.

Most real estate agencies have Web sites that provide extraordinary databases for property and other searches. Keep in mind that the NAR has adopted a new **Internet Listing Display Policy** that replaces the Virtual Office Web site (VOW) and the Internet Data Exchange (IDX) policies. The new NAR policy allows all MLS members to have equal rights to display MLS data, and it respects the rights of property owners and their listing real estate brokers to market a property as they wish. A *blanket opt-out* provision provides that those MLS participants interested in keeping their listings off of competitors' Web sites cannot then display other real estate brokers' listings. Real estate brokers who opt out of displaying their listings on competitors' Web sites can, at the direction of a seller, make an exception and display the seller's property on the MLS Web site.

Many real estate Web sites have **disclaimers** to indicate that the material on the site is solely for informational purposes and that no warranties or representations have been made.

Licensees can purchase Web site management tools to help with their marketing efforts. These tools help assess the effectiveness of Internet marketing by providing statistics on the number of page views, the number of people visiting the site, the most visited pages, the Web site page used to enter and exit, and the operating system and browser information of visitors, among other data.

E-mail   E-mail is yet another powerful tool making communication between real estate agents and consumers much more efficient. Gone are the days of playing phone tag. Instead, sending a quick e-mail message saves both agents and consumers valuable time. A real estate agent should be prepared for consumers who primarily want to communicate through the use of e-mail.

In communicating with clients or consumers via e-mail, the following are some suggestions: use the subject line in a useful and helpful manner; try to avoid spelling errors; respond promptly to all e-mail messages; be specific, to the point, and brief; and pay attention to the size of any attachments you send. Do not send unsolicited e-mails.

E-mail is an excellent opportunity for the ongoing marketing of your business. Make sure that all your contact information is up to date in your signature line, and use automated signatures. If you do use a lot of e-mail in your business, setting up an auto-responder is helpful when you are away for a period of time.

Internet Advertising

State laws vary regarding **Internet advertising**. It is important for you to check your own state's laws before engaging in Internet advertising. In addition to the Internet Listing Display Policy previously mentioned, some common Internet advertising laws include the following:

- All electronic communication by a real estate licensee must include the licensee's name, office address, and broker affiliation.
- Real estate professionals must disclose their status as a real estate broker or real estate salesperson on each page of a Web site that contains an advertisement.
- The listing of only a salesperson's name without the sponsoring broker's name in an advertisement is prohibited.
- An advertisement must be a true representation and not be misleading.

Electronic Contracting

Technology and the Internet have significantly changed the way in which real estate transactions are performed. As a result, **electronic contracting** is a growing field in real estate practice because it quickly and efficiently integrates information in a real estate transaction between clients, lenders, and title and closing agents. The transactions are conducted through e-mail or fax and can save a lot of time and money.

Two federal acts govern electronic contracting: the **Uniform Electronic Transactions Act (UETA)** and the **Electronic Signatures in Global and National Commerce Act (E-Sign)**.

UETA sets forth basic rules for entering an enforceable contract using electronic means and has been enacted in most states. The primary purpose of UETA is to remove barriers in electronic commerce that would otherwise prevent enforceability of contracts. UETA validates and effectuates electronic records and signatures in a procedural manner. It is intended to complement any state's digital signature statute. UETA does not in any way require parties to use electronic means. UETA's four key provisions are the following:

- A contract cannot be denied its legal effect just because an electronic record was used.
- A record or signature cannot be denied its legal effect just because it is in an electronic format.
- If a state's law requires a signature on a contract, an electronic signature is sufficient.
- If a state's law requires a written record, an electronic record is sufficient.

E-Sign functions as the electronic transactions law in states that have not enacted the UETA, and some sections of E-Sign apply to states that have enacted UETA.

The purpose of E-Sign is to make contracts (including signatures) and records legally enforceable, regardless of the medium in which they are created. For example, contracts formed using e-mail have the same legal significance as those formed on paper.

IN PRACTICE   When entering into a residential purchase sales agreement, it is important for the parties to feel comfortable with and clearly communicate the method chosen for transacting the agreement, whether by paper and ink or by e-mail.

National Do Not Call Registry

In 2003, federal *do-not-call* legislation was signed into law, and real estate licensees must comply with the provisions of the **National Do Not Call Registry**. The registry is managed by the Federal Trade Commission (FTC); it is a list of telephone numbers from consumers who have indicated their preference to limit the telemarketing calls they receive. The registry applies to any plan, program, or campaign to sell goods or services through interstate phone calls. The registry does not limit calls by political organizations, charities, collection agencies, or telephone surveyors.

Real estate licensees may call consumers with whom they have an established business relationship for up to 18 months after the consumer's last purchase, delivery, or payment, even if the consumer is listed on the National Do Not Call Registry. Also, a real estate licensee may call a consumer for up to three months after the consumer makes an inquiry or submits an application. Note that if a consumer asks a company not to call, despite the presence of an established business relationship, then the company must abide by the consumer's request, which stays in effect for five years.

To access the National Do Not Call Registry, visit *www.donotcall.gov*. Since January 2005, telemarketers and sellers are now required to search the registry at least once every 31 days and drop registered consumer phone numbers from their call lists.

Most states also have do-not-call rules or regulations. It is important to keep up to date with your own state's laws regarding do-not-call policies, as well as the national law.

■ KEY POINT REVIEW

All 50 states, Canadian provinces, and the District of Columbia have real estate license laws and rules with the force and effect of law that

- establish basic requirements for obtaining a real estate license,
- may require continuing education for license renewal,
- define which activities require licensing,
- describe acceptable standards of conduct and practice, and
- enforce standards through a disciplinary system.

A real estate broker is licensed to buy, sell, exchange, or lease real property for others for a fee and may operate as a

- sole proprietorship,
- partnership, or
- corporation.

The real estate **brokerage** may be independent or part of a regional or national franchise.

A real estate salesperson is licensed to perform real estate activities **only** on behalf of a licensed real estate broker.

A broker-employer is liable for the actions of the salesperson within the scope of the employment agreement.

An **independent contractor** is a real estate salesperson who

- usually receives a commission, with no withholding for Social Security, income tax, and other purposes;
- has the freedom to set hours and accomplish goals;
- does not relieve the broker of liability for related work activities of the salesperson; and
- must comply with Internal Revenue Service (IRS) requirements for a qualified real estate agent.

An **employee** is a salesperson

- who may receive salary in lieu of or in addition to commission;
- who may receive benefits, such as health insurance, profit-sharing, and workers' compensation;
- whose broker is required to withhold Social Security, income taxes, and other applicable federal and state taxes from earnings of the salesperson;
- whose broker sets hours, duties, and other specifics of day-to-day work; and
- whose broker has liability for related work activities of the salesperson.

A real estate assistant is

- a licensed employee of the employing broker, and
- if unlicensed, is limited in the activities that can be undertaken.

The Internet is invaluable for communication, research, marketing, and advertising of a brokerage and includes

- e-mail, as a quick and effective way to access most consumers;
- blogs to communicate with other agents and clients;
- vlogs (video blogs), which are becoming increasingly popular and helpful but tend to be expensive to produce;
- multiple listing services (MLSs), which may offer shared Web listings;
- real estate brokerage and real estate salesperson Web pages offering property details;
- Realtor.com, sponsored by the National Association of REALTORS®, and other popular Web sites to pull in prospective buyers and sellers; and
- effective advertising, which must comply with state and federal laws.

Electronic contracting includes

■ the **Uniform Electronic Transactions Act (UETA)**, which has been adopted in most states and does not require electronic communication, but if it is used, the
   — contract cannot be denied legal effect just because electronic record was used, and
   — the record or signature cannot be denied legal effect just because it is in electronic format;

■ the **Electronic Signatures in Global and National Commerce Act (E-Sign)**, which functions as **electronic transactions** law in states that have not enacted UETA and makes contracts (including signatures) and records legally enforceable, regardless of the medium in which they are created.

Broker's compensation must be agreed upon before agency relationship is established and can be a **commission** based on sales price, flat fee, or hourly rate:

■ **Fee for services** is based on charges for separate broker activities that the client desires (unbundling of services).

■ Some states now require **minimum services** to be offered by the broker.

■ The broker may set a minimum commission rate acceptable for the firm, but any attempt to impose a uniform commission rate would be a violation of state and federal antitrust laws.

■ *Entitled to* compensation means that an individual must be
   — a licensed real estate broker;
   — employed by the buyer or the seller under a valid contract; and
   — the **procuring cause** of the sale by starting or causing a chain of events that resulted in the sale.

■ The commission is earned when the seller accepts an offer from **ready, willing, and able buyer** prepared to buy on the seller's terms and ready to take positive steps toward consummation of the transaction.

A salesperson's compensation is set by mutual agreement of the employing broker and the salesperson.

Antitrust laws are both state and federal (**Sherman Antitrust Act**) that prohibit

■ monopolies; and

■ contracts, combinations, and conspiracies that unreasonably restrain trade, including
   — price-fixing;
   — group boycotting;
   — allocation of customers or markets; and
   — tie-in agreements (tying agreements) forcing customers to purchase a product when only another was wanted.

Penalties for antitrust violations include the following:

■ Under the Sherman Antitrust Act, violators face up to a $1 million fine and ten years in prison, with corporate fines as high as $100 million.

■ In a civil suit, the successful plaintiff may recover triple damages plus attorney's fees and costs.

Do-not-call legislation is found at federal and state levels:

- The **National Do Not Call Registry** (regulated by the Federal Trade Commission)
  — lists telephone numbers of consumers who have asked to be registered and
  — prohibits interstate calls to those numbers to sell goods or services.
- Many states provide their own do-not-call legislation for in-state calls.

■ RELATED WEB SITES

Association of Real Estate License Law Officials: *www.arello.org*
Internet Listing Display Policy: *www.realtor.org/ild/*
National Do Not Call Registry: *www.donotcall.gov*
Uniform Electronic Transactions Act:
    www.law.upenn.edu/bll/archives/ulc/fnact99/1990s/ueta99.htm
U.S. Department of Justice, Antitrust Division: *www.usdoj.gov/atr/*
U.S. Internal Revenue Service: *www.irs.gov*

CHAPTER 5 QUIZ

1. Which statement *BEST* explains the meaning of this sentence: "To recover a commission for brokerage services, a broker must *be employed* as the agent of the client"?
   a. The broker must work in a real estate office.
   b. The client must make an express or implied agreement to pay a commission to the broker.
   c. The broker must express an interest in representing the client.
   d. The broker must have a salesperson employed in the office.

2. Licensees who are paid in a lump sum and who are personally responsible for paying their own taxes are probably
   a. transactional brokers.
   b. buyer's agents.
   c. independent contractors.
   d. employees.

3. A licensed real estate salesperson entered a written contract with a broker, specifying that the salesperson is not an employee. In the past year, just less than half of the salesperson's income from real estate activities came from sales commissions. The remainder was based on an hourly wage paid by the broker. Using these facts, it is *MOST* likely that the IRS would classify the salesperson as which of the following for federal income tax purposes?
   a. Self-employed
   b. Employee
   c. Independent contractor
   d. Part-time real estate salesperson

    B p 75

4. When acting as an employee rather than an independent contractor, a salesperson may be obligated to
   a. list properties in his or her own name.
   b. work set hours.
   c. accept a commission from another broker.
   d. advertise property on his or her own behalf.

5. A real estate broker learns that her neighbor wishes to sell his house. The broker knows the property well and is able to persuade a customer-buyer to make an offer for the property. The broker then asks the neighbor if she can present an offer from the prospective buyer, and the neighbor agrees. At this point, which statement is *TRUE*? p.71
   a. The neighbor is not obligated to pay the broker a commission.
   b. The buyer is obligated to pay the broker for locating the property.
   c. The neighbor is obligated to pay the broker a commission for producing an offer to purchase.
   d. The broker may not be considered the procuring cause without a written contract.

6. A broker would have the right to dictate which of the following to an independent contractor?
   a. Number of hours the person would have to work
   b. Work schedule the person would have to follow
   c. Sales meetings the person would need to attend
   d. Compensation the person would receive

7. Two licensees were found guilty of conspiring with each other to allocate real estate brokerage markets. A woman suffered a $90,000 loss because of their activities. If the woman brings a civil suit against the two licensees, what can she expect to recover?
   a. Nothing, because a civil suit cannot be brought for damages resulting from antitrust activities
   b. Only $90,000—the amount of actual damages the woman suffered
   c. Actual damages plus attorney's fees and costs
   d. $270,000 plus attorney's fees and costs

8. Two salespeople who work for the same company agree to divide their town into a northern region and a southern region; one salesperson will handle listings in the northern region, and the other will handle listings in the southern region. Which statement is *TRUE* regarding this agreement?

    a. The agreement does not violate antitrust laws.

    b. The agreement constitutes illegal price-fixing.

    c. The two salespeople have violated the Sherman Antitrust Act and are liable for triple damages.

    d. The two salespeople are guilty of group boycotting with regard to other salespeople in their office.

9. A state has recently updated its *Rules and Regulations for the Real Estate Profession*. Assuming this state is like all other states and provinces, which statement is *TRUE* regarding this publication?

    a. The rules and regulations are state laws enacted by the legislature.

    b. The rules and regulations are a set of administrative rules adopted by the state real estate commission and do not have the same force and effect as the statutory license law.

    c. The rules and regulations are a set of administrative rules adopted by the state real estate commission that define the statutory license law and have the same force and effect as the license law itself.

    d. The rules and regulations create a suggested level of competence and behavior but are not enforceable against real estate licensees.

10. After a particularly challenging transaction finally closes, the client gives a salesperson a check for $500 "for all your extra work." Which statement is accurate?

    a. While such compensation is irregular, it is appropriate for the salesperson to accept the check.

    b. The salesperson may receive compensation only from the broker.

    c. The salesperson should accept the check and deposit it immediately in a special escrow account.

    d. The salesperson's broker is entitled to 80 percent of the check.

11. A broker has established the following office policy: "All listings taken by any salesperson associated with this real estate brokerage must include compensation based on a 7 percent commission. No lower commission rate is acceptable." If the broker attempts to impose this uniform commission requirement, which statement is *TRUE*?

    a. A homeowner may sue the broker for violating the antitrust law's prohibition against price-fixing.

    b. The salespeople associated with the brokerage will not be bound by the requirement and may negotiate any commission rate they choose.

    c. The broker must present the uniform commission policy to the local professional association for approval.

    d. The broker may, as a matter of office policy, legally set the minimum commission rate acceptable for the firm.

12. A real estate company has adopted a 100 percent commission plan. The monthly desk rent required of sales associates is $1,500, payable on the last day of the month. In August, a sales associate closed an $189,500 sale with a 6 percent commission and a $125,000 sale with a 5.5 percent commission. The salesperson's additional expenses for the month were $2,170. How much of the total monthly income did the salesperson keep?
    a. $14,575
    b. $16,075
    c. $16,745
    d. $18,245

13. A salesperson took a listing on a house that sold for $329,985. The commission rate was 8 percent. Another salesperson employed by another broker found the buyer. The listing broker received 60 percent of the commission on the sale; the buyer's broker received 40 percent. If the listing broker kept 30 percent and paid the listing salesperson the remainder, how much did the listing salesperson earn on this sale?
    a. $3,167.86
    b. $7,391.66
    c. $11,087.50
    d. $15,839.28

14. On the sale of any property, a salesperson's compensation is based on the total commission paid to the broker. The salesperson receives 30 percent of the first $2,500, 40 percent of any amount between $2,500 and $7,500, and 50 percent of any amount exceeding $7,500. If a property sells for $234,500 and the broker's commission rate is 6.5 percent, what is the salesperson's total compensation?
    a. $5,847.00
    b. $6,621.25
    c. $6,871.25
    d. $7,621.25

15. A broker helps a buyer and a seller with paperwork but does not represent either party. This is
    a. dual agency.
    b. prohibited in all states because a broker must always represent one party.
    c. transactional brokerage.
    d. designated agency.

16. The amount of commission paid to a salesperson is determined by
    a. state law.
    b. the local real estate board.
    c. mutual agreement with the broker.
    d. mutual agreement with the client.

17. A broker was accused of violating antitrust laws. Of the following, the broker was MOST likely accused of
    a. not having an equal housing opportunity sign in the office window.
    b. undisclosed dual agencies.
    c. price-fixing.
    d. dealing in unlicensed exchange services.

18. A real estate broker was responsible for a chain of events that resulted in the sale of one of a client's properties. This is referred to as
    a. pro forma.
    b. procuring cause.
    c. private offering.
    d. proffered offer.

19. A salesperson wants to be classified as a *qualified real estate agent*—the equivalent of holding independent contractor status. The salesperson must meet all of the following requirements *EXCEPT*
    a. receive substantially all income from the brokerage based on production, not time worked.
    b. be free from supervision by the broker and office manager.
    c. hold a current real estate license.
    d. have a written agreement with the broker stating that the salesperson will not be treated as an employee for federal tax purposes.

20. A real estate salesperson, classified by the IRS as an independent contractor, receives
    a. a monthly salary or hourly wage.
    b. company-provided health insurance.
    c. a company-provided automobile.
    d. negotiated commissions on transactions.

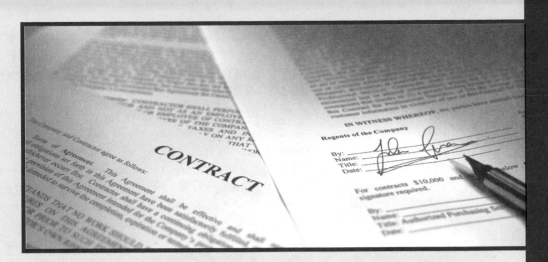

6 CHAPTER

Listing Agreements and Buyer Representation

■ **LEARNING OBJECTIVES** *When you have finished reading this chapter, you should be able to*

■ **identify** the different types of listing and buyer representation agreements and their terms;

■ **describe** the ways in which a listing may be terminated;

■ **explain** the listing process and the parts of the listing agreement;

■ **distinguish** between the characteristics of the various types of listing and buyer representation agreements; and

■ **define** the following *key terms:*

buyer agency agreement	exclusive-right-to-sell listing	net listing
exclusive-agency listing	multiple listing service (MLS)	open listing

LISTING AGREEMENTS AND BUYER REPRESENTATION

A listing agreement is an employment contract that creates a special agency between the property owner and the broker. The various types of listing agreements establish the basic relationship between the parties and provide different levels of rights and responsibilities for the listing broker. Perhaps most important, listings address the essential questions of how a property is marketed and how the agent will be compensated. A buyer representation agreement is an employment contract as well, because it establishes the rights and responsibilities of the broker as agent for the buyer. Various kinds of buyer representation agreements establish different levels of relationships between the agent and the buyer-principal.

In short, listing and buyer representation agreements are the fundamental, bedrock documents of the real estate profession. To understand who you are as a real estate professional, you must understand how these documents work, what they say, and what they mean to you.

LISTING AGREEMENTS

A listing agreement is an employment contract between a broker and a seller. It is a contract for the real estate professional services of the broker, not for the transfer of real estate. All states, either by their statutes of frauds or by specific rule from their real estate licensing authorities, require that the listing agreement be in writing to be enforceable in court.

As an agent, the broker is authorized to represent the principal (and the principal's real estate) to consumers. That authorization includes obtaining and submitting offers for the property. The real estate salesperson's authority to provide brokerage services originates with the broker. Even though the real estate salesperson may perform most, if not all, of the listing services, the listing remains with the broker.

Under both the law of agency and most state license laws, only a broker can act as agent to list, sell, rent, or purchase another person's real estate and provide other services to a principal. A salesperson who performs these acts does so only in the name and under the supervision of the broker (i.e., a salesperson is a general agent of the broker).

Types of Listing Agreements

Several types of listing agreements exist. The type of contract determines the specific rights and obligations of the parties. (See Table 6.1.)

Exclusive-Right-to-Sell Listing

- One authorized broker-agent receives a commission.
- Seller pays broker-agent regardless of who sells property.

Exclusive-right-to-sell listing   In an **exclusive-right-to-sell listing,** one broker is appointed as the seller's sole agent. The broker is given the exclusive right, or authorization, to market the seller's property. If the property is sold while the listing is in effect, the seller must pay the broker a commission, *regardless of who sells the property.* In other words, whether the seller finds a buyer with or without the broker's assistance, the seller *still* must pay the broker a commission. Sellers

	Exclusive-Right-to-Sell	Exclusive-Agency	Open Listing
TABLE 6.1	One broker	One broker	Multiple brokers
Types of Listing Agreements	Broker is paid regardless of who sells the house.	Broker is paid only if the broker is procuring cause.	Only selling broker is paid.
		Seller retains the right to sell without obligation.	Seller retains the right to sell without obligation.

benefit from this form of agreement because the broker feels freer to spend time and money actively marketing the property, making a timely and profitable sale more likely. From the broker's perspective, an exclusive-right-to-sell listing offers the greatest opportunity to receive a commission.

Exclusive-agency listing   In an **exclusive-agency listing**, one broker is authorized to act as the exclusive agent of the principal. However, *the seller retains the right to sell the property without the obligation to pay the broker*.

Open listing   In an **open listing** (also known in some areas as a nonexclusive listing), the seller retains the right to employ any number of brokers as agents. The brokers can act simultaneously, and the seller is obligated to pay a commission to only the broker who successfully produces a ready, willing, and able buyer. If the seller personally sells the property without the aid of any of the brokers, the seller is not obligated to pay a commission.

The terms of an open listing must still be negotiated, however. These negotiated terms should be in writing to protect the agent's ability to collect an agreed-on fee from the seller. Written terms may be in the form of a listing agreement (if the agent represents the seller) or a fee agreement (if the agent represents the buyer or the seller does not wish to be represented).

Special Listing Provisions

Multiple listing   A multiple-listing clause may be included in an exclusive listing. It is used by brokers who are members of the **multiple listing service (MLS)**. As previously discussed, the MLS is a marketing organization whose broker members make their own exclusive listings available through other brokers and gain access to other brokers' listed properties as well. (See Chapter 4.)

The MLS offers advantages to brokers, sellers, and buyers. Brokers develop a sizable inventory of properties to be sold and are assured a portion of the commission if they list property or participate in the sale of another broker's listing. Sellers gain because the property is exposed to a larger market. Buyers gain because of the variety of properties on the market.

The contractual obligations among the member brokers of an MLS vary widely. Most MLSs require that a broker turn over new listings to the service within a specific, fairly short period of time after the broker obtains the listing. The length of time during which the listing broker can offer a property exclusively without

Exclusive-Agency Listing

- There is one authorized agent.
- Brokers receive a commission only if they are the procuring cause.
- Seller retains the right to sell without obligation.

Open Listing

- There are multiple agents.
- Only the selling agent is entitled to a commission.
- Seller retains the right to sell independently without obligation.

notifying the other member brokers varies. Some MLSs, however, permit a broker up to five days before the listing must be submitted to the service.

Under the provisions of most MLSs, a participating broker makes a unilateral offer of cooperation and compensation to other member brokers. The broker must have the written consent of the seller to include the property in an MLS. If a broker chooses to be an agent for the buyer of a property in the MLS, that broker must notify the listing broker before any communication with the seller takes place. All brokers must determine the appropriate way to proceed to protect their clients.

IN PRACTICE Technology has enhanced the benefits of MLS membership. In addition to providing instant access to information about the status of listed properties, MLSs often offer a broad range of other useful information about mortgage loans, real estate taxes and assessments, and municipalities and school districts. They are equally helpful to the licensee who needs to make a competitive market analysis to determine the value of a particular property before suggesting an appropriate range of listing prices. Computer-assisted searches also help buyers select properties that best meet their needs.

> In a **net listing**, the broker is entitled to any amount exceeding the seller's stated net proceeds.

Net listing A **net listing** provision specifies that the seller will receive a net amount of money from any sale, with the excess going to the listing broker as commission. The broker is free to offer the property at any price greater than that net amount. Because a net listing can create a conflict of interest between the broker's fiduciary responsibility to the seller and the broker's profit motive, it is illegal in many states and discouraged in others.

■ TERMINATION OF LISTINGS

A listing agreement's success depends on the broker's professional efforts. Because the broker's services are unique, a listing cannot be assigned to another broker without the principal's written consent. The property owner cannot force the broker to perform, but the broker's failure to work diligently toward fulfilling the contract's terms constitutes a breach of the listing agreement. If the listing is canceled by the broker, the seller may be entitled to sue the broker for damages.

On the other hand, a property owner could be liable for damages to the broker by refusing to cooperate with the broker's reasonable requests, such as allowing the broker to show the property to prospective buyers or refusing to proceed with a complete sales contract.

A listing agreement may be terminated for the following reasons:

■ When the agreement's purpose is fulfilled, such as when a ready, willing, and able buyer has been found
■ When the agreement's term expires
■ If the property is destroyed or its use is changed by some force outside the owner's control, such as a zoning change or condemnation by eminent domain (See Chapter 7.)
■ If title to the property is transferred by operation of law, as in the case of the owner's bankruptcy or foreclosure

- If the broker and seller mutually agree to cancel the listing
- If either the broker or the seller dies or becomes incapacitated. If the salesperson dies or becomes incapacitated, the listing is still valid.

Expiration of Listing Period

All exclusive listings should specify a definite period during which the broker is to be employed. In most states, failing to specify a definite termination date in a listing is grounds for the suspension or revocation of a real estate license.

Courts have discouraged the use of *automatic extension clauses* in exclusive listings, such as a clause providing for a base period of 90 days that "continues thereafter until terminated by either party hereto by 30 days' notice in writing." Extension clauses are illegal in some states, and many listing contract forms specifically provide that there can be no automatic extensions of the agreement. Some courts have held that an extension clause actually creates an open listing rather than an exclusive-agency agreement.

Some listing contracts contain a *broker protection clause*. This clause provides that the property owner will pay the listing broker a commission if, within a specified number of days after the listing expires, the owner transfers the property to someone the broker originally introduced to the owner. This clause protects a broker who was the procuring cause from losing a commission because the transaction was completed after the listing expired.

■ THE LISTING PROCESS

Before signing a contract, the broker and the seller must discuss a variety of issues. The seller's main concerns typically are the selling price of the property and the net proceeds. The broker has tools to provide this information.

Common questions sellers may ask include "How quickly will the property sell?" and "What services will the broker provide during the listing period?" This is the broker's opportunity to explain the various types of listing agreements, the ramifications of different agency relationships, and the marketing services the broker provides. At the end of this discussion, the seller should feel comfortable with the decision to list with the broker.

Before the listing agreement is signed, the seller should provide comprehensive information about the property and any personal concerns. Based on this information, the broker can accept the listing with confidence that the seller's goals can be met in a profitable manner for both parties.

Information Needed for Listing Agreements

Obtaining as many facts as possible about the property ensures that most contingencies can be anticipated. This is particularly important when the listing will be shared with other brokers through the MLS and when the other licensees must rely on the information taken by the listing agent.

The information needed for a listing agreement generally includes the

- names and relationship, if any, of the owners;
- street address and legal description of the property;
- size, type, age, and construction of improvements;
- number of rooms and their sizes;
- dimensions of the lot;
- existing loans, including such information as the name and address of each lender, the type of loan, the loan number, the loan balance, the interest rate, the monthly payment which includes principal, interest, taxes, and insurance (PITI), whether the loan may be assumed by the buyer and under what circumstances, and whether the loan may be prepaid without penalty;
- possibility of seller financing;
- amount of any outstanding special assessments and whether they will be paid by the seller or assumed by the buyer;
- zoning classification of the property;
- current (or most recent year's) property taxes;
- neighborhood amenities (e.g., schools, parks and recreational areas, churches, and public transportation);
- real property, if any, to be removed from the premises by the seller and any personal property to be included in the sale for the buyer (both the listing contract and the subsequent purchase contract should be explicit on these points);
- any additional information that would make the property more appealing and marketable; and
- required disclosures regarding property conditions.

Disclosures

Most states have enacted laws requiring that agents disclose whose interests they legally represent. It is important that the seller be informed of the company's policies regarding single agency, dual agency, and buyer agency.

The seller must also disclose property conditions as required by law in most states. These disclosures cover a wide range of structural, mechanical, and other conditions that a prospective purchaser should know about in order to make an informed decision. Frequently, the laws require that the seller complete a standardized form. Licensees should caution sellers to make truthful disclosures to avoid litigation arising from fraudulent or careless misrepresentations.

■ THE LISTING CONTRACT FORM

A wide variety of listing contract forms is available. Some brokers have attorneys draft contracts for their firms, while others use forms prepared by the MLS or licensing authorities. State REALTOR® associations also create forms. Other brokers use a separate information sheet (also known as a profile or data sheet) for recording property features. That sheet is attached to a second form containing the contractual obligations between the seller and the broker: listing price, duration of the agreement, signatures of the parties, and so forth. A sample listing agreement appears in Figure 6.1.

MATH CONCEPTS

CALCULATING SALES PRICES, COMMISSIONS, AND NET TO SELLER

When a property sells, the sales price equals 100 percent of the money being transferred. Therefore, if a broker is to receive a 6 percent commission, 94 percent will remain for the seller's other expenses and equity. To calculate a commission using a sales price of $225,000 and a commission rate of 6 percent, multiply the sales price by the commission rate:

$225,000 × 6% = $225,000 × 0.06 = $13,500 commission

To calculate a sales price using a commission of $13,500 and a commission rate of 7 percent, divide the commission by the commission rate:

$13,500 ÷ 7% = $13,500 ÷ 0.07 = $192,857 sales price

To calculate a commission rate using a commission of $8,200 and a sales price of $164,000, divide the commission by the sales price:

$8,200 ÷ $164,000 = 0.05, or 5% commission rate

To calculate the net to the seller using a sales price of $125,000 and a commission rate of 8 percent, multiply the sales price by 100 percent minus the commission rate:

$125,000 × (100% − 8%) = $125,000 × (92%) = $125,000 × 0.92 = $115,000

The same result can be achieved by calculating the commission ($125,000 × 0.08 = $10,000) and deducting it from the sales price ($125,000 − $10,000 = $115,000); however, this involves unnecessary extra calculations.

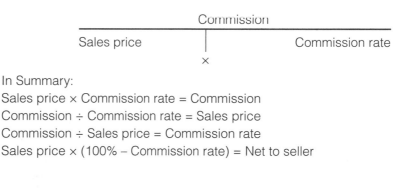

In Summary:
Sales price × Commission rate = Commission
Commission ÷ Commission rate = Sales price
Commission ÷ Sales price = Commission rate
Sales price × (100% − Commission rate) = Net to seller

F I G U R E   6.1

Sample Listing Agreement

VIRGINIA REGIONAL LISTING AGREEMENT - EXCLUSIVE RIGHT TO SELL

This Agreement is made on _____, _____, by and between
_____ ("Seller") and
_____ ("Broker").
("Firm Name")

In consideration of providing the services and facilities described herein, the Broker is hereby granted the exclusive right
to sell the Property known as: _____, Virginia
_____ ("Property"). Legal Description _____
Tax Map No./ ID#_____.

1. The Property is offered for sale at a selling price of $ _____, or such other price as later
agreed upon, which price includes the Broker's compensation. In the event of a sale, the Seller will sign a sales
contract enforceable in the Commonwealth of Virginia.

The Sales Price includes the following personal property and fixtures which shall be transferred free of liens: A. Any
existing built-in heating and central air conditioning equipment, plumbing and lighting fixtures, storm windows, storm
doors, screens, installed wall-to-wall carpeting, window shades, blinds, smoke and heat detectors, tv antennas, exterior
trees and shrubs and B. The items marked YES below as currently installed or offered:

YES	NO	ITEM	YES	NO	ITEM	YES	NO	ITEM	YES	NO	ITEM
☐	☐	Stove or Range	☐	☐	Disposer	☐	☐	Ceiling Fan(s) # ____	☐	☐	Alarm System
☐	☐	Cooktop	☐	☐	Freezer	☐	☐	Washer	☐	☐	Intercom
☐	☐	Wall Oven(s) # ___	☐	☐	Window Fan(s) # ____	☐	☐	Dryer	☐	☐	Storage Shed(s) # ___
☐	☐	Refrigerator(s) # ___	☐	☐	Window A/C Unit(s) # __	☐	☐	Furnace Humidifier	☐	☐	Garage Opener(s) #__
☐	☐	w/ ice maker	☐	☐	Pool, Equip. & Cover	☐	☐	Electronic Air Filter	☐	☐	w/ remote(s) #
☐	☐	Dishwasher	☐	☐	Hot Tub, Equip. & Cover	☐	☐	Central Vacuum	☐	☐	Playground Equipment
☐	☐	Built-in Microwave	☐	☐	Satellite Dish and Equip.	☐	☐	Water Treatment Sys	☐	☐	Wood Stove
☐	☐	Trash Compactor	☐	☐	Attic Fan(s)	☐	☐	Exhaust Fan(s)	☐	☐	Fireplace Screen/Drs
☐	☐	Sump Pump	☐	☐	Window Treatments						

EDUCATIONAL SAMPLE

Other inclusions or exclusions: _____
_____

WATER, SEWAGE, HEATING, AND CENTRAL AIR CONDITIONING: (Check all that apply)
Water Supply: ☐ Public   ☐ Well   ☐ Other _____   ☐ Hot Water: ☐ Oil   ☐ Gas   ☐ Elec.
Sewage Disposal: ☐ Public   ☐ Septic   ☐ # BR _____   ☐ Air Conditioning: ☐ Gas   ☐ Elec. ☐ Heat Pump
Heating: ☐ Oil   ☐ Gas   ☐ Elec.   ☐ Heat Pump   ☐ Other_____

The Seller will deliver the Property in substantially the same condition as on the Contract Date and in broom clean
condition with all trash and debris removed. The Seller will warrant to Buyer that the existing appliances, heating,
cooling, plumbing and electrical systems and equipment and smoke and heat detectors (as required) will be in normal
order as of the possession date.

2. **The Broker and the Sales Associate(s) shall promote the interests of the Seller by:**
A) performing the terms of this Agreement;
B) seeking a buyer at a price and terms agreed upon herein or otherwise acceptable to the Seller. However, the
Broker and the Sales Associate(s) shall not be obligated to seek additional offers to purchase the Property while the
Property is subject to a contract of sale, unless stated herein or as the contract of sale so provides;
C) presenting in a timely manner all written offers or counteroffers to and from the Seller even when the Property is

FIGURE 6.1

Sample Listing Agreement (Continued)

already subject to a contract of sale;
D) disclosing to the Seller all material facts related to the Property or concerning the transaction of which the Broker and Sales Associate(s) have actual knowledge;
E) accounting for in a timely manner all money and property received in which the Seller has or may have an interest.

Unless otherwise provided by law or the Seller consents in writing to the release of the information, the Broker and the Sales Associate(s) shall maintain the confidentiality of all personal and financial information and other matters identified as confidential by the Seller, if that information is received from the Seller during the brokerage relationship. In satisfying these duties, the Broker and the Sales Associate(s) shall exercise ordinary care, comply with all applicable laws and regulations and treat all prospective buyers honestly and not knowingly give them false information; and **the Broker and Sales Associate(s) shall disclose to prospective buyers all material adverse facts pertaining to the physical condition of the Property which are actually known by them.** In addition, the Broker and the Sales Associate(s) may provide assistance to a buyer or prospective buyer by performing ministerial acts that are not inconsistent with the Broker's and the Sales Associate's duties under this Agreement. The Seller acknowledges that the Broker and Sales Associate(s) and any cooperating brokers and sales associates may act on behalf of the Seller as the Seller's representatives.

Buyer representation occurs when buyers contract to use the services of their own broker (known as a buyer representative) to act on their behalf.

Designated representation occurs when a buyer and seller in one transaction are represented by different Sales Associate(s) affiliated with the same Broker. Each of these Sales Associates, known as a Designated Representative, represents fully the interests of a different client in the same transaction. Designated Representatives are not dual representatives if each represents only the buyer or only the seller in a specific real estate transaction. Except for disclosure of confidential information to the Broker, each Designated Representative is bound by the confidentiality requirements as above. The Broker remains a dual representative.   The Seller consents to designated representation **OR**   The Seller does not consent to designated representation which means the Seller does not allow the Property to be shown to a buyer represented by this Broker through another Designated Representative associated with the firm. The Broker will notify other associates within the firm via the MLS whether the Seller consents or does not consent.

Dual representation occurs when a buyer and seller in one transaction are represented by the same Broker and the same Sales Associate(s). When the parties agree to dual representation, the ability of the Broker and the Sales Associate(s) to represent either party fully and exclusively is limited. The confidentiality of all information of all clients shall be maintained as above.   The Seller consents to dual representation **OR**   The Seller does not consent to dual representation which means the Seller does not allow the Property to be shown to a buyer represented by this Broker through the same Sales Associate(s).

EDUCATIONAL SAMPLE

3.   The Broker and Sales Associate(s), in response to inquiries from buyers or cooperating brokers shall, with the Seller's approval, divulge the existence of offers on the property. Seller   does **OR**   does not authorize the Broker and Sales Associate to divulge such information to buyers or cooperating brokers.

4.   This Exclusive Right to Sell will expire at midnight on _____.

5.   This Property shall be shown and made available without regard to race, color, religion, sex, handicap, familial status or national origin as well as all classes protected by the laws of the United States, the Commonwealth of Virginia and applicable local jurisdictions.

6.   The Broker shall make a blanket unilateral offer of cooperation and compensation to other brokers in any Multiple Listing Service that the Broker deems appropriate. The Broker shall disseminate information regarding the Property, including the entry date, listing price(s), final price and all terms, and expired or withdrawn status, by printed form and/or electronic computer service, which may include the internet, during and after the expiration of this Agreement. The Broker shall enter the listing information into the MLS data base within 48 hours (unless otherwise instructed in writing by the Seller) after all Sellers= signatures have been obtained.

7.   A.   The Seller shall pay the Broker compensation of _____in cash if, during the term of this Agreement, anyone produces a buyer ready, willing and able to buy the Property. In addition to the Broker's compensation, an additional fee of _____ will be collected from the Seller payable to the Broker, at the time of settlement. The compensation is also earned if within _____ days after the expiration or termination of this

FIGURE 6.1

Sample Listing Agreement (Continued)

Agreement, a contract is ratified with a ready, willing and able buyer to whom the Property has been shown during the term of this Agreement; provided, however, that the compensation need not be paid if a contract is ratified on the Property while the Property is listed with another real estate company.

B.   The Broker acknowledges receipt of a retainer fee in the amount of _____, which ☐shall, **OR** ☐shall not be subtracted from any compensation due the Broker under this Agreement. The retainer is non-refundable and is earned when paid.

C.   The listing broker shall offer compensation to the selling broker as indicated:

Subagency Compensation _____   Buyer Agency Compensation _____   Non Agency Compensation _____

Note: Compensation shall be shown by a percentage of the gross selling price, a definite dollar amount or "N"for no compensation. No Multiple Listing Service or Association of REALTORS® is a party to this Agreement and no Multiple Listing Service or Association of REALTORS® sets, controls, recommends or suggests the amount of compensation for any brokerage service rendered pursuant to this Agreement.

8.   The Seller is participating in any type of employee relocation program ☐Yes **OR** ☐ No.

If "Yes": (a) the program is named: _____ , Contact #_____ and
(b) terms of the program are: _____
_____.

If "No" or the Seller has failed to list a specific employee relocation program, then the Broker shall have no obligation to cooperate with or compensate any undisclosed program.

9.   In consideration of the use of Broker's services and facilities and of the facilities of any REALTOR® Multiple Listing Service, the Seller and Seller's heirs and assigns hereby release the Broker, sales associates accompanying buyers or prospective buyers, any REALTORS® Multiple Listing Service and the directors, officers and employees thereof, including officials of any parent Association of REALTORS®, except for malfeasance on the part of such parties, from any liability to the Seller for vandalism, theft or damage of any nature whatsoever to the Property or its contents during the term of this Agreement, and that the Seller waives any and all rights, claims and causes of action against them and holds them harmless for any property damage or personal injury arising from the use or access to the Property by any person during the term of this Agreement.

10. The Seller retains full responsibility for the Property, including all utilities, maintenance, physical security and liability during the term of this Agreement and the sales contract period. Virginia licensed real estate salespersons and appraisers, inspectors and other persons shall be given access as needed to the Property to facilitate and/or consummate a sale. Authorization is granted to the Broker to show the Property during reasonable hours. Authority is granted to the Broker to:

A) Place a "For Sale" sign on the Property and to remove all other such signs
B) Place a common keysafe/lockbox on the Property containing keys and information necessary to obtain full access to the Property.

11. The Seller represents that the Property ☐is, **OR** ☐is not located within a development which is a Condominium or Cooperative. Condominiums or Cooperatives being offered for sale are subject to the receipt by buyers of the required Disclosures, and the Seller is responsible for payment of appropriate fees and for providing these disclosure documents to prospective buyers as prescribed in the Condominium Act, Section 55-79.39 et seq., and the Cooperative Act, Section 55-424, et seq., of the Code of Virginia.

12. The Seller represents that the Property   is, **OR**   is not located within a development(s) which is subject to the Virginia Property Owners ' Association Act, Sections 55-508 through 55-516 of the Code of Virginia. If the Property is within such a development, the Seller is responsible for payment of the appropriate fees and for providing these disclosure documents to the buyers.

13. The Seller acknowledges that the Broker has informed the Seller of the Seller=s rights and obligations under the Virginia Residential Property Disclosure Act. This Property ☐ is, **OR** ☐is not exempt from the Act. If not exempt, the Seller has completed and provided to the Broker: ☐a Residential Property Disclosure Statement where the Seller is making representations regarding the condition of the Property on which the buyer may rely, **OR** ☐a Residential Property Disclaimer Statement where the Seller is making no representations regarding the condition of the Property and is selling the Property "as is", except as may be provided otherwise in the sales contract.

FIGURE 6.1

Sample Listing Agreement (Continued)

14. The Seller represents that the residential dwelling(s) at the Property ☐were, **OR** ☐were not constructed before 1978. If the dwelling(s) were constructed before 1978, the Seller is subject to Federal law concerning disclosure of the possible presence of lead-based paint at the Property, and the Seller acknowledges that the Broker has informed the Seller of the Seller's obligations under the law. If the dwelling(s) were constructed before 1978, unless exempt under 42 U.S.C. 4852d, the Seller has completed and provided to the Broker the form, Sale: Disclosure And Acknowledgment Of Information On Lead-Based Paint And/Or Lead-Based Paint Hazards@ or equivalent form.

15.   The Property may be sold subject to existing Deed(s) of Trust, having a total unpaid balance of approximately $ _____.

16.   The Seller shall provide a _____ Deed of Trust Loan in the amount of $ _____ with further terms to be negotiated.

> **Sellers Proceeds:** The Seller acknowledges that Seller's proceeds may not be available at the time of settlement. The receipt of proceeds may be subject to the Virginia Wet Settlement Act, and may be subject to other laws, rules and regulations (e.g. Virginia estate statutes and the Foreign Investment Real Property Tax Act). Sellers are advised to seek legal and/or financial advice concerning these matters.

17. Other terms: _____
_____
_____

The terms and conditions of this Agreement must be used as a basis for presenting Property to prospective buyers, and, unless amended in writing, contain the final and entire Agreement between the parties hereto. The parties shall not be bound by any terms, conditions, oral statements, warranties, or representations not herein contained. Seen and agreed and receipt of a signed copy of this Agreement is hereby acknowledged.

_____ Date _____ Seller   _____ Broker
                                                                          (Firm)

_____ Date _____ Seller   _____
                                                                          (Address)

The Seller ☐is, **OR** ☐is not a licensed (active/inactive) real estate agent/broker

_____   _____, VA __

_____
(Seller's Mailing Address)

_____   Date: _____ By: _____
(City, State, and Zip Code)   (Broker/Sales Manager)

                                  Sales Associate: _____
                                                          (Designated Representative)

Phone (O) _____   Phone (O) _____

Phone (H) _____   Phone (H) _____

Fax #_____   Email _____   Fax #_____   Email _____

© 2003 Northern Virginia Association of REALTORS®, Inc.

Listing Agreement Issues

Regardless of which form of listing agreement is used, the same considerations arise in most real estate transactions. This means that all listing contracts require similar information. Nonetheless, licensees should review the specific forms used in their areas and refer to their states' laws for any specific requirements.

The broker's authority and responsibilities   The contract should specify whether the broker may place a sign on the property and advertise; it should address when the property can be shown, allowing reasonable notice to the seller. It should also address whether or not the broker may accept earnest money on behalf of the seller, and the responsibilities for holding the funds. The broker does not have the authority to sign any legal documents or contracts without first obtaining a power of attorney from the seller or the seller's representative.

The names of all parties to the contract   Anyone who has an ownership interest in the property must be identified and should sign the listing to validate it. If the property is owned under some form of co-ownership, that fact should be clearly established. (See Chapter 8.) If one or more of the owners is married, the spouse's consent and signature on the contract to release any marital rights is required in most states. If the property is in the possession of a tenant, that should be disclosed (along with the terms of the tenancy), and instructions should be included on how the property is to be shown to prospective buyers.

The brokerage firm   The brokerage company name, the employing broker, and if appropriate, the salesperson taking the listing must all be identified.

The listing price   This is the proposed sales price. The seller's proceeds will be reduced by unpaid real estate taxes, special assessments, mortgage debts, and any other outstanding obligations.

Real property and personal property   Any personal property that will be sold must be explicitly identified. Items of real property that the seller expects to remove at the time of the sale must be specified as well. Some items that may later become points of negotiation might include major appliances, swimming pool and spa equipment, fireplace accessories, storage sheds, window treatments, stacked firewood, and stored heating oil.

Leased equipment   It must be determined if leased equipment—security systems, cable television boxes, water softeners, special antennas—will be left with the property. If so, the seller is responsible for notifying the equipment's lessor of the change of property ownership.

The description of the premises   In addition to the street address, the legal description, lot size, and tax parcel number may be required for future purchase offers.

The proposed dates for the closing and the buyer's possession   These dates should be based on an anticipated closing date. The listing agreement should allow adequate time for the paperwork involved (including the buyer's qualification for any financing) and the move-in date to be arranged by the seller and the buyer.

The closing   An attorney, title company, or escrow company should be considered and retained as soon as possible. A designated party will be needed to complete the settlement statements, disburse the funds, and file the proper forms, such as documents to be recorded and documents to be sent to the IRS.

The evidence of ownership   A warranty deed, title insurance policy, or abstract of title with an attorney's opinion can be used for proof of title.

Encumbrances   All liens will be paid in full by the seller or be assumed by the buyer at the closing.

Home warranty program   It may be advisable for a buyer or a seller to purchase a home warranty with the property. A home warranty program covers such things as plumbing, electrical and heating systems, water heaters, duct work, and major appliances. A home warranty can be an attractive selling point. In most states, a home warranty program can be an option in the listing contract or an offer to purchase. Coverages, deductibles, limitations, and exclusions in the contract should be clearly specified.

The commission   The circumstances under which a commission will be paid must be specifically stated in the contract. The fee can be either a percentage or a flat rate and is usually paid at closing directly by the seller or the party handling the closing.

The termination of the contract   A contract should provide a way for the parties to terminate the agreement and should specify under what circumstances the contract can be terminated. Under certain circumstances, an agreement can be canceled if the seller arbitrarily refuses to sell or cooperate.

The broker protection clause   Brokers may be well advised to protect their interests against possible fraud or a reluctant buyer's change of heart. It is important to know the circumstances under which a broker will be entitled to a commission after the agreement terminates.

Warranties by the owner   The owner is responsible for certain assurances and disclosures. Is the property suitable for its intended purpose? Does it comply with the appropriate zoning and building codes? Will it be transferred to the buyer in essentially the same condition as it was originally presented, considering repairs or alterations to be made as provided for in a purchase contract? Are there any known defects?

Indemnification (hold harmless) wording   The seller and the broker may agree to hold each other harmless (i.e., not to sue one another) for any incorrect information supplied by one to the other. Indemnification may be offered, regardless of whether the inaccuracies are intentional or unintentional.

Nondiscrimination (equal opportunity) wording   The seller must understand that the property will be shown and offered without regard to the race, color, religion, national origin, family status, sex, or disability of the prospective buyer. Refer to other federal nondiscrimination laws and state and local fair housing laws for a complete listing of protected classes in your area. (See Chapter 20.)

Antitrust wording   The contract should indicate that all commissions have been negotiated between the seller and the broker. It is illegal for commissions to be set by any regulatory agency, trade association, or other industry organization.

The signatures of the parties   All parties identified in the contract must sign the contract, including all individuals who have a legal interest in the property.

The date the contract is signed   This date may be different from the date the contract actually becomes effective. For example, a salesperson takes the listing and then must have the broker sign the contract to accept employment under its terms.

■ BUYER AGENCY AGREEMENTS

Like a listing agreement, a **buyer agency agreement** is an employment contract. In this case, the broker is employed as the *buyer's* agent—the buyer, rather than the seller, is the principal. The purpose of the agreement is to find a suitable property. An agency agreement gives the buyer a degree of representation possible only in a fiduciary relationship. A buyer's broker must protect the buyer's interests at all points in the transaction. Figure 6.2 illustrates a typical buyer agency agreement.

Buyer Representation Issues

A number of issues must be discussed by a broker and a buyer before they sign a buyer agency agreement. For instance, the licensee should make the same disclosures to the buyer that the licensee would make to a seller in a listing agreement. The licensee should explain the forms of agency available and the parties' rights and responsibilities under each type. The specific services provided to a buyer-client should be clearly explained. Compensation issues need to be addressed as well. Buyer's agents may be compensated in the form of a flat fee for services, an hourly rate, or a percentage of the purchase price. The agent may require a *retainer fee* at the time the agreement is signed to cover initial expenses. The retainer may be applied as a credit toward any fees due at the closing. A buyer's agent may be compensated by sharing the commission paid by the seller.

As in any agency agreement, the source of compensation does not determine the relationship. A buyer's agent may be compensated by either the buyer or the seller. Issues of compensation are *always* negotiable.

FIGURE 6.2

Sample Buyer Agency Agreement

EXCLUSIVE RIGHT TO REPRESENT BUYER AGREEMENT

This Agreement is made on_____,_____ between
_____ ("Buyer") and _____("Broker").
(Name of brokerage firm)

In consideration of services and facilities, the Broker is hereby granted the right to represent the Buyer in the acquisition of real property. (As used in this Agreement, "acquisition of real property" shall include any purchase, option, exchange or lease of property or an agreement to do so.)

1. **BUYER'S REPRESENTATIONS**. The Buyer represents that as of the commencement date of this Agreement, the Buyer is not a party to a buyer representation agreement with any other brokerage firm. The Buyer further represents that the Buyer has disclosed to the Sales Associate information about any properties that the Buyer has previously visited at any new homes communities or resale Aopen houses@, or that the Buyer has been shown by any other real estate sales associate(s) in any area where the Buyer seeks to acquire property under this Agreement.

2. **TERM**. This Agreement commences when signed and, subject to Paragraph 7, expires at _____
☐ a.m. **OR** ☐ p.m. on _____,_____.

3. **RETAINER FEE**. The Broker, _____(Name of brokerage firm), acknowledges receipt of a retainer fee in the amount of_____, which ☐ shall **OR** ☐ shall not be subtracted from any compensation due the Broker under this Agreement. The retainer is non-refundable and is earned when paid.

4. **BROKER'S DUTIES**. The Broker and the Sales Associate shall promote the interests of the Buyer by:
    A) performing the terms of this Agreement;
    B) seeking property at a price and terms acceptable to the Buyer;
    C) presenting in a timely manner all written offers or counteroffers to and from the Buyer;
    D) disclosing to the Buyer all material facts related to the property or concerning the transaction of which they have actual knowledge;
    E) accounting for in a timely manner all money and property received in which the Buyer has or may have an interest.

Unless otherwise provided by law or the Buyer consents in writing to the release of the information, the Broker shall maintain the confidentiality of all personal and financial information and other matters identified as confidential by the Buyer, if that information is received from the Buyer during the brokerage relationship. In satisfying these duties, the Broker shall exercise ordinary care, comply with all applicable laws and regulations, treat all prospective sellers honestly and not knowingly give them false information, and disclose whether or not the Buyer's intent is to occupy the property as a principal residence. In addition, the Broker may: show the same property to other buyers; represent other buyers on the same or different properties; represent Sellers relative to other properties; or provide assistance to a seller or prospective seller by performing ministerial acts that are not inconsistent with the Broker's duties under this Agreement.

5. **BUYER'S DUTIES**. The Buyer shall: (a) work exclusively with the Broker during the term of this Agreement; (b) pay the Broker, directly or indirectly, the compensation set forth below; (c) comply with the reasonable requests of the Broker to supply any pertinent financial or personal data needed to fulfill the terms of this Agreement; (d) be available during the Broker=s regular working hours to view properties.

6. **PURPOSE**. The Buyer is retaining the Broker to acquire the following type of property: _____.

F I G U R E   6.2

Sample Buyer Agency Agreement (Continued)

7. **COMPENSATION.** In consideration of the time and effort expended by the Broker on behalf of the Buyer, and in further consideration of the advice and counsel provided to the Buyer, the Buyer shall pay compensation ("Broker's Fee") to the Broker as described below. The Broker's Fee, less the Retainer Fee if so indicated in Paragraph 3 above, shall be earned, due and payable under any of these circumstances whether the transaction is consummated through the services of the Broker or otherwise:

A) If the Buyer enters into a contract to acquire real property during the term of this Agreement and goes to settlement on that contract any time thereafter; **OR**

B) If, within_____ days after expiration or termination of this Agreement, the Buyer enters into a contract to acquire real property that has been described to or shown to the Buyer by the Broker during the term of this Agreement, unless the Buyer has entered into a subsequent "Exclusive Right to Represent Buyer" agreement with another real estate broker; **OR**

C) If, having entered into an enforceable contract to acquire real property during the term of this Agreement, the Buyer defaults under the terms of that contract.

The Broker's Fee shall be _____. In addition to the Broker's compensation, an additional fee of _____ will be collected from the Buyer payable to the Broker, at the time of settlement. If the seller or the seller's representative offers compensation to the Broker, then the Buyer authorizes the Broker to receive such compensation and the amount of such compensation shall be credited against the Buyer's obligation to pay the Broker's Fee. <u>The Broker may retain any additional compensation offered by the seller or seller's representative, even if this causes the compensation paid to the Broker to exceed the fees specified above. In no case shall the compensation be less than the fees specified above.</u>

Any obligation incurred under this Agreement on the part of the Buyer to pay the Broker's Fee shall survive the term of this Agreement.

8. The Buyer is participating in any type of employee relocation program☐Yes **OR** ☐No.

If "Yes": (a) the program is named: _____, and
(b) terms of the program are: _____
_____.

If "No" or the Buyer has failed to list a specific employee relocation program, then the Broker shall have no obligation to cooperate with or compensate any undisclosed program.

9. **DISCLOSED DUAL REPRESENTATION.** The Buyer acknowledges that in the normal course of business the Broker may represent sellers of properties in which the Buyer is interested. If the Buyer wishes to acquire any property listed with the Broker, then the Buyer will be represented in one of the two ways that are permitted under Virginia law in this situation. The written consent required from the parties in each case will be accomplished via execution of the appropriate disclosure form at the time of the contract offer.

Dual representation occurs when a buyer and seller in one transaction are represented by the same Broker and the same Sales Associate. When the parties agree to dual representation, the ability of the Broker and the Sales Associate to represent either party fully and exclusively is limited. The confidentiality of all clients shall be maintained as in Paragraph 4 above.

Designated representation occurs when a buyer and seller in one transaction are represented by different Sales Associates affiliated with the same Broker. Each of these Sales Associates, known as a Designated Representative, represents fully the interests of a different client in the same transaction. Designated Representatives are not dual representatives if each represents only the buyer or only the seller in a specific real estate transaction. Except for disclosure of confidential information to the Broker, each Designated Representative is bound by the confidentiality requirements in Paragraph 4 above. The Broker remains a dual representative.

CHECK ONE CHOICE IN EACH SECTION:

Dual representation: The Buyer ☐does **OR** ☐does not consent to be shown and to consider acquiring properties listed with the Broker through the Sales Associate.

FIGURE 6.2

Sample Buyer Agency Agreement (Continued)

Designated representation: The Buyer ☐ does **OR**   ☐ does not consent to be shown and to consider acquiring properties listed with the Broker through another Designated Representative associated with the firm.

10. **DISCLAIMER.** The buyer acknowledges that the Broker is being retained solely as a real estate agent and not as an attorney, tax advisor, lender, appraiser, surveyor, structural engineer, mold or air quality expert, home inspector or other professional service provider. The Buyer is advised to seek professional advice concerning the condition of the property or concerning legal and tax matters. The Buyer should exercise whatever due diligence the Buyer deems necessary with respect to information on any sexual offenders registered under Chapter 23 ('19.2-387 et. seq.) of Title 19.2. Such information may be obtained by contacting your local police department or the Department of State Police, Central Criminal Records Exchange, at (804)674-2000 or www.vsp.state.va.us.

11. **EQUAL OPPORTUNITY.** Properties shall be shown and made available to the Buyer without regard to race, color, religion, sex, handicap, familial status or national origin as well as all classes protected by the laws of the United States, the Commonwealth of Virginia and applicable local jurisdictions.

12. **OTHER PROVISIONS.** _____
_____
_____
_____

13. **MISCELLANEOUS.** This Agreement, any exhibits and any addenda signed by the parties constitute the entire agreement between the parties and supersedes any other written or oral agreements between the parties. This Agreement can only be modified in writing when signed by both parties. In any action or proceeding involving a dispute between the Buyer, the seller and/or the Broker, arising out of this Agreement, or to collect the Broker's Fee, the prevailing party shall be entitled to receive from the other party reasonable attorney's fees to be determined by the court or arbitrator(s).

(NOTE: The Buyer should consult with the Sales Associate before visiting any resale or new homes or contacting any other REALTORS® representing sellers, to avoid the possibility of confusion over the brokerage relationship and misunderstandings about liability for compensation.)

_____
Brokerage Firm

_____ _____ (SEAL)   _____
Date   Buyers Signature   Address

_____ _____ (SEAL)   _____
Date   Buyers Signature   City, State, Zip Code

The Buyer ☐ does **OR** ☐ does not hold an active or inactive Virginia real estate license.

_____   _____ _____ (SEAL)
Address   Date   Broker/Sales Manager's Signature

_____   _____
City, State, Zip Code   Sales Associate's/Designated Representative's Printed Name

Telephone: _____ _____   Telephone: _____ _____
           Work   Home   Work   Home

Fax: _____ Email: _____   Fax: _____ Email: _____

© 2004 Northern Virginia Association of REALTORS®, Inc.

■ KEY POINT REVIEW

A **listing agreement** is an **employment contract** between a broker and a seller. In all states, the agreement must be in writing to be enforceable in court.

As an **agent**, the **broker** is authorized to represent the **principal** and the principal's real estate to consumers. A real estate **salesperson** is a **general agent** of the broker and can carry out listing services only in the name of and under the supervision of the broker.

The characteristics of an **exclusive-right-to-sell listing** include the following:

- **One broker** is appointed as the seller's sole agent.
- If the property is sold while the listing is in effect, the broker is entitled to a commission, no matter who sells the property.

An **exclusive-agency listing**

- authorizes **one broker** to act as the sole agent of the seller, but
- allows the **seller** to retain the right to sell the property without obligation of payment to the broker.

In an **open listing** (also known as a **nonexclusive listing**),

- the seller retains the right to employ **any** number of brokers;
- the seller is obligated to pay a commission **only** to the broker who success-fully produces a **ready, willing, and able buyer**; and
- the seller is not obligated to pay a commission if the seller personally sells the property without the aid of any broker.

A **multiple-listing clause** permits cooperation with other brokers in the **multiple listing service (MLS)**.

A **net listing** has the following characteristics:

- The excess over the net from the sale will go to the listing broker as commission.
- The broker is free to offer the property at any price greater than the net amount.
- Net listings may be prohibited by state law.

A **listing agreement** may be **terminated** when

- the agreement's **purpose** is fulfilled,
- the agreement's term expires,
- the property is **destroyed**,
- **title** to the property is transferred by operation of law (e.g., bankruptcy),
- the broker and the seller **mutually agree** to end the listing,
- either party **dies** or becomes **incapacitated**, and
- either the broker or the seller **breaches** the contract.

The **broker protection clause** preserves a broker's commission if, within a certain number of days, the owner transfers the property to someone the broker introduced to them.

Disclosures of agency relationships and property condition are important consumer safeguards and may be required by state law.

CHAPTER 6 QUIZ

1. A listing taken by a real estate salesperson is technically an employment agreement between the seller and the
   a. broker.
   b. local multiple listing service.
   c. salesperson.
   d. salesperson and broker together.

2. Which of the following is a similarity between an exclusive-agency listing and an exclusive-right-to-sell listing?
   a. Under each, the seller retains the right to sell the real estate without the broker's help and without paying the broker a commission.
   b. Under each, the seller authorizes only one particular salesperson to show the property.
   c. Both types of listings give the responsibility of representing the seller to one broker only.
   d. Both types of listings are open listings.

3. The listing agreement on a residential property states that it expires on May 2. Which event would NOT terminate the listing?
   a. The agreement is not renewed prior to May 2.
   b. The owner dies on April 29.
   c. On April 15, the owner tells the listing broker that the broker's marketing efforts are not satisfactory.
   d. The house is destroyed by fire on April 25.

4. A seller has listed a property under an exclusive-agency listing with a broker. If the seller finds a buyer, the seller will owe the broker
   a. no commission.
   b. the full commission.
   c. a partial commission.
   d. only reimbursement for the broker's costs.

5. A broker sold a residence for $185,000 and received $12,950 as commission in accordance with the terms of the listing. What was the broker's commission rate?
   a. 6 percent
   b. 7 percent
   c. 7.25 percent
   d. 7.5 percent

6. Under a listing agreement, the broker is entitled to sell the property for any price, as long as the seller receives $85,000. The broker may keep any amount over $85,000 as a commission. This type of listing is called a(n)
   a. exclusive-right-to-sell listing.
   b. exclusive-agency listing.
   c. open listing.
   d. net listing.

7. Which of the following is a similarity between an open listing and an exclusive-agency listing?
   a. Under each, the seller avoids paying the broker a commission if the seller sells the property to someone the broker did not procure.
   b. Each grants a commission to any broker who procures a buyer for the seller's property.
   c. Under each, the broker earns a commission regardless of who sells the property, as long as it is sold within the listing period.
   d. Each grants the exclusive right to sell to whatever broker procures a buyer for the seller's property.

8. The final decision on a property's listed price should be made by the
   a. listing agent.
   b. appraised value.
   c. seller.
   d. seller's attorney.

9. Which statement is *TRUE* of a listing contract?

   a. It is an employment contract for the professional services of the broker.
   b. It obligates the seller to transfer the property if the broker procures a ready, willing, and able buyer.
   c. It obligates the broker to work diligently for both the seller and the buyer.
   d. It automatically binds the owner, the broker, and the MLS to its agreed provisions.

10. A broker sold a property and received a 6.5 percent commission. The broker gave the listing salesperson $3,575, which was 30 percent of the firm's commission. What was the selling price of the property?

    a. $55,000
    b. $95,775
    c. $152,580
    d. $183,333

11. A seller hired a broker under the terms of an open listing. While that listing was still in effect, the seller—without informing the broker—hired another broker from a separate firm. Under an exclusive-right-to-sell listing for the same property, if the first broker produces a buyer for the property whose offer the seller accepts, then the seller must pay a

    a. full commission only to the first broker.
    b. full commission only to the second broker.
    c. full commission to both brokers.
    d. half commission to both brokers.

12. A seller listed her residence with a broker. The broker brought an offer at full price and terms of the listing from buyers who are ready, willing, and able to pay cash for the property. However, the seller rejected the buyers' offer. In this situation, the seller

    a. must sell her property.
    b. owes a commission to the broker.
    c. is liable to the buyers for specific performance.
    d. is liable to the buyers for compensatory damages.

13. A buyer has signed an agreement with a broker to compensate the broker even if the buyer purchases the property from a relative. This is called an

    a. open buyer agency agreement.
    b. exclusive-agency buyer agency agreement.
    c. exclusive buyer agency agreement.
    d. invalid agreement.

14. A seller signs a listing agreement with a broker to sell a home. The agreement states that the broker will receive a 7 percent commission. The home sells for $220,000. What is the net amount that the seller will receive from the sale?

    a. $15,400
    b. $204,600
    c. $205,678
    d. $220,000

15. A seller has sold property to a neighbor without the services of a real estate broker. However, the seller still owes the broker a commission because the seller signed a(n)

    a. exclusive-agency listing.
    b. open listing.
    c. exclusive-right-to-sell listing.
    d. net listing.

16. Most states require that listing agreements contain a(n)

    a. multiple listing service (MLS) clause.
    b. definite contract termination date.
    c. automatic extension clause.
    d. broker protection clause.

17. Which type of listing is prohibited in some states?

    a. Exclusive-right-to-sell listing
    b. Net listing
    c. Buyer agency agreement
    d. Open listing

18. By executing a listing agreement with a seller, a real estate broker becomes

    a. a procuring cause.
    b. obligated to open a special trust account.
    c. the agent of the seller.
    d. responsible for sharing the commission.

19. The provision in a listing agreement that gives additional authority to the broker and obligates the broker to distribute the listing to other brokers is a(n)
    a. joint listing clause.
    b. multiple listing clause.
    c. net listing clause.
    d. open listing clause.

20. All of the following reasons are valid bases for terminating a listing agreement *EXCEPT*
    a. sale of the property.
    b. death of the salesperson.
    c. agreement of the parties.
    d. destruction of the premises.

Interests in Real Estate

LEARNING OBJECTIVES *When you have finished reading this chapter, you should be able to*

■ **identify** the kinds of limitations on ownership rights that are imposed by government action and the form of conveyance of property;

■ **describe** the various estates in land and the rights and limitations they convey;

■ **explain** concepts related to encumbrances and water rights;

■ **distinguish** the various types of governmental powers and how they are exercised; and

■ **define** the following *key terms*:

appurtenant easement	encumbrance	license
avulsion	escheat	lien
condemnation	estate in land	life estate
covenants, conditions, and restrictions (CC&Rs)	fee simple	littoral rights
	fee simple absolute	police power
	fee simple defeasible	prior appropriation
deed restrictions	fee simple determinable	pur autre vie
easement	fee simple subject to a condition subsequent	remainder interest
easement by necessity		reversionary interest
easement by prescription	freehold estate	riparian rights
easement in gross	future interest	taxation
eminent domain	homestead	
encroachment	legal life estate	

■ INTERESTS IN REAL ESTATE

Ownership of a parcel of real estate is not necessarily absolute; that is, it is dependent on the type of interest a person holds in the property Keep in mind that a landowner's power to control his or her property relates to the landowner having a title of the property and the bundle of legal rights that accompanies the title. Even the most complete ownership the law allows is limited by public and private restrictions. These restrictions are intended to ensure that one owner's use or enjoyment of his or her property does not interfere with others' use or enjoyment of their property or with the welfare of the general public. Licensees should have a working knowledge of the restrictions that might limit current or future owners. For example, a zoning ordinance that will not allow a doctor's office to coexist with a residence, a condo association bylaw prohibiting resale without board approval, or an easement allowing the neighbors to use the private beach may not only burden today's purchaser but also deter a future buyer.

■ GOVERNMENTAL POWERS

Individual ownership rights are subject to certain powers, or rights, held by federal, state, and local governments. These limitations on the ownership of real estate are imposed for the general welfare of the community and, therefore, supersede the rights or interests of the individual. Government powers include police power, eminent domain, taxation, and escheat.

Police Power

Every state has the power to enact legislation to preserve order, protect the public health and safety, and promote the general welfare of its citizens. That authority is known as a state's **police power**. The state's authority is passed on to municipalities and counties through legislation called enabling acts. What is identified as being in the public interest can vary considerably from state to state and region to region. For example, a police power is used to enact environmental protection laws, zoning ordinances, and building codes. Regulations that govern the use, occupancy, size, location, and construction of real estate also fall within the police powers.

Memory Tip

Four Government Powers

Police power
Eminent domain
Taxation
Escheat

Like the rights of ownership, the state's power to regulate land use is not absolute. The laws must be uniform and nondiscriminatory; that is, they may not operate to the advantage or disadvantage of any one particular owner or owners. (See Chapter 19.)

Eminent Domain

Eminent domain is the right of the government to acquire privately owned real estate for public use. **Condemnation** is the process by which the government exercises this right, by either judicial or administrative proceedings. In the taking of property, just compensation is to be paid to the owner, and the rights of the property owner are to be protected by due process of law. Ideally, the public agency and the owner of the property in question agree on compensation through direct negotiation, and the government purchases the property for a price considered fair by the owner. In some cases, the owner may simply dedicate the property to the government as a site for a school, park, or another beneficial use. Sometimes, however, in cases where the owner's consent cannot be obtained, the government agency can initiate condemnation proceedings to acquire the property.

Eminent domain is the government's right to acquire private property for public use; **condemnation** is the actual process of taking property.

Generally, states delegate their power of eminent domain to cities and counties or public entities for public services. For instance, a public housing authority might take privately owned land to build low-income housing, or the state's land-clearance commission or redevelopment authority could use the power of eminent domain to make way for urban renewal. If there were no other feasible way to do so, a railway, utility company, or state highway department might acquire farm-land to extend railroad tracks, bring electricity to a remote new development, or build a highway.

In the past, the proposed use for taking property was to be for the public good. However, in June 2005, the U.S. Supreme Court in *Kelo v. City of New London* significantly changed the definition of public use. The court held that local governments can condemn homes and businesses for private or economic development purposes.

In *Kelo v. City of New London*, a development agent, on behalf of the city, initiated condemnation proceedings on land owned by nine property owners who refused to have their property taken. The development plan involved land for commercial, residential, and recreational purposes. The court noted that the development plan was not going to benefit a particular class of identifiable individuals. Further, although the owners' properties were not blighted, the city determined that a program of economic rejuvenation was justified and entitled to deference. *Economic development* fit within the broad definition of *public purpose*. The court found that the city's proposed disposition of petitioners' properties qualified as a *public use* within the meaning of the Takings Clause of the Fifth Amendment of the U.S. Constitution.

In this case, the city had invoked a state statute that authorized the use of eminent domain to promote economic development. The court decision leaves it to the states to establish rules that cities must follow when exercising eminent domain powers. In response to this court decision, many state legislators are drafting legislation to impose a narrower definition of *public use* in eminent domain proceedings to stop condemnations justified on purely economic grounds.

Taxation

Taxation is a charge on real estate to raise funds to meet the public needs of a government. Taxes on real estate include annual real estate taxes assessed by local and area governmental entities, including school districts; taxes on income realized by individuals and corporations on the sale of property; and special fees that may be levied for special projects. Nonpayment of taxes may give government the power to claim an interest in the property. (See Chapter 10.)

Escheat

[handwritten: property reverts to county or state if owner dies and no heir exists]

Escheat (revert) is a process by which the state may acquire privately owned real or personal property. State laws provide for ownership to transfer, or **escheat**, to the state when an owner dies and leaves no heirs (as defined by the law) and there is no will or living trust instrument that directs how the real estate is to be distributed. In some states, real property escheats to the county where the land is located; in other states, it becomes the property of the state. Escheat is intended to prevent property from being ownerless or abandoned.

■ ESTATES IN LAND

An **estate in land** defines the degree, quantity, nature, and extent of an owner's interest in real property. Many types of estates exist, but not all *interests* in real estate are *estates*. To be an estate in land, an interest must allow possession, meaning the holding and enjoyment of the property either now or in the future, and must be measured according to time. Historically, estates in land have been classified primarily by their length of time of possession.

Estates are an ownership interest and are transferred using a deed.

Freehold estates last for an indeterminable length of time, such as for a lifetime or forever. A freehold estate continues for an indefinite period and may be passed along to the owner's heirs. A life estate is based on the lifetime of a person and ends when that individual dies. There are various types of freehold estates, which are illustrated in Figure 7.1.

Nonfreehold estates are those for which the length of time can be determined. These are called *leasehold estates*. (See Chapter 16.)

Fee Simple Estate

A **fee simple** estate, or **fee simple absolute**, is the highest interest in real estate recognized by law. Fee simple ownership is ownership in which the holder is entitled to all rights to the property by law. This estate is intended to run forever; upon the death of its owner, it passes to the owner's heirs. It is limited only by public and private restrictions, such as zoning laws and restrictive covenants. (See Chapter 19.)

Fee simple defeasible A **fee simple defeasible** estate is a qualified fee estate that is subject to the occurrence or nonoccurrence of some specified event. Two categories of defeasible estates exist: *fee simple determinable* and *fee simple subject to a condition subsequent.*

A **fee simple determinable** is a fee simple defeasible estate that may be inherited. This estate is qualified by a *special limitation* (which is an occurrence or event). The language used to distinguish a special limitation—words such as *so long as* or *while* or *during*—is the key to creating this special limitation. The former owner retains a *possibility of reverter*. If the limitation is violated, the former owner (or heirs or successors) can reacquire full ownership with no need go the court. The deed is automatically returned to the former owner.

FIGURE 7.1

Freehold Estates

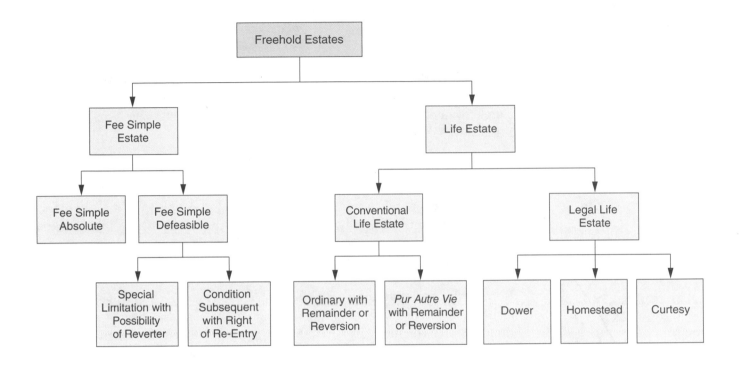

■ **FOR EXAMPLE**   When an owner gives land to a church, *so long as the land is used for only religious purposes*, it is known as a fee simple determinable. The church had the full bundle of rights possessed by a property owner, but one of the "sticks" in the bundle is a control "stick," in this case. If the church ever decides to use the land for a nonreligious purpose, the original owner has the right to reacquire the land without going to court.

A **fee simple subject to a condition subsequent**, the second type of fee simple defeasible estate, is similar to a fee simple determinable in that an owner gives real estate, *on condition of* ownership, but it differs in the way the estate will terminate if there is a violation to the condition. In fee simple determinable, the property reverts immediately to the original owner upon violation of the limitation. While in fee simple subject to a condition subsequent, the estate does not automatically terminate upon violation of the condition of ownership. The owner has the right of reentry but must go through the court to assert this right.

Fee simple *determinable*:
"So long as"
"While"
"During"

Fee simple subject to a condition subsequent:
"on condition that"

The *right of entry* and *possibility for reverter* may never take effect. If they do, it will only be at some time in the future. Therefore, each of these rights is considered a **future interest**.

■ **FOR EXAMPLE**   Land given *on the condition that* there be no consumption of alcohol on the premises is a fee simple subject to a condition subsequent. If alcohol is consumed on the property, the former owner has the right to reacquire full ownership. It will be necessary for the former owner (or the heirs or successors) to go to court to assert that right.

Life Estate

A **life estate** is a freehold estate limited in duration to the life of the owner or the life of some other designated person or persons. Unlike other freehold estates, a life estate is not inheritable. It passes to future owners according to the provisions of the life estate.

A life tenant is not a renter like a tenant associated with a lease. A life tenant is entitled to the rights of ownership and can benefit from both possession and ordinary use, and profits arising from ownership, just as if the individual were a fee simple owner. The life tenant's ownership may be sold, mortgaged, or leased, but it is always subject to the limitation of the life estate.

Pur autre vie   A life estate may also be based on the lifetime of a person other than the life tenant. Although a life estate is not considered an estate of inheritance, a life estate pur autre vie (for the life of another) provides for inheritance by the life tenant's heirs only until the death of the third party. A life estate pur autre vie is often created for people who are physically or mentally incapacitated in the hope of providing incentive for someone to care for them.

Remainder and reversion   The fee simple owner who creates a life estate must plan for its future ownership. When the life estate ends, it is replaced by a fee simple estate. The future owner of the fee simple estate may be designated in one of two ways:

- **Remainder interest**—The creator of the life estate may name a *remainderman* as the person to whom the property will pass when the life estate ends.

- **Reversionary interest**—The creator of the life estate may choose not to name a remainderman. In that case, ownership is said to *revert* to the original owner upon the end of the life estate.

Legal life estate   A **legal life estate** is not created voluntarily by an owner. Rather, it is a form of life estate established by state law. It becomes effective automatically when certain events occur. *Dower, curtesy,* and *homestead* are the legal life estates currently used in some states.

Dower and curtesy provide the nonowning spouse with a means of support after the death of the owning spouse. *Dower* is the life estate that a wife has in the real estate of her deceased husband. *Curtesy* is an identical interest that a husband has in the real estate of his deceased wife. (In some states, dower and curtesy are used interchangeably.)

Dower and curtesy provide that the nonowning spouse has a lifetime right to a one-half or one-third interest in the real estate, even if the owning spouse wills the estate to others. Because a nonowning spouse might claim an interest in the future, both spouses may have to sign the proper documents when real estate is conveyed. The signature of the nonowning spouse would be needed to release any *potential* common-law interests in the property being transferred.

Most states have abolished the common-law concepts of dower and curtesy in favor of the Uniform Probate Code (UPC). The UPC gives the surviving spouse a right to an elective share on the death of the other spouse. Community property states do not use dower and curtesy. (See Chapter 8.)

A **homestead** is a legal life estate in real estate occupied as the family home. In effect, the home (or at least some part of it) is protected from most creditors during the occupant's lifetime. In states that have homestead exemption laws, a portion of the acreage or value of the property occupied as the family home is exempt from certain judgments for debts, such as charge accounts and personal loans. The homestead is not protected from real estate taxes billed against the property or a mortgage for the purchase or cost of improvements; that is, if the debt is secured by the property, the property cannot be exempt from a judgment on that debt.

In some states, all that is required to establish a homestead is for the head of a household (which may be a single person) to own or lease the premises occupied by the family as a residence. In other states, the family is required by statute to file a notice of homestead rights. A family can have only one homestead at any given time.

How does the homestead exemption actually work? In most states, the homestead exemption merely reserves a certain amount of money for the family in the event of a court sale. In a few states, however, the entire homestead is protected from sale altogether. Once the sale occurs, any debts secured by the home (a mortgage, unpaid taxes, or mechanics' liens, for instance) will be paid from the proceeds. Then the family will receive the amount reserved by the homestead exemption. Finally, whatever remains will be applied to the family's unsecured debts.

■ ENCUMBRANCES

An **encumbrance** is a claim, charge, or liability that attaches to real estate. An encumbrance is not an estate, so it does not allow possession. An encumbrance may decrease the value or obstruct the use of the property. In essence, an encumbrance is a right or an interest held by someone other than the property owner that affects title to the real estate but does not necessarily prevent a transfer of title.

Encumbrances may be divided into two classifications:

- *Liens*—(usually monetary charges)
- *Encumbrance*—restrictions, easements, licenses, and encroachments that affect the condition or use of the property

Liens

A **lien** is a charge against property that provides security for a debt or an obligation of the property owner. If the obligation is not repaid, the lienholder is entitled to have the debt satisfied from the proceeds of a court-ordered or forced sale of the debtor's property. Real estate taxes, mortgages, judgments, and mechanics' liens all represent possible liens against an owner's real estate. (See Chapter 10.)

Deed Restrictions

Deed restrictions are private restrictions that affect the use of the land. Once placed in the deed by a previous owner, they "run with the land," limiting the use of the property and binding to all grantees.

Covenants, conditions, and restrictions (CC&Rs) are private agreements that affect land use. They may be enforced by an owner of real estate and included in the seller's deed to the buyer. Typically, however, restrictive covenants are imposed by a developer or subdivider to maintain specific standards in a subdivision. Such restrictive covenants are listed in the original development plans for the subdivision filed in the public record. (See Chapter 19.)

Easements

An **easement** is the right to use the land of another for a particular purpose. It may exist in any portion of the real estate, including the airspace above or a right-of-way across the land.

An **appurtenant easement** is attached to the ownership of one parcel and allows this owner the use of a neighbor's land. For an appurtenant easement to exist, two adjacent parcels of land must be owned by two different parties. The parcel over which the easement runs is known as the *servient tenement*; the neighboring parcel that benefits is known as the *dominant tenement*. (See Figure 7.2.)

An appurtenant easement is part of the dominant tenement, and if the dominant tenement is conveyed to another party, the easement transfers with the title. This type of easement is said to "run with the land." It is an encumbrance on

FIGURE 7.2

Easement Appurtenant

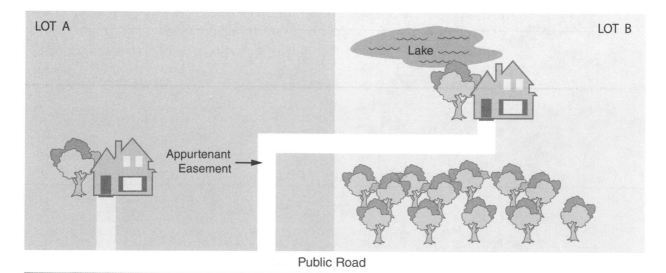

The owner of Lot B has an appurtenant easement across Lot A to gain access to his property from the public road. Lot B is dominant, and Lot A is servient.

FIGURE   7.3

Easement in Gross

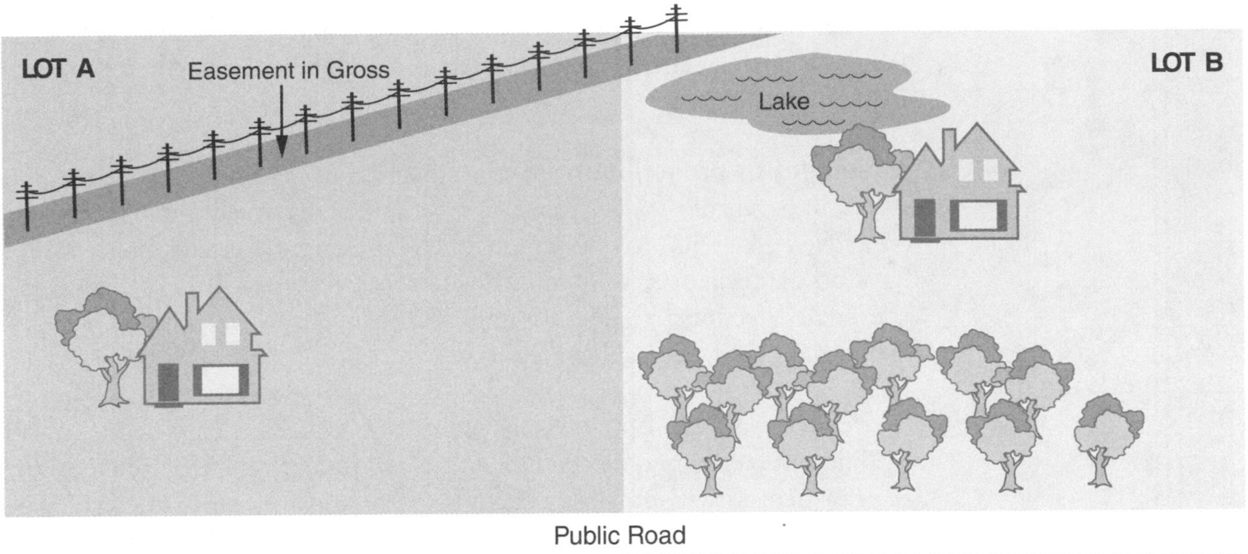

The utility company has an easement in gross across both parcels of land for its power lines.

property and will transfer with the deed of the dominant tenement forever, unless the holder of the dominant tenement legally releases that right.

A *party wall* can be an exterior wall of a building that straddles the boundary line between two lots, or it can be a commonly shared partition wall between two connected properties. Each lot owner owns the half of the wall on his or her lot, and each has an appurtenant easement in the other half of the wall. A written party wall agreement must be used to create the easement rights. Expenses to build and maintain the wall are usually shared. A fence built on the lot line is treated the same as a wall. A party driveway shared by and partly on the land of adjoining owners must also be created by written agreement, specifying responsibility for expenses.

An **easement in gross** is an *individual* or *company* interest in or right to use someone else's land. (See Figure 7.3.) A railroad's right-of-way is an easement in gross, as are the rights-of-way of utility easements (such as for a pipeline or high-tension power line). Commercial easements in gross may be assigned, conveyed, and inherited. Personal easements in gross are usually not assignable. Generally, a personal easement in gross terminates on the death of the easement owner.

Creating an easement   An easement is created by a written agreement between the parties that establishes the easement right. The creation of an easement always involves two separate parties, one of whom is the owner of the land over which the easement runs. Two other ways for an easement to be created are *easement by necessity* and *easement by prescription*.

Easement by necessity An easement that is created when an owner sells a parcel of land that has no access to a street or public way except over the seller's remaining land is an **easement by necessity**. An easement by necessity is created by court order based on the principle that owners must have the right to enter and exit their land—the right of *ingress* (*enter*) and *egress* (*exit*); they cannot be landlocked. Remember, this form of easement is called an *easement by necessity*; it is not merely for convenience.

Easement by prescription If the claimant has made use of another's land for a certain period of time as defined by state law, an **easement by prescription**, or a *prescriptive easement*, may be acquired. The prescriptive period ranges from 10 to 21 years. The claimant's use must have been continuous, exclusive, and without the owner's permission. The use must be visible, open, and notorious, and the owner must have been able to learn of it.

The concept of *tacking* provides that successive periods of continuous occupation by different parties may be combined (tacked) to reach the required total number of years necessary to establish a claim for a prescriptive easement. To tack on one person's possession to that of another, the parties must have been *successors in interest*, such as an ancestor and his or her heir, a landlord and a tenant, or seller and buyer.

■ **FOR EXAMPLE** A property is located in a state with a prescriptive period of 20 years. For the past 22 years, a neighbor has driven across the property's front yard several times a day to reach the neighbor's garage from a more comfortable angle. The neighbor has an *easement by prescription*.

For 25 years, another neighbor has driven across this same front yard two or three times a year to reach that neighbor's property when in a hurry. This neighbor does not have an easement by prescription because the use was not continuous.

For 15 years, the next-door neighbor parked a car on the same property, next to the garage. Six years ago, this neighbor sold the house to a person who continued to park a car next to garage. Last year, the new neighbor acquired an *easement by prescription* through *tacking*.

Terminating an easement An easement terminates

■ when the need no longer exists;
■ when the owner of either the dominant or the servient tenement becomes sole owner and the properties are merged under one legal description;
■ by the release of the right of easement to the owner of the servient tenement;
■ by the abandonment of the easement (the intention of the parties is the determining factor); or
■ by the nonuse of a prescriptive easement.

Note that an easement may not *automatically* terminate for these reasons. Certain legal steps may be required.

Licenses

A **license** is a personal privilege to enter the land of another for a specific purpose. A license differs from an easement in that *it can be terminated or canceled*. If the right to use another's property is given orally or informally, it generally is considered to be a license rather than an easement. A license ends with the death of either party or with the sale of the land.

Encroachments

Physical Encumbrances
- Restrictions
- Easements
- Licenses

When a building, fence, or driveway illegally extends beyond the land of its owner or legal building lines, an **encroachment** occurs. An encroachment is usually disclosed by either a physical inspection of the property or a spot survey. As a rule, a spot survey is more accurate and reliable than a simple physical inspection. If a building encroaches on adjoining land, the neighbor may be able to either recover damages or secure removal of the portion of the building that encroaches. Encroachments that exceed a state's prescriptive period, however, may give rise to easements by prescription.

■ WATER RIGHTS

Whether for agricultural, recreational, or other purposes, waterfront real estate has always been desirable. Each state has strict laws that govern the ownership and use of water as well as the adjacent land. The laws vary among the states, but all are closely linked to climactic and topographical conditions. Where water is plentiful, states may rely on the simple parameters set by the common-law doctrines of riparian and littoral rights. Where water is scarce, a state may control all but limited domestic use of water, according to the doctrine of prior appropriation.

Riparian Rights — *river, stream*

Riparian rights are common-law rights granted to owners of land along the course of a river, stream, or similar body of water. Although riparian rights are governed by laws that vary from state to state, they generally include the unrestricted right to use the water. As a rule, the only limitation on the owner's use is that such use cannot interrupt or alter the flow of the water or contaminate it in any way. In addition, an owner of land that borders a nonnavigable waterway, (i.e., a body of water unsuitable for commercial boat traffic) owns the land under the water to the exact center of the waterway. Land adjoining commercially navigable rivers, on the other hand, is usually owned to the water's edge, with the state holding title to the submerged land. (See Figure 7.4.) Navigable waters are considered public highways in which the public has an easement or right to travel.

Non-navigable — property extends halfway underneath water

Littoral Rights — *lake, sea, ocean*

Navigable — property stops at water's edge

Closely related to riparian rights are the **littoral rights** of owners whose land borders commercially navigable lakes, seas, and oceans. Owners with littoral rights enjoy unrestricted use of available waters but own the land adjacent to the water

Riparian Rights

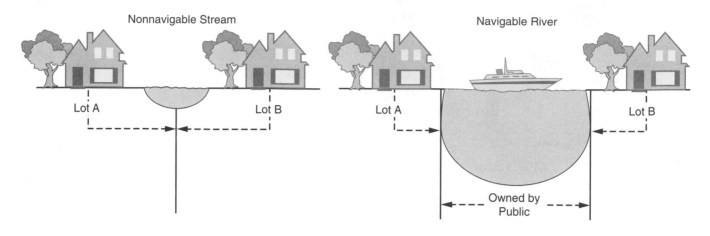

only up to the average high-water mark. All land below this point is owned by the government.

In some states, riparian and littoral rights are appurtenant (or attached) to the land and cannot be retained when the property is sold. The right to use the water belongs to whoever owns the bordering land and cannot be retained by a former owner after the land is sold.

Accretion, Erosion, and Avulsion

The amount of land an individual owns may be affected by the natural action of water. An owner is entitled to all land created through *accretion*—increases in the land resulting from the deposit of soil by the water's action.

On the other hand, an owner may lose land through *erosion*. Erosion is the gradual and imperceptible wearing away of the land by natural forces, such as wind, rain, and flowing water. Fortunately, erosion usually takes hundreds or even thousands of years to have any noticeable effect on a person's property. Flash floods or heavy winds, however, can increase the speed of erosion.

If erosion is a slow natural process, avulsion is its opposite. **Avulsion** is the sudden removal of soil by an act of nature. It is an event that causes the loss of land much less subtly than erosion. An earthquake or a mudslide, for instance, can cause an individual's landholding to become much smaller very quickly.

Doctrine of Prior Appropriation

In states where water is scarce, ownership and use of water are often determined by the doctrine of **prior appropriation**. Under this doctrine, the right to use any water, with the exception of limited domestic use, is controlled by the state rather than by the landowner adjacent to the water.

To secure water rights in prior appropriation states, a landowner must demonstrate to a state agency that the owner's plans are for *beneficial* use, such as crop irrigation. If the state's requirements are met, the landowner receives a permit to use a specified amount of water for the limited purpose of the beneficial use. Although statutes governing prior appropriation vary from state to state, the priority of water rights is usually determined by the oldest recorded permit date.

Under some state laws, once granted, water rights attach to the land of the permit holder. The permit holder may sell a water right to another party. Issuance of a water permit does not grant access to the water source. All access rights-of-way over the land of another (easements) must be obtained from the property owner.

■ KEY POINT REVIEW

Government powers can be recalled by using the letters PETE:

■ **Police power** is the state's authority—passed down to municipalities and counties through **enabling acts**—to enact nondiscriminatory legislation to
  — preserve order,
  — protect the public health and safety, and
  — promote the general welfare of citizens.
■ **Eminent domain** is the government's right to acquire privately owned real estate for a public or economically beneficial use through
  — **condemnation**, a process that begins with a judicial or an administrative proceeding, or
  — **just compensation**, which must be paid to the property owner.
■ **Taxation** is a charge on real estate to raise funds to meet public needs.
■ **Escheat** occurs when the deceased has no will or lawful heirs.

A **freehold estate** lasts for an indeterminable length of time:

■ **Fee simple** is the highest estate recognized by law.
■ **Fee simple defeasible** is a qualified estate subject to occurrence or nonoccurrence of some specified event.
■ **Life estate** is based on the lifetime of a person.

An **encumbrance** is a claim, charge, or liability that attaches to real estate and may be one of the following:

■ **Liens** are charges against property that provide security for a debt or obligation of the property owner.
■ **Covenants, conditions, and restrictions (CC&Rs)** are private agreements that affect the use of land.

Easements are rights to use the land of another:

■ An **appurtenant easement** is said to **run with the land** when title is transferred.
■ An **easement in gross** is an individual or company interest in or right to use another's land.
■ An easement is usually created by **written agreement** between the parties.

- An **easement by necessity** arises when land has no access to a street or public way.
- An **easement by prescription** is acquired when a claimant has used another's land for 10 to 21 years. The use must be visible, open, and notorious.

An easement is **terminated**

- when the need no longer exists,
- when the owner of either the dominant or the servient tenement becomes the sole owner,
- when the owner of a servient tenement **releases** the right of easement,
- if the easement is **abandoned**, or
- by the **nonuse** of prescriptive easement.

License is a personal privilege to enter the land of another for a specific purpose.

Encroachment occurs when all or part of a structure illegally intrudes on the land of another or beyond legal building lines.

Water rights are determined by common law and statute:

- **Riparian rights** are common-law rights granted to owners of land along rivers, streams, or similar bodies of water.
- **Littoral rights** belong to owners of land that borders commercially navigable lakes, seas, and oceans.
- The **doctrine of prior appropriation** in some states provides that water use, aside from limited domestic use, is controlled by the state rather than the landowner adjacent to the water; to use the water, the landowner must demonstrate **beneficial use** of the water, such as irrigation of crops.

■ RELATED WEB SITES

Eminent Domain: *www.realtor.org/realtororg.nsf/pages/EminentDomain/*
Interests in Real Estate: *http://topics.law.cornell.edu/wex/Real_property/*

CHAPTER 7 QUIZ

1. The right of a government body to take owner-ship of real estate for public use is called
   a. escheat.
   b. eminent domain.
   c. condemnation.
   d. police power.

2. A purchaser of real estate learns that his owner-ship rights could continue forever and that no other person can claim to be the owner or has any ownership control over the property. This person owns a
   a. fee simple interest.
   b. life estate.
   c. determinable fee.
   d. condition subsequent.

3. A person owned the fee simple title to a vacant lot adjacent to a hospital and was per-suaded to make a gift of the lot. She wanted to have some control over its use, so her attor-ney prepared her a deed to convey ownership of the lot to the hospital "so long as it is used for hospital purposes." After completion of the gift, the hospital will own a
   a. fee simple absolute estate.
   b. license.
   c. fee simple determinable.
   d. leasehold estate.

4. Your neighbors use your driveway to reach their garage, which is on their property. Your attorney explains that ownership of the neighbors' real estate includes an easement appurtenant giving them the right to do this. Your property is the
   a. leasehold interest.
   b. dominant tenement.
   c. servient tenement.
   d. license property.

5. A *license* is an example of a(n)
   a. appurtenant easement.
   b. encroachment.
   c. personal privilege.
   d. restriction.

6. An appurtenant easement
   a. terminates with the sale of the property.
   b. is a right-of-way for a utility company.
   c. is revocable.
   d. runs with the land.

7. A property owner wants to use water from a river that runs through the property to irrigate a potato field. To do so, the owner is required by state law to submit an application to the Department of Water Resources describing in detail the plan for beneficial use of the water. If the department approves the owner's appli-cation, it will issue a permit allowing a limited amount of river water to be diverted onto the property. Based on these facts, it can be assumed that this property owner's state relies on which rule of law?
   a. Riparian rights
   b. Littoral rights
   c. Doctrine of prior appropriation
   d. Doctrine of highest and best use

8. Which of the following is NOT an example of governmental power?
   a. Dedication
   b. Police power
   c. Eminent domain
   d. Taxation

9. A property owner who has the legal right to use a neighbor's land holds a(n)
   a. estate in land.
   b. easement.
   c. police power.
   d. encroachment.

10. Which of the following is a legal life estate?
    a. Leasehold
    b. Fee simple absolute
    c. Homestead
    d. Determinable fee

11. An owner conveys ownership of her residence to her church but reserves for herself a life estate in the residence. The future interest held by the church is a

a. pur autre vie.
b. remainder.
c. reversion.
d. leasehold.

12. An owner has a fence on his property. By mistake, the fence extends one foot over the lot line onto a neighbor's property. The fence is an example of a(n)

a. license.
b. encroachment.
c. easement by necessity.
d. easement by prescription.

13. A homeowner may be allowed certain protection from judgments of creditors as a result of the state's

a. littoral rights.
b. curtesy rights.
c. homestead rights.
d. dower rights.

14. A person has permission from a property owner to hike on the owner's property during the autumn months. The hiker has

a. an easement by necessity.
b. an easement by condemnation.
c. riparian rights.
d. a license.

15. A tenant who rents an apartment from the owner of the property holds a(n)

a. easement.
b. license.
c. freehold interest.
d. leasehold interest.

16. Because a homeowner failed to pay the real estate taxes on time, the taxing authority imposed a claim against the homeowner's property. This claim is known as a(n)

a. deed restriction.
b. lien.
c. easement.
d. reversionary interest.

17. The type of easement that is a right-of-way for a utility company's power lines is a(n)

a. easement in gross.
b. easement by necessity.
c. easement by prescription.
d. nonassignable easement.

18. The water rights of an owner of property located along the banks of a river are called

a. littoral rights.
b. prior appropriation rights.
c. riparian rights.
d. hereditaments.

19. A landowner has divided much of his land into smaller parcels and has recently sold a tract near a nature preserve that is landlocked and cannot be entered except through one of the other tracts. The buyer of that property will probably be granted what type of easement by court action?

a. Easement by necessity
b. Easement in gross
c. Easement by prescription
d. Easement by condemnation

20. All of the following will terminate an easement EXCEPT

a. need no longer exists.
b. nonuse of a prescriptive easement.
c. abandonment of easement.
d. release of the right of easement to the dominant tenement.

124

CHAPTER 8

Forms of Real Estate Ownership

■ LEARNING OBJECTIVES *When you have finished reading this chapter, you should be able to*

■ **identify** the four basic forms of co-ownership;

■ **describe** the ways in which various business organizations may own property;

■ **explain** how a tenancy in common, joint tenancy, and tenancy by the entirety are created and how they may be terminated;

■ **distinguish** cooperative ownership from condominium ownership; and

■ **define** the following *key terms*:

common elements	limited liability company (LLC)	severalty
community property		tenancy by the entirety
condominium	limited partnership	tenancy in common
cooperative	partition	time-share
co-ownership	partnership	town house
corporation	PITT	trust
general partnership	right of survivorship	
joint tenancy	separate property	

FORMS OF REAL ESTATE OWNERSHIP

Licensees provide buyers the information necessary for them to determine the type of ownership that best fit their needs. The choice of ownership will affect the ability to transfer the real estate, has tax implications, and decides rights to future claims.

Although the forms of ownership available are controlled by state laws, a fee simple estate may be held in three basic ways:

- In severalty, where title is held by one individual or corporation
- In co-ownership, where title is held by two or more individuals
- In trust, where a neutral individual holds title for the benefit of another

OWNERSHIP IN SEVERALTY

Ownership in **severalty** occurs when property is owned by one individual or corporation. The term comes from the fact that a sole owner is *severed* or *cut off* from other owners. The severalty owner has sole rights to the ownership and sole discretion to sell, will, lease, or otherwise transfer part or all of the ownership rights to another person.

CO-OWNERSHIP

When title to one parcel of real estate is held by two or more individuals, those parties are called *co-owners* or *concurrent owners*. Most states commonly recognize various forms of **co-ownership**. Individuals may co-own property as tenants in common, joint tenants, or tenants by the entirety, or they may co-own it as community property. There is no apparent difference between the various types of ownership during the lifetime of the co-owners. Only when the property is conveyed or one of the owners dies do the differences become apparent.

Tenancy in Common

A parcel of real estate may be owned by two or more people as tenants in common. In a **tenancy in common** each tenant holds an *undivided fractional interest* in the property. A tenant in common may hold one-half or one-third interest in a property. The physical property is not divided into a specific half or third. The co-owners have *unity of possession*, meaning that they are entitled to possession of the whole property. It is the *ownership* interest, not the property that is divided.

Forms of Co-ownership
- Tenancy in common
- Joint tenancy
- Tenancy by the entirety
- Community property

The deed creating a tenancy in common may or may not state the fractional interest held by each co-owner. If no fractions are stated, the tenants are presumed to hold equal shares. For example, if five people hold title, each would own an undivided one-fifth interest.

Because the co-owners own separate interests, they can sell, convey, mortgage, or transfer their individual interest without the consent of the other co-owners.

FIGURE 8.1

Tenancy in Common

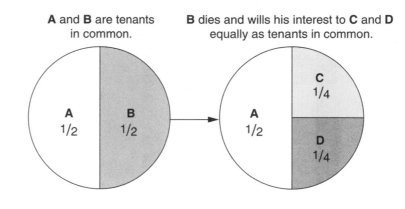

A and B are tenants in common.

B dies and wills his interest to C and D equally as tenants in common.

A 1/2   B 1/2

A 1/2   C 1/4   D 1/4

However, no individual tenant may transfer the ownership of the entire property. When one co-owner dies, the tenant's undivided interest passes according to the co-owner's will, heirs, or living trust. (See Figure 8.1.)

When two or more people acquire title to real estate and the deed does not indicate the form of the tenancy, the new owners are usually determined to have acquired title as tenants in common.

Joint Tenancy

Most states recognize some form of **joint tenancy** in property owned by two or more people.

Joint tenancy is the **right of survivorship**. Upon the death of a joint tenant, the deceased's interest transfers directly to the surviving joint tenant or tenants. Essentially, there is one less owner.

With each successive joint tenant death, the surviving joint tenants keep acquiring the deceased tenant's interest. The last survivor takes title in severalty and has all the rights of sole ownership, including the right to pass the property to any heirs. (See Figure 8.2.)

IN PRACTICE   The form under which title should be taken should be discussed with an attorney. Remember that licensees may not give legal advice or engage in the practice of law.

Creating joint tenancies   A joint tenancy can be created only by the intentional act of conveying a deed or giving the property by will or living trust. It cannot be implied or created by operation of law. The deed must specifically state the parties' intention to create a joint tenancy, and the parties must be explicitly identified as joint tenants.

To create joint tenancy, four groups or unities are needed:

- Unity of *possession*—all joint tenants holding an undivided right to possession
- Unity of *interest*—all joint tenants holding equal ownership interests

Memory Tip

The Four Unities

The four unities necessary to create a joint tenancy may be remembered by the acronym **PITT**:
- Possession
- Interest
- Time
- Title

FIGURE   8.2

Joint Tenancy with Right of Survivorship

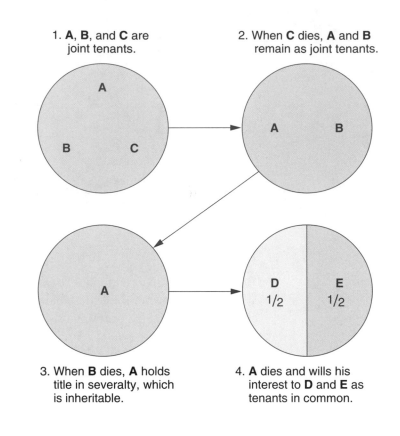

1. **A**, **B**, and **C** are joint tenants.

2. When **C** dies, **A** and **B** remain as joint tenants.

3. When **B** dies, **A** holds title in severalty, which is inheritable.

4. **A** dies and wills his interest to **D** and **E** as tenants in common.

- Unity of *time*—all joint tenants acquiring their interests at the same time
- Unity of *title*—all joint tenants acquiring their interests by the same document

The four requirements for unities are the following:

- Title is acquired by one deed.
- The deed is executed, signed, and delivered at one time.
- The deed conveys equal interests to all of the parties.
- The parties hold undivided possession of the property as joint tenants.

Terminating joint tenancies   A joint tenancy is destroyed when any one of the four unities of joint tenancy is terminated. A joint tenant is free to convey interest in the jointly held property, but doing so destroys the unities of time and title. The new owner cannot become a joint tenant. Rights of other joint tenants, however, are unaffected. For example, if A, B, and C hold title as joint tenants and A conveys her interest to D, then D will own an undivided one-third interest in severalty as tenant in common with B and C, who continue to own their undivided two-thirds interest as joint tenants. (See Figure 8.3.)

Termination of Co-ownership by Partition Suit

Partition is a legal way to dissolve the relationship when the parties do not voluntarily agree to its termination. If the court determines that the land cannot be divided physically into separate parcels without destroying its value, the court will

FIGURE 8.3

Combination of Tenancies

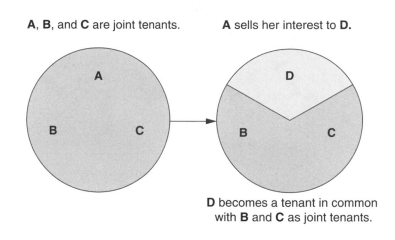

A, B, and C are joint tenants.

A sells her interest to D.

D becomes a tenant in common with B and C as joint tenants.

order the real estate sold. The proceeds of the sale will then be divided among the co-owners according to their fractional interests.

Ownership by Married Couples

Tenancy by the entirety is a special form of co-ownership used in some states that allows the husband or the wife to inherit the other spouse's ownership interest upon death. In this form of ownership, each spouse has an equal, undivided interest in the property. (The term *entirety* refers to the fact that the owners are considered one indivisible unit because early common law viewed a married couple as one legal person.) A husband and wife who are tenants by the entirety have rights of survivorship. During their lives, they can convey title only by a deed signed by both parties. One party cannot convey a one-half interest, and generally they have no right to partition or divide.

Community property rights   Community property laws are based on the idea that a husband and wife, rather than merging into one entity, are equal partners in the marriage. Under community property laws, any property acquired during a marriage is considered to be obtained by mutual effort. As of 2010, nine states have adopted this concept. However, community property law varies widely among the states, but they all recognize two kinds of property: separate property and community property.

Separate property is real or personal property that was owned solely by either spouse before the marriage, acquired by gift or inheritance during the marriage, as well as purchased with separate funds during the marriage. Any income earned from a person's separate property remains part of his or her separate property. Separate property can be mortgaged or conveyed by the owning spouse without the signature of the nonowning spouse.

Community property consists of real and personal property acquired by either spouse during the marriage. Any conveyance or encumbrance of community property requires the signatures of *both* spouses. Spouses can will their half of the community property to whomever they desire, but upon the death of one spouse, the

	Co-ownerships	Property Held	Property Conveyed
TABLE 8.1 **Forms of Co-ownership**	Tenancy in Common	Each tenant holds a fractional undivided interest.	The tenants can convey or devise their individual interest, but not the entire interest.
	Joint Tenancy	Unity of ownership. Created by intentional act; unities of possession, interest, time, title.	Right of survivorship; cannot be conveyed to heirs.
	Tenants by the Entirety	Husband and wife have equal undivided interest in property.	Right of survivorship; convey by deed signed by both parties. One party can't convey one-half interest.
	Community Property	Husband and wife are equal partners in marriage. Real or personal property acquired during marriage is community property.	Conveyance requires signature of both spouses. No right of survivorship; when one spouse dies, survivor owns one-half of community property. Other one-half is distributed according to will or, if no will, according to state law.

surviving spouse automatically owns one-half of the remaining property. If one spouse dies without a will, the other half is inherited by the surviving spouse or by the decedent's other heirs, depending on state law. Community property does *not* provide an automatic right of survivorship as joint tenancy does.

■ TRUSTS

A **trust** is a device by which one person transfers ownership of property to someone else to hold or manage for the benefit of a third party. Perhaps a grandfather wishes to ensure the college education of his granddaughter, so he transfers his oil field to the grandchild's mother. He instructs the mother to use its income to pay for the grandchild's college tuition. In this case, the grandfather is the *trustor*—the person who creates the trust. The granddaughter is the *beneficiary*—the person who benefits from the trust. The mother is the *trustee*—the party who holds legal title to the property and is entrusted with carrying out the trustor's instructions regarding the purpose of the trust. The trustee is a *fiduciary*, who acts in confidence or trust and has a special legal relationship with the beneficiary. The trustee's power and authority are limited by the terms of the trust agreement, will, or deed in trust.

IN PRACTICE The legal and tax implications of setting up a trust are complex and vary widely from state to state. Attorneys and tax experts should always be consulted on the subject of trusts.

Most states allow real estate to be held in trust. Depending on the type of trust and its purpose, the trustor, trustee, and beneficiary can all be either people or legal entities, such as corporations. *Trust companies* are corporations set up for this specific purpose.

Real estate can be owned under living or testamentary trusts and land trusts. It can also be held by investors in a real estate investment trust (REIT). (See Chapter 23.)

Living and Testamentary Trusts

Property owners may provide for their own financial care or for that of their family by establishing a trust. This trust may be created by agreement during the property owner's lifetime (a *living trust*) or established by will after the owner's death (a *testamentary trust*). (Note that neither of these is related to the so-called living will, which deals with the right to refuse medical treatment.)

The person who creates the trust conveys real or personal property to a trustee (usually a corporate trustee), with the understanding that the trustee will assume certain duties. These duties may include the care and investment of the trust assets to produce an income. After paying the trust's operating expenses and trustee's fees, the income is paid to or used for the benefit of the beneficiary. The trust may continue for the beneficiary's lifetime, or the assets may be distributed when the beneficiary reaches a certain age or when other conditions are met.

In recent years, living trusts have become a major estate planning tool used to minimize the time and costs of probate. In a living trust, the property owner (trustor, grantor, or settler) transfers ownership of real and personal property to a trustee. The trustee is often the trustor. In this way, the owner continues to control the assets of the trust. The trustee may transfer property into and out of the trust, subject to the trust agreement. Upon the death of the trustee, the property passes to the beneficiary or beneficiaries without the need for probate. In the case of community property, the husband and wife may transfer real and personal property into a trust and name themselves as joint trustees with rights of survivorship. Upon the death of the surviving trustee, the estate is distributed to the beneficiary or beneficiaries.

Land Trusts

In the creation of *land trusts*, real estate is the only asset. As in all trusts, the title to the property is conveyed to a trustee, and the beneficial interest belongs to the beneficiary. In the case of land trusts, however, the beneficiary is usually also the trustor. While the beneficial interest is *personal property*, the beneficiary retains management and control of the real property and has the right of possession and the right to any income or proceeds from its sale. Land trusts are frequently created for the conservation of farmland, forests, coastal land, and scenic vistas.

One of the distinguishing characteristics of a land trust is that the *public records usually do not name the beneficiary*. A land trust may be used for secrecy when assembling separate parcels. There are other benefits as well. A beneficial interest can be transferred by assignment, making the formalities of a deed unnecessary.

The beneficial interest in property can be pledged as security for a loan without having a mortgage recorded. Because the beneficiary's interest is personal, it passes at the beneficiary's death under the laws of the state in which the beneficiary lived. If the deceased owned property in several states, additional probate costs and inheritance taxes can be avoided.

A land trust ordinarily continues for a definite term, such as 20 years. If the beneficiary does not extend the trust term when it expires, the trustee is usually obligated to sell the real estate and return the net proceeds to the beneficiary.

■ OWNERSHIP OF REAL ESTATE BY BUSINESS ORGANIZATIONS

A business organization is a legal entity that exists independently of its members. Ownership by a business organization makes it possible for many people to hold an interest in the same parcel of real estate. Investors may be organized to finance a real estate project in various ways. Some provide for the real estate to be owned by the entity; others provide for direct ownership by the investors.

Partnership

A **partnership** is an association of two or more persons who carry on a business for profit as co-owners. In a **general partnership** all the partners participate in the operation and management of the business and share full liability for business losses and obligations. A **limited partnership** consists of one or more general partners and limited partners. The business is run by the general partner or partners. The limited partners are not legally permitted to participate, and each can be held liable for business losses only to the amount invested. The limited partnership is a popular method of organizing investors because it permits investors with small amounts of capital to participate in large real estate projects with minimum personal risk.

General partnerships are dissolved and must be reorganized if one partner dies, withdraws, or goes bankrupt. In a limited partnership, however, the partnership agreement may provide for the continuation of the organization following the death or withdrawal of one of the partners.

Corporations

A **corporation** is a legal entity—an artificial person—created under the authority of the laws of the state from which it receives its charter. A corporation is managed and operated by its *board of directors*. The charter sets forth the powers of the corporation, including its right to buy and sell real estate (based on a resolution by the board of directors). Because the corporation is a legal entity, it can own real estate in *severalty* or as a *tenant in common*. Some corporations are permitted by their charters to purchase real estate for any purpose; others are limited to purchasing only the land necessary to fulfill the entities' corporate purposes.

As a legal entity, a corporation continues to exist until it is formally dissolved. The death of one of the officers or directors does not affect title to property owned by the corporation.

Limited Liability Companies

The **limited liability company (LLC)** is a relatively recent form of business organization. An LLC combines the most attractive features of limited partnerships and corporations. The members of an LLC enjoy the limited liability offered by a corporate form of ownership and the tax advantages of a partnership. In addition, the LLC offers flexible management structures without the complicated requirements of corporations or the restrictions of limited partnerships. The structure and methods of establishing a new LLC, or of converting an existing entity to the LLC form, vary from state to state.

■ CONDOMINIUMS, COOPERATIVES, TOWN HOUSES, AND TIME-SHARES

A growing urban population, diverse lifestyles, changing family structures, and heightened mobility have created a demand for new forms of ownership. Condominiums, cooperatives, town houses, and time-share arrangements are four types of property ownership that have arisen in residential, commercial, and industrial markets to address our society's changing real estate needs.

See Table 8.2 for a comparison chart of these types of property ownership.

Condominium Ownership

The **condominium** form of ownership has become increasingly popular throughout the United States. Condominium laws, often called *horizontal property acts,* have been enacted in every state. Under these laws, the owner of each unit holds a *fee simple title* to the unit. The individual unit owners also own a specified share of the undivided interest in the remainder of the building and land, known as **common elements** Common elements typically include such items as land, courtyards, lobbies, the exterior structure, hallways, elevators, stairways, and the roof, as well as recreational facilities such as swimming pools, tennis courts, and golf courses. (See Figure 8.4.) The individual unit owners own these common elements as *tenants in common.* State law usually provides, however, that unit owners do not have the same right to partition that other tenants in common have. Condominium ownership is not restricted to high-rise buildings. Low-rises and detached structures can also be condominiums.

Owning a condominium   Once the property is established as a condominium, each unit becomes a separate parcel of real estate that is owned in fee simple and may be held by one or more persons in any type of ownership or tenancy recognized by state law. A condominium unit may be mortgaged like any other parcel of real estate. The unit can usually be sold or transferred to whomever the owner chooses, unless the condominium association provides for a *right of first refusal.* In this case, the owner is required to offer the unit at the same price to the other owners in the condominium or the association before accepting an outside purchase offer.

TABLE 8.2

Four Types of Property Ownership

Type	Condominium	Cooperative	Town House	Time-Share
Description	Single units are located in low-rise and high-rise complexes.	Single units are located in low-rise and high-rise complexes.	Two-floor units share common walls; units are usually clustered together.	Multiple purchasers buy interests in real estate—usually resort or hotel property. Each purchaser has right to use unit for set time each year.
Ownership	Owners have fee title to interior space of units and share title to common areas.	Tenants own shares in a corporation, partnership, or trust that holds title to the building. Tenants have proprietary leases and the right to occupy their respective units.	Owners have fee title to dwelling unit and lot. They share title to common areas. Town houses are often organized as associations.	Time-share estate is a fee simple interest. Time-share use agreement is personal property that expires after a specified time period.
Transfer	Single units are transferred by deed, will, or living trust.	Shares are personal property. Shareholders may sell or transfer shares. Transfer of shares may be restricted by bylaws.	Single units conveyed by deed or will.	An interest in a time-share estate may be conveyed by deed or will by the owner. An interest in time-share use is personal property that may or may not be transferable according to the contract.
Governed By	Declaration of condominium and elected board of directors (HOA)	Bylaws of the corporation and elected board of directors or trustees	Elected board of directors (condominiums) or homeowners' association	Developer

FIGURE 8.4

Condominium Ownership

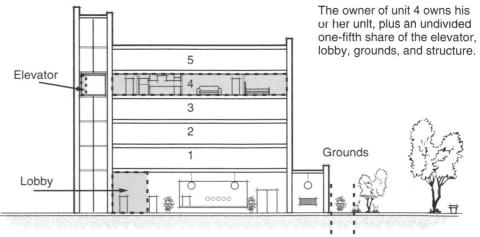

The owner of unit 4 owns his or her unit, plus an undivided one-fifth share of the elevator, lobby, grounds, and structure.

Real estate taxes are assessed and collected on each unit as an individual property. Default in the payment of taxes or a mortgage loan by one unit owner may result in a foreclosure sale of that owner's unit. An owner's default, however, does not affect the other unit owners.

IN PRACTICE   Before buying a condominium, the buyer should do as much background research as possible. Examining association fees and rules are critical so the buyer understands condominium ownership.

Operation and administration   The condominium property is administered by a homeowners' association (HOA), which is made up of unit owners. The association may be governed by a board of directors or another official entity, and it may manage the property on its own or hire a property manager.

The association must enforce any rules it adopts regarding the operation and use of the property. The association is responsible for the maintenance, repair, cleaning, and sanitation of the common elements and structural portions of the property. It must also maintain fire, extended-coverage, and liability insurance.

The expenses of maintaining and operating the building are paid by the unit owners in the form of fees and assessments. Both fees and assessments are imposed and collected by the homeowners' association. Recurring fees (referred to as *condo fees*) are paid by each unit owner. The fees may be due monthly, quarterly, semi-annually, or annually, depending on the provisions of the bylaws. If the fees are not paid, the association may seek a court-ordered judgment to have the delinquent owner's unit sold to cover the outstanding amount or place a lien on the property.

Assessments are special payments required of unit owners to address some specific expense, such as a new roof. Assessments are structured like condo fees: Owners of larger units pay proportionately higher assessments than smaller units.

Cooperative Ownership

In a **cooperative** a corporation holds title to the land and the building. The corporation then offers *shares of stock* to prospective tenants. The price the corporation sets for each apartment becomes the price of the stock. The purchaser becomes a shareholder in the corporation by virtue of stock ownership and receives a *proprietary lease* to the apartment for the life of the corporation. Because stock is personal property, the cooperative tenant-owners do not own real estate, as is the case with condominiums. Instead, they own an interest in a corporation that has only one asset: the building.

Operation and management   The operation and management of a cooperative are determined by the corporation's bylaws. Through their control of the corporation, the shareholders of a cooperative control the property and its operation. They elect officers and directors who are responsible for operating the corporation and its real estate assets. Individual shareholders are obligated to abide by the corporation's bylaws.

An important issue in most cooperatives is the method by which shares in the corporation may be transferred to new owners. For instance, the bylaws may require that the board of directors approve any prospective shareholders. In some cooperatives, a tenant-owner must sell the stock back to the corporation at the original purchase price so that the corporation realizes any profits when the shares are resold.

■ **FOR EXAMPLE** In often publicized events, a controversial celebrity may attempt to move into a highly exclusive cooperative apartment building and is blocked by the cooperative's board. In refusing to allow a controversial personality to purchase shares, the board can cite the unwanted publicity and media attention other celebrity tenants might suffer.

Unlike in a condominium association, which has the authority to impose a lien on the title owned by someone who defaults on maintenance payments, the burden of any defaulted payment in a cooperative falls on the remaining shareholders. Each shareholder is affected by the financial ability of the others. For this reason, approval of prospective tenants by the board of directors frequently involves financial evaluation. If the corporation is unable to make mortgage and tax payments because of shareholder defaults, the property might be sold by court order in a foreclosure suit. This would destroy the interests of all shareholders, including those who have paid their assessments.

Advantages Cooperative ownership, despite its risks, has become more desirable in recent years for several reasons. Lending institutions view the shares of stock as acceptable collateral for financing. The availability of financing expands the transferability of shares beyond wealthy cash buyers. As a tenant-owner, rather than a tenant who pays rent to a landlord, the shareholder has some control over the property. Tenants in cooperatives also enjoy certain income tax advantages. The IRS treats cooperatives as it does fee simple interest in single homes or condominiums in regard to deductibility of loan interest, property taxes, and home-sellers' tax exclusions. Finally, owners enjoy freedom from maintenance.

IN PRACTICE The laws in some states may prohibit real estate licensees from listing or selling cooperative interests because the owners own only personal property. Individuals who participate in these transactions may need a securities license appropriate for the type of cooperative interest involved.

Town House Ownership

A **town house** is a popular form of housing in urban areas. The term *town house* is often used to describe any type of housing connected by common walls. In fact, the town-house concept is a cross between single-family houses and apartments. Normally, each town house has two floors and is located on a small lot.

Title to each unit and lot is vested in the individual owner. Each owner also has a fractional interest in the common areas. Common areas include open spaces, recreational facilities, driveways, and sidewalks. The owner may sell, lease, will, or otherwise transfer the dwelling unit. The rights to the use of common areas pass with title. Town-house ownership, which is typically fee simple ownership, should not be confused with condominium interest, where the land is held as part of the general common elements.

Time-Share Ownership

Time-share ownership permits multiple purchasers to buy interests in real estate; time-shares are most common with resort property ownership. Each purchaser receives the right to use the facilities for a certain period. A *time-share estate* includes a real property interest in condominium ownership; a *time-share use* is a contract right under which the developer owns the real estate.

A time-share *estate* is a fee simple interest. The owner's occupancy and use of the property are limited to the contractual period purchased—for instance, the 17th complete week, Sunday through Saturday, of each calendar year. The owner is assessed for maintenance and common area expenses based on the ratio of the ownership period to the total number of ownership periods in the property. Time-share estates theoretically never end because they are real property interests. However, the physical life of the improvements is limited and must be looked at carefully when considering such a purchase.

The principal difference between a time-share *estate* and a time-share *use* lies in the interest transferred to an owner by the developer of the project. A time-share use consists of the right to occupy and use the facilities for a certain number of years. At the end of that time, the owner's rights in the property terminate. In effect, the developer has sold only a right of occupancy and use to the owner, not a fee simple interest.

Some time-sharing programs specify certain months or weeks of the year during which the owner can use the property. Others provide a rotation system under which the owner can occupy the unit during different times of the year in different years. Some include a swapping privilege for transferring the ownership period to another property to provide some variety for the owner. Time-shared properties typically are used 50 weeks each year, with the remaining two weeks reserved for maintenance of the improvements.

Membership camping is similar to time-share use. The owner purchases the right to use the developer's facilities, which usually consist of an open area with minimal improvements (such as camper and trailer hookups and restrooms). Normally, the owner is not limited to a specific time for using the property; use is limited only by weather and access.

A newer type of time-share program is *"vacation ownership,"* often known as vacation or holiday clubs. Resorts offer consumers condominium-style vacations with flexible opportunities. Most ownerships are either fee simple (giving a title to a fraction of a unit, in perpetuity) or right-to-use contracts (entitled to use but includes no ownership interest and is for a predetermined number of years). Other options include fixed weeks, floating weeks, and point clubs. Many of the larger resorts are structured on an annual allotment of points based on the size of the real estate interest purchased. Vacation point value is determined by the type of room and timing of the stay.

IN PRACTICE   The laws governing the development and sale of time-share units are complex and vary substantially from state to state. In addition, the sale of time-share properties may be subject to federal securities laws, as well as a state's real estate commission oversight. In many states, time-share properties are now subject to subdivision requirements. Several states have adopted versions of the Model Real Estate Time-Share Act. The act contains provisions for the termination of time-share units. It also deals with the management of time-share units and provides consumer protection for purchasers of time-shares.

■ KEY POINT REVIEW

Ownership in severalty, title held by one individual, has the following characteristics:

- Sole rights to ownership
- Sole discretion to transfer part or all ownership rights to another person
- May be a single individual or an artificial person, such as a corporation

Co-ownership, title held by two or more individuals, may be one of four forms:

1. **Tenancy in common**, where

   - each tenant holds an **undivided fractional interest**;
   - co-owners have **unity of possession**—right to occupy entire property;
   - each interest can be sold, conveyed, mortgaged, or transferred; and
   - interest passes by will when a co-owner dies.

2. **Joint tenancy** is where tenants enjoy the four unities (**PITT**):

   - **Unity of possession**—all joint tenants have undivided right to possession.
   - **Unity of interest**—all joint tenants own an equal interest.
   - **Unity of time**—all joint tenants acquire their interest at the same time.
   - **Unity of title**—title is conveyed to all joint tenants by the same document.

Joint tenants also enjoy the **right of survivorship**; upon the death of a joint tenant, interest passes to the other joint tenant or tenants.

Termination of joint tenancy is by

- **death** of all but one joint **tenant**, who then owns the property in severalty;
- **conveyance** of a joint **tenant's** interest, but only as to that interest; or
- **partition**, which can be **brought** to force division or sale of property.

3. **Tenancy by the entirety**, recognized by some states, has the following characteristics:

   - Only available to husband **and wife**
   - Title conveyed only by **deed signed by both**
   - Carries **right of survivorship**; survivor becomes owner in severalty

4. **Community property**, recognized by nine states as of 2010, is generally property acquired during marriage that is not separate property.

   ■ **Separate** property is property owned by one spouse before marriage, or by inheritance or gift or with proceeds of separate property.
   ■ **Community property** requires the signatures of both spouses to be conveyed.
   ■ **Separate** property of one spouse requires only that spouse's signature to be conveyed.
   ■ On the **death** of one spouse, the other spouse owns one-half of community property and other half is distributed according to deceased spouse's will or according to state law.

A **partnership** is an association of two or more persons who carry on a business for profit as co-owners in general or a limited partnership, as provided by state law.

   ■ In a **general partnership**,
     — all partners **participate** in operation and management, and
     — partners share **full liability** for business losses and obligations.
   ■ A **limited partnership** has both general partners and limited partners.
   ■ **General partners** run the business.
   ■ **Limited partners** do not participate in running the business and are liable for business losses only up to the amount of the individual's investment.

A **limited liability company (LLC)** may be permitted by state law and offers its members the following benefits:

   ■ **Limited liability** offered by a corporate form of ownership
   ■ **Tax advantages** of a partnership (no double taxation)
   ■ **Flexible management structure** without corporation requirements or restrictions on limited partnership

Condominium laws of each state define the following:

   ■ The condominium owner holds fee simple title to the airspace of a unit as well as an undivided share in the remainder of the building and land, known as the common elements.
   ■ **Common elements** are owned by condominium unit owners as tenants in common.
   ■ The condominium is administered by a **homeowners' association** of unit owners that may decide to hire an outside property management firm.
   ■ **Maintenance** of common elements is funded by **fees** charged to each unit owner.
   ■ Unit owners have no right to partition common elements.
   ■ Condominium units may be mortgaged; default on payment does not affect other unit owners.
   ■ The condominium association may have a **right of first refusal** when a unit owner wants to sell.

In a **cooperative**, title to the land and the building is held by a corporation, which sells shares of stock to prospective tenants.

- A purchaser of stock becomes a **shareholder** in the corporation and receives a **proprietary lease** to the apartment for the life of the corporation.
- Stock is owned as personal property and not real estate.
- The **lender** may accept stock as collateral for financing, which expands the pool of potential owners.
- The **IRS** treats a cooperative the same as houses or condominiums for tax purposes.

In a **town house**, a form of ownership in which houses share common vertical walls, **titles** to individual units include a fractional interest in common areas.

A **time-share** permits the sale of a leasehold interest (time-share use) or deeded ownership (time-share estate) that allows occupancy during a specific period of time, typically weekly.

Time-share ownership permits multiple purchasers to buy interests in real estate, a form of ownership most commonly found with resort property.

The **Model Real Estate Time-Share Act** deals with time-share management and protections for purchasers of units.

■ RELATED WEB SITES

The Official Business Link to the U.S. Government: *www.business.gov*
Legal Information Institute: Uniform Condominium Act:
   www.law.cornell.edu/uniform/vol7.html#condo
U.S. Small Business Administration: *www.sba.gov*

CHAPTER 8 QUIZ

PITT

1. The four unities of <u>possession</u>, <u>interest</u>, <u>time</u>, and <u>title</u> are associated with which of the following?
   a. Community property
   b. Severalty ownership
   c. Tenants in common
   d. Joint tenancy

2. A parcel of property was purchased by two friends. The deed they received from the seller at closing transferred the property without further explanation. The two friends took title as which of the following?
   a. Joint tenants
   b. Tenants in common
   c. Tenants by the entirety
   d. Community property owners

126 *B*

3. Three people are joint tenants with rights of survivorship in a tract of land. One owner conveys interest to a friend. Which statement is *TRUE*?
   a. The first two owners remain joint tenants.
   b. The new owner has severalty ownership.
   c. They all become tenants in common.
   d. They all become joint tenants.

4. A man owns one of 20 units in a building in fee simple, along with a 5 percent ownership share in the parking facilities, recreation center, and grounds. What kind of property does he own?
   a. Cooperative
   b. Condominium
   c. Time-share
   d. Land trust

5. A trust is a legal arrangement in which title to property is held for the benefit of a third party by a(n)
   a. beneficiary.
   b. trustor.
   c. trustee.
   d. attorney-in-fact.

6. According to some states, any real property that either spouse of a married couple owns at the time of the marriage remains separate property. Further, any real property acquired by either spouse during the marriage (except by gift or inheritance) belongs to both of them equally. What is this form of ownership called?

    P. 129 D
   a. Partnership
   b. Joint tenancy
   c. Tenancy by the entirety
   d. Community property

7. Three women were concurrent owners of a parcel of real estate. When one woman died, her interest, according to her will, became part of the estate. The deceased was a

   B *P. 126*
   a. joint tenant.
   b. tenant in common.
   c. tenant by the entirety.
   d. severalty owner.

8. A legal arrangement under which the title to real property is held to protect the interests of a beneficiary is a
   a. trust.
   b. corporation.
   c. limited partnership.
   d. general partnership.

9. A person lives in an apartment building. The land and structures are owned by a corporation, with one mortgage loan securing the entire property. Like the other residents, this person owns stock in the corporation and has a lease to the apartment. This type of ownership is called
   a. condominium.
   b. planned unit development.
   c. time-share.
   d. cooperative.

10. An owner purchased an interest in a house. The owner is entitled to the right of possession only between July 10 and August 4 of each year. Which of the following is MOST likely the type of ownership that has been purchased?

    a. Cooperative
    b. Condominium
    c. Time-share
    d. Town house

11. A corporation is a legal entity, an artificial person according to state law. Property owned by the corporation is owned in

    a. trust.
    b. partnership.
    c. severalty.
    d. survivorship tenancy.

12. Which of the following refers to ownership by one person?

    a. Tenancy by the entirety
    b. Community property
    c. Tenancy in common
    d. Severalty

13. A married couple co-owns a farm and has right of survivorship. This arrangement is MOST likely

    a. severalty ownership.
    b. community property.
    c. a tenancy in common.
    d. an estate by the entirety.

14. All of the following can be classified as real property EXCEPT

    a. ownership in severalty.
    b. cooperative unit ownership.
    c. condominium unit ownership.
    d. a tenancy in common.

15. Two people are co-owners of a small office building with the right of survivorship. One of the co-owners dies intestate and leaves nothing to be distributed to his heirs. Which of the following would explain why the second co-owner acquired the deceased's interest?

    a. Adverse possession
    b. Joint tenancy
    c. Reversionary interest
    d. Foreclosure

16. Which of the following is MOST likely evidence of ownership in a cooperative?

    a. Tax bill for an individual unit
    b. Existence of a reverter clause
    c. Shareholder's stock
    d. Right of first refusal

17. An ownership interest that is based on annual occupancy intervals is a

    a. leasehold.
    b. time-share.
    c. condominium.
    d. cooperative.

18. Which statement applies to both joint tenancy and tenancy by the entirety?

    a. There is no right to file a partition suit.
    b. The last survivor becomes a severalty owner.
    c. A deed signed by one owner will convey a fractional interest.
    d. A deed will not convey any interest unless signed by both spouses.

19. Which of the following is NOT a form of co-ownership?

    a. Tenancy in common
    b. Ownership in severalty
    c. Tenancy by the entirety
    d. Community property

20. If property is held by two or more owners as joint tenants, the interest of the deceased co-owners will be passed to the

    a. surviving owner or owners.
    b. heirs of the deceased.
    c. state, under the law of escheat.
    d. trust under which the property was owned.

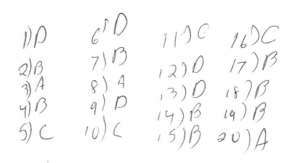

1) D   6) D   11) C   16) C
2) B   7) B   12) D   17) B
3) A   8) A   13) D   18) B
4) B   9) D   14) B   19) B
5) C   10) C   15) B   20) A

CHAPTER 9

Legal Descriptions

■ LEGAL DESCRIPTIONS

Consumers expect to become owners of every bit of land to which they are entitled. Ownership of land purchased must be precisely described in the legal documents. Though lawyers review the legal descriptions for accuracy, the licensee needs to understand how the land is described and the reasoning behind that description.

■ DESCRIBING LAND

A street address, while usually enough to find the location of a particular building, is not precise enough to describe legal ownership. Addresses change as streets are renamed, or rural roads might become public streets in growing communities. Sales contracts, deeds, and mortgages require a more specific (or *legally sufficient*) description of property to be binding.

A **legal description** is a detailed way of describing a parcel of land for documents such as deeds and mortgages that will be accepted in a court of law. The description is based on information collected through a **survey**—the process by which boundaries are measured by calculating the dimensions and area to determine the exact location of a piece of land. Courts have stated that a description is *legally sufficient* if it allows a surveyor to *locate* the parcel. In this context, *locate* means that the surveyor must be able to define the exact boundaries of the property. A street address will not tell a surveyor how large the property is or where it begins and ends. Several alternative systems of identification have been developed to express a **legal description** of real estate.

■ METHODS OF DESCRIBING REAL ESTATE

Three basic methods can be used to describe real estate:

- Metes and bounds
- Rectangular (or government) survey
- Lot and block (recorded plat)

Although each method can be used independently, the methods may be combined in some situations. Some states use only one method; others use all three.

Metes-and-bounds descriptions were used in the original thirteen colonies and in those states that were being settled while the rectangular survey system was being developed. Today, as technology allows for greater precision and expanded record keeping, there is greater integration of land description information. Currently, the Federal Bureau of Land Management and the USDA Forest Service are developing the National Integrated Land System (NILS) in cooperation with states, counties, and private industry. This new system of land description is designed to be compatible with both the metes-and-bounds description and the rectangular survey system. The NILS has unified the worlds of surveying into the Graphic Information System (GIS) for the management of *cadastral* (public survey records) and land parcel information.

Metes-and-Bounds Method

The **metes-and-bounds description** is the oldest type of legal description. *Metes* means to measure, and *bounds* means linear directions. The method relies on a property's physical features to determine the boundaries and measurements of the parcel. A metes-and-bounds description starts at a designated place on the parcel, called the **point of beginning (POB)**. The POB is also the **point of ending (POE)**, but often only the POB is used in describing the property. From there, the surveyor proceeds around the property's boundaries. The boundaries are recorded by referring to linear measurements, natural and artificial landmarks (called *monuments*), and directions. A metes-and-bounds description always ends back at the POB so that the tract being described is completely enclosed.

Monuments are fixed objects used to identify the POB, all corners of the parcel or ends of boundary segments, and the location of intersecting boundaries. In colonial times, a monument might have been a natural object such as a stone, a large tree, a lake, or a stream. It also may have been a street, a fence, or other marker. Today, monuments are iron pins or concrete posts placed by the U.S. Corps of Engineers, other government departments, or trained private surveyors. Measurements often include the words *more or less* because the location of the monuments is more important than the distances between them. The actual distance between monuments takes precedence over any linear measurements in the description. Because monuments can be moved, surveyors give their final metes-and-bounds reference in terms of cardinal points and distance. They include the statement "to the point of beginning (POB)" to ensure closure and to remove questions if an error in footage prevents closure.

An example of a historical metes-and-bounds description of a parcel of land (pictured in Figure 9.1) follows:

> A tract of land located in Red Skull, Boone County, Virginia, described as follows: Beginning at the intersection of the east line of Jones Road and the south line of Skull Drive; then east along the south line of Skull Drive 200 feet; then south 15° east 216.5 feet, more or less, to the center thread of Red Skull Creek then northwesterly along the center line of said creek to its intersection with the east line of Jones Road; then north 105 feet, more or less, along the east line of Jones Road to the point of beginning.

When used to describe property within a town or city, a metes-and-bounds description may begin as follows:

> Beginning at a point on the southerly side of Kent Street, 100 feet easterly from the corner formed by the intersection of the southerly side of Kent Street and the easterly side of Broadway; then ...

In this description, the POB is given by reference to the corner intersection. *Again, the description must close by returning to the POB.*

An example of a technically assisted metes-and-bounds description follows:

> Beginning at a point (POB) on the North side of Newberry Street 100.50 feet East from the corner formed by the intersection of the East boundary of Peter Road and the North boundary of Newberry Street; then East 90

FIGURE 9.1

Metes-and-Bounds Tract

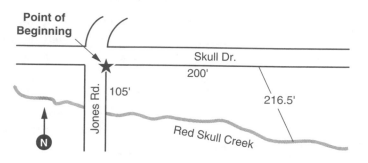

degrees, 15 minutes, 200.22 feet; then North 1 degree, 3 minutes, 2 seconds 300 feet; then West 89 degrees, 10 minutes, 3 seconds, 200.05 feet; then direct to the POB.

Metes-and-bounds descriptions are complicated. They can be difficult to understand when they include detailed compass directions or concave and convex lines. Sometimes the lines are curved on an arc or radius that becomes part of the description. Natural deterioration or destruction of the monuments in a description can make boundaries difficult to identify.

Technological advances, such as the use of computers, lasers, satellites, and global positioning systems, have meant a resurgence in property descriptions using points of reference or metes-and-bounds descriptions.

Rectangular (Government) Survey System

The **rectangular survey system**, sometimes called the *government survey system*, was established by Congress in 1785 to standardize the description of land acquired by the newly formed federal government. By dividing the land into rectangles, the survey provided land descriptions by describing the rectangle(s) in which the land was located. The system is based on two sets of intersecting lines: principal meridians and base lines. The **principal meridians** run north and south, and the base lines run east and west. Both are located by reference to degrees of longitude and latitude. Each principal meridian has a name or number and is crossed by a base line. Each principal meridian and its corresponding base line are used to survey a definite area of land, indicated on the map by boundary lines. There are 37 principal meridians in the United States.

Each principal meridian describes only specific areas of land by boundaries. No parcel of land is described by reference to more than one principal meridian. The meridian used may not necessarily be the nearest one.

Ranges   The land on either side of a principal meridian is divided into six-mile-wide strips by lines that run north and south, *parallel to the meridian*. These north-south strips of land are called **ranges**. (See Figure 9.3.) They are designated by consecutive numbers east or west of the principal meridian. For example, Range 3 East would be a strip of land between 12 and 18 miles east of its principal meridian.

The directions of township lines and range lines may be easily remembered by thinking of the words this way:

Township lines
Range lines

FIGURE 9.2

Township Lines

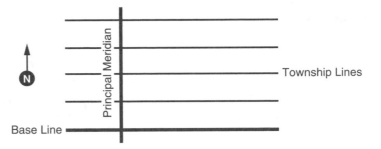

Township tiers   Lines running east and west, *parallel to the base line* and six miles apart, are referred to as **township lines**. (See Figure 9.2.) They form strips of land called **township tiers**. These township tiers are designated by consecutive numbers north or south of the base line. For instance, the strip of land between 6 and 12 miles north of a base line is Township 2 North.

Townships are numbered the same way a field is plowed. Remember: *right to left, left to right, right to left.*

Township squares   When the horizontal township lines and the vertical range lines intersect, they form squares. These *township* squares are the basic units of the rectangular survey system. (See Figure 9.4.) **Townships** are 6 miles square and contain 36 square miles (23,040 acres).

Each township is given a legal description. The township's description includes the following:

■ Designation of the township tier in which the township is located
■ Designation of the range strip
■ Name or number of the principal meridian for that area

■ **FOR EXAMPLE**   In Figure 9.4, the shaded township is described as Township 3 North, Range 4 East of the Principal Meridian. This township is the third strip, or tier, north of the base line, and it designates the township number and direction. The township is also located in the fourth range strip (those running north and south) east

FIGURE 9.3

Range Lines

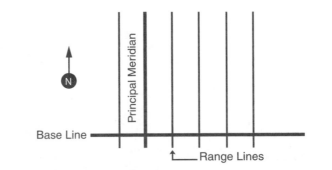

**Townships in the
Rectangular Survey
System**

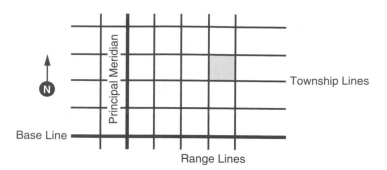

of the principal meridian. Finally, reference is made to the principal meridian because the land being described is within the boundary of land surveyed from that meridian. This description is abbreviated as *T3N, R4E 4th Principal Meridian.*

Sections   Township squares are subdivided into sections and subsections called halves and quarters, which can be further divided. Each township contains 36 **sections**. Each section is one square mile or 640 acres, with 43,560 square feet in each acre. Sections are numbered 1 through 36, as shown in Figure 9.5. Section 1 is always in the northeast, or upper right-hand, corner. The numbering proceeds right to left to the upper left-hand corner. From there, the numbers drop down to the next tier and continue from left to right, then back from right to left. By law, each Section 16 was set aside for school purposes, and the sale or rental proceeds from this land were originally available for township school use. The schoolhouse was usually located in this section so it would be centrally located for all the students in the township. As a result, Section 16 is commonly referred to as a *school section.*

Sections are divided into *halves* (320 acres) and *quarters* (160 acres). In turn, each of those parts is further divided into halves and quarters. The southeast quarter of a section, which is a 160-acre tract, is abbreviated SE¼. The SE¼ of SE¼ of

> **Math Shortcut**
>
> To calculate acres in a survey system description, multiply all the denominators and divide that number into 640 acres. For instance, the SE¼ of SE¼ of SE¼ of Section 1 = 4 × 4 × 4 = 64; 640 ÷ 64 = 10 acres.

Sections in a Township

Section 16

School Section

	N				
6	5	4	3	2	1
7	8	9	10	11	12
18	17	16	15	14	13
19	20	21	22	23	24
30	29	28	27	26	25
31	32	33	34	35	36

W   E

S

F I G U R E 9.6

A Section

	5,280 Feet		
1,320 20 Chains	1,320 20 Chains	2,640 40 Chains 160 Rods	
W¹/₂ of NW¹/₄ (80 Acres)	E¹/₂ of NW¹/₄ (80 Acres)	NE¹/₄ (160 Acres)	

(Figure 9.6 — A Section diagram showing subdivisions:)

- 5,280 Feet (top measurement)
- Left edge: 2,640 / 1,320 / 1,320
- Top cells: W¹/₂ of NW¹/₄ (80 Acres); E¹/₂ of NW¹/₄ (80 Acres); NE¹/₄ (160 Acres)
- Middle row: NW¹/₄ of SW¹/₄ (40 Acres); NE¹/₄ of SW¹/₄ (40 Acres); N¹/₂ of NW¹/₄ of SE¹/₄ (20 Acres) — 20 Acres; W¹/₂ of NE¹/₄ of SE¹/₄ (20 Acres) 1 Furlong; 20 Acres
- Bottom row: SW¹/₄ of SW¹/₄ (40 Acres) 80 Rods; 40 Acres 440 Yards; (10 Acres) 660 Feet; (10 Acres) 660 Feet; 5 Acres / 5 Acres; 5 Acs. / 5 Acs. — SE¹/₄ of SE¹/₄ of SE¹/₄ 10 Acres

SE¹/₄ of Section 1 would be a 10-acre square in the lower right-hand corner of Section 1. (See Figure 9.6; the old measurements in chains and rods are defined in Table 9.1: Units of Land Measurements.)

The rectangular survey system sometimes uses a shorthand method in its descriptions. For instance, a comma may be used in place of the word *of*: SE¹/₄, SE¹/₄, SE¹/₄, Section 1. It is possible to combine portions of a section, such as NE¹/₄ of SW¹/₄ and N¹/₂ of NW¹/₄ of SE¹/₄ of Section 1, which could also be written NE¹/₄, SW¹/₄; N¹/₂, NW¹/₄, SE¹/₄ of Section 1. A semicolon means *and*. Because of the semicolon in this description, the area is 60 acres.

Starting with township and range lines, Figure 9.7 illustrates how sections are created and subdivided.

Reading a rectangular survey description   To determine the location and size of a property described in the rectangular or government survey style, *start at the end* and work backward to the beginning, *reading from right to left*. For example, consider the following description (see Figure 9.6):

> The S¹/₂ of the NW¹/₄ of the SE¹/₄ of Section 11, Township 8 North, Range 6 West of the Fourth Principal Meridian.

To locate this tract of land from the citation alone, first search for the fourth principal meridian on a map of the United States and note its base line. Then, on a regional map, find the township in which the property is located by counting six range strips west of the fourth principal meridian and eight townships north of its corresponding base line. After locating Section 11, divide the section into

FIGURE 9.7

Parts of a Township

Township Lines
(Six miles lines running east and west)

Range Lines
(Six miles lines running north and south)

Township
(The squares formed by the intersections of the lines to form the basic units of the rectangular systems)

Section in a Township
(Each township is divided into 36 sections)

A Section
(The various subdivisions into which a 640 acre sections may be divided)

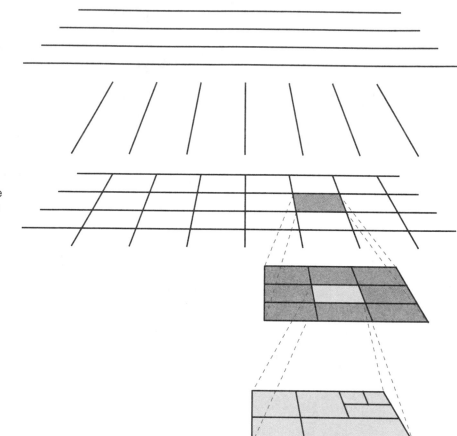

quarters. Then divide the SE¼ into quarters, and then the NW¼ of that into halves. The S½ of that NW¼ contains the property in question.

Legal descriptions should always include the name of the county and state in which the land is located because meridians often relate to more than one state and occasionally relate to two base lines. For example, the description "the southwest quarter of Section 10, Township 4 North, Range 1 West of the Fourth Principal Meridian" could refer to land in either Illinois or Wisconsin.

Metes-and-bounds descriptions within the rectangular survey system
Land in states that use the rectangular survey system may also require a metes-and-bounds description. This usually occurs in one of three situations: (1) when describing an irregular tract; (2) when a tract is too small to be described by quarter-sections; or (3) when a tract does not follow the lot or block lines of a recorded subdivision or section, quarter-section lines, or other fractional section lines.

Lot-and-Block System

The third method of legal description is the lot-and-block (recorded plat) system. This system uses lot and block numbers referred to in a plat map filed in the public records of the county where the land is located. The plat map is a map of a town, a section, or a subdivision, indicating the location and boundaries of individual properties. The lot-and-block system is used mostly in subdivisions and urban areas.

A lot-and-block survey is performed in two steps. First, a large parcel of land is described either by the metes-and-bounds method or by rectangular survey. Once this large parcel is surveyed, it is broken into smaller parcels. As a result, a lot-and-block legal description always refers to a prior metes-and-bounds or rectangular survey description. For each parcel described under the lot-and-block system, the *lot* refers to the numerical designation of any particular parcel. The *block* refers to the name of the subdivision under which the map is recorded. The block reference is drawn from the early 1900s, when a city block was the most common type of subdivided property.

The lot-and-block system starts with the preparation of a *subdivision plat* by a licensed surveyor or an engineer. (See Figure 9.8.) On this plat, the land is divided into numbered or lettered lots and blocks, and streets or access roads for public use are indicated. Lot sizes and street details must be described completely and

FIGURE   9.8

Subdivision Plat Map of Block A

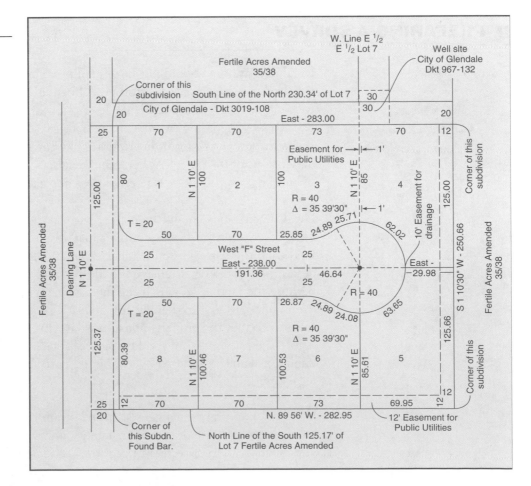

must comply with all local ordinances and requirements. When properly signed and approved, the subdivision plat is recorded in the county in which the land is located. The plat becomes part of the legal description. In describing a lot from a recorded subdivision plat, three identifiers are used:

1. Lot and block number
2. Name or number of the subdivision plat
3. Name of the county and state

The following is an example of a lot-and-block description:

> Lot 71, Happy Valley Estates 2, located in a portion of the southeast quarter of Section 23, Township 7 North, Range 4 East of the Seward Principal Meridian in _____ County, _____ [state].

Anyone who wants to locate this parcel would start with the map of the Seward principal meridian to identify the township and range reference. Then that person would consult the township map of Township 7 North, Range 4 East, and the section map of Section 23. From there, the quarter-section map of the southeast quarter would be looked at. The quarter-section map would refer to the plat map for the subdivision known as the second unit (second parcel subdivided) under the name of Happy Valley Estates.

Some lot-and-block descriptions are not dependent on a government survey system and may refer to the plat recording in the land records of the county.

■ PREPARING A SURVEY

Legal descriptions should not be altered or combined without adequate information from a surveyor or title attorney. A licensed surveyor is trained and authorized to locate and determine the legal description of any parcel of land. The surveyor does this by preparing two documents: a survey and a survey sketch. The *survey* states the property's legal description. The *survey sketch* shows the location and dimensions of the parcel. When a survey also shows the location, size, and shape of buildings on the lot, it is referred to as a *spot survey*.

Legal descriptions should be copied with extreme care. An incorrectly worded legal description in a sales contract may result in a conveyance of more or less land than the parties intended. For example, damages suffered from an incorrect description could be extensive if buildings and improvements need to be moved because the land upon which the improvements were made is not owned. Often, even punctuation is extremely critical. Title problems can arise for the buyer who seeks to convey the property at a future date. Even if the contract can be corrected before the sale is closed, the licensee risks losing a commission and may be held liable for damages suffered by an injured party because of an improperly worded legal description.

It is very important for licensees to be aware of various surveys and their uses. Not all surveys include surveyor liability and warranties of accuracy. Some surveys, such as an Improvement Location Certificate (ILC) are not full surveys. It is prepared in a shorter time frame and at less cost. It provides only the location of the structures and improvements as related to property boundaries.

IN PRACTICE   Because legal descriptions, once recorded, affect title to real estate, they should be prepared only by a professional surveyor. Real estate licensees who attempt to draft legal descriptions create potential risks for themselves and their clients and customers.

■ MEASURING ELEVATIONS

Just as surface rights must be identified, surveyed, and described, so must rights to the property above the earth's surface. Recall from Chapter 2 that *land* includes the space above the ground. In the same way land may be measured and divided into parcels, the air may be divided. An owner may subdivide the air above her land into **air lots**. Air lots are composed of the airspace within specific boundaries located over a parcel of land.

The *condominium laws* passed in all states require that a registered land surveyor prepare a plat map that shows the elevations of floor and ceiling surfaces and the vertical boundaries of each unit with reference to an official *datum* (discussed later in this chapter). (See Chapter 8.) A unit's floor, for instance, might be 60 feet above the datum and its ceiling, 69 feet. Typically, a separate plat is prepared for each floor in the condominium building.

The following is an example of the legal description of a condominium apartment unit that includes a fractional share of the common elements of the building and land:

> UNIT _____, Level ___, as delineated on survey of the following described parcel of real estate (hereinafter referred to as Development Parcel): The north 99 feet of the west ½ of Block 4 (except that part, if any, taken and used for street), in Sutton's Division Number 5 in the east ½ of the southeast ¼ of Section 24, Township 3 South, Range 68 West of the Sixth Principal Meridian, in Denver County, Colorado, which survey is attached as Exhibit A to Declaration made by Colorado National Bank as Trustee under Trust No. 1250, recorded in the Recorder's Office of Denver County, Colorado, as Document No. 475637; together with an undivided _____% interest in said Development Parcel (excepting from said Development Parcel all the property and space comprising all the units thereof as defined and set forth in said Declaration and Survey).

Subsurface rights can be legally described in the same manner as air rights. However, they are measured *below* the datum rather than above it. Subsurface rights are used not only for coal mining, petroleum drilling, and utility line location but also for multistory condominiums—both residential and commercial—that have several floors below ground level.

Datum

A datum is a point, line, or surface from which elevations are measured or indicated. For the purpose of the United States Geological Survey (USGS), *datum* is defined as the mean sea level at New York Harbor. But virtually all large cities have a local official datum that is used instead of the USGS datum. A surveyor would use a datum in determining the height of a structure or establishing the grade of a street.

Monuments   Monuments are traditionally used to mark surface measurements between points. A monument could be a marker set in concrete, a piece of steel-reinforcing bar (rebar), a metal pipe driven into the soil, or simply a wooden stake stuck in the dirt. Because such items are subject to the whims of nature and vandals, their accuracy is sometimes suspect. As a result, surveyors rely most heavily on *benchmarks* to mark their work accurately and permanently.

Benchmarks are permanent reference points that have been established throughout the United States. They are usually embossed brass markers set into solid concrete or asphalt bases. While used to some degree for surface measurements, their principal reference use is for marking datums.

IN PRACTICE   All large cities have established a local official datum used in place of the USGS datum. For instance, the official datum for Chicago is known as the *Chicago City Datum*. It is a horizontal plane that corresponds to the low-water level of Lake Michigan in 1847 (the year in which the datum was established) and is considered to be at zero elevation. Although a surveyor's measurement of elevation based on the USGS datum will differ from one computed according to a local datum, it can be translated to an elevation based on the USGS.

Land acquisition costs   Cities with local datums also have designated official local benchmarks, which are assigned permanent identifying numbers. Local benchmarks simplify surveyors' work because the basic benchmarks may be miles away.

MATH CONCEPTS

LAND ACQUISITION COSTS

To calculate the cost of purchasing land, use the same unit in which the cost is given. Costs quoted per square foot must be multiplied by the proper number of square feet; costs quoted per acre must be multiplied by the proper number of acres; and so on.

To calculate the cost of a parcel of land of three acres at $1.10 per square foot, convert the acreage to square feet before multiplying:

43,560 square feet per acre × 3 acres = 130,680 square feet

130,680 square feet × $1.10 per square foot = $143,748

To calculate the cost of a parcel of land of 17,500 square feet at $60,000 per acre, convert the cost per acre into the cost per square foot before multiplying by the number of square feet in the parcel:

$60,000 per acre ÷ 43,560 square feet per acre = $1.38 (rounded) per square foot

17,500 square feet × $1.38 per square foot = $24,150

	Unit	Measurement
TABLE 9.1 **Units of Land Measurement**	mile	5,280 feet; 1,760 yards; 320 rods
	rod	16.5 feet; 5.50 yards
	square mile	640 acres (5,280 × 5,280 = 27,878,400 ÷ 43,560)
	acre	43,560 square feet
	cubic yard	27 cubic feet
	square yard	9 square feet
	square foot	144 square inches
	chain	66 feet; 4 rods; 100 links

■ LAND UNITS AND MEASUREMENTS

It is important to understand land units and measurements because they are integral parts of legal descriptions. Some historical measurements are listed in Table 9.1. Today, the terms *rods, cubic yards,* and *chains* are not often used.

■ KEY POINT REVIEW

The three methods of legal description of land are the following:

The **metes-and-bounds method**

■ measures distances (**metes**);
■ starts from a **point of beginning (POB)**;
■ follows compass directions or angles (**bounds**);
■ arrives at the **point of ending (POE)**, which must be the same as the POB; and
■ uses **monuments** (fixed objects or markers) to identify the POB and corners or places where boundary lines change direction.

The **rectangular survey system (government survey system)**

■ divides land into **rectangles**;
■ is measured from the intersection of **principal meridians** and **base lines**;
■ is referenced by degrees of **longitude and latitude**;
■ uses **township lines,** which run east to west parallel to and counted from base lines that are
  — **6 miles** apart,
  — in units called **townships** of 36 square miles each,
  — in rows of townships called **tiers,** and
  — arranged so each township is divided into **36 sections** of one mile square (640 acres), counted from northeast and running right to left, then left to right, and so on; and
■ uses **range lines,** which run north to south parallel to (and counted from) **principal meridian,** that are
  — **6 miles** apart and
  — in rows called **ranges.**

The **lot-and-block (recorded plat) system**

- divides a larger parcel further into **block** (subdivision) and **lot** (individual parcel) **numbers** and
- references all data in a subdivision **plat map**, noting lot sizes, street names, and other required information that is
  - — **approved** by the governing body, and
  - — filed **in public records** of the county where the land is located.

Survey preparation includes both a **legal description** and a **survey sketch**. Legal description must be transcribed **exactly** as written to avoid future problems over incorrect boundaries.

Elevations must be measured if **air lots** above the surface or **subsurface rights** are to be described and conveyed, with

- distances noted as above or below **datum**, defined by U.S. Geological Survey (USGS) as **mean sea level at New York Harbor**, and making use of
  - — permanent **benchmarks** often based on a **local official datum,** and
  - — **monuments** marking surface measurements between points.

The most common units of **land measurement** include the

- **mile** of 5,280 feet,
- **acre** of 43,560 square feet (approximately 207 × 207 feet), and
- **square mile** of 640 acres.

■ RELATED WEB SITE

U.S. Geological Survey: *www.usgs.gov*

CHAPTER 9 QUIZ

1. What is the proper description of this shaded area of a section using the rectangular government survey?

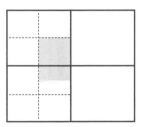

   a. SW¼ of the NE¼ and the N½ of the SE¼ of the SW¼
   b. N½ of the NE¼ of the SW¼ and the SE¼ of the NW¼
   c. SW¼ of the SE¼ of the NW¼ and the N½ of the NE¼ of the SW¼
   d. S½ of the SW¼ of the NE¼ and the NE¼ of the NW¼ of the SE¼

2. When surveying land, a surveyor refers to the principal meridian that is
   a. nearest the land being surveyed.
   b. in the same state as the land being surveyed.
   c. not more than 40 townships or 15 ranges distant from the land being surveyed.
   d. within the rectangular survey system area in which the land being surveyed is located.

D
146

3. The N½ of the SW¼ of a section contains how many acres? 
   a. 20
   b. 40
   c. 60
   d. 80

4. In describing real estate, the system that may use a property's physical features to determine boundaries and measurements is
   a. rectangular survey.
   b. metes-and-bounds.
   c. government survey.
   d. lot-and-block.

Questions 5 through 8 refer to the following illustration of a whole township and parts of the adjacent townships.

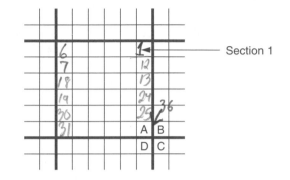

Section 1

5. The section marked A is which of the following?
   a. School section
   b. Section 31
   c. Section 36
   d. Government lot

6. Which of the following is Section 6?
   a. A
   b. B
   c. C
   d. D

7. The section directly below C is
   a. Section 7.
   b. Section 12.
   c. Section 25.
   d. Section 30.

8. Which of the following is Section D?
   a. Section 1
   b. Section 6
   c. Section 31
   d. Section 36

9. Which of these shaded areas of a section depicts the NE¼ of the SE¼ of the SW¼?

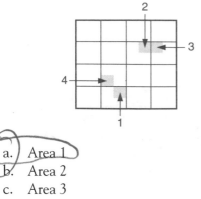

a. Area 1
b. Area 2
c. Area 3
d. Area 4

10. A buyer purchased a half-acre parcel for $2.15 per square foot. What was the selling price of the parcel?

acre = 43,560 SF

a. $774
b. $46,827
c. $1,376
d. $93,654

11. How many acres are contained in the tract described as "beginning at the NW corner of the SW¼, then south along the west line to the SW corner of the section, then east along the south line of the section 2,640 feet, more or less, to the SE corner of the said SW¼, then in a straight line to the POB"?

a. 80 acres
b. 90 acres
c. 100 acres
d. 160 acres

12. If a farm described as "the NW¼ of the SE¼ of Section 10, Township 2 North, Range 3 West of the 6th. P.M." sold for $1,500 an acre, what would the total sales price be?

a. $15,000
b. $30,000
c. $45,000
d. $60,000

13. As a legal description, "the northwest ¼ of the southwest ¼ of Section 6, Township 4 North, Range 7 West" is defective because it contains no reference to

pub

a. lot numbers.
b. boundary lines.
c. a principal meridian.
d. a record of survey.

14. A man buys 4.5 acres of land for $78,400. An adjoining owner wants to purchase a strip of this land measuring 150 feet by 100 feet. What should this strip cost the adjoining owner if the owner sells it for the same price per square foot he originally paid for it?

a. $3,000
b. $6,000
c. $7,800
d. $9,400

43,560
× 4.5

150×100
= 15000 SF

196,020 SF = $0.40/SF

.40 × 15,000

15. Which of the following are NOT basic components of metes-and-bounds descriptions?

a. Tangible and intangible monuments
b. Base lines, principal meridians, and townships
c. Degrees, minutes, and seconds
d. Points of beginning

16. A property contains ten acres. How many lots of not less than 50 feet by 100 feet can be subdivided from the property if 26,000 square feet were dedicated for roads?

a. 80
b. 81
c. 82
d. 83

43,560 × 10 =
435,600
- 26,000
404,600

17. A parcel of land is 400 feet by 640 feet. The parcel is cut in half diagonally by a stream. How many acres are in each half of the parcel?

a. 2.75
b. 2.94
c. 5.51
d. 5.88

40 acres

18. What is the shortest distance between Section 1 and Section 36 in the same township?

   a. Three miles
   b. Four miles
   c. Five miles
   d. Six miles

19. In any township, what is the number of the section designated as the school section?

   a. 1
   b. 16
   c. 25
   d. 36

20. The *LEAST* specific method for identifying real property is

   a. rectangular survey.
   b. metes-and-bounds.
   c. street address.
   d. lot-and-block.

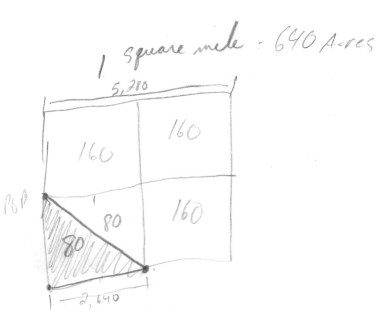

1 square mile - 640 Acres

5,280

160   160

POB   80   160

80

2,640

11)

14) 4.5 Acres for 78,400/4.5

$17,422/Acre

100 × 150 = 15,000 square

× .39999 = Approx

$0.39/square foot

$6,000

10

Real Estate Taxes and Liens

■ **identify** the various classifications of liens;

■ **describe** how real estate taxes are applied through assessments, tax liens, and the use of equalization ratios;

■ **explain** how nontax liens, such as mechanics' liens, mortgage liens, and judgment liens are applied and enforced;

■ **distinguish** the characteristics of voluntary, involuntary, statutory, and equitable liens; and

■ **define** the following *key terms*:

ad valorem tax	general real estate tax	redemption
assessment	inheritance taxes	special assessments
attachment	involuntary lien	specific liens
equalization factor	judgment	statutory lien
equitable lien	lien	subordination agreements
equitable right of redemption	lis pendens	tax sale
	mechanic's lien	vendor's lien
estate tax	mill	voluntary lien
general liens	mortgage lien	

■ REAL ESTATE TAXES AND LIENS

The ownership of real estate is subject to certain obligations imposed by governmental powers, usually in the form of taxes. Creditors and courts can also make claim against property to secure payment for debts, by way of a *lien*.

■ LIENS

A **lien** is a charge or claim against a person's property made to enforce the payment of money. Whenever someone borrows money, the lender generally requires some form of *security*. Security (also referred to as *collateral*) is something of value that the borrower promises to give the lender if the borrower fails to repay the debt. When the lender's security is in the form of real estate, the security is called a lien.

Liens are not limited to security for borrowed money. Liens can be enforced against property by a government agency to recover taxes owed by the owner. A lien can be used to force the payment of an assessment or other special charge. In these ways, a person or an entity can use another's property to ensure payment for work performed, services rendered, or debts incurred. If a lien is not paid in the allotted time, the lienholder may foreclose on the lien, potentially forcing the sale of the property according to a particular state's statute.

All liens are encumbrances, but not all encumbrances are liens.

A lien represents an interest only in ownership; it does not constitute actual ownership of the property. It is an encumbrance on the owner's title. An *encumbrance* is any charge or claim that attaches to real property and lessens its value or impairs its use. An encumbrance does not necessarily prevent the transfer or conveyance of the property, but because an encumbrance is *attached* to the property, it transfers along with it. Liens differ from other encumbrances because they are financial or monetary in nature and attach to the property because of a debt. Other encumbrances may be physical in nature and may affect the owner's use of the property, such as easements or encroachments. (See Chapter 7.)

Generally, a lienholder must initiate a legal action to force the sale of the property or acquire title. The debt is then paid out of the proceeds.

Memory Tip

Four Ways to Create a Lien (VISE):

■ Voluntary
■ Involuntary
■ Statutory
■ Equitable

There are many different types of liens. (See Figure 10.1.) One way that liens are classified is by how they are created. A **voluntary lien** is created *intentionally* by the property owner's action, such as when someone takes out a mortgage loan. An **involuntary lien** is not a matter of choice; it is created by law and may be either statutory or equitable. A **statutory lien** is created by statute. A real estate tax lien, for example, is an involuntary, statutory lien. It is created by statute without any action by the property owner. An **equitable lien** arises out of common law. A court-ordered judgment that requires a debtor to pay the balance on a delinquent charge account would be an involuntary, equitable lien on the debtor's real estate.

Types of Liens

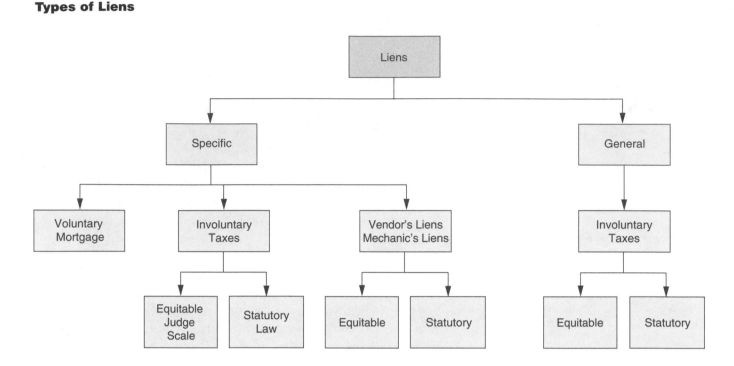

Liens may be classified according to the type of property involved. **General liens** affect all the property, both real and personal, of a debtor. This includes judgments, estate and inheritance taxes, decedent's debts, corporate franchise taxes, and Internal Revenue Service taxes. A lien on real estate differs from a lien on personal property. A lien attaches to real property *at the moment it is filed and recorded.* In contrast, a lien does not attach to personal property *until the personal property is seized.*

Specific liens are secured by specific property and affect only that particular property. Specific liens on real estate include vendors' liens, mechanics' liens, mortgage liens, real estate tax liens, and liens for special assessments and utilities. A **vendor's lien** is a lien belonging to a vendor (or seller of a property) for the unpaid purchase price of the property, where the vendor or the seller has not taken any other lien or security, such as a mortgage, beyond the personal obligation of the purchaser. Vendors' liens in real estate are uncommon and arise out of the use of owner financing to sell property.

Effects of Liens on Title

The existence of a lien does not necessarily prevent a property owner from transferring title to someone else. The lien might reduce the value of the real estate because few buyers will take on the risk of a property that has a lien on it. Because the lien attaches to the property, not the property owner, a new owner might lose the property if the creditors take court action to enforce payment. Once in place, a lien *runs with the land* and will bind all successive owners until the lien is paid and cleared.

IN PRACTICE A buyer should insist on a title search before closing a real estate transaction so that any recorded liens are revealed. If liens are present, the buyer may decide to purchase at a lower price or at better terms, require that the liens be paid, or refuse to purchase.

Priority of liens *Priority of liens* refers to the order in which claims against the property will be *satisfied*. In general, the rule for priority of liens is *first to record, first in right (priority)*. The priority of payment is from the date the liens are recorded in the public records of the county in which the property is located. A lien's priority is also in accordance with state law, which varies from state to state.

There are some notable exceptions to this rule. For instance, real estate taxes and special assessments generally take priority over all other liens, regardless of the order in which the liens are recorded. This means that outstanding real estate taxes and special assessments are paid from the proceeds of a court-ordered sale *first*.

Subordination agreements are written agreements between lienholders to change the priority of mortgage, judgment and other liens. Under a subordination agreement, the holder of a superior or prior lien agrees to permit a junior lienholder's interest to move ahead of the superior or prior lien.

■ REAL ESTATE TAX LIENS

There are two types of real estate taxes: general real estate taxes (also called *ad valorem taxes*) and special assessments or improvement taxes. Both are levied against specific parcels of property and automatically become liens on those properties.

The ownership of real estate is subject to certain governmental powers. (See Chapter 7.) One of these is the right of state and local governments to impose (levy) taxes to pay for their functions. Because the location of real estate is permanently fixed, the government can levy taxes with a high degree of certainty that the taxes will be collected. The annual taxes levied on real estate usually have priority over previously recorded liens, so they may be enforced by a court-ordered sale.

Ad Valorem Tax

The **general real estate tax** is an **ad valorem tax**. *Ad valorem* is Latin for "according to value." Ad valorem taxes are based on the value of the property being taxed and are specific, involuntary, statutory liens. They are charged by various government agencies and municipalities, including

- states;
- counties;
- cities, towns, boroughs, and villages;
- school districts (local elementary and high schools, publicly funded junior colleges, and community colleges);
- drainage districts;
- hospital districts;

- water districts;
- sanitary districts; and
- parks, forest preserves, and recreation districts.

Real estate property taxes are a favored source of revenue for local governments because real estate cannot be hidden and is relatively easy to value. Property taxes pay for a wide range of government services and programs.

Exemptions from general taxes   Most state laws exempt certain real estate from taxation. Such property must be used for tax-exempt purposes, as defined in the statutes. The most common exempt properties are owned by

- cities,
- various municipal organizations (such as schools, parks, and playgrounds),
- state and federal governments,
- religious and charitable organizations,
- hospitals, and
- educational institutions.

Many state laws also allow special exemptions to reduce real estate tax bills for certain property owners or land uses. For instance, senior citizens and veterans are frequently granted reductions in the assessed values of their homes. Some state and local governments offer real estate tax reductions to attract industries and sports franchises. Many states also offer tax reductions for agricultural land.

Assessment   Real estate is valued for tax purposes by county or township assessors or appraisers. This official valuation process is called **assessment**. A property's *assessed value* is generally based on the sales prices of comparable properties, although practices may vary. Land values may be assessed separately from buildings or other improvements, and different valuation methods may be used for different types of property. State laws may provide for property to be periodically reassessed.

Sometimes, a property owner believes that an error was made in determining the assessed property value—usually that the assessment is too high in comparison with the assessments of neighboring properties. Such owners may present their objections to a local board of appeal or board of review. Protests or appeals regarding tax assessments may ultimately be taken to court.

Equalization   In some jurisdictions, when it is necessary to correct inequalities in statewide tax assessments, an **equalization factor** is used to achieve uniformity. An equalization factor may be applied to raise or lower assessments in a particular district or county. The assessed value of each property in the area is multiplied by the equalization factor and the tax rate is then applied to the *equalized assessment*.

Tax rates   The process of arriving at a real estate tax rate begins with the *adoption of a budget* by each taxing district. Each budget covers the financial requirements of the taxing body for the coming fiscal year. The fiscal year may be the January through December calendar year or some other 12-month period designated by statute. The budget must include an estimate of all expenditures for the year.

The next step is *appropriation*. Appropriation is the way a taxing body authorizes the expenditure of funds and provides for the sources of the funding. Appropriation generally involves the adoption of an ordinance or the passage of a law that states the specific terms of the proposed taxation.

The amount to be raised from the general real estate tax is then imposed on property owners through a *tax levy*. A *tax levy* is the formal action taken to impose the tax, usually by a vote of the taxing district's governing body.

The *tax rate* for each taxing body is computed separately. To arrive at a tax rate, the total monies needed for the coming fiscal year are divided by the total assessments of all real estate located within the taxing body's jurisdiction.

The *tax rate* may be stated in a number of ways. In many areas, it is expressed in mills. A **mill** is *1/1,000 of a dollar*, or *$0.001*. The tax rate may be expressed as a mill-per-dollar ratio—for instance, in dollars per hundred or in dollars per thousand. A tax rate of 0.032, or 3.2 percent, could be expressed as 32 mills, or $3.20 per $100 of assessed value or $32 per $1,000 of assessed value.

Tax bills   A property owner's tax bill is computed by applying the tax rate to the assessed valuation of the property.

■ **FOR EXAMPLE**   If a property is assessed for tax purposes at $160,000, at a tax rate of 3 percent, or 30 mills, the tax will be $4,800 ($160,000 × 0.03).

If an equalization factor is used, the computation with an equalization factor of 120 percent will be $5,760 ($160,000 × 1.20 = $192,000, then $192,000 × 0.03 = $5,760).

The due dates for tax payments (also called the *penalty dates*) are set by statute. Taxes may be payable in 2 installments (semiannually), 4 installments (quarterly), or 12 installments (monthly). In some areas, taxes become due at the beginning of the current tax year and must be paid in advance (e.g., the year 2010 taxes must be paid at the beginning of 2009). In other areas, taxes are payable during the year after the taxes are levied (e.g., 2010 taxes are paid throughout 2010). In some states, taxes are paid one year in arrears, and you cannot pay any portion of the ad valorem taxes during the current year (e.g., 2009 taxes could not be paid until the tax books open in 2010). In still other areas, a partial payment is due in the year of the tax, with the balance due in the following year (e.g., 2010 taxes are payable partly during 2010 and partly during 2011).

Some states offer discounts and monthly payment plans to encourage prompt payment of real estate taxes. Penalties, in the form of monthly interest charges on overdue taxes, are added to all taxes that are not paid when due.

Enforcement of tax liens   Real estate taxes must be valid to be enforceable. That means they must be charged properly, must be used for a legal purpose, and must be applied equitably to all property. Tax liens usually are given priority over all other liens against a property. Real estate taxes that have remained delinquent for the statutory period can be collected through a **tax sale**. While the methods and details of the various states' tax sale procedures differ substantially, the results are the same.

Generally, the delinquent taxpayer can redeem the property any time before the tax sale. The taxpayer exercises this **equitable right of redemption** by paying the delinquent taxes plus interest and charges (any court costs or attorney's fees). In those states that permit **redemption**, the bidding at a tax sale is based on the interest rate the defaulted taxpayer would have to pay to redeem the property; that is, the person who bids the lowest redemption rate (the one most beneficial for the taxpayer) becomes the successful bidder. That interest rate theoretically would be the easiest for the taxpayer to pay to redeem the property.

A tax sale is usually held according to a published notice after a court has rendered a judgment for overdue taxes, penalties, and administrative costs and has ordered that the property be sold. A tax sale is advertised in local newspapers, and a notice of sale is posted on the affected property. The county sheriff or other public official then holds a public sale of the property. Because a specific amount of delinquent tax and penalty must be collected, the purchaser at a tax sale must pay at least that amount. A *certificate of sale* is usually given to the highest bidder when that bidder pays the delinquent tax amount in cash. The certificate of sale gives the holder the right to take possession of the property.

The holder of the certificate of sale may be required to wait for a while after the sale to receive the deed to the property. Some states grant a period of redemption *after the tax sale*. In this case, the defaulted owner (or the defaulted owner's creditors) may redeem the property by paying the amount collected at the tax sale plus interest and charges (including any taxes levied since the sale). This is known as a *statutory right of redemption*. (See Chapter 14.) If the property is not redeemed within the statutory period, the certificate holder can apply for a *tax deed (sheriff's deed)*. The quality of the title conveyed by a tax deed varies from state to state.

In some states, the delinquent taxpayer may redeem the property any time before the tax sale. The taxpayer exercises this *equitable right of redemption* by paying the delinquent taxes plus interest and charges (any court costs or attorney's fees). An owner who does not exercise this right may force a sale.

Special Assessments and Local Improvement District Taxes

Special assessments are taxes charged on real estate to fund public improvements to the property. Property owners in the improvement area are required to pay for the improvements because their properties benefit directly from them. For example, the construction of paved streets, curbs, gutters, sidewalks, storm sewers, or street lighting increases the property value. Essentially, the homeowners' property taxes pay for the improvements.

Special assessments are generally paid in equal annual installments over a period of years. The first installment is usually due during the year following the public authority's approval of the assessment. The first bill includes one year's interest on the property owner's share of the entire assessment. Subsequent bills include one year's interest on the unpaid balance. Property owners have the right to prepay any or all installments to avoid future interest charges.

For large-scale improvement projects such as streets, sidewalks, and water or sewer construction, a local improvement district (LID) may be created. An LID is a specific geographical area formed by a group of property owners working together to fund needed capital improvements. LID taxation is simply a financing method available for the design and construction of public improvements.

In some parts of the country, strict subdivision regulations and LIDs have just about eliminated special assessments. Most items for which assessments have traditionally been levied are now required to be installed at the time of construction as a condition of a subdivision's approval.

Homeowner Tax Relief

In 2008, the value of many homes throughout the United States decreased. In an effort to avoid an increase in home foreclosures, some states have subsidized low-income homeowners' tax bills. The federal government has also extended assistance by offering tax credits for first-time homebuyers and loan modification options for existing mortgages. Through these combined efforts, both governments have saved millions of homeowners from loss and helped the overall economy from a catastrophic collapse.

■ OTHER LIENS ON REAL PROPERTY

In addition to real estate tax and special assessment liens, a variety of other liens may be charged against real property.

Mortgage Liens (Deed of Trust Liens)

A **mortgage lien**, sometimes called a *deed of trust lien*, is a voluntary lien on real estate given to a lender by a borrower as security for a real estate loan. It becomes a lien on real property when the lender records the documents in the county where the property is located. Lenders generally require a preferred lien, referred to as a *first mortgage lien*. This means that no other liens against the property (aside from real estate taxes) can take priority over the mortgage lien. Subsequent liens are referred to as *junior liens*. (See Chapter 14.)

Mechanics' Liens

A **mechanic's lien** is a specific, involuntary lien that gives security to persons or companies that perform labor or furnish material to improve real property. A mechanic's lien is available to contractors, subcontractors, architects, equipment lessors, surveyors, laborers, and other providers. This type of lien is filed when the owner has not fully paid for the work or when the general contractor has been compensated but has not paid the subcontractors or suppliers of materials. Statutes in some states prohibit subcontractors from placing liens directly on certain types of property, such as owner-occupied residences. While laws regarding mechanics' liens vary from state to state, there are many similarities.

To be entitled to a mechanic's lien, the person who did the work must have had a contract with the owner or the owner's authorized representative, such as a general contractor. A person claiming a mechanic's lien must file a notice of lien in the public record of the county where the property is located within a certain time after the work has been completed. A lien waiver is required for a contractor to receive a payment from the owner's construction loan. Once the work is completed, the owner will ask for a release of satisfaction of lien for future interests.

According to state law, priority of a mechanic's lien may be established as of the date the construction began or materials were first furnished; the date the work was completed; the date the individual subcontractor's work was either commenced or completed; the date the contract was signed or work was ordered; or the date a notice of the lien was recorded, filed, posted, or served. In some states, mechanics' liens may be given priority over previously recorded liens, such as mortgages.

If improvements that were not ordered by the property owner have commenced, the property owner should execute a document called a *notice of nonresponsibility* to be relieved from possible mechanics' liens. By posting this notice in some conspicuous place on the property and recording a verified copy of it in the public record, the owner gives notice that he or she is not responsible for the work done. This may prevent the filing of mechanics' liens on the property.

IN PRACTICE   In most states, a mechanic's lien takes priority from the time it attaches. Nonetheless, a claimant's notice of lien will not be filed in the public record until some time after that. A prospective purchaser of property that has been recently constructed, altered, or repaired should be cautious about possible unrecorded mechanics' liens against the property.

Judgments

A **judgment** is a decree issued by a court. When the decree establishes the amount a debtor owes and provides for money to be awarded, it is referred to as a *money judgment*. These often result from damages caused to one person by another person through a wrongful act, breach of contract, or nonpayment of a debt.

A judgment is a general, involuntary, equitable lien on both real and personal property owned by the debtor. A judgment is not the same as a mortgage because no specific parcel of real estate was given as security at the time the debt was created. A lien usually covers only property located within the county in which the judgment is issued. As a result, a notice of the lien must be filed in any county to which a creditor wishes to extend the lien coverage. Judgments expire after a number of years but, in some states, can be renewed indefinitely by the judgment creditor.

To enforce a judgment, the creditor must obtain a *writ of execution* from the court. A writ of execution directs the sheriff to seize and sell as much of the debtor's property as is necessary to pay both the debt and the expenses of the sale. A judgment does not become a lien against the personal property of a debtor until the creditor orders the sheriff to assess the property and the charge is actually made.

A judgment lien's priority is established by one of or a combination of the following (as provided by state law):

- Date the judgment was entered by the court
- Date the judgment was filed in the recorder's office
- Date a writ of execution was issued

When real property is sold to satisfy a debt, the debtor should demand a legal document known as a *satisfaction of judgment* (or *satisfaction piece*). In those states using a deed of trust, a deed of reconveyance must be filed with either the clerk of the court or, in some states, the recorder of deeds. Filing the satisfaction of judgment clears the record of the lien.

Lis pendens   There is often a considerable delay between the time a lawsuit is filed and the time final judgment is rendered. When any suit that affects title to real estate is filed, a special notice, known as a **lis pendens** (Latin for *litigation pending*), is recorded. A lis pendens is not itself a lien, but rather *notice of a possible future lien*. Recording a lis pendens notifies prospective purchasers and lenders that there is a potential claim against the property. It also establishes a priority for the later lien: The lien is backdated to the recording date of the lis pendens.

Attachments   To prevent a debtor from conveying title to such previously unsecured real estate while a court suit is being decided, a creditor may seek a writ of **attachment**. A writ of attachment is a court order against the property of another person that directs the sheriff or other officer of the court to seize or take control of a property. By this writ, the court retains custody of the property until the suit concludes. Most attachments arise from an action for payment of an unsecured debt. For example, a plaintiff in a lawsuit may attach a defendant's property to gain a security interest in order to foreclose the property, or to prevent the defendant from disposing of the property that may be needed to pay a judgment.

Estate and Inheritance Tax Liens

Federal **estate taxes** and state **inheritance taxes** (as well as the debts of decedents) are general, statutory, involuntary liens that encumber a deceased person's real and personal property. These taxes and debts are normally paid or cleared in probate court proceedings. (See Chapter 12.)

Liens for Municipal Utilities

Municipalities often have the right to impose a specific, equitable, involuntary lien on the property of an owner who refuses to pay bills for municipal utility services.

Bail Bond Lien

A real estate owner who is charged with a crime that will result in a trial may post bail in the form of real estate rather than cash. The execution and recording of such a bail bond creates a specific, statutory, voluntary lien against the owner's real estate. If the accused fails to appear in court, the lien may be enforced by the sheriff or another court officer.

Corporation Franchise Tax Lien

State governments generally levy a corporation franchise tax on corporations as a condition of allowing them to do business in the state. Such a tax is a general, statutory, involuntary lien on all real and personal property owned by the corporation.

IRS Tax Lien

A federal tax lien, or *Internal Revenue Service (IRS) tax lien*, results from a person's failure to pay any portion of federal taxes, such as income and withholding taxes. A federal tax lien is a general, statutory, involuntary lien on all real and personal property held by the delinquent taxpayer. Its priority, however, is based on the date of filing or recording; it does not supersede previously recorded liens. The same rules apply to most state income tax liens.

■ KEY POINT REVIEW

A **lien** is a claim of a creditor or taxing authority against the **real property** of a debtor that is used as **security** to ensure repayment of the debt. Note the following:

■ A lien is not an ownership interest in real estate; it is an **encumbrance** that transfers with it (**runs with the land**) and lessens its value or impairs its use because it binds all successive owners until paid and cleared.
■ If a debtor **defaults** in payment of debt, a **lienholder** must bring legal action to
  — force the **sale** of the property, or
  — **acquire title**.

Creation of a lien may be **VISE,** an acronym for the following:

■ **Voluntary,** if it is created by action of the property owner, such as a mortgage
■ **Involuntary,** if it is created without the property owner's express permission
■ **Statutory,** if it is created by statute
■ **Equitable,** if it is created by a court based on the common law

A lien is either of the following:

■ **General**—affects all of a debtor's property, both real and personal. General liens include judgments, estate and inheritance taxes, decedent's debts, corporate franchise taxes, and Internal Revenue Service taxes.
■ **Specific**—affects only identified property. Specific liens include a vendor's lien, a mechanic's lien, a mortgage lien, a real estate tax lien, and a lien for special assessments and utilities.

Priority of liens determines the order in which claims will be **satisfied** (paid off):

■ Generally, **first to record is first in right.**
■ Real estate taxes and special assessments take **priority** over all other liens.
■ A **subordination agreement** between **lienholders** can be used to change order of priority.

Real estate taxes include the following:

- **Ad valorem** taxes, based on value of property taxed, are
  — specific, involuntary, statutory liens; and
  — levied by states, counties, municipalities, school districts, utility districts, parks and recreation districts, and others.
- **Exemptions** may be available for schools, parks, hospitals, or property owned by municipal, state, or federal governments, or religious or charitable organizations.
- **Reductions** in tax may be made for certain homeowners, including low-income homeowners, senior citizens, and veterans, or for property owned by industries, sports franchises, or farmers.
- Property **assessments** (valuations) are conducted by county or township tax **assessors** or appraisers.
  — **Assessed value** is generally based on sales prices of comparable properties. Land value may be assessed separately from building value and improvements, and different valuation methods may be used for different types of property.
  — **Equalization factor** may be applied to correct inequalities in statewide tax assessments.
- **Tax rates** for each taxing body are computed separately (and may be expressed in mills—1/1,000 of a dollar, or $0.001). Mills may be shown as dollars per hundred or thousand dollars of assessed value.

Enforcement of tax liens is as follows:

- **Delinquent** taxes can be collected through a **tax sale**.
- Statutory **notice** requirements must be followed before a tax sale.
- The **taxpayer** usually has **equitable right of redemption** any time before a tax sale.
- The **bidder** at a tax sale who bids the lowest **redemption interest rate** receives the **certificate of sale**.
- The state may allow a **statutory right of redemption** following a tax sale.
- If there are **no bidders** at the tax sale, property may be forfeited to the state.

Levied on property that benefits from public improvements, **special assessments**

- are always specific and statutory,
- may be voluntary or involuntary, and
- are usually paid in annual installments over a period of years.

A **mortgage or deed of trust lien is a** voluntary lien given to a lender by a borrower as security for a real estate loan. The lien takes effect when the lender **records** the documents in the county where the property is located.

- A **first mortgage lien** on a property, when recorded, has **priority** over other liens (except for tax liens); subsequent liens are **junior liens**.

A **mechanic's lien** is a specific, involuntary lien that gives security to persons or companies that perform labor or furnish material to improve real property.

- A mechanic's lien is **filed** when an **owner** has not fully paid for work or the **general contractor** has been compensated but has not paid subcontractors or suppliers of materials.
- In some states, mechanics' liens have priority over previously recorded liens such as mortgages.

A **judgment**, a decree issued by a court, is a general, involuntary, equitable lien on both real and personal property owned by a debtor that must be filed in **every county** in which the judgment debtor owns property.

- While a lawsuit is pending,
  - **lis pendens** can be filed to give notice of a possible future lien and establish priority of the claimant, and
  - **writ of attachment** can be sought from the court to authorize the sheriff to seize the property that the debtor may attempt to transfer.

Estate and inheritance tax liens are general, statutory, involuntary liens that encumber a deceased person's real and personal property and are normally paid or cleared in probate proceeding.

A **lien for municipal utilities** is a specific, equitable, involuntary lien on the property of the owner who refuses to pay bills for municipal utility services.

A **corporation franchise tax lien** is a general, statutory, involuntary lien on real and personal property owned by the corporation.

An **IRS tax lien** is a general, statutory, involuntary lien on all real and personal property held by a delinquent taxpayer; it does **not** supersede previously recorded liens (which is also true of most state income tax liens).

■ RELATED WEB SITE

U.S. Internal Revenue Service: *www.irs.gov*

CHAPTER 10 QUIZ

1. Which lien affects all real and personal property of a debtor?
   a. Specific
   b. Voluntary
   c. Involuntary
   d. General

2. Priority of liens refers to which of the following?
   a. Order in which a debtor assumes responsibility for payment of obligations
   b. Order in which liens will be paid if property is sold to satisfy a debt
   c. Dates liens are filed for record
   d. Fact that specific liens have greater priority than general liens

3. A lien on real estate made to secure payment for a specific municipal improvement project is which of the following?
   a. Mechanic's lien
   b. Special assessment
   c. Ad valorem
   d. Utility lien

4. Which of the following would be classified as a general lien?
   a. Mechanic's lien
   b. Bail bond lien
   c. Judgment
   d. Real estate taxes

5. Which lien usually would be given highest priority in disbursing funds from a foreclosure sale?
   a. Mortgage dated last year
   b. Real estate taxes due
   c. Mechanic's lien for work started before the mortgage was made
   d. Judgment rendered the day before foreclosure

6. A specific parcel of real estate has a market value of $160,000 and is assessed for tax purposes at 75 percent of market value. The tax rate for the county in which the property is located is 40 mills. The tax bill will be
   a. $6,400.
   b. $5,000.
   c. $5,200.
   d. $4,800.

7. Which tax would target homeowners in particular?
   a. Personal property tax
   b. Sales tax
   c. Real property tax
   d. Luxury tax

8. A mechanic's lien claim arises when a contractor has performed work or provided material to improve a parcel of real estate on the owner's order and the work has not been paid for. Such a contractor has a right to
   a. tear out the work.
   b. record a notice of the lien.
   c. record a notice of the lien and file a court suit within the time required by state law.
   d. have personal property of the owner sold to satisfy the lien.

9. What is the annual real estate tax on a property valued at $135,000 and assessed for tax purposes at $47,250, with an equalization factor of 125 percent, when the tax rate is 25 mills?
   a. $945
   b. $1,181
   c. $1,418
   d. $1,477

10. Which of the following is a voluntary, specific lien?
    a. IRS tax lien
    b. Mechanic's lien
    c. Mortgage lien
    d. Seller's lien

11. A seller sold a buyer a parcel of real estate. Title has passed, but to date the buyer has not paid the purchase price in full, as originally agreed. If the seller wants to force payment, which remedy would the seller be entitled to seek?

    a. Attachment
    b. Mechanic's lien
    c. Lis pendens
    d. Judgment

12. A general contractor recently filed suit against a homeowner for nonpayment. The contractor now learns that the homeowner has listed the property for sale with a real estate broker. In this situation, which of the following will the contractor's attorney use to protect the contractor's interest?

    a. Seller's lien
    b. Buyer's lien
    c. Assessment
    d. Lis pendens

13. Which statement MOST accurately describes special assessment liens?

    a. They are general liens.
    b. They are paid on a monthly basis.
    c. They take priority over mechanics' liens.
    d. They cannot be prepaid in full without penalty.

14. Which of the following creates a lien on real estate?

    a. Easement running with the land
    b. Unpaid mortgage loan
    c. License
    d. Encroachment

15. Which statement is TRUE of both a mortgage lien and a judgment lien?

    a. They must be entered by the court.
    b. They involve a debtor-creditor relationship.
    c. They are general liens.
    d. They are involuntary liens.

16. A mechanic's lien would be available to all of the following EXCEPT a

    a. subcontractor.
    b. contractor.
    c. surveyor.
    d. broker.

17. The right of a defaulted taxpayer to recover property before its sale for unpaid taxes is the

    a. statutory right of reinstatement.
    b. equitable right of appeal.
    c. statutory right of assessment.
    d. equitable right of redemption.

18. Which of the following is a specific, involuntary, statutory lien?

    a. Real estate tax lien
    b. Income tax lien
    c. Estate tax lien
    d. Judgment lien

19. General real estate taxes levied for the operation of the government are called

    a. assessment taxes.
    b. ad valorem taxes.
    c. special taxes.
    d. improvement taxes.

20. All of the following probably would be exempt from real estate taxes EXCEPT a(n)

    a. public hospital.
    b. golf course operated by the park district.
    c. community church.
    d. apartment building.

1) D
2) B
3) B
4) C
5) D
6) D
7) C
8) C
9) D
10) C
11) D
12) D
13) C
14) B
15) B
16) D
17) D
18) A
19) B
20) D

CHAPTER 11

Real Estate Contracts

■ **LEARNING OBJECTIVES** *When you have finished reading this chapter, you should be able to*

■ **identify** the requirements for a valid contract;

■ **describe** the various types of contracts used in the real estate business;

■ **explain** how contracts may be discharged;

■ **distinguish** among bilateral and unilateral, executed and executory, and valid, void, and voidable contracts; and

■ **define** the following *key terms:*

addendum	equitable title	rescission
amendment	escrow contract	statute of frauds
assignment	executed contract	suit for specific performance
bilateral contract	executory contract	
breach of contract	express contract	time is of the essence
consideration	implied contract	unenforceable contract
contingencies	land contract	unilateral contract
contract	liquidated damages	valid contract
counteroffer	novation	void contract
disclosure	offer and acceptance	voidable contract
earnest money	option	

■ REAL ESTATE CONTRACTS

The real estate market is driven by contracts. Both listing and buyer representation agreements are contracts. Options are contracts—and an offer in the first half of a sales contract. Leases and escrows are contracts. Wherever you go as a real estate professional, whatever aspect of the real estate business you find yourself in, you will be dealing with contracts. It is important for a licensee to know how a contract is created, what it means, what is required for the parties, and what kinds of actions can end it.

■ CONTRACT LAW

A **contract** is a voluntary agreement or promise between legally competent parties, supported by legal consideration, to perform (or refrain from performing) some legal act. The definition may be easier to understand if its various parts are examined separately.

> A **contract** is a voluntary, legally enforceable promise between two competent parties to *perform* (or *not perform*) some legal act in exchange for consideration.

A contract must be

- *voluntary*—no one may be forced into a contract;
- *an agreement or a promise*—a contract is essentially a promise or set of promises;
- made by *legally competent parties*—the parties must be viewed by the law as capable of making a legally binding promise;
- supported by *legal consideration*—a contract must be supported by some valuable thing that induces a party to enter into the contract and that must be legally sufficient to support a contract; and
- for a *legal act*—no one may enter a legal contract for something illegal.

Licensees use many types of contracts and agreements to carry out their responsibilities to sellers, buyers, and the general public. The area of law that governs such agreements is known as *contract law*.

IN PRACTICE Real estate licensees are advised to use preprinted and pre-approved forms provided by their associations or employing brokers. Remember that licensees cannot practice law without a license. Both the buyer and the seller have the option of selecting their own attorney.

Express and Implied Contracts

Depending on how a contract is created, it is either express or implied. In an **express contract**, the parties state the terms and show their intentions in words, either oral or written. The majority of real estate contracts are express contracts; they have been committed to writing. Under the **statute of frauds**, certain types of contracts must be in writing to be enforceable in a court of law. In an **implied contract**, the agreement of the parties is demonstrated by their acts and conduct.

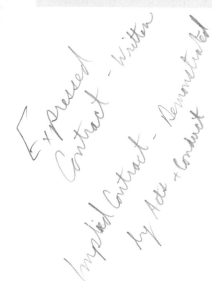

Bilateral and Unilateral Contracts

Contracts are classified as either bilateral or unilateral. In a **bilateral contract**, both parties promise to do something; one promise is given in exchange for another. A real estate sales contract is a bilateral contract because the seller promises to sell a parcel of real estate and transfer title to the property to the buyer, who promises to pay a certain sum of money for the property. An exclusive-right-to-sell listing contract is a bilateral contract.

A **unilateral contract**, on the other hand, is a one-sided agreement. One party makes a promise to entice a second party to do something. The second party is not legally obligated to act. However, if the second party does comply, the first party is obligated to keep the promise.

For instance, a law enforcement agency might offer a monetary payment to anyone who can aid in the capture of a criminal. Only if someone actually aids in the capture is the reward paid.

■ **FOR EXAMPLE**   A homeowner offers to pay a commission to a broker to find a buyer for a property. The broker is not obligated to find a buyer. The property owner is only obligated to pay a commission to the broker who finds a buyer. This is a unilateral contract.

> **Bilateral** contract
> *Bi* means *two*—must have two promises.
>
> **Unilateral** contract
> *Uni* means *one*—has only one promise.

Executed and Executory Contracts

Executory – not fulfilled

A contract may be classified as either executed or executory, depending on whether the agreement is performed. An **executed contract** is one in which all parties have fulfilled their promises; the contract has been performed. An **executory contract** exists when one or both parties still have an act to perform. A sales contract is an executory contract from the time it is signed until closing; ownership has not yet changed hands, and the seller has not received the sales price. At closing, the sales contract is executed.

Table 11.1 highlights the issues involved in the formation of a contract—issues talked about in detail in this chapter.

Essential Elements of a Valid Contract

A contract must meet certain minimum requirements to be considered legally valid. The following are the basic essential elements of a contract.

Offer and acceptance   There must be an offer by one party that is accepted by the other. The person who makes the offer is the *offeror*. The person to whom an offer is made is the *offeree*. This requirement is also called mutual assent. It means that there must be a *meeting of the minds*; that is, there must be complete agreement between the parties about the purpose and terms of the contract. Courts look to the *objective intent of the parties* to determine whether they intended to enter into a binding agreement. Most states require that the **offer and acceptance** be in writing. The wording of the contract must express all the agreed terms and must be clearly understood by the parties.

	Preformation	Formation	Postformation
TABLE 11.1 **Contract Issues**	**Essential Elements**	**Classification**	**Discharge**
	Offer and acceptance, consideration, legal purpose, consent, legal capacity	Valid, void, voidable, enforceable, unenforceable, express, implied, unilateral, bilateral, executory, executed	Performance, breach, remedies (damages, specific performance, rescission)

Elements of a Contract

- Offer and acceptance
- Consideration
- Legally competent parties
- Consent
- Legal purpose

An *offer* is a promise made by one party, requesting something in exchange for that promise. The offer is made with the intention that the offeror will be bound to the terms if the offer is accepted. The terms of the offer must be definite and specific and must be communicated to the offeree.

An *acceptance* is a promise by the offeree to be bound by the *exact* terms proposed by the offeror. The acceptance must be communicated by the offeror. Proposing any deviation from the terms of the offer is considered a rejection of the original offer. This is known as a counteroffer. The counteroffer must be accepted by both parties for a contract to exist.

Besides being terminated by a counteroffer, an offer may be terminated by the offeree's outright rejection of it. Alternatively, an offeree may fail to accept the offer before it expires. The offeror may revoke the offer at any time before acceptance. This revocation must be communicated to the offeree by the offeror, either directly or through the parties' agents. The offer is revoked if the offeree learns of the revocation and observes the offeror acting in a manner that indicates that the offer no longer exists. For example, if a buyer gives a seller three days to accept an offer and on the third day the buyer's broker calls the seller's broker and cancels the offer, the offer is now void.

Consideration The contract must be based on consideration. **Consideration** is something of legal value offered by one party and accepted by another as an inducement to perform or to refrain from performing some act. There must be a definite statement of consideration in a contract to show that something of value was given in exchange for the promise. Consideration is some interest or benefit accruing to one party, or some loss or responsibility by the other party.

Consideration must be *good and valuable* between the parties. The courts do not inquire into the adequacy of consideration. Adequate consideration ranges from as little as a promise of *love and affection* to a substantial sum of money. Anything that has been bargained for and exchanged is legally sufficient to satisfy the requirement for consideration. The only requirements are that the parties agree and that no undue influence or fraud has occurred.

Consent A contract that complies with all the basic requirements may still be either void or voidable. A contract must be entered into by consent as a free and voluntary act of each party. Each party must be able to make a prudent and knowledgeable decision without undue influence. A mistake, misrepresentation, fraud, undue influence, or duress would deprive a person of that ability. If any of these circumstances is present, the contract is voidable by the injured party. If the other party were to sue for breach, the injured party could use lack of voluntary assent as a defense.

Legal purpose   A contract must be for a legal purpose—that is, even with all the other elements (consent, competent parties, consideration, and offer and acceptance). A contract for an illegal purpose or an act against public policies is not a valid contract.

Legally competent parties   All parties to the contract must have *legal capacity;* meaning they must be of legal age and have enough mental capacity to understand the nature or consequences of their actions in the contract. In most states, 18 is the age of contractual capacity.

Validity of contracts   A contract can be described as valid, void, voidable, or unenforceable, depending on the circumstances.

A **valid contract** meets all the essential elements that make it legally sufficient, or enforceable, and is binding in a court of law.

A **void contract** has no legal force or effect because it lacks some or all the essential elements of a contract. A contract that is void was never a legal contract. For example, the use of a forged name in a listing contract would make the contract void.

A **voidable contract** appears on the surface to be valid but may be rescinded or disaffirmed by one or both parties based on some legal principle. A voidable contract is considered by the courts to be valid if the party who has the option to disaffirm the agreement does not do so within a period of time. A contract with a minor, for instance, is voidable. A contract entered into by a mentally ill person is usually voidable during the mental illness and for a reasonable period after the person is cured. If a contract was made under duress, with misrepresentation, under the influence, and with intent to defraud, it is also voidable.

IN PRACTICE   Mental capacity to enter into a contract is not the same as medical sanity. The test is whether the individual in question is capable of understanding his or her actions. A person may suffer from a mental illness but clearly understand the significance of his or her actions. Such psychological questions require consultation with experts.

An **unenforceable contract** may also appear on the surface to be valid; however, neither party can sue the other to force performance. For example, an oral agreement for the sale of a parcel of real estate would be unenforceable. Because the statute of frauds requires that real estate sales contracts be in writing, the defaulting party could not be taken to court and forced to perform. There is, however, a distinction between a suit to force performance and a suit for damages, which is permissible in an oral agreement. An unenforceable contract is said to be *valid as between the parties.* This means that once the agreement is fully executed and both parties are satisfied, neither has reason to initiate a lawsuit to force performance.

A contract may be

- valid—has all legal elements and is fully enforceable;
- void—lacks one or all elements and has no legal force or effect;
- voidable—has all legal elements and may be rescinded or disaffirmed; or
- unenforceable—has all legal elements and is enforceable only between the parties.

■ DISCHARGE OF CONTRACTS

A contract is *discharged* when the agreement is terminated. The most desirable case is when a contract terminates because it was completely performed, with all its terms fulfilled. Contracts may be terminated for other reasons, such as a party's breach or default.

Performance of a Contract

Each party has certain rights and duties to fulfill. The question of *when* a contract must be performed is an important factor. Many contracts call for a specific time by which the agreed acts must be completely performed. Furthermore, some contracts provide that **time is of the essence**, which means that the contract must be performed within a specified time. A party who fails to perform on time is liable for breach of contract.

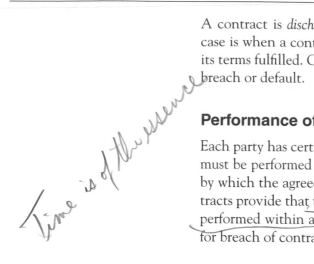

IN PRACTICE When a *time is of the essence* clause is used in a contract, the parties should consult an attorney. The ramifications of a breach of a contract in which *time is of the essence* is used can be significant. For example, a buyer might lose escrow funds, or the seller might lose the right to enforce the contract.

When a contract does not specify a date for performance, the acts it requires should be performed within a reasonable time. The interpretation of what constitutes a reasonable time depends on the situation. Courts have sometimes declared contracts to be invalid because they did not contain a time or date for performance.

Assignment

> **Assignment** =
> Substitution of parties
> **Novation** = Substitution
> of a new contract

Assignment refers to a transfer of rights or duties under a contract. Generally rights and obligations may be assigned to a third party. Obligations may be delegated, but the original party remains primarily liable unless specifically released. The majority of contracts have a clause to either allow or forbid assignment.

Novation

Substitution of a new contract for an existing contract is called **novation**. The new agreement may be between the same parties, or a new party may be substituted for either (this is *novation of the parties*). The parties' intent must be to discharge the old obligation. For instance, when a real estate purchaser assumes the seller's existing mortgage loan, the lender may choose to release the seller and substitute the buyer as the party primarily liable for the mortgage debt. Or when there are many changes to a real estate contract and it is faxed several times, the contract may no longer be legible. Novation occurs when a new, clear contract with all the accepted changes is signed by all the parties.

Breach of Contract

A contract may be terminated if it is breached by one of the parties. A **breach of contract** is a violation of any of the terms or conditions of a contract without legal reason. A seller who fails to deliver title to the buyer breaches a sales contract.

The breaching or defaulting party assumes certain burdens, and the nondefaulting party has certain legal remedies.

If the seller breaches a real estate sales contract, the buyer may sue for *specific performance* unless the contract specifically states otherwise. In a **suit for specific performance**, the buyer asks the court to force the seller to go through with the sale and transfer the property as previously agreed. The buyer may choose to sue for damages, in which case the seller is asked to pay for any costs and hardships suffered by the buyer as a result of the seller's breach.

If the buyer defaults, the seller can sue for damages or sue for the purchase price. A suit for the purchase price is essentially a suit for specific performance: The seller tenders the deed and asks that the buyer be required to pay the agreed price.

The contract may limit the remedies available to the parties. A liquidated damages clause in a real estate purchase contract specifies the amount of money to which the seller is entitled if the buyer breaches the contract.

Statute of limitations   Every state limits the time during which parties to a contract may bring legal suit to enforce their rights. The statute of limitations varies for different legal actions, and any rights not enforced within the applicable time period are lost.

Other reasons for termination   Contracts may also be discharged or terminated when any of the following occurs:

- *Partial performance of the terms, along with a written acceptance* by the party for whom acts have not been done or to whom money is owed. For instance, if the parties agree that the work performed is close enough to completion, they can agree that the contract is discharged even if some minor elements remain unperformed.
- *Substantial performance*, in which one party has substantially performed on the contract but does not complete all the details exactly as the contract requires. Such performance may be enough to force payment, with certain adjustments for any damages suffered by the other party. For example, where a newly constructed addition to a home is finished except for polishing the brass doorknobs, the contractor is entitled to the final payment.
- *Impossibility of performance*, in which an act required by the contract cannot be legally accomplished.
- *Mutual agreement* of the parties to cancel the contract.
- *Operation of law*—such as in the voiding of a contract by a minor—as a result of fraud, due to the expiration of the statute of limitations, or because a contract was altered without the written consent of all parties involved.
- *Rescission*—one party may cancel or terminate the contract as though it had never been made. Cancellation terminates a contract without a return to the original position. **Rescission**, however, returns the parties to their original positions before the contract, so any monies exchanged must be returned. Rescission is normally a contractual remedy for a breach, but a contract may also be rescinded by the mutual agreement of the parties.

■ CONTRACTS USED IN THE REAL ESTATE BUSINESS

The written agreements most commonly used by licensees are

- ■ listing agreements and buyer agency agreements,
- ■ real estate sales contracts,
- ■ options agreements,
- ■ escrow agreements,
- ■ leases, and
- ■ land contracts or contracts for deed.

Many states have specific guidelines for when and how real estate licensees may prepare contracts for their consumers. These guidelines are created by state real estate officials, court decisions, or statutes. A licensee may be permitted to fill in the blanks on certain approved preprinted documents, such as sales contracts, as directed by the client. No separate fee may be charged for completing the forms. The practice of law includes preparing legal documents, such as deeds and mortgages, and offering advice on legal matters; a real licensee who is not a licensed attorney cannot practice law.

Contract forms   Because so many real estate transactions are very similar in nature, preprinted forms are available for most kinds of contracts. The use of preprinted forms raises three problems: (1) what to write in the blanks, (2) what words and phrases should be ruled out by drawing lines through them because they don't apply, and (3) what additional clauses or agreements (called *riders* or *addenda*) should be added. All changes and additions are usually initialed in the margin or on the rider by both parties when a contract is signed.

IN PRACTICE   It is essential that both parties to a contract understand exactly what they are agreeing to. Poorly drafted documents, especially those containing extensive legal language, may be subject to various interpretations and lead to litigation. The parties to a real estate transaction should be advised to have sales contracts and other legal documents examined by their lawyers before they sign them to ensure that the agreements accurately reflect their intentions. When preprinted forms do not sufficiently cover special provisions in a transaction, the parties should have an attorney draft an appropriate contract.

Listing and Buyer Agency Agreements

A listing agreement is an employment contract. It establishes the rights and obligations of the broker as agent and the seller as principal. A buyer agency contract establishes the relationship between a buyer and the buyer's agent.

Some states suggest or require the use of specific forms of listing contracts. Oral listing contracts for a period of less than one year are recognized in some states, while in other states, only written listing contracts are recognized.

IN PRACTICE   If a contract contains any ambiguity, the courts generally interpret the agreement against the party who prepared it.

Sales Contracts

The real estate sales contract is the most important document in the sale of real estate. It establishes the legal rights and obligations of the buyer and seller. Depending upon the area, the contract may be referred to as an offer to purchase, a contract of purchase and sale, a purchase agreement, an earnest money agreement, or a deposit receipt.

A real estate sales contract contains the complete agreement between a buyer of a parcel of real estate and the seller. It is an offer to purchase real estate as soon as it has been prepared and signed by the purchaser. If the document is accepted and signed by the seller, it becomes a contract of sale.

In addition to the essential elements of a contract, several details frequently appear in contracts. These include

- the sales price and terms;
- a legal description of the land;
- a statement of the kind and condition of the title and the form of deed to be delivered by the seller;
- the kind of title evidence required, who will provide it, and how many defects in the title will be eliminated; and
- a statement of all the terms and conditions of the agreement between the parties, and any contingencies.

Offer　A licensee lists an owner's real estate for sale at whatever price and conditions the owner sets. When a prospective buyer is found, the licensee helps that consumer prepare an offer to purchase. The offer is signed by the prospective buyer and presented by the licensee to the seller.

> A **counteroffer** is a *new* offer; it rejects the original offer.

Counteroffer　Any change by the seller to the terms proposed by the buyer creates a **counteroffer**. The original offer ceases to exist because the seller has rejected it. The buyer may accept or reject the seller's counteroffer. If the buyer desires, the process may continue by making another counteroffer. Any change in the last offer may result in a counteroffer until either the parties reach agreement or one party walks away.

An offer or counteroffer *may be withdrawn at any time before it has been accepted,* even if the person making the offer or counteroffer agreed to keep the offer open for a set period.

Acceptance　If the seller agrees to the original offer or a later counteroffer *exactly* as it is made and signs the document, the offer has been accepted and a contract is formed. The licensee must advise the buyer of the seller's acceptance and obtain the approval of the parties' attorneys if the contract calls for it. A copy of the contract must be provided to each party.

An offer is not considered accepted until the person making the offer has been *notified of the other party's acceptance.* When the parties communicate through an agent or at a distance, questions may arise regarding whether an acceptance, rejection, or counteroffer has occurred. Though current technology allows for fast communication, a signed agreement that is faxed, for instance, would not necessarily constitute adequate communication. The licensee must transmit all offers, acceptances, or other responses as soon as possible to avoid questions of proper communication.

Binder   In some states, licensees may prepare a shorter document known as a binder, instead of a complete sales contract. The binder states the essential terms of the offer and acknowledges that the licensee has received the purchaser's deposit. A more formal and complete contract of sale is drawn up by an attorney once the seller accepts and signs the binder. A binder might also be used where the details of the transaction are too complex for the standard sales contract form.

Earnest money deposits   It is customary, although not essential, for a purchaser to provide a deposit when making an offer to purchase real estate. This deposit, usually in the form of a check, is referred to as **earnest money**. The earnest money deposit is evidence of the buyer's intention to carry out the terms of the contract in good faith. The check is given to the broker, who usually holds it for the parties in a special account. An **escrow contract** is an agreement between a buyer, a seller, and an escrow holder setting forth the rights and responsibilities of each. An escrow contract is entered into when earnest money is deposited in a broker's escrow account. In some areas, it is common practice for deposits to be held in escrow by the seller's attorney. If the offer is not accepted, the earnest money deposit is immediately returned to the would-be buyer.

The amount of the deposit is a matter to be agreed on by the parties. Under the terms of most listing agreements, a real estate broker is required to accept a *reasonable amount* as earnest money. As a rule, the deposit should be an amount sufficient to

- discourage the buyer from defaulting,
- compensate the seller for taking the property off the market, and
- cover any expenses the seller might incur if the buyer defaults.

This money cannot be mixed with a broker's personal funds (called *commingling*). Brokers may not use earnest money funds for their personal use (called *conversion*). A separate escrow account does not have to be opened for each earnest money deposit received; all deposits may be kept in one account. A broker must maintain full, complete, and accurate records of all earnest money deposits. Real estate licenses may be revoked or suspended if deposits are not managed properly.

The special account may or may not pay interest, depending on state law. If the account bears interest, there must be some provision in the contract for how the interest earned will be distributed. The broker must provide the parties with an accounting of the amount and dates of interest payments. Often, a check for the interest amount is given to the buyer at closing. On the other hand, the contract may provide for the interest to be paid to the seller as part of the purchase price.

Equitable title   When a buyer signs a contract to purchase real estate, the buyer does not receive title to the land. Title transfers only upon delivery and acceptance of a deed. However, after both buyer and seller have executed a sales contract, the buyer acquires an *interest* in the land. This interest is known as **equitable**

title. A person who holds equitable title has rights that vary from state to state. Equitable title may give the buyer an insurable interest in the property.

Destruction of premises　In many states, once the sales contract is signed by both parties, the buyer assumes the risk of any damage to the property that may occur before closing the contract. However, laws and court decisions in many states have placed the risk of loss on the seller. The Uniform Vendor and Purchaser Risk Act specifically provides that the seller bear any loss that occurs before the title passes or the buyer takes possession.

Liquidated damages　To avoid a lawsuit if one party breaches the contract, the parties may agree on a certain amount of money that will compensate the nonbreaching party. Such money is called **liquidated damages**. If a sales contract specifies that the earnest money deposit is to serve as liquidated damages in case the buyer defaults, the seller will be entitled to keep the deposit if the buyer refuses to perform without good reason. The seller who keeps the deposit as liquidated damages may not sue for any further damages if the contract provides that the deposit is the seller's sole remedy.

Parts of a sales contract　All real estate sales contracts can be divided into a number of separate parts. Although each form of contract contains these divisions, their location within a particular contract may vary. Most sales contracts include the following information:

- The purchaser's name and a statement of the purchaser's obligation to purchase the property, including how the purchaser intends to take title
- An adequate description of the property, such as the street address (While a street address is adequate for a sales contract, it is not adequate for a legal description.) (See Chapter 9.)
- The seller's name and a statement of the type of deed a seller agrees to give, including any covenants, conditions, and restrictions
- The purchase price and how the purchaser intends to pay for the property, including earnest money deposits, additional cash from the purchaser, and the conditions of any mortgage financing
- The amount and form of the down payment toward the loan and earnest money deposit and whether the payments will be in the form of a check or promissory note
- A provision for the closing of the transaction and the transfer of possession of the property to the purchaser by a specific date
- A provision of title evidence
- The method by which real estate taxes, rents, fuel costs, and other expenses are to be prorated
- A provision for the completion of the contract should the property be damaged or destroyed between the time of signing and the closing date
- A liquidated damages clause, specific performance clause, or other statement of remedies available in the event of default
- Contingency clauses (such as the buyer's obtaining financing or selling a currently owned property, the seller's acquisition of another desired property or clearing of the title; attorney approval and home inspection are other commonly included contingencies)

- The dated signatures of all parties (In some states, the seller's nonowning spouse may be required to release potential marital or homestead rights.)
- In most states, an agency disclosure statement

Additional provisions   Many sales contracts provide for the following:

- Any personal property to be left with the premises for the purchaser (such as major appliances or lawn and garden equipment)
- Any real property to be removed by the seller before the closing (such as a storage shed)
- The transfer of any applicable warranties on items such as heating and cooling systems or built-in appliances
- The identification of any leased equipment that must be transferred to the purchaser or returned to the lessor (such as security systems, cable television boxes, and water softeners)
- The appointment of a closing or settlement agent
- Closing or settlement instructions
- The transfer or payment of any outstanding special assessments
- The purchaser's right to inspect the property shortly before the closing or settlement (often called the walkthrough)
- The agreement as to what documents will be provided by each party and when and where they will be delivered

Contingencies   Additional conditions that must be satisfied before a sales contract is fully enforceable are called **contingencies**. A contingency includes the following three elements:

- The actions necessary to satisfy the contingency
- The time frame within which the actions must be performed
- Who is responsible for paying any costs involved

The most common contingencies include the following:

- A *mortgage contingency*, which protects the buyer's earnest money until a lender commits the mortgage loan funds.
- An *inspection contingency*; a sales contract may be contingent on the buyer's obtaining certain inspections of the property. Inspections may include those for wood-boring insects, lead-based paint, structural and mechanical systems, sewage facilities, and radon or other toxic materials.
- A *property sale contingency*, where buyers may make the sales contract contingent on the sale of their current home. This protects the buyers from owning two homes at the same time and also helps ensure the availability of cash for the purchase.

The seller may insist on an *escape clause*, which permits the seller to continue to market the property until all the buyer's contingencies have been satisfied or removed. The buyer may retain the right to eliminate the contingencies if the seller receives a more favorable offer. (Note that contingencies create a *voidable contract*; if the contingencies are rejected or not satisfied, the contract is void.)

Amendments and addendums   An **amendment** is a change or modification to the existing content of a contract. Any time words or provisions are added to or deleted from the body of the contract, the contract has been amended. For instance, a form contract's provision requiring closing in 90 days might be crossed out and replaced with a 60-day period. Amendments must be initialed or signed by all parties.

An **addendum** is any provision added to an existing contract without altering the content of the original. An addendum is essentially a new contract between parties that includes the original contract's provisions *by reference*, meaning the addendum mentions the original contract. An addendum must be signed by all parties. For example, an addendum might be an agreement to split the cost of repairing certain items discovered in a home inspection.

Disclosures   Many states have enacted mandatory **disclosure** laws, which help consumers make informed decisions. (See Chapters 4 and 6.) Many licensees have instituted procedures for making disclosures and recommending technical experts to ensure that purchasers have accurate information about real estate. Disclosure of property conditions may be included as part of a sales contract, or it may be a separate form. Many states require separate forms for disclosing environmental problems. (See Chapter 21.) In addition, disclosure of the licensee's agency relationship may also be required by state law. (See Chapter 4.)

Options

An **option** is a contract by which an *optionor* (generally an owner) gives an *optionee* (a prospective purchaser or lessee) the right to buy or lease the owner's property at a fixed price within a certain period of time. The optionee pays a fee (the agreed actual consideration) for this option right. The optionee has to decide to either exercise the option right or allow the option to expire. An option is enforceable by the optionee only (a unilateral contract). Options must contain all the terms and provisions required for a valid contract.

A common application of an option is a lease that includes an option for the tenant to purchase the property. Options on commercial real estate frequently depend on some specific conditions being fulfilled, such as obtaining a zoning change or a building permit. The optionee may be obligated to exercise the option if the conditions are met. Similar terms could also be included in a sales contract.

Land Contracts

A real estate sale can be made under a **land contract**, also called a *contract for deed*, a *bond for title*, an *installment contract*, a *land sales contract*, or *articles of agreement for warranty deed*. Under a typical land contract, the seller (also known as the *vendor*) retains legal title. The buyer (called the vendee) takes possession and gets equitable title to the property. The buyer agrees to give the seller a down payment and pay regular monthly installments of principal and interest over a number of years. The buyer also agrees to pay real estate taxes, insurance premiums, repairs, and upkeep on the property. Although the buyer obtains possession under the contract, *the seller is not obligated to execute and deliver a deed to the buyer until the terms* *of the contract have been satisfied.* This frequently occurs when the buyer has made enough payments to obtain a mortgage loan and pay off the balance due on the contract. Although a land contract is usually assumable by subsequent purchasers, it generally must be approved by the seller.

■ KEY POINT REVIEW

Following are characteristics of a **valid contract**:

- A **voluntary agreement** based on **consent**
  — If a mistake, misrepresentation, fraud, undue influence, or duress occurs, it is **voidable** by the injured party.
- The **agreement** or **promise** is based on an **offer** by one party (**offeror**) that is **accepted** by the other (**offeree**).
  — **Mutual assent** or meeting of the minds exists.
  — **Acceptance** and **revocation** must be communicated by offeree to offeror.
  — A **counteroffer** terminates the original offer and initiates a new offer.
- Made by **legally competent parties between** parties of **legal age** who are able to understand the nature or consequences of their actions
  — A contract with a minor is **voidable**.
- Supported by **legal consideration**,
  — something of legal value, which could be *love* and *affection*, and
  — free of **undue influence** or **fraud**
- Concerned with a **legal act**

A contract may be

- **express** or **implied** by conduct of parties;
- required to be **in writing** to be **enforceable** in a court of law;
- **bilateral** (having obligations on both sides) or **unilateral** (a promise by one side that can be accepted or rejected by the other side);
- **executed** (all parties have fulfilled their promises) or **executory** (one or both parties still have an act to perform);
- **void** if one of the essential elements is missing; or
- **voidable**, if it may be **rescinded** or **disaffirmed** by one or both parties.

Contracts may be **discharged** (completed) by the following:

- **Performance**, which completes the contract terms
- **Partial performance**, if agreeable to both parties
- **Substantial performance**, depending on circumstances
- **Impossibility of performance** (required acts cannot be legally accomplished)
- **Assignment** (transfer of rights to **assignee** or **delegation** of duties)
- **Novation** (substitutes a new contract or party for the original)
- **Breach** by one of the parties without legal cause
  — **Liquidated damages clause** may specify the amount the seller will receive if the buyer defaults.
- Failure to enforce contract within **statute of limitations**
- **Mutual agreement** of parties
- **Operation of law**, as when a contract is void from inception
- **Rescission (cancellation)** by one or both parties

Real estate contracts may be completed by real estate licensees if preprinted, standard contract forms are used. **Real estate licensees who are not licensed attorneys may not practice law.** Standard forms may include the following:

- **Real estate sales contract**
  - Usually accompanied by an **earnest money deposit** held in **trust** or **escrow account** to avoid **commingling** with broker's own funds
  - **Contingencies** to the sale (such as mortgage, inspection, and property sale contingencies) that must be stated in the contract
  - May provide for the purchaser's right to inspect the property
  - **Disclosures** required by state law that must be made
- **Land contract**—**contract for deed, bond for title, installment contract, land sales contract, articles of agreement for warranty deed**
- **Escrow agreement** between buyer, seller, and escrow holder

■ RELATED WEB SITE

FindLaw: Contract Law: *www.findlaw.com/01topics/07contracts/*

CHAPTER 11 QUIZ

1. A legally enforceable agreement under which two parties promise to do something for each other is known as a(n)
   a. escrow agreement.
   b. legal pledge.
   c. bilateral contract.
   d. option agreement.

2. A person approaches an owner and says, "I'd like to buy your house." The owner says, "Sure," and they agree on a price. What kind of contract is this?
   a. Implied
   b. Unenforceable
   c. Void
   d. No contract

3. A contract is said to be *bilateral* if
   a. one of the parties is a minor.
   b. the contract has yet to be fully performed.
   c. only one party to the agreement is bound to act.
   d. all parties to the contract exchange binding promises.

4. During the period of time after a real estate sales contract is signed, but before title actually passes, the status of the contract is
   a. voidable.
   b. executory.
   c. unilateral.
   d. implied.

5. A contract for the sale of real estate that does NOT state the consideration and is NOT signed by the parties is considered to be
   a. voidable.
   b. executory.
   c. void.
   d. enforceable.

6. A buyer and a seller sign a contract to purchase. The seller backs out, and the buyer sues for specific performance. What is the buyer seeking in this lawsuit?
   a. Money damages
   b. New contract
   c. Deficiency judgment
   d. Transfer of the property

7. In a standard sales contract, several words were crossed out or inserted by the parties. To eliminate future controversy as to whether the changes were made before or after the contract was signed, the usual procedure is to
   a. write a letter to each party listing the changes.
   b. have each party write a letter to the other approving the changes.
   c. redraw the entire contract.
   d. have both parties initial or sign in the margin near each change.

8. A buyer makes an offer on a seller's house and the seller accepts. Both parties sign the sales contract. At this point, the buyer has what type of title to the property?
   a. Equitable
   b. Voidable
   c. Escrow
   d. Contract

9. The sales contract says the buyer will purchase only if an attorney approves the sale by the following Saturday. The attorney's approval is a
   a. contingency.
   b. reservation.
   c. warranty.
   d. consideration.

10. A broker uses earnest money placed in the company trust account to pay for the rent owed on the broker's office. Using escrow funds for this purpose is

    a. commingling of funds and is illegal.

    b. legal if the trust account is reimbursed by the end of the calendar month.

    c. legal if the seller gives consent in writing.

    d. conversion of funds and is illegal.

11. An option to purchase binds which of the following parties?

    a. Buyer only

    b. Seller only

    c. Neither buyer nor seller

    d. Both buyer and seller

12. A buyer and a seller enter into a real estate sales contract. Under the contract's terms, the buyer will pay the seller $500 a month for ten years. The seller will continue to hold legal title, while the buyer will live in the home and pay all real estate taxes, insurance premiums, and regular upkeep costs. What kind of contract do the buyer and seller have?

    a. Option contract

    b. Contract for mortgage

    c. Unilateral contract

    d. Land or installment contract

13. The purchaser of real estate under an installment contract

    a. generally pays no interest charge.

    b. receives title immediately.

    c. is not required to pay property taxes for the duration of the contract.

    d. has only an equitable interest in the property's title.

14. Under the statute of frauds, all contracts for the sale of real estate must be

    a. originated by a real estate broker.

    b. on preprinted forms.

    c. in writing to be enforceable.

    d. accompanied by earnest money deposits.

15. If, upon the receipt of an offer to purchase a property subject to certain conditions, the seller makes a counteroffer, the prospective buyer is

    a. bound by the original offer.

    b. bound to accept the counteroffer.

    c. bound by whichever offer is lower.

    d. relieved of the original offer.

16. A buyer makes an offer to purchase certain property listed with a licensee and leaves an escrow deposit with the licensee to show good faith. The broker should

    a. immediately apply the deposit to the listing expenses.

    b. put the deposit in an account, as provided by state law.

    c. give the deposit to the seller when the offer is presented.

    d. put the deposit in the broker's personal checking account.

17. While suffering from a mental illness that caused delusions, hallucinations, and loss of memory, a person signed a contract to purchase real estate. Which statement regarding the contract to purchase is *TRUE*?

    a. The contract is voidable.

    b. The contract is void.

    c. The contract lacks consent.

    d. The contract is fully valid and enforceable.

18. A licensee has found a buyer for a seller's home. The buyer has indicated in writing a willingness to buy the property for $1,000 less than the asking price and has deposited $5,000 in earnest money with the licensee. The seller is out of town for the weekend, and the licensee has been unable to inform the seller of the signed document. At this point, the buyer has signed a(n)

    a. voidable contract.

    b. offer.

    c. executory agreement.

    d. implied contract.

19. A buyer and a seller agree to the purchase of a house for $200,000. The contract contains a clause stating that time is of the essence. Which statement is *TRUE*?

a. The closing must take place within a reasonable period before the stated date.

b. A "time is of the essence" clause is not binding on either party.

c. The closing date must be stated as a particular calendar date, and not simply as a formula, such as "two weeks after loan approval."

d. If the closing date passes and no closing takes place, the contract may be rescinded by the party who was ready to settle on the scheduled date.

20. A buyer signs a contract under which he is given the right to purchase a property for $30,000 any time in the next three months. The buyer pays the current owner $500 at the time that contract is signed. Which of the following *BEST* describes this agreement?

a. Contingency

b. Option

c. Installment

d. Sales

CHAPTER

12

Transfer of Title

When you have finished reading this chapter, you should be able to

- ■ **identify** the basic requirements for a valid deed;
- ■ **describe** the fundamental types of deeds;
- ■ **explain** how property may be transferred through involuntary alienation;
- ■ **distinguish** transfers of title by will from transfers by intestacy; and
- ■ **define** the following *key terms*:

acknowledgment	grantor	testate
adverse possession	habendum clause	testator
bargain and sale deed	heirs	title
deed	intestate	transfer tax
deed of trust	involuntary alienation	trustee's deed
devise	probate	voluntary alienation
general warranty deed	quitclaim deed	will
grantee	reconveyance deed	
granting clause	special warranty deed	

■ TRANSFER OF TITLE

Transfer of title is an aspect of the real estate transaction generally handled by lawyers and title companies, rarely by the licensee. Nonetheless, as with other legal aspects of the transaction, a licensee who is aware of the fundamentals of deeds and title issues will know what kind of questions to ask. An informed licensee will know how to direct consumers to professionals to avoid potential title problems.

■ TITLE

Title / not a document

The term *title* has two functions. **Title** to real estate means the *right to or ownership of the land*; it represents the owner's bundle of legal rights. (See Chapter 2.) Title also serves as *evidence* of that ownership. A person who holds the title, if challenged in court, would be able to recover or retain ownership or possession of a parcel of real estate. Title is just a way of referring to ownership; it is not an actual printed document.

Real estate may be transferred voluntarily by sale or gift. Alternatively, it may be transferred involuntarily by operation of law. Real estate may be transferred while the owner lives or by will or descent after the owner dies.

■ VOLUNTARY ALIENATION — *gift or sell property, etc.*

Deed - real document

Voluntary alienation is the legal term for the voluntary transfer of title. The owner may voluntarily transfer title by either making a gift or selling the property. To transfer during his or her lifetime, the owner must use some form of document to show the conveyance.

A **grantor** conveys property to a grantee.
A **grantee** receives property from a grantor.
A **deed** is the instrument that conveys property from a grantor to a grantee.

A **deed** is the written instrument by which an owner of real estate intentionally conveys the right, title, or interest in the parcel of real estate to someone else. The statute of frauds requires that all deeds be in writing. The owner who transfers the title is referred to as the **grantor,** and the person who acquires the title is called the **grantee.** A deed is executed (or signed) by the grantor. To be able to execute a valid deed, the grantor must have legal capacity. (See Table 12.1.)

Requirements for a Valid Deed

Although formal requirements vary, most states require that a valid deed contain the following elements:

- Grantor who has the legal competency to execute (sign) the deed
- Grantee named with reasonable certainty to be identified
- Statement of consideration
- Granting clause (words of conveyance)
- Habendum clause (to define ownership taken by the grantee)
- Accurate legal description of the property conveyed
- Any relevant exceptions or reservations
- Signature of the grantor, which must be acknowledged (notarization)
- Delivery of the deed and acceptance by the grantee to pass title

T A B L E   12.1

Remembering Legal Terminology: "OR" Versus "EE"

Throughout this book, we will be referring to people as *grantor* and *grantee*, *trustor* and *trustee*, *mortgagor* and *mortgagee*, and so forth. This table may help you remember the terminology of who's who in a transaction.

Product	Person Giving the Product	Person Receiving the Product
Devise	Devisor	Devisee
Deed	Grantor	Grantee
Legacy	Legator	Legatee
Lease	Lessor	Lessee
Mortgage*	Mortgagor	Mortgagee
Offer	Offeror	Offeree
Option	Optionor	Optionee
Sublease	Sublessor	Sublessee
Trust	Trustor	Trustee

*Note: In a mortgage, the product being transferred is the real estate itself. Therefore, the mortgagor is the borrower and the mortgagee is the lender.

A deed also may include a description of any *limitations* on the conveyance of a full fee simple estate and a statement of any *exceptions and reservations* (also known as *"subject to" clauses*) that affect title to the property.

Grantor   A grantor must be of lawful age, usually at least 18 years old. A deed executed by a minor is generally voidable.

A grantor also must be of *sound mind*. Generally, any grantor who can understand the action is viewed as mentally capable of executing a valid deed. A deed executed by someone who was mentally impaired at the time is voidable, but it is not void. If, however, the grantor has been judged legally incompetent, the deed will be void. Real estate owned by someone who is legally incompetent can be conveyed only with a court's approval.

The grantor's name must be spelled correctly and consistently throughout the deed. If the grantor's name has changed since the title was acquired, as when a person's name changes with marriage, both names should be shown—for example, "Mary Smith, formerly Mary Jones."

Grantee   To be valid, a deed must name a grantee. The grantee must be specifically named so that the person to whom the property is being conveyed can be readily identified from the deed itself.

■ **F O R   E X A M P L E**   Olive wanted to convey Whiteacre to her nephew, Jack Jackson. In the deed, Olive wrote the following words of conveyance: "I, Olive Burbank, hereby convey to Jack all my interest in Whiteacre." The only problem was that Olive also had a son named Jack, a cousin Jack, and a neighbor Jack. The grantee's identity could not be discerned from the deed itself. Olive should have conveyed Whiteacre "to my nephew, Jack Jackson."

If more than one grantee is involved, the granting clause should specify their rights in the property. For instance, the clause might state that the grantees will take title as joint tenants or tenants in common. This is especially important when specific wording is necessary to create a joint tenancy.

Consideration   A valid deed must contain a clause acknowledging that the grantor has received consideration. Generally, the amount of consideration is stated in dollars. When a deed conveys real estate as a gift to a relative, love and affection may be sufficient consideration. In most states it is customary to recite a nominal consideration, such as "$10 and other good and valuable consideration."

Granting Clause (Words of Conveyance)

A deed must contain a **granting clause** that states the grantor's intention to convey the property. Depending on the type of deed and the obligations agreed to by the grantor, the wording would be similar to one of the following:

- "I, *JKL*, convey and warrant ..."
- "I, *JKL*, remise, release, alienate, and convey ..."
- "I, *JKL*, grant, bargain, and sell ..."
- "I, *JKL*, remise, release, and quitclaim ..."

A deed that conveys the grantor's entire fee simple interest usually contains wording such as "to *ABC* and to her heirs and assigns forever." If less than the grantor's complete interest is conveyed, such as a life estate, the wording must indicate this limitation—for example, "to *ABC* for the duration of her natural life."

Habendum clause   When it is necessary to define or explain the ownership to be enjoyed by the grantee, a **habendum clause** may follow the granting clause. The habendum clause begins with the words *to have and to hold*. Its provisions must agree with those stated in the granting clause. For example, if a grantor conveys a time-share interest or an interest less than fee simple absolute, the habendum clause would specify the owner's rights as well as how those rights are limited (a specific time frame or certain prohibited activities, for instance).

Legal description of real estate   To be valid, a deed must contain an accurate legal description of the real estate conveyed. Land is considered adequately described if a professional surveyor can locate the property using the description.

Exceptions and reservations   A valid deed must specifically note any encumbrances, reservations, or limitations that affect the title being conveyed. This might include such things as restrictions and easements that run with the land. In addition to citing existing encumbrances, a grantor may reserve some right in the land, such as an easement, for the grantor's use. A grantor may also place certain restrictions on a grantee's use of the property. Developers often restrict the number of houses that may be built on each lot in a subdivision. Such private restrictions must be stated in the deed or contained in a previously recorded document, such as the subdivider's master deed, that is expressly referred to in the deed. Many of these deed restrictions have time limits and often include renewal clauses.

Signature of grantor   To be valid, a deed must be signed by all grantors named in the deed. Some states also require witnesses to or notarization of the grantor's signature.

Most states permit a power of attorney (written specific authority) to sign legal documents for a grantor. (A power of attorney is not necessarily an attorney-at-law.) The person having *power of attorney* has written authority to execute and sign one or more legal instruments for another person. Usually, the power of attorney must be recorded in the county where the property is located.

In some states, a grantor's spouse is required to sign any deed of conveyance to waive any marital or homestead rights. This requirement varies according to state law and depends on the manner in which title to real estate is held.

Many states still require a *seal* (or simply the word *seal*) to be written or printed after an individual grantor's signature. The corporate seal may be required of a corporate grantor.

Acknowledgment   An **acknowledgment** is a formal declaration under oath that the person who signs a written document does so *voluntarily* and that the signature is genuine. The declaration is made before a registered notary public or an authorized public officer, such as a judge, justice of the peace, or some other person as prescribed by state law. An acknowledgment usually states that the person signing the deed or other document is known to the officer or has produced sufficient identification to prevent a forgery. After verifying the person's information, the notary public will sign and stamp the form, which allows the person to be able to record the document, completely satisfying the instrument.

An acknowledgment (that is, a formal declaration before a notary public) is not essential to the validity of the deed unless it is required by state statute. However, a deed that is not acknowledged is not a completely satisfactory instrument. In most states, an unacknowledged deed is not eligible for recording.

Delivery and acceptance   A title is not considered transferred until the deed is actually *delivered* to and *accepted* by the grantee. The grantor may deliver the deed to the grantee either personally or through a third party.

> Transfer of title requires both delivery and acceptance of the deed.

Title is said to "pass" only when a deed is delivered and accepted. The effective date of the transfer of title from the grantor to the grantee is the date of delivery of the deed itself. Delivery and acceptance are usually presumed if the deed has been examined and registered by the county clerk.

Execution of Corporate Deeds

The laws governing a corporation's right to convey real estate vary from state to state. However, two basic rules must be followed:

- A corporation can convey real estate only by authority granted in its *bylaws* or on a proper resolution passed by its *board of directors*. If all or a substantial portion of a corporation's real estate is being conveyed, usually a resolution authorizing the sale must be secured from the *shareholders*.
- Deeds to real estate can be signed *only by an authorized officer*.

Rules pertaining to religious corporations and not-for-profit corporations vary even more widely. Because the legal requirements must be followed exactly, an attorney should be consulted for all corporate conveyances.

Types of Deeds

A deed can take several forms, depending on the extent of the grantor's promises to the grantee. Regardless of any guarantees the deed offers, the grantee will want additional assurance that the grantor has the right to offer what the deed conveys. To obtain this protection, grantees commonly seek evidence of title. (See Chapter 13.)

The most common deeds are the following:

- General warranty deed
- Special warranty deed
- Bargain and sale deed
- Quitclaim deed

General warranty deed   A **general warranty deed** provides the greatest protection to the buyer because the grantor is legally bound by certain covenants (promises) or warranties. In most states, the warranties are implied by the use of certain words specified by statute. In some states, the grantor's warranties are expressly written into the deed itself. Each state law should be examined, but some of the specific words include convey and warrant or warrant generally. The basic warranties are as follows:

General Warranty Deed

Five covenants:
- Covenant of seisin
- Covenant against encumbrances
- Covenant of quiet enjoyment
- Covenant of further assurance
- Covenant of warranty forever

- *Covenant of seisin*: Grantors warrant that they own the property and have the right to convey title to it. (*Seisin* simply means *possession*.) The grantee may recover damages up to the full purchase price if this covenant is broken.
- *Covenant against encumbrances*: The grantor warrants that the property is free from liens or encumbrances, except for any specifically stated in the deed. Encumbrances generally include mortgages, mechanics' liens, and easements. If this covenant is breached, the grantee may sue for the cost of removing the encumbrances.
- *Covenant of quiet enjoyment*: The grantor guarantees that the grantee's title will be good against third parties who might bring court actions to establish superior title to the property. If the grantee's title is found to be inferior, the grantor is liable for damages.
- *Covenant of further assurance*: The grantor promises to obtain and deliver any instrument needed to make the title good. For example, if the grantor's spouse has failed to sign away dower rights, the grantor must deliver a quitclaim deed to clear the title.
- *Covenant of warranty forever*: The grantor promises to compensate the grantee for the loss sustained if the title fails at any time in the future.

These covenants in a general warranty deed are not limited to matters that occurred during the time the grantor owned the property; they extend back to its origins. The grantor defends the title against both himself or herself and *all those who previously held title.*

Special warranty deed   A **special warranty deed** contains two basic warranties:

■ That the grantor received title
■ That the property was not encumbered *during the time the grantor held title*, except as otherwise noted in the deed

Special Warranty Deed

Two warranties:
■ Warranty that grantor received title
■ Warranty that property was unencumbered by grantor

In effect, grantors defend the title against themselves. The granting clause generally contains these words: "Grantor remises, releases, alienates, and conveys." The grantor may include additional warranties, but they must be specifically stated in the deed. In areas where a special warranty deed is more commonly used, the purchase of title insurance is viewed as providing adequate protection to the grantee.

A special warranty deed may be used by fiduciaries such as trustees, executors, and corporations. A special warranty deed is appropriate for fiduciaries because they lack the authority to warrant against acts of *predecessors in title* (i.e., the former owners). A fiduciary may hold title for a limited time without having a personal interest in the proceeds. Sometimes a special warranty deed is used by a grantor who has acquired title at a tax sale.

Bargain and Sale Deed

No express warranties:
■ Implication that grantor holds title and possession

Bargain and sale deed   A **bargain and sale deed** contains no express warranties against encumbrances. However, it does *imply* that the grantor holds title and possession of the property. The granting clause usually states a person's name or name of an entity and the words *grants and releases* or *grants, bargains,* and *sells.* Because the warranty is not specifically stated, the grantee has little legal recourse if title defects appear later. In some areas, this deed is used in foreclosures and tax sales. The buyer should purchase, or the seller provide, title insurance for protection.

A covenant against encumbrances initiated by the grantor may be added to a standard bargain and sale deed to create a *bargain and sale deed with covenant against the grantor's acts.* This deed is closely equivalent to a special warranty deed. Warranties used in general warranty deeds may be inserted in a bargain and sale deed to give the grantee similar protection.

Quitclaim Deed

No express or implied covenants or warranties:
■ Used primarily to convey less than fee simple or to cure a title defect

Quitclaim deed   A **quitclaim deed** provides the grantee with the least protection of any deed. It carries *no covenants or warranties* and generally conveys only whatever interest the grantor may have when the deed is delivered. If the grantor has no interest, the grantee will acquire nothing. Nor will the grantee acquire any right of warranty claim against the grantor. A quitclaim deed can convey title as effectively as a warranty deed if the grantor has good title when the deed is delivered, but it provides none of the guarantees of a warranty deed. Through a quitclaim deed, the grantor only "remises, releases, and quitclaims" the grantor's interest in the property, if any.

Usually, a quitclaim deed is the only type of deed that may be used to convey less than a fee simple estate. This is because a quitclaim deed conveys only the grantor's right, title, or interest.

A quitclaim deed is frequently used to cure a defect, called a *cloud on the title*. For example, if the name of the grantee is misspelled on a warranty deed filed in the public record, a quitclaim deed with the correct spelling may be executed to the grantee to perfect the title.

A quitclaim deed is also used when a grantor allegedly *inherits* property but is not certain that the decedent's title was valid. A warranty deed in such an instance could carry with it obligations of warranty, while a quitclaim deed would convey only the grantor's interest, whatever it may be.

One of the most common uses of the quitclaim deed is as a simple transfer of property from one family member to another.

Deed of trust   A deed of trust (or *deed in trust* in some states) is the means by which a *trustor* conveys real estate to a *trustee* for the benefit of a *beneficiary*. The real estate is held by the trustee to fulfill the purpose of the trust. (See Figure 12.1.)

Reconveyance deed   A reconveyance deed is used by a trustee to return title to the trustor. For example, when a loan secured by a deed of trust has been fully paid, the beneficiary notifies the trustee. The trustee then reconveys the property to the trustor. As with any document of title, a reconveyance deed should be recorded to prevent title problems in the future.

Trustee's deed   A deed executed by a trustee is a **trustee's deed**. It is used when a trustee conveys real estate held in the trust to anyone *other than the trustor*. The trustee's deed must state that the trustee is executing the instrument in accordance with the powers and authority granted by the trust instrument.

Deed executed pursuant to a court order   Executors' and administrators' deeds, masters' deeds, sheriffs' deeds, and many other types are all *deeds executed pursuant to a court order*. These deeds are established by state statute and are used to convey title to property that is transferred by court order or by will. The form of such a deed must conform to the laws of the state in which the property is located.

One common characteristic of deeds executed pursuant to court order is that the *full consideration* is usually stated in the deed. Instead of "$10 and other valuable consideration," for example, the deed would list the actual sales price.

Deed of Trust

Conveyance from trustor to trustee

Reconveyance Deed

Conveyance from trustee back to trustor

Trustee's Deed

Conveyance from trustee to third party

F I G U R E   12.1

Trust Deeds

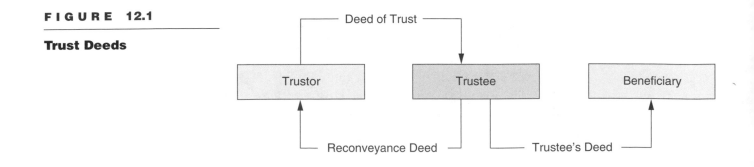

Transfer Tax Stamps

Many states have enacted laws providing for a state **transfer tax** (also referred to in some states as a *grantor's tax*) on conveyances of real estate. In these states, the tax is usually payable when the deed is recorded. In some states, the taxpayer purchases *stamps* from the recorder of the county in which the deed is recorded. The stamps must be affixed to deeds and conveyances before the documents can be recorded. In other states, the taxpayer simply pays the clerk of court or county recorder the appropriate transfer tax amount in accordance with state and local law.

The transfer tax may be paid by either the seller or the buyer, or split between them, depending on local custom or agreement in the sales contract. The actual *tax rate* varies and may be imposed at the state, county, or city level. For example, the rate might be calculated as $1.10 for every $1,000 of the sales price, as $0.26 for every $500, or as a simple percentage.

MATH CONCEPTS

CALCULATING TRANSFER TAXES

A state has a transfer tax of $1.50 for each $500 (or fraction of $500) of the sales price of any parcel of real estate. The transfer tax is paid by the seller. To calculate the transfer tax due in the sale of a $300,000 house, use the following formula:

(Value ÷ Unit) × Rate per unit = Tax

In this example:

$300,000 ÷ $500 = 600 taxable units

600 × $1.50 = $900

The seller in this transaction must pay a transfer tax of $900 to the state.

In many states, a *transfer declaration form* (or *transfer statement* or *affidavit of real property value*) must be signed by both the buyer and the seller or their agents. The transfer declaration states

- the full sales price of the property;
- its legal description;
- the type of improvement;
- the address, date, and type of deed; and
- whether the transfer is between relatives or in accordance with a court order.

Certain deeds may be *exempted* from the tax, such as the following:

- Gifts of real estate
- Deeds not made in connection with a sale (such as a change in the form of co-ownership)
- Conveyances to, from, or between government bodies
- Deeds by charitable, religious, or educational institutions
- Deeds securing debts or releasing property as security for a debt
- Partitions
- Tax deeds
- Deeds pursuant to mergers of corporations
- Deeds from subsidiary to parent corporations for cancellations of stock

■ INVOLUNTARY ALIENATION

[handwritten: — Foreclose — Delinquent tax or mortgage, etc.]

Title to property may be transferred without the owner's consent by **involuntary alienation**. (See Figure 12.2.) Involuntary transfers are usually carried out by operation of law—such as by condemnation or a sale to satisfy delinquent tax or mortgage liens. When a person dies intestate (with no will), the title to the real estate passes to the state by the state's power of escheat because there are no heirs. Land may be acquired through the process of accretion or actually lost through erosion. (See Chapter 7.) Other acts of nature, such as earthquakes, hurricanes, sinkholes, and mudslides, may create or eliminate a landowner's holdings.

Transfer by Adverse Possession

Adverse possession is another means of involuntary transfer. An individual who makes a claim to certain property, takes possession of it and, most important, uses it, may take title away from an owner who fails to use or inspect the property for a period of years. The law recognizes that the use of land is an important function of its ownership.

Usually the possession by the claimant must be all of the following:

- *Open* (i.e., obvious to anyone who looks)
- *Notorious* (i.e., known by others)
- *Continuous* and uninterrupted
- *Hostile* (i.e., without the true owner's consent)
- *Adverse* to the true owner's possession

The necessary period of uninterrupted possession is a matter of state law. The statutory periods range from as few as 5 years in some states to as many as 30 years in others.

In order to establish title by adverse possession, there must be proof of nonpermissive use that is actual, open, notorious, exclusive, and adverse for the statutorily prescribed period. To claim title, the adverse possessor normally files an action in court to receive undisputed title.

IN PRACTICE   The right of adverse possession is a statutory right. State requirements must be followed carefully to ensure the successful transfer of title. The parties to a transaction that might involve adverse possession should seek legal counsel.

■ CONVEYANCE OF A DECEDENT'S PROPERTY

A person who dies **testate** has prepared a will indicating how the deceased's property will be disposed of. In contrast, when a person dies **intestate** (without a will), real estate and personal property pass to the decedent's heirs according to the state's statute of descent and distribution. In effect, the state makes a will for an intestate decedent.

FIGURE 12.2

Involuntary Alienation

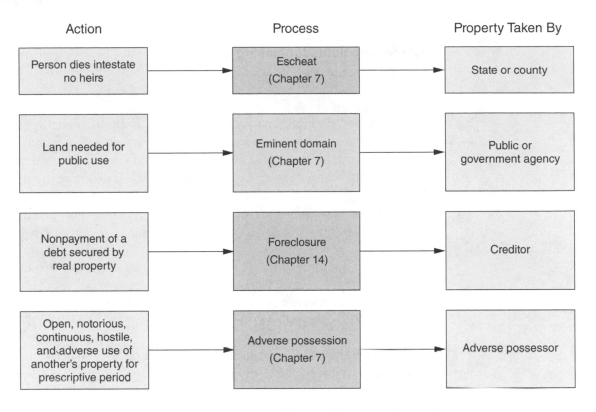

Legally, when a person dies, ownership of real estate immediately passes either to the heirs by descent or to the persons named in the will. Before these individuals can take full title and possession of the property, the estate must go through a judicial process called probate, and all claims against the estate must be satisfied.

Transfer of Title by Will

A **will** is made by an owner to convey title to real or personal property after the owner's death. This differs from a deed, which *must* be delivered during the lifetime of the grantor and which conveys a present interest in property. While the **testator**, the person who makes a will, is alive, any property included in the will can still be conveyed by the owner. The parties named in a will have no rights or interests as long as the party who made the will is alive; they acquire interest or title only after the owner's death.

Only property owned by the testator at the time of the testator's death may be transferred by will. The gift of real property by will is known as a **devise**, and a person who receives real property by will is known as a *devisee*. The other two gifts by will are a bequest, which is a gift of personal property, and a legacy, which is a gift of money.

For title to pass to the devisees, state laws require that on the death of a testator, the will must be filed with the court and probated. Probate is a legal procedure for verifying the validity of a will and accounting for the decedent's assets. The process can take several months to complete. Probate is the formal judicial process.

A will cannot supersede the state laws of dower and curtesy, which were enacted to protect the inheritance rights of a surviving spouse. When a will does not provide a spouse with the minimum statutory inheritance, the spouse may demand it from the estate.

Legal requirements for making a will   A will must be executed and prepared according to the laws of the state in which the real estate is located. Only a valid and probated will can effectively convey title to real estate.

A testator must have legal capacity to make a will. There are no rigid tests to determine legal capacity. Usually, a person must be of *legal age* and of *sound mind*. Legal age varies from state to state. To demonstrate sound mind, the testator must have sufficient mental capacity to understand the nature and extent of the property the testator owns. A testator must understand the identity of his or her natural heirs and that the property will go to those persons named in the will. The drawing of a will must be a voluntary act, free of any undue influence by other people.

In most states, a written will must be signed by its testator before two or more witnesses, who must also sign the document. The witnesses should not be individuals who are named as devisees in the will. Some states do not permit real property to be conveyed by oral (*nuncupative*) wills or handwritten (*holographic*) wills.

A testator may alter a will any time. Any modification, amendment, or addition to a previously executed will is contained in a separate document called a *codicil*.

Transfer of Title by Descent

Under a state's statute of descent and distribution, the primary **heirs** of the deceased are the surviving spouse and close blood relatives (such as children, parents, brothers, sisters, aunts, uncles, and, in some cases, first and second cousins). The right to inherit under laws of descent varies from state to state, and intestate property is distributed according to the laws of the state in which the property is located. (See Table 12.2.)

Probate Proceedings

Probate is a formal judicial process that

- proves or confirms the validity of a will,
- determines the precise assets of the deceased person, and
- identifies the people to whom the assets are to pass.

The purpose of probate is to see that the assets are distributed correctly. All assets must be accounted for, and the decedent's debts must be satisfied before any property is distributed to the heirs or devisee. In addition, estate taxes must be paid before any distribution. The laws of each state govern the probate proceedings and the functions of the individuals appointed to administer the decedent's affairs.

Assets that are distributed through probate are those that do not otherwise distribute themselves. For instance, property held in joint tenancy or tenancy by the

TABLE 12.2

Sample Statutory Distributions

This table illustrates how a state's statute of descent and distribution might provide for an intestate's estate. The specific persons entitled to property, and the various percentages involved, vary from state to state. Remember: *Licensees should never try to determine descent or ownership status without consulting with legal counsel.*

Decedent Status	Family Status	How Property Passes
Married, surviving spouse[1]	No children No other relatives	100% to surviving spouse
Married, surviving spouse	Children	50% to surviving spouse 50% shared by children or descendants of deceased child
Married, no surviving spouse	Children	Children share equally, with descendants of a deceased child taking their parent's share
Unmarried, no children	Relatives	100% to father or mother, brothers or sisters, or other relatives (such as grandparents or great-grandparents; uncles or aunts; nieces or nephews; first or second cousins) in order of priority
	No relatives or heirs as defined by state law	100% to state by escheat

[1]Some states allow the decedent's spouse the right to elect a life estate of dower or curtesy in place of the share provided for in the law of descent. (See Chapter 7.)

entirety passes immediately. Probate proceedings take place in the county *in which the decedent resided.* If the decedent owned real estate in another county, probate would occur in that county as well.

The person who has possession of the will—normally the person designated in the will as *executor*—presents it for filing with the court. The court is responsible for determining that the will meets the statutory requirements for its form and execution. If the will was modified or if more than one will exists, the court will decide how these documents should be probated.

The court must rule on a challenge if a will is contested. Once the will is upheld, the assets can be distributed according to its provisions. Probate courts distribute assets according to statute only when no other reasonable alternative exists.

When a person dies intestate, the court determines who inherits the assets by reviewing proof from relatives of the decedent and their entitlement under the statute of descent and distribution. Once the heirs have been determined, the court appoints an *administrator* or *personal representative* to administer the affairs of the estate—the role usually taken by an executor.

IN PRACTICE   A broker entering into a listing agreement with the executor or administrator of an estate in probate should be aware that the amount of commission is approved by the court and that the commission is payable only from the proceeds of the sale. The broker will not be able to collect a commission unless the court approves the sale.

■ KEY POINT REVIEW

Title is **ownership**, or the right to ownership, of land and **evidence** of that ownership.

Voluntary alienation is the voluntary transfer of title to real estate by **gift** or **sale**, using some form of **deed**.

- **Grantor** (person who transfers title) must be of legal age and legally competent to execute (sign) a deed. A deed executed by a **minor** is **voidable**.
    — **Mental impairment** at time of signing deed makes the deed **voidable**.
    — If the grantor has been declared **incompetent by a judge**, the deed is **void**.
    — All names the grantor has used should be provided.
- **Grantee** must be identifiable with sufficient certainty.
- **Consideration** (payment) of some form must be stated.
- **Granting clause** (words of conveyance) must be used.
- **Habendum clause** must define ownership interest taken by the grantee; it specifies limits on ownership, such as with a time-share.
- **Legal description** of the property conveyed is essential.
- **Exceptions** or **reservations** of any relevance must be included.
- **Signature of the grantor(s)** must be **acknowledged** by a notary public or other official authorized by the state in which the property is located.
- **Delivery** of the deed **and acceptance** by the grantee are necessary.

Types of deeds include the following:

- **General warranty deed** provides the greatest protection to the grantee and includes
    — **covenant of seisin**—warrants the grantor has the right to convey title;
    — **covenant against encumbrances**—warrants the property is free from liens or encumbrances, unless expressly stated;
    — **covenant of quiet enjoyment**—makes the grantor liable for damages if the grantee's title is found to be inferior;
    — **covenant of further assurance**—the grantor's promise to obtain any other document necessary to convey good title; and
    — **covenant of warranty forever**—the grantor's promise to compensate the grantee if title fails at any future time.
- **Special warranty deed** includes the warranties that the grantor received title and that the property was not encumbered during the time the grantor held title, except as otherwise noted.
- **Bargain and sale deed** implies that the grantor holds title and possession of the property, and there are no express warranties against encumbrances.

- **Quitclaim deed** provides the least protection of any deed, carries no covenants or warranties, and conveys only whatever interest the grantor may have when the deed is delivered.

Transfer tax stamps may be required to be affixed to deeds and conveyances before being recorded, with the tax rate depending on state, county, and city requirements.

Involuntary alienation (transfer) of title to property is usually by operation of law.

- **Escheat**—property taken by state when deceased has no heirs
- **Eminent domain**—property taken by public or government agency
- **Foreclosure**—property taken by creditor for nonpayment of debt secured by real property
- **Adverse possession**—property seizure occurring when someone who is not the lawful owner takes possession of property for the length of time specified by state law and usually in a way that is <u>O</u>pen, <u>N</u>otorious, <u>C</u>ontinuous, <u>H</u>ostile, and <u>A</u>dverse

Transfer of title by will occurs when the deceased dies **testate** (leaving a will), prepared as required by state law that generally includes the following:

- Wills take effect only after death and can be changed by **codicil** or revoked while the **testator** is still alive.
- **Devise** is a gift of real property by will to the **devisee**.
- **Bequest** is a gift of personal property.
- **Legacy** is a gift of money.
- To pass title to property on death, the will must be **filed with the court** and **probated**.
- Wills cannot supersede state laws protecting inheritance rights of the surviving wife (**dower**) or husband (**curtesy**).

Transfer of title under a state's **statute of descent and distribution** occurs when a person dies **intestate** (without a will). **Probate** proceedings must have an administrator appointed, and laws of the state where the real property is **located** govern property distribution.

CHAPTER 12 QUIZ

1. The basic requirements for a valid conveyance are governed by
   a. state law.
   b. local custom.
   c. national law.
   d. the law of descent.

2. Every deed must be signed by the
   a. grantor.
   b. grantee.
   c. grantor and grantee.
   d. devisee.

3. A 15-year-old boy recently inherited many parcels of real estate from his late father and has decided to sell one of them. If the boy entered into a deed conveying his interest in the property to a purchaser, such a conveyance would be
   a. valid.
   b. void.
   c. invalid.
   d. voidable.

4. A form authorizing one person to act for another is called a
   a. power of attorney.
   b. release deed.
   c. quitclaim deed.
   d. power to represent.

5. The grantee receives greatest protection with what type of deed?
   a. Quitclaim
   b. General warranty
   c. Bargain and sale with covenant
   d. Executor's

6. A man receives a deed from a woman. The granting clause of the deed states, "I hereby remise, release, alienate, and convey to the man the real property." What type of deed has the man received?
   a. Special warranty
   b. Quitclaim
   c. General warranty
   d. Bargain and sale

7. Under the covenant of quiet enjoyment, the grantor
   a. promises to obtain and deliver any instrument needed to make the title good.
   b. guarantees to compensate the grantee if the title fails in the future.
   c. warrants that he or she is the owner and has the right to convey title to the property.
   d. ensures that the title will be good against the title claims of third parties.

8. Which type of deed merely implies but does *NOT* specifically warrant that the grantor holds good title to the property?
   a. Special warranty
   b. Bargain and sale
   c. Quitclaim
   d. Trust deed

9. Step 1: A decided to convey a house to B. Step 2: A signed a deed transferring title to B. Step 3: A gave the signed deed to B, who accepted it. Step 4: B took the deed to the county recorder's office and had it recorded. At which step did title to the house actually transfer or pass to B?
   a. Step 1
   b. Step 2
   c. Step 3
   d. Step 4

10. A man signed a deed transferring ownership of his house to a woman. To provide evidence that his signature was genuine, the man executed a declaration before a notary. This declaration is known as an
    a. affidavit.
    b. acknowledgment.
    c. affirmation.
    d. estoppel.

11. Title to real estate may be transferred during a person's lifetime by
    a. devise.
    b. descent.
    c. involuntary alienation.
    d. escheat.

12. A woman bought acreage in a distant county, never went to see the acreage, and did not use the ground. A man moved his mobile home onto the land, had a water well drilled, and lived there for 22 years. The man may become the owner of the land if he has complied with the state law regarding

a. requirements for a valid conveyance.
b. adverse possession.
c. avulsion.
d. voluntary alienation.

13. Eminent domain and escheat are two examples of

a. voluntary alienation.
b. adverse possession.
c. transfers of title by descent.
d. involuntary alienation.

14. A deed contains a promise that the title conveyed is good and a promise to obtain and deliver any documents necessary to ensure good title. This promise is an example of which covenant?

a. Further assurance
b. Seisin
c. Quiet enjoyment
d. Warranty forever

15. A deed contains a guarantee that the grantor will compensate the grantee for any loss resulting from the title's failure in the future. This is an example of which type of covenant?

a. Warranty forever
b. Further assurance
c. Quiet enjoyment
d. Seisin

16. A person who has died without a will has died

a. testate.
b. in valid conveyance.
c. intestate.
d. under the acknowledgment clause.

17. Title to real estate can be transferred upon death by what type of document?

a. Warranty deed
b. Special warranty deed
c. Quitclaim deed
d. Will

18. An owner of real estate was declared legally incompetent and was committed to a state mental institution. While institutionalized, the owner wrote and executed a will. The owner later died and was survived by a spouse and three children. The real estate will pass

a. to the owner's spouse.
b. to the heirs mentioned in the owner's will.
c. according to the state laws of descent.
d. to the state.

19. Generally, where does a probate proceeding involving real property take place?

a. Only in the county in which the property is located
b. Only in the county in which the decedent resided
c. In both the county where the decedent resided and the county in which the property is located
d. In the county in which the executor or the beneficiary resides

20. A deed states that the grantors are conveying all their rights and interests to the grantees to have and to hold. This is communicated in the

a. acknowledgment clause.
b. restriction clause.
c. covenant of seisen.
d. habendum clause.

13

Title Records

When you have finished reading this chapter, you should be able to

■ **identify** the various proofs of ownership;

■ **describe** recording, notice, and chain of title issues;

■ **explain** the process and purpose of a title search;

■ **distinguish** constructive and actual notice; and

■ **define** the following *key terms*:

abstract of title	chain of title	recording
actual notice	constructive notice	suit to quiet title
attorney's opinion of title	marketable title	title insurance
certificate of title	priority	title search

■ TITLE RECORDS

Public records are just that—records that are open to the public—which means that anyone interested in a particular property can review the records to learn about the documents, claims, and other details that affect its ownership. A prospective buyer, for example, needs to be sure that the seller can convey title to the property. If the property is subject to any liens or other encumbrances, a prospective buyer or lender needs to know. An attorney or title company typically performs a search of the public records to ensure that good title is being conveyed. Nonetheless, it is important for a real estate licensee to understand what is in the public record and what the searchers are likely to find.

■ PUBLIC RECORDS

Public records contain detailed information about each parcel of real estate in a city or county. These records are crucial in establishing ownership, giving notice of encumbrances, and establishing priority of liens. They protect the interests of real estate owners, taxing bodies, creditors, and the general public. The real estate recording system includes written documents that affect title, such as deeds and mortgages. Public records regarding taxes, judgments, probate, and marriage also may offer important information about the title to a particular property.

Public records are maintained by

- recorders of deeds,
- county clerks,
- county treasurers,
- city clerks,
- collectors, and
- clerks of court.

IN PRACTICE   Prospective buyers rarely search public records for evidence of title or encumbrances themselves. Instead, *title companies,* attorneys, and lenders conduct the searches.

Recording

Recording is the act of placing documents in the public record. The specific rules for recording documents are a matter of state law. Although the details may vary, all recording acts essentially provide that any written document that affects any estate, right, title, or interest in land *must be recorded in the county (or, in some states, the town) where the land is located* to serve as public notice. This way, anyone interested in the title to a parcel of property will know where to look to discover the various interests of all other parties. Recording acts also generally give legal priority to those interests recorded first—the *first in time, first in right* or *first come, first served* principle. (See Chapter 10.)

> In most states, written documents that affect land *must be recorded in the county where the land is located.*

To be *eligible for recording,* a document must be drawn and executed according to the recording acts of the state in which the real estate is located. For instance, a state may require that the parties' names be typed below their signatures or that the document be acknowledged before a notary public. In some states, the document must be witnessed. Others require that the name of the person who prepared the document appear on it. States may have specific rules about the size of documents and the color and quality of paper they are printed on. Electronic recording—using computers or fax machines, for instance—is permitted in a growing number of localities. Some states require a certificate of real estate value and the payment of current property taxes due for recording.

Notice

Anyone with an interest in a parcel of real estate can take certain steps, called *giving notice*, to ensure that the interest is available to the public. The two basic types of notice are constructive notice and actual notice.

Constructive notice is the legal presumption that information may be obtained by an individual through due diligence. Properly recording documents in the public record serves as constructive notice to the world of an individual's rights or interest, as does the physical possession of a property. Because the information or evidence is readily available to the world, a prospective purchaser or lender is responsible for discovering the interest.

Actual notice means not only that the information available but also that someone has been given the information and actually knows it. An individual who has searched the public records and inspected the property has actual notice, also known as *direct knowledge*. If it can be proved that an individual has had actual notice of information, that person cannot use a lack of constructive notice (such as an unrecorded deed) to justify a claim.

Priority

Priority refers to the order of when documents or liens were recorded. Many complicated situations can affect the priority of rights in a parcel of real estate—who recorded first, which party was in possession first, or who had actual or constructive notice. How the courts rule in any situation depends, of course, on the specific facts of the case. These are strictly legal questions that should be referred to the parties' attorneys.

■ **FOR EXAMPLE** Buyer A purchased a property from Seller B and received a deed. Buyer A did not record the deed but took possession of the property in June. In November, Seller B sold the same property to Buyer C who received a deed which Buyer C promptly recorded. Buyer C never inspected the property to determine if someone was in possession of it. By taking possession of the property, Buyer A has the superior right to the property even though Buyer A did not record the deed.

Unrecorded Documents

Certain types of liens are not recorded. Real estate taxes and special assessments are liens on specific parcels of real estate and are not usually recorded until some time after the taxes or assessments are past due. Inheritance taxes and franchise taxes are statutory liens and are placed against all real estate owned by a decedent at the time of death or by a corporation at the time the franchise taxes became a lien. Like real estate taxes, they are not recorded.

Notice of these liens must be gained from sources other than the recorder's office. Evidence of the payment of real estate taxes, special assessments, municipal utilities, and other taxes can be gathered from paid tax receipts and letters from municipalities. Creative measures are often required to get information about *off the record* liens.

Chain of Title

Chain of title is the record of a property's ownership. Beginning with the earliest owner, a title may pass to many individuals. Each owner is linked to the next so that a chain is formed. An unbroken chain of title can be traced through linking conveyances from the present owner back to the earliest recorded owner. Chain of title does not include liens and encumbrances or any other document not directly related to ownership.

If ownership cannot be traced through an unbroken chain, a gap or cloud in the chain of title is said to exist. In these cases, the cloud on the title makes it necessary to establish ownership by a court action called a **suit to quiet title**. For instance, a suit might be required when a grantor acquired title under one name and conveyed it under another name. Or there may be a forged deed in the chain, after which no subsequent grantee acquired legal title.

Title Search and Abstract of Title

A **title search** is an examination of all of the public records to determine whether any defects exist in the chain of title. The records of the conveyances of ownership are examined, beginning with the present owner. Then the title is traced backward to its origin (or 40 to 60 years or some definite period of time, depending on state statute). The time beyond which the title must be searched is limited in states that have adopted the Marketable Title Act. This law extinguishes certain interests and cures certain defects arising before the *root of the title*—the conveyance that establishes the source of the chain of title.

Other public records are examined to identify wills, judicial proceedings, and other encumbrances that may affect title. These include a variety of taxes, special assessments, and other recorded liens.

An **abstract of title** is a summary report of what the title search found in the public record. A person who prepares this report is called an *abstractor*. The abstractor searches all the public records and then summarizes the various events and proceedings that affected the title throughout its history. The report begins with the original grant (or root) and then provides a chronological list of recorded instruments. All recorded liens and encumbrances are included, along with their current status. A list of all of the public records examined is also provided as evidence of the scope of the search.

IN PRACTICE An abstract of title is a condensed history of those items that can be found in public records. It does not reveal such items as encroachments or forgeries or any interests or conveyances that have not been recorded.

Marketable Title

Under the terms of the typical real estate sales contract, the seller is required to deliver **marketable title** to the buyer at the closing. To be marketable, a title must

- disclose no serious defects and not depend on doubtful questions of law or fact to prove its validity;
- not expose a purchaser to the hazard of litigation or threaten the quiet enjoyment of the property; and
- convince a reasonably well-informed and prudent purchaser, acting on business principles and with knowledge of the facts and their legal significance, that the purchaser could sell or mortgage the property at a later time.

Although a title that does not meet these requirements still can be transferred, it contains certain defects that may limit or restrict its ownership. A buyer cannot be forced to accept a conveyance that is materially different from the one bargained for in the sales contract. However, questions of marketable title must be raised by a buyer *before acceptance of the deed.* Once a buyer has accepted a deed with unmarketable title, the only available legal recourse is to sue the seller under any covenants of warranty contained in the deed.

In some states, a preliminary title search is conducted as soon as an offer to purchase has been accepted. In fact, it may be customary to include a contingency in the sales contract that gives the buyer the right to review and approve the title report before proceeding with the purchase. A preliminary title report also benefits the seller by giving the seller an early opportunity to cure title defects.

■ PROOF OF OWNERSHIP

Proof of ownership is evidence that title is marketable. A deed by itself is not considered sufficient evidence of ownership. Even though a warranty deed conveys the grantor's interest, it contains no proof of the condition of the grantor's title at the time of the conveyance. The grantee needs some assurance that ownership is actually being acquired and that the title is marketable. A certificate of title, title insurance, or a Torrens certificate is commonly used to prove ownership.

Certificate of Title

A **certificate of title** is a statement of opinion of the title's status on the date the certificate is issued. *A certificate of title is not a guarantee of ownership.* Rather, it certifies the condition of the title based on an examination of the public records—a title search. The certificate may be prepared by a title company, licensed abstractor, or attorney. An owner, mortgage lender, or buyer may request the certificate.

Although a certificate of title is used as evidence of ownership, it is not perfect. Unrecorded liens or rights of parties in possession cannot be discovered by a search of the public records. Hidden defects, such as transfers involving forged documents, incorrect marital information, incompetent parties, minors, or fraud, cannot be detected. A certificate offers no defense against these defects because they are unknown. The person who prepares the certificate is liable only for negligence in preparing the certificate.

IN PRACTICE   You may have heard the phrase *under color of title*. This phrase refers to a situation in which title is conveyed in a transaction by a written instrument (such as a deed or will) that is actually inadequate to legally transfer ownership, whether because it was incorrectly executed or because it was executed by someone who did not, in fact, hold title in the first place.

An abstract and **attorney's opinion of title** are used in some areas of the country as evidence of title. It is an opinion of the status of the title based on a review of the abstract. Similar to a certificate of title, the opinion of title does not protect against defects that cannot be discovered from the public records. Many buyers purchase title insurance to defend the title from these defects.

Title Insurance

Title insurance is a contract under which the policyholder is protected from losses arising from defects in the title. A title insurance company determines whether the title is insurable, based on a review of the public records. If so, a policy is issued. Unlike other insurance policies that insure against *future losses*, title insurance protects the insured from an event that occurred *before* the policy was issued. Title insurance is considered the best defense of title: the title insurance company will defend any lawsuit based on an insurable defect and pay claims if the title proves to be defective.

After examining the public records, the title company usually issues what may be called a *preliminary report of title* or a *commitment* to issue a title policy. This describes the type of policy that will be issued and includes

- the name of the insured party;
- the legal description of the real estate;
- the estate or interest covered;
- conditions and stipulations under which the policy is issued; and
- a schedule of all exceptions, including encumbrances and defects found in the public records and any known unrecorded defects.

The *premium* for the policy is paid once, at closing. The maximum loss for which the company may be liable cannot exceed the face amount of the policy (unless the amount of coverage has been extended by use of an *inflation rider*).

Coverage   Exactly which defects the title company will defend depends on the type of policy. (See Table 13.1.) A *standard coverage policy* normally insures the title as it is known from the public records. In addition, the standard policy insures against such hidden defects as forged documents, conveyances by incompetent grantors, incorrect marital statements, and improperly delivered deeds.

Extended coverage as provided by an American Land Title Association (ALTA) policy includes the protections of a standard policy plus additional protections. An extended policy protects the homeowner against defects that may be discovered

	Standard Coverage	Extended Coverage	Not Covered by Either Policy
TABLE 13.1 **Owner's Title Insurance Policy**	■ Defects found in public records ■ Forged documents ■ Incompetent grantors ■ Incorrect marital statements ■ Improperly delivered deeds	Standard coverage plus defects discoverable through the following: ■ Property inspection, including unrecorded rights of persons in possession ■ Examination of survey ■ Unrecorded liens not known by policyholder	■ Defects and liens listed in policy ■ Defects known to buyer ■ Changes in land use brought about by zoning ordinances

by inspection of the property: rights of parties in possession, examination of a survey, and certain unrecorded liens.

Title insurance does not offer guaranteed protection against all defects. A title company will not insure a bad title or offer protection against defects that clearly appear in a title search. The policy generally names certain uninsurable losses, called *exclusions*. These exclusions include zoning ordinances, restrictive covenants, easements, certain water rights, and current taxes and special assessments.

Types of policies   The different types of policies depend on who is named as the insured. An *owner's policy* is issued for the benefit of the owner (new buyer) and the owner's heirs or devisees. A *lender's policy* is issued for the benefit of the mortgage company. The amount of the coverage depends on the amount of the mortgage loan.

The Torrens System   The Torrens title system is a legal registration system used to verify ownership and encumbrances. Registration in the Torrens system provides evidence of title without the need for an additional search of the public records. Under the Torrens system, an owner of real property submits a written application to register a title. The application is submitted to the court clerk of the county in which the real estate is located. If the applicant proves ownership, the court enters an order to register the real estate. The registrar of titles is directed to issue a certificate of title. The original Torrens certificate of title in the registrar's office reveals the owner of the land and all mortgages, judgments, and similar liens. It does not, however, reveal federal or state taxes and some other items. The Torrens title system of registration relies on the physical title document itself; a person acquires title only when it is registered.

■ KEY POINT REVIEW

To serve as **constructive notice**, and with **priority** over subsequent documents, a **written document** is needed that

- affects an **estate**, **right**, **title**, or **interest** in **land** (such as deeds; mortgages, tax liens, and judgments; and marriage, probate, and other proceedings that may affect title);
- must be **drafted** and **executed** (signed);
- is written according to state law (**recording acts**); and
- is recorded in the **public records** that are maintained by the designated **official**, such as the recorder of deeds, county clerk, or city clerk, and held in the **county** (or city) in which the **property is located**.

Public records are typically **searched** by **title companies** that provide **title insurance** to prospective purchasers based on the findings of the title search.

Constructive notice of a document is assumed when **due diligence** (such as a search of public records and inspection of the property) would reveal its existence. **Actual notice** means that an individual has **direct knowledge** of documents in the public records and facts revealed by an inspection of the property.

Unrecorded documents that may affect title, such as a tax lien, may not be recorded immediately, yet are still given priority by law and require a search of tax records and other sources.

Chain of title is a record of property ownership, but it does not include liens and other encumbrances:

- A **gap** in the chain or other dispute of ownership creates a **cloud on the title**.
- A cloud on title is resolved by **suit to quiet title**.

An **abstract of title**, prepared by an **abstractor** or an **attorney**, is a **summary** report of what the title search reveals. It includes all **recorded liens and encumbrances** and lists **records searched** but does not indicate forgeries and interests that are unrecorded or could be discovered by property inspection.

A **marketable title** is one that must

- **not have serious defects**, nor rely on doubtful questions of law or fact to prove its validity;
- not expose the purchaser to litigation or threaten **quiet enjoyment** of property; and
- convince a reasonably well-informed and prudent purchaser that the property could be sold or mortgaged at a later time.

Proof of ownership may be established by **certificate of title**, but it will not reveal unrecorded liens or rights of parties in possession.

Title insurance, issued as an **owner's policy** or **mortgagee's (lender) policy** under which the insured is protected from losses arising from defects in title, insures against hidden defects and identifies **exclusions** that include readily apparent title defects, zoning, and others.

The **Torrens system**, used in fewer than ten states, provides confirmed **certificate of title** by the county clerk that requires no further search to validate.

CHAPTER 13 QUIZ

1. A title search in the public records may be conducted by
   a. anyone.
   b. attorneys and abstractors only.
   c. attorneys, abstractors, and real estate licensees only.
   d. anyone who obtains a court order under the Freedom of Information Act.

2. Which statement *BEST* explains why instruments affecting real estate are recorded?
   a. Recording gives constructive notice to the world of the rights and interests claimed by a party in a particular parcel of real estate.
   b. Failing to record will void the transfer.
   c. The instruments must be recorded to comply with the terms of the statute of frauds.
   d. Recording proves the execution of the instrument.

3. A purchaser went to the county building to check the recorder's records, which showed that the seller was the grantee in the last recorded deed and that no mortgage was on record against the property. The purchaser may assume which of the following?
   a. All taxes are paid and no judgments are outstanding.
   b. The seller has good title.
   c. The seller did not mortgage the property.
   d. No one else is occupying the property.

4. The date and time a document was recorded help establish which of the following?
   a. Priority
   b. Abstract of title
   c. Subrogation
   d. Marketable title

5. A buyer bought a house, received a deed, and moved into the residence but neglected to record the document. One week later, the seller died and the heirs in another city, unaware that the property had been sold, conveyed title to a relative, who recorded the deed. Who owns the property?
   a. The buyer
   b. The relative
   c. The seller's heirs
   d. Both the buyer and the relative

6. A property with encumbrances that will outlast the closing
   a. cannot be sold.
   b. can be sold only if title insurance is provided.
   c. cannot have a deed recorded without a survey.
   d. can be sold if a buyer agrees to take it subject to the encumbrances.

7. Which of the following would *NOT* be acceptable evidence of ownership?
   a. Attorney's opinion
   b. Title insurance policy
   c. Abstract
   d. Deed signed by the last seller

8. Chain of title is *MOST* accurately defined as a(n)
   a. summary or history of all documents and legal proceedings affecting a specific parcel of land.
   b. report of the contents of the public record regarding a particular property.
   c. instrument or document that protects the insured parties (subject to specific exceptions) against defects in the examination of the record and hidden risks such as forgeries, undisclosed heirs, errors in the public records, and so forth.
   d. record of a property's ownership.

9. A seller delivered title to a buyer at closing. A title search had disclosed no serious defects, and the title did not appear to be based on doubtful questions of law or fact or to expose the buyer to possible litigation. The seller's title did not appear to present a threat to the buyer's quiet enjoyment, and the title insurance policy provided was sufficient to convince a reasonably well-informed person that the property could be resold. The title conveyed would commonly be referred to as a(n)

    a. certificate of title.
    b. abstract of title.
    c. marketable title.
    d. attorney's opinion of title.

10. The person who prepares an abstract of title for a parcel of real estate

    a. searches the public records and then summarizes the events and proceedings that affect title.
    b. insures the condition of the title.
    c. inspects the property.
    d. issues title insurance.

11. Homeowners are frantic because they want to sell their property and the deed is missing. Which of the following is TRUE?

    a. They may need to sue for quiet title.
    b. They must buy title insurance.
    c. They do not need the original deed if it has been recorded.
    d. They should execute a replacement deed to themselves.

12. Mortgagee title policies protect which parties against loss?

    a. Buyers
    b. Sellers
    c. Mortgagees
    d. Buyers and lenders

13. Which of the following are traditionally covered by a standard title insurance policy?

    a. Unrecorded rights of persons in possession
    b. Improperly delivered deeds
    c. Changes in land use due to zoning ordinances
    d. Unrecorded liens not known to the policyholder

14. A written summary of the history of all conveyances and legal proceedings affecting a specific parcel of real estate is called a(n)

    a. affidavit of title.
    b. certificate of title.
    c. abstract of title.
    d. title insurance policy.

15. Which of the following is NOT covered by a standard title insurance policy?

    a. Forged documents
    b. Incorrect marital statements
    c. Unrecorded rights of parties in possession
    d. Incompetent grantors

16. Documents referred to as title evidence include

    a. policies of title insurance.
    b. general warranty deeds.
    c. security agreements.
    d. special warranty deeds.

17. All of the following are true regarding public records EXCEPT they

    a. give notice of encumbrances.
    b. establish priority of liens.
    c. guarantee marketable title.
    d. provide constructive notice about interests in the property.

18. A sells a portion of property to B. B promptly records the deed in the appropriate county office. If A tries to sell the same portion of property to C, which of the following statements is TRUE?

    a. C has been given constructive notice of the prior sale because B promptly recorded the deed.
    b. C has been given actual notice of the prior sale because B promptly recorded the deed.
    c. Because C's purchase of the property is the more recent, it will have priority over B's interest, regardless of when B recorded the deed.
    d. Because C purchased the property from its rightful owner, C is presumed by law to be aware of B's prior interest.

19. The *BEST* reason for a buyer to obtain title insurance is

  a. that the mortgage lender requires it.
  b. to ensure that the seller can deliver marketable title.
  c. to ensure that the abstractor has prepared a complete summary of title.
  d. to pay future liens that may be filed.

20. The mortgagee received a title insurance policy on the property a buyer is pledging as security for the mortgage loan. Which of the following is *TRUE*?

  a. The policy is issued for the benefit of the buyer.
  b. The policy guarantees that the buyer's equity will be protected.
  c. The amount of coverage is commensurate with the loan amount.
  d. The amount of coverage increases as the borrower's equity increases.

CHAPTER 14

Real Estate Financing: Principles

■ **LEARNING OBJECTIVES**   *When you have finished reading this chapter, you should be able to*

■ **identify** the basic provisions of security and debt instruments: promissory notes, mortgage documents, deeds of trust, and land contracts;

■ **describe** the effect of discount points on yield;

■ **explain** the procedures involved in a foreclosure;

■ **distinguish** between lien and title theories;

■ **explain** the three methods of foreclosure; and

■ **define** the following *key terms:*

acceleration clause	foreclosure	owner financing
alienation clause	hypothecation	prepayment penalty
assume	interest	promissory note
beneficiary	lien theory	release deed
deed in lieu of foreclosure	loan origination fee	satisfaction
deed of trust	mortgage	statutory right of
defeasance clause	mortgagee	redemption
deficiency judgment	mortgagor	subject to
discount points	negotiable instrument	title theory
equitable right of	note	trustor
redemption	novation	usury

■ REAL ESTATE FINANCING PRINCIPLES

Perhaps the most important investment decision your clients will ever make is the one you help them with: buying a home. In the United States, relatively few homes are purchased for cash. Most homes are bought with borrowed money, and a huge lending industry has been built to service the financial requirements of homebuyers. Knowing how real estate financing works, then, is especially important to become a successful licensee. If the buyer can't get funding to purchase the property, there can be no transaction.

Chapters 14 and 15 will help you understand how to guide your customers through a process that enables them to buy or sell their property. A borrower and a lender can tailor financing instruments to suit the type of transaction and the financial needs of both parties.

IN PRACTICE Although it is best for licensees to refer consumers to a lender to be preapproved for a loan prior to writing a real estate sales contract, it is important for the licensee to be knowledgeable about real estate financing programs and products in order to provide quality service, especially when serving as buyer agents.

■ MORTGAGE LAW

A **mortgage** is a lien or encumbrance on the real property of a debtor, called a mortgagor. The borrower, or **mortgagor**, receives a loan and in return gives a note and mortgage to the lender, called the **mortgagee**. When the loan is paid in full, the mortgagee issues a satisfaction of mortgage. The mortgage is a voluntary, specific lien. If the debtor defaults, the lender can sue on the note and foreclose on the mortgage.

In **title theory** states, the mortgagor actually gives *legal title* to the mortgagee (or some other designated individual) and retains *equitable title*. Legal title is returned to the mortgagor only when the debt is paid in full (or some other obligation is performed). In theory, the lender actually owns the property until the debt is paid. The lender allows the borrower to have all the usual rights of ownership, such as possession and use. In effect, because the lender actually holds legal title, the lender has the right to immediate possession of the real estate and rents from the mortgaged property if the mortgagor defaults.

In **lien theory** states, the mortgagor retains both legal and equitable title. The mortgagee simply has a lien on the property as security for the mortgage debt. The mortgage, or deed of trust, is nothing more than collateral for the loan. If the mortgagor defaults, the mortgagee must go through a formal foreclosure proceeding to obtain legal title. The property is offered for sale at public auction, and the funds from the sale are used to pay the balance of the remaining debt. In some states, a defaulting mortgagor may *redeem* (buy back) the property during a certain period *after the sale*. A borrower who fails to redeem the property during that time loses the property irrevocably.

IN PRACTICE In reality, the differences between the parties' rights in a lien theory state and those in a title theory state are more technical than actual. Regardless of the theory practiced in any particular state, all borrowers and lenders observe the same general requirements to protect themselves in a loan transaction. As with any contract, the parties must be legally competent, their signatures valid and attested, and adequate consideration exchanged.

SECURITY AND DEBT

A basic principle of property law is that no one can convey more than he or she actually owns. This principle also applies to mortgages. The owner of a fee simple estate can mortgage the fee. The owner of a leasehold or subleasehold can mortgage that leasehold interest. The owner of a condominium unit can mortgage the fee interest in the condominium. Even the owner of a cooperative interest may be able to offer that personal property interest as collateral for a loan.

A mortgage loan, like all loans, creates a relationship between a debtor and a creditor. In the relationship, the creditor loans the debtor money for some purpose, and the debtor agrees to pay or pledges to pay the principal and interest according to an agreed schedule. The debtor agrees to offer some property or collateral to the creditor if the loan is not repaid.

Mortgage loans are secured loans. Mortgage loans have two parts: the debt itself and the security for the debt. When a property is mortgaged, the owner must *execute* (sign) two separate instruments—a promissory note stating the amount owed and a security document, either a mortgage or deed of trust, specifying the collateral used to secure the loan.

Hypothecation In mortgage lending practice, a borrower is required to pledge specific real property as security (collateral) for the loan. The debtor retains the right of possession and control, while the creditor receives an underlying equitable right in the pledged property. This type of pledging is termed **hypothecation**. The right to foreclose on the pledged property in the event a borrower defaults is contained in a security agreement, such as a mortgage or a deed of trust.

PROMISSORY NOTES

The **promissory note**, referred to as the *note* or *financing instrument*, is the borrower's personal promise to repay a debt according to agreed terms. The note exposes all the borrower's assets to claims by secured creditors. The mortgagor executes one or more promissory notes to total the amount of the debt.

A promissory note executed by a borrower (known as the *maker* or *payor*) is a contract complete in itself. It generally states the amount of the debt, the time and method of payment, and the rate of interest. When signed by the borrowers and other necessary parties, the note becomes a legally enforceable and fully negotiable instrument of debt. When the terms of the note are satisfied, the debt is discharged. If the terms of the note are not met, the lender may choose to sue to collect on the note or to foreclose.

A note need not be tied to a mortgage or a deed of trust. A note used as a debt instrument without any related collateral is called an unsecured note. Unsecured notes are used by banks and other lenders to extend short-term personal loans.

A **note** is a **negotiable instrument** like a check or bank draft. The lender who holds the note is referred to as the *payee* and may transfer the right to receive payment to a third party in one of two ways:

- By signing the instrument over (that is, by *assigning* it) to the third party
- By delivering the instrument to the third party

IN PRACTICE   All notes should be clearly dated. Accurate dates are essential because *time is of the essence* in every real estate contract. Also, the dates of the notes may be necessary to determine the chronological order of priority rights.

Interest

Interest is a charge for the use of money. A lender charges a percent of interest on the principal over the time of loan. Interest may be due at either the end or the beginning of each payment period. Payments made at the end of a period are known as payments *in arrears*. This payment method is the general practice, and mortgages often call for end-of-period payments due on the first of the following month. Payments may also be made at the beginning of each period and are known as payments *in advance*. Whether interest is charged in arrears or in advance is specified in the note. This distinction is important if the property is sold before the debt is repaid in full.

Usury   Charging interest in excess of the maximum rate allowed by law is called **usury**. To protect consumers from unscrupulous lenders, many states have enacted laws limiting the interest rate that may be charged on loans. In some states, the legal maximum rate is a fixed amount. In others, it is a floating interest rate, which is adjusted up or down at specific intervals based on a certain economic standard, such as the prime lending rate or the rate of return on government bonds.

Whichever approach is taken, lenders are penalized for making usurious loans. In some states, a lender that makes a usurious loan is permitted to collect the borrowed money, but only at the legal rate of interest. In others, a usurious lender may lose the right to collect any interest or may lose the entire amount of the loan in addition to the interest.

Loan origination fee   The processing of a mortgage application is known as *loan origination*. When a mortgage loan is originated, a **loan origination fee**, or transfer fee, is charged by most lenders to cover the expenses involved in generating the loan. These expenses include the loan officer's salary, paperwork, and the lender's other costs of doing business. A loan origination fee is not prepaid interest; rather, it is a charge that must be paid to the lender. The typical loan origination fee is 1 percent of the loan amount, although origination fees may range from one to three points (*one point* equals 1 percent of the loan amount).

IN PRACTICE Because many real estate loans are made by private loan companies that may not be covered by federal regulations, it is important that borrowers insist on receiving a statement in advance from their lender that clearly states the total amount of the loan closing costs and the effective interest rate, in order to avoid unpleasant surprises at closing.

Discount points are used to increase the lender's yield (rate of return) on its investment. For example, the interest rate that a lender charges for a loan might be less than the yield an investor demands. To make up the difference, the lender charges the borrower discount points. The number of points charged depends on two factors:

- The difference between the loan's stated interest rate and the yield required by the lender
- How long the lender expects it will take the borrower to pay off the loan

> A **point** is 1 percent of the amount being borrowed; it is *not* 1 percent of the purchase price.

For borrowers, one discount point equals 1 percent of the loan amount and is charged as prepaid interest at the closing. For instance, three discount points charged on a $100,000 loan would be $3,000 ($100,000 × 3 percent, or 0.03). If a house sells for $100,000 and the borrower seeks an $80,000 loan, each point would be $800, *not* $1,000. In some cases, however, the points in a new acquisition may be paid in cash at closing by the buyer (or, of course, by the seller on the buyer's behalf) rather than being financed as part of the total loan amount.

To figure how many points are charged on a loan, divide the total dollar amount of the points by the amount of the loan. For example, if the loan amount is $350,000 and the charge for points is $9,275, how many points are being charged?

$9,275 ÷ $350,000 = 0.0265 or 2.65% or 2.65 points

Prepayment penalty Most mortgage loans are paid in installments over a long period of time. As a result, the total interest paid by the borrower may add up to more than the principal amount of the loan. That does not come as a surprise to the lender; the total amount of accrued interest is carefully calculated during the origination phase to determine the profitability of each loan. If the borrower repays the loan before the end of the term, the lender collects less than the anticipated interest. For this reason, some mortgage notes contain a *prepayment clause*. This clause requires that the borrower pay a **prepayment penalty** against the unearned portion of the interest for any payments made ahead of schedule.

The penalty may be as little as 1 percent of the balance due at the time of prepayment or as much as all the interest due for the first ten years of the loan. Some lenders allow the borrower to pay off a certain percentage of the original loan without paying a penalty. However, if the loan is paid in full, the borrower may be charged a percentage of the principal paid in excess of that allowance. *Lenders may not charge prepayment penalties on mortgage loans insured or guaranteed by the federal government or on those loans that have been sold to Fannie Mae or Freddie Mac.*

IN PRACTICE   Some states limit the amount of prepayment penalty that lenders may impose, while others prohibit lenders from charging any penalty at all on prepaid residential mortgage or deed of trust loans. Some states allow lenders to charge a prepayment penalty *only* if the loan is paid off with funds borrowed from another source.

■ MORTGAGES OR DEEDS OF TRUST

In some situations, lenders may prefer to use a three-party instrument known as a **deed of trust**. A trust deed conveys naked title or bare legal title—that is, title without the right of possession. The deed is given as security for the loan to a third party, called the *trustee*. The trustee holds bare title on behalf of the lender, who is known as the **beneficiary**. The beneficiary is the holder of the note. The conveyance establishes the actions that the trustee' may take if the borrower, the **trustor**, defaults under any of the deed of trust terms. (See Figures 14.1 and 14.2 for a comparison of mortgages and deeds of trust.) In states where deeds of trust are generally preferred, foreclosure procedures for default are usually simpler and faster than for mortgage loans.

Usually, the lender chooses the trustee and reserves the right to substitute trustees in the event of death or dismissal. State law usually dictates who may serve as trustee. Although the deed of trust is particularly popular in certain states, it is used all over the country. For example, in the financing of a commercial or an industrial real estate venture that involves a large loan and several lenders, the borrower generally executes a single deed of trust to secure as many notes as necessary.

A mortgage or deed of trust must clearly establish that the property is security for a debt, identify the lender and the borrower, and include an accurate legal description of the property. Both instruments incorporate the terms of the note by reference. They should be signed by all parties who have an interest in the real estate. Common provisions of both instruments are discussed in the following paragraphs.

FIGURE 14.1

Mortgages

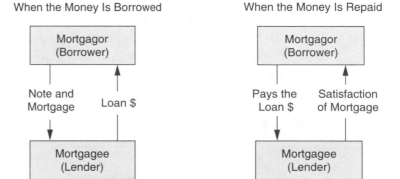

Mortgage —Two Parties

When the Money Is Borrowed

When the Money Is Repaid

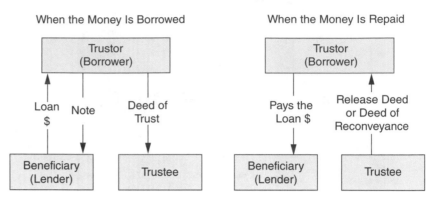

Deed of Trust—Three Parties

Duties of the Mortgagor or Trustor

The borrower is required to fulfill certain obligations created by the mortgage or deed of trust. These usually include the following:

- Payment of the debt in accordance with the terms of the note
- Payment of all real estate taxes on the property given as security
- Maintenance of adequate insurance to protect the lender if the property is destroyed or damaged by fire, windstorm, or other hazard
- Maintenance of the property in good repair at all times
- Receipt of lender authorization before making any major alterations on the property

Failure to meet any of these obligations can result in a borrower's default. The loan documents may, however, provide for a grace period (such as 30 days) during which the borrower can meet the obligation and cure the default. If the borrower does not do so, the lender has the right to foreclose the mortgage or deed of trust and collect on the note.

Provisions for Default

The mortgage or deed of trust typically includes an **acceleration clause** to assist the lender in foreclosure. If a borrower defaults, the lender has the right to accelerate the maturity of the debt. This means the lender may declare the *entire* debt due and payable *immediately*. Without an acceleration clause, the lender would have to sue the borrower every time a payment was overdue.

Other provisions in a mortgage or deed of trust enable the lender to take care of the property in the event of the borrower's negligence or default. If the borrower does not pay taxes or insurance premiums, or fails to make necessary repairs on the property, the lender may step in and do so. The lender has the power to protect the security (the real estate).

I N P R A C T I C E In financing real estate sales, lenders seldom accept unsecured promissory notes because there would be no security for the loans. If borrowers defaulted, the lender would be forced to sue for a money judgment. In the meantime, the debtor might dispose of the property and hide assets. In some states, a money judgment cannot be used to foreclose on a debtor's personal residence. Because of these, and other reasons, lenders prefer a security interest in real property. The mortgage (or deed of trust) is known as the security instrument. The security instrument creates the lien on the property. The mortgage allows the lender to sue for foreclosure in the event the borrower defaults.

Assignment of the Mortgage

Without changing the provisions of a contract, a note may be sold to a third party, such as an investor or another mortgage company. The original mortgagee endorses the note to the third party and executes an *assignment of mortgage*. The assignee becomes the new owner of the debt and security instrument. When the debt is paid in full (or satisfied), the assignee is required to execute the satisfaction (or release) of the security instrument.

Release of the Mortgage Lien or Deed of Trust

When all loan payments have been made and the note has been paid in full, the borrower will want the public record to show that the debt has been satisfied and that the lender is divested of all rights conveyed under the mortgage or deed of trust. By the provisions of the **defeasance clause** in the document, the lender is required to execute a **satisfaction** (also known as a *release* or *discharge*) when the note has been fully paid. This document returns to the borrower all interest in the real estate originally conveyed to the lender. Entering this release in the public record shows that the debt has been removed from the property.

The release must be executed and recorded by the assignee or mortgagee when the mortgage or deed of trust has been assigned.

When a real estate loan secured by a deed of trust has been completely repaid, the beneficiary must make a written request that the trustee convey the title to the property back to the grantor. The trustee executes and delivers a **release deed** (sometimes called a *deed of reconveyance*) to the trustor. The release deed conveys the same rights and powers that the trustee was given under the deed of trust. The release deed should be acknowledged (notarized) and recorded in the public records of the county in which the property is located.

Tax and Insurance Reserves

Many lenders require that borrowers provide a reserve fund to meet future real estate taxes and property insurance premiums. This fund is called an *impound* or *escrow account*. When the mortgage or deed of trust loan is made, the borrower starts the reserve by depositing funds to cover the amount of unpaid real estate taxes. If a new insurance policy has just been purchased, the insurance premium reserve will be started with the deposit of one-twelfth of the insurance premium liability. The borrower's monthly loan payments will include PITI: principal, interest, taxes, and insurance. Other costs are included, such as flood insurance. Federal regulations limit the total amount of reserves that a lender may require.

> The basic recurring components of a borrower's monthly loan payment may be remembered as **PITI**: Principal, Interest, Taxes, and Insurance

Flood insurance reserves   The National Flood Insurance Reform Act of 1994 imposes certain mandatory obligations on lenders and loan servicers to set aside (*escrow*) funds for flood insurance on new loans for property in flood-prone areas. This means that if a lender or servicer discovers that a secured property is in a flood hazard area, it must notify the borrower. The borrower then has 45 days to purchase flood insurance. If the borrower fails to procure flood insurance, the lender must purchase the insurance on the borrower's behalf. The cost of the insurance may be charged back to the borrower.

Buying "Subject to" or Assuming a Seller's Mortgage or Deed of Trust

When a person purchases real estate that has an outstanding mortgage or deed of trust, the buyer may take the property in one of two ways. The property may be purchased **subject to** the mortgage or deed of trust, or the buyer may **assume** the mortgage or deed of trust and agree to pay the debt. This technical distinction becomes important if the buyer defaults and the mortgage or deed of trust is foreclosed.

When the property is sold *subject to* the mortgage, the buyer is not personally obligated to pay the debt in full. The buyer takes title to the real estate knowing that he or she must make payments on the existing loan. Upon default, the lender forecloses and the property is sold by court order to pay the debt. If the sale does not pay off the entire debt, the purchaser is not liable for the difference. In some circumstances, however, the original seller might continue to be liable.

In contrast, a buyer who purchases a property and assumes the seller's debt becomes personally obligated for the payment of the entire debt. If a seller wants to be completely free of the original mortgage loan, the seller(s), buyer(s), and lender must execute a **novation** agreement in writing. The novation makes the buyer solely responsible for any default on the loan. The original borrower (seller) is freed of any liability for the loan.

The existence of a lien does not prevent the transfer of property; however, when a secured loan is assumed, the mortgagee or beneficiary must approve the assumption and any release of liability of the original mortgagor or trustor. Because a loan may not be assumed without lender approval, the lending institution would require the assumer to qualify financially, and many lending institutions charge a transfer fee to cover the costs of changing the records. This charge can be paid by either the buyer or the seller.

Alienation clause   The lender may want to prevent a future purchaser of the property from being able to assume the loan, particularly if the original interest rate is low. For this reason, most lenders include an **alienation clause** (also known as a *resale clause*, *due-on-sale clause*, or *call clause*) in the note. An alienation clause provides that when the property is sold, the lender may either declare the entire debt due immediately or permit the buyer to assume the loan at an interest rate acceptable to the lender. Land contracts that involve a due-on-sale clause also limit the assumption of the contract.

Recording a Mortgage or Deed of Trust

The mortgage document or deed of trust must be recorded in the recorder's office of the county in which the real estate is located. Recording gives constructive notice to the world of the borrower's obligations. Recording also establishes the lien's priority. (See Chapter 10.) If the property is registered in the Torrens system, notice of the lien must be entered on the original Torrens certificate.

Priority of a Mortgage or Deed of Trust

Priority of mortgages and other liens normally is determined by the order in which they were recorded. A mortgage or deed of trust on land that has no prior mortgage lien is a *first mortgage* or *deed of trust*. If the owner later executes another loan for additional funds, the new loan becomes a *second mortgage* or *deed of trust* (or a *junior lien*) when it is recorded. Second loans represent greater risk to the lender, and they usually have a higher interest rate.

In the event that a second lien has a higher amount than the first, the lender may require a *subordination agreement*, in which the first lender subordinates or lowers its lien position to that of the second lender. To be valid, both lenders must sign the agreement.

▪ PROVISIONS OF LAND CONTRACTS AND OWNER FINANCING

Real estate can be purchased under a land contract, also known as a *contract for deed* or an *installment contract*. (See Chapter 11.) Real estate is usually sold on contract for specific financial reasons. For instance, mortgage financing may be unavailable to a borrower for some reason. High interest rates may make borrowing too expensive. Or the purchaser may not have a sufficient down payment to cover the difference between a mortgage loan and the selling price.

Under a land contract, the buyer (called the *vendee*) agrees to make a down payment and a monthly loan payment that includes interest and principal. The payment may also include real estate tax and insurance reserves. The seller (called the *vendor*) retains legal title to the property during the contract term, and the buyer is granted equitable title and possession. At the end of the loan term, the seller delivers clear title. The contract usually permits the seller to evict the buyer in the event of default. In that case, the seller may keep any money the buyer has already paid, which is construed as rent. Many states now offer some legal protection to a defaulting buyer under a land contract.

While land contracts or **owner financing** can occur with residential or commercial properties, they are more common with unimproved acreage and farmland sales. Sometimes the seller is the primary lender, and at other times, the seller may be in a secondary position. In either case, the sellers would want to secure their interest either by the use of a deed, note and mortgage, deed of trust, or perhaps the use of a contract for deed instrument.

FORECLOSURE

When a borrower defaults on the payments or fails to fulfill any of the other obligations set forth in the mortgage or deed of trust, the lender's rights can be enforced through foreclosure. **Foreclosure** is a legal procedure in which property pledged as security is sold to satisfy the debt. The foreclosure procedure brings the rights of the parties and all junior lienholders to a conclusion. It passes title to either the person holding the mortgage document or deed of trust or to a third party who purchases the property at a *foreclosure sale*. The purchaser could be the mortgagee. The property is sold *free of the foreclosing mortgage and all junior liens.*

Methods of Foreclosure

There are three general types of foreclosure proceedings—judicial, nonjudicial, and strict foreclosure. The specific provisions and procedures depend on state law.

Judicial foreclosure   Judicial foreclosure allows the property to be sold by court order after the mortgagee has given sufficient public notice. When a borrower defaults, the lender may *accelerate* the due date of the remaining principal balance, along with all overdue monthly payments and interest, penalties, and administrative costs. The lender's attorney can then file a suit to foreclose the lien. After presentation of the facts in court, the property is ordered sold. A public sale is advertised and held, and the real estate is sold to the highest bidder.

Nonjudicial foreclosure   Some states allow nonjudicial foreclosure procedures to be used when the security instrument contains a *power-of-sale clause*. In nonjudicial foreclosure, no court action is required. In those states that recognize deed of trust loans, the trustee is generally given the power of sale. Some states allow a similar power of sale to be used with a mortgage loan.

To institute a nonjudicial foreclosure, the trustee or mortgagee may be required to record a notice of default at the county recorder's office. The default must be recorded within a designated period to give notice to the public of the intended auction. The notice is generally provided by newspaper advertisements that state the total amount due and the date of the public sale. After selling the property, the trustee or mortgagee may be required to file a copy of a notice of sale or an affidavit of foreclosure.

Strict foreclosure   Although judicial foreclosure is the prevalent practice, it is still possible in some states for a lender to acquire mortgaged property through a *strict foreclosure* process. First, appropriate notice must be given to the delinquent borrower. Once the proper papers have been prepared and recorded, the court establishes a deadline for the balance of the defaulted debt to be paid in full. If the borrower does not pay off the loan by that date, the court simply awards full legal title to the lender. No sale takes place.

Deed in Lieu of Foreclosure

As an alternative to foreclosure, a lender may accept a **deed in lieu of foreclosure** from the borrower. This is sometimes known as a *friendly foreclosure* because it is carried out by mutual agreement rather than by lawsuit. The disadvantage of the deed in lieu of foreclosure is to the lender because it does not eliminate junior liens. In a foreclosure action, all junior liens are eliminated. Also, by accepting a deed in lieu of foreclosure, the lender usually loses any rights pertaining to FHA or private mortgage insurance or to VA guarantees. Finally, it should be pointed out that a deed in lieu of foreclosure is still considered an adverse element in the borrower's credit history.

Redemption

Most states give defaulting borrowers a chance to redeem their property through the **equitable right of redemption**. (See Chapter 10.) If, after default *but before the foreclosure sale*, the borrower (or any other person who has an interest in the real estate, such as another creditor) pays the lender the amount in default, plus costs, the debt will be reinstated. In some cases, the person who redeems may be required to repay the accelerated loan in full. If some person other than the mortgagor or trustor redeems the real estate, the borrower becomes responsible to that person for the amount of the redemption.

Certain states also allow defaulted borrowers a period in which to redeem their real estate after the sale. During this period (which may be as long as one year), the borrower has a **statutory right of redemption**. The mortgagor who can raise the necessary funds to redeem the property within the statutory period pays the redemption money to the court. Because the debt was paid from the proceeds of the sale, the borrower can take possession free and clear of the former defaulted loan. The court may appoint a receiver to take charge of the property, collect rents, and pay operating expenses during the redemption period. (See Figure 14.3.)

Deed to Purchaser at Sale

If redemption is not made or if state law does not provide for a redemption period, the successful bidder at the sale receives a deed to the real estate. Officials such as a sheriff, an officer of the court, or a trustee executes this deed to the purchaser to *convey whatever title the borrower had.*

FIGURE 14.3

Redemption

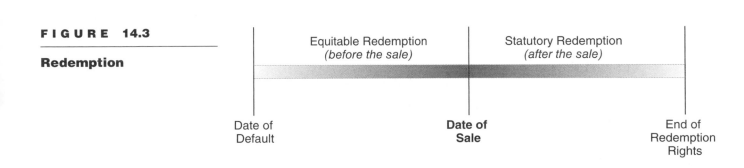

| Equitable Redemption *(before the sale)* | Statutory Redemption *(after the sale)* |

Date of Default   Date of **Sale**   End of Redemption Rights

Deficiency Judgment

The foreclosure sale may not produce enough cash to pay the loan balance in full after deducting expenses and accrued unpaid interest. In this case, the mortgagee may be entitled to a *personal judgment* against the borrower for the unpaid balance. Such a judgment is a **deficiency judgment**. It may also be obtained against any endorsers or guarantors of the note and against any owners of the mortgaged property who assumed the debt by written agreement. However, if any money remains from the foreclosure sale after paying the debt and any other liens (such as a second mortgage or a mechanic's lien), expenses, and interest, these proceeds are paid to the borrower.

■ KEY POINT REVIEW

In a **mortgage**, the **mortgagor** (owner) borrows money from the **mortgagee** (lender), and the real estate is used as **security** for the debt.

The term **mortgage** refers to any **financing instrument** by which real estate is used as **security** for a debt. The mortgage can take the form of either a **mortgage lien** or a **deed of trust**.

A **mortgage lien** on property is the common-law form of mortgage with the following characteristics:

- **Lien-theory** states have specific requirements that must be met.
- A **mortgage document** is executed by the borrower and **recorded** in the county in which the property is located.
- When a loan is paid in full, a **defeasance clause** requires the lender to execute a **satisfaction** (**release** or **discharge**) that is **recorded** to clear title.
- If the borrower **defaults**, the lender can **accelerate** the due date of the remaining principal balance and all other payments and costs.
- If the borrower continues in default, the lender can bring court action called **judicial foreclosure** where
  — the **judge** orders the property sold;
  — the **public sale** is advertised and the real estate is sold to the **highest bidder**;
  — the borrower has **equitable right of redemption** within a time period (before and/or after sale) allowed by state law;
  — no court action is necessary to begin the sale process if the mortgage or deed of trust has a **power-of-sale** clause;
  — the mortgagee may have the right to a **deficiency judgment** against the borrower for an unpaid balance, **when allowed by state law**, if the sale proceeds are less than the amount owed;
  — the court can **award title** to the **lender** and no sale occurs if it is a **strict foreclosure**; and
  — the lender may accept a **deed in lieu of foreclosure** from a defaulting borrower, but title is **subject to junior liens** that are eliminated in a foreclosure.

A **deed of trust** transfers **title** from the **trustor** (property owner) to a **trustee,** who holds it on behalf of a **beneficiary** (lender). Note the following:

- **Title-theory** states have specific requirements that must be met.
- A **deed of trust** executed by the borrower is **recorded** in the county in which property is located.
- The **mortgagor** transfers **legal title** to the **mortgagee** but retains **equitable title** and has the right to **possession and use** of the mortgaged property.
- When the loan is paid in full, a **defeasance clause** requires the beneficiary to request the **trustee** to execute and deliver to the trustor a **release deed (deed of reconveyance)** to return legal title to the trustor.
- If the borrower **defaults**, the lender can **accelerate** the due date of the remaining principal balance and all overdue costs.
- If the borrower continues in default, a **deed of trust with power of sale** allows the beneficiary (lender) to ask the trustee to conduct the **trustee's sale** without court action.

Priority of mortgages and other liens is determined by the order in which they were recorded. **Priority** may be changed by **subordination agreement**.

An impound (escrow) account may be required to create a reserve fund to ensure that future tax, property insurance, and other payments are made.

- **Borrower** funds the account through an increase in loan payment that can be remembered as **PITI**: **P**rincipal, **I**nterest, **T**axes, and **I**nsurance.
- **Lender** makes tax, insurance, and other payments on the **borrower's behalf**.
- The **National Flood Insurance Reform Act of 1994** imposes obligations on lenders and loan servicers to set aside escrow funds for flood insurance on new loans for property in flood-prone areas.

When property with an **outstanding mortgage or deed of trust** is conveyed, the new owner may take title in one of two ways, if allowed by the loan document:

1. **"Subject to"**—the **new owner** makes payments on existing loans but is **not personally liable** if the property is sold on default and proceeds of the sale do not satisfy debt. "Subject to" is no longer in use.
2. **Assuming** the existing mortgage or deed of trust and agreeing to pay the debt, where the **new owner** takes personal responsibility for existing loans and is subject to a **deficiency judgment** if the property is sold on default and proceeds of the sale do not satisfy the debt.

An **alienation clause (due-on-sale clause)** in a loan document will prevent future purchasers of the property from assuming the loan.

A **novation** agreement may be used to release the seller from any future liability on loans secured by the real estate.

■ RELATED WEB SITE

Legal Information Institute: Mortgages:
http://topics.law.cornell.edu/wex/Mortgage/

CHAPTER 14 QUIZ

1. A charge of three discount points on a $120,000 loan equals
    a. $450.
    b. $3,600.
    c. $4,500.
    d. $116,400.

2. A prospective buyer needs to borrow money to buy a house. The buyer applies for and obtains a real estate loan from a mortgage company. Then the buyer signs a note and a mortgage. In this example, the buyer is referred to as the
    a. mortgagor.
    b. beneficiary.
    c. mortgagee.
    d. vendor.

3. In the previous question, the mortgage company is the
    a. mortgagor.
    b. beneficiary.
    c. mortgagee.
    d. vendor.

4. The borrower under a deed of trust is known as the
    a. trustor.
    b. trustee.
    c. beneficiary.
    d. vendee.

5. In a land contract, the vendee
    a. is not responsible for the real estate taxes on the property.
    b. does not pay interest and principal.
    c. has possession during the term of the contract.
    d. obtains legal title at closing.

6. A state law provides that lenders cannot charge more than 24 percent interest on any loan. This kind of law is called
    a. trustee law.
    b. a usury law.
    c. the statute of frauds.
    d. contract law.

7. After the foreclosure sale, a borrower who has defaulted on a loan may seek to pay off the mortgage debt plus any accrued interest and costs under what right?
    a. Equitable redemption
    b. Defeasance
    c. Usury
    d. Statutory redemption

8. Which clause would give a lender the right to have all future installments become due upon default?
    a. Escalation
    b. Defeasance
    c. Alienation
    d. Acceleration

9. What document is available to the mortgagor when the mortgage debt is completely repaid?
    a. Satisfaction of mortgage
    b. Defeasance certificate
    c. Deed of trust
    d. Mortgage estoppel

10. Under a typical land contract, when does the vendor give the deed to the vendee?
    a. When the contract is fulfilled and all payments have been made
    b. At the closing
    c. When the contract for deed is approved by the parties
    d. After the first year's real estate taxes are paid

11. A land contract provides for the
    a. sale of unimproved land only.
    b. sale of real property under an option agreement.
    c. conveyance of legal title at a future date.
    d. immediate transfer of reversionary rights.

12. All the following clauses in a loan agreement enable the lender to demand that the entire remaining debt be paid immediately *EXCEPT* a(n)

    a. due-on-sale clause.
    b. defeasance clause.
    c. acceleration clause.
    d. alienation clause.

13. Which of the following allows a mortgagee to proceed to a foreclosure sale without going to court first?

    a. Waiver of redemption right
    b. Power of sale
    c. Alienation clause
    d. Possession rights

14. The mortgagee foreclosed on a property after the borrower defaulted on the loan payments. At the foreclosure sale, however, the house sold for only $129,000. The unpaid balance of the loan at the time of the sale was $140,000. What must the lender do to recover the $11,000 the borrower still owes?

    a. Sue for damages
    b. Sue for specific performance
    c. Seek a judgment by default
    d. Seek a deficiency judgment

15. Discount points on a mortgage are computed as a percentage of the

    a. selling price.
    b. loan amount.
    c. closing costs.
    d. down payment.

16. In one state, a mortgagee holds legal title to real property offered as collateral for a loan, and the mortgagor retains the rights of possession and use. If the borrower defaults, the lender is entitled to immediate possession and rents. This state can be *BEST* characterized as what kind of state?

    a. Lien theory
    b. Mortgage theory
    c. Intermediate theory
    d. Title theory

17. In another state, a mortgagee holds a lien on real property offered as collateral for a loan. The mortgagor retains both legal and equitable title to real property. If the borrower defaults on the loan, the lender must go through formal fore-closure proceedings to recover the debt. This state can be *BEST* characterized as what kind of state?

    a. Lien theory
    b. Mortgage theory
    c. Intermediate theory
    d. Title theory

18. The seller agrees to sell the house to the buyer for $100,000. The buyer is unable to qualify for a mortgage loan for this amount, so the seller and the buyer enter into a contract for deed. The interest the buyer has in the property under a contract for deed is

    a. legal title.
    b. equitable title.
    c. joint title.
    d. mortgagee in possession.

19. A junior lien may become first in priority if the original lender agrees to execute a

    a. deed of trust.
    b. subordination agreement.
    c. second mortgage agreement.
    d. call clause.

20. A buyer purchased a home under an agreement that made the buyer personally obligated to continue making payments under the seller's existing mortgage. If the buyer defaults and the court sale of the property does not satisfy the debt, the buyer will be liable for making up the difference. The buyer has

    a. purchased the home subject to the seller's mortgage.
    b. assumed the seller's mortgage.
    c. benefited from the alienation clause in the seller's mortgage.
    d. benefited from the defeasance clause in the seller's mortgage.

15 CHAPTER

Real Estate Financing: Practice

■ **LEARNING OBJECTIVES** *When you have finished reading this chapter, you should be able to*

■ **identify** the types of institutions in the primary and secondary mortgage markets;

■ **describe** the various types of financing techniques available to real estate purchasers and the role of government financing regulations;

■ **explain** the requirements and qualifications for conventional, FHA, and VA loan programs;

■ **distinguish** among the different types of financing techniques that address borrowers' different needs; and

■ **define** the following *key terms*:

adjustable-rate mortgage (ARM)

amortized loan

balloon payment

blanket loan

buydown

certificate of reasonable value (CRV)

Community Reinvestment Act of 1977 (CRA)

computerized loan origination (CLO)

construction loan

conventional loan

Equal Credit Opportunity Act (ECOA)

Fannie Mae

Federal Deposit Insurance Corporation (FDIC)

Federal Reserve System (Fed)

FHA loan

Freddie Mac

Ginnie Mae

growing-equity mortgage

home equity loan

index

interest-only mortgage

loan-to-value (LTV) ratio

margin

mortgage insurance premium (MIP)

open-end loan

package loan

primary mortgage market

private mortgage insurance (PMI)

purchase-money mortgage (PMM)

Real Estate Settlement Procedures Act (RESPA)

Regulation Z

reverse mortgage

sale-and-leaseback

secondary mortgage market

straight loan

trigger terms

Truth in Lending Act

VA loan

wraparound loan

■ REAL ESTATE FINANCING: PRACTICE

Most real estate transactions require some form of financing. The real estate lending and borrowing environment is complex. As economic conditions change, the forces of supply and demand create a rapidly evolving mortgage market. The challenge for today's licensees is to maintain a working knowledge of the various financing options. By understanding financing techniques and payment options, licensees can be valuable participants in helping buyers reach their real estate goals.

■ INTRODUCTION TO THE REAL ESTATE FINANCING MARKET

The real estate financing market has the following three basic components:

■ Government influences, primarily the Federal Reserve System
■ The primary mortgage market
■ The secondary mortgage market

Under the umbrella of the financial policies set by the Federal Reserve System, the primary mortgage market originates loans that are bought, sold, and traded in the secondary mortgage market. Before turning to the specific types of mortgage options available to consumers, it is important to have a clear understanding of the bigger picture: the market in which those mortgages exist.

The Federal Reserve System

The role of the **Federal Reserve System** (the **Fed**) is to maintain sound credit conditions, help counteract inflationary and deflationary trends, and create a favorable economic climate. The Federal Reserve System divides the country into 12 federal reserve districts, each served by a federal reserve bank. All nationally chartered banks must join the Fed and purchase stock in its district reserve banks. The Federal Reserve System regulates the flow of money and interest rates in the marketplace through its member banks by controlling their *reserve requirements* and *discount rates*.

The Primary Mortgage Market

The **primary mortgage market** is made up of the lenders that originate mortgage loans. These lenders make money available directly to borrowers. From a borrower's point of view, a loan is a means of financing an expenditure; from a lender's point of view, a loan is an investment. All investors look for profitable returns on their investments. Income on the loan is realized from the following two sources:

■ *Finance charges* collected at closing, such as loan origination fees and discount points
■ *Recurring income*, the interest collected during the term of the loan

In addition to the income directly related to loans, some lenders derive income from servicing loans for other mortgage lenders or investors who have purchased the loans. Servicing involves

- collecting payments (including taxes and insurance),
- accounting,
- bookkeeping,
- preparing insurance and tax records,
- processing payments of taxes and insurance, and
- following up on loan payment and delinquency.

Some of the major lenders in the primary market include the following:

- *Thrifts, savings associations, and commercial banks.* These institutions are known as *fiduciary lenders* because of their fiduciary obligations to protect and preserve their depositors' funds. *Thrifts* is a generic term for the savings associations. Mortgage loans are perceived as secure investments for generating income and enable these institutions to pay interest to their depositors. Fiduciary lenders are subject to standards and regulations established by government agencies such as the **Federal Deposit Insurance Corporation (FDIC)**. The various government regulations (which include reserve fund, reporting, and insurance requirements) are intended to protect depositors against the reckless lending that characterized the savings and loan industry in the 1980s.
- *Insurance companies.* Insurance companies accumulate large sums of money from the premiums paid by their policyholders. While part of this money is held in reserve to satisfy claims and cover operating expenses, much of it is free to be invested in profit-earning enterprises, such as long-term real estate loans.
- *Credit unions.* Credit unions are cooperative organizations whose members place money in savings accounts. In the past, credit unions made only short-term consumer and home improvement loans. Now, they routinely originate longer-term first and second mortgage and deed of trust loans.
- *Pension funds.* Pension funds usually have large amounts of money available for investment. Because of the comparatively high yields and low risks offered by mortgages, pension funds have begun to participate actively in financing real estate projects. Most real estate activity for pension funds is handled through mortgage bankers and mortgage brokers.
- *Endowment funds.* Many commercial banks and mortgage bankers handle investments for endowment funds. The endowments of hospitals, universities, colleges, charitable foundations, and other institutions provide a good source of financing for low-risk commercial and industrial properties.
- *Investment group financing.* Large real estate projects, such as high-rise apartment buildings, office complexes, and shopping centers, are often financed as joint ventures through group financing arrangements like syndicates, limited partnerships, and real estate investment trusts.
- *Mortgage banking companies.* Mortgage banking companies originate mortgage loans with money belonging to insurance companies, pension funds, and individuals, and with funds of their own. They make real estate loans with the intention of selling them to investors and receiving a fee for

Primary Mortgage Market

- Thrifts
- Savings associations
- Commercial banks
- Insurance companies
- Credit unions
- Pension funds
- Endowment funds
- Investment group financing
- Mortgage banking companies

servicing the loans. Mortgage banking companies are generally organized as stock companies. As a source of real estate financing, they are subject to fewer lending restrictions than are commercial banks or savings associations. They are *not* mortgage brokers.

■ *Mortgage brokers.* Mortgage brokers are not lenders. They are intermediaries who bring borrowers and lenders together. Mortgage brokers locate potential borrowers, process preliminary loan applications, and submit the applications to lenders for final approval. They do not service loans once the loans are made. Mortgage brokers also may be real estate brokers who offer these financing services in addition to their regular real estate brokerage activities. Many state governments are establishing separate licensure requirements for mortgage brokers to regulate their activities.

IN PRACTICE   A growing number of consumers apply for mortgage loans via the Internet. Many major lenders have Web sites that offer information to potential borrowers regarding their current loan programs and requirements. In addition, online brokerages link lenders with potential borrowers. Some borrowers prefer the Internet for its convenience in shopping for the best rates and terms, accessing a wide variety of loan programs, and speeding up the loan approval process.

The Secondary Mortgage Market

In addition to the primary mortgage market, where loans are originated, there is a **secondary mortgage market**. The secondary mortgage market helps lenders raise capital to continue making mortgage loans. Furthermore, the secondary market is especially useful when money is in short supply; it stimulates both the housing construction market and the mortgage market by expanding the types of loans available.

In the secondary mortgage market, loans are bought and sold only after they have been funded. Lenders routinely sell loans to avoid interest rate risks and to realize profits on the sales. This secondary market activity helps lenders raise capital to continue making mortgage loans. Secondary market activity is especially desirable when money is in short supply; it stimulates both the housing construction market and the mortgage market by expanding the types of loans available. Growth in the use of secondary markets has greatly increased the standardization of loans. When a loan is sold, the original lender may continue to collect the payments from the borrower. The lender then passes the payments along to the investor who purchased the loan. The investor is charged a fee for servicing of the loan.

In the secondary market, various agencies purchase a number of mortgage loans and assemble them into packages (called *pools*). These agencies purchase the mortgages from banks and savings associations. Securities that represent shares in these pooled mortgages are then sold to investors or other agencies. (See Table 15.1.)

Fannie Mae   In September 2008, **Fannie Mae** (Federal National Mortgage Association) became a government-owned enterprise. Until that time, it was organized as a completely privately owned corporation that issued its own stock. Then, as now, it provides a secondary market for mortgage loans. Fannie Mae deals

TABLE 15.1	Institution	Secondary Market Function
Secondary Mortgage Market	Fannie Mae	Conventional, VA, FHA loans
	Freddie Mac	Mostly conventional loans
	Ginnie Mae	Special assistance loans

in conventional and Federal Housing Administration (FHA) and Department of Veterans Affairs (VA) loans. Fannie Mae buys from a lender a *block* or *pool* of mortgages that may then be used as collateral for *mortgage-backed securities* that are sold on the global market.

Freddie Mac Freddie Mac (Federal Home Loan Mortgage Corporation) is also now a government-owned enterprise, similar to Fannie Mae, that provides a secondary market for mortgage loans, primarily conventional loans.

Many lenders use the standardized forms and follow the guidelines issued by Fannie Mae and Freddie Mac. In fact, the use of such forms is mandatory for lenders that wish to sell mortgages in the agencies' secondary mortgage market. The standardized documents include loan applications, credit reports, and appraisal forms.

Ginnie Mae Ginnie Mae (Government National Mortgage Association) has always been a governmental agency. Ginnie Mae is a division of the Department of Housing and Urban Development (HUD), organized as a corporation without capital stock. Ginnie Mae administers special-assistance programs and guarantees mortgage-backed securities using FHA and VA loans as collateral. Ginnie Mae guarantees investment securities issued by private offerors (such as banks, mortgage companies, and savings and loan associations) and backed by pools of FHA and VA mortgage loans. The *Ginnie Mae pass-through certificate* is a security interest in a pool of mortgages that provides for a monthly pass-through of principal and interest payments directly to the certificate holder. Such certificates are guaranteed by Ginnie Mae.

■ FINANCING TECHNIQUES

Real estate financing comes in a wide variety of forms. While the payment plans described in the following sections are commonly referred to as *mortgages*, they are really *loans* secured by either a mortgage or a deed of trust.

Straight Loans

A **straight loan** (also known as a *term loan* or *interest-only loan*) essentially divides the loan into two amounts to be paid off separately. The borrower makes periodic payments of interest only, followed by the payment of the principal *in full at the end of the term*. Straight loans were once the only form of mortgage available. Today, they are generally used for home improvements and second mortgages rather than for residential first mortgage loans.

Interest-Only Mortgage

An **interest-only mortgage** is a mortgage that requires the payment of interest only for a stated period of time with the principal balance due at the end of the term. In the past, interest-only mortgages have been used for short-term financing. But today, interest-only mortgages have become a popular option, not only for home improvements and second mortgages, but also for long-term first mortgages. The InterestFirst™ mortgage requires payment of interest only for 10 years or 15 years, with the principal balance plus interest recalculated over the remaining years of the loan.

Balloon Payment Loan

When the periodic payments are not enough to fully amortize the loan by the time the final payment is due, the final payment is larger than the others. This final payment is called a **balloon payment**. It is a *partially amortized loan* because some of the principal is still owed at the end of the term.

MATH CONCEPTS

BALLOON PAYMENT LOAN

Consider a loan with the following terms: $130,000 at 6 percent interest, with interest only payable monthly and the loan fully repayable in 15 years. The following illustrates how to calculate the amount of the final balloon payment:

$130,000 × 0.06 = $7,800 annual interest

$7,800 annual interest ÷ 12 months = $650 monthly interest payment

$130,000 principal payment + $650 final month's interest

= $130,650 final balloon payment

It is frequently assumed that if payments are made promptly, the lender will extend the balloon payment for another limited term. The lender, however, is not legally obligated to grant this extension and can require payment in full when the note is due.

Amortized Loans

Unlike a straight loan payment, the payment in an **amortized loan** partially pays off both principal and interest. Most mortgage and deed in trust loans are amortized loans. The word *amortizes* literally means to kill off. They are paid off slowly, over time, in equal payments. Regular periodic payments are made over a term of years. The most common periods are 15 years or 30 years, although 20-year mortgages are also available. Each payment is applied first to the interest owed; the balance of the payment is then applied to the principal amount. At the end of the term, the full amount of the principal and all interest due is reduced to zero. Such loans are known as *direct reduction loans*.

Most amortized mortgage and deed of trust loans are paid in monthly installments. However, some are payable quarterly (four times a year) or semiannually (twice a year).

Different payment plans tend alternately to gain and lose favor with lenders and borrowers as the cost and availability of mortgage money fluctuate. The most frequently used plan is the *fully amortized loan*, or *level-payment loan*. The mortgagor pays a *constant amount*, usually monthly. The lender credits each payment first to the interest due, then to the principal amount of the loan. As a result, while each payment remains the same, the portion applied to repayment of the principal grows and the interest due declines as the unpaid balance of the loan is reduced. If the borrower pays additional amounts that are applied directly to the principal, the loan will amortize more quickly. This benefits the borrower who will then pay less interest if the loan is paid off before the end of its term. Of course, lenders are aware of this, too, and may guard against unprofitable loans by including penalties for early payment.

If you know what the monthly payment and interest rates are, you can determine the amount of the constant payment of an amortized loan from a prepared mortgage payment book or a mortgage factor chart. The mortgage factor chart indicates the amount of monthly payment per $1,000 of loan, depending on the term and interest rate. This factor is multiplied by the number of thousands (and fractions of thousands) of the amount borrowed.

IN PRACTICE Financial calculators can accurately perform most of the standard mortgage lending calculations, and most commercial lenders provide mortgage calculators on their Web sites. Nonetheless, it's valuable to understand how the calculations are performed.

Adjustable-Rate Mortgages (ARMs)

Adjustable-rate mortgages (ARMs) generally originate at one rate of interest, then fluctuate up or down during the loan term, based on an objective economic indicator. Because the interest rate may change, so may mortgagor's loan repayments. Details of how and when the interest rate will change are included in the note. Common components of an ARM include the following:

- The **index** is an undeterminable economic indicator that is used to adjust the interest rate in the loan. Most indexes are tied to U.S. Treasury securities.
- Usually, the interest rate is the index rate plus a premium, called the **margin**. The margin represents the lender's cost of doing business.
- *Rate caps* limit the amount the interest rate may change. Most ARMs have two types of rate caps—periodic and life-of-the-loan (or aggregate). A periodic rate cap limits the amount the rate may increase, usually over a year. A life-of-the-loan rate cap limits the amount the rate may increase over the entire life of the loan.
- The mortgagor is protected from unaffordable individual payments by the *payment cap*. The payment cap sets a maximum amount for payments.
- The adjustment establishes how often the rate may be changed, whether it be monthly, quarterly, or annually.
- Lenders may offer a conversion option that permits the mortgagor to convert from an adjustable-rate to a fixed-rate loan at certain intervals during the life of the mortgage.

T A B L E   15.2

Mortgage Factor Chart

Rate	Term 15 Years	Term 30 Years
6	8.44	6.00
6⅛	8.51	6.08
6¼	8.57	6.16
6⅜	8.64	6.24
6½	8.71	6.32
6⅝	8.78	6.40
6¾	8.85	6.49
6⅞	8.92	6.57
7	8.98	6.65
7⅛	9.06	6.74
7¼	9.12	6.82
7⅜	9.20	6.91
7½	9.27	6.99
7⅝	9.34	7.08
7¾	9.41	7.16
7⅞	9.48	7.25
8	9.56	7.34
8⅛	9.63	7.43
8¼	9.71	7.52
8⅜	9.78	7.61
8½	9.85	7.69
8⅝	9.93	7.78
8¾	10.00	7.87
8⅞	10.07	7.96
9	10.15	8.05

How To Use This Chart

To use this chart, start by finding the appropriate interest rate. Then follow that row over to the column for the appropriate loan term. This number is the *interest rate factor* required each month to amortize a $1,000 loan. To calculate the principal and interest (PI) payment, multiply the interest rate factor by the number of 1,000s in the total loan.

For example, if the interest rate is 8 percent for a term of 30 years, the interest rate factor is 7.34. If the total loan is $100,000, the loan contains 100 1,000s. Therefore, 100 × 7.34 = $734 PI only.

Growing-Equity Mortgage

A **growing-equity mortgage** is also known as a *rapid-payoff mortgage*. The growing-equity mortgage uses a fixed interest rate, but payments of principal are increased according to an index or a schedule. Thus, the total payment increases, and the loan is paid off more quickly. A growing-equity mortgage is most frequently used when the borrower's income is expected to keep pace with the increasing loan payments.

THE MORTGAGE AMORTIZATION TRIANGLE

If you know what the monthly payment and interest rate are, you can easily track how much of each month's payment is being applied toward principal and how much is applied toward interest.

Begin in the lower-left box and follow the arrows to perform the calculations described in each box for each month's calculation. Your result will show how much of a given month's mortgage payment goes to pay principal and what portion pays interest on the loan to the lender. For instance, if you wanted to see how much the loan principal would be reduced after three months, you would "go around the triangle" three times.

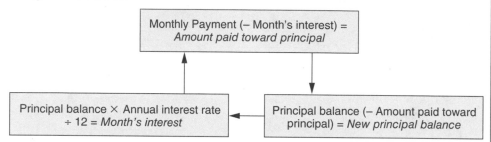

For example, using the Mortgage Factor Chart in Table 15.2, assume a 30-year mortgage loan for $150,000 at a 7.75% annual interest rate and a monthly payment of $1,074 ($150,000 \div 1,000 \times 7.16 = \$1,074$). You can see how the triangle can help you determine the amount of principal and interest in each payment for the first two months of the loan (shown in each box as "1" and "2").

The principal balance on the loan at the end of the second month (the beginning of the third month) is $149,788.84.

What is the principal balance on this loan at the end of the third month?

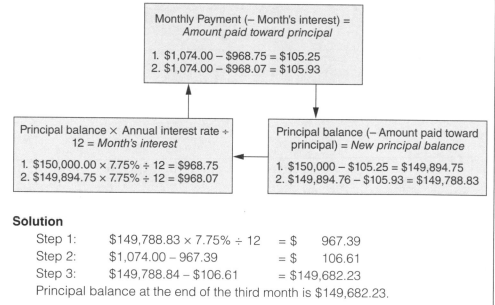

Solution

Step 1:	$149,788.83 \times 7.75\% \div 12$	= $	967.39
Step 2:	$1,074.00 - 967.39$	= $	106.61
Step 3:	$149,788.84 - $106.61	= $	149,682.23

Principal balance at the end of the third month is $149,682.23.

Reverse Mortgage

A **reverse mortgage** allows people 62 or older to borrow money against the equity they have built in their home. Reverse mortgages are the opposite of conventional mortgages in that the homeowner's equity diminishes as the loan amount increases. The money may be used for any purpose and the borrowers decide if they want to receive the money in a lump sum, fixed monthly payments, an open line of credit, or other options. The borrower is charged a fixed rate of interest and no payments are due until the property is sold or the borrower defaults, moves, or dies. Though reverse mortgages have been available for almost 30 years, they have become more widespread as people live longer and need more money. The FHA home equity conversion mortgage (HECM) is one of the more common reverse mortgages.

■ LOAN PROGRAMS

Mortgage loans are generally classified based on their **loan-to-value (LTV) ratio**. The LTV is the ratio of debt to value of the property. Value is the sales price or the appraisal value, whichever is less. The *lower* the ratio of debt to value, the *higher* the down payment by the borrower. For the lender, the higher down payment means a more secure loan, which minimizes the lender's risk.

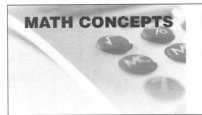

MATH CONCEPTS

DETERMINING LTV

If a property has an appraised value of $200,000, secured by an $180,000 loan, the LTV is 90 percent:

$180,000 ÷ $200,000 = 90%

Conventional Loans

Conventional loans are viewed as the most secure loans because their loan-to-value ratios are often lowest. Traditionally, the ratio is 80 percent of the value of the property or less because the borrower makes a down payment of at least 20 percent. The security for the loan is provided solely by the mortgage; the payment of the debt rests on the ability of the borrower to pay. In making such a loan, the lender relies primarily on its appraisal of the property. Information from credit reports that indicate the reliability of the prospective borrower is also important. Usually with a 20 percent down payment and a conventional loan, no additional insurance or guarantee on the loan is necessary to protect the lender's interest. A conventional loan is not government-insured or guaranteed, in contrast to FHA-insured and VA-guaranteed loans.

Lenders can set criteria by which a borrower and the collateral are evaluated to qualify for a loan. Today, the secondary mortgage market has a significant impact on borrower qualifications, standards for the collateral, and documentation procedures followed by lenders. Loans must meet strict criteria to be sold to Fannie Mae and Freddie Mac. Lenders still can be flexible in their lending decisions, but they may not be able to sell unusual loans in the secondary market.

To qualify for a conventional loan under Fannie Mae guidelines, for instance, the borrower's monthly housing expenses, including PITI (principal, interest, taxes, and insurance), must not exceed 28 percent of total monthly gross income. Also, the borrower's total monthly obligations, including housing costs plus other regular monthly payments, must not exceed 36 percent of total monthly gross income (80 percent LTV loans). Loans that meet these criteria are called *conforming loans* and are eligible to be sold in the secondary market.

IN PRACTICE   The Federal Housing Finance Agency (FHFA) publishes the maximum loan limits for loans sold to Fannie Mae. In 2010, the maximum loan limit for a single-family home ranges from $417,000 to $729,750 in high-cost areas. Specific loan limits are established for each county (or equivalent), and the loan limit may be lower for each specific high-cost area. The upper loan limit for loans that Freddie Mac will buy is $625,500.

Loans that exceed the limits are referred to as *nonconforming loans* and are not marketable, but they must be held in the lender's investment portfolio.

■ **FOR EXAMPLE**   Following is the qualifying math for a $160,000 loan at 7.5 percent interest for 30 years with payments of $1,200 per month in principal and interest:

Combined Monthly Gross Income $8,000

Monthly Housing Expenses:
Principal and Interest	1,200
Property Taxes	400
Hazard Insurance	50
PMI Insurance	90
Homeowners' Association Dues	+ 30
Total Housing Expense	$1,770

$1,770 ÷ 8,000 = 22%

Debt Expense:
Installment Payments	$200
Revolving Charges	80
Auto Loan	250
Child Care	300
Other	+ 200
Total Debt Expense	$1,030
Plus Housing	+ $1,770
Grand Total	$2,800

$2,800 ÷ 8,000 = 35%

These borrowers will qualify for this loan under conventional loan guidelines of 28 percent and 36 percent.

Private Mortgage Insurance

One way a borrower can obtain a conventional mortgage loan with a lower down payment is by obtaining **private mortgage insurance (PMI)**. In a PMI program, the buyer purchases an insurance policy that provides the lender with funds in the

Low LTV =
High down payment

High down payment =
Low lender risk

event that the borrower defaults on the loan. This allows the lender to assume more risk so that the loan-to-value ratio is higher than for other conventional loans. The borrower purchases insurance from a private mortgage insurance company as additional security to insure the lender against borrower default. In 2010, LTVs of up to 95 percent of the appraised value of the property are possible with mortgage insurance, although these percentages change.

PMI protects the top portion of a loan, usually 20 percent to 30 percent, against borrower default. The borrower pays a monthly premium or fee while the insurance is in force. The premium may be financed within the loan. When a borrower has limited funds available for an initial investment, these alternative methods of reducing closing costs are very important. Because only a portion of the loan is insured, once the loan is repaid to a certain level, the lender may agree to allow the borrower to terminate the PMI coverage. Practices for termination vary from lender to lender.

IN PRACTICE   On loans originating after July 1999, federal law requires that PMI automatically terminate if a borrower has accumulated at least 22 percent equity in the home *and* is current on mortgage payments. The 22 percent of equity is based on the purchase price of the home.

The requirement to automatically terminate does not take into consideration any credit given for appreciation of the property. Borrowers do have other options, however. The first option is to pay down the loan by making extra payments to bring the equity to 22 percent of the original purchase price. But, if the home is located in an area where homes have appreciated and/or if home improvements have been added, borrowers can petition that the lender drop the PMI. Most lenders require an appraisal, at the borrower's expense, that documents that the property has indeed risen in value. Lenders consider the payment history as well as the appraised value when deciding whether to drop PMI.

FHA-Insured Loans

The Federal Housing Administration (FHA), which operates under HUD, neither builds homes nor lends money. The common term **FHA loan** refers to a loan that is *insured* by the agency. These loans must be made by FHA-approved lending institutions. The FHA insurance provides security to the lender, in addition to the real estate. As with private mortgage insurance, the FHA insures lenders against loss from borrower default.

The most popular FHA program is Title II, Section 203(b), fixed-interest-rate loans for 10 years to 30 years on one- to four-family residences. Rates are competitive with other types of loans, even though they are high-LTV loans. According to the FHA Web site (in 2010), the borrower is eligible for approximately 96.5 percent financing for one- to four-unit structures. Certain technical requirements must be met before the FHA will insure the loans. These requirements include the following:

■ The borrower must pay a down payment of at least 3.5 percent of the purchase price, but most of the closing costs and fees can be included in the loan.

■ The borrower is charged a **mortgage insurance premium (MIP)** for all FHA loans. The *up-front premium* is charged at closing and can be financed into the mortgage loan. The borrower is also responsible for paying an annual premium that is usually charged monthly. The up-front premium is charged on all FHA loans, except those for the purchase of a condominium, which require only a monthly MIP.

■ The mortgaged real estate must be appraised by an *approved FHA appraiser*.

■ The FHA sets maximum mortgage limits for various regions of the country.

■ The borrower must meet standard FHA credit qualifications.

■ Financing for manufactured homes and factory-built housing is also available, both for those who own the land that the home is on and also for manufactured homes that are, or will be, located on another plot of land.

If the purchase price exceeds the FHA-appraised value, the buyer may pay the difference in cash as part of the down payment. Some exceptions are made for special programs, such as the Good Neighbor Program.

Other types of FHA loans are available, including one-year adjustable-rate mortgages, home improvement and rehabilitation loans, and loans for the purchase of condominiums. Specific standards for condominium complexes and the ratio of owner-occupants to renters must be met for a loan on a condominium unit to be financed through the FHA insurance programs.

A qualified buyer may assume an existing FHA-insured loan. The application consists of a credit check to demonstrate that the person assuming the loan is financially qualified. The process is quicker and less expensive than applying for a new loan. Sometimes, the older loan has a lower interest rate and no appraisal is required.

IN PRACTICE The FHA sets lending limits for single-unit and multiple-unit properties. The limits vary significantly, depending on the average cost of housing in different regions of the country. In addition, the FHA changes its regulations for various programs from time to time. Contact your local FHA office or mortgage lender for loan amounts in your area and for specific loan requirements, or visit *www.hud.gov/ buying/loans.cfm.*

Assumption rules The assumption rules for FHA-insured loans vary, depending on the dates the loans were originated, as follows:

■ FHA loans originating before December 1986 generally have no restrictions on their assumptions.

■ For an FHA loan originating between December 1, 1986, and December 15, 1989, a creditworthiness review of the prospective assumer is required. If the original loan was for the purchase of a principal residence, this review is required during the first 12 months of the loan's existence. If the original loan was for the purchase of an investment property, the review is required during the first 24 months of the loan.

■ For FHA loans originating on December 15, 1989, and later, no assumptions are permitted without complete buyer qualification.

Discount points   The lender of an FHA-insured loan may charge discount points in addition to a loan origination fee. The payment of points is a matter of negotiation between the seller and the buyer. As of November 2009, if the seller pays more than 6 percent of the costs normally paid by the buyer (such as discount points, the loan origination fee, the mortgage insurance premium, buydown fees, prepaid items, and impound or escrow amounts), the lender will treat the payments as a reduction in sales price and recalculate the mortgage amount accordingly.

VA-Guaranteed Loans

The Department of Veterans Affairs (VA) is authorized to guarantee loans to purchase or construct homes for eligible veterans and their spouses (including unremarried spouses of veterans whose deaths were service-related). The VA also guarantees loans to purchase manufactured homes and lots on which to place them. A veteran who meets any of the following time-in-service criteria is eligible for a VA loan:

- 90 days of active service for veterans of World War II, the Korean War, the Vietnam conflict, and the Persian Gulf War
- A minimum of 181 days of active service during interconflict periods between July 26, 1947, and September 6, 1980
- Two full years of service during any peacetime period since 1980 for enlisted and since 1981 for officers
- Six or more years of continuous duty as a reservist in the Army, Navy, Air Force, Marine Corps, or Coast Guard, or as a member of the Army or Air National Guard

The VA assists veterans in financing the purchase of homes with little or no down payments at market interest rates. The VA issues rules and regulations that set forth the qualifications, limitations, and conditions under which a loan may be guaranteed. The owner must live on the property.

Like the term *FHA loan*, **VA loan** is something of a misnomer. The VA does not normally lend money; it guarantees loans made by lending institutions approved by the agency. The term *VA loan* refers to a loan that is not made by the agency but is guaranteed by it.

There is no VA dollar limit on the amount of the loan a veteran can obtain; this limit is determined by the lender and the qualification of the buyer. The VA limits the amount of the loan it will guarantee.

IN PRACTICE   The VA loan guarantee is tied to the current conforming loan limit for Fannie Mae and Freddie Mac. Typically, lenders will loan four times the guarantee (e.g., a conforming loan of $417,000 ÷ 4 = $104,250 VA guarantee).

To determine what portion of a mortgage loan the VA will guarantee, the veteran must apply for a *certificate of eligibility*. This certificate does not mean that the veteran automatically receives a mortgage. It merely sets forth the maximum guarantee to which the veteran is entitled. For individuals with full eligibility, no down payment is required for a loan up to the maximum guarantee limit.

The VA also issues a **certificate of reasonable value (CRV)** for the property being purchased. The CRV states the property's current market value based on a VA-approved appraisal. The CRV places a ceiling on the amount of a VA loan allowed for the property. If the purchase price is greater than the amount cited in the CRV, the veteran may pay the difference in cash. The CRV is based on an appraisal.

New VA regulations allow only one active VA loan at a time, and a veteran may own only two properties that were acquired using VA loan benefits. VA benefits will never expire as long as the previous benefits have been paid in full.

The VA borrower pays a loan origination fee to the lender, as well as a funding fee (2 percent to 3 percent, depending on the down payment amount) to the Department of Veterans Affairs. The funding fee depends on the down payment. With no down payment, the funding fee depends on whether it is first-time use (2.15 percent) or a subsequent use (3.15 percent). The funding fee drops with down payments of 5 percent or more. Reservists and National Guard veterans pay higher funding fees. Reasonable discount points may be charged on a VA-guaranteed loan, and either the veteran or the seller may pay them.

Prepayment privileges   As with an FHA loan, the borrower under a VA loan can prepay the debt at any time without penalty.

Assumption rules   VA loans made before March 1, 1988, are freely assumable, although an assumption processing fee will be charged. For loans made on or after March 1, 1988, the VA must approve the buyer and the assumption agreement. The original veteran borrower remains personally liable for the repayment of the loan unless the VA approves a *release of liability*. The release of liability will be issued by the VA only if

- the buyer assumes all the veteran's liabilities on the loan, and
- the VA or the lender approves both the buyer and the assumption agreement.

Releases are also possible if veterans use their own entitlement in assuming another veteran's loan.

IN PRACTICE   A release of liability issued by the VA does not release the veteran's liability to the lender. This must be obtained separately from the lender. Real estate licensees should contact their local mortgage lenders for specific requirements for obtaining or assuming VA-guaranteed loans. The programs change from time to time.

Agricultural Loan Programs

The Farm Service Agency (FSA) is a federal agency of the Department of Agriculture. The FSA offers programs to help families purchase or operate family farms. Through the Rural Housing and Community Development Service (RHCDS), it also provides loans to help families purchase or improve single-family homes in rural areas (generally areas with populations of fewer than 10,000 people). FSA loan programs fall into two categories: guaranteed loans, made and serviced by private lenders and guaranteed for a specific percentage by the FSA, and loans made directly by the FSA.

The Farm Credit System (Farm Credit) provides loans to farmers, ranchers, rural homeowners, agricultural cooperatives, rural utility systems, and agribusinesses. Unlike commercial banks, Farm Credit System banks and associations do not take deposits. Instead, loanable funds are raised through the system-wide sale of bonds and notes in the nation's capital markets.

Farmer Mac (formerly the Federal Agricultural Mortgage Corporation, or FAMC) is another government-sponsored enterprise (GSE) that operates similarly to Fannie Mae and Freddie Mac but in a context of agricultural loans. It was created to improve the availability of long-term credit at stable interest rates to America's farmers, ranchers, and rural homeowners, businesses, and communities. Farmer Mac pools or bundles agricultural loans from lenders for sale as mortgage-backed securities.

■ OTHER FINANCING TECHNIQUES

Because borrowers often have different needs, a variety of other financing techniques have been created. Other techniques apply to various types of property.

Purchase-Money Mortgages

A **purchase-money mortgage (PMM)** is created when the seller agrees to finance all or part of the purchase price and consists of a first or junior lien depending on whether prior mortgage liens exist. Often referred to as seller financing or owner financing, a PMM is often used when the buyer does not qualify for a typical lender loan. The buyer/borrower executes a note and mortgage at the time of purchase; the seller records the mortgage against the property. Payments are made to the seller, according to the terms of the note; if the buyer stops making payments, the seller has recourse to foreclose on the property.

■ **FOR EXAMPLE** A man wants to buy a farm for $200,000. He has a $40,000 down payment and agrees to assume an existing mortgage of $80,000. Because the buyer might not qualify for a new mortgage under the circumstances, the owner agrees to finance a purchase-money second mortgage in the amount of $80,000. At the closing, the buyer will execute a mortgage and note in favor of the owner, who will convey title to the buyer.

Package Loans

A **package loan** includes real and personal property. In recent years, these kinds of loans have been very popular with developers and purchasers of unfurnished condominiums. Package loans usually include furniture, drapes, the kitchen range, refrigerator, dishwasher, washer, dryer, food freezer, and other appliances as part of the sales price of the home.

Blanket Loans

A **blanket loan** covers more than one parcel or lot. It is usually used to finance subdivision developments. However, it can finance the purchase of improved properties or consolidate loans as well. A blanket loan usually includes a provision known as a *partial release clause*. This clause permits the borrower to obtain the release of any one lot or parcel from the blanket lien by repaying a certain amount of the loan. The lender issues a partial release for each parcel released from the mortgage lien. The release form includes a provision that the lien will continue to cover all other unreleased lots.

Wraparound Loans

A **wraparound loan** enables a borrower with an existing mortgage or deed of trust loan to obtain additional financing from a second lender without paying off the first loan. The second lender gives the borrower a new, increased loan at a higher interest rate and assumes payment of the existing loan. The total amount of the new loan includes the existing loan as well as the additional funds needed by the borrower. The borrower makes payments to the new lender on the larger loan. The new lender makes payments on the original loan out of the borrower's payments.

A wraparound mortgage can be used to refinance real property or to finance the purchase of real property when an existing mortgage cannot be prepaid. The buyer executes a wraparound mortgage to the seller or lender, who collects payments on the new loan and continues to make payments on the old loan. It also can finance the sale of real estate when the buyer wishes to invest a minimum amount of initial cash. A wraparound loan is possible only if the original loan permits it. For instance, an acceleration and alienation or a due-on-sale clause in the original loan documents may prevent a sale under a wraparound loan.

IN PRACTICE To protect themselves against a seller's default on a previous loan, buyers should require that protective clauses be included in any wraparound document to grant buyers the right to make payments directly to the original lender.

Open-End Loans

An **open-end loan** secures a *note* executed by the borrower to the lender. It also secures any future *advances* of funds made by the lender to the borrower. The interest rate on the initial amount borrowed is fixed, but interest on future advances may be charged at the market rate in effect. An open-end loan is often a less costly alternative to a home improvement loan. It allows the borrower to *open* the mortgage or deed of trust to increase the debt to its original amount, or the amount stated in the note, after the debt has been reduced by payments over a period of time. The mortgage usually states the maximum amount that can be secured, the terms and conditions under which the loan can be opened, and the provisions for repayment.

Construction Loans

A **construction loan** is made to finance the construction of improvements on real estate such as homes, apartments, and office buildings. The lender commits to the full amount of the loan but disburses the funds in payments during construction. These payments are also known as *draws*. Draws are made to the general contractor or the owner for that part of the construction work that has been completed since the previous payment. Before each payment, the lender inspects the work. The general contractor must provide the lender with adequate waivers that release all mechanics' lien rights for the work covered by the payment.

Construction loans are generally *short-term* or *interim financing*. The borrower pays interest only on the monies that have actually been disbursed. The borrower is expected to arrange for a permanent loan, also known as an *end loan* or *take-out loan*, which will repay or *take out* the construction financing lender when the work is completed.

Sale-and-Leaseback

Sale-and-leaseback arrangements are used to finance large commercial or industrial properties. The land and the building, usually used by the seller for business purposes, are sold to an investor. The real estate then is leased back by the investor to the seller, who continues to conduct business on the property as a tenant. The buyer becomes the landlord, and the original owner becomes the tenant. This enables a business to free money tied up in real estate to be used as working capital.

Buydowns

A **buydown** is a way to temporarily (or permanently) lower the interest rate on a mortgage or deed of trust loan. Perhaps a homebuilder wishes to stimulate sales by offering a lower-than-market rate. Or a first-time residential buyer may have trouble qualifying for a loan at the prevailing rates. Relatives or the sellers might want to help the buyer qualify. In any case, a lump sum is paid in cash to the lender at the closing. The payment offsets (and so reduces) the interest rate and monthly payments during the mortgage's first few years. Typical buydown arrangements reduce the interest rate by 1 percent to 2 percent over the first one to two years of the loan term. After that, the rate rises. The assumption is that the borrower's income will also increase, making it more likely that the borrower will be able to pay the increased monthly payments. In a permanent buydown, a larger up-front payment reduces the effective interest rate for the life of the loan.

Home Equity Loans

Home equity loans are a source of funds using the equity built up in a home. The original mortgage loan remains in place; the home equity loan is junior to the original lien. It is an alternative to refinancing and can be used for a variety of financial needs, such as to

- finance the purchase of expensive items;
- consolidate existing installment loans or credit card debt; and
- pay medical, education, home improvement, or other expenses.

The original mortgage loan remains in place; the home equity loan is junior to the original lien. If the homeowner completely refinances, the original mortgage loan and the home equity loan are paid off and replaced by a new loan. (This strategy is an alternative way to borrow the equity and is not really a home equity loan.)

A home equity loan can be taken out as a fixed loan amount or as an equity line of credit. With the *home equity line of credit*, referred to as a *HELOC*, the lender extends a line of credit that the borrower can use at will.

IN PRACTICE The homeowner must consider a number of factors before deciding on a home equity loan, including

- the costs involved in obtaining a new mortgage loan or a home equity loan,
- current interest rates,
- total monthly payments, and
- income tax consequences.

■ FINANCING LEGISLATION

The federal government regulates the lending practices of mortgage lenders through the Truth in Lending Act, the Equal Credit Opportunity Act, Community Reinvestment Act of 1977, and the Real Estate Settlement Procedures Act (RESPA).

Truth in Lending Act and Regulation Z

Regulation Z, which was enacted pursuant to the **Truth in Lending Act** by the Federal Trade Commission (FTC), requires that credit institutions inform borrowers of the true cost of obtaining credit. With proper disclosures, borrowers can compare the costs of various lenders to avoid the uninformed use of credit. Regardless of the amount, however, *Regulation Z generally applies when a credit transaction is secured by a residence*. The regulation does *not* apply to business or commercial loans or to agricultural loans of any amount.

Under the Truth in Lending Act, a consumer must be fully informed of all finance charges and the true interest rate before a transaction is completed. The finance charge disclosure must include any loan fees, finder's fees, service charges and points, as well as interest. In the case of a mortgage loan made to finance the purchase of a dwelling, the lender must compute and disclose the *annual percentage rate (APR)*.

Creditor A *creditor*, for purposes of Regulation Z, is any person who extends consumer credit more than 25 times each year or more than 5 times each year if the transactions involve dwellings as security. The credit must be subject to a finance charge or payable in more than four installments by written agreement.

Three-day right of rescission In the case of most consumer credit transactions covered by Regulation Z, the borrower has three days in which to rescind (cancel) the transaction by notifying the lender. *This right of rescission does not apply to owner-occupied residential purchase-money or first mortgage or deed of trust loans.* It does, however, apply to refinancing a home mortgage or to a home equity loan.

Advertising   Regulation Z provides strict regulation of real estate advertisements (in all media, including newspapers, flyers, signs, billboards, Web sites, radio or television ads, and direct mailings) that refer to mortgage financing terms. General phrases like "flexible terms available" may be used, but if details are given, they must comply with the act. The APR—which is calculated based on all charges rather than the interest rate alone—must be stated.

Advertisements for buydowns or reduced-rate mortgages must show both the limited term to which the interest rate applies and the annual percentage rate. If a variable-rate mortgage is advertised, the advertisement must include

- the number and timing of payments,
- the amount of the largest and smallest payments, and
- a statement of the fact that the actual payments will vary between these two extremes.

Specific credit terms, such as down payment, monthly payment, dollar amount of the finance charge, or term of the loan, are referred to as **trigger terms**. These terms may not be advertised unless the advertisement includes the following information:

- Cash price
- Required down payment
- Number, amounts, and due dates of all payments
- Annual percentage rate
- Total of all payments to be made over the term of the mortgage (unless the advertised credit refers to a first mortgage or deed of trust to finance the acquisition of a dwelling)

Penalties   Regulation Z provides penalties for noncompliance. The penalty for violation of an administrative order enforcing Regulation Z is $10,000 for each day the violation continues. A fine of up to $10,000 may be imposed for engaging in an unfair or a deceptive practice. In addition, a creditor may be liable to a consumer for twice the amount of the finance charge, for a minimum of $100 and a maximum of $1,000, plus court costs, attorney's fees, and any actual damages. Willful violation is a misdemeanor punishable by a fine of up to $5,000, one year's imprisonment, or both.

Equal Credit Opportunity Act

The federal **Equal Credit Opportunity Act (ECOA)** prohibits lenders and others who grant or arrange credit to consumers from discriminating against credit applicants on the basis of

- race,
- color,
- religion,
- national origin,
- sex,
- marital status,
- age (provided the applicant is of legal age), or
- dependence on public assistance.

Furthermore, lenders and other creditors must inform all rejected credit applicants of the principal reasons for the denial or termination of credit. The notice must be provided in writing within 30 days. The federal ECOA also provides that a borrower is entitled to a copy of the appraisal report if the borrower paid for the appraisal.

Community Reinvestment Act of 1977 (CRA)

Community reinvestment refers to the responsibility of financial institutions to help meet their communities' needs for low-income and moderate-income housing. In 1977, Congress passed the **Community Reinvestment Act of 1977 (CRA)**. Under the CRA, financial institutions are expected to meet the deposit and credit needs of their communities; participate and invest in local community development and rehabilitation projects; and participate in loan programs for housing, small businesses, and small farms.

The law requires any federally regulated financial institution to prepare a statement containing

- a definition of the geographic boundaries of its community;
- an identification of the types of community reinvestment credit offered, such as residential housing loans, housing rehabilitation loans, small-business loans, commercial loans, and consumer loans; and
- comments from the public about the institution's performance in meeting its community's needs.

Financial institutions are periodically reviewed by one of three federal financial regulatory agencies: the Comptroller of the Currency, the Federal Reserve's Board of Governors, or the Federal Deposit Insurance Corporation. The institutions must post a public notice that their community reinvestment activities are subject to federal review, and they must make the results of these reviews public.

Real Estate Settlement Procedures Act

The federal **Real Estate Settlement Procedures Act (RESPA)** applies to any residential real estate transaction involving a new first mortgage loan. RESPA is designed to ensure that the buyer and the seller are both fully informed of all settlement costs. (See Chapter 22.)

■ COMPUTERIZED LOAN ORIGINATION (CLO)

A **computerized loan origination (CLO)** system is an electronic network for handling loan applications through remote computer terminals linked to several lenders' computers. With a CLO, a real estate broker or salesperson can call up a menu of mortgage lenders, interest rates, and loan terms and then help a buyer select a lender and apply for a loan right from the brokerage office.

The licensee may assist the applicant in answering the on-screen questions and in understanding the services offered. The broker in whose office the terminal is located may earn fees of up to one-half point of the loan amount. The *borrower*, not the mortgage broker or lender, *must pay the fee*. The fee amount may be financed, however. While multiple lenders may be represented on an office's CLO computer, consumers must be informed that other lenders are available. An applicant's ability to comparison shop for a loan may be enhanced by a CLO system; the range of options may not be limited. (See Chapter 22.)

On the lenders' side, new automated underwriting procedures can shorten loan approvals from weeks to minutes. Automated underwriting also tends to lower the cost of loan application and approval by reducing lenders' time spent on the approval process by as much as 60 percent. Freddie Mac uses a system called *Loan Prospector*. Fannie Mae has a system called *Desktop Underwriter*, which reduces approval time to minutes, based on the borrower's credit report, a paycheck stub, and a drive-by appraisal of the property. Complex or difficult mortgages can be processed in less than 72 hours. Through automated underwriting, one of a borrower's biggest headaches in buying a home—waiting for loan approval—is eliminated. In addition, prospective buyers can strengthen their purchase offer by including proof of loan approval.

Scoring and automated underwriting   Lenders have been using credit scoring systems to predict prospective borrowers' likelihood of default for many years. When used as a part of traditional *manual* evaluation of applicants, credit scoring provides a useful objective standard against which to balance the loan officer's more subjective professional judgment. When used in automated underwriting systems, however, the application of credit scores has become somewhat controversial. Critics of scoring are concerned that they may not be accurate or fair, and in the absence of human discretion, they could result in making it more difficult for low-income and minority borrowers to obtain mortgages.

Freddie Mac has the following to say about automated underwriting:

> *Whether using traditional or automated methods, underwriters must consider all three areas of underwriting—collateral, credit reputation, and capacity. When reviewing collateral, underwriters look at house value, down payment, and property type. Income, debt, cash reserves, and product type are considered when underwriters are looking at capacity. Credit scores are simply one consideration when underwriters are reviewing credit reputation. Even lenders who use an automated underwriting system such as Loan Prospector, still rely on human judgment when the scoring system indicates that the loan application is a higher risk.*

◼ KEY POINT REVIEW

The **Federal Reserve System (Fed)** consists of 12 federal reserve district banks.

The **primary mortgage market** consists of lenders that originate mortgage loans based on

- ◼ **finance charges** collected at loan closing, including
  - — **loan origination fees,** and
  - — discount points;
- ◼ **recurring income**—interest collected during the term of loan, if kept;

■ funds generated by **sale of loans** on the **secondary mortgage market**; and

■ fees for **loan servicing** for other mortgage lenders or investors who have purchased the loans.

The **primary mortgage market lenders** include the following:

■ **Fiduciary lenders**—thrifts, savings associations, commercial banks—subject to the
— **Federal Deposit Insurance Corporation (FDIC)**

■ **Insurance companies**—generally investing in long-term commercial, industrial, and large multifamily properties

■ Credit unions

■ Pension funds

■ **Endowment funds** of universities, colleges, and other institutions

■ **Investment group financing**—joint ventures, syndicates, limited partnerships, and real estate investment trusts (REITs)

■ **Mortgage banking companies**

■ **Mortgage brokers**

The **secondary mortgage market**, where loans are bought and sold after being funded, does the following:

■ Provides **additional income** to lenders and **frees up funds** to make more loans, with lenders often retaining servicing functions for a fee

■ Purchases mortgage loans through agencies, assembles them into packages called **pools**, and sells them as **shares (securitized)** to investors or other agencies

Fannie Mae (Federal National Mortgage Association) is

■ government-owned with privately issued common stock;

■ creates **mortgage-backed securities** using pool of mortgages as collateral; and

■ deals in conventional, FHA, and VA loans.

Freddie Mac (Federal Home Loan Mortgage Corporation) is

■ government–owned, and

■ has authority to purchase mortgages, pool them, and use them as security for bonds sold on the open market but does not guarantee payment of mortgages.

Ginnie Mae (Government National Mortgage Association) is entirely a government agency, a division of the **Department of Housing and Urban Development (HUD)**, organized as a corporation but without corporate stock, that

■ administers **special-assistance programs,** and

■ guarantees **mortgage-backed securities** using FHA and VA loans as collateral.

Following are **types of financing**:

■ **Straight loan (term loan or interest-only loan)**—periodic payments of interest only for the life of the loan, with payment of principal in full at the end of the loan term

- **Balloon payment (partially amortized) loan**—periodic payments of interest and principal are not great enough to pay down entire amount borrowed by end of loan term, resulting in a larger final payment
- **Amortized (fully amortized) loan**—equal periodic payments of interest and principal result in complete payment of amount borrowed over the term of the loan
- **Adjustable-rate mortgage (ARM)**—lower initial rate of interest that may change over the life of the loan based on a specified index, usually tied to U.S. Treasury securities
- **Growing equity (rapid-payoff) mortgage**—fixed interest rate but payments of principal increased according to an index or schedule so that the loan is paid off more quickly
- **Reverse mortgage**—payments made by the lender to the borrower, at regular intervals (such as monthly), in a lump sum, or as a line of credit to be drawn against, allowing the borrower to remain in the home while receiving income

Conventional loans are the most secure loans. Note the following:

- The **loan-to-value ratio (LTV)** is often lowest for these loans—traditionally 80 percent—meaning the down payment is 20 percent, but the LTV may be as high as 100 percent.
- Conventional loans are **not** government-insured or guaranteed.
- Conventional loans meet all the requirements of the secondary market, set by Fannie Mae and Freddie Mac, for **conforming loans**, including the following:
  — The borrower's **monthly housing expenses**, including PITI, should be no more than 28 percent of total monthly gross income.
  — The borrower's **total monthly obligations**, including housing costs and other regular monthly payments, must not exceed 36 percent of the total monthly gross income.
- **Nonconforming loans** must be retained in the lender's investment portfolio.
- **Private mortgage insurance (PMI)** may be required for LTVs higher than 80 percent (i.e., down payments of less than 20 percent). Note the following PMI conditions:
  — Federal law requires PMI to **automatically** terminate if the borrower has accumulated 22 percent equity in the home (based on purchase price) *and* is current on mortgage payments.
  — **Fannie Mae** and **Freddie Mac** have extended the automatic termination option to all loans that are in good standing and have had no additional financing added to the original loan.

FHA-insured loans are backed by the **Federal Housing Administration (FHA)**, which is part of HUD. FHA does not make loans but insures loans made by an FHA-approved lending institution.

Mortgage insurance premium (MIP) has an up-front fee along with monthly installments. The premium can be financed within the loan.

VA-guaranteed loans are backed by the **Department of Veterans Affairs** and are available to eligible veterans and spouses.

The **Farm Service Agency (FSA),** formerly **Farmers Home Administration**, is part of the Department of Agriculture and has the following programs to help families purchase or operate family farms:

- Rural Housing and Community Development Service (RHCDS)
- **Farm Credit System (Farm Credit)**
- **Farmer Mac** (formerly **Federal Agricultural Mortgage Corporation**)

Other types of loans include the following:

- A **purchase-money mortgage** is a note and mortgage created at the time of purchase.
- The **package loan** includes all personal property and appliances as well as real estate.
- A **blanket loan** covers more than one parcel or lot, and a **partial release clause** allows a borrower to pay off part of a loan to remove the liens from one parcel or lot at a time.
- **Wraparound loans** allow the borrower to obtain additional financing, retaining the first loan on the property.
- An **open-end loan** secures the current loan to the borrower and future advances made by the lender to the borrower.
- **Construction loans** finance construction of property improvements.
- **Sale-and-leaseback loans** are used to finance large commercial or industrial properties.
- A **buydown** is a payment made at closing to reduce the interest rate on the loan.
- A **home equity loan (home equity line of credit** or **HELOC)** is junior to the original lien.

The **Truth in Lending Act, Regulation Z** of the **Federal Trade Commission (FTC)**, requires that when a loan is secured by a residence, lenders inform borrowers of the true cost of obtaining credit, within the following rules:

- The borrower has a **three-day right of rescission**.
- **Advertising** is strictly regulated.
- There is a **$10,000 penalty** for each day the violation continues.

The **Equal Credit Opportunity Act (ECOA)** prohibits **discrimination** in granting or arranging credit on the basis of race, color, religion, national origin, sex, marital status, age (as long as the applicant is not a minor), or dependence on public assistance.

Computerized loan origination (CLO) allows real estate brokers and salespersons to assist loan applicants in surveying lenders and providing information.

Automated underwriting (loan processing) programs include Fannie Mae's Desktop Underwriter and Freddie Mac's Loan Prospector.

A credit score may be used as part of a loan application evaluation process.

■ RELATED WEB SITES

Fannie Mae: *www.fanniemae.com/kb/*

Farm Credit Network: *www.farmcreditnetwork.com*

Federal Reserve Board: *www.federalreserve.gov*

Freddie Mac: *www.freddiemac.com*

Ginnie Mae: *www.ginniemae.gov*

Mortgage Banker's Association: *www.mbaa.org*

National Association of Mortgage Bankers: *www.namb.org*

National Reverse Mortgage Lenders Association: *www.reversemortgage.org*

U.S. Department of Agriculture Rural Development Agency:
    www.rurdev.usda.gov

U.S. Department of Housing and Urban Development: *www.hud.gov*

U.S. Department of Veterans Affairs: *www.va.gov*

U.S. Farm Service Agency: *www.fsa.usda.gov*

CHAPTER 15 QUIZ

1. The buyers purchased a residence for $195,000. They made a down payment of $25,000 and agreed to assume the seller's existing mortgage, which had a current balance of $123,000. The buyers financed the remaining $47,000 of the purchase price by executing a mortgage and note to the seller. This type of loan, by which the seller becomes the mortgagee, is called a
   a. wraparound mortgage.
   b. package mortgage.
   c. balloon note.
   d. purchase-money mortgage.

2. A buyer purchased a new residence for $175,000. The buyer made a down payment of $15,000 and obtained a $160,000 mortgage loan. The builder of the house paid the lender 3 percent of the loan balance for the first year and 2 percent for the second year. This represented a total savings for the buyer of $8,000. What type of mortgage arrangement is this?
   a. Wraparound
   b. Package
   c. Blanket
   d. Buydown

3. Which of the following is NOT a participant in the secondary market?
   a. Fannie Mae
   b. Ginnie Mae
   c. Credit union
   d. Freddie Mac

4. A buyer purchased a home for cash 30 years ago. Today the buyer receives monthly checks from a mortgage lender that supplement her retirement income. The buyer MOST likely has obtained a(n)
   a. purchase-money mortgage.
   b. adjustable-rate mortgage.
   c. reverse mortgage.
   d. overriding deed of trust.

5. If buyers seek a mortgage on a single-family house, they would be LEAST likely to obtain the mortgage from a
   a. mutual savings bank.
   b. life insurance company.
   c. credit union.
   d. commercial bank.

6. Which characteristic of a fixed-rate home loan that is amortized according to the original payment schedule is TRUE?
   a. The amount of interest to be paid is predetermined.
   b. The loan cannot be sold in the secondary market.
   c. The monthly payment amount will fluctuate each month.
   d. The interest rate change may be based on an index.

7. In a loan that requires periodic payments that do not fully amortize the loan balance by the final payment, what term BEST describes the final payment?
   a. Adjustment
   b. Acceleration
   c. Balloon
   d. Variable

8. A developer received a loan that covers five parcels of real estate and provides for the release of the mortgage lien on each parcel when certain payments are made on the loan. This type of loan arrangement is called a
   a. purchase-money loan.
   b. blanket loan.
   c. package loan.
   d. wraparound loan.

9. Funds for Federal Housing Administration (FHA) loans are usually provided by
   a. the FHA.
   b. the Federal Reserve.
   c. approved lenders.
   d. the seller.

10. The provisions of the Truth in Lending Act (Regulation Z) require all of the following to be disclosed to a residential buyer *EXCEPT*

   a. discount points.
   b. the real estate brokerage commission.
   c. a loan origination fee.
   d. the loan interest rate.

11. A home is purchased using a fixed-rate, fully amortized mortgage loan. Which statement regarding this mortgage is *TRUE*?

   a. A balloon payment will be made at the end of the loan.
   b. Each mortgage payment amount is the same.
   c. Each mortgage payment reduces the principal by the same amount.
   d. The principal amount in each payment is greater than the interest amount.

12. Which statement about interest on a fully amortized mortgage or deed of trust loan is *TRUE*?

   a. Interest may be paid in arrears—that is, at the end of each period for which it is earned.
   b. The interest portion of each payment increases throughout the term of the loan.
   c. Only interest is paid each period.
   d. The final interest payment will be determined after the last payment is made.

13. The primary activity of Freddic Mac is to

   a. guarantee mortgages with the full faith and credit of the federal government.
   b. buy and pool blocks of conventional mortgages.
   c. act in tandem with Ginnie Mae to provide special assistance in times of tight money.
   d. buy and sell VA and FHA mortgages.

14. The federal Equal Credit Opportunity Act allows lenders to discriminate against potential borrowers on the basis of

   a. race.
   b. sex.
   c. age.
   d. amount of income.

15. A borrower obtains a $100,000 mortgage loan for 30 years at 6 percent interest. If the monthly payments of $575 are credited first to interest and then to principal, what will be the balance of the principal after the borrower makes the first payment?

   a. $99,425
   b. $99,925
   c. $99,500
   d. $100,000

16. The buyer borrowed $85,000, to be repaid in monthly installments of $530.20 at 7 percent annual interest. How much of the buyer's first month's payment was applied to reducing the principal amount of the loan?

   a. $40.00
   b. $34.37
   c. $530.20
   d. $495.83

17. If a lender agrees to make a loan based on an 80 percent LTV, what is the amount of the loan if the property appraises for $114,500 and the sales price is $116,900?

   a. $83,200
   b. $91,300
   c. $91,600
   d. $92,900

18. In which type of loan is the loan amount divided into two parts, to be paid off separately by periodic interest payments followed by payment of the principal in full at the end of the term?

   a. Amortized
   b. Straight
   c. ARM
   d. Balloon

19. In an adjustable-rate mortgage, the interest rate is tied to an objective economic indicator called a(n)

   a. mortgage factor.
   b. discount rate.
   c. index.
   d. reserve requirement.

20. Which law requires that all advertising that references mortgage financing terms contain certain disclosures?

    a. Equal Credit Opportunity Act
    b. Fair Housing Act
    c. Community Reinvestment Act
    d. Truth in Lending Act (Regulation Z)

CHAPTER 16

Leases

■ **LEARNING OBJECTIVES**   *When you have finished reading this chapter, you should be able to*

■ **identify** the four types of leasehold estates;

■ **describe** the requirements and general conditions of a valid lease and how a lease may be discharged;

■ **explain** the rights of landlords and tenants in an eviction proceeding and the effect of protenant legislation and civil rights laws on the landlord-tenant relationship;

■ **distinguish** the various types of leases; and

■ **define** the following *key terms:*

actual eviction	ground lease	nondisturbance clause
assignment	holdover tenancy	percentage lease
constructive eviction	lease	purchase option
estate at sufferance	leasehold estate	renewal option
estate at will	lease purchase	reversionary right
estate for years	lessee	right of first refusal
estate from period to period	lessor	sale-and-leaseback
	month-to-month tenancy	security deposit
gross lease	net lease	sublease

■ LEASES

By the end of 2009, more than 35 million occupied residential units were rentals. Although some owners manage their own properties (a real estate license is not required to do so), most are professionally managed. In many states, property managers are required to hold a real estate or property manager license. Licensees should be aware of their local rental market to better assist buyers who may not qualify to buy their own property, to locate an appropriate property for an investor-buyer, or to manage their own portfolios. In any case, licensees should be aware of leases, management agreements, landlord-tenant issues, and more.

■ LEASING REAL ESTATE

A **lease** is a contract between an owner of real estate (the **lessor**) and a tenant (the **lessee**). A lease is a contract to transfer the lessor's rights to exclusive possession and use of the property to the tenant for a specified period of time. The lease establishes the length of time the contract is to run and the amount the lessee is to pay for use of the property. Other rights and obligations of the parties are also set forth.

In effect, the lease agreement combines two contracts. A lease is (1) a conveyance of a possession of the real estate and (2) a contract to pay rent and assume other obligations. The lessor grants the lessee the right to occupy the real estate and use it for purposes stated in the lease. In return, the landlord receives payment for use of the premises and retains a **reversionary right** to possession after the lease term expires.

The statute of frauds in most states requires lease agreements for more than one year to be in writing to be enforceable. In general, oral leases for one year or less that can be performed within a year of their making are enforceable. Written leases should be signed by both the lessor and the lessee.

IN PRACTICE Even though an oral lease may be enforceable, such as a lease for one year commencing from the day of agreement, it is always better practice to put lease agreements in writing. A written lease provides concrete evidence of the terms and conditions to which the parties have agreed. Any written agreement should be signed by both the landlord and tenant.

■ LEASEHOLD ESTATES

A tenant's right to possess real estate for the term of the lease is called a **leasehold** (less-than-freehold) **estate**. A leasehold is generally considered personal property. When the tenant assumes many of the landowner's obligations under a lease for life or for more than 99 years, certain states give the tenant some of the benefits and privileges of ownership. Just as there are several types of freehold (ownership) estates, there are different kinds of leasehold estates. (See Figure 16.1.)

FIGURE 16.1

Leasehold Estates

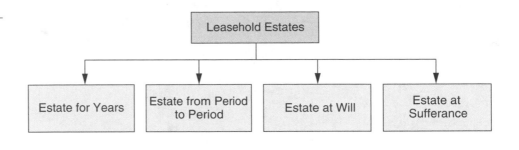

Estate for Years

An **estate** (tenancy) **for years** is a leasehold estate that continues for a definite period. That period may be years, months, weeks, or even days. An estate for years (sometimes referred to as an *estate for term*) always has specific starting and ending dates. When the estate expires, the lessee is required to vacate the premises and surrender possession to the lessor. *No notice is required to terminate the estate for years* because the lease agreement states a specific expiration date. When the date comes, the lease expires, and the tenant's rights are extinguished.

If both parties agree, the lease for years may be terminated before the expiration date. Otherwise, neither party may terminate without showing that the lease agreement has been breached. Any extension of the tenancy requires that a new contract be negotiated.

> **Estate (tenancy) for years**
> = *Any definite period*

As is characteristic of all leases, a tenancy for years gives the lessee the right to occupy and use the leased property according to the terms and covenants contained in the lease agreement. Remember that a lessee has the right to use the premises for the entire lease term. That right is unaffected by the original lessor's death or the sale of the property, unless the lease states otherwise. If the original lease provides for an option to renew, no further negotiation is required; the tenant merely exercises the option.

Estate from Period to Period – *no specific expiration*

An **estate from period to period**, or *periodic tenancy*, is created when the landlord and tenant enter into an agreement for an indefinite time—that is, the lease does not contain a specific expiration date. Such a tenancy is created initially to run for a definite amount of time—for instance, month to month, week to week, or year to year—but the tenancy continues indefinitely until proper notice of termination is given. Rent is payable at definite intervals. A periodic tenancy is characterized by *continuity* because it is automatically renewable under the original terms of the agreement until one of the parties gives notice to terminate. In effect, the payment and acceptance of rent extend the lease for another period. A **month-to-month tenancy**, for example, is created when a tenant takes possession with no definite termination date and pays monthly rent. Periodic tenancy is often used in residential leases.

■ **FOR EXAMPLE**   A landlord and a tenant have agreed that the apartment can be rented by the month without specifying the number of months the lease will run. The lease simply continues until either the landlord or the tenant gives proper notice to terminate.

Estate from period to period (periodic tenancy) = *Indefinite term; automatically renewing*

If the original agreement provides for the conversion from an estate for years to a periodic tenancy, no negotiations are necessary; the tenant simply exercises the option.

An estate from period to period also might be created when a tenant with an estate for years remains in possession, or holds over, after the lease term expires. If no new lease agreement has been made, a **holdover tenancy** is created. The landlord may evict the tenant or treat the holdover tenant as one who holds a periodic tenancy. The landlord's acceptance of rent usually is considered conclusive proof of acceptance of the periodic tenancy. The courts customarily rule that a tenant who holds over can do so for a term equal to the term of the original lease, provided the period is for one year or less. For example, a tenant with a lease for six months would be entitled to a new six-month tenancy. However, if the original lease were for five years, the holdover tenancy could not exceed one year. Some leases stipulate that in the absence of a renewal agreement, a tenant who holds over does so as a month-to-month tenant.

To *terminate* a periodic estate, either the landlord or the tenant must *give proper notice*. The form and timing of the notice may be established by state statute. Normally, the notice must be given *one period in advance*. For example, to terminate an estate from week to week, one week's notice is required; to terminate an estate from month to month, one month's notice is required. For an estate from year to year, however, the notice requirements vary from two months to six months.

Estate at Will

Estate (tenancy) at will = *Indefinite term; possession with landlord's consent*

An **estate** (tenancy) **at will** gives the tenant the right to possess property with the landlord's consent for an unspecified or uncertain term. An estate at will is a tenancy of indefinite duration; it continues until it is terminated by either party giving proper notice. No definite initial period is specified, as is the case in a periodic tenancy. An estate at will is automatically terminated by the death of either the landlord or the tenant. It may be created by express agreement or by operation of law. During the existence of a tenancy at will, the tenant has all the rights and obligations of a lessor-lessee relationship, including the duty to pay rent at regular intervals. As a practical matter, tenancy at will is rarely used in a written agreement and is viewed skeptically by the courts.

■ **FOR EXAMPLE**   A landlord tells a tenant that at the end of the lease someone else will be moving into the apartment. The landlord gives the tenant the option to continue to rent until the new tenant is ready to move. If the tenant agrees, a tenancy at will is created.

tenant refuses to leave after expiration of lease

Estate at Sufferance

An **estate (tenancy) at sufferance** arises when a tenant who lawfully possessed real property continues in possession of the premises *without the landlord's consent* after the rights expire. This estate can arise when a tenant for years fails to surrender possession at the lease's expiration.

> **Estate (tenancy) at sufferance** = *Tenant's previously lawful possession continued without landlord's consent*

When a tenant fails to surrender possession, or *holds over*, the tenant is responsible for the payment of monthly rent at existing terms and rate. If a lease contains a holdover clause, that lease governs the rights of both the landlord and the tenant. If a lease does not contain such a clause, then a state's law governs and typically offers three options:

- The landlord can accept rent offered by the tenant, thereby creating a new tenancy under conditions of the original lease, a *holdover tenancy*. If the original lease term was greater than one year, generally the new tenancy is limited to one year.
- The landlord can treat the tenant as a *tenant at sufferance* by either objecting to the tenant holding over or informing the tenant of such treatment, thus creating a month-to-month or periodic tenancy. The landlord receives rent, and both parties have to provide notice within a certain period of terminating the arrangement.
- The landlord can treat the tenant as a trespasser and proceed with an eviction and damages action. Under this situation, the landlord must comply with the *notice to quit* requirements in the lease and the state laws regarding the landlord-tenant relationship.

■ LEASE AGREEMENTS

Most states require no special wording to establish the landlord-tenant relationship. The lease may be written, oral, or implied, depending on the circumstances and the requirements of the statute of frauds. The law of the state where the real estate is located must be followed to ensure the validity of the lease. Figure 16.2 is an example of a typical residential lease.

Requirements of a Valid Lease

A lease is a contract between the lessor (landlord) and the lessee (tenant). To be valid, a lease must meet the following requirements, which are essentially the same as in any other contract:

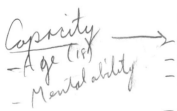

- *Capacity to contract.* The parties must have the legal capacity to contract.
- *Legal objectives.* The objectives of the lease must be legal.
- *Offer and acceptance.* The parties must reach a mutual agreement on all the terms of the contract.
- *Consideration.* The lease must be supported by valid consideration, an exchange of promises. The landlord promises to provide occupancy and the tenant promises to pay rent. Rent is typically monetary, although the tenant could provide agreed-upon labor in maintaining or fixing up the property. Because a lease is a contract, the rent and other terms may not be changed unless both parties agree to the changes in writing and executed in the same manner as the original lease.

F I G U R E   16.2

Sample Residential Lease

RESIDENTIAL LEASE AGREEMENT

1. **IDENTIFICATION OF PARTIES AND PREMISES**   This Agreement is made and entered into this _____ day of _____, 20___, between the following named persons:

    _____   _____

    _____   _____

    (herein called "Tenants") and _____ (herein called "Landlord"). Subject to the terms and conditions set forth in this Agreement, Landlord rents to Tenants, and Tenants rent from Landlord, the premises located at _____, California (herein called "the premises"). The premises shall be occupied only by the above mentioned Tenants. Tenants shall use the premises for residential purposes only and for no other purpose without Landlord's prior written consent. Occupancy by guests for more than ten days in any six-month period is prohibited without Landlord's written consent and shall be considered a breach of this Agreement.

2. **INDIVIDUAL LIABILITY**   Each tenant who signs this Agreement, whether or not said person is or remains in possession, shall be jointly and severally liable for the full performance of each and every obligation of this Agreement, but not limited to, the payment of all rent due and the payment of costs to remedy damages to the premises regardless of whether such damages were caused by a Tenant or invitee of a Tenant.

3. **TERM OF THE TENANCY**   The term of this Agreement shall commence on _____, 20____, and shall continue from that date
    - ❑   a. on a month-to-month basis. This Agreement will continue for successive terms of one month each until either Landlord or Tenants terminate the tenancy by giving the other thirty (30) days written notice of an intention to terminate the premises. In the event such notice is given, Tenants agree to pay all rent up to and including the notice period.
    - ❑   b. for a period of _____ months expiring on _____, 20____. Should Tenants vacate before the expiration of the term, Tenants shall be liable for the balance of the rent for the remainder of the term, less any rent Landlord collects or could have collected from a replacement tenant by reasonably attempting to re-rent. Tenants who vacate before expiration of the term are also responsible for Landlord's costs of advertising for a replacement tenant. In the event Tenants fail to give written notice of an intention to vacate the premises at the end of the term, the tenancy shall become one of month-to-month on all terms specified in section (a) of this clause.

4. **PAYMENT OF RENT**   Tenants shall pay Landlord rent of $ _____ per month, payable in advance on the _____ day of each month. If that day falls on a weekend or legal holiday, the rent is due on the next business day. Rent shall be paid by personal check, money order or cashier's check only, to _____ at, _____ _____, or at such other place as Landlord shall designate from time to time.

5. **LATE CHARGES AND RETURNED CHECKS**   If rent is paid after the _____ day of the month, there will be a late charge of $ _____ assessed. If any check given by Tenants to Landlord for the payment of rent or for any other sum due under this Agreement is returned for insufficient funds, a "stop payment" or any other reason, Tenants shall pay Landlord a returned check charge of $ _____ .

6. **FAILURE TO PAY**   As required by law, Tenants are hereby notified that a negative credit report reflecting on Tenants' credit history may be submitted to a credit reporting agency if Tenants fail to fulfill the terms of their credit obligations, such as their financial obligations under the terms of this Agreement.

7. **SECURITY DEPOSIT**   Before the commencement of this Agreement, Tenants shall pay Landlord $_____ as a security deposit. Landlord may use therefrom such amounts as are reasonably necessary to remedy Tenants' default in the payment of rent, repair damages to the premises exclusive of ordinary wear and tear, and to clean the premises if necessary. Landlord shall refund Tenants the balance of the security deposit after such deductions within

F I G U R E   16.2

Sample Residential Lease (Continued)

twenty-one (21) days after the expiration of this Agreement. If deductions have been made, Landlord shall provide Tenants with an itemized account of each deduction including the reasons for and the dollar amount of each deduction.

Interest payments on security deposits accrue as follows:
- ❑ a. Local law does not require Landlord to pay interest on security deposits.
- ❑ b. Local law requires Landlord to pay Tenants interest payments on security deposits as follows:

_____

_____

8. <u>UTILITIES</u> Tenants shall pay directly for all utilities, services and charges provided to the premises, including any and all deposits required, except for the following, which shall be paid by Landlord:
- ❑ a. None.
- ❑ b. _____

9. <u>PARKING</u> Tenants are assigned parking as follows:
- ❑ a. None.
- ❑ b. _____
    This space shall be used for the parking of _____ car(s) only. Tenants may not repair vehicles of any kind in any parking space or anywhere else on or about the property. Grease, oil and any other drippings must be cleaned by Tenants when they occur and at Tenants' expense. Cars are not to be washed on or about the premises. In addition to rent, Tenants shall pay Landlord a parking fee of $ _____ per month. This fee is payable in advance along with the rent and shall be paid at the same address as designated by Landlord for payment of rent.

10. <u>PETS</u> No animal, bird or other pet shall be brought on or kept on the premises without Landlord's prior written consent, except for the following:
- ❑ a. None.
- ❑ b. _____

11. <u>QUIET ENJOYMENT</u> Tenants shall be entitled to quiet enjoyment of the premises. Tenants shall not use the premises in such a way as to violate any law or ordinance, commit waste or nuisance, or annoy, disturb, inconvenience, or interfere with the quiet enjoyment of any other or nearby resident.

12. <u>ASSIGNMENT AND SUBLETTING</u> No portion of the premises shall be sublet nor this Agreement assigned without the prior written consent of the Landlord. Any attempted subletting or assignment by Tenants shall, at the election of Landlord, be an irremediable breach of this Agreement and cause for immediate termination as provided here and by law.

13. <u>POSSESSION OF THE PREMISES</u> The failure of Tenants to take possession of the premises shall not relieve them of their obligation to pay rent. If Landlord is unable to deliver possession of the premises for any reason not within Landlord's control, Landlord shall not be liable for any damage caused thereby, nor will this Agreement be void or voidable, but Tenants shall not be liable for any rent until possession is delivered.   If Landlord is unable to deliver possession within _____ calendar days after the agreed commencement date, Tenants may terminate this Agreement by giving written notice to Landlord, and shall receive a refund of all rent and security deposits paid.

14. <u>CONDITION OF THE PREMISES</u> Tenants agree to
- (i) properly use, operate and safeguard the premises and all furniture and furnishings, appliances and fixtures within the premises,
- (ii) maintain the premises in clean and sanitary condition, and upon termination of the tenancy, to surrender the premises to Landlord in the same condition as when Tenants first took occupancy, except for ordinary wear and tear,
- (iii) if the surrounding grounds are part of the premises and for exclusive use of Tenants, Tenants agree to irrigate and maintain the surrounding grounds in a clean and safe manner, keeping the grounds clear of rubbish and weeds and trimming all grass and shrubbery as necessary to effect a neat and orderly appearance to the property,

F I G U R E   16.2

Sample Residential Lease (Continued)

(iv)   notify Landlord in writing upon discovery of any damages, defects or dangerous conditions in and about the premises; and

(v)   reimburse Landlord for the cost of any repairs to the premises of damages caused by misuse or negligence of Tenants or their guests or invitees.

Tenants acknowledge that they have examined the entire interior and exterior of the premises, including plumbing, heating and electrical appliances, smoke detector(s), fixtures, carpets, drapes and paint, and have found them to be in good, safe and clean condition and repair, with the following exceptions: (Specify "none" if there are no exceptions)

_____

_____

_____

_____

15. **REPAIRS, ALTERATIONS AND DAMAGES** Except as provided by law or as authorized by the prior written consent of Landlord, Tenants shall not make any repairs or alterations to the premises, including but not limited to, painting the walls, installing wallpaper, murals, paneling, tile, or hanging posters or pictures weighing in excess of twenty pounds.

If the premises are damaged or destroyed as to render them uninhabitable, then either Landlord or Tenants shall have the right to terminate this Agreement as of the date on which such damage occurs, through written notice to the other party to be given within fifteen days of occurrence of such damage. However, if such damage should occur as the result of the conduct or negligence of Tenants or Tenants' guests or invitees, Landlord only shall have the right to termination and Tenants shall be responsible for all losses, including, but not limited to, damage and repair costs as well as loss of rental income.

16. **EMERGENCY ENTRY AND INSPECTION** Tenants shall make the premises available to Landlord or Landlord's agents for the purposes of making repairs or improvements, or to supply agreed services or show the premises to prospective buyers or tenants, or in case of emergency. Except in case of emergency, Landlord shall give Tenants reasonable notice of intent to enter. For these purposes, twenty-four (24) hour written notice shall be deemed reasonable, and reasonable hours shall be defined as _____ to _____ Monday through Friday and _____ to _____ on Saturdays. In order to facilitate Landlord's right of access, Tenants shall not, without Landlord's prior written consent, add, alter or re-key any locks to the premises. At all times Landlord shall be provided with a key or keys capable of unlocking all such locks and gaining entry. Tenants further agree to notify Landlord in writing if Tenants install any burglar alarm system, including instructions on how to disarm it in case of emergency entry.

17. **EXTENDED ABSENCES AND ABANDONMENT** In the event Tenants will be away from the premises for more than _____ consecutive days, Tenants agree to notify Landlord in writing of the absence. During such absence, Landlord may enter the premises at times reasonably necessary to maintain the property and inspect for damages and needed repairs.

Abandonment is defined as absence of the Tenants from the premises, for at least _____ consecutive days without notice to Landlord. If the rent is outstanding and unpaid for fourteen (14) days and there is no reasonable evidence, other than the presence of the Tenants' personal property, that the Tenants are occupying the unit, Landlord may at Landlord's option terminate this agreement and regain possession in the manner prescribed by law.

18. **INSURANCE DISCLAIMERS** Tenants assume full responsibility for all personal property placed, stored or located on or about the premises. Tenants' personal property is not insured by Landlord. Landlord recommends that Tenants obtain insurance to protect against risk of loss from harm to Tenants' personal property. Landlord shall not be responsible for any harm to Tenants' property resulting from fire, theft, burglary, strikes, riots, orders or acts of public authorities, acts of nature or any other circumstance or event beyond Landlord's control.

19. **HOLD HARMLESS** Tenants expressly release Landlord from any and all liability for any damages or injury to Tenants, or any other person, or to any property, occurring on the premises unless such damage is the direct result of the negligence or unlawful act of Landlord or Landlord's agents.

20. **SMOKE DETECTORS** The premises are equipped with a smoke detection device(s), and Tenants shall be responsible for reporting any problems, maintenance or repairs to Landlord. Replacing batteries is the responsibility of Tenants.

FIGURE 16.2

Sample Residential Lease (Continued)

21. **LEAD BASED PAINT DISCLOSURE** By initialing, Tenant acknowledges receipt of disclosure of information on lead-based paint and lead-based paint hazards. Landlord has no reports or knowledge of lead-based paint on the premises.

   Tenants initial here: _____ _____ _____ _____

22. **LIQUID-FILLED FURNITURE** Tenant shall not use or have any liquid-filled furniture on the premises without Landlord's prior written consent.

23. **ADDITIONAL PROVISIONS** (Specify "none" if there are no additional provisions)

   _____

   _____

   _____

   _____

   _____

   _____

24. **ENTIRE AGREEMENT** This document constitutes the entire Agreement between the Tenants and Landlord. This Agreement cannot be modified except in writing and must be signed by all parties. Neither Landlord nor Tenants have made any promises or representations, other than those set forth in this Agreement and those implied by law. The failure of Tenants or their guests or invitees to comply with any term of this Agreement is grounds for termination of the tenancy, with appropriate notice to Tenants and procedures as required by law.

   _____   _____
   Landlord/Manager   Date

   _____

   Landlord/Manager's Street Address, City, State & ZIP

   _____   _____
   Tenant   Date

   _____   _____
   Tenant   Date

   _____   _____
   Tenant   Date

   _____   _____
   Tenant   Date

The leased premises should be clearly described. For most residential leases, the street address or the apartment number is usually sufficient. If supplemental space is part of the rental, it should be clearly identified. If the lease covers land, such as a ground lease, then a legal description should be used. There should be no ambiguity.

IN PRACTICE Preprinted lease agreements are usually better suited to residential leases. Commercial leases are generally more complex, have different legal requirements, and may include complicated calculations of rent and maintenance costs. Drafting a commercial lease—or even a complex residential lease, for that matter—may constitute the practice of law. Unless the real estate licensee is also an attorney, legal counsel should be sought.

Possession of Premises

The lessor, as the owner of the real estate, is usually bound by the *covenant of quiet enjoyment* that the lessee can occupy the premises without interference from the owner or anyone else. Quiet enjoyment does not have anything to do with barking dogs or late-night motorcycles. The lease usually stipulates the conditions under which the landlord may enter the property to perform maintenance, to make repairs, or for other stated purposes. Except in emergencies, the tenant's permission is usually required, which may be stipulated in the lease or by state law.

Use of Premises

A lessor may restrict a lessee's use of the premises through provisions included in the lease. As per Figure 16.2, Section 1, "The premises shall be occupied only by the above mentioned Tenants. Tenants shall use the premises for residential purposes only and for no other purpose without Landlord's prior written consent." Use restrictions are particularly common in leases for stores or commercial space. For example, a lease may provide that the leased premises are to be used only as a real estate office *and for no other purpose*. In the absence of such clear limitations, a lessee may use the premises for any *lawful* purpose.

Term of Lease

The term of a lease, the period for which the lease will run, should be stated precisely, including the beginning and ending dates together with a statement of the total period of the lease. For instance, a lease might run "for a term of 30 years beginning June 1, 2010, and ending May 31, 2040." A perpetual lease for an inordinate amount of time or an indefinite term usually will be ruled invalid. However, if the language of the lease and the surrounding circumstances clearly indicate that the parties intended such a term, the lease will be binding on the parties. Some states prohibit leases that run for 100 years or more.

Security Deposit

Tenants are often required to provide a **security deposit**, which is held by the landlord during the lease term. The security deposit is used if the tenant defaults on payment of rent or destroys the premises. Licensees should be aware of local state laws that govern security deposits: how they may be held, maximum amounts, whether interest must be paid, and how and when they are returned. To safeguard against nonpayment of rent, landlords may require an advance rental payment or a contract for a lien on the tenant's property or may require the tenant to have a third-person guarantee payment.

IN PRACTICE A lease should specify whether a payment is a security deposit or an advance on rent. If it is a security deposit, the tenant is usually not entitled to apply it to the final month's rent. If it is an advance on rent, the landlord must treat it as income for tax purposes.

Improvements

Neither the landlord nor the tenant is required to make any improvements to the leased property. The tenant may, however, make improvements with the landlord's permission. In most residential properties, any alterations become the property of the landlord. However, in many commercial leases, tenants are permitted to install trade fixtures, those articles attached to a rental space that are required by tenants to conduct their businesses. Trade fixtures may be removed before the lease expires, provided the tenant restores the premises to the previous condition, with allowance for the wear and tear of normal use.

Accessibility   The federal Fair Housing Act makes it illegal to discriminate against prospective tenants on the basis of physical disability. (See Chapter 20.) Tenants with disabilities must be permitted to make reasonable modifications to a property at their own expense. However, if the modifications would interfere with a future tenant's use, the landlord may require that the premises be restored to their original condition at the end of the lease term.

Maintenance of Premises

Most states require a lessor of residential property to maintain dwelling units in a habitable condition. Landlords must make any necessary repairs to common areas, such as hallways, stairs, and elevators, and maintain safety features, such as fire sprinklers and smoke alarms. The tenant does not have to make any repairs but must return the premises in the same condition they were received, with allowances for ordinary wear and tear. However, lessees of commercial and industrial properties usually maintain the premises and are often responsible for making their own repairs.

Destruction of Premises

The obligation to pay rent for damaged or destroyed premises differs depending on the type of property and the lease. Usually, residential tenants are permitted to reduce their rent payments in proportion to the amount of space they are unable to use. Likewise, tenants who lease only part of a building, such as office or commercial space, generally are not required to continue to pay rent after the leased premises are destroyed. In fact, in some states, if the property was destroyed as a result of the landlord's negligence, the tenant can recover damages.

On the other hand, tenants who have constructed buildings on leased land, often agricultural or industrial land, are still obligated for the payment of rent if the improvements are damaged or destroyed. If the buildings are destroyed, these tenants must turn to their insurance companies to deal with their loss of the improvement.

Assignment and Subleasing

When a tenant transfers all leasehold interests to another person, the lease has been assigned. The new tenant is legally obligated for all the promises the original tenant made in the lease.

When a tenant transfers less than all the leasehold interests by leasing them to a new tenant, the original tenant has *subleased* (or sublet) the property. The original tenant remains responsible for rent being paid by the new tenant and for any damage done to the rental during the lease term. The new tenant is responsible only to the original tenant to pay the rent due.

Assignment and subleasing are only allowed when a lease specifically permits them. In both assignments and subleases, details of the new arrangements should be in writing.

In most cases, the **sublease** or **assignment** of a lease does not relieve the original lessee of the obligation to pay rent. The landlord may, however, agree to waive the former tenant's liability. Most leases prohibit a lessee from assigning or subletting without the lessor's consent. This permits the lessor to retain control over the occupancy of the leased premises. As a rule, the lessor must not unreasonably withhold consent. The sublessor's (original lessee's) interest in the real estate is known as a *sandwich lease*.

Recording a Lease

Anyone who inspects the property receives actual notice. For these reasons, it is usually considered unnecessary to record a lease. However, most states allow a lease to be recorded in the county in which the property is located. Furthermore, leases of three years or longer often are recorded as a matter of course. Some states *require* that long-term leases be recorded, especially when the lessees intend to mortgage the leasehold interests.

Nondisturbance Clause

A **nondisturbance clause** is a mortgage clause stating that the mortgagee agrees not to terminate the tenancies of lessees who pay their rent should the mortgagee foreclose on the mortgagor-lessor's building.

Options

A lease may contain a clause that grants the lessee the privilege of renewing the lease (called a **renewal option**). The lessee must, however, give notice of intent to exercise the option. Some leases grant the lessee the option to purchase the leased premises (called a **purchase option**). This option normally gives the tenant the right to purchase the property at a predetermined price within a certain period, possibly the lease term. The lease might also contain a **right of first refusal** clause, allowing the tenant the opportunity to buy the property before the owner accepts an offer from another party. Although not required, the owner may give the tenant credit toward the purchase price for some percentage of the rent paid. The lease agreement is a primary contract over the option to purchase.

IN PRACTICE   All the general statements concerning provisions of a lease are controlled largely by the terms of the agreement and state law. Landlord-tenant laws also vary from state to state. Great care must be exercised in reading the entire lease document before signing it because every clause in the lease has an economic and legal impact on either the landlord or the tenant. Although preprinted lease forms are available, there is no such thing as a standard lease. When complicated lease situations arise, legal counsel should be sought.

■ TYPES OF LEASES

The manner in which rent is determined indicates the type of lease that is put into effect. There are three basic types of leases; the gross lease, the net lease, and the percentage lease. (See Table 16.1.)

Gross Lease

In a **gross lease**, the tenant pays a fixed rent, and the landlord pays all taxes, insurance, repairs, utilities, and maintenance connected with the property (usually called *property charges* or *operating expenses*). Residential and commercial office leases are most often gross leases.

Net Lease

In a **net lease**, the tenant pays all or most of the property charges in addition to the rent. The monthly rental is net income for the landlord after operating costs have been paid. This lease is most often associated with large commercial and industrial leases.

Percentage Lease

Either a gross lease or a net lease may be a **percentage lease**. This type of lease is generally used for retail business leases. The rent is based on a minimum fixed rental fee plus a percentage of the gross income received by the tenant doing

TABLE 16.1 **Types of Leases**	**Type of Lease**	**Lessee**	**Lessor**
	Gross lease	Pays basic rent	Pays property charges (taxes, repairs, insurance, etc.)
	Net lease	Pays basic rent plus all or most property charges	May pay some property charges
	Percentage lease (commercial and industrial)	Pays basic rent plus percent of gross sales (may pay property costs)	Lessor often pays property charges (taxes, repairs, insurance, etc.)

business on the leased property. The percentage charged is negotiable and varies depending on the nature of the business, location of the property, and general economic conditions.

Other Types of Leases

Variable lease   Several types of leases allow for increases in the rental charges during the lease periods. A *graduated lease* provides for specified rent increases at set future dates. Another is the *index lease*, which allows rent to be increased or decreased periodically based on changes in the consumer price index or some other indicator.

Ground lease   When a landowner leases unimproved land to a tenant who agrees to erect a building on the land, the lease is usually referred to as a **ground lease**. It is most often used in commercial property development. Ground leases typically involve separate ownership of the land and the buildings. These leases must be for a long enough term to make the transaction desirable to the tenant investing in the building. They often run for terms of 50 to 99 years. Ground leases are generally *net leases*: the lessee must pay rent on the ground as well as real estate taxes, insurance, upkeep, and repairs.

Oil and gas lease   When an oil company leases land to explore for oil and gas, a special lease agreement must be negotiated. Usually, the landowner receives a cash payment for executing the lease. If no well is drilled within the period stated in the lease, the lease expires. However, most oil and gas leases permit the oil company to continue its rights for another year by paying another flat rental fee. Such rentals may be paid annually until a well is produced. If oil or gas is found, the landowner usually receives a percentage of its value as a royalty. As long as oil or gas is obtained in significant quantities, the lease continues indefinitely.

A **lease purchase** is used when a tenant wants to purchase the property but is unable to do so. Perhaps the tenant cannot obtain favorable financing or clear title, or the tax consequences of a current purchase would be unfavorable. In this arrangement, the purchase agreement is the primary consideration, and the lease is secondary. Part of the periodic rent is applied toward the purchase price of the property until it is reduced to an amount for which the tenant can obtain financing or purchase the property outright, depending on the terms of the lease purchase agreement.

A **sale-and-leaseback** is the arrangement whereby the owners of property sell the property and then lease it back again for an agreed period and rental. A sale-and-leaseback is often used when extra capital is needed on a construction project. The original owners pull out their equity to use on other projects and reduce their taxable income when they pay rent to the new owner. The new owner now has a reliable source of rental income for an extended time.

■ DISCHARGE OF LEASES

As with any contract, a lease is discharged when the contract terminates. Termination can occur when all parties have fully performed their obligations under the agreement. In addition, the parties may agree to cancel the lease. If the tenant, for instance, offers to surrender the leasehold interest, and if the landlord accepts the tenant's offer, the lease is terminated. A tenant who simply abandons leased property, however, remains liable for the terms of the lease—including the rent. The terms of the lease will usually indicate whether the landlord is obligated to try to rerent the space. If the landlord intends to sue for unpaid rent, however, most states require an attempt to mitigate damages by rerenting the premises to limit the amount owed.

The lease does not terminate if the parties die or if the property is sold. There are two exceptions to this general rule. First, a lease from the owner of a life estate ends when the tenant's life ends. The death of either party terminates a tenancy at will. Second, in all other cases, the heirs of a deceased landlord are bound by the terms of existing valid leases.

If leased real estate is sold or otherwise conveyed, the new landlord takes the property subject to the rights of the tenants. A lease agreement may, however, contain language that permits a new landlord to terminate existing leases. The clause, commonly known as a *sale clause*, requires that the tenants be given some period of notice before the termination. Because the new owner has taken title subject to the rights of the tenants, the sale clause enables the new landlord to claim possession and negotiate new leases under the new owner's terms and conditions. A tenancy may also be terminated by operation of law, as in a bankruptcy or condemnation proceeding.

Breach of Lease

When a tenant breaches any lease provision, the landlord may sue the tenant to obtain a judgment to cover past-due rent, damages to the premises, or other defaults. Likewise, when a landlord breaches any lease provision, the tenant is entitled to certain remedies. The rights and responsibilities of the landlord-tenant relationship are governed by state law.

Suit for possession—actual eviction   When a tenant breaches a lease or improperly retains leased premises, the landlord may regain possession through a legal process known as **actual eviction**. The landlord must serve notice on the tenant before commencing the lawsuit. Most lease terms require at least a ten-day notice in the case of default. In many states, however, only a five-day notice is necessary when the tenant defaults in the payment of rent. When a court issues a judgment for possession to a landlord, the tenant must vacate the property. If the tenant fails to leave, the landlord can have the judgment enforced by a court officer, who forcibly removes the tenant and the tenant's possessions. The landlord then has the right to re-enter and regain possession of the property. In some states, in cases of nonpayment of rent, a landlord also has the right to distrain, that is, to seize the tenant's property for rent in arrears, generally by changing the locks and giving notice. Most states require a court order for distraint.

Tenants' remedies—constructive eviction If a landlord breaches any clause of a lease agreement, the tenant has the right to sue and recover damages against the landlord. If the leased premises become unusable for the purpose stated in the lease, the tenant may have the right to abandon them. This action, called **constructive eviction**, terminates the lease agreement. The tenant must prove that the premises have become unusable because of the conscious neglect of the landlord. To claim constructive eviction, the tenant must leave the premises while the conditions that made the premises uninhabitable exist.

■ **FOR EXAMPLE** A tenant's lease requires that the landlord furnish heat. The landlord fails to repair a defective furnace, and no heat is provided to the tenant's apartment during the winter months. The tenant is forced to abandon the apartment. Because the lack of heat was due to the landlord's negligence, the tenant has been constructively evicted.

Protenant Legislation

For the most part, leases are drawn up primarily for the benefit of the landlord. However, due to tenants' rights movements and increased consumer awareness, several states have adopted some variation of the Uniform Residential Landlord and Tenant Act. This model law addresses the need for both parties to a lease to fulfill certain basic obligations. The act addresses such issues as

■ the landlord's right of entry,
■ maintenance of the premises,
■ the tenant's protection against retaliation by the landlord for complaints, and
■ the disclosure of the property owners' names and addresses to the tenants.

The act further establishes the specific remedies available to both the landlord and the tenant if a breach of the lease agreement occurs.

■ FAIR HOUSING AND CIVIL RIGHTS LAWS

The federal fair housing and civil rights laws affect landlords and tenants just as they do sellers and purchasers. All persons must have access to housing of their choice without any differentiation in the terms and conditions because of their race, color, religion, national origin, sex, disability, or familial status. State and local municipalities have their own fair housing laws that add protected classes such as age and sexual orientation. Withholding an apartment that is available for rent, segregating certain people in separate sections of an apartment complex or parts of a building, and charging people in the protected classes different amounts for rent or security deposits all constitute violations of the law.

It is important that landlords realize that changes in the laws stemming from the federal Fair Housing Amendments Act of 1988 significantly alter past practices, particularly as they affect individuals with disabilities and families with children. The fair housing laws require that the same tenant criteria be applied to families with children that are applied to adults. A landlord cannot charge a different amount of rent or security deposit because one of the tenants is a child. While landlords have historically argued that children are noisy and destructive, the fact is that many adults are noisy and destructive as well.

■ KEY POINT REVIEW

A **lease** is a contract between the **lessor** (the owner of real estate) and the **lessee** that transfers **possession and use** of the property, lasts for a **specified period**, and is made in return for **consideration** (possession and payment).

The **statute of frauds** in most states requires that leases for more than one year be **in writing to be enforceable.**

The lessor (**landlord**) has a **reversionary right** to possession of property when a lease expires.

The lessee (**tenant**) has a **leasehold** estate that can be one of the following:

■ **Estate for years (tenancy for years)**—continues for a definite period
■ **Estate from period to period (periodic tenancy)**—has no specific expiration date, but rent is payable at definite intervals
  — Has continuity because it automatically renews
  — **Month-to-month tenancy**—a common form of residential lease
  — **Holdover tenancy**—may be created when a tenant with an estate for years stays on after the lease term expires and the landlord accepts rent payment
■ **Estate at will (tenancy at will)**—has no specified initial term, is created by **express agreement** or **operation of law**, and can be **terminated** by the landlord or the tenant at any time on proper notice
■ **Estate at sufferance (tenancy at sufferance)**—created when the tenant stays on without the landlord's consent after termination
  — The landlord's acceptance of rent creates a **holdover tenancy.**
  — The landlord can treat a tenant as a **trespasser** and begin eviction proceedings and action for damages under state laws.

A **valid lease** requires parties with **CLOAC** (**C**apacity to contract, **L**egal objectives, **O**ffer and **A**cceptance, and valid **C**onsideration) and includes the following:

■ **Description** of leased premises
■ Implied **covenant of quiet enjoyment**
■ Limitations on tenant's **use** of the property and the term (length) of the lease
■ **Security deposit,** which must comply with state law
■ Whether **improvements** may be made by the tenant:
  — Fixtures generally become the landlord's property.
  — **Federal fair housing law** requires that the landlord allow a tenant with a physical disability to make reasonable modifications.
  — **Americans with Disabilities Act (ADA)** requires that commercial nonresidential property be free of barriers or that reasonable accommodations be provided.
■ **Maintenance** of premises by landlord in compliance with state law
■ **Assignment** of lease that relieves tenant of further obligation
■ **Sublease** provisions
■ **Recording** of lease that may be required by state law
■ **Nondisturbance** clause
■ **Option** that may give the tenant the **right to renew** the lease, **right to purchase** property, or **right of first refusal** before landlord can sell the property

A **gross lease** requires the tenant to pay basic rent and the landlord to pay expenses of ownership.

A **net lease** requires the tenant to pay basic rent plus all or most property expenses and the landlord to pay some property expenses.

In a **percentage lease**, the tenant pays basic rent plus a percentage of gross sales and may pay property expenses.

A **variable lease** allows an increase in rent during the lease period. A **graduated lease** states specific rent increases. An **index lease** allows rent changes (up or down) based on the consumer price index or other indicator.

A **ground lease** involves separate ownership of the land and the buildings.

An **oil and gas lease** allows exploration for and removal of oil and gas.

In a **lease purchase,** part of the rent may be applied to the purchase price.

A **sale-and-leaseback** allows the original owner to use the property while freeing up capital for other business purposes.

The remedies for **breach** of a lease are governed by state law and include the following:

- The landlord may bring **suit for possession (actual eviction)**.
- The tenant may claim **constructive eviction** if the premises are unusable.

The **Uniform Residential Landlord and Tenant Act** has been adopted by some states.

The **Fair Housing Amendments Act of 1988** prohibits discrimination on the basis of race, color, religion, national origin, sex, disability, or familial status. State and local governments may add more protected groups.

■ RELATED WEB SITE

Legal Information Institute: Landlord-Tenant Law:
   http://topics.law.cornell.edu/wex/landlord-tenant_law/

CHAPTER 16 QUIZ

1. Which transaction would *BEST* be described as involving a ground lease?
   a. A landowner agrees to let a tenant drill for oil on a property for 75 years.
   b. A tenant agrees to pay proportionate, increased rental based on annual appraisals of the rented property.
   c. A landlord charges a commercial tenant separate amounts for the rented land and for the leased building.
   d. A tenant pays a base amount for the property plus a percentage of business-generated income.

2. A tenant enters into a commercial lease that requires a monthly rent of a minimum fixed amount, plus an additional amount determined by the tenant's gross receipts exceeding $5,000. This type of lease is called a
   a. standard lease.
   b. gross lease.
   c. percentage lease.
   d. net lease.

3. If a tenant moved out of a rented store building because access to the building was blocked as a result of the landlord's negligence, the
   a. tenant might have no legal recourse against the landlord.
   b. landlord may be liable for the rent until the expiration date of the lease.
   c. landlord may have to provide substitute space.
   d. tenant may be entitled to recover damages from the landlord.

4. A tenant moves a pet into an apartment community that has a no-pets policy. The landlord wishes to remove the tenant due to the breach. The legal process to remove a tenant is known as
   a. constructive eviction.
   b. eminent domain.
   c. actual eviction.
   d. partial eviction.

5. A tenant still has five months remaining on a one-year apartment lease. When the tenant moves to another city, he transfers possession of the apartment to a friend for the entire remaining term of the lease. The friend pays rent directly to the tenant. In this situation, the tenant has become a(n)
   a. assignor.
   b. sublessor.
   c. sublessee.
   d. lessor.

6. Which of the following is *TRUE* about a holdover tenant?
   a. The landlord must accept additional rent if the tenant remains on the premises.
   b. The tenant must give the landlord a 30-day notice to vacate.
   c. The tenant may continue to occupy the premises without permission of the landlord.
   d. The landlord may evict the tenant.

7. A tenant's tenancy for years will expire in two weeks. The tenant plans to move to a larger apartment across town when the current tenancy expires. In order to terminate this agreement, the tenant must
   a. give the landlord immediate notice or the lease will automatically renew.
   b. give the landlord one week's prior notice or the lease will automatically renew.
   c. do nothing because the agreement will terminate automatically at the end of the current term.
   d. sign a lease for the new apartment, which will automatically terminate the existing lease.

8. When a tenant holds possession of a landlord's property without a current lease agreement and without the landlord's approval, the
   a. tenant is maintaining a gross lease.
   b. landlord can file suit for possession.
   c. tenant has no obligation to pay rent.
   d. landlord may be subject to a constructive eviction.

9. Under the negotiated terms of a certain residential lease, the landlord is required to maintain the water heater. If the tenant is unable to get hot water because of a faulty water heater that the landlord has failed to repair after repeated notification, the tenant could do all of the following EXCEPT
   a. sue the landlord for damages.
   b. sue the landlord for breach of the covenant of seisin.
   c. abandon the premises claiming constructive eviction.
   d. terminate the lease agreement.

10. A person has a one-year leasehold interest in a house. The interest automatically renews itself at the end of each year. The person's interest is referred to as a tenancy
    a. for years.
    b. from period to period.
    c. at will.
    d. at sufferance.

11. Rent would BEST be defined as
    a. contractual consideration to a third party.
    b. consideration for the use of real property.
    c. all monies paid by the lessor to the lessee.
    d. the total balance owed under the terms of a lease.

12. Which of the following would automatically terminate a residential lease?
    a. Total destruction of the property
    b. Sale of the property
    c. Failure of the tenant to pay rent
    d. Death of the tenant

13. Which of the following describes a net lease?
    a. An agreement in which the tenant pays a fixed rent and the landlord pays all taxes, insurance, and expenses related to the property
    b. A lease in which the tenant pays rent, plus some—or all—of the operating expenses related to the property
    c. A lease in which the tenant pays the landlord a percentage of the monthly income derived from the property
    d. An agreement granting an individual a leasehold interest in fishing rights for shoreline properties

14. A tenancy in which the tenant continues in possession after the lease has expired, without the landlord's permission, is a
    a. tenancy for years.
    b. periodic tenancy.
    c. tenancy at will.
    d. tenancy at sufferance.

15. A percentage lease calls for a minimum rent of $1,200 per month plus additional annual rent of 4 percent of the year's gross business exceeding $150,000. If the business generated $270,000, how much annual rent does the tenant owe?
    a. $10,800
    b. $14,400
    c. $19,200
    d. $25,200

16. Which of the following describes a gross lease?
    a. An agreement in which the tenant pays a fixed rent and the landlord pays all taxes, insurance, and expenses related to the property
    b. A lease in which the tenant pays rent plus some of the operating expenses related to the property
    c. A lease in which the tenant pays the landlord a percentage of the monthly income derived from the property
    d. An agreement allowing the tenant to terminate the lease if certain conditions near the premises become unbearable

17. A tenant signs a lease that includes a schedule of rent increases on specific dates over the course of the lease term. What kind of lease has this tenant signed?
    a. Percentage
    b. Net
    c. Graduated
    d. Index

18. A tenant signs a lease that includes the following clause: "The stated rent under this agreement will be increased or decreased every three months based on the percentage increase in the consumer price index (CPI) for that period." What kind of lease has this tenant signed?
    a. Percentage
    b. Net
    c. Graduated
    d. Index

19. The death of either the landlord or the tenant will terminate the lease and the parties' heirs will NOT be bound by its terms under which of the following tenancies?
    a. Tenancy for years
    b. Periodic tenancy
    c. Tenancy at will
    d. Tenancy at sufferance

20. The tenant leases a heated apartment, but the landlord fails to provide heat because of a defective central heating plant. The tenant vacates the premises and refuses to pay any rent. This is an example of
    a. abandonment.
    b. actual eviction.
    c. constructive eviction.
    d. lessor negligence.

PART II

PRACTICE

CHAPTER 17

Property Management

■ **LEARNING OBJECTIVES** *When you have finished reading this chapter, you should be able to*

■ **identify** the basic elements of a management agreement;

■ **describe** a property manager's functions;

■ **explain** the role of environmental regulations and the Americans with Disabilities Act in the property manager's job;

■ **distinguish** the various types of risk management; and

■ **define** the following *key terms*:

budget comparison statement	multiperil policies	routine maintenance
cash flow report	operating budget	surety bonds
corrective maintenance	preventive maintenance	tenant improvements
management agreement	profit and loss statement	workers' compensation acts
management plan	property manager	
	risk management	

PROPERTY MANAGEMENT

As a specialized field, property management is one of the fastest growing areas of real estate. Many mortgage lenders require that investors hire a professional property manager to manage their properties. Property management involves the leasing, managing, marketing, and overall maintenance of real estate owned by others, usually rental property.

THE PROPERTY MANAGER

A property manager must
- achieve the goals of the owners,
- generate income for the owners, and
- preserve and increase the value of the property.

The role of the **property manager** is complex, requiring the manager to wear many hats. It is not unusual for a property manager to be a market analyst, salesperson, accountant, advertising specialist, and maintenance person—all in the same day. In addition, the property manager frequently interacts with people in various professions, including lawyers, environmental engineers, and accountants. The three principal responsibilities of the property manager are to

- achieve the objectives of the property owners,
- generate income for the owners, and
- preserve and/or increase the value of the investment property.

The property manager carries out the goals of the property owners. In the process, the property manager is responsible for maintaining the owner's investment and making sure the property earns income. These goals can be accomplished in several ways. The physical property must be maintained in good condition. Suitable tenants must be found, rent must be collected, and employees must be hired and supervised. The property manager is responsible for budgeting and controlling expenses, keeping proper accounts, and making periodic reports to the owner. In all of these activities, the manager's primary goal is to operate and maintain the physical property in such a way as to preserve and enhance the owner's capital investment.

Some property managers work for property management companies. These firms manage properties for a number of owners under management agreements. Others are independent contractors in an agency relationship with the owner that involves greater authority and discretion over management than an employee would have. A property manager or an owner may employ building managers to supervise the daily operations of a building. In some cases, these individuals might be residents of the building.

IN PRACTICE In most states, licensed real estate brokers are permitted to manage properties for others. Some states have instituted separate property management licenses When directly employed by the owner, nonlicensed individuals are permitted by some states to manage properties. While some states require licensing in order to manage condominium or cooperative homeowners' associations, others do not. Some states require an on-site manager for residential income-producing properties having more than a certain number of units (e.g., California requires a manager on-site for residential properties of 16 or more units).

Securing Management Business

Possible sources of a property management business include

- corporate owners,
- apartment buildings,
- owners of small rental residential properties,
- homeowners' associations,
- investment syndicates,
- trusts, and
- owners of office buildings.

A good reputation is often the manager's best advertising. A manager who consistently demonstrates the ability to increase property income over previous levels should have little difficulty finding new business.

Before contracting to manage any property, however, the professional property manager should be certain that the building owner has realistic income expectations. Necessary maintenance, unexpected repairs, and effective marketing all take time and money. In addition, most states have landlord-tenant laws that require the landlord-owner to keep the property repaired and make sure it complies with building codes. Through the agency relationship with the owner, the property manager becomes responsible for repairs and the building's condition.

New Opportunities

Specialization has opened a range of new opportunities. Well-trained specialists are needed to manage shopping centers, commercial buildings, and industrial parks in addition to the more visible management of residential properties. Here are just a few of the specialties looking for a few good people:

Community association management   The prevalence of homeowners' and condominium associations combined with complex planning and development codes have placed new demands on property managers. Working as part of a team, property managers assist in providing a comprehensive array of services to volunteer boards. Many states now require at least a real estate license or an association management license for those who specialize in managing associations.

Housing for the near-elderly and elderly   Opportunities abound in managing housing for the near-elderly (55+) and elderly (62+), many of which are federally assisted housing programs. In addition to marketing, these property managers are often responsible for the operations of the facility, as well as housekeeping, meal service, social event planning, and medical emergency planning. Since subsidized housing is involved, these property managers need to be familiar with state and federal rules pertaining to eligibility requirements and income verification.

Manufactured homes (i.e., mobile home parks)   Homes built in factories meeting HUD specifications are called manufactured homes (incorrectly, mobile homes). These homes may be placed on individually owned land, but more than a third are sited in communities. The tenants may be renting only the "pad," the land on which the home is sited, or the home itself. Many communities are geared toward the near-elderly and elderly; these managers must be effective at building community spirit.

Resort housing Managing second-home and resort rentals presents specific challenges. These managers must be able to care for and maintain often-vacant properties and be able to attract and manage short-term tenants. Many of these properties are located in high-risk areas for natural disasters such as hurricanes, so the manager must be ready to work with insurance adjusters as well.

Concierge services A new area for property managers to specialize in is the training and managing of concierge staff for office buildings and other settings. Concierge staff are responsible for anything from arranging for taxi rides to assisting with visual aids equipment for a conference.

Asset management Asset managers monitor a portfolio of properties similar to a securities portfolio by analyzing the performance of the properties and making recommendations to the owners of the properties. Real property asset management helps clients decide what type of real estate to invest in—commercial or residential, which property is best to purchase, the best financial sources for a real estate purchase, and when to dispose of property.

Corporate property managers Corporate property managers manage properties for corporations that invest in real estate. Because these corporations do not usually deal in real estate, they are not necessarily knowledgeable about property management. Hiring a corporate property manager allows a corporation to invest in real estate and increase its capital without needing the specialized knowledge of property management. Typically, corporate property managers are employees of the corporation and not independent contractors.

Leasing agents Leasing agents are usually independent contractors working on a commission basis and are in high demand because of their skill in securing lessees.

Professional Associations

Most metropolitan areas have local associations of building and property owners and managers that are affiliates of regional and national associations. Many of these professional organizations provide information and contacts for all aspects of property management.

Here is a list of some well-known associations:

- Building Owners and Managers Association International (BOMA): commercial real estate
- Building Owners and Managers Institute International (BOMI): education programs for commercial property and facility management industries
- Community Associations Institute (CAI): homeowners' associations, condominiums, and other planned communities
- Institute of Real Estate Management (IREM): multifamily and commercial real estate designation
- International Council of Shopping Centers (ICSC): shopping centers worldwide
- National Apartment Association (NAA): multifamily housing industry

- National Association of Home Builders (NAHB): all aspects of home building
- National Association of Residential Property Managers (NARPM): single-family and small residential properties

THE MANAGEMENT PLAN AND AGREEMENT

The Management Plan

Property management begins with a **management plan** prepared by the property manager. A management plan outlines the details of the owner's objectives with the property, as well as what the property manager expects to accomplish and how, including all financial objectives. In preparing a management plan, a property manager analyzes three factors: the owner's objectives, the regional and neighborhood market, and the specific property. Occupancy, absorption rates, and new starts are critical indicators. The plan also includes a budgetary section on sources of revenue and anticipated expenses. While the management plan is a document for the present, it is forward-looking in determining the feasibility of a property owner's long-term goals for a specific property.

The Management Agreement

The first step in taking over the management of any property is to enter into a **management agreement,** a contract creating a general agency relationship between the owner and the property manager; it defines the duties and responsibilities of each party. It is also a guide used in operating the property, as well as a reference in case of any future disputes.

The management agreement creates an agency relationship between the owner and the property manager. The property manager usually is considered to be a *general agent.* As an agent, the property manager is charged with the fiduciary responsibilities of care, obedience, accounting, loyalty, and disclosure. Property managers are usually empowered to make many more decisions on behalf of the owner than a broker can make on behalf of a seller or buyer. After entering into an agreement with a property owner, a manager handles the property the same way the owner would. In all activities, the manager's first responsibility is to realize the highest return on the property in a manner consistent with the owner's instructions. As in any other contract involving real estate, the management agreement should be in writing, and it should include the following points:

- *Description* of the property
- *Time period* the agreement covers and specific provisions for termination
- *Definition of the management's responsibilities.* All the manager's duties should be specifically stated in the contract. Any limitations or restrictions on what the manager may do should be clearly stated.

- *Statement of the owner's purpose and responsibilities.* The owner should clearly state what the manager is to accomplish. One owner may want to maximize net income, while another may want to increase the capital value of the investment. What the manager does depends on the owner's long-term goals for the property. The agreement should list the owner's responsibilities for management expenses, such as payroll, advertising, insurance, and management fees.

- *Extent of the manager's authority.* This provision should state what authority the manager is to have in matters such as hiring, firing, and supervising employees; fixing rental rates for space; and making expenditures and authorizing repairs. Repairs that exceed a certain expense limit may require the owner's written approval.

- *Reporting.* The frequency and detail of the manager's periodic reports on operations and financial position should be agreed on. These reports serve as a means for the owner to monitor the manager's work. They also form a basis for both the owner and the manager to spot trends that are important in shaping management policy. In general, state real estate commissions have rules concerning reporting that must be followed.

- *Compensation.* The management fee or other form of compensation may be based on a percentage of gross or net income, a fixed fee, or some combination of these and other factors. The compensation provision of the agreement should state the base fee, as well as any leasing fees, supervision fees, or other commissions or compensations. Finally, the agreement should require that the manager be included as an additional insured on the property liability policy.

- *Allocation of costs.* The agreement should state which of the property manager's expenses—such as office rent, office help, telephone, advertising, and association fees—will be paid by the manager. Other costs will be paid by the owner.

- *Antitrust provisions.* Management fees are subject to the same antitrust considerations as sales commissions. They cannot be standardized in the marketplace, because standardization would be considered as price-fixing. The fee must be negotiated between the agent and the principal. In addition, the property manager may be entitled to a commission on new rentals and renewed leases.

- *Equal opportunity statement.* Residential property management agreements should include a statement that the property will be shown, rented, and otherwise made available to all persons, regardless of race, color, religion, sex, disability, national origin, or family status, and to any class of person protected by state or federal law.

MATH CONCEPTS

RENTAL COMMISSIONS

Residential property managers often earn commissions when they find tenants for a property. Rental commissions are usually based on the annual rent from a property. For example, if an apartment unit rents for $1,200 per month and the commission payable is 8 percent, the commission is calculated as follows:

$1,200 per month × 12 months = $14,400

$14,400 × 0.08 (8%) = $1,152

■ THE PROPERTY MANAGER'S RESPONSIBILITIES

A property manager's responsibilities are determined by the management agreement. Certain duties, however, are found in most agreements. These duties may include creating financial reports, renting property, selecting tenants, maintaining good relations with tenants, marketing, and maintaining the property.

Financial Reports

One of the primary responsibilities of a property manager is maintaining financial reports, including an operating budget, cash flow report, profit and loss statement, and budget comparison statement. While there are no standard formats for these reports, there is some similarity among the reports, and it is important for the property manager to adapt a report to meet an owner's needs.

Operating budget An **operating budget** is the projection of income and expense for the operation of a property over a one-year period. This budget, developed before attempting to rent property, is based on anticipated revenues and expenses and provides the owner the amount of anticipated profit. The property uses the operating budget as a guide for the property's financial performance in the present and future.

Once a property manager has managed a property for a length of time, an operating budget may be developed based on the results of the profit and loss statement in comparison to the original budget (actual versus projected). After making the comparison, a new operating budget is prepared for a new time period in the future.

Cash flow report A **cash flow report** is a monthly statement that details the financial status of the property. Sources of income and expenses are noted, as well as net operating income, and net cash flow. The cash flow report is the most important financial report because it provides a picture of the current financial status of a property.

Income Income includes gross rentals collected, delinquent rental payments, utilities, vending, contracts, late fees, and storage charges. Any losses from uncollected rental payments or evictions are deducted from the total gross to arrive at the total adjusted income.

In some properties, there is space that is not income producing, such as the property manager's office. The rental value of the property that is not producing income is subtracted from the gross rental income to equal the gross collectible, or billable, rental income.

Expenses Fixed and variable expenses include administrative costs (including building personnel), operating expenses, and maintenance costs. Fixed expenses that remain constant and do not change include employee wages, utilities, and other basic operating costs. Variable expenses may be recurring or nonrecurring, and can include capital improvements, building repairs, and landscaping.

The formula for arriving at cash flow is as follows:

> Gross rental income + Other income – Losses incurred = Total income
> Total income – Operating expenses = Net operating income before debt service (e.g., mortgage payments)
> Net operating income before debt service – Debt service – Reserves = Cash flow

A **profit and loss statement** is a financial picture of the revenues and expenses used to determine whether the business has made money or suffered a loss. It may be prepared monthly, quarterly, semiannually, or annually. The statement is created from the monthly cash flow reports and does not include itemized information. A formula for profit and loss statement looks like this:

> Gross receipts – Operating expenses – Total mortgage payment + Mortgage loan principal = Net profit

Budget comparison statement The **budget comparison statement** compares the actual results with the original budget, often giving either percentages or a numerical variance of actual versus projected income and expenses. Budget comparisons are especially helpful in identifying trends in order to help with future budget planning.

Renting the Property

Effective rental of the property is essential to ensure the long-term financial health of the property. Although the property manager may use the services of a leasing agent, the broker acting as leasing agent is concerned solely with renting space but is not responsible for maintaining and managing the property.

Setting rental rates Because rental rates are influenced primarily by supply and demand, property managers should conduct a detailed survey of the competitive space available in the neighborhood, emphasizing similar properties. In establishing rental rates, property managers must consider the following:

- The rental income must be sufficient to cover the property's fixed charges and operating expenses.
- The rental income must provide a return on the owner's investment.
- The rental rate should be comparable with prevailing rates in comparable buildings in the area; it may be slightly higher or slightly lower, depending on the strength of the property.
- The current vacancy rate in the property is a good indicator of how much of a rent increase might be advisable. A building with a low vacancy rate is a better candidate for an increase than one with a high vacancy rate.

A rental rate for residential space is usually stated as the monthly rate *per unit.* Commercial leases—including office, retail, and industrial space rentals—are usually stated according to either annual or monthly rates *per square foot.*

An elevated level of vacancy may indicate poor management, a defective or undesirable property, or rental rates that are too high for the market or the property. A high occupancy rate may mean that rental rates are too low. Before adjusting the rental rates, the manager should investigate the rental market to determine whether a rent increase is warranted.

Marketing

To ensure that a property generates income, the property manager must attract the best tenants. The marketing strategy must take into consideration the property itself, the supply and demand in the area where the property is located, and the amount of money available for advertising.

Advertising   All advertising and promotional activities must comply with federal, state, and local nondiscriminatory laws. The content cannot market to one protected class, such as race, color, religion, sex, national origin, family status, or physical disabilities. To ensure that a property generates income, the property manager must attract the best tenants. The marketing strategy must take into consideration the property itself, the supply and demand in the area where the property is located, and the amount of money available for advertising.

Advertising methods are numerous and include newspaper advertising, brochures, and direct-mail pieces, and on Web sites, radio, television, and billboards.

Management activities   Because property management firms are often known by reputation, it is important for a firm to maintain good public relations. One way to cultivate public relations is through community involvement and charitable giving.

Firms can also write and issue public service announcements (PSAs or press releases) regarding special projects. These announcements can attract the attention of the media and, ultimately, prospective tenants.

Marketing costs   A cost-benefit analysis helps a property manager assess whether a particular advertising method worked to attract new tenants. Property marketing expenses are usually figured on a cost-per-prospect-per-lease basis. For example, if a three-bedroom apartment rents for $1,500 and is typically viewed by 10 prospects before it is leased, an $800 newspaper advertisement would cost $80 per prospect.

The Internet has significantly expanded a property manager's ability to reach consumers. Online apartment vacancy listing sites include *www.craigslist.com*, *www.apartmentfinder.com*, *www.forrent.com*, and *www.apartmentguide.com*.

Selecting Tenants

Proper selection is the first step in establishing and maintaining sound, long-term relationships with tenants. The manager should be sure that the premises are suitable for the tenant in terms of size, location, and amenities, and that the tenant can afford the space. A commercial tenant's business should be compatible not only with the building but also with the businesses of the other tenants. Some commercial leases prohibit the introduction of similar businesses, but in any event, introduction of competitors into the same property should be undertaken with care. Managers should always ask commercial tenants about the potential for expansion. Because the property may not have enough room for expansion, the manager could soon lose the tenant to a larger space.

The residential property manager must be sure to comply with all federal, state, and local fair housing laws in selecting tenants. (See Chapters 16 and 20.) Although fair housing laws do not apply to commercial properties, commercial property managers need to be aware of federal, state, and local antidiscrimination and equal opportunity laws that may govern industrial or retail properties.

Most states have strict requirements as to how security deposits should be handled by the property manager: how soon they must be deposited, into what kind of account, and when they must be refunded. In general, funds belonging to others, such as security deposits and collected rents, should be placed into a trust or escrow account. Property managers should not use any of these funds personally (conversion) or mix the funds into personal accounts (commingling).

MATH CONCEPTS

CALCULATING MONTHLY RENT PER SQUARE FOOT (COMMERCIAL)

1. Determine the total square footage of the rental premises (generally floor space only).

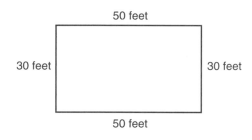

50 feet

30 feet   30 feet

50 feet

   50 feet × 30 feet = 1,500 square feet

2. Find the total annual rent.

   $2,500 per month × 12 months = $30,000 per year

3. Divide the total annual rent by the total square feet to determine the annual rate per square foot.

   $30,000 ÷ 1,500 square feet = $20 per square foot

4. Convert the annual rate to a monthly rate.

   $20 ÷ 12 months = $1.67 per square foot

Collecting rents   A property manager should accept only those tenants who can be expected to meet their financial obligations. The manager should investigate financial references, check with local credit bureaus, and when possible, interview a prospective tenant's former landlord to ensure the tenant is able to meet the financial obligations.

The terms of rental payment should be spelled out in the lease agreement, including

■ time and place of payment,
■ provisions and penalties for late payment and returned checks, and
■ provisions for cancellation and damages in case of nonpayment.

The property manager should establish a firm and consistent collection plan. The plan should include a system of notices and records that complies with state and local law.

Every attempt must be made to collect rent without resorting to legal action. Legal action is costly, and time consuming, and does not contribute to good tenant relations. In some cases, however, legal action is unavoidable. In these instances, a property manager must be prepared to initiate and follow through with the necessary legal steps. Obviously, legal action must be taken in cooperation with the property owner's or management firm's legal counsel.

Maintaining Good Relations with Tenants

The ultimate success of a property manager depends on the ability to maintain good relations with tenants. Dissatisfied tenants are more likely to vacate the property early. A high tenant turnover rate results in greater expenses for advertising and redecorating and less profit for the owner due to uncollected rents.

An effective property manager establishes a good communication system with tenants. Regular newsletters or posted memoranda help keep tenants informed and involved. Maintenance and service requests must be attended to promptly, and all lease terms and building rules must be enforced consistently and fairly. A manager who fails to treat all tenants the same in terms of rent collection and enforcement of lease terms or rule and regulations might be violating fair housing laws. A good manager is tactful and decisive, and acts to benefit both owner and occupants.

The property manager must be able to address residents who do not pay their rents on time or who violate building regulations. When one tenant fails to follow the rules, the other tenants often become frustrated and dissatisfied. Careful record keeping shows whether rent is remitted promptly and in the proper amount. Records of all lease renewal dates should be kept so that the manager can anticipate expiration and retain good tenants who might otherwise move when their leases end.

Maintaining the Property

One of the most important functions of a property manager is the supervision of property maintenance. A manager must learn to balance the services provided with their costs—that is, to satisfy tenants' needs while minimizing operating expenses.

To maintain the property efficiently, the manager must be able to assess the building's needs and how best to meet those needs. Because staffing and scheduling requirements vary with the type, size, and geographic location of the property, the owner and the manager usually agree in advance on maintenance objectives. In some cases, the best plan may be to operate a low-rent property, with minimal expenditures for services and maintenance. Another property may be more lucrative if kept in top condition and operated with all possible tenant services. A well-maintained, high-service property can command premium rental rates.

A primary maintenance objective is to protect the physical integrity of the property over the long term. For example, preserving the property by repainting the exterior or replacing the heating system helps decrease long-term maintenance costs. Keeping the property in good condition involves the following three types of maintenance:

> **Three Types of Maintenance**
> - Preventive
> - Repair or corrective
> - Routine

- Preventive
- Repair or corrective
- Routine

Preventive maintenance includes regularly scheduled activities such as painting and seasonal servicing of appliances and systems. Preventive maintenance preserves the long-range value and physical integrity of the building. This is both the most critical and the most neglected maintenance responsibility. Failure to perform preventive maintenance invariably leads to greater expense in other areas of maintenance.

> **Preventive maintenance** helps prevent problems and expenses. **Corrective maintenance** corrects problems after they've occurred.

Repair or **corrective maintenance** involves the actual repairs that keep the building's equipment, utilities, and amenities functioning. Repairing a toilet, fixing a leaky faucet, and replacing a broken air-conditioning unit are acts of corrective maintenance.

A property manager also must supervise the **routine maintenance** of the building. Routine maintenance includes such day-to-day duties as performing minor carpentry and plumbing repairs, and providing regularly scheduled upkeep of heating, air-conditioning, and landscaping.

IN PRACTICE One of the major decisions a property manager faces is whether to contract for maintenance services from an outside firm or to hire on-site employees. The property manager will make the decision on what is most cost-effective for the owner. This decision should be based on a number of factors, including the

> **Construction** involves making a property meet a tenant's needs.

- size of the building,
- complexity of the tenants' requirements,
- time and expense involved, and
- availability of suitable labor.

A commercial or industrial property manager often is called on to make **tenant improvements** (or *build-outs*). These are construction alterations to the interior of the building to meet a tenant's particular space needs. Such alterations range from

simply repainting or recarpeting to completely gutting the interior
the space by erecting new walls, partitions, and electrical systems.
ments are especially important when renting new buildings. In n
the interiors are usually left incomplete so that they can be ada
of individual tenants. One matter that must be clarified is which improvements
will be considered trade fixtures (personal property belonging to the tenant) and
which will belong to the owner of the real estate. (See Chapter 2.)

Modernization or renovation of buildings that have become functionally obsolete
and thus unsuited to today's building needs is also important. (See Chapter 18.)
The renovation of a building often enhances the building's marketability and
increases its potential income.

FEDERAL LAWS AFFECTING PROPERTY MANAGEMENT

Several federal laws affect the property management profession. The Americans
with Disabilities Act, the Equal Credit Opportunity Act, and the Fair Housing
Act all help to ensure that consumer rights are not violated and whether those
rights involve the need to make accommodations for people with disabilities or
the need to treat all housing applicants the same.

The Americans with Disabilities Act

The Americans with Disabilities Act (ADA) has had a significant impact on the
responsibilities of the property manager, in both building amenities and employment issues.

Title I of the ADA provides for the employment of qualified job applicants,
regardless of their disability. Any employer with 15 or more employees must adopt
nondiscriminatory employment procedures. In addition, employers must make
reasonable accommodations to enable individuals with disabilities to perform
essential job functions.

Property managers also must be familiar with Title III of the ADA, which prohibits discrimination in commercial properties and public accommodations. The
ADA requires that managers ensure that people with disabilities have full and
equal access to facilities and services. (See Figure 17.1.)

■ FOR EXAMPLE   A prospective tenant is visually impaired. The property
manager should be prepared to provide a lease agreement that is in enlarged, easy-
to-read type or that is printed in Braille.

The property manager typically is responsible for determining whether a building meets the ADA's accessibility requirements. The property manager also must
prepare a plan for retrofitting a building that is not in compliance when removal
of existing barriers is readily achievable and can be performed without much difficulty or expense. Some tax advantages may be available to help offset the expense
of ADA compliance. ADA experts may be consulted, as well as architectural
designers who specialize in accessibility issues.

IGURE   17.1

Reasonable Modifications to Public Facilities or Services

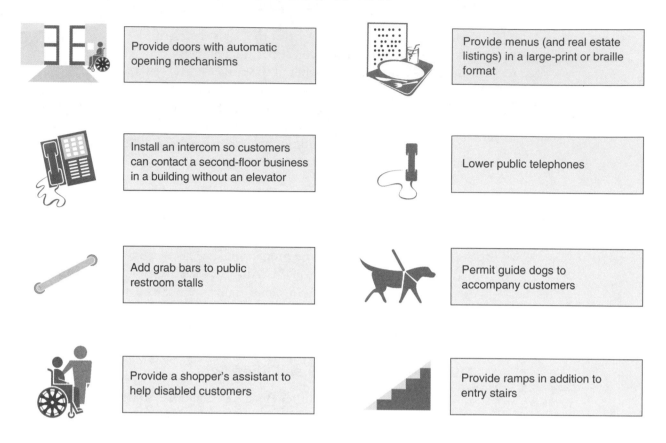

Provide doors with automatic opening mechanisms

Provide menus (and real estate listings) in a large-print or braille format

Install an intercom so customers can contact a second-floor business in a building without an elevator

Lower public telephones

Add grab bars to public restroom stalls

Permit guide dogs to accompany customers

Provide a shopper's assistant to help disabled customers

Provide ramps in addition to entry stairs

To protect owners of existing structures from the massive expense of extensive remodeling, the ADA recommends reasonably achievable accommodations to provide access to the facilities and services. New construction and remodeling, however, must meet higher standards of accessibility and usability because it costs less to incorporate accessible features in the design than to retrofit. Though the law intends to provide for people with disabilities, many of the accessible design features and accommodations benefit everyone.

IN   PRACTICE   The U.S. Department of Justice has ADA specialists available to answer general information questions about compliance issues. The ADA Information Line is 800-514-0301 (TTY: 800-514-0383).

Existing barriers must be removed when this can be accomplished in a readily achievable manner with little difficulty and at low cost. The following are typical examples of readily achievable modifications:

- Ramping or removing an obstacle from an otherwise accessible entrance
- Lowering wall-mounted public telephones
- Adding raised letters and Braille markings on elevator buttons
- Installing auditory signals in elevators
- Reversing the direction in which doors open

Alternative methods can be used to provide reasonable accommodations if extensive restructuring is impractical or if retrofitting is unduly expensive. For instance, installing a cup dispenser at a water fountain, which is too high for a person in a wheelchair, may be more practical than installing a lower water fountain.

IN PRACTICE Federal, state, and local laws may provide additional requirements for accommodating people with disabilities. Licensees should be aware of the full range of laws to ensure that their practices are in compliance.

Equal Credit Opportunity Act

Guiding principle: what you do for one, do for all.

The Equal Credit Opportunity Act (ECOA) prohibits a lender from denying a loan based on a person's race, color, religion, national origin, sex, marital status, age, and receipt of public assistance. The ECOA affects the property manager in several ways. A manager should use the same lease application for every applicant. If a manager requires a credit report from one applicant, the manager should require credit reports from all applicants. The manager should be consistent in evaluating the income and debt of applicants and in determining whether to rent to an applicant.

Fair Housing Act

The federal Fair Housing Act and its amendments prohibit discrimination in the sale, rental, or financing of housing based on race, color, religion, national origin, sex, familial status, or disability. (See Chapter 20.) Property managers need to ensure that their practices of attracting tenants do not violate fair housing laws. For example, blockbusting and steering are prohibited. *Blockbusting* is encouraging people to rent or to sell a property by claiming that the entry of a protected class of people will have a negative impact on property values. *Steering* is the channeling of protected class members to certain buildings or neighborhoods.

IN PRACTICE Many of the fair housing complaints are related to property management issues.

■ RISK MANAGEMENT AND ENVIRONMENTAL ISSUES RELATED TO PROPERTY MANAGEMENT

Enormous monetary losses can result from certain unexpected or catastrophic events. As a result, one of the most critical areas of responsibility for a property manager is **risk management**.

Security of Tenants

The physical safety of tenants of the leased premises is an important issue for property managers and owners. Recent court decisions in several parts of the country have held owners and their agents responsible for physical harm that was inflicted on tenants by intruders. These decisions have prompted property managers and owners to think about how to protect tenants and secure apartments from intruders. There is also the concern of wrongdoing or criminal behavior inflicted by tenants on other tenants in the building. Many leases now have a crime-free provision that makes criminal activity, such as drug use or assault, grounds for eviction.

Risk Management Techniques

Risk management involves answering the question, What happens if something goes wrong? The perils of any risk must be evaluated in terms of options. In considering the possibility of a loss, the property manager must decide whether it is better to

- *avoid it* by removing the source of risk (e.g., a swimming pool may pose an unacceptable risk);
- *control it* by preparing for an emergency before it happens (by installing sprinklers, fire doors, and security systems);
- *transfer it* by shifting the risk onto another party (by taking out an insurance policy); or
- *retain it* by deciding that the chances of the event occurring are too small to justify the expense of any other response (an alternative might be to take out an insurance policy with a large deductible, which usually is considerably less expensive).

Types of Insurance

Insurance is a first line of defense in risk management for property owners and managers. (See Chapter 3.) Numerous forms of insurance policies are available, covering a wide range of possible events that might result in devastating loss. A single policy may cover risks in one or more categories.

Tenant's insurance The property manager should notify tenants that in order to protect personal belongings, they must obtain renter's insurance, known as HO-4, in order to protect their personal belongings. The owner can only insure what the owner owns (i.e., the building); the owner cannot insure the property of the tenants. Residential tenants need an HO-4 or renter's policy to insure their personal property. Business tenants can obtain their own business or commercial policy. These policies are offered through the personal lines marketplace.

Commercial insurance An insurance audit should be performed by a competent, reliable insurance agent who is familiar with insurance issues for the type of property involved. The audit will indicate areas in which greater or lesser coverage is recommended and will highlight particular risks. The final decision, however, must be made by the property owner.

Common types of coverage available to income property owners and managers include the following:

- *Fire and hazard.* Fire insurance policies provide coverage against direct loss or damage to property from a fire on the premises. Standard fire coverage can be extended to include other hazards such as windstorm, hail, smoke damage, or civil insurrection.
- *Flood.* Flood insurance is always a separate policy from home, rental, or building insurance policies. A flood insurance policy is available to any property located in a community participating in the National Flood Insurance Program (NFIP). It covers flooding caused by heavy rains, melting snow, inadequate drainage systems, or failed levees or dams. Consult *www.fema.gov/business/nfip/*.

- *Consequential loss, use, and occupancy.* Also known as *loss of rent* or *business interruption insurance*, consequential loss insurance covers the results, or consequences, of a disaster. Consequential loss can include the loss of rent or revenue to a business that occurs if the business's property cannot be used.
- *Contents and personal property.* This type of insurance covers building contents and personal property during periods when they are not actually located on the premises.
- *Liability.* Public liability insurance covers the risks an owner assumes whenever the public enters the building. A claim paid under this coverage is used for medical expenses incurred by a person who is injured in the building or on the property as a result of the owner's negligence. Claims for medical or hospital payments for injuries sustained by building employees hurt in the course of their employment are covered by state laws known as **workers' compensation acts**.
- *Casualty.* Casualty insurance policies include coverage against theft, burglary, vandalism, and machinery damage, as well as health and accident insurance.
- *Surety bonds.* Surety bonds cover an owner against financial losses resulting from an employee's criminal acts or negligence while performing assigned duties.

Many insurance companies offer **multiperil policies** for apartment buildings. Such a policy offers the property manager an insurance package that includes standard types of commercial coverage, such as fire, hazard, public liability, and casualty. Special coverage for terrorism, earthquakes, and floods is also available. Remember that flood insurance is always a separate policy.

Condominium associations carry insurance on all the *common elements*, and cooperatives carry insurance on the building. Condominium owners and proprietary lease owners must carry their own casualty and liability insurance. If a condominium owner rents out space to tenants, those tenants must carry their own insurance.

The property manager may also want to carry insurance to cover the office, its contents, and any professional malpractice problems. For example, a property manager may want to consider purchasing errors and omissions (E&O) insurance to protect against any financial management mistakes.

Claims

Two possible methods can be used to determine the amount of a claim under an insurance policy. One is the depreciated or actual cash value of the damaged property; the property is not insured for what it would cost to replace it but rather for what it was originally worth, less the depreciation in value that results from use and the passage of time. The other method is *current replacement cost*. In this policy, the building or property is insured for what it would cost to rebuild or replace it today. When purchasing insurance, a manager must decide whether a property should be insured at full replacement cost or at a depreciated cost. Full replacement cost coverage is generally more expensive than depreciated cost.

As with the homeowners' insurance policies, commercial policies include *coinsurance clauses* that require the insured to carry fire coverage, usually in an amount equal to 80 percent of a building's replacement value.

Property managers can encounter legal issues with insurance claims. For example, if the property owner is not present in order to file an insurance claim, the property manager must have proper authorization, such as a power of attorney.

Handling Environmental Concerns

The environment is an increasingly important property management issue. A variety of environmental issues, from waste disposal to air quality, must be addressed by the property manager. Tenant concerns, as well as federal, state, and local regulations, determine the extent of the manager's environmental responsibilities. Property managers are not expected to be experts in all of the disciplines necessary to operate a property; they are expected to be knowledgeable in many diverse subjects, most of which are technical in nature. Environmental concerns are one such subject.

Though recycling facilities are not required by law, the manager may want to provide them for tenants. Hazardous wastes produced by employees or tenants must be properly disposed of. Even the normally nonhazardous waste of an office building must be controlled to avoid violation of laws requiring segregation and recycling of types of waste. Residential property managers of buildings constructed before 1978 must provide lead-based paint disclosure forms to all new tenants. Environmental audits also identify issues relating to asbestos, radon, and mold.

Air quality issues are a key concern for those involved in property management and design. Building-related illness (BRI) and sick building syndrome (SBS) are illnesses that are more prevalent today because of energy and efficiency standards used in construction that make buildings more airtight with less ventilation. BRI is a clinically diagnosed condition that can be attributed directly to airborne building contaminants. Symptoms include asthma, hypersensitivity, and some allergies. SBS is more typical in an office building, and symptoms include fatigue, nausea, dizziness, headache, and sensitivity to odors. Often, increasing ventilation or replacing interior features, such as carpeting, can solve air quality problems.

■ KEY POINT REVIEW

A **property manager**, whether an individual or a company, acts as the **general agent** of the investment property owner and has fiduciary duties to the owner of <u>c</u>are, <u>o</u>bedience, <u>a</u>ccounting, <u>c</u>onfidentiality, <u>l</u>oyalty, and <u>d</u>isclosure in administering the property to accomplish the following:

- Achieve the **objectives** of the owner
- Generate **income** for the owner
- Preserve and increase the property's **value**

Property management functions may require a real estate broker's or property manager's **license**, as provided by state law.

Property managers may undertake **asset management** by helping the owner to decide the

- **type** of real estate in which to invest—residential or commercial,
- **best** property to purchase,
- **financial resources** to fund the purchase, and
- best time to **dispose** of the property.

A **leasing agent** is usually a state-licensed real estate broker working as an **independent contractor** or property manager on a commission basis.

A **corporate property manager** is usually an **employee** of the corporation.

A **management plan** and **management agreement** should include the following:

- **Description** of the property
- **Time period** of the agreement
- Method of **termination** of the agreement
- Definition of the **management's responsibilities**, including limitations and restrictions
- Statement of the **owner's purpose**—long-term goals
- **Owner's responsibilities** for management expenses
- Extent of the **manager's authority**
- **Reporting requirements** of the owner and the state
- **Compensation** to the manager
- **Compliance with applicable federal, state, and local laws**
- **Financial reports**
- Periodic **profit and loss statement** providing general financial information as expressed by the following formula:

  Net Profit
  Gross Receipts – Operating Expenses – Total Mortgage Payment + Mortgage Loan Principal
- **Budget comparison statement**, comparing actual results with original budget

The building manager **sets rents** that are

- sufficient to cover fixed charges and operating expenses and a **fair return** on the owner's investment,
- in line with the **prevailing rates** in comparable buildings,
- a reflection of the current **vacancy rate** of the property,
- determined at a **monthly rate per unit** for residential property, and
- calculated at a **monthly rate per square foot** for commercial property.

A building manager **selects tenants** within certain parameters, while complying with all applicable federal, state, and local fair housing, antidiscrimination, and equal opportunity laws.

Commercial tenant considerations typically include the following:

- **Suitability** of the building in size, location, and amenities
- **Compatibility** with the building and other tenants
- **Availability** of space for expansion, if necessary

The building manager should establish a firm and consistent **collection plan** for rents. Lease agreements should spell out the

- **time and place** of payment,
- **penalties** for late payment and bounced checks, and
- **cancellation** procedures and **damages** in case of nonpayment.

Building managers maintain **good relations with tenants** with tact and uniformity through good **communication**, fair and consistent **enforcement** of rules, prompt attention to **maintenance and service** requests, and careful **record keeping**, with attention to lease renewal dates.

To find and retain reliable tenants, a building manager must devise an **effective marketing strategy**.

Following are the federal laws affecting property management:

- **Americans with Disabilities Act (ADA)**, which includes
  - **Title I**—applies to **employers** with 15 or more employees and provides for employment of qualified job applicants, regardless of disability, with reasonable accommodations; and
  - **Title III**—prohibits discrimination in **commercial properties and public accommodations** and requires that access to facilities and services be provided when reasonably achievable in existing buildings, with a higher standard for new construction or remodeling
- **Equal Credit Opportunity Act (ECOA)**, which prohibits lenders from denying a loan based on a person's race, color, religion, national origin, sex, marital status, age, and receipt of public assistance; additional protections may be added by state or local laws
- **Fair Housing Act** and amendments, which prohibit discrimination in the sale, rental, or financing of housing based on race, color, religion, national origin, sex, familial status, or disability; additional protected individuals may be added by state or local laws

Risk management includes treatment of risk by deciding whether to <u>a</u>void it, <u>c</u>ontrol it, <u>t</u>ransfer it, <u>or</u> <u>r</u>etain it (**ACTOR**) and focuses on tenant security and types of insurance available.

The **environmental concerns** that require attention of the property manager include the following:

- Disposal of **hazardous wastes**
- **Lead-based paint** disclosure for residential property constructed before 1978

■ RELATED WEB SITES

American Management Association: *www.amanet.org*

Building Owners and Managers Association International: *www.boma.org*

Independent Institute for Property and Facility Management Education:
www.bomi.org

Institute of Real Estate Management: *www.irem.org/home.cfm*

National Association of Home Builders: *www.nahb.com*

National Association of Residential Property Managers: *www.narpm.org*

U.S. Department of Justice, Civil Rights Division:
www.justice.gov/crt/drs/drshome.php

CHAPTER 17 QUIZ

1. Which type of insurance coverage insures an employer against MOST claims for job-related injuries?
   a. Consequential loss
   b. Workers' compensation
   c. Casualty
   d. Surety bond

2. Avoid, control, transfer, or retain are the four alternative techniques of
   a. tenant relations.
   b. acquiring insurance.
   c. risk management.
   d. property management.

3. Adaptations of property specifications to suit tenant requirements are
   a. tax-exempt improvements.
   b. tenant improvements.
   c. prohibited by most nonresidential leases.
   d. generally not a good idea.

4. A guest slips on an icy apartment building stair and is hospitalized. A claim against the building owner for medical expenses may be paid under which of the following policies held by the owner?
   a. Workers' compensation
   b. Casualty
   c. Liability
   d. Fire and hazard

5. All of the following should be included in a management agreement EXCEPT
   a. a description of the property.
   b. compensation.
   c. restrictions regarding ages of children.
   d. the extent of the manager's authority.

6. A property manager is offered a choice of three insurance policies with different deductibles. If the property manager selects the policy with the highest deductible, which risk management technique is being used?
   a. Avoiding risk
   b. Retaining risk
   c. Controlling risk
   d. Transferring risk

7. Asbestos, SBS, and lead paint are all examples of
   a. issues beyond the scope of a property manager's job description.
   b. problems faced only by newly constructed properties.
   c. issues that arise under the ADA.
   d. environmental concerns that a property manager may have to address.

8. The manager of a commercial building has many responsibilities in connection with the operation and maintenance of the structure. The manager would normally be considered the agent of
   a. the building's owner.
   b. the building's tenants.
   c. both the owner and the tenants.
   d. neither the owner nor the tenants.

9. Which of the following would be considered a variable expense when a manager develops an operating budget?
   a. Employee wages
   b. Utilities
   c. Building repairs
   d. Basic operating costs

10. In MOST market areas, rents are determined by
    a. supply and demand factors.
    b. the local apartment owners' association.
    c. HUD.
    d. a tenants' union.

11. A high-rise apartment building burns to the ground. What type of insurance covers the landlord against the resulting loss of rent?
    a. Fire and hazard
    b. Liability
    c. Consequential loss, use, and occupancy
    d. Casualty

12. A property manager hires a full-time maintenance person. While repairing a faucet in one of the apartments, the maintenance person steals a television set, and the tenant sues the owner. The property manager could protect the owner against this type of loss by purchasing

    a. liability insurance.
    b. workers' compensation insurance.
    c. a surety bond.
    d. casualty insurance.

13. Residential leases are usually expressed as a(n)

    a. annual or monthly rate per square foot.
    b. percentage of total space available.
    c. monthly rate per unit.
    d. annual rate per room.

14. A property manager repairs a leaking sink. This is classified as which type of maintenance?

    a. Preventive
    b. Corrective
    c. Routine
    d. Construction

15. A property manager who enters into a management agreement with an owner is usually a

    a. special agent.
    b. general agent.
    c. universal agent.
    d. designated agent.

16. A semiannual statement sent to an owner that does not reflect the entire debt service as an expense is called a(n)

    a. cash flow report.
    b. profit and loss statement.
    c. budget comparison statement.
    d. operating budget statement.

17. An insurance policy package that includes standard commercial property coverage such as fire, hazard, public liability, and casualty is referred to as what kind of policy?

    a. Coinsurance
    b. Multiperil
    c. Universal
    d. Surety

18. Removing existing barriers when readily achievable in public buildings, such as adding Braille markings to elevator buttons, is a requirement of which law?

    a. Fair Housing Act
    b. Equal Credit Opportunity Act
    c. Americans with Disabilities Act
    d. Regulation Z

19. Title III of the Americans with Disabilities Act (ADA) impacts which type of property?

    a. Residential
    b. Industrial
    c. Commercial and public accommodations
    d. Privately owned

20. In evaluating rental applications, it is important for the property manager to establish consistent criteria for acceptable debt and income ratios to be in compliance with

    a. federal antitrust laws.
    b. the Americans with Disabilities Act.
    c. Regulation Z.
    d. the Equal Credit Opportunity Act.

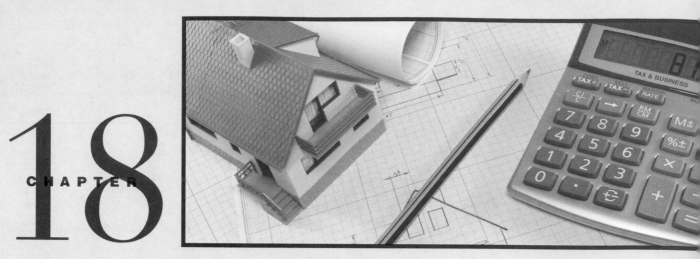

CHAPTER 18

Real Estate Appraisal

■ **LEARNING OBJECTIVES**   *When you have finished reading this chapter, you should be able to*

■ **identify** the different types and basic principles of value;

■ **describe** the three basic valuation approaches used by appraisers;

■ **explain** the steps in the appraisal process;

■ **distinguish** the four methods of determining reproduction or replacement cost; and

■ **define** the following *key terms*:

accrued depreciation

anticipation

appraisal

assemblage

broker's price opinion
(BPO)

capitalization rate

change

competitive market
analysis (CMA)

competition

conformity

contribution

cost approach

depreciation

economic life

external obsolescence

functional obsolescence

gross income multiplier
(GIM)

gross rent multiplier
(GRM)

highest and best use

income approach

law of diminishing returns

law of increasing returns

market data approach

market value

net operating income
(NOI)

physical deterioration

plottage

progression

reconciliation

regression

replacement cost new

reproduction cost

sales comparison
approach

sales price

substitution

supply and demand

*Uniform Standards of
Professional Appraisal
Practice* (*USPAP*)

value

■ REAL ESTATE APPRAISAL

Appraisal is a distinct area of specialization within the world of real estate professionals. Appraisal provides a clearer understanding about the market's response to a subject property. Real estate licensees must be aware of the fundamental principles of valuation in order to complete an accurate and effective competitive market analysis (CMA) that assists seller clients in arriving at a reasonable asking price and buyer clients to make appropriate offers based on current market conditions. Furthermore, knowledge of the appraisal process allows the licensee to recognize an unacceptable appraisal.

■ APPRAISING

An **appraisal** is an estimate or opinion of value based on supportable evidence and approved methods. An *appraisal report* is an opinion of market value on a property given to a lender or client with detailed and accurate information. An appraiser is an independent professional trained to provide an *unbiased* estimate of value in an impartial and objective manner, according to the appraisal process. Appraising is a professional service performed for a fee.

Regulation of Appraisal Activities

Title XI of the Financial Institutions Reform, Recovery, and Enforcement Act of 1989 (FIRREA) requires that any appraisal used in connection with a federally related transaction be performed by a competent individual whose professional conduct is subject to supervision and regulation. Federal law requires that appraisers be licensed or certified according to individual state law. State qualifications must conform to the federal requirements that, in turn, follow the criteria for certification established by the Appraiser Qualifications Board of the Appraisal Foundation. The Appraisal Foundation is a national body composed of representatives of the major appraisal and related organizations. Appraisers are also expected to follow the **Uniform Standards of Professional Appraisal Practice (USPAP)** established by the foundation's Appraisal Standards Board.

A federally related transaction is any real estate–related financial transaction in which a federal financial institution or regulatory agency is engaged. These transactions involve the sale, lease, purchase, investment, or exchange of real property. They also include the financing, refinancing, or use of real property as security for a loan or an investment, including mortgage-backed securities. Appraisals of residential property valued at $250,000 or less are exempt and need not be performed by licensed or certified appraisers. Nonresidential properties valued at more than $250,000 require a certified appraiser.

Competitive Market Analysis

Not all estimates of value are made by professional appraisers. Licensees prepare a **competitive market analysis (CMA)** for their sellers and buyers. A CMA is distinctly different from an appraisal report offered by a licensed appraiser. An appraisal is based on an analysis of properties that have actually sold; in contrast, the CMA features properties similar to the subject property in size, location, and amenities. The CMA analysis is based on

- recently closed properties (solds),
- properties currently on the market (competition for the subject property), and
- properties that did not sell (expired listings in the area).

Broker's Price Opinion (BPO)

A **broker's price opinion (BPO)** is a less-expensive alternative of valuating property often used by lenders working with home equity lines, refinancing, portfolio management, loss mitigation, and collections. Both Fannie Mae and Freddie Mac provide forms that are used by real estate licensees who perform BPOs for a fee. Although some BPOs are more extensive, including information about the neighborhood and interior analysis, many are simply "drive bys" that verify the existence of the property, along with a listing of comparable sales. A BPO should not be confused with an appraisal, which consists of more in-depth analysis of gathered information and which may be performed only by a licensed appraiser. A BPO cannot be used if the matter involves a federally related transaction that requires an appraisal and/or the transaction occurs in a state that requires an appraiser's license.

■ THE APPRAISAL PROCESS

Although appraising is not an exact or precise science, the key to an accurate appraisal lies in the methodical collection and analysis of data. The appraisal process is an orderly set of procedures used to collect and analyze data to arrive at a reasonable market value conclusion. The data are divided into two basic classes:

1. *General data*, which covers the nation, region, city, and neighborhood. Of particular importance is the neighborhood, where an appraiser finds the physical, economic, social, and political influences that directly affect the value and potential of the subject property.
2. *Specific data*, which covers details of the subject property, as well as comparative data relating to costs, sales, income, and expenses of properties similar to and competitive with the subject property

Figure 18.1 outlines the steps an appraiser takes in carrying out an appraisal assignment.

Once the approaches have been reconciled and an opinion of value has been reached, the appraiser prepares a report for the client. The report should

- identify the real estate and real property interest being appraised;
- state the purpose and intended use of the appraisal;
- define the value to be estimated;
- state the effective date of the value and the date of the report;
- state the extent of the process of collecting, confirming, and reporting the data;
- list all assumptions and limiting conditions that affect the analysis, opinion, and conclusions of value;

FIGURE   18.1

The Appraisal Process

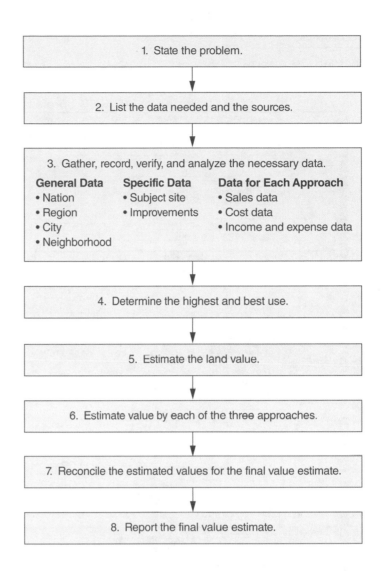

1. State the problem.

2. List the data needed and the sources.

3. Gather, record, verify, and analyze the necessary data.

General Data	**Specific Data**	**Data for Each Approach**
• Nation	• Subject site	• Sales data
• Region	• Improvements	• Cost data
• City		• Income and expense data
• Neighborhood		

4. Determine the highest and best use.

5. Estimate the land value.

6. Estimate value by each of the three approaches.

7. Reconcile the estimated values for the final value estimate.

8. Report the final value estimate.

- describe the information considered, the appraisal procedures followed, and the reasoning that supports the report's conclusions (if an approach was excluded, the report should explain why);

- describe the appraiser's opinion of the highest and best use of the real estate;

- describe any additional information that may be appropriate to show compliance with the specific guidelines established in the *Uniform Standards of Professional Appraisal Practice* (*USPAP*) or to clearly identify and explain any departures from these guidelines; and

- include a signed certification, as required by the Uniform Standards.

Figure 18.2 shows the Uniform Residential Appraisal Report, the form required by many government agencies. It illustrates the types of detailed information required of an appraisal of residential property.

FIGURE 18.2

Uniform Residential Appraisal Report

Uniform Residential Appraisal Report
File #

The purpose of this summary appraisal report is to provide the lender/client with an accurate, and adequately supported, opinion of the market value of the subject property.

SUBJECT

Property Address		City	State	Zip Code

Borrower | Owner of Public Record | County

Legal Description

Assessor's Parcel # | Tax Year | R.E. Taxes $

Neighborhood Name | Map Reference | Census Tract

Occupant ☐ Owner ☐ Tenant ☐ Vacant | Special Assessments $ | ☐ PUD | HOA $ | ☐ per year ☐ per month

Property Rights Appraised ☐ Fee Simple ☐ Leasehold ☐ Other (describe)

Assignment Type ☐ Purchase Transaction ☐ Refinance Transaction ☐ Other (describe)

Lender/Client | Address

Is the subject property currently offered for sale or has it been offered for sale in the twelve months prior to the effective date of this appraisal? ☐ Yes ☐ No

Report data source(s) used, offering price(s), and date(s).

CONTRACT

I ☐ did ☐ did not analyze the contract for sale for the subject purchase transaction. Explain the results of the analysis of the contract for sale or why the analysis was not performed.

Contract Price $ | Date of Contract | Is the property seller the owner of public record? ☐ Yes ☐ No Data Source(s)

Is there any financial assistance (loan charges, sale concessions, gift or downpayment assistance, etc.) to be paid by any party on behalf of the borrower? ☐ Yes ☐ No
If Yes, report the total dollar amount and describe the items to be paid.

NEIGHBORHOOD

Note: Race and the racial composition of the neighborhood are not appraisal factors.

Neighborhood Characteristics			One-Unit Housing Trends			One-Unit Housing		Present Land Use %	
Location ☐ Urban ☐ Suburban ☐ Rural			Property Values ☐ Increasing ☐ Stable ☐ Declining			PRICE	AGE	One-Unit	%
Built-Up ☐ Over 75% ☐ 25–75% ☐ Under 25%			Demand/Supply ☐ Shortage ☐ In Balance ☐ Over Supply			$ (000)	(yrs)	2-4 Unit	%
Growth ☐ Rapid ☐ Stable ☐ Slow			Marketing Time ☐ Under 3 mths ☐ 3–6 mths ☐ Over 6 mths			Low		Multi-Family	%
Neighborhood Boundaries						High		Commercial	%
						Pred.		Other	%

Neighborhood Description

Market Conditions (including support for the above conclusions)

SITE

Dimensions | Area | Shape | View

Specific Zoning Classification | Zoning Description

Zoning Compliance ☐ Legal ☐ Legal Nonconforming (Grandfathered Use) ☐ No Zoning ☐ Illegal (describe)

Is the highest and best use of the subject property as improved (or as proposed per plans and specifications) the present use? ☐ Yes ☐ No If No, describe

Utilities	Public	Other (describe)		Public	Other (describe)	Off-site Improvements—Type	Public	Private
Electricity	☐	☐	Water	☐	☐	Street	☐	☐
Gas	☐	☐	Sanitary Sewer	☐	☐	Alley	☐	☐

FEMA Special Flood Hazard Area ☐ Yes ☐ No FEMA Flood Zone | FEMA Map # | FEMA Map Date

Are the utilities and off-site improvements typical for the market area? ☐ Yes ☐ No If No, describe

Are there any adverse site conditions or external factors (easements, encroachments, environmental conditions, land uses, etc.)? ☐ Yes ☐ No If Yes, describe

IMPROVEMENTS

General Description		Foundation		Exterior Description	materials/condition	Interior	materials/condition
Units ☐ One ☐ One with Accessory Unit		☐ Concrete Slab ☐ Crawl Space		Foundation Walls		Floors	
# of Stories		☐ Full Basement ☐ Partial Basement		Exterior Walls		Walls	
Type ☐ Det. ☐ Att. ☐ S-Det./End Unit		Basement Area sq. ft.		Roof Surface		Trim/Finish	
☐ Existing ☐ Proposed ☐ Under Const.		Basement Finish %		Gutters & Downspouts		Bath Floor	
Design (Style)		☐ Outside Entry/Exit ☐ Sump Pump		Window Type		Bath Wainscot	
Year Built		Evidence of ☐ Infestation		Storm Sash/Insulated		Car Storage ☐ None	
Effective Age (Yrs)		☐ Dampness ☐ Settlement		Screens		☐ Driveway # of Cars	
Attic ☐ None		Heating ☐ FWA ☐ HWBB ☐ Radiant		Amenities ☐ Woodstove(s) #		Driveway Surface	
☐ Drop Stair ☐ Stairs		☐ Other Fuel		☐ Fireplace(s) # ☐ Fence		☐ Garage # of Cars	
☐ Floor ☐ Scuttle		Cooling ☐ Central Air Conditioning		☐ Patio/Deck ☐ Porch		☐ Carport # of Cars	
☐ Finished ☐ Heated		☐ Individual ☐ Other		☐ Pool ☐ Other		☐ Att. ☐ Det. ☐ Built-in	

Appliances ☐ Refrigerator ☐ Range/Oven ☐ Dishwasher ☐ Disposal ☐ Microwave ☐ Washer/Dryer ☐ Other (describe)

Finished area **above** grade contains: Rooms | Bedrooms | Bath(s) | Square Feet of Gross Living Area Above Grade

Additional features (special energy efficient items, etc.)

Describe the condition of the property (including needed repairs, deterioration, renovations, remodeling, etc.).

Are there any physical deficiencies or adverse conditions that affect the livability, soundness, or structural integrity of the property? ☐ Yes ☐ No If Yes, describe

Does the property generally conform to the neighborhood (functional utility, style, condition, use, construction, etc.)? ☐ Yes ☐ No If No, describe

Freddie Mac Form 70 March 2005 | Page 1 of 6 | Fannie Mae Form 1004 March 2005

FIGURE 18.2

Uniform Residential Appraisal Report (Continued)

Uniform Residential Appraisal Report   File

| There are | comparable properties currently offered for sale in the subject neighborhood ranging in price from $ | | to $ | . |
| There are | comparable sales in the subject neighborhood within the past twelve months ranging in sale price from $ | | to $ | . |

FEATURE	SUBJECT	COMPARABLE SALE # 1		COMPARABLE SALE # 2		COMPARABLE SALE # 3	
Address							
Proximity to Subject							
Sale Price	$		$		$		$
Sale Price/Gross Liv. Area	$ sq. ft.	$ sq. ft.		$ sq. ft.		$ sq. ft.	
Data Source(s)							
Verification Source(s)							
VALUE ADJUSTMENTS	DESCRIPTION	DESCRIPTION	+(-) $ Adjustment	DESCRIPTION	+(-) $ Adjustment	DESCRIPTION	+(-) $ Adjustment
Sale or Financing Concessions							
Date of Sale/Time							
Location							
Leasehold/Fee Simple							
Site							
View							
Design (Style)							
Quality of Construction							
Actual Age							
Condition							
Above Grade	Total Bdrms. Baths	Total Bdrms. Baths		Total Bdrms. Baths		Total Bdrms. Baths	
Room Count							
Gross Living Area	sq. ft.	sq. ft.		sq. ft.		sq. ft.	
Basement & Finished Rooms Below Grade							
Functional Utility							
Heating/Cooling							
Energy Efficient Items							
Garage/Carport							
Porch/Patio/Deck							
Net Adjustment (Total)		☐ + ☐ -	$	☐ + ☐ -	$	☐ + ☐ -	$
Adjusted Sale Price of Comparables		Net Adj. % Gross Adj. %	$	Net Adj % Gross Adj. %	$	Net Adj. % Gross Adj. %	$

I ☐ did ☐ did not research the sale or transfer history of the subject property and comparable sales. If not, explain

My research ☐ did ☐ did not reveal any prior sales or transfers of the subject property for the three years prior to the effective date of this appraisal.

Data source(s)

My research ☐ did ☐ did not reveal any prior sales or transfers of the comparable sales for the year prior to the date of sale of the comparable sale.

Data source(s)

Report the results of the research and analysis of the prior sale or transfer history of the subject property and comparable sales (report additional prior sales on page 3).

ITEM	SUBJECT	COMPARABLE SALE # 1	COMPARABLE SALE # 2	COMPARABLE SALE # 3
Date of Prior Sale/Transfer				
Price of Prior Sale/Transfer				
Data Source(s)				
Effective Date of Data Source(s)				

Analysis of prior sale or transfer history of the subject property and comparable sales

Summary of Sales Comparison Approach

Indicated Value by Sales Comparison Approach $

Indicated Value by: Sales Comparison Approach $ Cost Approach (if developed) $ Income Approach (if developed) $

This appraisal is made ☐ "as is", ☐ subject to completion per plans and specifications on the basis of a hypothetical condition that the improvements have been completed, ☐ subject to the following repairs or alterations on the basis of a hypothetical condition that the repairs or alterations have been completed, or ☐ subject to the following required inspection based on the extraordinary assumption that the condition or deficiency does not require alteration or repair:

Based on a complete visual inspection of the interior and exterior areas of the subject property, defined scope of work, statement of assumptions and limiting conditions, and appraiser's certification, my (our) opinion of the market value, as defined, of the real property that is the subject of this report is $, as of   , which is the date of inspection and the effective date of this appraisal.

FIGURE 18.2

Uniform Residential Appraisal Report (Continued)

Uniform Residential Appraisal Report   File

ADDITIONAL COMMENTS

COST APPROACH TO VALUE (not required by Fannie Mae)

Provide adequate information for the lender/client to replicate the below cost figures and calculations.

Support for the opinion of site value (summary of comparable land sales or other methods for estimating site value)

ESTIMATED ☐ REPRODUCTION OR ☐ REPLACEMENT COST NEW	OPINION OF SITE VALUE .... = $
Source of cost data	Dwelling Sq. Ft. @ $ .... =$
Quality rating from cost service Effective date of cost data	Sq. Ft. @ $ .... =$
Comments on Cost Approach (gross living area calculations, depreciation, etc.)	
	Garage/Carport Sq. Ft. @ $ .... =$
	Total Estimate of Cost-New .... = $
	Less Physical Functional External
	Depreciation =$( )
	Depreciated Cost of Improvements........................ =$
	"As-is" Value of Site Improvements....................... =$
Estimated Remaining Economic Life (HUD and VA only) Years	Indicated Value By Cost Approach .... =$

INCOME APPROACH TO VALUE (not required by Fannie Mae)

Estimated Monthly Market Rent $ X Gross Rent Multiplier   = $ Indicated Value by Income Approach

Summary of Income Approach (including support for market rent and GRM)

PROJECT INFORMATION FOR PUDs (if applicable)

Is the developer/builder in control of the Homeowners' Association (HOA)? ☐ Yes ☐ No   Unit type(s) ☐ Detached ☐ Attached

Provide the following information for PUDs ONLY if the developer/builder is in control of the HOA and the subject property is an attached dwelling unit.

Legal name of project

Total number of phases   Total number of units   Total number of units sold

Total number of units rented   Total number of units for sale   Data source(s)

Was the project created by the conversion of an existing building(s) into a PUD? ☐ Yes ☐ No   If Yes, date of conversion

Does the project contain any multi-dwelling units? ☐ Yes ☐ No   Data source(s)

Are the units, common elements, and recreation facilities complete? ☐ Yes ☐ No   If No, describe the status of completion.

Are the common elements leased to or by the Homeowners' Association? ☐ Yes ☐ No   If Yes, describe the rental terms and options.

Describe common elements and recreational facilities

FIGURE   18.2

Uniform Residential Appraisal Report (Continued)

Uniform Residential Appraisal Report   File

This report form is designed to report an appraisal of a one-unit property or a one-unit property with an accessory unit; including a unit in a planned unit development (PUD). This report form is not designed to report an appraisal of a manufactured home or a unit in a condominium or cooperative project.

This appraisal report is subject to the following scope of work, intended use, intended user, definition of market value, statement of assumptions and limiting conditions, and certifications. Modifications, additions, or deletions to the intended use, intended user, definition of market value, or assumptions and limiting conditions are not permitted. The appraiser may expand the scope of work to include any additional research or analysis necessary based on the complexity of this appraisal assignment. Modifications or deletions to the certifications are also not permitted. However, additional certifications that do not constitute material alterations to this appraisal report, such as those required by law or those related to the appraiser's continuing education or membership in an appraisal organization, are permitted.

SCOPE OF WORK: The scope of work for this appraisal is defined by the complexity of this appraisal assignment and the reporting requirements of this appraisal report form, including the following definition of market value, statement of assumptions and limiting conditions, and certifications. The appraiser must, at a minimum: (1) perform a complete visual inspection of the interior and exterior areas of the subject property, (2) inspect the neighborhood, (3) inspect each of the comparable sales from at least the street, (4) research, verify, and analyze data from reliable public and/or private sources, and (5) report his or her analysis, opinions, and conclusions in this appraisal report.

INTENDED USE: The intended use of this appraisal report is for the lender/client to evaluate the property that is the subject of this appraisal for a mortgage finance transaction.

INTENDED USER: The intended user of this appraisal report is the lender/client.

DEFINITION OF MARKET VALUE: The most probable price which a property should bring in a competitive and open market under all conditions requisite to a fair sale, the buyer and seller, each acting prudently, knowledgeably and assuming the price is not affected by undue stimulus. Implicit in this definition is the consummation of a sale as of a specified date and the passing of title from seller to buyer under conditions whereby: (1) buyer and seller are typically motivated; (2) both parties are well informed or well advised, and each acting in what he or she considers his or her own best interest; (3) a reasonable time is allowed for exposure in the open market; (4) payment is made in terms of cash in U. S. dollars or in terms of financial arrangements comparable thereto; and (5) the price represents the normal consideration for the property sold unaffected by special or creative financing or sales concessions* granted by anyone associated with the sale.

*Adjustments to the comparables must be made for special or creative financing or sales concessions. No adjustments are necessary for those costs which are normally paid by sellers as a result of tradition or law in a market area; these costs are readily identifiable since the seller pays these costs in virtually all sales transactions. Special or creative financing adjustments can be made to the comparable property by comparisons to financing terms offered by a third party institutional lender that is not already involved in the property or transaction. Any adjustment should not be calculated on a mechanical dollar for dollar cost of the financing or concession but the dollar amount of any adjustment should approximate the market's reaction to the financing or concessions based on the appraiser's judgment.

STATEMENT OF ASSUMPTIONS AND LIMITING CONDITIONS: The appraiser's certification in this report is subject to the following assumptions and limiting conditions:

1. The appraiser will not be responsible for matters of a legal nature that affect either the property being appraised or the title to it, except for information that he or she became aware of during the research involved in performing this appraisal. The appraiser assumes that the title is good and marketable and will not render any opinions about the title.

2. The appraiser has provided a sketch in this appraisal report to show the approximate dimensions of the improvements. The sketch is included only to assist the reader in visualizing the property and understanding the appraiser's determination of its size.

3. The appraiser has examined the available flood maps that are provided by the Federal Emergency Management Agency (or other data sources) and has noted in this appraisal report whether any portion of the subject site is located in an identified Special Flood Hazard Area. Because the appraiser is not a surveyor, he or she makes no guarantees, express or implied, regarding this determination.

4. The appraiser will not give testimony or appear in court because he or she made an appraisal of the property in question, unless specific arrangements to do so have been made beforehand, or as otherwise required by law.

5. The appraiser has noted in this appraisal report any adverse conditions (such as needed repairs, deterioration, the presence of hazardous wastes, toxic substances, etc.) observed during the inspection of the subject property or that he or she became aware of during the research involved in performing this appraisal. Unless otherwise stated in this appraisal report, the appraiser has no knowledge of any hidden or unapparent physical deficiencies or adverse conditions of the property (such as, but not limited to, needed repairs, deterioration, the presence of hazardous wastes, toxic substances, adverse environmental conditions, etc.) that would make the property less valuable, and has assumed that there are no such conditions and makes no guarantees or warranties, express or implied. The appraiser will not be responsible for any such conditions that do exist or for any engineering or testing that might be required to discover whether such conditions exist. Because the appraiser is not an expert in the field of environmental hazards, this appraisal report must not be considered as an environmental assessment of the property.

6. The appraiser has based his or her appraisal report and valuation conclusion for an appraisal that is subject to satisfactory completion, repairs, or alterations on the assumption that the completion, repairs, or alterations of the subject property will be performed in a professional manner.

FIGURE 18.2

FIGURE 18.2

Uniform Residential Appraisal Report (Continued)

Uniform Residential Appraisal Report   File

APPRAISER'S CERTIFICATION: The Appraiser certifies and agrees that:

1. I have, at a minimum, developed and reported this appraisal in accordance with the scope of work requirements stated in this appraisal report.

2. I performed a complete visual inspection of the interior and exterior areas of the subject property. I reported the condition of the improvements in factual, specific terms. I identified and reported the physical deficiencies that could affect the livability, soundness, or structural integrity of the property.

3. I performed this appraisal in accordance with the requirements of the Uniform Standards of Professional Appraisal Practice that were adopted and promulgated by the Appraisal Standards Board of The Appraisal Foundation and that were in place at the time this appraisal report was prepared.

4. I developed my opinion of the market value of the real property that is the subject of this report based on the sales comparison approach to value. I have adequate comparable market data to develop a reliable sales comparison approach for this appraisal assignment. I further certify that I considered the cost and income approaches to value but did not develop them, unless otherwise indicated in this report.

5. I researched, verified, analyzed, and reported on any current agreement for sale for the subject property, any offering for sale of the subject property in the twelve months prior to the effective date of this appraisal, and the prior sales of the subject property for a minimum of three years prior to the effective date of this appraisal, unless otherwise indicated in this report.

6. I researched, verified, analyzed, and reported on the prior sales of the comparable sales for a minimum of one year prior to the date of sale of the comparable sale, unless otherwise indicated in this report.

7. I selected and used comparable sales that are locationally, physically, and functionally the most similar to the subject property.

8. I have not used comparable sales that were the result of combining a land sale with the contract purchase price of a home that has been built or will be built on the land.

9. I have reported adjustments to the comparable sales that reflect the market's reaction to the differences between the subject property and the comparable sales.

10. I verified, from a disinterested source, all information in this report that was provided by parties who have a financial interest in the sale or financing of the subject property.

11. I have knowledge and experience in appraising this type of property in this market area.

12. I am aware of, and have access to, the necessary and appropriate public and private data sources, such as multiple listing services, tax assessment records, public land records and other such data sources for the area in which the property is located.

13. I obtained the information, estimates, and opinions furnished by other parties and expressed in this appraisal report from reliable sources that I believe to be true and correct.

14. I have taken into consideration the factors that have an impact on value with respect to the subject neighborhood, subject property, and the proximity of the subject property to adverse influences in the development of my opinion of market value. I have noted in this appraisal report any adverse conditions (such as, but not limited to, needed repairs, deterioration, the presence of hazardous wastes, toxic substances, adverse environmental conditions, etc.) observed during the inspection of the subject property or that I became aware of during the research involved in performing this appraisal. I have considered these adverse conditions in my analysis of the property value, and have reported on the effect of the conditions on the value and marketability of the subject property.

15. I have not knowingly withheld any significant information from this appraisal report and, to the best of my knowledge, all statements and information in this appraisal report are true and correct.

16. I stated in this appraisal report my own personal, unbiased, and professional analysis, opinions, and conclusions, which are subject only to the assumptions and limiting conditions in this appraisal report.

17. I have no present or prospective interest in the property that is the subject of this report, and I have no present or prospective personal interest or bias with respect to the participants in the transaction. I did not base, either partially or completely, my analysis and/or opinion of market value in this appraisal report on the race, color, religion, sex, age, marital status, handicap, familial status, or national origin of either the prospective owners or occupants of the subject property or of the present owners or occupants of the properties in the vicinity of the subject property or on any other basis prohibited by law.

18. My employment and/or compensation for performing this appraisal or any future or anticipated appraisals was not conditioned on any agreement or understanding, written or otherwise, that I would report (or present analysis supporting) a predetermined specific value, a predetermined minimum value, a range or direction in value, a value that favors the cause of any party, or the attainment of a specific result or occurrence of a specific subsequent event (such as approval of a pending mortgage loan application).

19. I personally prepared all conclusions and opinions about the real estate that were set forth in this appraisal report. If I relied on significant real property appraisal assistance from any individual or individuals in the performance of this appraisal or the preparation of this appraisal report, I have named such individual(s) and disclosed the specific tasks performed in this appraisal report. I certify that any individual so named is qualified to perform the tasks. I have not authorized anyone to make a change to any item in this appraisal report; therefore, any change made to this appraisal is unauthorized and I will take no responsibility for it.

20. I identified the lender/client in this appraisal report who is the individual, organization, or agent for the organization that ordered and will receive this appraisal report.

Freddie Mac Form 70 March 2005   Page 5 of 6   Fannie Mae Form 1004 March 2005

FIGURE 18.2

Uniform Residential Appraisal Report (Continued)

Uniform Residential Appraisal Report   File

21. The lender/client may disclose or distribute this appraisal report to: the borrower; another lender at the request of the borrower; the mortgagee or its successors and assigns; mortgage insurers; government sponsored enterprises; other secondary market participants; data collection or reporting services; professional appraisal organizations; any department, agency, or instrumentality of the United States; and any state, the District of Columbia, or other jurisdictions; without having to obtain the appraiser's or supervisory appraiser's (if applicable) consent. Such consent must be obtained before this appraisal report may be disclosed or distributed to any other party (including, but not limited to, the public through advertising, public relations, news, sales, or other media).

22. I am aware that any disclosure or distribution of this appraisal report by me or the lender/client may be subject to certain laws and regulations. Further, I am also subject to the provisions of the Uniform Standards of Professional Appraisal Practice that pertain to disclosure or distribution by me.

23. The borrower, another lender at the request of the borrower, the mortgagee or its successors and assigns, mortgage insurers, government sponsored enterprises, and other secondary market participants may rely on this appraisal report as part of any mortgage finance transaction that involves any one or more of these parties.

24. If this appraisal report was transmitted as an "electronic record" containing my "electronic signature," as those terms are defined in applicable federal and/or state laws (excluding audio and video recordings), or a facsimile transmission of this appraisal report containing a copy or representation of my signature, the appraisal report shall be as effective, enforceable and valid as if a paper version of this appraisal report were delivered containing my original hand written signature.

25. Any intentional or negligent misrepresentation(s) contained in this appraisal report may result in civil liability and/or criminal penalties including, but not limited to, fine or imprisonment or both under the provisions of Title 18, United States Code, Section 1001, et seq., or similar state laws.

SUPERVISORY APPRAISER'S CERTIFICATION: The Supervisory Appraiser certifies and agrees that:

1. I directly supervised the appraiser for this appraisal assignment, have read the appraisal report, and agree with the appraiser's analysis, opinions, statements, conclusions, and the appraiser's certification.

2. I accept full responsibility for the contents of this appraisal report including, but not limited to, the appraiser's analysis, opinions, statements, conclusions, and the appraiser's certification.

3. The appraiser identified in this appraisal report is either a sub-contractor or an employee of the supervisory appraiser (or the appraisal firm), is qualified to perform this appraisal, and is acceptable to perform this appraisal under the applicable state law.

4. This appraisal report complies with the Uniform Standards of Professional Appraisal Practice that were adopted and promulgated by the Appraisal Standards Board of The Appraisal Foundation and that were in place at the time this appraisal report was prepared.

5. If this appraisal report was transmitted as an "electronic record" containing my "electronic signature," as those terms are defined in applicable federal and/or state laws (excluding audio and video recordings), or a facsimile transmission of this appraisal report containing a copy or representation of my signature, the appraisal report shall be as effective, enforceable and valid as if a paper version of this appraisal report were delivered containing my original hand written signature.

APPRAISER

Signature_____

Name _____

Company Name _____

Company Address_____

_____

Telephone Number _____

Email Address_____

Date of Signature and Report_____

Effective Date of Appraisal _____

State Certification #_____

or State License # _____

or Other (describe) _____ State # _____

State _____

Expiration Date of Certification or License _____

ADDRESS OF PROPERTY APPRAISED

_____

_____

APPRAISED VALUE OF SUBJECT PROPERTY $ _____

LENDER/CLIENT

Name _____

Company Name _____

Company Address_____

_____

Email Address_____

SUPERVISORY APPRAISER (ONLY IF REQUIRED)

Signature _____

Name_____

Company Name _____

Company Address_____

Telephone Number _____

Email Address_____

Date of Signature _____

State Certification #_____

or State License # _____

State _____

Expiration Date of Certification or License _____

SUBJECT PROPERTY

☐ Did not inspect subject property

☐ Did inspect exterior of subject property from street

   Date of Inspection _____

☐ Did inspect interior and exterior of subject property

   Date of Inspection _____

COMPARABLE SALES

☐ Did not inspect exterior of comparable sales from street

☐ Did inspect exterior of comparable sales from street

   Date of Inspection _____

Freddie Mac Form 70 March 2005   Page 6 of 6   Fannie Mae Form 1004 March 2005

IN PRACTICE   While the appraiser does not determine value, neither is value determined by what the seller wants to get, what the buyer wants to pay, or what the real estate licensee recommends. The appraiser, relying on experience and expertise in valuation theories, develops a supportable and objective report called an appraisal that verifies the value indicated by the market. Sellers and licensees may not agree with the appraiser's value, and may argue that it is lower than they think that it should be. However, since most appraisals are ordered by lenders, who base their loan on this value, the appraiser must be able to back up the appraisal report with quantifiable conclusions; in the event of a loan default, at what value can the property most probably be sold for the lender to recover the remaining loan balance?

■ VALUE

Memory Tip

The characteristics of value **DUST**:
Demand
Utility
Scarcity
Transferability

To have **value** in the real estate market—that is, monetary worth based on desirability—a property must have the following characteristics:

- *Demand*: the need or desire for possession or ownership backed by the financial means to satisfy that need
- *Utility*: the property's usefulness for its intended purposes
- *Scarcity*: a finite supply
- *Transferability*: the relative ease with which ownership rights are transferred from one person to another

Market Value

The goal of an appraiser is to estimate or express an opinion of market value. The **market value** of real estate is the most probable price that a property should bring in a fair sale. This definition makes three assumptions. First, it presumes a competitive and open market. Second, the buyer and the seller are both assumed to be acting prudently and knowledgeably. Third, market value depends on the price not being affected by unusual circumstances.

The following are essential to determining market value:

- The *most probable* price is not the average or highest price.
- The buyer and the seller must be unrelated and acting without *undue pressure*.
- Both the buyer and the seller must be *well informed* about the property's use and potential, including both its defects and its advantages.
- A *reasonable time* must be allowed for exposure in the open market.
- Payment must be made in cash or its equivalent.
- The price must represent a normal market price for the property sold, unaffected by special financing amounts or terms, services, fees, costs, or credits incurred in the market transaction.

Market value—a reasonable opinion of a property's worth

Market price—the actual selling price of a property

Market value versus market price   *Market value* is an opinion of value based on an analysis of data. The data may include not only an analysis of comparable sales but also an analysis of potential income, expenses, and replacement costs. *Market price*, on the other hand, is what a property actually sells for—its sales price.

Market value versus cost   An important distinction can be made between market value and cost. One of the most common misconceptions about valuing property is that cost represents market value. Cost and market value may be the same. In fact, when the improvements on a property are new, cost and value are likely to be equal. But more often, cost does not equal market value. For example, a homeowner may install a swimming pool for $20,000; however, the cost of the improvement may not add $20,000 to the value of the property.

Basic Principles of Value

A number of economic principles can affect the value of real estate. The most important are defined in the text that follows.

Anticipation   According to the principle of **anticipation**, value is created by the expectation that certain events will occur. For instance, the value of a house may be affected if rumors circulate that an adjacent property may be converted to commercial use in the near future. If the property is neglected, it is possible that the neighboring home's value will increase. On the other hand, if the vacant property had been perceived as a park or play area that added to the neighborhood's quiet atmosphere, the news of its replacement might cause the house's value to decline. The principle of anticipation is the foundation on which the income approach to value is based.

Change   No physical or economic condition remains constant; this is the principle of **change**. Real estate is subject to natural phenomena such as tornadoes, fires, and routine wear and tear. The real estate business is subject to market demands, like any other business. An appraiser must be knowledgeable about both the past and the predictable future effects of natural phenomena and the behavior of the marketplace.

Competition   **Competition** is the interaction of supply and demand. Excess profits tend to attract competition. For example, the success of a retail store may cause investors to open similar stores in the area. This tends to mean less profit for all stores concerned unless the purchasing power in the area substantially increases.

Conformity   The principle of **conformity** means that maximum value is created when a property is in harmony with its surroundings. Maximum value is realized if the use of land conforms to existing neighborhood standards. In single-family residential neighborhoods, for instance, buildings should be similar in design, construction, size, and age.

Contribution   Under the principle of **contribution**, the value of any part of a property is measured by its effect on the value of the whole parcel. Installing a swimming pool, greenhouse, or private bowling alley may not add value to the property equal to the cost, but remodeling an outdated kitchen or bathroom might.

Highest and best use   The most profitable single use of a property that is legal and feasible, and will bring the most money over time, is known as the **highest and best use**. The use must be

- physically possible,
- legally permitted,
- economically or financially feasible, and
- the most profitable or maximally productive.

The highest and best use of a site can change with social, political, and economic forces. A parking lot in a busy downtown area, for example, may not maximize the land's profitability to the same extent an office would.

Increasing and diminishing returns   The addition of improvements to land and structures increases value only to the assets' maximum value. Beyond that point, additional improvements no longer affect a property's value. As long as money spent on improvements produces an increase in income or value, the **law of increasing returns** applies. At the point where additional improvements do not increase income or value, the **law of diminishing returns** applies. No matter how much money is spent on the property, the property's value does not keep pace with the expenditures. A remodeled kitchen or bathroom might increase the value of a house; adding restaurant-quality appliances and gold faucets, however, would be a cost that the owner probably would not be able to recover.

Plottage: The individual value of two adjacent properties may be greater if they are combined than if each is sold separately.

Plottage   The principle of **plottage** holds that merging or consolidating adjacent lots into a single larger one produces a greater total land value than the sum of the two sites valued separately. For example, two adjacent lots valued at $35,000 each might have a combined value of $90,000 if consolidated. The process of merging two separately owned lots under one owner is known as **assemblage**. *Plottage* is the amount that value is increased by successful assemblage.

Regression and progression   In general, the worth of a better-quality property is adversely affected by the presence of a lesser-quality property. This is known as the principle of **regression**. Thus, in a neighborhood of modest homes, a structure that is larger, better maintained, or more luxurious would tend to be valued in the same range as the less lavish homes. Conversely, under the principle of **progression**, the value of a modest home would be higher if it were located among larger, fancier properties.

Substitution   The principle of **substitution** says that the maximum value of a property tends to be set by how much it would cost to purchase an equally desirable and valuable substitute property. Substitution is the foundation of the sales comparison approach.

Supply and demand   The principle of **supply and demand** says the value of a property depends on the number of properties available in the marketplace—the supply of the product. When supply increases, value decreases and when demand increases, value increases. Other factors include the prices of other properties, the number of prospective purchasers, and the price buyers will pay.

■ THE THREE APPROACHES TO VALUE

To arrive at an accurate estimate of value, appraisers traditionally use three basic valuation techniques: the sales comparison approach, the cost approach, and the income approach. The three methods serve as checks against each other. Using them narrows the range of the final value estimate. Each method addresses a specific type of property.

The Sales Comparison Approach

In the **sales comparison approach** (also known as the **market data approach**), an estimate of value is obtained by comparing the property being appraised—the subject property—with recently sold comparable properties—properties similar to the subject. Because no two parcels of real estate are exactly alike, each comparable property must be analyzed for differences and similarities between it and the subject property. This approach is a good example of the principle of substitution, discussed above. The **sales prices** of the comparables must be adjusted for any differences. The elements of comparison for which adjustments must be made include the following:

■ *Property rights.* An adjustment must be made when less than fee simple, the full legal bundle of rights, is involved. This includes land leases, ground leases, life estates, easements, deed restrictions, and encroachments.

■ *Financing concessions.* The financing terms must be considered, including adjustments for differences such as mortgage loan terms and owner financing or buydowns by a builder-developer.

■ *Market conditions.* Interest rates, supply and demand, and other economic indicators must be analyzed.

■ *Conditions of sale.* Adjustments must be made for motivational factors that would affect the sale, such as foreclosure, a sale between family members, or some nonmonetary incentive.

■ *Market conditions since the date of sale.* An adjustment must be made if economic changes occur between the date of sale of the comparable property and the date of the appraisal.

■ *Location, or area preference.* Similar properties might differ in price from neighborhood to neighborhood or even between locations within the same neighborhood.

■ *Physical features and amenities.* Physical features, such as the structure's age, size, and condition, may require adjustments.

The sales comparison approach is usually considered the most reliable of the three approaches in appraising single-family homes, where the intangible benefits may be difficult to measure otherwise. Most appraisals include a minimum of three comparable sales reflective of the subject property. (See Table 18.1.)

The Cost Approach

The **cost approach** to value also is based on the principle of substitution. The cost approach consists of five steps:

1. Estimate the value of the land as though it were vacant and available to be put to its highest and best use.

TABLE 18.1

Sales Comparison Approach to Value

	Subject Property	Comparable Properties		
		A	B	C
Sales price		$260,000	$252,000	$265,000
Financing concessions	none	none	none	none
Date of sale		current	current	current
Location	good	same	poorer +6,500	same
Age	6 years	same	same	same
Size of lot	60' × 135'	same	same	larger –5,000
Landscaping	good	same	same	same
Construction	brick	same	same	same
Style	ranch	same	same	same
No. of rooms	6	same	same	same
No. of bedrooms	3	same	poorer +500	same
No. of baths	1½	same	same	better –500
Sq. ft. of living space	1,500	same	same	better –1,000
Other space (basement)	full basement	same	same	same
Condition—exterior	average	better –1,500	poorer +1,000	better –1,500
Condition—interior	good	same	same	better –500
Garage	2-car attached	same	same	same
Other improvements	none	none	none	none
Net adjustments		–1,500	+8,000	–8,500
Adjusted value		$258,500	$260,000	$256,500

Note: The value of a feature that is present in the subject but not in the comparable property is *added* to the sales price of the comparable. Likewise, the value of a feature that is present in the comparable but not in the subject property is *subtracted*. A good way to remember this is: CBS stands for "comp better subtract"; and CPA stands for "comp poorer add." The adjusted sales prices of the comparables represent the probable range of value of the subject property. From this range, a single market value estimate can be selected.

2. Estimate the current cost of constructing buildings and improvements.
3. Estimate the amount of **accrued depreciation** (loss in value) resulting from the property's physical deterioration, external depreciation, and functional obsolescence.
4. Deduct the accrued depreciation (Step 3) from the construction cost (Step 2).
5. Add the estimated land value (Step 1) to the depreciated cost of the building and site improvements (Step 4) to arrive at the total property value.

■ **FOR EXAMPLE**

Value of the land	=	$50,000
Current cost of construction	=	$180,000
Accrued depreciation	=	$20,000
$180,000 – $20,000	=	$160,000
$50,000 + $160,000	=	$210,000

In this example, the total property value is $210,000.

There are two ways to look at the construction cost of a building for appraisal purposes: reproduction cost and replacement cost. **Reproduction cost** is the construction cost at current prices of an exact duplicate of the subject improvement, including both the benefits and the drawbacks of the property. **Replacement cost new** is the cost to construct an improvement similar to the subject property, using current construction methods and materials but not necessarily an exact duplicate. Replacement cost new is more frequently used in appraising older structures because it eliminates obsolete features and takes advantage of current construction materials and techniques.

An example of the cost approach to value, applied to the same property as in Table 18.1, is shown in Table 18.2.

Determining reproduction or replacement cost new An appraiser using the cost approach computes the reproduction or replacement cost of a building using one of the following four methods:

- *Square-foot method.* The cost per square foot of a recently built comparable structure is multiplied by the number of square feet (using exterior dimensions) in the subject building. The square-foot method is the most common and easiest method of cost estimation. Table 18.2 uses the square-foot method, which is also referred to as the comparison method. For some, usually nonresidential, properties such as warehouse space, the cost per cubic foot of a recently built comparable structure is multiplied by the number of cubic feet in the subject structure.
- *Unit-in-place method.* In the unit-in-place method, the replacement cost of a structure is estimated based on the construction cost per unit of measure of individual building components, including material, labor, overhead, and builder's profit. Most components are measured in square feet, although items such as plumbing fixtures are estimated by cost. The sum of the components is the cost of the new structure.
- *Quantity-survey method.* The quantity and quality of all materials (such as lumber, brick, and plaster) and the labor are estimated on a unit-cost basis. These factors are added to indirect costs (e.g., building permit, survey, payroll, taxes, and builder's profit) to arrive at the total cost of the structure. Because it is so detailed and time consuming, the quantity-survey method is usually used only in appraising historical properties. However, it is the most accurate method of appraising new construction.
- *Index method.* A factor representing the percentage increase of construction costs up to the present time is applied to the original cost of the subject property. Because this method fails to take into account individual property variables, it is useful only as a check of the estimate reached by one of the other methods.

Depreciation In a real estate appraisal, **depreciation** is a loss in value for any reason. It refers to a condition that adversely affects the value of an improvement to real property. Remember: Land does not depreciate; it retains its value indefinitely, except in such rare cases as downzoned urban parcels, improperly developed land, or misused farmland. Depreciation is the result of a negative condition that affects real property.

TABLE 18.2	**Subject Property**		
Cost Approach to Value	**Land valuation**: Size 60' × 135' @ $450 per front foot	=	$ 27,000
	Plus site improvements: driveway, walks, landscaping, etc.	=	8,000
	Total		$ 35,000

Building valuation: replacement cost
1,500 sq. ft. @ $85 per sq. ft. = $127,500

Less depreciation:
Physical depreciation
  Curable
    (items of deferred maintenance)
    exterior painting $4,000
  Incurable (structural deterioration)   9,750
Functional obsolescence   2,000
External obsolescence   0
Total depreciation $15,750

Depreciated value of building	$111,750
Indicated value by cost approach	$146,750

Depreciation is considered to be curable or incurable, depending on the amount of the contribution to the value of the property. For appraisal purposes, depreciation is divided into three classes, according to cause:

- **Physical deterioration.** A curable item is one in need of repair, such as painting (deferred maintenance), that is economically feasible and would result in an increase in value equal to or exceeding the cost. An item is incurable if it is a defect caused by physical wear and tear and its correction would not be economically feasible or contribute a comparable value to the building, such as a crack in the foundation. The cost of a major repair may not warrant the financial investment.

- **Functional obsolescence.** Obsolescence means a loss in value from the market's response to the item. Outmoded or unacceptable physical or design features that are no longer considered desirable by purchasers are curable. Such features could be replaced or redesigned at a cost that would be offset by the anticipated increase in ultimate value. Outmoded plumbing, for instance, is usually easily replaced. Room function may be redefined at no cost if the basic room layout allows for it. A bedroom adjacent to a kitchen, for example, may be converted to a family room. However, currently undesirable physical or design features that cannot be easily remedied because the cost of the cure would be greater than its resulting increase in value are considered incurable. An office building that cannot be air-conditioned economically, for example, suffers from incurable functional obsolescence if the cost of adding air-conditioning is greater than its contribution to the building's value.

- **External obsolescence.** If caused by negative factors not on the subject property, such as environmental, social, or economic forces, the depreciation is always incurable. The loss in value cannot be reversed by spending money on the property. For example, close proximity to a polluting factory or a deteriorating neighborhood is one factor that could not be cured by the owner of the subject property.

The easiest but least precise way to determine depreciation is the straight-line method, also called the economic age-life method. Depreciation is assumed to occur at an even rate over a structure's **economic life**, the period during which it is expected to remain useful for its original intended purpose. The property's cost is divided by the number of years of its expected economic life to derive the amount of annual depreciation.

For instance, a $420,000 property may have a land value of $240,000 and an improvement value of $180,000. If the improvement is expected to last 60 years, the annual straight-line depreciation would be $3,000 ($180,000 divided by 60 years). Such depreciation can be calculated as an annual dollar amount or as a percentage of a property's improvements.

The cost approach is most useful in the appraisal of newer or special-purpose buildings such as schools, churches, and public buildings. Such properties are difficult to appraise using other methods because there are seldom enough local sales to use as comparables and because the properties do not ordinarily generate income.

Much of the functional obsolescence and all the external obsolescence can be evaluated only by considering the actions of buyers in the marketplace.

The Income Approach

The **income approach** to value is based on the present value of the rights to future income. It assumes that the income generated by a property will determine the property's value. The income approach is used for valuation of income-producing properties such as apartment buildings, office buildings, and shopping centers and is based on anticipation. In estimating value using the income approach, an appraiser must take the following five steps:

**Memory Tip
Income Approach**

Gross
Income
Vacancy
Expenses
Net operating income

1. Estimate annual potential gross income. An estimate of economic rental income must be made based on market studies. Current rental income may not reflect the current market rental rates, especially in the case of short-term leases or leases about to terminate. Potential income includes other income to the property from such sources as vending machines, parking fees, and laundry machines.
2. Deduct an appropriate allowance for vacancy and rent loss, based on the appraiser's experience, and arrive at the effective gross income.
3. Deduct the annual operating expenses, enumerated in Table 18.3, from the effective gross income to arrive at the annual **net operating income (NOI)**. Management costs are always included, even if the current owner manages the property. Mortgage payments (principal and interest) are debt service and are not considered operating expenses. Capital expenditures are not considered expenses; however, an allowance can be calculated representing the annual usage of each major capital item.
4. Estimate the price a typical investor would pay for the income produced by this particular type and class of property. This is done by estimating the rate of return (or yield) that an investor will demand for the investment of capital in this type of building. This rate of return is called the **capitalization rate** (or "cap" rate) and is determined by comparing the relationship of net operating income with the sales prices of similar properties

TABLE 18.3	Potential gross annual income Market rent (100% capacity)	$60,000
Income Capitalization Approach to Value	Income from other sources (vending machines and pay phones)	+600
		$60,600
	Less vacancy and collection losses (estimated) @ 4%	−2,424
	Effective gross income	$58,176

Expenses:

Real estate taxes	$9,000
Insurance	1,000
Heat	2,500
Maintenance	6,400
Utilities, electricity, water, gas	800
Repairs	1,200
Decorating	1,400
Replacement of equipment	800
Legal and accounting	600
Advertising	300
Management	3,000
Total	$27,000
Annual net operating income	$31,176

Capitalization rate = 10% (overall rate)

Capitalization of annual net income: $31,176 ÷ 0.10 = $311,760
Income value by income approach = $311,760

that have sold in the current market. For example, a comparable property that is producing an annual net income of $15,000 is sold for $187,500. The capitalization rate is $15,000 divided by $187,500, or 8 percent. If other comparable properties sold at prices that yielded substantially the same rate, it may be concluded that 8 percent is the rate that the appraiser should apply to the subject property.

5. Apply the capitalization rate to the property's annual net operating income to arrive at the estimate of the property's value.

With the appropriate capitalization rate and the projected annual net operating income, the appraiser can obtain an estimate of value by the income approach.

This formula and its variations are important in dealing with income property:

Income ÷ Rate = Value
Income ÷ Value = Rate
Value × Rate = Income

For example:

Net Operating Income ÷ Capitalization Rate = Value
Example: $18,000 income ÷ 9% cap rate = $200,000 value or
$18,000 income ÷ 8% cap rate = $225,000 value

Note the relationship between the rate and value. As the rate goes down, the value increases.

A simplified version of the computations used in applying the income approach is illustrated in Table 18.3.

Gross rent or gross income multipliers   If a buyer is interested in purchasing a one- to four-unit residential rental property, the **gross rent multiplier (GRM)** would be used for the appraisal value. If the buyer is interested in purchasing five or more units, a commercial **gross income multiplier (GIM)** would be used for the appraisal value.

Because single-family residences usually produce only rental incomes, the gross rent multiplier is used. This relates a sales price to monthly rental income. However, commercial and industrial properties generate income from many other sources (rent, concessions, escalator clause income, and so forth), and they are valued using their annual income from all sources.

The formulas are as follows:

- For one to four residential units:
  Sales price ÷ Monthly gross rent = Gross rent multiplier (GRM)
- For five or more units and commercial:
  Sales price ÷ Annual gross income = Gross income multiplier (GIM)

For example, if a home recently sold for $155,000 and its monthly rental income was $1,250, the GRM for the property would be computed as follows:

$155,000 ÷ $1,250 = 124 GRM

If a commercial property recently sold for $155,000 and its annual rental income was $15,000, the GIM for the property would be computed as follows:

$155,000 ÷ $15000 = 10.33 GIM

To establish an accurate GRM, an appraiser must have recent sales and rental data from at least four properties that are similar to the subject property. The resulting GRM can then be applied to the estimated fair market rental of the subject property to arrive at its market value. The formula would be as follows:

Rental income × GRM = Estimated market value

Table 18.4 shows some examples of GRM comparisons.

Reconciliation

When the three approaches to value are applied to the same property, they normally produce three separate indications of value. (Compare Table 18.1 with Table 18.2.) **Reconciliation** is the act of analyzing and effectively weighing the findings from the three approaches. In reconciliation, an appraiser explains not only the appropriateness of each approach but also the relative reliability of the data within each approach in line with the type of value sought. The appraiser should also explain how the data reflect the market functions.

TABLE 18.4

Gross Rent Multiplier

Comparable No.	Sales Price	Monthly Rent	GRM
1	$280,000	$1,800	155.55
2	243,000	1,350	180.00
3	287,000	2,000	143.50
4	262,500	1,675	156.72
Subject	?	1,750	?

Note: Based on an analysis of these comparisons, comparables 2 and 3 show extremes. Based on monthly rent between comparables 1 and 4, a GRM of 156.72 seems reasonable for homes in this area. In the opinion of an appraiser, the estimated value of the subject property would be $1,750 × 156.72, or $274,260.

The process of reconciliation is not simply taking the average of the three estimates of value. An average implies that the data and logic applied in each of the approaches are equally valid and reliable and should, therefore, be given equal weight. In fact, however, certain approaches are more valid and reliable with some kinds of properties than with others.

For example, in appraising a home, the income approach is rarely valid, and the cost approach is of limited value unless the home is relatively new. Therefore, the sales comparison approach is usually given greatest weight in valuing single-family residences. In the appraisal of income or investment property, the income approach normally is given the greatest weight. In the appraisal of churches, libraries, museums, schools, and other special-use properties, where little or no income or sales revenue is generated, the cost approach usually is assigned the greatest weight. From this analysis, or reconciliation, a single estimate of market value is produced.

■ KEY POINT REVIEW

Appraisal is an estimate or opinion of **value** based on supportable evidence and appraisal methods, defined by the **Uniform Standards of Appraisal Practice (USPAP)** and set by the Appraisal Foundation's Appraisal Standards Board.

An **appraiser** must be state-licensed or certified for an appraisal performed as part of a federally related transaction.

A **competitive market analysis (CMA)** is a report by a real estate salesperson of market statistics, but it is not an appraisal.

A **broker's price opinion (BPO)** may be used in a non-federally related transaction: home equity lines, refinancing, portfolio management, loss mitigation, and collections.

Value is created by **d**emand, **u**tility, **s**carcity, and **t**ransferability of property (**DUST**). **Market value** is the most probable price that property should bring in a fair sale, but not necessarily the same as **price** paid or **cost** to construct.

A **sales comparison approach** (**market data approach**) makes use of sales of properties comparable (referred to as **comps**) to the property that is the subject of the appraisal by adding or subtracting the value of a feature present or absent in the subject property versus the comparable.

The **cost approach** estimates current **reproduction** or **replacement cost** of constructing building and other property improvements using the square-foot method, the unit-in-place method, the quantity-survey method, or the index method; and

- estimates **accrued depreciation** using the straight-line method (**economic age-life method**), or
- by estimating items of **physical deterioration, functional obsolescence,** or **external obsolescence.**

The **income approach** is based on the present value of the right to future income and uses the following five steps:

1. Estimate annual potential **gross income.**
2. Deduct allowance for vacancy and rent loss to find **effective gross income.**
3. Deduct annual operating expenses to find **net operating income (NOI).**
4. Estimate **rate of return** (**capitalization rate** or **cap rate**) for subject by analyzing cap rates of similar properties.
5. Derive estimate of subject's market value by applying cap rate to annual NOI using this formula: **Net operating income ÷ Capitalization rate = Value.**

Reconciliation is the process by which the validity and reliability of the results of the approaches to value are weighed objectively to determine the appraiser's final opinion of value.

■ RELATED WEB SITES

American Society of Appraisers: *www.appraisers.org*
American Society of Farm Managers and Rural Appraisers, Inc.: *www.asfmra.org*
Appraisal Foundation: *www.appraisalfoundation.org*
Appraisal Institute: *www.appraisalinstitute.org*
International Right of Way Association: *www.irwaonline.org*
National Association of Independent Fee Appraisers: *www.naifa.com*

CHAPTER 18 QUIZ

1. Which appraisal method uses a rate of investment return?
   a. Sales comparison approach
   b. Cost approach
   c. Income approach
   d. Gross income multiplier method

2. The characteristics of value include which of the following?
   a. Competition
   b. Scarcity
   c. Anticipation
   d. Balance

3. There are two vacant adjacent lots, each worth approximately $50,000. If their owner sells them as a single lot, however, the combined parcel will be worth $120,000. What principle does this illustrate?
   a. Substitution
   b. Plottage
   c. Regression
   d. Progression

4. The amount of money a property commands in the marketplace is its
   a. intrinsic value.
   b. market price.
   c. subjective value.
   d. book value.

5. A homeowner constructs an eight-bedroom brick house with a tennis court, a greenhouse, and an indoor pool in a neighborhood of modest two-bedroom and three-bedroom frame houses on narrow lots. The value of this house is MOST likely to be affected by what principle?
   a. Progression
   b. Assemblage
   c. Change
   d. Regression

6. In Question 5, the owners of the lesser-valued houses in the neighborhood may find that the values of their homes are affected by what principle?
   a. Progression
   b. Increasing returns
   c. Competition
   d. Regression

7. For appraisal purposes, accrued depreciation is NOT caused by
   a. functional obsolescence.
   b. physical deterioration.
   c. external obsolescence.
   d. accelerated depreciation.

8. The term reconciliation refers to which of the following?
   a. Loss of value due to any cause
   b. Separating the value of the land from the total value of the property to compute depreciation
   c. Analyzing the results obtained by the different approaches to value to estimate a final estimate of value
   d. The process by which an appraiser determines the highest and best use for a parcel of land

9. If a property's annual net income is $24,000 and it is valued at $300,000, what is its capitalization rate?
   a. 8 percent
   b. 10.5 percent
   c. 12 percent
   d. 15 percent

10. Which of the following is NOT used by an appraiser applying the income approach to value?
    a. Annual net operating income
    b. Capitalization rate
    c. Accrued depreciation
    d. Annual gross income

11. An appraiser asked to estimate the value of an existing strip shopping center would probably give the MOST weight to which approach to value?

    a. Cost approach
    b. Sales comparison approach
    c. Income approach
    d. Index method

12. The market value of a parcel of real estate is

    a. an estimate of its future benefits.
    b. the amount of money paid for the property.
    c. an estimate of the most probable price it should bring.
    d. its value without improvements.

13. Capitalization is the process by which annual net operating income is used to

    a. determine cost.
    b. estimate value.
    c. establish depreciation.
    d. determine potential tax value.

14. From the reproduction or replacement cost of a building, the appraiser deducts depreciation, which represents

    a. the remaining economic life of the building.
    b. remodeling costs to increase rentals.
    c. loss of value due to any reason.
    d. costs to modernize the building.

15. All of the following factors would be important in comparing properties under the sales comparison approach to value EXCEPT differences in

    a. dates of sale.
    b. financing terms.
    c. appearance and condition.
    d. original cost.

16. A building was purchased five years ago for $240,000. It currently has an estimated remaining useful life of 55 years. What is the property's total depreciation to date?

    a. $14,364
    b. $20,000
    c. $48,000
    d. $54,000

17. In Question 16, what is the current value of the building?

    a. $235,636
    b. $220,000
    c. $192,000
    d. $186,000

18. The appraised value of a residence with four bedrooms and one bathroom would probably be reduced because of

    a. external obsolescence.
    b. functional obsolescence.
    c. curable physical deterioration.
    d. incurable physical deterioration.

19. Which principle of value indicates that a developer's very profitable real estate project will attract others to engage in similar activity in the same area and thus drive down profits?

    a. Anticipation
    b. Competition
    c. Value
    d. Progression

20. Change, contribution, plottage, and substitution are some of the basic principles that affect what aspect of real estate?

    a. Demand
    b. Depreciation
    c. Value
    d. Supply

CHAPTER 19

Land-Use Controls and Property Development

■ LEARNING OBJECTIVES   *When you have finished reading this chapter, you should be able to*

- **identify** the various types of public and private land-use controls;

- **describe** how a comprehensive plan influences local real estate development;

- **explain** the various issues involved in subdivision;

- **distinguish** the function and characteristics of building codes and zoning ordinances; and

- **define** the following *key terms:*

buffer zone	density zoning	plat
building code	developer	restrictive covenants
certificate of occupancy	enabling acts	subdivider
comprehensive plan	Interstate Land Sales Full	subdivision
conditional-use permit	Disclosure Act	variance
covenants, conditions,	inverse condemnation	zoning
and restrictions	nonconforming use	zoning ordinance
(CC&Rs)	planned unit development	
	(PUD)	

■ LAND-USE CONTROLS AND PROPERTY DEVELOPMENT

Over the years, the government's policy has been to encourage private ownership of land, but this does not always mean that owners can do whatever they want with their properties. In most areas of the United States, local municipalities have developed comprehensive planning that restricts how land may be used, with the goal of orderly and planned growth.

Real estate licensees must be knowledgeable about local land-use restrictions in order to avoid placing their buyers in properties that they cannot use as they intended, especially when working with buyers who are looking for properties to develop for specific commercial or residential uses. Moreover, buyers of homes within a residential community association are also subject to specific rules. While no one expects a real estate licensee to become an "expert" in land use, licensees are still expected to be aware of these issues and to be able to direct their clients to appropriate sources of additional information.

■ LAND-USE CONTROLS

Land use is controlled and regulated through public and private restrictions and through the direct ownership of land by federal, state, and local governments. Over the years, the government's policy has been to encourage private ownership of land.

It is necessary for a certain amount of land to be owned by the government for such uses as municipal buildings, state government buildings, schools, and military bases. Government ownership may also serve the public interest through urban renewal efforts, public housing, and streets and highways. Often, the only way to ensure that enough land is set aside for recreational and conservation purposes is through direct government ownership in the form of national and state parks and forest preserves. Beyond this sort of direct ownership of land, most government controls on property occur at the local level.

The states' *police power* is their inherent authority to create regulations needed to protect the public health, safety, and welfare. Through enabling acts, states delegate to counties and local municipalities the authority to enact ordinances in keeping with general laws. (See Chapter 2.) The increasing demands placed on finite natural resources have made it necessary for cities, towns, and villages to increase their limitations on the private use of real estate. There are now controls over noise, air, and water pollution as well as population density.

■ THE COMPREHENSIVE PLAN

Local governments, municipalities, and counties establish development goals by creating a **comprehensive plan**. The comprehensive plan, also known as a master plan, is not a regulatory document, but rather a guide to planning for change rather than reacting to proposals. The comprehensive plan usually is long term, perhaps 20 years or longer, and often includes (a) general plan that can be revised and updated more frequently, (b) plans for specific areas, and (c) strategic plans. Systematic planning for orderly growth consists of the following basic elements:

- Land use—determining how much land may be proposed for residence, industry, business, agriculture, traffic and transit facilities, utilities, community facilities, parks and recreational facilities, floodplains, and areas of special hazards
- Housing needs of present and anticipated residents, including rehabilitation of declining neighborhoods, as well as new residential developments
- Movement of people and goods, including highways and public transit, parking facilities, and pedestrian and bikeway systems
- Community facilities and utilities such as schools, libraries, hospitals, recreational facilities, fire and police stations, water resources, sewerage, waste treatment and disposal, storm drainage, and flood management
- Energy conservation to reduce energy consumption and promote the use of renewable energy sources

The preparation of a comprehensive plan involves surveys, studies, and analyses of housing, demographic, and economic characteristics and trends. The municipality's planning activities may be coordinated with other government bodies and private interests to achieve orderly growth and development.

■ **FOR EXAMPLE**   After the Great Chicago Fire of 1871 reduced most of the city's downtown to rubble and ash, the city engaged planner Daniel Burnham to lay out a design for Chicago's future. The resulting Burnham Plan of orderly boulevards linking a park along Lake Michigan with other large parks and public spaces throughout the city established an ideal urban space. The plan is still being implemented today.

■ ZONING

Zoning is a regulatory tool that helps communities regulate and control how land is used for the protection of public health, safety, and welfare. **Zoning ordinances** implement the comprehensive plan and regulate and control of the use of land and structures within designated land-use districts, in part by separating conflicting land uses. If the comprehensive plan is the big picture, zoning is the details.

Although no nationwide or statewide zoning ordinances exist, the state's **enabling acts** confer zoning powers to local municipal governments. State and federal governments may, however, regulate land use through special legislation such as scenic easements, coastal management, and environmental laws.

Zoning affects such things as

- permitted uses of each parcel of land,
- lot sizes,
- types of structures,
- building heights,
- setbacks (the minimum distance away from streets or sidewalks that structures may be built),

- style and appearance of structures,
- density (the ratio of land area to structure area), and
- protection of natural resources.

Zoning ordinances cannot be static; they must remain flexible to meet the changing needs of society.

■ **FOR EXAMPLE**   In many large cities, factories and warehouses sit empty. Some cities have begun changing the zoning ordinances for such properties to permit new residential or commercial developments in areas once zoned strictly for heavy industrial use. Coupled with tax incentives, the changes lure developers back into the cities. The resulting housing is modern, conveniently located, and affordable. Simple zoning changes can help revitalize whole neighborhoods in big cities.

Zoning Classifications

Land is divided into zones. The zones are identified by a coding system that outlines how the land may be used according to the code. Common zoning classifications include C for commercial, R for residential, and A for agricultural. There are subcategories in the classifications, and some land may be zoned for mixed use.

A **planned unit development (PUD)** is a development where land is set aside for mixed-use purposes, such as residential, commercial, and public areas. Zoning regulations may be modified for PUDs.

Zoning Ordinances

Zoning ordinances have traditionally classified land use into residential, commercial, industrial, and agricultural. These land-use areas are further divided into subclasses. For example, residential areas may be subdivided to provide for detached single-family dwellings, semidetached structures containing not more than four dwelling units, walkup apartments, and high-rise apartments.

To meet both the growing demand for a variety of housing types and the need for innovative residential and nonresidential development, municipalities are adopting ordinances for subdivisions and planned residential developments. Some municipalities also use **buffer zones**, to ease transition from one use to another. A buffer zone is typically a strip of land separating land dedicated to one use from land dedicated to another use. For example, landscaped parks and playgrounds, and hiking trails are used to screen residential areas from nonresidential zones. Certain types of zoning that focus on special land-use objectives are used in some areas. These include

- *bulk zoning* to control density and avoid overcrowding by imposing restrictions such as setbacks, building heights, and percentage of open area or by restricting new construction projects;
- *aesthetic zoning* to specify certain types of architecture for new buildings; and
- *incentive zoning* to ensure that certain uses are incorporated into developments, such as requiring the street floor of an office building to house retail establishments.

Constitutional issues and zoning ordinances   Zoning can be a highly controversial issue and often raises questions of constitutional law. The preamble of the U.S. Constitution provides for the promotion of the general welfare. More specifically, the Fourteenth Amendment prevents the states from depriving "any person of life, liberty, or property, without due process of law." The ongoing question is how a local government can enact zoning ordinances that protect public safety and welfare without violating the constitutional rights of property owners. The government provides a forum for the citizens to discuss zoning ordinances before they are enacted; these are called public hearings.

Any land-use legislation that is destructive, unreasonable, arbitrary, or confiscatory usually is considered void. Furthermore, zoning ordinances must not violate the various provisions of the state's constitution. Commonly applied tests in determining the validity of ordinances require that

- power be exercised in a reasonable manner;
- provisions be clear and specific;
- ordinances be nondiscriminatory;
- ordinances promote public health, safety, and general welfare under the police power concept; and
- ordinances apply to all property in a similar manner.

Taking   The concept of *taking* is similar to eminent domain in that it comes from the takings clause of the Fifth Amendment to the U.S. Constitution. The clause reads "nor shall private property be taken for public use, without just compensation," meaning that when land is taken for public use through the government's power of eminent domain or condemnation, the owner must be compensated. In general, no land is exempt from government seizure. However, the rule is that the government cannot seize land without paying for it. This payment is referred to as just or fair compensation.

Inverse condemnation is an action brought by a property owner seeking just compensation for land taken for a public use where it appears that the taker of the property does not intend to bring eminent domain proceedings. The property is condemned because its use and value have been diminished due to an adjacent property's public use. For example, property along a newly constructed highway may be inversely condemned. While the property itself was not used in constructing the highway, the property value may be significantly diminished due to the construction of the highway close to the property. The property owner may bring an inverse condemnation action to be compensated for the loss. (See Chapter 7.)

It is sometimes very difficult to determine what level of compensation is fair in any particular situation. The compensation may be negotiated between the owner and the government, or the owner may seek a court judgment setting the amount.

IN PRACTICE   One method used to determine just compensation is the before-and-after method. This method is used primarily where a portion of an owner's property is seized for public use. The value of the owner's remaining property after the taking is subtracted from the value of the whole parcel before the taking. The result is the total amount of compensation due to the owner.

Zoning Permits

Compliance with zoning can be monitored by requiring that property owners obtain permits before they begin any development. A permit will not be issued unless a proposed development conforms to the permitted zoning, among other requirements. Zoning permits are usually required before building permits can be issued.

Zoning hearing board Most communities have established zoning hearing boards (or zoning boards of appeal) to hear testimony about the effects a zoning ordinance may have on specific parcels of property. Petitions for variances or exceptions to the zoning law may be presented to an appeal board.

Nonconforming use Frequently, a lot or an improvement does not conform to the zoning use because it existed before the enactment or amendment of the zoning ordinance. Such a **nonconforming use** may be allowed to continue legally as long as it complies with the regulations governing nonconformities in the local ordinance, until the improvement is destroyed or torn down, or until the current use is abandoned. If the nonconforming use is allowed to continue indefinitely, it is considered to be grandfathered into the new zoning.

Licensees should never assume, nor allow their clients to assume, that the existing nonconforming use will be allowed to continue. Buyers should verify with the local zoning authorities the conditions under which the use is allowed to remain or whether changes are permitted.

■ **FOR EXAMPLE** Under the city's old zoning ordinances, a grocery store was well within a commercial zone. When the zoning map was changed to accommodate an increased need for residential housing, the grocery store was grandfathered into the new zoning; that is, it was allowed to continue its successful operations, even though it did not fit the new zoning rules.

Conditional-use permits allow nonconforming but related land uses.

Variances permit prohibited land uses to avoid undue hardship.

Variances and conditional-use permits Once a plan or zoning ordinance is enacted, property owners and developers know what they can and cannot do on their property. However, they may want to propose changes to the existing zoning in order to use their property somewhat differently. Generally these owners may appeal for either a **conditional-use permit** or a variance to allow a use that does not meet current zoning requirements.

A conditional-use permit (also known as a special-use permit) is usually granted to a property owner to allow a special use of property that is defined as an allowable conditional use within that zone, such as a house of worship or daycare center in a residential district. For a conditional-use permit to be appropriate, the intended use must meet certain standards set by the municipality.

Variances provide relief if zoning regulations deprive an owner of the reasonable use of the property. To qualify for a variance, the owner must demonstrate the unique circumstances that make the variance necessary. In addition, the owner must prove that the regulations have caused harm or created a burden.

A variance might also be sought to provide relief if existing zoning regulations create a physical hardship for the development of a specific property. For example, if an owner's lot is level next to a road but slopes steeply 30 feet away from the road, the zoning board may allow a variance so the owner can build closer to the road than the setback allows.

Both variances and conditional-use permits are issued by zoning boards only after public hearings. The neighbors of a proposed use must be given an opportunity to voice their opinions.

A property owner also can seek a change in the zoning classification of a parcel of real estate by obtaining an amendment to the district map or a zoning ordinance for that area; that is, the owner can attempt to have the zoning changed to accommodate an intended use of the property.

■ BUILDING CODES AND CERTIFICATES OF OCCUPANCY

Most municipalities have enacted ordinances to specify construction standards that must be met when repairing or erecting buildings. These are called **building codes,** and they set many requirements for such things as materials and standards of workmanship, sanitary equipment, electrical wiring, and fire prevention.

A property owner who wants to build a structure or alter or repair an existing building usually must obtain a building permit. Through the permit requirement, municipal officials are made aware of new construction or alterations and can verify compliance with building codes and zoning ordinances. Inspectors will closely examine the plans and conduct periodic inspections of the work. Once the completed structure has been inspected and found satisfactory, the municipal inspector issues a **certificate of occupancy** or occupancy permit.

If a building use has been converted from another use to residential or a new home has been constructed, the municipal inspector must ensure that the construction complies with relevant ordinances and codes. A certificate of occupancy or occupancy permit indicating that the property is suitable for habitation by meeting certain safety and health standards must be issued before anyone moves in and often before a lender will allow closing.

If the construction of a building or an alteration violates a deed restriction, the issuance of a building permit will not cure this violation. A building permit is merely evidence of the applicant's compliance with municipal regulations.

Similarly, communities with historic districts, or those that are interested in maintaining a particular look or character, may have aesthetic ordinances. These laws require that all new construction or restorations be approved by a special board. The board ensures that the new structures will blend in with existing building styles. Owners of existing properties may need to obtain approval to have their homes painted or remodeled.

IN PRACTICE   The subject of planning, zoning, and restricting the use of real estate is extremely technical, and the interpretation of the law is not always clear. Questions concerning any of these subjects in relation to real estate transactions should be referred to legal counsel. Furthermore, the landowner should be aware of the costs for various permits.

■ SUBDIVISION

Most communities have adopted **subdivision** and land development ordinances as part of their comprehensive plans. An ordinance includes provisions for submitting and processing subdivision plats. A major advantage of subdivision ordinances is that they encourage flexibility, economy, and ingenuity in the use of land. A **subdivider** is a person who buys undeveloped acreage and divides it into smaller lots for sale to individuals or developers or for the subdivider's own use. A **developer**, who may also be a subdivider, improves the land, constructs homes or other buildings on the lots, and sells them. Developing is generally a much more extensive activity than subdividing.

Regulation of Land Development

Just as no national zoning ordinance exists, no uniform planning and land development legislation affects the entire country. Laws governing subdividing and land planning are controlled by the state and local governing bodies where the land is located. Rules and regulations developed by government agencies have, however, provided certain minimum standards. Many local governments have established standards that are higher than the minimum standards.

> **Subdividers** split up land into parcels.
>
> **Developers** construct improvements on the subdivided parcels.

Land development plan   Before the actual subdividing can begin, the subdivider must go through the process of land planning. The resulting land development plan must comply with the municipality's comprehensive plan. Although comprehensive plans and zoning ordinances are not necessarily inflexible, a plan that requires them to be changed must undergo long, expensive, and frequently complicated hearings.

Plats   From the land development and subdivision plans, the subdivider draws plats. A **plat** is a detailed map that illustrates the geographic boundaries of individual lots. It shows the blocks, sections, streets, public easements, and monuments in the prospective subdivision. (See Figure 9.8 in Chapter 9 for an example of a subdivision plat map.) A plat may also include engineering data and restrictive covenants. The plats must be approved by the municipality before they can be recorded. Once a plat is properly recorded, it may be used as an adequate description of real property. A developer is often required to submit an environmental impact report with the application for subdivision approval. This report explains what effect the proposed development will have on the surrounding area.

Subdivision Plans

In plotting out a subdivision according to local planning and zoning controls, a subdivider usually determines the size as well as the location of the individual lots.

The maximum or minimum size of a lot is generally regulated by local ordinances and must be considered carefully.

The land itself must be studied, usually in cooperation with a surveyor, so that the subdivision takes advantage of natural drainage and land contours. A subdivider should provide for utility easements as well as easements for water and sewer mains.

Most subdivisions are laid out by use of lots and blocks. An area of land is designated as a block, and the area making up this block is divided into lots.

One negative aspect of subdivision development is the potential for increased tax burdens on all residents, both inside and outside the subdivision. To protect local taxpayers against the costs of a heightened demand for public services, many local governments strictly regulate nearly all aspects of subdivision development and may impose impact fees. *Impact fees* are charges made in advance to cover anticipated expenses involving off-site capital improvements such as expanding water and sewer facilities, additional roads, and school expansions.

Subdivision Density

Zoning ordinances control land use. Such control often includes minimum lot sizes and population density requirements for subdivisions and land developments. For example, a typical zoning restriction may set the minimum lot area on which a subdivider can build a single-family housing unit at 10,000 square feet. This means that the subdivider can build four houses per acre. Many zoning authorities establish special **density zoning** standards for certain subdivisions. Density zoning ordinances restrict the average maximum number of houses per acre that may be built within a particular subdivision. If the area is density zoned at an average maximum of four houses per acre, for instance, the subdivider may choose to cluster building lots to achieve an open effect. Regardless of lot size or number of units, the subdivider will be consistent with the ordinance as long as the average number of units in the development remains at or below the maximum density. This average is called gross density.

■ PRIVATE LAND-USE CONTROLS

Not all restrictions on the use of land are imposed by government bodies. Certain restrictions to control and maintain the desirable quality and character of a property or subdivision may be created by private entities, including the property owners themselves. These restrictions are separate from and in addition to the land-use controls exercised by the government. No private restriction can violate a local, state, or federal law.

Restrictive covenants   **Restrictive covenants** are limitations to the use of property imposed by a past owner or the current owner and are binding on future grantees.

On the other hand, **covenants, conditions, and restrictions (CC&Rs)** are private rules set up by the developer that set standards for all the parcels within the defined subdivision. The developer's restrictions may be imposed through a covenant in the deed or by a separate recorded declaration. CC&Rs typically govern the type, height, and size of buildings that individual owners can erect, as well as land use, architectural style, construction methods, setbacks, and square footage. CC&Rs are enforced by the homeowners' association.

Unlike most deed restrictions, many CC&Rs have time limitations; for example, a restriction might state that it is "effective for a period of 25 years from this date." After this time, it becomes inoperative or it may be extended if approved by the required number of owners. Many developers also include methods by which a required number of homeowners may change a CC&R.

Restrictive covenants are usually considered valid if they are reasonable restraints that benefit all property owners in the subdivision; that is, they protect property values or safety. If the terms of the restrictions are too broad, they may be construed as preventing the free transfer of property. If a restrictive covenant or condition is judged unenforceable by a court, the estate will stand free from the invalid covenant or condition. Restrictive covenants cannot be used for illegal purposes, such as for the exclusion of members of certain races, nationalities, or religions.

Private land-use controls may be more restrictive of an owner's use than the local zoning ordinances. The rule is that the more restrictive of the two takes precedence.

Private restrictions can be enforced in court when one lot owner applies to the court for an injunction to prevent a neighboring lot owner from violating the recorded restrictions. The court injunction will direct the violator to stop or remove the violation. The court retains the power to punish the violator for failing to obey. If adjoining lot owners stand idly by while a violation is committed, they can lose the right to an injunction by their inaction. The court might claim their right was lost through laches—that is, the legal principle that a right may be lost through undue delay or failure to assert it.

■ REGULATION OF LAND SALES

Just as the sale and use of property within a state are controlled by state and local governments, the sale of property in one state to buyers in another state is subject to strict federal and state regulations.

Interstate Land Sales Full Disclosure Act

The U.S Congress created the **Interstate Land Sales Full Disclosure Act** to prevent fraudulent marketing schemes that may arise when land is sold without being seen by the purchasers. The act is administered by the secretary of Housing and Urban Development (HUD) through the office of Interstate Land Sales registration. The seller is required to file statements of record with HUD before they can offer unimproved lots in interstate commerce by telephone or through the mail. The statements of record must contain numerous disclosures about the property.

Developers are also required to provide each purchaser or lessee of property with a printed report before the purchaser or lessee signs a purchase contract or lease. The report must disclose specific information about the land, including the

- type of title being transferred to the buyer,
- number of homes currently occupied on the site,
- availability of recreation facilities,
- distance to nearby communities,
- utility services and charges, and
- soil conditions and foundation or construction problems.

If the purchaser or lessee does not receive a copy of the report before signing the purchase contract or lease, the consumer may have grounds to void the contract.

The act provides a number of exemptions. For instance, it does not apply to subdivisions consisting of fewer than 25 lots or to those in which each lot is 20 acres or more. Lots offered for sale solely to developers also are exempt from the act's requirements, as are lots on which buildings exist or where a seller is obligated to construct a building within two years.

State Subdivided Land Sales Laws

Many state legislatures have enacted their own subdivided land sales laws. Some affect only the sale to state residents of land located outside the state. Other states' laws regulate sales of land located both inside and outside the states. These state land sales laws tend to be stricter and more detailed than the federal law. Licensees should be aware of the laws in their states and how they compare with federal law.

■ KEY POINT REVIEW

Land use is controlled and regulated through

- **public restrictions**—planning, zoning, building codes, subdivision plans;
- **private restrictions** imposed by deed; and
- direct ownership of land by federal, state, and local governments.

The **police power** of the state is its authority to create regulations to protect the public health, safety, and welfare. State enabling acts allow the power to enact laws authorized by the state's police power to be passed down to municipalities and other local governing authorities. Such regulations must be

- exercised in a reasonable manner,
- clear and specific,
- nondiscriminatory, and
- applicable to all property in a similar manner.

Land may be taken for public use through the government's **power of eminent domain** or **condemnation**, with the following limits:

■ When a taking of property occurs, the Fifth Amendment to the U.S. Constitution requires that the owner be given just (fair) compensation.

■ A property owner may claim compensation under **inverse condemnation** if an adjacent public land use diminishes the value of the owner's property but the property has not been condemned for public use.

A **comprehensive plan (master plan)** created by a local government usually covers land use, housing needs, movement of people and goods, community facilities and utilities, and energy conservation.

Zoning ordinances are local laws implementing the land uses designated in the comprehensive plan and typically cover items such as **permitted uses**, lot sizes, types of structures, building heights, setbacks, style and appearance of structures, density, and protection of natural resources.

Zoning classifies property by uses and types, such as commercial, industrial, residential, agricultural, and **planned unit developments (PUDs)**.

Other ways in which zoning is used include

■ **buffer zones** separating residential from nonresidential areas,
■ bulk zoning to control density,
■ aesthetic zoning to specify certain types of architecture for new buildings, and
■ incentive zoning to require certain uses in developments.

Zoning is enforced through the use of **permits**, and an individual case may be considered by a **zoning hearing board (or zoning board of appeals)**, which may decide to

■ allow a **nonconforming use** to continue,
■ grant a **variance** from a zoning ordinance to permit a prohibited land use to avoid undue hardship, or
■ grant a **conditional-use permit (special-use permit)**.

Building codes require permits for new construction and remodeling of or additions to existing construction.

A **certificate of occupancy (occupancy permit)** is issued upon satisfactory completion of work for which the permit was issued.

Subdivision and land development ordinances may be created by the state or may be made part of a local government's comprehensive plan. These ordinances usually include the following:

■ **Subdividers**, who buy undeveloped acreage and divide it into smaller lots for sale to individuals or developers
■ **Developers**, who improve the land, construct homes or other buildings, and sell them

- **Plat map (subdivision map)**, which shows geographic boundaries of separate land parcels, usually by showing **blocks** of land divided into individual **lots**
- **Subdivision plan**, which describes subdivision features and compliance with zoning and other laws, including utility easements, and density zoning
- **Private** land-use controls, such as **restrictive covenants (deed restrictions)**, which are placed in deeds to all property owners in a subdivision and cannot impose an illegal covenant or condition and may be enforced by injunction against property owner in violation of covenant or restriction
  — If in conflict with local zoning, the **more restrictive** controls apply.

The **Federal Interstate Land Sales Full Disclosure Act** regulates the interstate sale of unimproved lots in subdivisions of 25 or more lots of less than 20 acres each. The law does not apply to subdivisions sold solely to developers. **State subdivision laws** may also apply to sales within the state of subdivisions located either inside or outside the state.

■ RELATED WEB SITES

U.S. Department of Housing and Urban Development: Housing Discrimination:
   http://portal.hud.gov/portal/page/portal/HUD/topics/housing_discrimination/
U.S. Department of Housing and Urban Development: Office of Housing:
   http://portal.hud.gov/portal/page/portal/HUD/program_offices/housing/

CHAPTER 19 QUIZ

1. A subdivision declaration reads, "No property within this subdivision may be further subdivided for sale or otherwise, and no property may be used for other than single-family housing." This is an example of
   a. a restrictive covenant.
   b. an illegal reverter clause.
   c. R-1 zoning.
   d. a conditional-use clause.

2. A landowner who wants to use property in a manner that is prohibited by a local zoning ordinance but would benefit the community can apply for which of the following?
   a. Conditional-use permit
   b. Prescriptive easement
   c. Occupancy permit
   d. Property dedication

3. What is NOT included in public land-use controls?
   a. Subdivision regulations
   b. Restrictive covenants
   c. Environmental protection laws
   d. Comprehensive plan specifications

4. Under its police powers, a municipality may regulate all of the following about housing in a development EXCEPT
   a. lot sizes.
   b. building heights.
   c. identity of ownership.
   d. type of structure.

5. The purpose of a building permit is to
   a. assert a deed's restrictive covenant.
   b. maintain municipal control over the volume of building.
   c. provide evidence of compliance with municipal regulations.
   d. show compliance with restrictive covenants.

6. Zoning powers are conferred on municipal governments in which of the following ways?
   a. By state enabling acts
   b. Through the master plan
   c. By popular local vote
   d. Through city charters

7. A town enacts a new zoning code. Under the new code, commercial buildings are not permitted within 1,000 feet of the lake. A commercial building that is permitted to continue in its former use even though it is built on the lakeshore is an example of
   a. nonconforming use.
   b. variance.
   c. special use.
   d. adverse possession.

8. To determine whether a location can be put to future use as a retail store, one would examine the
   a. building code.
   b. list of permitted nonconforming uses.
   c. housing code.
   d. zoning ordinance.

9. All of the following are legal deed restrictions EXCEPT the
   a. types of buildings that may be constructed.
   b. allowable ethnic origins of purchasers.
   c. activities that are not to be conducted at the site.
   d. minimum size of buildings to be constructed.

10. A restriction in a seller's deed may be enforced by which of the following?
    a. Court injunction
    b. Zoning board of appeal
    c. City building commission
    d. State legislature

11. A buyer owns a large tract of land. After an adequate study of all the relevant facts, the buyer legally divides the land into 30 lots suitable for the construction of residences. In this situation, the buyer is acting as a(n)

    a. subdivider.
    b. developer.
    c. land planner.
    d. urban planner.

12. A map illustrating the sizes and locations of streets and lots in a subdivision is called a

    a. gridiron plan.
    b. survey.
    c. plat of subdivision.
    d. property report.

13. In one city, developers are limited by law to constructing no more than an average of three houses per acre in any subdivision. What does this restriction regulate?

    a. Clustering
    b. Gross density
    c. Out-lots
    d. Covenants

14. Which of the following is a variance?

    a. An exception to a zoning ordinance
    b. A court order prohibiting certain activities
    c. A reversion of ownership
    d. A nullification of an easement

15. Permitted land uses and set-asides, housing projections, transportation issues, and objectives for implementing future controlled development would all be found in a community's

    a. zoning ordinance.
    b. comprehensive plan.
    c. enabling act.
    d. land-control law.

16. Which of the following items would usually NOT be shown on the plat for a new subdivision?

    a. Easements for sewer and water mains
    b. Land to be used for streets
    c. Numbered lots and blocks
    d. Prices of residential and commercial lots

17. A plat for a proposed subdivision is submitted to the

    a. municipality.
    b. property owners.
    c. developer.
    d. state.

18. Restrictive covenants

    a. are no longer effective when the title is transferred.
    b. apply only until the developer has conveyed the title.
    c. can be removed by a court of competent jurisdiction.
    d. apply to and bind successive owners of the property.

19. To protect the public from fraudulent interstate land sales, a developer involved in interstate land sales of 25 or more lots must

    a. provide each purchaser with a printed report disclosing details of the property.
    b. pay the prospective buyer's expenses to see the property involved.
    c. provide preferential financing.
    d. allow a 30-day cancellation period.

20. When is a certificate of occupancy issued?

    a. When the owner of a multifamily residential property wishes to limit the number of individuals who may live in a single unit
    b. At the time a property owner applies for a building permit
    c. After a newly constructed building has been inspected and found satisfactory by the municipal inspector
    d. When an application for a variance or conditional-use permit has been granted by the zoning board

CHAPTER

Fair Housing and Ethical Practices

■ FAIR HOUSING AND ETHICAL PRACTICES

Licensees and their clients and customers today reflect the changing diversity in American society: those for whom English is a second language, people from a wide range of cultural backgrounds, people of various age and religious preferences, and people with disabilities, to name just a few. Although some differences are protected by state and federal laws, others are not. Understanding and working within the context of equal opportunity is critical to creating and maintaining a more diverse, vibrant, and ultimately profitable real estate market for everyone. When challenged to meet consumers on their terms, successful licensees recognize that embracing diversity is a good business practice, does the right thing, and builds bridges not barriers.

■ EQUAL OPPORTUNITY IN HOUSING

The civil rights laws that affect the real estate industry ensure that everyone has the opportunity to live where they choose. Federal, state, and local fair housing or equal opportunity laws affect every phase of a real estate transaction, from listing to closing.

The U.S. Congress and the U.S. Supreme Court have created a legal framework that preserves the constitutional rights of all citizens. However, while the passage of laws may establish a code for public conduct, centuries of discriminatory practices and attitudes are not so easily changed. Real estate licensees cannot allow their own prejudices to interfere with the ethical and legal conduct of their profession; nor can they allow discriminatory attitudes of property owners or property seekers to affect compliance with fair housing laws. Complying with fair housing laws is not always easy, but it is important to remember that failure to comply with fair housing laws is both a civil and a criminal violation and constitutes grounds for disciplinary action against a licensee.

IN PRACTICE Licensees must have a thorough knowledge of both state and federal fair housing laws. State laws may be stricter than the federal requirements, may provide protections for more classes of persons, and may be applicable to all real property transactions, not just residential. State licensing rules may provide for fines as well as for the suspension or revocation of an offender's license.

The federal government's effort to guarantee equal housing opportunities to all U.S. citizens began with the passage of the **Civil Rights Act of 1866.** This law prohibits any type of discrimination based on race.

The U.S. Supreme Court's 1896 decision in *Plessy v. Ferguson* established the separate but equal doctrine of legalized racial segregation. A series of court decisions and federal laws between 1948 and 1968 attempted to address the inequities in housing that were the result of *Plessy.* Those efforts tended to address only certain aspects of the housing market, such as federally funded housing programs. As a result, their impact was limited. Title VIII of the Civil Rights Act of 1968, however, prohibits specific discriminatory practices throughout the real estate industry.

■ FAIR HOUSING ACT

Title VIII of the Civil Rights Act of 1968 prohibits discrimination in housing based on race, color, religion, or national origin. In 1974, the Housing and Community Development Act added sex to the list of protected classes. In 1988, the Fair Housing Amendments Act included disability and familial status (i.e., households with children). Today, these laws are known as the federal Fair Housing Act. (See Table 20.1.) The **Fair Housing Act** prohibits discrimination on the basis of race, color, religion, sex, disability, familial status, or national origin. The act also prohibits discrimination against individuals because of their *association* with persons in the protected classes.

The Fair Housing Act is administered by the **Department of Housing and Urban Development (HUD)**. HUD has established rules and regulations that further interpret the practices affected by the law. In addition, HUD distributes an equal housing opportunity poster. (See Figure 20.1.) The poster declares that the office in which it is displayed promises to adhere to the Fair Housing Act and pledges support for affirmative marketing and advertising programs.

In 1988, Congress passed the **Fair Housing Amendments Act** that expanded federal civil rights protections to include families with children and people with physical or mental disabilities, in addition to race, color, religion, and national origin. The act also changed the penalties, making them more severe, and added damages, such as those for noneconomic injuries (humiliation, embarrassment, inconvenience, and mental anguish).

T A B L E   20.1

Federal Fair Housing Laws

Legislation	Race	Color	Religion	National Origin	Sex	Age	Marital Status	Disability	Familial Status	Public Assistance Income
Civil Rights Act of 1866	•	•								
Fair Housing Act of 1968 (Title VIII)	•	•	•	•						
Housing and Community Development Act of 1974					•					
Fair Housing Amendments Act of 1988								•	•	
Equal Credit Opportunity Act of 1974 (lending)	•	•	•	•	•	•	•			•

FIGURE 20.1

Equal Opportunity Housing Poster

U.S. Department of Housing and Urban Development

EQUAL HOUSING
OPPORTUNITY

We Do Business in Accordance With the Federal Fair Housing Law

(The Fair Housing Amendments Act of 1988)

> ## It is Illegal to Discriminate Against Any Person Because of Race, Color, Religion, Sex, Handicap, Familial Status, or National Origin

- In the sale or rental of housing or residential lots
- In advertising the sale or rental of housing
- In the financing of housing

- In the provision of real estate brokerage services
- In the appraisal of housing
- Blockbusting is also illegal

Anyone who feels he or she has been discriminated against may file a complaint of housing discrimination:
    1-800-669-9777 (Toll Free)
    1-800-927-9275 (TDD)

**U.S. Department of Housing and Urban Development
Assistant Secretary for Fair Housing and Equal Opportunity
Washington, D.C. 20410**

Previous editions are obsolete

form HUD-928.1A (2/2003)

In 1995, Congress passed the Housing for Older Persons Act (HOPA), which repealed the requirement that 55-and-older housing have "significant facilities and services" designed for seniors. HOPA still requires that at least 80 percent of occupied units have one person age 55 or older living there. The act prohibits the awarding of monetary damages against those who, in good faith, reasonably believed that property designated as housing for older persons was exempt from familial status provisions of the Fair Housing Act.

IN PRACTICE   When HUD investigates a broker for discriminatory practices, it may consider failure to prominently display the equal housing opportunity poster in the broker's place of business as evidence of discrimination.

Definitions

HUD's regulations provide specific definitions that clarify the scope of the Fair Housing Act.

Housing   The regulations define *housing* as a *dwelling* that includes any building or part of a building designed for occupancy as a residence by one or more families. This includes a single-family house, a condominium, a cooperative, and manufactured housing, as well as vacant land on which any of these structures will be built.

> **The Fair Housing Act prohibits discrimination** based on
> - race,
> - color,
> - religion,
> - sex,
> - disability,
> - familial status, and
> - national origin.

Familial status   *Familial status* is defined as one or more individuals under age 18 living with a parent or guardian. It also includes a woman who is pregnant and anyone who is in the process of assuming custody of a child under age 18. Housing that qualifies for older people is exempt. Otherwise, single or multifamily housing must be made available to families with children under the same terms and conditions applied to anyone else. It is illegal to advertise properties as being for adults only or to indicate a preference for a certain number of children. Landlords and condominiums/cooperatives cannot restrict the number of occupants with the intent of eliminating families with children. Any occupancy standards must be based on objective factors, such as sanitation or safety.

■ **FOR EXAMPLE**   A man owned an apartment building. One of his elderly tenants was terminally ill. The tenant requested that no children be allowed in the vacant apartment next door because the children's noise would make the situation more difficult. The owner of the apartment building agreed and refused to rent to families with children. Although the intent was to make things easier for a dying tenant, the owner was nonetheless found to have violated the Fair Housing Act by discriminating on the basis of familial status.

Disability   A *disability* is a physical or mental impairment. It is unlawful to discriminate against prospective buyers or tenants on the basis of disability. The term includes those having a history of, or being regarded as having, an impairment that substantially limits one or more major life activities. Persons who have AIDS are protected by the fair housing laws under this classification.

IN PRACTICE   The federal Fair Housing Act's protection of disabled people does not include those who are current users of illegal or controlled substances. Individuals who have been convicted of the illegal manufacture or distribution of a controlled substance are also not protected under this law. However, the law does prohibit discrimination against those who are participating in addiction recovery programs. For instance, a landlord could lawfully discriminate against a cocaine addict but not against a member of Alcoholics Anonymous.

Landlords must make reasonable accommodations to existing policies, practices, or services to permit persons with disabilities to have equal enjoyment of the premises. It would be reasonable for a landlord to permit support animals (such as guide dogs) in a normally no-pets building or to provide a designated handicap parking space in a generally unreserved lot.

People with disabilities must be permitted to make reasonable modifications to the premises at their own expense. Such modifications might include lowering door handles or installing bath rails to accommodate a person in a wheelchair. Failure to permit reasonable modification constitutes discrimination.

The law does recognize that some reasonable modifications might make a rental property undesirable to the general population. In such a case, the landlord is allowed to require that the property be restored to its previous condition when the lease period ends, aside from reasonable wear and tear. Where it is necessary to ensure with reasonable certainty that funds will be available to pay for the restorations at the end of the tenancy, the landlord may negotiate, as part of a restoration agreement, a provision requiring that the tenant pay into an interest-bearing escrow account, over a reasonable period, a reasonable amount of money not to exceed the cost of the restorations. The interest in the account accrues to the benefit of the tenant. A landlord may not increase the required security deposit for a people with a disabilities.

The law does not prohibit restricting occupancy exclusively to persons with handicaps in dwellings that are designed specifically for their accommodation.

In newly constructed multifamily buildings with an elevator and four or more units, the public and common areas must be accessible to persons with disabilities, and doors and hallways must be wide enough for wheelchairs. The entrance to each unit must be accessible, as well as the light switches, electrical outlets, thermostats, and other environmental controls. People in wheelchairs should be able to use the kitchen and bathrooms; bathroom walls should be reinforced to accommodate later installation of grab bars. Ground-floor units must meet these requirements in buildings that do not have an elevator. Licensees should be aware that state and local laws may require stricter standards.

Racial discrimination: *Jones v. Mayer* In 1968, the Supreme Court heard the case of *Jones v. Alfred H. Mayer Company* (392 U.S. 409 (1968)). The court's decision upheld the Civil Rights Act of 1866. This decision is important because although the federal Fair Housing Act exempts individual homeowners and certain groups, the 1866 law prohibits all racial discrimination without exception. Racial discrimination is prohibited in the sale or rental of publicly or privately held property, whether facilitated by a real estate agent or sold or rented by the owner. Where race is involved, no exceptions apply.

The U.S. Supreme Court has expanded the definition of the term *race* to include ancestral and ethnic characteristics, including certain physical, cultural, or linguistic traits that are shared by a group with a common national origin. These rulings are significant because discrimination on the basis of race, as it is now defined, affords due process of complaints under the provisions of the Civil Rights Act of 1866.

IN PRACTICE   A real estate agent or broker is not obligated to provide ethnic-diversity information to homebuyers. At issue in a 2001 case from Ohio, *Hannah v. Sibcy Cline Realtors*, was whether an agent or broker had the fiduciary duty to (1) inform a client whether a neighborhood was ethnically diverse or (2) direct the client to resources that provided such information. The court concluded that while licensees might choose to provide such information to clients or direct clients to resources about the ethnic diversity of a particular area, the licensees do so at their own risk and there is no fiduciary duty to do so.

Exemptions to the Fair Housing Act

The federal Fair Housing Act covers most housing. However, in some circumstances, it provides for certain exemptions. The Fair Housing Act exempts

- owner-occupied buildings with no more than four units,
- single-family housing sold or rented without the use of a licensee, and
- housing operated by organizations and private clubs that limit occupancy to members.

The sale or rental of a single-family home is exempt when

- the home is owned by an individual who does not own more than three such homes at one time (and who does not sell more than one every two years),
- a real estate licensee is *not* involved in the transaction, and
- discriminatory advertising is not used.

The rental of rooms or units in an owner-occupied one- to four-family dwelling is exempt from the Fair Housing Act.

Furthermore, housing owned by religious organizations may be restricted to people of the same religion if membership in the organization is not restricted on the basis of race, color, or national origin. A private club that is not open to the public may restrict the rental or occupancy of lodgings that it owns to its members as long as the lodgings are not operated commercially. Membership in a private club must be open to people of all races, colors, and national origins.

The Fair Housing Act does not require that housing be made available to any individual whose tenancy would constitute a direct threat to the health or safety of other individuals or would result in substantial physical damage to the property of others.

Housing for older persons   While the Fair Housing Act protects families with children, certain properties can be restricted to occupancy by elderly persons. Housing intended for persons age 62 or older or housing occupied by at least one person 55 years of age or older per unit (where 80 percent of the units are occupied by individuals 55 or older) is exempt from the familial status protection.

Megan's Law   Federal legislation, known as Megan's Law, promotes the establishment of state registration systems to maintain residential information on every person who kidnaps children, commits sexual crimes against children, or commits sexually violent crimes. Upon release from prison, offenders must register their name with state authorities and indicate where they will be residing. Local law enforcement agencies may release relevant information about such an offender upon request if they deem it necessary for the protection of the public.

Megan's Law affects a licensee's duty of disclosure. In accordance with state law, a licensee may need to request that a customer sign a form indicating where the customer may obtain information about the sex offender registry. An index to sex offender registries in all 50 states can be found at *www.prevent-abuse-now .com/register.htm*. Depending on the state, a licensee may be required to disclose information regarding a released offender if the licensee is aware that officials have informed individuals, groups, or the public that a sex offender resides in a particular area. Megan's Law, in effect, creates another category of stigmatized property. (See Chapter 4.)

Equal Credit Opportunity Act

> **The Equal Credit Opportunity Act prohibits discrimination** in granting credit based on
> - race,
> - color,
> - religion,
> - national origin,
> - sex,
> - receipt of public assistance,
> - marital status, and
> - age.

The federal **Equal Credit Opportunity Act (ECOA)** prohibits discrimination in the lending process based on race, color, religion, national origin, sex, marital status, or age or the receipt of public assistance in the granting of credit. The ECOA requires that credit applications be considered only on the basis of income, net worth, job stability, and credit rating.

The protections offered by ECOA are both similar (race, color, religion, and national origin) and different from those of the Federal Fair Housing Act (ECOA includes age, marital status, and receipt of public assistance). Real estate licensees should be aware of the protections offered by this law because their clients should not face discrimination when applying for a loan to buy a property or when applying to rent one.

A creditor may not consider age unless the applicant is too young to legally sign a contract, which is usually 18, although the creditor may consider age if determining if income will drop due to retirement. Lenders are prohibited from discriminating against recipients of public assistance programs such as food stamps and Social Security. Lenders may not ask questions about a spouse, unless the spouse is also applying for credit; they may not discount a woman's income or assume that she will leave the workforce to raise children.

The agency that enforces ECOA depends on the type of financial institution. In general, the ECOA is enforced by the Federal Trade Commission (FTC) and the Department of Justice as well as other agencies.

Americans with Disabilities Act

Although the **Americans with Disabilities Act (ADA)** is not a housing or credit law, it still has a significant effect on the real estate industry. The ADA requires reasonable accommodations in employment and access to goods, services, and public buildings. The ADA is important because real estate brokers are often employers, and their offices are public spaces. The ADA's goal is to enable individuals with disabilities to become part of the economic and social mainstream of society. (See Chapter 17.)

Title I of the ADA requires that employers, including real estate licensees, make *reasonable accommodations* that enable an individual with a disability to perform essential job functions. Reasonable accommodations include making the work site accessible, restructuring a job, providing part-time or flexible work schedules, and modifying equipment that is used on the job. The provisions of the ADA apply to any employer with 15 or more employees.

Title III of the ADA requires that individuals with disabilities have full accessibility to businesses, goods, and public services. As a result, building owners and managers of commercial spaces must be constantly alert to ensure that obstacles are removed. The Americans with Disabilities Act Accessibility Guidelines (ADAAG) contain detailed specifications for designing parking spaces, curb ramps, elevators, drinking fountains, toilet facilities, and directional signs to ensure maximum accessibility. Unless the licensee is a qualified ADA expert, it is best to advise commercial clients to seek the services of an attorney, an architect, or a consultant who specializes in ADA issues.

IN PRACTICE   In 1999, the U.S. Supreme Court strictly limited the definition of *persons with disabilities* protected by the ADA. The decision excludes individuals whose disability, such as nearsightedness, can be corrected. In 2002, the U.S. Supreme Court narrowed the definition even further by stating that in determining whether a person is disabled, you may ask whether the impairment(s) prevent or restrict the person from performing tasks that are of central importance to most people's daily lives.

ADA and the Fair Housing Act   The ADA exempts the following two types of property from its requirements:

- Property that is covered by the Fair Housing Act
- Property that is exempt from coverage by the Fair Housing Act

Some properties are subject to both laws. For example, in an apartment complex, the rental office is a place of public accommodation. As such, it is covered by the ADA and must be accessible to persons with disabilities at the owner's expense. Individual rental units would be covered by the Fair Housing Act. A tenant who wished to modify the unit to make it accessible would be responsible for the cost.

Issues of housing and disability discrimination are often litigated in the courts. For example, in a 2005 case, *Wells v. State Manufactured Homes*, the landlord ordered the owner of a manufactured housing unit to move from the community because he claimed she violated the no-pets provision of her rental agreement. The landlord refused to make a reasonable accommodation for the owner's emotional disability by not permitting her to keep a dog. She filed suit under the ADA and Fair Housing Act. The court held that there was no violation of the Fair Housing Act or the ADA. The court said she failed to establish that her mental impairment substantially limited a major life activity and that she was not disabled under the ADA.

IN PRACTICE Real estate licensees need a general knowledge of the ADA's provisions. It is necessary for a broker's workplace and employment policies to comply with the law. Amendments to the ADA are periodically introduced in the U.S. Congress, and it is important to be aware of changes in the law. Also, licensees who are building managers must ensure that the properties are legally accessible. However, ADA compliance questions may arise with regard to a client's property, too. Unless the agent is a qualified ADA expert, it is best to advise commercial clients to seek the services of an attorney, an architect, or a consultant who specializes in ADA issues. It is possible that an appraiser may be liable for failing to identify and account for a property's noncompliance.

■ FAIR HOUSING PRACTICES

For the civil rights laws to accomplish their goal of eliminating discrimination, licensees must apply them routinely. Compliance also means that licensees avoid violating both the laws and the ethical standards of the profession. The following discussion examines the ethical and legal issues that confront real estate licensees.

Blockbusting

Blockbusting is the act of encouraging people to sell or rent their homes by claiming that the entry of a protected class of people into the neighborhood will have some sort of negative impact on property values. Blockbusting was a common practice during the 1950s and 1960s when unscrupulous real estate licensees profited by fueling "white flight" from cities to suburbs. Any message, however subtle, that property should be sold or rented because the neighborhood is "undergoing changes" is considered blockbusting. It is illegal to assert that the presence of certain persons will cause property values to decline, crime or antisocial behavior to increase, and the quality of schools to suffer.

A critical element in blockbusting, according to HUD, is the profit motive. A property owner may be intimidated into selling a property at a depressed price to the blockbuster, who in turn sells the property to another person at a higher price. Another term for this activity is *panic selling*. To avoid accusations of blockbusting, licensees should use good judgment when choosing locations and methods for marketing their services and soliciting listings.

Steering

Steering is the channeling of homeseekers to particular neighborhoods or by discouraging potential buyers from considering some areas. In the rental process, steering occurs when the landlord puts members of a protected class on a certain floor or building. Another form of steering occurs when the landlord tells a prospective tenant that no vacancy exists when, in fact, there is a vacancy. When the misstatement is made on the basis of a protected class, the prospect is steered away from that building. In any case, it is an illegal limitation of a purchaser's or renter's options.

	Category	Rule	Permitted	Not Permitted
TABLE 20.2 **HUD's Advertising Guidelines**	Race Color National origin	No discriminatory limitation/ preference may be expressed	"master bedroom" "good neighborhood"	"white neighborhood" "no French"
	Religion	No religious preference/ limitation	"chapel on premises" "kosher meals available" "Merry Christmas"	"no Muslims" "nice Christian family" "near great Catholic school"
	Sex	No explicit preference based on sex	"mother-in-law suite" "master bedroom" "female roommate sought"	"great house for a man" "wife's dream kitchen"
	Disability	No exclusions or limitations based on disability	"wheelchair ramp" "walk to shopping"	"no wheelchairs" "able-bodied tenants only"
	Familial status	No preference or limitation based on family size or nature	"two-bedroom" "family room" "quiet neighborhood"	"married couple only" "no more than two children" "retiree's dream house"
	Photographs or illustrations of people	People should be clearly representative and nonexclusive	Illustrations showing multiple ethnicities, family groups, singles, etc.	Illustrations showing only singles, African American families, elderly white adults, etc.

Advertising

Advertisements of property for sale or rent may not include language indicating a preference or limitation. No exception to this rule exists, regardless of how subtle the choice of words. HUD's regulations cite examples that are considered discriminatory. (See Table 20.2.) However, an advertisement that is gender specific, such as "female roommate sought," is allowed as long as the advertiser seeks to share living quarters with someone of the same gender. The media used for promoting property or real estate services cannot target one population to the exclusion of others. The selective use of media, whether by language or geography, may have discriminatory impact. For instance, advertising property only in a Korean-language newspaper tends to discriminate against non-Koreans. Similarly, limiting advertising to a cable television channel available only to white suburbanites may be construed as a discriminatory act. However, if an advertisement appears in general-circulation media as well, it may be legal.

IN PRACTICE   The Fair Housing Council of Oregon filed a complaint against a local multiple listing service (MLS), charging that the phrase "adults only over 40" was included in the "Remarks" section of a condominium listing. While the condominium association's bylaws actually did contain the age restriction, the Fair Housing Council argued that including the phrase in the listing constituted discrimination against families with children in violation of the Fair Housing Act. The MLS paid $30,000 to settle with HUD, $20,000 of which went to support the antidiscrimination efforts of the Fair Housing Council of Oregon. The MLS also agreed to conduct regular computerized searches of its database for 67 different discriminatory words and phrases.

Appraising

Those who prepare appraisals or any statements of valuation—whether formal or informal, oral or written (including a competitive market analysis)—may consider any factors that affect value. However, race, color, religion, national origin, sex, disability, and familial status are not factors that may be considered.

Redlining

The practice of refusing to make mortgage loans or issue insurance policies in specific areas for reasons other than the economic qualifications of the applicants is known as **redlining**. Redlining refers to literally drawing a line around particular areas. This practice is often a major contributor to the deterioration of older neighborhoods. Redlining is frequently based on racial grounds rather than on any real objection to an applicant's creditworthiness. The federal Fair Housing Act prohibits discrimination in mortgage lending and covers not only the actions of primary lenders but also activities in the secondary mortgage market. A lending institution, however, can refuse a loan solely on sound economic grounds.

Intent and Effect

If an owner or real estate licensee purposely sets out to engage in blockbusting, steering, or other unfair activities, the intent to discriminate is obvious. However, owners and licensees must examine their activities and policies carefully to determine whether they have unintentional discriminatory effects. Whenever policies or practices result in unequal treatment of people in the protected classes, they are considered discriminatory, regardless of any innocent intent. This "effects" test is applied by regulatory agencies to determine whether an individual has been discriminated against.

Response to Concerns of Terrorism

In response to the concern of future terrorist attacks, landlords and property managers have been developing new security procedures. These procedures have focused on protecting buildings and residents. Landlords and property managers are also educating residents on signs of possible terrorist activity and how and where to report it. At the same time, landlords and property managers need to ensure that their procedures and education do not infringe on the fair housing rights of others.

For screening and rental procedures, it is unlawful to screen housing applicants on the basis of race, color, religion, sex, national origin, disability, or familial status. According to HUD, landlords and property managers have been inquiring about whether they can screen applicants on the basis of citizenship status. The Fair Housing Act does not specifically prohibit discrimination based solely on a person's citizenship status. Therefore, asking applicants for citizenship documentation or immigration status papers during the screening process does not violate the Fair Housing Act. For many years, the federal government has been asking for these documents in screening applicants for federally assisted housing. There is, however, a specific procedure for collecting and verifying citizenship papers provided by HUD.

■ **FOR EXAMPLE**   In an interview with a landlord, a woman mentions that she left her native country to study at the local university. The landlord is concerned about the woman's visa and whether it will expire during the lease term. The landlord asks the woman for documentation to determine how long she can legally live in the United States. The landlord asks for this information, regardless of her race or national origin. The landlord has not violated the Fair Housing Act.

■ ENFORCEMENT OF THE FAIR HOUSING ACT

The federal Fair Housing Act is administered by the Office of Fair Housing and Equal Opportunity under the direction of the secretary of HUD. Any aggrieved person who believes illegal discrimination has occurred may file a complaint with HUD within one year of the alleged act. HUD also may initiate its own complaint. Complaints may be reported to the Office of Fair Housing and Equal Opportunity, Department of Housing and Urban Development, Washington, DC 20410, or to the Office of Fair Housing and Equal Opportunity in care of the nearest HUD regional office. Complaints may also be submitted directly to HUD using an online form available on the HUD Web site.

Upon receiving a complaint, HUD initiates an investigation. Within 100 days of the filing of the complaint, HUD either determines that reasonable cause exists to bring a charge of illegal discrimination or dismisses the complaint. During this investigation period, HUD can attempt to resolve the dispute informally through conciliation. Conciliation is the resolution of a complaint by obtaining assurance that the person against whom the complaint was filed (the respondent) will remedy any violation that may have occurred. The respondent further agrees to take steps to eliminate or prevent discriminatory practices in the future. If necessary, these agreements can be enforced through civil action.

The aggrieved person has the right to seek relief through administrative proceedings. Administrative proceedings are hearings held before *administrative law judges (ALJs)*. An ALJ has the authority to award actual damages to the aggrieved parties and, if it is believed the public interest will be served, to impose monetary penalties. The penalties range from up to $11,000 for the first offense to $27,500 for a second violation within five years and $55,000 for further violations within seven years. The ALJ also has the authority to issue an injunction to order the offender to either do something (such as rent an apartment to the complaining party) or refrain from doing something (such as acting in a discriminatory manner).

The parties may elect civil action in federal court at any time within two years of the discriminatory act. For cases heard in federal court, unlimited punitive damages can be awarded in addition to actual damages. The court can also issue injunctions.

The attorney general, upon finding reasonable cause to believe that any person or group is engaged in a pattern or practice of resistance to the full enjoyment of any of the rights granted by the federal fair housing laws, may file a civil action in any federal district court. Civil penalties may result in an amount not to exceed $50,000 for a first violation and an amount not to exceed $100,000 for second and subsequent violations.

Complaints brought under the Civil Rights Act of 1866 are taken directly to federal courts. The only time limit for action is a state's statute of limitations for torts (injuries one individual inflicts on another).

IN PRACTICE In July 2009, HUD charged a landlord and the real estate company with two separate acts of housing discrimination for refusing to rent to families with children. Not only was their initial ad discriminatory—"This is an immaculate, spacious three-bedroom house for rent … No cats, dogs, or children please"—but when two different families with children called, the agent refused to show the home to them stating that "the owner would not rent to families with children" (*Colon v. Bill, Wetherbee*, and others).

State and Local Enforcement Agencies

Many states and municipalities have their own fair housing laws. If a state or local law is substantially equivalent to the federal law, all complaints filed with HUD are referred to the local enforcement agencies. To be considered substantially equivalent, the local law and its related regulations must contain prohibitions comparable to those in the federal law. In addition, the state or locality must show that its local enforcement agency takes sufficient affirmative action in processing and investigating complaints and in finding remedies for discriminatory practices. It is important for all licensees to be aware of their states' fair housing laws, as well as applicable local ordinances.

Threats or Acts of Violence

Being a real estate agent is not generally considered a dangerous occupation. Some licensees find themselves the targets of threats or violence merely for complying with fair housing laws. The federal Fair Housing Act of 1968 protects the rights of those who seek the benefits of the open housing law. It also protects owners and licensees who aid or encourage the enjoyment of open housing rights. Threats, coercion, and intimidation are punishable by criminal action. In such a case, the victim should report the incident immediately to law enforcement officials.

■ IMPLICATIONS FOR BROKERS AND SALESPEOPLE

The real estate industry is largely responsible for creating and maintaining an open housing market. Licensees are a community's real estate experts. With the privilege of profiting from real estate transactions comes the social and legal responsibilities to ensure that everyone's civil rights are protected. Establishing relationships with community and fair housing groups to discuss common concerns and find solutions to problems is a worthwhile activity. Licensees who actively work to improve their community will earn a reputation for being concerned citizens, which may well translate into a larger consumer base.

Fair housing *is* the law. The consequences for anyone who violates the law are serious. In addition to the financial penalties, the livelihood of real estate licensees may be in jeopardy if their license is suspended or revoked. That the offense was unintentional is no defense. Licensees must scrutinize their practices and be particularly careful not to fall victim to clients or customers who expect to discriminate.

■ PROFESSIONAL ETHICS

Professional conduct involves more than just complying with the law. In real estate, state licensing laws establish which activities are illegal and, therefore, prohibited. Merely complying with the letter of the law may not be enough: licensees may perform legally yet not ethically. **Ethics** refers to a system of moral principles, rules, and standards of conduct. The ethical system of a profession establishes conduct that goes beyond merely complying with the law. These moral principles address the following two sides of a profession:

- They establish standards for integrity and competence in dealing with consumers of an industry's services.
- They define a code of conduct for relations within the industry among its professionals.

Code of Ethics

One way that many organizations address ethics among their members or in their respective businesses is by adopting codes of professional conduct. A **code of ethics** is a written system of standards for ethical conduct. The code contains statements designed to advise, guide, and regulate behavior. To be effective, a code of ethics must be specific by dictating rules that either prohibit or demand certain behavior. By including sanctions for violators, a code of ethics becomes more effective.

The National Association of REALTORS® (NAR), the largest trade association in the country, with over one million members, adopted a code of ethics for its members in 1913. REALTORS® are expected to subscribe to this strict code of conduct. Not all licensees are REALTORS®—only those who are members of NAR. NAR has established procedures for professional standards committees at the local, state, and national levels of the organization to administer compliance. Practical applications of the articles of the code are known as Standards of Practice. The NAR Code of Ethics has proved helpful because it contains practical applications of business ethics. Many other professional organizations in the real estate industry have codes of ethics as well. In addition, many state real estate commissions are required by law to establish codes or canons of ethical behavior for their states' licensees.

■ KEY POINT REVIEW

Equal opportunity in housing is intended to create a marketplace in which all persons of similar financial means have a similar range of housing choices. Equal opportunity laws apply to owners, real estate licensees, apartment management companies, real estate organizations, lending agencies, builders, and developers.

The **Civil Rights Act of 1866**

■ guaranteed **equal housing opportunities** to all U.S. citizens,
■ was upheld in *Jones v. Mayer*, 1968, and
■ prohibits all racial discrimination with no exceptions.

Race was defined by the U.S. Supreme Court to include ancestral and ethnic characteristics, including certain physical, cultural, or linguistic traits that are shared by a group with a common national origin.

The **federal Fair Housing Act** is Title VIII of the **Civil Rights Act of 1968** and

■ prohibits discrimination in housing based on **race**, **color**, **religion**, or **national origin**;
■ does not prohibit discrimination based solely on a person's citizenship status; and
■ prohibits illegal activities that include **steering**, **blockbusting**, and **redlining**.

The **Housing and Community Development Act of 1974** added **sex** to list of protected classes.

The **Fair Housing Amendments Act of 1988,** which added **disability** and **familial status** (families with children) to protected classes,

■ prohibits discrimination against individuals because of their association with people in the protected classes; and
■ is administered by HUD, which
    — establishes rules and regulations to further clarify the law, and
    — created the **equal housing opportunity poster**.

The 1995 Fair Housing Amendment repealed facilities and services requirements designed for older persons and prohibited an award of monetary damages against those who reasonably rely in good faith on property designated as housing for older persons as being exempt from familial status provisions of the Fair Housing Act.

Exemptions from the Fair Housing Act (but not the Civil Rights Act of 1866) include

■ rentals in **owner-occupied buildings** with no more than four units;
■ housing operated by organizations and private clubs that limit occupancy to members; and
■ the sale or rental of a **single-family home** when fewer than three homes are owned by an **individual**, discriminatory advertising is not used, and a real estate licensee is not involved in the transaction.

Housing is **exempt** from familial status protection if it is restricted to persons age **62** or older, or if 80 percent of the units are occupied by persons over age **55**.

The **Equal Credit Opportunity Act** of 1974 prohibits discrimination in lending on the basis of **race, color, religion, national origin, sex, age, marital status,** and **public assistance**.

Familial status extends fair housing protections to families with children, meaning a family in which one or more individuals under the age of 18 live with either a parent or a guardian, or a woman who is pregnant, including the following:

- Families with children must be considered under the same terms and conditions as anyone else.
- The property cannot be advertised as adults only, and the ads cannot indicate limitation on the number of children accepted.
- Limitations on the number of people permitted to reside in a house or apartment must be based on objective factors such as sanitation or safety.

A **disability** is a physical or mental impairment that substantially limits one or more of an individual's major life activities.
- Persons with AIDS are considered disabled.
- The law **does not** protect individuals who are **current users** of illegal or controlled substances or who have been **convicted** of the illegal manufacture or distribution of a controlled substance. However, the law **does** protect individuals who are participating in addiction recovery programs.
- **Reasonable modifications** to property to make it usable by an individual with a disability must be allowed, but the individual must return the property to its former condition on vacating it.

The **Americans with Disabilities Act (ADA)** prohibits discrimination in employment and public accommodations; access to facilities and services in commercial properties must be provided when **reasonably achievable** in existing buildings, with higher standards for new construction/remodeling. Exempt properties include those covered by federal fair housing laws.

Megan's Law requires that certain sex offenders register their home location. Although licensees are not required to provide this information, they may be required to inform buyers where the information can be obtained.

HUD enforces the Fair Housing Act in the following manner:

- A **complaint** must be brought within **one year** of the alleged act of discrimination.
- Within **100 days** of filing a complaint that is not referred by HUD to a local enforcement agency, HUD dismisses or goes forward with a charge of illegal discrimination.
  - Conciliation is the resolution of a complaint in the 100-day period when a respondent promises to remedy any violation.

■ A complaint may be heard by an administrative law judge (ALJ), whose remedies include the following **penalties**:
— **U**p to **$11,000** for the first offense
— **$27,500** for the **second** violation within five years
— **$55,000** for further violations within seven years
— **Injunction** may also be issued.
■ **Civil action** may be brought in federal court within **two years** of discriminatory act.

The **attorney general** may bring civil action in federal court, and **penalties** may include a fine not to exceed

■ **$50,000** for the first violation, and
■ **$100,000** for second and subsequent violations.

Complaints under the Civil Rights Act of 1866 go directly to federal court.

Real estate licensees must act legally and ethically to ensure equal access to housing.

■ RELATED WEB SITES

Legal Information Institute: *www.law.cornell.edu*

National Association of REALTORS®: Code of Ethics:
    www.realtor.org/mempolweb.nsf/pages/code/

National Fair Housing Advocate Online: *www.fairhousing.com*

U.S. Department of Housing and Urban Development: 2004-2010 HUD
    charges: *www.hud.gov/offices/fheo/enforcement/2009hudcharges.cfm*

U.S. Department of Housing and Urban Development: Department of Justice
    charges: *www.hud.gov/offices/fheo/DOJCharges.cfm*

U.S. Department of Housing and Urban Development: Fair Housing:
    http://portal.hud.gov/portal/page/portal/HUD/groups/fairhousing

U.S. Department of Housing and Urban Development: Fair Housing Laws and
    Presidential Executive Orders: *www.hud.gov/offices/fheo/FHLaws/index.cfm*

U.S. Department of Housing and Urban Development: Fair Housing Library:
    http://portal.hud.gov/portal/page/portal/HUD/library/bookshelf09/

U.S. Department of Housing and Urban Development: Fair Housing
    Logo: *www.hud.gov/library/bookshelf15/hudgraphics/fheologo.cfm*

U.S. Department of Housing and Urban Development: Housing Discrimination
    Complaints: *www.hud.gov/offices/fheo/complaint-process.cfm*

U.S. Department of Housing and Urban Development: Non-Discrimination and
    Accessibility for Persons with Disabilities:
    http://portal.hud.gov/portal/page/portal/HUD/program_offices/administration/
    hudclips/notices/pih/files/10-02pihn.doc

U.S. Department of Housing and Urban Development: People With Disabilities
    Frequently Asked Questions: *www.hud.gov/offices/fheo/disabilities/*
    sect504faq.cfm

U.S. Department of Housing and Urban Development: Public Service
    Announcements: *www.hud.gov/offices/fheo/adcampaign.cfm*

CHAPTER 20 QUIZ

1. Under the Fair Housing Act, which action is legally permitted?
   a. Advertising property for sale only to a special group
   b. Altering the terms of a loan for a member of a minority group
   c. Refusing to make a mortgage loan to a minority individual because of a poor credit history
   d. Telling an individual that an apartment has been rented when in fact it has not

2. Complaints relating to the Civil Rights Act of 1866
   a. must be taken directly to federal courts.
   b. are no longer reviewed in the courts.
   c. are handled by HUD.
   d. are handled by state enforcement agencies.

3. Why is the Civil Rights Act of 1866 unique?
   a. It has been broadened to protect the aged.
   b. It adds welfare recipients as a protected class.
   c. It contains "choose your neighbor" provisions.
   d. It provides no exceptions that would permit racial discrimination.

4. "I hear *they're* moving in. There goes the neighborhood! Better put your house on the market before values drop!" This is an example of what illegal practice?
   a. Steering
   b. Blockbusting
   c. Redlining
   d. Fraudulent advertising

5. The act of directing homeseekers toward or away from particular areas, either to maintain or to change the character of the neighborhood, is
   a. blockbusting.
   b. redlining.
   c. steering.
   d. permitted under the Fair Housing Act of 1968.

6. A lender's refusal to lend money to potential homeowners attempting to purchase properties located in predominantly African American neighborhoods is known as
   a. redlining.
   b. blockbusting.
   c. steering.
   d. prequalifying.

7. All of the following would be permitted under the federal Fair Housing Act *EXCEPT*
   a. an expensive club in New York rents rooms only to members who are graduates of a particular university.
   b. the owner of a 20-unit residential apartment building rents to men only.
   c. a Catholic convent refuses to furnish housing for a Jewish man.
   d. an owner refuses to rent the other side of her duplex to a family with children.

8. It is illegal for a lending institution to refuse to make a residential real estate loan in a particular area only because of the
   a. questionable economic situation of the applicant.
   b. physical location of the property.
   c. applicant not being of legal age.
   d. deteriorated condition of the premises.

9. If a mortgage lender discriminates against a loan applicant on the basis of marital status, what law is violated?
   a. ADA
   b. Civil Rights Act of 1866
   c. ECOA
   d. Fair Housing Act

10. Housing that qualifies for exemption from familial status provisions

    a. includes housing intended for persons 50 years old or older.

    b. includes a restriction that 80 percent of the units be occupied by persons 55 or older.

    c. is not permitted under the federal Fair Housing Act.

    d. is permitted for owner-occupied buildings with four or more units.

11. Which statement describes the Supreme Court's decision in the case of *Jones v. Alfred H. Mayer Company*?

    a. Racial discrimination is prohibited by any party in the sale or rental of real estate.

    b. Sales by individual residential homeowners are exempted, provided the owners do not use brokers.

    c. Laws against discrimination apply only to federally related transactions.

    d. Persons with disabilities are a protected class.

12. After a licensee takes a sale listing of a residence, the owners specify that they will not sell the home to any Asian family. The broker should do which of the following?

    a. Advertise the property exclusively in Asian-language newspapers.

    b. Explain to the owner that the instruction violates federal law and that the broker cannot comply with it.

    c. Abide by the principal's directions despite the fact that they conflict with the fair housing laws.

    d. Require that the owner sign a separate legal document stating the additional instruction as an amendment to the listing agreement.

13. The fine for a first violation of the federal Fair Housing Act could be as much as

    a. $5,000.

    b. $27,500.

    c. $55,000.

    d. $11,000.

14. A single man with two small children has been told by a real estate licensee that homes for sale in a condominium complex are available only to married couples with no children. Which statement is *TRUE*?

    a. Because a single-parent family can be disruptive if the parent provides little supervision of the children, the condominium is permitted to discriminate against the family under the principle of rational basis.

    b. Condominium complexes are exempt from the fair housing laws and can therefore restrict children.

    c. The man may file a complaint alleging discrimination on the basis of familial status.

    d. Restrictive covenants in a condominium take precedence over the fair housing laws.

15. The following ad appeared in the newspaper: "For sale: 4 BR brick home; Redwood School District; excellent Elm Street location; short walk to St. John's Church; and right on the bus line. Move-in condition; priced to sell." Which statement is *TRUE*?

    a. The ad describes the property for sale and is very appropriate.

    b. The fair housing laws do not apply to newspaper advertising.

    c. The ad should state that the property is available to families with children.

    d. The ad should not mention St. John's Church.

16. A discrimination suit may be filed in federal court by

    a. a person aggrieved by racial discrimination.

    b. the Department of Housing and Urban Development.

    c. the state or county nondiscrimination officer.

    d. the Federal Housing Administration.

17. The federal Fair Housing Act does *NOT* prohibit

    a. blockbusting.

    b. discriminatory advertising.

    c. redlining.

    d. discriminating on the basis of marital status.

18. Which of the following would be considered legal?
    a. Charging a family with children a higher security deposit than those with no children
    b. Requiring a person with a disability to establish an escrow account for the costs to restore a property after it has been modified
    c. Picturing only white people in a brochure as the "happy residents" in a housing development
    d. Refusing to sell a house to a person who has a history of mental illness

19. The landlord's lease prohibits tenants from altering the property in any way. A young woman who uses a wheelchair cannot maneuver over the doorstep into her apartment by herself. In addition, she cannot access the bathroom facilities in her wheelchair. Which of the following is *TRUE*?
    a. The landlord is responsible for making all apartments accessible to people with disabilities.
    b. The tenant cannot remedy these conditions because of the terms of the lease.
    c. The landlord should not have rented this apartment to the tenant.
    d. The tenant is entitled to make the necessary alterations.

20. The provisions of the Fair Housing Act apply
    a. in all states.
    b. only in those states that have ratified the act.
    c. only in those states that do not have substantially equivalent laws.
    d. only in those states that do not have specific state fair housing laws.

Environmental Issues and the Real Estate Transaction

■ **LEARNING OBJECTIVES** *When you have finished reading this chapter, you should be able to*

■ **identify** the basic environmental hazards an agent should be aware of in order to protect the client's interests;

■ **describe** the warning signs, characteristics, causes, and solutions for the various environmental hazards most commonly found in real estate transactions;

■ **explain** the fundamental liability issues arising under environmental protection laws;

■ **distinguish** lead-based paint issues from other environmental issues; and

■ **define** the following *key terms:*

asbestos	encapsulation	radon
brownfields	environmental impact	Small Business Liability
carbon monoxide (CO)	statement (EIS)	Relief and Brownfields
chlorofluorocarbons	environmental site	Revitalization Act
(CFCs)	assessment (ESA)	Superfund Amendments
Comprehensive	formaldehyde	and Reauthorization Act
Environmental	groundwater	(SARA)
Response,	lead	underground storage
Compensation, and	mold	tanks (USTs)
Liability Act (CERCLA)	polychlorinated biphenyls	urea-formaldehyde foam
electromagnetic fields	(PCBs)	insulation (UFFI)
(EMFs)		water table

■ ENVIRONMENTAL ISSUES

As a growing number of homebuyers base their decisions in part on the desire for fresh air, clean water, and outdoor recreational opportunities, many states recognize that preservation of a state's environment both enhances the quality of life and helps strengthen property values. The legitimate commercial use of land must be balanced with the need to preserve vital resources and protect the quality of the states' air, water, and soil. The prevention and cleanup of pollutants and toxic wastes not only revitalize the land but create greater opportunities for responsible development and ensure that the interests of all parties involved in real estate transactions are protected.

Environmental issues are health issues, and health issues based on environmental hazards have become real estate issues. Although licensees are not expected to have the technical expertise necessary to determine whether a hazardous substance is present, they should be familiar with state and federal environmental laws and the regulatory agencies that enforce them. Licensees can help prospective purchasers find authoritative information about hazardous substances so that the buyers can make informed decisions.

A state-mandated disclosure is usually required by a seller only for transactions involving property with one to four dwelling units. In the past, licensees tended to accept seller-supplied disclosure forms without question, trusting that all was accurate and complete. Today that trust is risky business. In fact, some states impose a burden on the licensee to discover problems and ask questions. Similarly, licensees should inform buyers of the need to ask and discover and not rely on disclosure forms as a warranty or guarantee. Sellers are to disclose what they are aware of, and buyers are put on notice to discover hazards they are concerned about.

IN PRACTICE It is important that licensees and sellers provide property disclosures to prospective buyers when required by law. For example, in the 2003 case *Saiz v. Horn*, homebuyers found substantial defects in the home they purchased. The buyers learned that the seller had in the past given prospective buyers a disclosure statement revealing the defects but had not provided it to the buyers. The court found that the real estate licensee should have told the homebuyers that the sellers had a legal duty to provide them with a disclosure statement.

■ HAZARDOUS SUBSTANCES

Pollution and hazardous substances in the environment are of interest to real estate licensees because they affect the attractiveness, safety, desirability, and market value of cities, neighborhoods, and backyards. No one wants to live in a toxic environment. (See Figure 21.1.)

Asbestos

Asbestos is a fire-resistant mineral that was once used extensively as insulation and to strengthen other materials. A component of more than 3,000 types of building materials, asbestos was found in most construction, including residential,

Environmental Hazards

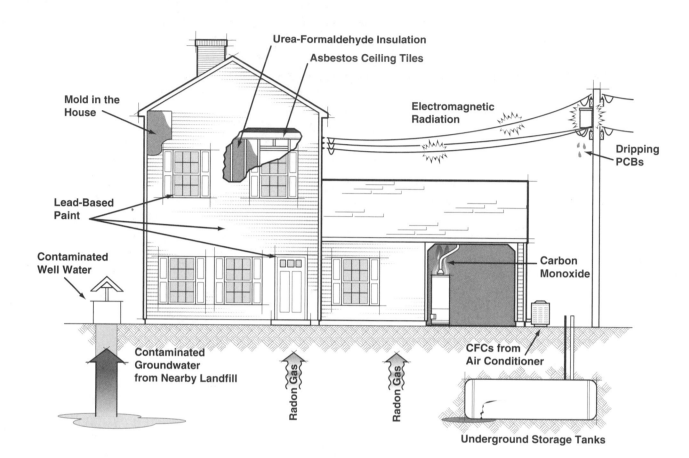

Mold in the House
Urea-Formaldehyde Insulation
Asbestos Ceiling Tiles
Electromagnetic Radiation
Dripping PCBs
Lead-Based Paint
Contaminated Well Water
Carbon Monoxide
Contaminated Groundwater from Nearby Landfill
Radon Gas
Radon Gas
CFCs from Air Conditioner
Underground Storage Tanks

until 1978, when its use was banned. The Environmental Protection Agency (EPA) estimates that, even today, about 20 percent of the nation's commercial and public buildings have asbestos-containing materials (ACMs).

Asbestos insulation can create airborne contaminants that may result in respiratory diseases.

Asbestos was used to cover pipes, ducts, and heating and hot water units. Its fire-resistant properties made it a popular material for use in floor tile, exterior siding, roofing products, linoleum flooring materials, joint compounds, wallboard material, backing, and mastics. Though some ACMs are easy to identify (e.g., insulation around heating and water pipes), identifying asbestos may be more difficult when it is behind walls or under floors.

Asbestos is highly *friable*, meaning that as it ages, asbestos fibers easily break down into tiny filaments. This makes asbestos especially harmful when it is disturbed or exposed and becomes airborne, as often occurs during renovation or remodeling. Those who have inhaled asbestos fibers often develop serious and deadly respiratory diseases decades later. While federal regulations establish guidelines for owners of public and commercial buildings to test for asbestos-containing materials, there are no guidelines regarding the presence of asbestos in residential properties.

Because improper removal procedures may further contaminate the air within the structure, the process requires state-licensed technicians and specially sealed environments. The waste generated must be disposed of at a licensed facility, which further adds to the cost of removal. **Encapsulation,** or the sealing off of disintegrating asbestos, is an alternate method of asbestos control that may be preferable to removal in certain circumstances. However, an owner must periodically monitor the condition of the encapsulated asbestos to make sure it is not disintegrating.

Only a certified asbestos inspector should perform an asbestos inspection of a structure to identify which building materials may contain asbestos. The inspector can also provide recommendations and costs associated with remediation. Buyers should be aware of where ACMs are located so that they are not disturbed during any repair, remodeling, demolition, or even routine use. Appraisers also should be aware of the possible presence of asbestos.

More information on asbestos-related issues is available from the EPA at 202-554-1404. The EPA has numerous publications that provide guidance, information, and assistance with asbestos issues.

Lead-Based Paint and Other Lead Hazards

Lead was used as a pigment and drying agent in alkyd oil-based paint. Lead-based paint may be on any interior or exterior surface, but it is particularly common on doors, windows, and other woodwork. The federal government estimates that lead is present in about 75 percent of all private housing built before 1978; that's approximately 57 million homes, ranging from low-income apartments to million-dollar mansions.

Children younger than six are the most vulnerable to damage from excessive lead levels. Elevated levels of lead in children cause learning disabilities, developmental delays, reduced height, and poor hearing, and the effects are generally irreversible. Excessive exposure in adults can induce anemia and hypertension, trigger gallbladder problems, and cause reproductive problems in both men and women.

Lead dust can be ingested from the hands by a crawling infant, inhaled by any occupant of a structure, or ingested from the water supply because of lead pipes or lead solder. Soil and groundwater may be contaminated by everything from lead plumbing in leaking landfills to discarded skeets and bullets from an old shooting range. High levels of lead have been found in the soil near waste-to-energy incinerators.

In 1996, the EPA and the Department of Housing and Urban Development (HUD) issued final regulations, known as the Lead-Based Paint Hazard Reduction Act (LBPHRA) of 1992, requiring disclosure of the presence of any known lead-based paint hazards to potential buyers or renters. The federal law does not require that anyone test for the presence of lead-based paint.

Lead from paint or other sources can result in damage to the brain, nervous system, kidneys, and blood. Children under the age of six are particularly vulnerable.

LBPHRA requires the following from sellers and landlords of residential dwellings built before 1978:

- Landlords must disclose known information on lead-based paint and hazards before leases take effect. Leases must include a disclosure form regarding lead-based paint.
- Sellers have to disclose known information on lead-based paint and hazards prior to an execution of a contract for sale. Sales contracts must include a completed disclosure form about lead-based paint. (See Figure 21.2.) This is the form for sellers and is slightly different from the form for landlords. Licensees should use EPA-written disclosure forms rather than creating their own forms.
- Buyers have up to ten days to conduct a risk assessment or an inspection for the presence of lead-based paint hazards.
- Licensees provide buyers and lessees with "Protect Your Family from Lead in Your Home," the pamphlet created by the EPA, HUD, and the U.S. Consumer Product Safety Commission.
- Renovators must give homeowners the "Protect Your Family from Lead in Your Home" pamphlet before starting any renovation work.
- Beginning April 2010, federal law requires anyone who is paid to perform work that disturbs paint in housing and child-occupied facilities to be trained and certified in the EPA's new lead-based work practices. This includes residential rental property owners/managers, general contractors, and special trade contractors (e.g., painters, plumbers, carpenters, electricians). The Renovation, Repair, and Painting (RR&P) program involves pre-renovation education. This education includes distribution of the pamphlet "Renovate Right" to the property owners before work commences.
- Licensees must ensure that all parties comply with the law.
- Sellers, lessors, and renovators are required to disclose any prior test results or any knowledge of lead-based paint hazards. With only a very narrow exception, all real estate licensees (subagent, buyer's agent, facilitator) are required to advise sellers to make the required disclosures. Only buyer's agents who are paid entirely by the buyer are exempt.

IN PRACTICE Nearly 20 years after the law took effect, serious problems with notifications still exist. However, the EPA and HUD are serious about enforcement. In early 2008, a Boston property management company agreed to pay a $28,000 penalty and spend nearly $290,000 to replace windows containing lead-based paint. A year later, a large, nonprofit corporation that develops, finances, and manages affordable, mixed-income housing and nearly two dozen associated property owners agreed to pay a $200,000 penalty and to spend more than $2 million in lead-paint abatement at their residential properties. In the fall of 2009, a New York City property management company and 20 affiliated owners of federally assisted multifamily properties in Brooklyn agreed to pay a $20,000 penalty and to perform lead-based paint hazard reduction work in 639 units in 17 properties.

A home can be inspected for lead hazards in the following ways:

- *Paint inspection.* A paint inspection will provide the lead content of every different type of painted surface in a home. This inspection will not indicate whether the paint is a hazard or how the homeowner should deal with it.

F I G U R E   21.2

Disclosure of Lead-Based Paint and Lead-Based Paint Hazards

Disclosure of Information on Lead-Based Paint and/or Lead-Based Paint Hazards

Lead Warning Statement

Every purchaser of any interest in residential real property on which a residential dwelling was built prior to 1978 is notified that such property may present exposure to lead from lead-based paint that may place young children at risk of developing lead poisoning. Lead poisoning in young children may produce permanent neurological damage, including learning disabilities, reduced intelligence quotient, behavioral problems, and impaired memory. Lead poisoning also poses a particular risk to pregnant women. The seller of any interest in residential real property is required to provide the buyer with any information on lead-based paint hazards from risk assessments or inspections in the seller's possession and notify the buyer of any known lead-based paint hazards. A risk assessment or inspection for possible lead-based paint hazards is recommended prior to purchase.

Seller's Disclosure

(a) Presence of lead-based paint and/or lead-based paint hazards (check (i) or (ii) below):

   (i) _____ Known lead-based paint and/or lead-based paint hazards are present in the housing (explain).

   _____

   (ii) _____ Seller has no knowledge of lead-based paint and/or lead-based paint hazards in the housing.

(b) Records and reports available to the seller (check (i) or (ii) below):

   (i) _____ Seller has provided the purchaser with all available records and reports pertaining to lead-based paint and/or lead-based paint hazards in the housing (list documents below).

   _____

   (ii) _____ Seller has no reports or records pertaining to lead-based paint and/or lead-based paint hazards in the housing.

Purchaser's Acknowledgment (initial)

(c) _____ Purchaser has received copies of all information listed above.

(d) _____ Purchaser has received the pamphlet *Protect Your Family from Lead in Your Home.*

(e) Purchaser has (check (i) or (ii) below):

   (i) _____ received a 10-day opportunity (or mutually agreed upon period) to conduct a risk assessment or inspection for the presence of lead-based paint and/or lead-based paint hazards; or

   (ii) _____ waived the opportunity to conduct a risk assessment or inspection for the presence of lead-based paint and/or lead-based paint hazards.

Agent's Acknowledgment (initial)

(f) _____ Agent has informed the seller of the seller's obligations under 42 U.S.C. 4852(d) and is aware of his/her responsibility to ensure compliance.

Certification of Accuracy

The following parties have reviewed the information above and certify, to the best of their knowledge, that the information they have provided is true and accurate.

Seller	Date	Seller	Date
Purchaser	Date	Purchaser	Date
Agent	Date	Agent	Date

■ *Risk assessment.* A risk assessment indicates whether there are any sources of serious lead exposure, such as peeling paint or lead dust. It also describes what actions can be taken to address the hazards.

EPA guidance pamphlets, a list of professionals qualified to inspect or assess for lead-based paint, and other information about lead-based hazards are available from the National Lead Information Center at 800-424-5323.

Radon

Radon is a naturally occurring, colorless, odorless, tasteless, radioactive gas produced by the decay of other radioactive substances. Radon is measured in picocuries (a unit of radiation) contained in a liter of air (i.e., pCi/L). Radon is found in every state and territory with radon levels in the outdoor air averaging 0.4 pCi/L. Fans and thermal "stack effects" (i.e., rising hot air draws cooler air in from the ground through cracks in the basement and foundation walls) pulls radon into buildings.

The potential for developing lung cancer from exposure to radon is a function of the extent and the length of a person's exposure to radon. Radon has been classified as a "Class A" known human carcinogen. Furthermore, smokers have a risk factor 15 times greater than nonsmokers.

Because neither the EPA nor current scientific consensus has been able to establish a "threshold" safe level of radon exposure, the EPA suggests an "action" level of 4 pCi/L. The action level of 4 was chosen because 95 percent of the time, current technology can bring the level below 4, and 75 percent of the time, levels can be reduced to 2 pCi/L. Radon mitigation is less expensive when the system is installed during construction; mitigation consists of removing the radon before it seeps into the house. A fan is installed in a pipe running from the basement to the attic to draw the radon up and out.

Home testing may be done with passive devices, such as alpha track detectors and a charcoal canister. Continuous monitors require electrical power and usually a trained technician. Test results are normally received within 10 days or so when using a passive device (immediately when using an electric continuous monitor). Although a 90-day testing period is most accurate, the EPA developed a 48-hour procedure that can be used in a real estate transaction. The 48-hour test can satisfactorily predict whether a home's annual average is at or above 4 pCi/L in 94 percent of cases.

Because one out of every 15 homes probably needs mitigation, before looking at properties, licensees should discuss radon concerns with their buyers. Licensees can direct buyers to the EPA Web site for the pamphlet "A Citizen's Guide to Radon" and for additional information about testing and mitigation methods.

Formaldehyde

Formaldehyde, a colorless chemical with a strong, pronounced odor, is used widely in the manufacture of building materials and many household products because of its preservative characteristics. Often emitted as a gas, formaldehyde is one of the most common and problematic volatile organic compounds (VOCs) and is one of the few indoor air pollutants that can be measured. Formaldehyde was listed as a hazardous air pollutant in the Clean Air Act Amendments of 1990.

Formaldehyde is classified as a "probable human carcinogen" (i.e., causing cancer in animals and probably in humans). For the 10 to 20 percent of the population that is "sensitive" to formaldehyde, formaldehyde may trigger respiratory problems (shortness of breath, wheezing, chest tightness, asthma) as well as eye and skin irritations (burning sensations in the eyes and throat). It is a major contributor to sick building syndrome (SBS), discussed in Chapter 17, in commercial properties.

The largest source of formaldehyde in any building is likely to be the off-gassing from pressed-wood products made from using adhesives that contain urea-formaldehyde (UF) resins. Pressed-wood products include particleboard, hardwood plywood paneling, and medium-density fiberboard. It is also used in carpeting and ceiling tiles. Since 1985, the Department of Housing and Urban Development (HUD) has regulated the use of plywood and particleboard so that they conform to specified formaldehyde-emission levels in the construction of prefabricated homes and manufactured housing (mobile homes).

Urea-formaldehyde foam insulation (UFFI), once popular, then banned, and now legal again, is rarely used. When incorrectly mixed, UFFI never properly cures, resulting in strong emissions shortly after installation. Studies have shown that formaldehyde emissions generally decrease over time, so homes where UFFI was installed many years ago are unlikely to have high levels of formaldehyde now unless the insulation is exposed to extreme heat or moisture. Still, licensees should check their state's property disclosure form to see if UFFI must be disclosed. Appraisers should also be aware of the presence of formaldehyde.

Carbon Monoxide

Carbon monoxide (CO) is a colorless, odorless, and tasteless gas that occurs as a by-product of burning fuels such as wood, oil, and natural gas, owing to incomplete combustion. Carbon monoxide is quickly absorbed by the body, where it inhibits the blood's ability to transport oxygen, resulting in dizziness and nausea. As CO concentrations increase, the symptoms become more severe, and death may occur within a short time. More than 300 deaths from carbon monoxide poisoning occur each year, with thousands of others requiring hospital emergency room care.

Furnaces, water heaters, space heaters, fireplaces, and wood stoves all produce CO as a natural result of their combustion of fuel. When these units are functioning properly and properly ventilated, their CO emissions are not a problem. However, those with improper ventilation or equipment malfunctions allow large quantities of CO to be released into a residence or commercial structure. CO is a problem often encountered by property managers if tenants use kerosene heaters.

Carbon monoxide detectors are available, and their use is mandatory in some areas. Annual maintenance of heating systems helps avoid CO exposure.

Polychlorinated Biphenyls

Polychlorinated biphenyls (PCBs) consist of more than 200 chemical compounds that are not found naturally in nature. Flame resistant, they were often used in electrical equipment, such as transformers, electrical motors in refrigerators, caulking compounds, and hydraulic oil in older equipment. The EPA has classified PCBs as reasonably carcinogenic and they have been implicated in lower fertility and shortened life spans. Although the commercial distribution of PCBs was banned in 1979, PCBs remain in the environment because burning them at more than 2,400 degrees in a closed environment is the only known way to destroy them.

PCBs are most likely a concern for commercial and industrial property managers. These managers should ask the local utility company to identify and remove any type of transformer that might be a source of PCBs. If the PCBs leak into the environment, penalties and removal methods are expensive.

Chlorofluorocarbons

Chlorofluorocarbons (CFCs) are nontoxic, nonflammable chemicals used as refrigerants in air conditioners, refrigerators, and freezers. CFCs are also used in aerosol sprays, paints, solvents, and foam-blowing applications. Although CFCs are safe in most applications and are inert in the lower atmosphere, once CFC vapors rise to the upper atmosphere, where they may survive from 2 to 150 years, they are broken down by ultraviolet light into chemicals that deplete the ozone layer.

Global treaties have sought to reduce the production levels of CFCs. The manufacture of these chemicals ended for the most part in 1996, with exceptions for production in developing countries, medical products (e.g., asthma inhalers), and research.

Although newer air conditioners use a different product, older appliances may leak CFCs and should be properly disposed of to prevent further leakage. Licensees may wish to advise their buyers to consider upgrading to newer, more energy-efficient and environmentally safe appliances.

Only EPA-certified technicians should do any work on a refrigeration system, especially the larger systems found in commercial and industrial buildings. Approved equipment should carry a label reading "This equipment has been certified by ARI/UL to meet EPA's minimum requirements for recycling and recovery equipment."

Mold

Mold can be found almost anywhere and can grow on almost any organic substance, so long as moisture, oxygen, and an organic food source are present. Moisture feeds mold growth. If a moisture problem is not discovered or addressed, mold growth can gradually destroy what it is growing on.

In addition, some molds can cause serious health problems. They can trigger allergic reactions and asthma attacks. Some molds are known to produce potent toxins and/or irritants.

Some moisture problems in homes and buildings have been directly linked to recent changes in construction practices. Some of these practices have resulted in buildings that are too tightly sealed, preventing adequate ventilation. Building materials, such as drywall, may not allow moisture to escape easily. The material used in drywall wicks moisture to the nutrition source of glue and paper. Vinyl wallpaper and exterior insulation finish systems (EIFS), also known as synthetic stucco, also do not allow moisture to escape. Other moisture problems include roof leaks, unvented combustion appliances, and landscaping or gutters that direct water to the building.

The EPA has published guidelines for the remediation and/or cleanup of mold and moisture problems in schools and commercial buildings. See the list of EPA Web sites at the end of this chapter for these guidelines.

Mold is an important issue for licensees. Initially, lawsuits were brought against construction and insurance companies until the insurance companies started amending their homeowners' insurance policies to exclude mold from coverage. Now, plaintiffs name sellers, landlords, property management companies, and real estate licensees as defendants, in addition to construction and insurance companies.

■ **FOR EXAMPLE**   In a 2005 case, *Eddy v. B.S.T.V., Inc.*, a couple sued a real estate company for failing to disclose mold contamination in the home they purchased. The real estate company's insurers refused to provide coverage, stating that the insurance policies had specific exclusion clauses that would not cover property damage arising out of a real estate agent's failure to render professional services. The issue in the case was whether the professional-services exclusion clause in the insurance policy issued to the real estate company applied to the couple's claims. The couple alleged that the real estate agents breached the real estate company's professional-service responsibilities and that, therefore, the exclusions applied. The real estate company tried to argue that because its real estate agents were trained in identifying mold-related hazards, the claim did not fit the exclusion clause. The court did not agree, and the real estate company was held liable. The court held that the exclusion clauses in the policies prevented insurance coverage for the injuries.

In light of this case and other court decisions on this topic, real estate companies and licensees will find it difficult to know what to do when mold is suspected or found on a property. There are no federal requirements to disclose mold contamination at this time, and only a few states require disclosure. Licensees should remind buyers that sellers cannot disclose what they do not know. Also, licensees should advise buyers that they have not only the right but also the burden to discover.

Licensees may need to take extra steps to protect themselves from liability. Licensees who suspect that mold is present in a home should ask many questions about leaks, floods, and prior damage and remind the sellers to honestly and truthfully disclose any insurance claims regarding mold and other water issues.

Electromagnetic Fields

Electromagnetic fields (EMFs) are generated by the movement of electrical currents by any electrical appliance: clock radios, blow dryers, televisions, and computers. The EMFs produced by high-voltage lines, as well as by secondary distribution lines and transformers, have been suspected of causing cancer, hormonal changes, and behavioral abnormalities. There is considerable controversy (and much conflicting evidence) about whether EMFs pose a health hazard. Buyers who are aware of the controversy may, however, be unwilling to purchase property near power lines or transformers. Licensees are cautioned to remain neutral, letting buyers draw their own conclusions.

■ GROUNDWATER PROTECTION

Groundwater, water that exists under the earth's surface within the tiny spaces or crevices in geological formations, forms the **water table**, the natural level at which the ground is saturated. The water table may be several hundred feet underground or near the surface. When the earth's natural filtering systems are inadequate to ensure the availability of pure water, any contamination of underground water threatens the supply of pure, clean water for private wells or public water systems. Numerous state and federal laws have been enacted to preserve and protect the water supply.

Groundwater can be contaminated from a number of sources, including runoff from waste disposal sites, leaking underground storage tanks, septic systems, dry wells, and storm drains, as well as the illegal disposal of hazardous materials and regular use of insecticides and herbicides. Because water flows from one place to another, contamination can spread far from its source. Once the contamination has been identified, its source can be eliminated. Although the water may eventually become clean, the process can be time consuming and extremely expensive.

The Safe Drinking Water Act (SDWA) was passed to protect public health by regulating the nation's public drinking water supply. The SDWA authorizes the EPA to set national health-based standards for drinking water. Later amendments strengthened the law by increasing source water protection, operator training, funding for water system improvements, and public information. For example, the EPA now requires that water suppliers report any health risk situation within 24 hours, instead of the 72 hours mandated in the past.

Many property disclosure forms require sellers to identify the property's water source, such as well water, municipal water supply, or some other source. Anything other than a municipal water supply should be tested. Also, sellers are generally required to identify the type of septic system because an incorrectly placed or poorly functioning system can contaminate the water source.

IN PRACTICE   Real estate licensees should educate their sellers about full and honest disclosure concerning the property's water supply and septic systems. Buyers should be educated about potential groundwater contamination sources both on and off a property. Licensees should always recommend testing the water supply when it is not part of a municipal source.

■ UNDERGROUND STORAGE TANKS

Underground storage tanks (USTs) are commonly found on sites where petroleum products are used or where gas stations and auto repair shops are or were located. They also may be found in a number of other commercial and industrial establishments, including printing and chemical plants, wood treatment plants, paper mills, paint manufacturers, dry cleaners, food processing plants, and chemical storage or process waste plants. Military bases and airports are also common sites for underground tanks. In residential areas, tanks are used to store heating oil.

Some tanks are currently in use, but many are long forgotten. Over time, neglected tanks may leak hazardous substances into the environment, permitting contaminants to pollute not only the soil around the tank but also adjacent parcels and groundwater. In addition to being aware of possible noncompliance with state and federal regulations, the parties to a real estate transaction should be aware that many older tanks have never been registered. Exempt tanks are not required to be registered, and there may be no visible sign of their presence.

State and federal laws impose strict requirements on landowners whose property contains underground storage tanks. The federal UST program is regulated by the EPA. The regulations apply to tanks that contain hazardous substances or liquid petroleum products and that store at least 10 percent of their volume underground. Some states have adopted laws regulating underground storage tanks that are more stringent than the federal laws. UST owners are required to register their tanks and adhere to strict technical and administrative requirements that govern

- installation,
- maintenance,
- corrosion prevention,
- overspill prevention,
- monitoring, and
- record keeping.

Owners are also required to demonstrate that they have sufficient financial resources to cover any damage that might result from leaks.

The following types of tanks are among those that are exempt from the federal regulations:

- Tanks that hold less than 110 gallons
- Farm and residential tanks that hold 1,100 gallons or less of motor fuel used for noncommercial purposes
- Tanks that store heating oil burned on the premises
- Tanks on or above the floor of underground areas, such as basements or tunnels
- Septic tanks and systems for collecting storm water and wastewater

Most seller property disclosures are required only for residential properties. However, most of the problematic USTs are found in commercial and industrial properties, thereby placing the duty of discovery squarely on the buyer. Because many of the older tanks have never been registered and exempt tanks are not required to be registered, licensees and their buyers should be particularly alert to the presence of fill pipes, vent lines, stained soil, and fumes or odors, any of which may indicate the presence of a UST. Detection, removal, and cleanup of surrounding contaminated soil can be expensive, so it is important to deal with these issues before, not after, closing.

■ WASTE DISPOSAL SITES

Federal, state, and local regulations govern the location, construction, content, and maintenance of landfill sites built to accommodate the vast quantities of garbage produced every day in America. A *landfill* is an enormous hole, either excavated for the purpose of waste disposal or left over from surface mining operations. The hole is lined with clay or a synthetic liner to prevent leakage of waste material into the water supply. A system of underground drainage pipes permits the monitoring of leaks and leaching. Waste is laid on the liner at the bottom of the excavation, and a layer of topsoil is then compacted onto the waste. The layering procedure is repeated until the landfill is full, with the layers mounded up sometimes as high as several hundred feet.

Capping is the process of laying two to four feet of soil over the top of the site and then planting grass on it to enhance the landfill's aesthetic value and prevent erosion. A ventilation pipe runs from the landfill's base through the cap to vent off accumulated natural gases created by the decomposing waste. Test wells around landfill operations are installed to constantly monitor the groundwater in the surrounding area, and soil analyses test for contamination.

Capped landfills have been used as parks and golf courses. Rapid suburban growth has resulted in many housing developments and office campuses being built on landfill sites. Most newer landfill sites are well documented, but the locations of many older landfill sites are no longer known.

Special hazardous waste disposal sites contain radioactive waste from nuclear power plants, toxic chemicals, and waste materials produced by medical, scientific, and industrial processes. Additional waste disposal sites used as on-site garbage dumps are located on rural property, such as farms, ranches, and residences. Some materials, such as radioactive waste, are sealed in containers buried deep underground and placed in *tombs* designed to last thousands of years. These disposal sites are usually limited to extremely remote locations, well away from populated areas or farmland.

Hazardous and radioactive waste disposal sites are subject to strict state and federal regulation to prevent the escape of toxic substances.

■ BROWNFIELDS

Brownfields are defunct, derelict, or abandoned commercial or industrial sites, many of which are suspected to contain toxic wastes. According to the U.S. General Accounting Office, several hundred thousand brownfields plague communities as eyesores and potentially dangerous and hazardous properties, often contributing to the decline of urban property values.

The **Small Business Liability Relief and Brownfields Revitalization Act** (or Brownfields Law) was signed into law in 2002. The Brownfields Law provides funds to assess and clean up brownfields, clarifies liability protections, and provides tax incentives toward enhancing state and tribal response programs. The law is also important for property owners and developers because it shields innocent developers from liability for toxic wastes that existed at a site prior to the purchase of property. In effect, a property owner who neither caused nor contributed to the contamination is not liable for the cleanup.

Significantly, the law encourages the development of abandoned properties, some of which are located in prime urban real estate areas.

IN PRACTICE Since 1979, the U.S Department of Energy has attempted to gain approval to store spent nuclear fuel and high-level radioactive wastes, currently stored at 121 sites around the nation, in one repository built on Yucca Mountain, Nye County, Nevada. These materials are a result of nuclear power generation and national defense programs. The proposal has been challenged repeatedly by environmentalists and nearby residents as well as by the communities through which the waste material would be transported. Approval, which seemed certain in 2002, is less sure today.

ENVIRONMENTAL PROTECTION

Over the past four decades, federal laws have been passed to deal with environmental problems. The Environmental Protection Agency (EPA), created in 1970, works with other federal agencies to oversee and implement many of the laws passed to protect and improve the environment. Most federal laws encourage state and local governments to enact their own legislation.

Comprehensive Environmental Response, Compensation, and Liability Act

The **Comprehensive Environmental Response, Compensation, and Liability Act (CERCLA)** was created in 1980. It established a fund of $9 billion, called the Superfund, to clean up uncontrolled hazardous waste sites and to respond to spills. The act created a process for identifying potential responsible parties (PRPs) and for ordering them to take responsibility for the cleanup action. CERCLA is administered and enforced by the EPA.

Liability Landowners are liable under CERCLA when a release or a threat of release of a hazardous substance has occurred on their property. Regardless of whether the contamination is the result of the landowner's actions or those of others, the owner can be held responsible for the cleanup. This liability includes the cleanup not only of the landowner's property but also of any neighboring property that has been contaminated. A landowner who is not responsible for the contamination can seek reimbursement for the cleanup costs from previous landowners, any other responsible party, or the Superfund. However, if other parties are not available, even a landowner who did not cause the problem could be solely responsible for the cleanup costs.

Once the EPA determines that hazardous material has been released into the environment, the agency is authorized to begin remedial action. First, it attempts to identify the potentially responsible parties (PRPs). If the PRPs agree to cooperate in the cleanup, they must also agree about how to divide the cost. If the PRPs do not voluntarily undertake the cleanup, the EPA may hire its own contractors to do the necessary work. The EPA then bills the PRPs for the cost. If the PRPs refuse to pay, the EPA can seek damages in court for up to three times the actual cost of the cleanup.

Liability under the Superfund is considered to be strict, joint and several, and retroactive. Strict liability means that the owner is responsible to the injured party without excuse. Joint and several liability means that each of the individual owners is personally responsible for the total damages. If only one of the owners is financially able to handle the total damages, that owner must pay the total and collect the proportionate shares from the other owners whenever possible. Retroactive liability means that the liability is not limited to the current owner but includes people who have owned the site in the past.

Superfund Amendments and Reauthorization Act

The **Superfund Amendments and Reauthorization Act (SARA)** created an "innocent landowner" immunity status. It recognized that, in certain cases, a landowner in the chain of ownership was completely innocent of all wrongdoing and therefore should not be held liable. The innocent landowner immunity clause established the criteria by which to judge whether a person or business could be exempted from liability. The criteria included the following:

- The pollution was caused by a third party.
- The property was acquired after the fact.
- The landowner had no actual or constructive knowledge of the damage.
- Due care was exercised when the property was purchased (the landowner made a reasonable search, called an environmental or Phase I site assessment) to determine that no damage to the property existed.
- Reasonable precautions were taken in the exercise of ownership rights.

IN PRACTICE   The EPA has conducted a number of studies to determine the impact on surrounding property values with regard to proximity to landfills and hazardous waste sites. In the report "Challenges in Applying Property Value Studies to Assess the Benefits of the Superfund Program," released January 2009, the EPA concluded the following:

- Impacts on surrounding residential property values vary in size and direction.
- Expected declines have been found, but increases in property values around Superfund sites have also been found.
- The direction of the price effect on surrounding home values appears to vary significantly with individual sites.
- Remedial action can reverse the decline at some sites.
- Delays in cleanup result in a more permanent decline in value.

The most serious problems associated with value involve the presence of undisclosed landfills and hazardous waste sites. Licensees can encourage buyers to consult *www.epa.gov/superfund/sites/index.htm* to determine whether a property of interest is located near a Superfund site. Buyers should also speak with neighbors. Many buyers of commercial and industrial properties hire an environmental engineer to conduct detailed studies prior to closing. In other words, the parties should do everything possible to avoid surprises.

■ LIABILITY OF REAL ESTATE PROFESSIONALS

A real estate licensee can avoid liability with environmental issues by
- becoming familiar with common environmental problems in the licensee's area;
- looking for signs of environmental contamination;
- suggesting (and including as a contingency) an environmental audit if the licensee suspects contamination; and
- giving no advice on environmental issues.

Environmental law is relatively new. Although federal and state laws have defined many of the liabilities involved, common law is being used for further interpretation. The real estate professional and all others involved in a real estate transaction must be aware of both actual and potential liability.

Sellers often carry the most exposure to liability. Innocent landowners might be held responsible even though they did not know about the presence of environmental hazards. Purchasers may be held liable even if they didn't cause the contamination. Lenders may end up owning worthless assets if owners default on the loans rather than undertaking expensive cleanup efforts. Real estate licensees could be held liable for improper disclosure; therefore, it is necessary to be aware of the potential environmental risks from neighboring properties, such as gas stations, manufacturing plants, or even funeral homes.

Additional exposure is created for individuals involved in other aspects of real estate transactions. For example, real estate appraisers must identify and adjust for environmental problems. Adjustments to market value typically reflect the cleanup cost plus a factor of the degree of panic and suspicion that exists in the current market. Although the sales price can be affected dramatically, the underlying market value might possibly remain relatively equal to others in the neighborhood. The real estate appraiser's greatest responsibility is to the lender, which depends on the appraiser to identify values affected by environmental hazards. Although the lender may be protected under certain conditions by virtue of the 1986 amendments to the Superfund Act, the lender must be aware of any potential problems and may require additional environmental reports.

Insurance carriers also might be affected in the transactions. Mortgage insurance companies protect lenders' mortgage investments and might be required to carry part of the ultimate responsibility in cases of loss. More important, hazard insurance carriers might be directly responsible for damages if such coverage was included in the initial policy.

Discovery of Environmental Hazards

Real estate licensees are not expected to have the technical expertise necessary to discover the presence of environmental hazards. They are presumed by the public to have special knowledge about real estate, so licensees must be aware of possible hazards and where to seek professional help.

The most appropriate people on whom a licensee can rely for sound environmental information are scientific or technical experts. Environmental auditors (or *environmental assessors*) are scientific or technical experts who can provide the most comprehensive studies. Developers and purchasers of commercial and industrial properties often rely on an environmental assessment that includes the property's history of use, a current-use review, and an investigation into the existence of reported or known contamination sources in the subject area that may affect the property. Testing of soil, water, air, and structures can be conducted, if warranted.

Not only do environmental experts detect environmental problems, they can usually offer guidance about how best to resolve the conditions. Although environmental audits or assessments may occur at any stage in a transaction, they are most frequently a contingency that must be satisfied prior to closing.

IN PRACTICE   Environmental assessments and tests conducted by environmental consultants can take time. Licensees should be aware of the time involved and contact environmental consultants as soon as they know such tests are needed, in order to prevent delays in closing a transaction.

Environmental Site Assessments

An **environmental site assessment (ESA)** is often performed on a property to show that due care was exercised in determining whether any environmental impairments exist. The assessment can help prevent parties from becoming involved in contaminated property and work as a defense to liability. It is often requested by a lending institution, developer, or a potential buyer. The assessment is commonly performed in phases, such as Phase 1 or Phase 2. A Phase 1 Environmental Report is requested first to determine if any potential environmental problems exist at or near the subject property that may cause impairment. There are no federal regulations that define what an environmental assessment must include.

Environmental Impact Statements

A federally funded project requires that an **environmental impact statement (EIS)** be performed. These statements detail the impact the project will have on the environment. They can include information about air quality, noise, public health and safety, energy consumption, population density, wildlife, vegetation, and the need for sewer and water facilities. Increasingly, these statements are also being required for private development.

Disclosure of Environmental Hazards

Most state laws address the issue of disclosure of known material facts regarding a residential property. In some states, a real estate licensee may be liable if the licensee should have known of a condition, even if the seller neglected to make the disclosure. Very few states require disclosure of environmental issues with commercial and industrial property. Real estate licensees specializing in these properties should emphasize to their buyers the importance of professional environmental audits in the absence of required disclosures.

■ KEY POINT REVIEW

Asbestos is a mineral composed of fibers that have fireproofing and insulating qualities. Note the following:

■ Asbestos is a health hazard when fibers break down and are inhaled.
■ Asbestos has been banned for use in insulation since 1978.
■ Encapsulation can prevent asbestos fibers from becoming airborne.

Lead can be found in pipes, pipe solder, paints, air, and soil. Note the following:

■ **Lead-based paint** is found in many of the housing units built before 1978.
■ Lead accumulates in the body and can damage the brain, nervous system, kidneys, and blood.
■ The Lead-Based Paint Hazard Reduction Act of 1992 (LBPHRA) requires disclosure of known lead-based paint hazards to potential buyers or renters.
   — **Real estate licensees** provide buyers and lessees with "Protect Your Family from Lead in Your Home," a pamphlet created by EPA, HUD, and the U.S. Consumer Product Safety Commission.

Radon is an odorless, tasteless, **radioactive gas** produced by the natural decay of radioactive substances in the ground and is found throughout the United States. Radon gas may cause lung cancer. Testing for radon in buildings is not a federal requirement.

Formaldehyde, described as a hazardous air pollutant in the Clean Air Act Amendments of 1990, is used for building and household products, such as **urea-formaldehyde foam insulation (UFFI)**, and may cause respiratory problems, eye and skin irritations, and possibly cancer. Since 1985, it has been regulated by HUD for use in wood products.

Real estate licensees should check state formaldehyde disclosure requirements, and appraisers should note the presence of formaldehyde.

Carbon monoxide (CO), a colorless, odorless gas that is by-product of fuel burning,

■ is produced by furnaces, water heaters, space heaters (including kerosene heaters), fireplaces, and wood stoves;
■ may cause carbon monoxide poisoning, which can result in death unless the gas is properly vented; and
■ is detectable with available carbon monoxide detectors, which may be required by state law.

Polychlorinated biphenyls (PCBs) may be found in electrical equipment. Note the following:

■ PCBs are suspected of causing health problems.
■ The manufacture of PCBs has been banned since January 1, 1979.
■ The commercial distribution of PCBs has been banned since July 1, 1979.

Chlorofluorocarbons (CFCs), used in refrigerators, aerosol sprays, paints, solvents, and foam applications, are no longer manufactured worldwide, for the most part since 1996, and have been replaced by available environmentally friendly substitutes for home appliances.

Mold is present in the air everywhere and grows in the presence of moisture, oxygen, and a cellulosic (organic) food source. Note the following:

- Some molds can cause serious health problems.
- The **EPA** has guidelines for remediation and/or cleanup of mold and moisture problems in schools and commercial buildings.
- **Real estate licensees** should recommend a **mold inspection** if mold is evident or suspected because of water problems.

Electromagnetic fields (EMFs) are produced by all electrical appliances. High-voltage electrical lines producing EMFs are under investigation for health risks.

Groundwater is found under the earth's surface and forms the water table. The Safe Drinking Water Act (SDWA) of 1974 regulates the public drinking water supply. On property transfers, any water source other than a municipal supply should be tested, as should any septic system.

Underground storage tanks (USTs), which contain petroleum products, industrial chemicals, and other substances, are a concern because the leakage may imperil both public and private water sources. Note the following:

- USTs are subject to federal law and state law, which is sometimes stronger than federal law.
- The EPA regulates the federal UST program.
- When a property purchase is being considered, a careful inspection of any property on which USTs are suspected should be conducted.

Waste disposal sites can be owned by municipalities, be part of commercial enterprises, or be found on farms and other rural properties. Note the following:

- A landfill disposal site, whether excavated or making use of previously mined property, is
  — lined to prevent seepage,
  — capped with soil for aesthetic reasons, and
  — vented to release gases created by decomposing waste.

Brownfields legislation encourages development of abandoned properties by shielding innocent developers from liability for toxic wastes that existed at a site prior to purchase.

The **Comprehensive Environmental Response, Compensation, and Liability Act (CERCLA)** is administered and enforced by the EPA. CERCLA

- established a Superfund to clean up uncontrolled hazardous waste sites;
- identifies potential responsible parties (PRPs);

■ established liability as follows:
— Strict liability where the landowner has no defense to the responsibility for cleanup
— Joint and several liability in which each of several landowners is responsible for the entire cleanup
— Retroactive liability where the present owner and previous owners are responsible
■ defined when "innocent landowner" immunity applies.

Environmental liability issues for real estate professionals include the following:

■ Discovery of environmental hazards that includes
— questioning the owner,
— recommending an environmental audit (environmental site assessment), and
— an **environmental impact statement (EIS)**, as required for federally funded projects and by the state or locality, if required.

Disclosure of environmental hazards—state laws cover disclosure of known material facts regarding property condition.

■ RELATED WEB SITES

Consumer Product Safety Commission: *www.cpsc.gov*
Legal Information Institute: Court Opinions: *www.law.cornell.edu/co.html*
National Safety Council Environmental Health Center: Lead:
    www.nsc.org/news_resources/Resources/Documents/Lead_Poisoning.pdf
U.S. Environmental Protection Agency: *www.epa.gov*
U.S. Environmental Protection Agency: Asbestos: *www.epa.gov/oppt/asbestos/*
U.S. Environmental Protection Agency: CERCLA/Superfund:
    www.epa.gov/superfund/policy/cercla.htm
U.S. Environmental Protection Agency: Compliance and Enforcement:
    www.epa.gov/compliance/
U.S. Environmental Protection Agency: Formaldehyde:
    www.epa.gov/iaq/formalde.html
U.S. Environmental Protection Agency: Indoor Air Quality: Mold:
    www.epa.gov/mold/
U.S. Environmental Protection Agency: Indoor Air Quality: Radon:
    www.epa.gov/radon/
U.S. Environmental Protection Agency: Lead: *www.epa.gov/lead/*
U.S. Environmental Protection Agency: Lead-Based Paint Disclosure
    Forms: *www.epa.gov/lead/pubs/leadbase.htm*
U.S. Environmental Protection Agency: Mold Remediation:
    www.epa.gov/mold/mold_remediation.html

CHAPTER 21 QUIZ

1. Under the federal Lead-Based Paint Hazard Reduction Act, which statement is *TRUE*?

   a. All residential housing built prior to 1978 must be tested for the presence of lead-based paint before being listed for sale or rent.

   b. A disclosure statement must be attached to all sales contracts and leases involving residential properties built prior to 1978.

   c. A lead-hazard pamphlet must be distributed to all prospective buyers but not to tenants.

   d. Purchasers of housing built before 1978 must be given five days to test the property for the presence of lead-based paint.

2. The term *encapsulation* refers to the

   a. process of sealing a landfill with three to four feet of topsoil.

   b. way in which insulation is applied to pipes and wiring systems.

   c. method of sealing disintegrating asbestos.

   d. way in which lead-based paint particles become airborne.

3. A real estate licensee showed a pre-World War I house to a prospective buyer. The buyer has two toddlers and is worried about potential health hazards. Which of the following is *TRUE*?

   a. There is a risk that urea-foam insulation was used in the original construction.

   b. As a real estate licensee, the licensee can offer to personally inspect for lead and remove any lead risks.

   c. Because of the age of the house, there is a good likelihood of the presence of lead-based paint.

   d. Removal of lead-based paint and asbestos hazards is covered by standard title insurance policies.

4. Which of the following is *TRUE* regarding asbestos?

   a. Improper removal of asbestos can cause further contamination of a building.

   b. Asbestos causes health problems only when it is eaten.

   c. The level of asbestos in a building is affected by weather conditions.

   d. HUD requires that all asbestos-containing materials be removed from all residential buildings.

5. All of the following may contribute to the growth of mold *EXCEPT*

   a. low humidity.

   b. EIFS.

   c. roof leaks.

   d. improperly installed gutters.

6. Federal underground storage tank (UST) regulations require that

   a. home fuel oil tanks in basements be registered with the EPA.

   b. septic tanks be pumped every five years.

   c. liquid petroleum tanks that store at least 10 percent of their volume underground be in compliance.

   d. states not develop regulations more stringent than the federal requirements.

7. Which of the following describes the process of creating a landfill site?

   a. Waste is liquefied, treated, and pumped through pipes to *tombs* under the water table.

   b. Waste and topsoil are layered in a pit, mounded up, and then covered with dirt and plants.

   c. Waste is compacted and sealed in a container, then placed in a *tomb* designed to last several thousand years.

   d. Waste is buried in an underground concrete vault.

8. Liability under the Superfund is
   a. limited to the owner of record.
   b. joint and several and retroactive, but not strict.
   c. voluntary.
   d. strict, joint and several, and retroactive.

9. Radon poses the greatest potential health risk to people when it is
   a. contained in insulation material used in residential properties during the 1970s.
   b. found in high concentrations in unimproved land.
   c. trapped and concentrated in inadequately ventilated areas.
   d. emitted by malfunctioning or inadequately ventilated appliances.

10. What do UFFI, lead-based paint, and asbestos have in common?
   a. They all pose a risk to humans because they may emit harmful gases.
   b. They all were banned in 1978.
   c. All three were used in insulating materials.
   d. They were all used at one time in residential construction.

11. A method of scaling off disintegrating asbestos is called
   a. capping.
   b. encapsulation.
   c. containment.
   d. contamination closure.

12. All of the following are true about asbestos EXCEPT
   a. it was commonly used as insulation.
   b. removal can cause further contamination of a building.
   c. HUD requires all residential buildings be tested for asbestos-containing materials.
   d. it is most dangerous when airborne.

13. The most common source of harmful lead in older residential properties is in
   a. asbestos.
   b. basements.
   c. appliances.
   d. alkyd oil-based paint.

14. Urea-formaldehyde is found in residential properties in
   a. lead-based paints.
   b. insulating foam.
   c. home appliances.
   d. electromagnetic fields.

15. In regulations regarding lead-based paints, HUD requires that
   a. homeowners test for its presence.
   b. paint be removed from surfaces before selling.
   c. known paint hazards be disclosed.
   d. only licensed contractors deal with its removal.

16. Radon is
   a. only found in the eastern United States.
   b. easy to detect because of its odor.
   c. a known human carcinogen.
   d. not found in older homes.

17. Contamination from underground storage tanks is
   a. found only in petroleum stations.
   b. addressed by EPA regulations.
   c. only caused by tanks currently in use.
   d. easily detected and eliminated.

18. All of the following are true about underground water contamination EXCEPT
   a. it is a minor problem in the United States.
   b. any contamination of underground water can threaten the supply of pure, clean water from private wells and public water systems.
   c. protective state and federal laws concerning water supply have been enacted.
   d. real estate licensees need to be aware of potential contamination sources.

19. CERCLA regulations for administration of the Superfund, which helps pay for cleanup of uncontrolled hazardous waste sites,
   a. exempt from responsibility those sites that contaminate neighboring properties.
   b. release from liability those owners of contaminated property who did not actually cause the contamination.
   c. make no provision for recovering Superfund expenses incurred in cleanup operations.
   d. impose strict, joint and several, and retroactive liability on potentially responsible parties.

20. Asbestos dust can cause
   a. lung disease.
   b. radiation sickness.
   c. skin cancer.
   d. AIDS.

CHAPTER 22

Closing the Real Estate Transaction

■ **LEARNING OBJECTIVES** *When you have finished reading this chapter, you should be able to*

■ **identify** the issues of particular interest to the buyer and the seller as a real estate transaction closes;

■ **describe** the steps involved in preparing a closing statement;

■ **explain** the general rules for prorating;

■ **distinguish** the procedures involved in face-to-face closings from those in escrow closings; and

■ **define** the following *key terms:*

accrued items	escrow account	prepaid items
closing	escrow closing	prorations
closing statement	Good Faith Estimate	Real Estate Settlement
controlled business	(GFE)	Procedures Act
arrangement (CBA)	impound account	(RESPA)
credit	Mortgage Disclosure	survey
debit	Improvement Act	Uniform Settlement
	(MDIA)	Statement (HUD-1)

■ CLOSING THE REAL ESTATE TRANSACTION

The conclusion of the real estate transaction is the **closing**, the culmination of many efforts—finding clients, negotiating offers, solving problems, coordinating inspections, and much more. At the closing, title to the real estate is transferred in exchange for payment of the purchase price. It's also a complicated time because until closing preparations begin, the licensee's relationship is primarily with the buyer or the seller. During the closing period, new players come on the scene: appraisers, inspectors, loan officers, insurance agents, and lawyers. Negotiations continue, sometimes right up until the property is finally transferred. A thorough knowledge of the process is the best defense against the risk of a transaction failing.

■ PRECLOSING PROCEDURES

Closing involves two major events. First, the promises made in the sales contract are fulfilled; second, the mortgage funds are distributed to the buyer. Before the property changes hands, however, important issues must be resolved. Many real estate licensees maintain lists of events that must take place prior to the actual closing in order to avoid surprises that might lead to delays. Each party—buyer and seller—has specific concerns that must be addressed.

Buyer's Issues

Both the buyers and their lenders must be sure that the seller can deliver the title that was promised in the purchase agreement and that the property is now in essentially the same condition it was in when the buyers and the sellers agreed to the sale. This involves inspecting

> **Closing** is the point at which ownership of a property is transferred in exchange for the payment of the selling price.

- the title evidence;
- the sellers deed;
- any documents demonstrating the removal of undesired liens and encumbrances;
- the survey;
- the results of any inspections, such as termite or structural inspections, or required repairs; and
- any leases, if tenants reside on the premises.

IN PRACTICE   Although the "For Your Protection, Get a Home Inspection" pamphlet is required only for FHA loans, the information is valuable for all buyers. The pamphlet emphasizes the difference between an appraisal and a home inspection. (See Figure 22.1.)

Final property inspection   In the real estate contract, the buyer usually reserves the right to make a *final inspection*, often referred to as a *walk-through*, shortly before the closing takes place. Accompanied by the licensee, the buyer verifies that necessary repairs have been made, that the property has been well maintained, that all fixtures are in place, and that no unauthorized removal or alteration of any part of the improvements has taken place. It is not an opportunity to reopen negotiations.

FIGURE 22.1

For Your Protection, Get a Home Inspection

CAUTION

U.S. Department of Housing
and Urban Development
Federal Housing Administration (FHA)

OMB Approval No: 2502-0538
(exp. 07/31/2009)

For Your Protection: Get a Home Inspection

Why a Buyer Needs a Home Inspection

A home inspection gives the buyer more detailed information about the overall condition of the home prior to purchase. In a home inspection, a qualified inspector takes an in-depth, unbiased look at your potential new home to:

- ✔ Evaluate the physical condition: structure, construction, and mechanical systems;
- ✔ Identify items that need to be repaired or replaced; and
- ✔ Estimate the remaining useful life of the major systems, equipment, structure, and finishes.

Appraisals are Different from Home Inspections

An appraisal is different from a home inspection. Appraisals are for lenders; home inspections are for buyers. An appraisal is required to:

- ✔ Estimate the market value of a house;
- ✔ Make sure that the house meets FHA minimum property standards/requirements; and
- ✔ Make sure that the property is marketable.

FHA Does Not Guarantee the Value or Condition of your Potential New Home

If you find problems with your new home after closing, FHA can not give or lend you money for repairs, and FHA can not buy the home back from you. That is why it is so important for you, the buyer, to get an independent home inspection. Ask a qualified home inspector to inspect your potential new home and give you the information you need to make a wise decision.

Radon Gas Testing

The United States Environmental Protection Agency and the Surgeon General of the United States have recommended that all houses should be tested for radon. For more information on radon testing, call the toll-free National Radon Information Line at 1-800-SOS-Radon or 1-800-767-7236. As with a home inspection, if you decide to test for radon, you may do so before signing your contract, or you may do so after signing the contract as long as your contract states the sale of the home depends on your satisfaction with the results of the radon test.

Be an Informed Buyer

It is your responsibility to be an informed buyer. Be sure that what you buy is satisfactory in every respect. You have the right to carefully examine your potential new home with a qualified home inspector. You may arrange to do so before signing your contract, or may do so after signing the contract as long as your contract states that the sale of the home depends on the inspection.

EQUAL HOUSING
OPPORTUNITY

HUD-92564-CN (6/06)

FHA
HOMEOWNERSHIP

CAUTION

Survey A **survey** provides information about the exact location and size of the property. Typically, the survey indicates the location of all buildings, driveways, fences, and other improvements located on the premises. The survey should also indicate any existing easements and encroachments. The cost of the survey is negotiated in the contract.

IN PRACTICE Relying on old surveys is not necessarily a good idea; the property should be resurveyed prior to closing by a competent surveyor, whether or not the title company or lender requires it. A current survey confirms that the property purchased is exactly what the buyer wants.

Seller's Issues

Obviously, the seller's main interest is to receive payment for the property. Sellers want assurance that the buyer has obtained the necessary financing and has sufficient funds to complete the sale. In turn, sellers should review the purchase agreement to ensure they have completed their tasks. Both parties, accompanied by their attorneys or real estate licensees, will want to inspect the closing statement to make sure that all monies involved in the transaction have been accounted for properly.

Title Procedures

Buyers and their lenders require that the seller's title complies with the terms of the real estate contract. Although practices vary from state to state, most require that the seller produce a current abstract of title or title commitment from the title insurance company. When an abstract of title is used, the purchaser's attorney examines it and issues an opinion of title. The attorney's opinion of title is a statement of the quality of the seller's title, and it lists all liens, encumbrances, easements, conditions, and restrictions that appear on the record and to which the seller's title is subject. The attorney's opinion is not a guarantee of title.

> The *title* or *opinion of title* discloses all liens, encumbrances, easements, conditions, and restrictions on the property.

When the purchaser pays cash or obtains a new loan to purchase the property, the seller's existing loan is paid in full and satisfied on the record. The exact amount required to pay the existing loan is provided in a current *payoff statement* from the lender, effective the date of closing. This payoff statement notes the unpaid amount of principal, the interest due through the date of payment, the fee for issuing the certificate of satisfaction or release deed, credits (if any) for tax and insurance reserves, and the amount of any prepayment penalties. The same procedure is followed for any other liens that must be released before the buyer takes title.

When the buyer assumes the seller's existing mortgage loan, the buyer needs to know the exact balance of the loan as of the closing date. Usually, the lender is required to provide the buyer with a *mortgage reduction certificate*, which certifies the amount owed on the mortgage loan, the interest rate, and the date and amount of the last interest payment.

The closing agent examines the title commitment or the abstract that was issued several days or weeks before the closing. Because liens may have been filed during the interval, two searches of the public record are often made. The first search shows the status of the seller's title on that date. The second search, known as a *bring down*, is made after the closing and before any new documents are filed.

As part of the later search, the sellers may be required to execute an *affidavit of title*. This affidavit is a sworn statement in which the sellers assure the title insurance company (and the buyer) that no other defects in the title have occurred since the date of the title examination (e.g., judgments, bankruptcies, divorces, unrecorded deeds or contracts, unpaid repairs or improvements that might lead to mechanics' liens). The affidavit gives the title insurance company a basis on which to sue the sellers should their statements in the affidavit be incorrect.

In areas where real estate sales transactions are customarily closed through an escrow, the escrow instructions usually provide for an extended coverage policy to be issued to the buyer effective the date of closing. The seller has no need to execute an affidavit of title.

IN PRACTICE   Licensees often assist in preclosing arrangements as part of their service to customers. In some states, licensees are required to advise the parties of the approximate expenses involved in closing when a real estate sales contract is signed. In other states, licensees have a statutory duty to coordinate and supervise closing activities. Aside from state laws on this issue, a licensee without a specific role in the closing may still be the person with the most knowledge about the transaction. Because of this, many licensees feel it is part of their fiduciary duty to be present at a face-to-face closing.

■ CONDUCTING THE CLOSING

Closing is known by many names. For instance, in some areas, closing is called *settlement and transfer*. In some parts of the country, the parties in the transaction sit around a table and exchange copies of documents, a process known as *passing papers*. ("We passed papers on the new house Wednesday morning.") In other regions, the buyer and the seller never meet; the paperwork is handled by an escrow agent in a process known as *closing escrow*. ("We'll close escrow on our house next week.") The main concerns are that the buyer receives marketable title and that the seller receives the purchase price.

In a *face-to-face closing*, the parties meet face to face.

Face-to-Face Closing

Face-to-face closings may be held at the office of the title company, the lending institution, an attorney for one of the parties, the broker, the county recorder, or the escrow company. Those attending a closing *may* include

- the buyer;
- the seller;
- the real estate salespeople or brokers (both the buyer's and the seller's agents);
- the seller's and the buyer's attorneys;
- representatives of the lending institutions involved with the buyer's new mortgage loan, the buyer's assumption of the seller's existing loan, or the seller's payoff of an existing loan; and
- a representative of the title insurance company.

Closing agent or closing officer A closing agent may be a representative of the title company, the lender, the real estate broker, or the buyer's or seller's attorney. Some title companies and law firms employ paralegal assistants who conduct closings for their firms.

The closing agent orders and reviews the title insurance policy or title certificate, surveys, property insurance policies, and other items. After reviewing the agreement of sale (purchase agreement), the agent prepares a closing statement indicating the division of income and expenses between the parties. Finally, the time and place of closing must be arranged.

The exchange The exchange is made when the parties are satisfied that everything is in order. The seller delivers the signed deed to the buyer, who accepts it. All pertinent documents are then recorded in the correct order to ensure continuity of title. For instance, if the seller pays off an existing loan and the buyer obtains a new loan, the seller's satisfaction of mortgage must be recorded before the seller's deed to the buyer. Because the buyer cannot pledge the property as security for the new loan until ownership has been transferred, the buyer's new mortgage or deed of trust is recorded after the deed.

Closing in Escrow

> In an *escrow closing*, a third party coordinates the closing activities on behalf of the buyer and the seller.

In an **escrow closing**, a disinterested third party is authorized to act as escrow agent (escrow holder) and to coordinate the closing activities. The escrow agent may be an attorney, a title company, a trust company, an escrow company, or the escrow department of a lending institution. Although a few states do not permit certain transactions to be closed in escrow, escrow closings are used to some extent in most states.

Escrow procedure After the sales contract is signed, the buyer and the seller execute escrow instructions to the escrow agent. The selection of the escrow agent is often determined by negotiation, custom, or state law. The broker turns over the earnest money to the escrow agent, who deposits it in a special trust, or escrow, account.

The buyer and the seller deposit all pertinent documents and other items with the escrow agent before the specified date of closing.

The seller usually deposits

- the deed conveying the property to the buyer;
- title evidence (abstract and attorney's opinion of title, certificate of title, title insurance, or Torrens certificate);
- existing hazard insurance policies;
- a letter or mortgage reduction certificate from the lender stating the exact principal remaining (if the buyer is assuming the seller's loan);
- affidavits of title (if required);
- a payoff statement (if the seller's loan is to be paid off); and
- other instruments or documents necessary to clear the title or to complete the transaction.

The buyer deposits

- the balance of the cash needed to complete the purchase, usually in the form of a certified check;
- loan documents (if the buyer secures a new loan);
- proof of hazard insurance, including (where required) flood insurance; and
- other necessary documents, such as inspection reports required by the lender.

The escrow agent has the authority to examine the title evidence. When marketable title is shown in the name of the buyer and all other conditions of the escrow agreement have been met, the agent is authorized to disburse the purchase price to the seller, minus all charges and expenses. The agent then records the deed and mortgage or deed of trust (if a new loan has been obtained by the purchaser).

If the escrow agent's examination of the title discloses liens, a portion of the purchase price can be withheld from the seller. The withheld portion is used to pay the liens to clear the title.

If the seller cannot clear the title, or if for any reason the sale cannot be consummated, the escrow instructions usually provide that the parties be returned to their former status, as if no sale occurred. The escrow agent reconveys title to the seller and returns the purchase money to the buyer.

Internal Revenue Service Reporting Requirements

Certain real estate closings must be reported to the Internal Revenue Service (IRS) on Form 1099-S. The affected properties include sales or exchanges of

- land (improved or unimproved), including air space;
- an inherently permanent structure, including any residential, commercial, or industrial building;
- a condominium unit and its appurtenant fixtures and common elements (including land); or
- shares in a cooperative housing corporation.

Information to be reported includes the sales price, the amount of property tax reimbursement credited to the seller, and the seller's Social Security number. If the closing agent does not notify the IRS, the responsibility for filing the form falls on the mortgage lender, although the brokers or the parties to the transaction ultimately could be held liable.

Broker's Role at Closing

Depending on local practice, the licensee's role at closing can vary from simply collecting the commission to conducting the proceedings. In the states that require an attorney's participation, a licensee's responsibility is essentially finished as soon as the real estate contract is signed. Even so, most licensees continue to be involved all the way through closing because it is also in their best interest that the transactions move successfully and smoothly to a conclusion. On behalf of their clients, licensees take care of all details so that the closing can proceed smoothly. This may mean actively arranging for title evidence, surveys, appraisals, and inspections or repairs related to structural conditions, water supplies, sewerage facilities, or toxic substances.

Although real estate licensees do not always conduct closing proceedings, they usually attend. Often, the parties look to their agents for guidance, assistance, and information during what can be a stressful experience. Licensees must be thoroughly familiar with the process and the procedures involved in preparing a closing statement, which includes the expenses and prorations of costs to close the transaction.

IN PRACTICE Licensees should avoid *recommending* sources for any inspection or testing services. If a buyer suffers any injury as a result of a provider's negligence, the licensee might also be named in any lawsuit. The better practice is to give clients the names of several professionals who offer high-quality services. In addition, licensees who receive any compensation or reward from a source they recommend to a client must disclose such an arrangement to the client. Licensees must never receive compensation from an attorney or a lender.

Lender's Interest in Closing

Whether a buyer obtains new financing or assumes the seller's existing loan, the lender wants to protect its security interest in the property and ensure that its mortgage liens have priority over other liens. Therefore lenders may require a survey, a pest control or another inspection report, or a certificate of occupancy (for a newly constructed building). In order to ensure that the buyer takes good and marketable title at closing, lenders generally require a mortgagee's title insurance policy.

The buyer must also provide a fire and hazard insurance policy (along with a receipt for the premium). A lender usually requests that a reserve account be established for tax and insurance payments so that these payments are maintained. Lenders sometimes even require representation by their own attorneys at closing.

Mortgage Disclosure Improvement Act

Since its effective date of July 31, 2009, the **Mortgage Disclosure Improvement Act (MDIA)** has changed how buyers and sellers, lenders, mortgage brokers, title agents, and real estate licensees prepare for a closing. The timeliness of certain disclosures now affects the date of closings. Lenders and licensees should keep in mind the numbers 3, 7, and 3:

- 3 business days from application to provide the truth-in-lending statement (TIL) and good-faith estimate (GFE)
- 7 business days before the signing of loan documents, after the borrower receives the final truth-in-lending statement and good-faith estimate
- 3 business days to wait for closing if the APR has changed more than 0.125 percent from the original or most recent TIL and GFE

Until the applicant/borrower receives the GFE and the TIL, the lender may collect only a reasonable fee for accessing the applicant's credit history. Plus, the Home Valuation Code of Conduct (HVCC) requires that the borrower be provided with a copy of the home's appraisal within three business days of closing.

Lenders must provide a statement to the applicants indicating that they are not obligated to complete the transaction simply because disclosures were provided or because they applied for a loan. If the annual percentage rate increases more than 0.125 percent from the original TIL, then creditors must provide new disclosures with a revised annual percentage rate (APR) and then wait an additional three business days before closing the loan. Consumers are permitted to accelerate the process if a personal emergency, such as a foreclosure, exists.

The intent of this law is to prevent consumers from receiving an enticing low rate at the initial application and then learning at settlement that the lender is charging more in fees. Licensees should encourage their buyers to discuss all loan options with their lenders before signing a contract so that lenders can provide the disclosures in a timely fashion. Borrowers should lock in interest rates with a date that is about ten days from an anticipated settlement. Any change to the interest rate, loan amount, loan product, or lender's or escrow fees can affect the APR, which may then require a redisclosure. Redisclosures can potentially delay settlement.

Before closing, everyone involved in the real estate transaction should check and double-check that the GFE and TIL forms are consistent with the original application. No one—buyers, sellers, or real estate agents—should schedule closings that do not account for the seven-day waiting period.

■ REAL ESTATE SETTLEMENT PROCEDURES ACT (RESPA)

The **Real Estate Settlement Procedures Act (RESPA)** is a federal consumer law that requires certain disclosures about the mortgage and settlement process and prohibits certain practices that increase the costs of settlement services, such as kickbacks and referral fees that can increase settlement costs for home buyers.

RESPA regulations apply to first-lien residential mortgage loans made to finance the purchases of one- to four-family homes, cooperatives, and condominiums, for either investment or occupancy, as well as second or subordinate liens for home equity loans when a purchase is financed by a federally related mortgage loan. Federally related loans are those made by banks, savings and loan associations, or other lenders whose deposits are insured by federal agencies; loans insured by the FHA and guaranteed by the VA; loans administered by HUD; and loans intended to be sold by the lenders to Fannie Mae, Ginnie Mae, or Freddie Mac. RESPA is administered by HUD.

RESPA does not apply to the following settlements:

- Loans on large properties (i.e., more than 25 acres)
- Loans for business or agricultural purposes
- Construction loans or other temporary financing
- Vacant land (unless a dwelling will be placed on the lot within two years)
- A transaction financed solely by a purchase-money mortgage taken back by the seller

- An installment contract (contract for deed)
- A buyer's assumption of a seller's existing loan (If the terms of the assumed loan are modified, or if the lender charges more than $50 for the assumption, the transaction is subject to RESPA regulations.)

RESPA prohibits certain practices that increase the cost of settlement services:

- Section 8 prohibits kickbacks and fee-splitting for referrals of settlement services, and unearned fees for services not actually performed. Violations are subject to criminal and civil penalties, including fines up to $10,000 and/or imprisonment up to one year. Consumers may privately pursue a violator in court; the violator may be liable for an amount up to three times the amount of the charge paid for the service.
- Section 9 prohibits homesellers from requiring that homebuyers buy title insurance from a particular company. Buyers may sue the seller for such a violation; violators are liable for up to three times the amount of all charges paid for the title insurance.
- Section 10 prohibits lenders from requiring excessive escrow account deposits, money set aside to pay taxes, hazard insurance, and other charges related to the property.

Sweeping changes required by January 1, 2010, include the mandatory use of the new Good Faith Estimate (GFE) and the modified HUD-1 form. Although the burden of implementing the new reforms is the responsibility of the lender, real estate licensees should be aware of the requirements because failure to meet the standards can and will delay closings. To make it easier for borrowers to understand costs, the new rules and forms require lenders to provide a standard Good Faith Estimate (GFE), provided by HUD, that clearly discloses key loan terms and closing costs. More important, most of these disclosed costs cannot vary greatly between the time that the GFE is issued and closing.

IN PRACTICE Although RESPA's requirements are aimed primarily at lenders, real estate licensees fall under RESPA when they refer buyers to particular lenders, title companies, attorneys, or other providers of settlement services. Licensees who offer computerized loan origination (CLO) are also subject to regulation. Remember: Buyers have the right to select their own providers of settlement services.

Controlled Business Arrangements

To streamline the settlement process, a real estate firm, title insurance company, mortgage broker, home inspection company, or even a moving company may agree to offer a package of services to consumers, a system known as a **controlled business arrangement (CBA)**. RESPA permits a CBA as long as a consumer is clearly informed of the relationship among the service providers, that participation is not required, that other providers are available, and that the only thing of value received by one business entity from others, in addition to permitted payments for services provided, is a return on ownership interest or franchise relationship.

Fees must be reasonably related to the value of the services provided and not be fees exchanged among the affiliated companies simply for referring business to one another. This referral-fee prohibition may be a particularly important issue for licensees who offer **computerized loan origination (CLO)** services to their clients and customers. (See Chapter 15.) CLOs that provide services to consumers may charge for the services provided; the fees must be disclosed on the settlement statement. While a borrower's ability to comparison shop for a loan may be enhanced by a CLO system, the range of choices must not be limited. Consumers must be informed of the availability and costs of other lenders.

Disclosure Requirements

Lenders and settlement agents have the following disclosure obligations at the time of loan application and loan closing or within three business days of receiving the loan application. If the lender denies the loan within three days, then RESPA does not require that the lender provide the following documents:

Special information booklet   This HUD booklet, which must be given at the time of application or provided within three days of loan application, provides the borrower with general information about settlement (closing) costs. It also explains the various provisions of RESPA, including a line-by-line description of the Uniform Settlement Statement.

Good-faith estimate of settlement costs   The new three-page **Good Faith Estimate (GFE)** must contain the exact language specified by HUD, making it easier for borrowers to compare loan conditions from one lender to another. (See Figure 22.2.)

The only fee that the lender may collect before the applicant receives the GFE is for a credit report. Once the GFE is issued, lenders are committed and may only modify the GFE in certain specific instances. If certain information or circumstances change after the original GFE is issued, then a new GFE must be issued. Issuing a new GFE triggers a new three-day waiting period; in which case, closing may not occur until after three days have passed.

The new GFE indicates which closing costs may or may not change prior to settlement and, if they do, by how much. The fees are divided into three categories:

- *No tolerance*—fees that may not increase before closing: lender charges for taking, underwriting, and processing the loan application, including points, origination fees, and yield spread premiums
- *10 percent tolerance*—fees that cannot increase by more than 10 percent in any given category: settlement services for which the lender selects the provider or for which the borrower selects the provider from the lender's list, title services and title insurance if the lender selects the provider, and recording fees
- *Unlimited tolerance*—fees for services that are out of the lender's control: services for which the borrower chooses the provider (such as escrow and title insurance), impounds for taxes, mortgage interest, and the cost of homeowners' insurance

F I G U R E   22.2

Good Faith Estimate

OMB Approval No. 2502-0265

Good Faith Estimate (GFE)

Name of Originator		Borrower	
Originator Address		Property Address	
Originator Phone Number			
Originator Email		Date of GFE	

Purpose

This GFE gives you an estimate of your settlement charges and loan terms if you are approved for this loan. For more information, see HUD's *Special Information Booklet* on settlement charges, your *Truth-in-Lending Disclosures*, and other consumer information at www.hud.gov/respa. If you decide you would like to proceed with this loan, contact us.

Shopping for your loan

Only you can shop for the best loan for you. Compare this GFE with other loan offers, so you can find the best loan. Use the shopping chart on page 3 to compare all the offers you receive.

Important dates

1. The interest rate for this GFE is available through _____ . After this time, the interest rate, some of your loan Origination Charges, and the monthly payment shown below can change until you lock your interest rate.

2. This estimate for all other settlement charges is available through _____ .

3. After you lock your interest rate, you must go to settlement within ☐ days (your rate lock period) to receive the locked interest rate.

4. You must lock the interest rate at least ☐ days before settlement.

Summary of your loan

Your initial loan amount is	$
Your loan term is	years
Your initial interest rate is	%
Your initial monthly amount owed for principal, interest, and any mortgage insurance is	$ per month
Can your interest rate rise?	☐ No ☐ Yes, it can rise to a maximum of %. The first change will be in .
Even if you make payments on time, can your loan balance rise?	☐ No ☐ Yes, it can rise to a maximum of $
Even if you make payments on time, can your monthly amount owed for principal, interest, and any mortgage insurance rise?	☐ No ☐ Yes, the first increase can be in and the monthly amount owed can rise to $. The maximum it can ever rise to is $.
Does your loan have a prepayment penalty?	☐ No ☐ Yes, your maximum prepayment penalty is $.
Does your loan have a balloon payment?	☐ No ☐ Yes, you have a balloon payment of $ due in years.

Escrow account information

Some lenders require an escrow account to hold funds for paying property taxes or other property-related charges in addition to your monthly amount owed of $ _____ .
Do we require you to have an escrow account for your loan?
☐ No, you do not have an escrow account. You must pay these charges directly when due.
☐ Yes, you have an escrow account. It may or may not cover all of these charges. Ask us.

Summary of your settlement charges

A	Your Adjusted Origination Charges *(See page 2.)*	$
B	Your Charges for All Other Settlement Services *(See page 2.)*	$
A + B	Total Estimated Settlement Charges	$

F I G U R E   22.2

Good Faith Estimate (Continued)

Understanding
your estimated
settlement charges

Your Adjusted Origination Charges	
1. Our origination charge This charge is for getting this loan for you.	
2. Your credit or charge (points) for the specific interest rate chosen ☐ The credit or charge for the interest rate of [____] % is included in "Our origination charge." (See item 1 above.) ☐ You receive a credit of $[_____] for this interest rate of [____] %. This credit **reduces** your settlement charges. ☐ You pay a charge of $[_____] for this interest rate of [____] %. This charge (points) **increases** your total settlement charges. The tradeoff table on page 3 shows that you can change your total settlement charges by choosing a different interest rate for this loan.	
A Your Adjusted Origination Charges	$

Some of these charges can change at settlement. See the top of page 3 for more information.

Your Charges for All Other Settlement Services	
3. Required services that we select These charges are for services we require to complete your settlement. We will choose the providers of these services. *Service* *Charge*	
4. Title services and lender's title insurance This charge includes the services of a title or settlement agent, for example, and title insurance to protect the lender, if required.	
5. Owner's title insurance You may purchase an owner's title insurance policy to protect your interest in the property.	
6. Required services that you can shop for These charges are for other services that are required to complete your settlement. We can identify providers of these services or you can shop for them yourself. Our estimates for providing these services are below. *Service* *Charge*	
7. Government recording charges These charges are for state and local fees to record your loan and title documents.	
8. Transfer taxes These charges are for state and local fees on mortgages and home sales.	
9. Initial deposit for your escrow account This charge is held in an escrow account to pay future recurring charges on your property and includes ☐ all property taxes, ☐ all insurance, and ☐ other [_____].	
10. Daily interest charges This charge is for the daily interest on your loan from the day of your settlement until the first day of the next month or the first day of your normal mortgage payment cycle. This amount is $[_____] per day for [____] days (if your settlement is [_____]).	
11. Homeowner's insurance This charge is for the insurance you must buy for the property to protect from a loss, such as fire. *Policy* *Charge*	
B Your Charges for All Other Settlement Services	$
A + B Total Estimated Settlement Charges	$

 Good Faith Estimate (HUD-GFE) 2

FIGURE 22.2

Good Faith Estimate (Continued)

Instructions

Understanding which charges can change at settlement

This GFE estimates your settlement charges. At your settlement, you will receive a HUD-1, a form that lists your actual costs. Compare the charges on the HUD-1 with the charges on this GFE. Charges can change if you select your own provider and do not use the companies we identify. (See below for details.)

These charges **cannot increase** at settlement:	The total of these charges **can increase up to 10%** at settlement:	These charges **can change** at settlement:
▪ Our origination charge ▪ Your credit or charge (points) for the specific interest rate chosen (after you lock in your interest rate) ▪ Your adjusted origination charges (after you lock in your interest rate) ▪ Transfer taxes	▪ Required services that we select ▪ Title services and lender's title insurance (if we select them or you use companies we identify) ▪ Owner's title insurance (if you use companies we identify) ▪ Required services that you can shop for (if you use companies we identify) ▪ Government recording charges	▪ Required services that you can shop for (if you do not use companies we identify) ▪ Title services and lender's title insurance (if you do not use companies we identify) ▪ Owner's title insurance (if you do not use companies we identify) ▪ Initial deposit for your escrow account ▪ Daily interest charges ▪ Homeowner's insurance

Using the tradeoff table

In this GFE, we offered you this loan with a particular interest rate and estimated settlement charges. However:

▪ If you want to choose this same loan with **lower settlement charges,** then you will have a **higher interest rate.**
▪ If you want to choose this same loan with a **lower interest rate,** then you will have **higher settlement charges.**

If you would like to choose an available option, you must ask us for a new GFE.

Loan originators have the option to complete this table. Please ask for additional information if the table is not completed.

	The loan in this GFE	The same loan with lower settlement charges	The same loan with a lower interest rate
Your initial loan amount	$	$	$
Your initial interest rate[1]	%	%	%
Your initial monthly amount owed	$	$	$
Change in the monthly amount owed from this GFE	No change	You will pay $ **more** every month	You will pay $ **less** every month
Change in the amount you will pay at settlement with this interest rate	No change	Your settlement charges will be **reduced** by $	Your settlement charges will **increase** by $
How much your total estimated settlement charges will be	$	$	$

[1] *For an adjustable rate loan, the comparisons above are for the initial interest rate before adjustments are made.*

Using the shopping chart

Use this chart to compare GFEs from different loan originators. Fill in the information by using a different column for each GFE you receive. By comparing loan offers, you can shop for the best loan.

	This loan	Loan 2	Loan 3	Loan 4
Loan originator name				
Initial loan amount				
Loan term				
Initial interest rate				
Initial monthly amount owed				
Rate lock period				
Can interest rate rise?				
Can loan balance rise?				
Can monthly amount owed rise?				
Prepayment penalty?				
Balloon payment?				
Total Estimated Settlement Charges				

If your loan is sold in the future

Some lenders may sell your loan after settlement. Any fees lenders receive in the future cannot change the loan you receive or the charges you paid at settlement.

Mortgage servicing disclosure statement   This statement tells the borrower whether the lender intends to service the loan or to transfer it to another lender. It will also provide information about resolving complaints.

The last page of the GFE is a worksheet consumers can use to compare different loans and terms to aid in price shopping. The lender is responsible for the accuracy of the GFE and the actual costs that the lender charges on the HUD-1.

Uniform Settlement Statement (HUD-1)   RESPA requires that the Uniform Settlement Statement itemize all charges that are normally paid by a borrower and a seller in connection with settlement, whether required by the lender or another party, or paid by the lender or any other person. Charges required by the lender that are paid before closing are indicated as paid outside of closing (POC). The third page of the new HUD-1 form provides for a comparison of the original GFE estimates to the actual charges appearing on the HUD-1. Lenders are permitted to "correct" any violation of the tolerances by reimbursing the borrower within 30 days of settlement.

RESPA's Consumer Protections

- CLO regulation
- CBA disclosure
- Settlement cost booklet
- Good-faith estimate of settlement costs
- Uniform Settlement Statement
- Prohibition of kickbacks and unearned fees

RESPA prohibits lenders from requiring borrowers to deposit amounts in escrow accounts for taxes and insurance that exceed certain limits, thus preventing the lenders from taking advantage of the borrowers. While RESPA does not require that escrow accounts be set up, certain government loan programs and some lenders require escrow accounts as a condition of the loan. RESPA places limits on the amounts that a lender may require: on a monthly basis, the lender may require only one-twelfth of the total of the disbursements for the year, plus an amount necessary to cover a shortage in the account. No more than one-sixth of the year's total disbursements may be held as a cushion (a cushion is not required). Once a year, the lender must perform an escrow account analysis and return any amount over $50 to the borrower. (See Figure 22.3)

By law, borrowers have the right to inspect a completed HUD-1 form, to the extent that the figures are available, one business day before the closing. (Sellers are not entitled to this privilege.) Lenders must retain these statements for two years after the dates of closing date. In addition, state laws generally require that licensees retain all records of a transaction for a specific period.

Kickbacks and referral fees   RESPA prohibits the payment of kickbacks, or unearned fees, in any real estate settlement service. It prohibits referral fees *when no services are actually rendered*. The *payment* or *receipt* of a fee, a kickback, or anything of value for referrals for settlement services includes activities such as mortgage loans, title searches, title insurance, attorney services, surveys, credit reports, and appraisals.

■ PREPARATION OF CLOSING STATEMENTS

A typical real estate transaction requires accounting for the expenses incurred by either party, generally on the HUD-1, a form required for any federally related closing. All expenses must be itemized to arrive at the exact amount of cash required from the buyer and the net proceeds to the seller. These include prorated items—those prepaid by the sellers for which they must be reimbursed (such as taxes) and expenses the seller has incurred but for which the buyer will be billed (such as mortgage interest paid in arrears when a loan is assumed).

How the Closing Statement Works

The **closing statement** is an accounting of the parties' debits and credits. A **debit** is a charge—an amount that a party owes and must pay at closing. A **credit** is an amount entered in a person's favor—an amount that has already been paid, an amount being reimbursed, or an amount the buyer promises to pay in the form of a loan.

A **debit** is an amount to be paid by the buyer or the seller.

A **credit** is an amount payable to the buyer or the seller.

To determine the amount a buyer must bring to closing, any buyer expenses and prorated amounts for items prepaid by the seller are added to the purchase price. Then the buyer's credits are totaled. Credits to the buyer include the earnest money (already paid), the balance of the loan the buyer obtains or assumes, and the seller's share of any prorated items the buyer will pay in the future.

Finally, the total of the buyer's credits is subtracted from the total debits to arrive at the actual amount of cash the buyer must bring to closing. The buyer usually brings a cashier's or certified check.

A similar procedure is followed to determine the net proceeds to the seller. The seller's debits are subtracted from the seller's credits. Seller credits include the purchase price plus the buyer's share of any prorated items that the seller has prepaid. The seller's debits include expenses, the seller's share of prorated items to be paid by the buyer, and the balance of any mortgage loan or other lien that the seller must satisfy. (See Table 22.1.)

Broker's commission The responsibility for paying the broker's commission will have been determined by previous agreement. If the broker is the agent for the seller, the seller is normally responsible for paying the commission. If an agency agreement exists between a broker and the buyer or if two agents are involved, one for the seller and one for the buyer, the commission *may* be distributed as an expense between both parties or according to some other arrangement.

Attorney's fees If either of the parties' attorneys will be paid from the closing proceeds, that party will be charged with the expense in the closing statement. This expense may include fees for the preparation or review of documents or for representing the parties at settlement.

Recording expenses The seller usually pays for any recording charges (filing fees) necessary to clear all defects and furnish the purchaser with a marketable title. Items customarily charged to the seller include the recording of release deeds or satisfaction of mortgages, quitclaim deeds, affidavits, and satisfaction of mechanics' liens. The buyer pays for recording charges that arise from the actual transfer of title. Usually, such items include recording the deed that conveys title to the purchaser and a mortgage or deed of trust executed by the buyer.

Transfer tax Most states, counties, and local municipalities require some form of transfer tax, conveyance fee, or tax stamps on real estate conveyances. Responsibility for these charges varies according to local practice and by agreement in the sales contract.

Title expenses Responsibility for title expenses varies according to local custom. In most areas, the seller is required to furnish evidence of good title and pay for the title search. If the buyer's attorney inspects the evidence or if the buyer purchases title insurance policies, the buyer is charged for the expense.

Loan fees The discussion of loan fees becomes even more critical with the new good-faith estimate form associated with the new HUD-1 form. For a new loan, the lender generally charges an origination fee and possibly discount points, if the borrower wants a below-market interest rate. These lender charges for taking, underwriting, and processing the loan application, including points and origination fees, may not increase prior to closing. If they do, the lender may elect to reissue a new GFE, thereby triggering a three-day waiting period to closing (to allow the buyer time to "shop" for a new loan) or to "correct" the problem with a reimbursement within 30 days of closing. If the buyer assumes the seller's existing financing, the buyer may be required to pay an assumption fee. Also, under the terms of some mortgage loans, the seller may be required to pay a prepayment charge or penalty for paying off the mortgage loan before its due date.

Tax Reserves and insurance reserves (escrow or impound accounts) Most mortgage lenders require that borrowers provide funds to pay future real estate taxes and insurance premiums. These funds are held in an **escrow account** or **impound account**. A borrower starts the account at closing by depositing funds to cover at least the amount of unpaid real estate taxes from the date of the lien to the end of the current month. (The buyer receives a credit from the seller at closing for any unpaid taxes.) Afterward, an amount equal to one month's portion of the estimated taxes is included in the borrower's monthly mortgage payment.

The borrower is responsible for maintaining adequate fire or hazard insurance as a condition of the mortgage loan. Generally, the first year's premium is paid in full at closing. An amount equal to one month's premium is paid after that. The borrower's monthly loan payment includes the principal and interest on the loan, plus one-twelfth of the estimated taxes and insurance (PITI). The taxes and insurance are held by the lender in the escrow or impound account until the bills are due.

IN PRACTICE RESPA permits lenders to maintain a cushion equal to one-sixth of the total estimated amount of annual taxes and insurance. However, if state law or mortgage documents allow for a smaller cushion, the lesser amount prevails.

Appraisal fees Either the seller or the purchaser pays the appraisal fees, depending on who orders the appraisal. When the buyer obtains a mortgage, it is customary for the lender to require an appraisal. In this case, the buyer usually bears the cost, although this is always a negotiable item. If the fee is paid at the time of the loan application, it is reflected on the closing statement as having been paid outside of closing (POC).

Survey fees   The purchaser who obtains new mortgage financing customarily pays the survey fees. The sales contract may require that the seller furnish a survey.

Additional fees   An FHA borrower owes a lump sum for payment of the mortgage insurance premium (MIP) if it is not financed as part of the loan. A VA mortgagor pays a funding fee directly to the Department of Veterans Affairs at closing. If a conventional loan carries private mortgage insurance (PMI), the buyer prepays one year's insurance premium at closing.

Accounting for Expenses

Expenses paid out of the closing proceeds are debited only to the party making the payment. Occasionally, an expense item (e.g., an escrow fee, a settlement fee, or a transfer tax) may be shared by the buyer and the seller. In this case, each party is debited for its share of the expense.

■ PRORATIONS

Most closings involve the division of financial responsibility between the buyer and the seller for such items as loan interest, taxes, rents, fuel, and utility bills. These allowances are called **prorations**. Prorations are necessary to ensure that expenses are divided fairly between the seller and the buyer. For example, the seller may owe current taxes that have not been billed; the buyer would want this item settled at the closing. When taxes must be paid in advance, the seller is entitled to a rebate at the closing. If the buyer assumes the seller's existing mortgage or deed of trust, the seller usually owes the buyer an allowance for accrued interest through the date of closing.

Accrued items =
Buyer credits

Prepaid items =
Seller credits

Accrued items are expenses to be prorated (such as water bills and interest on an assumed mortgage) that are owed by the seller but will be paid late by the buyer. The seller, therefore, pays for these items by giving the buyer credits for them at closing.

Prepaid items are expenses to be prorated (such as fuel oil in a tank) that have been prepaid by the seller but not fully used up. They are, therefore, credits to the seller.

The Arithmetic of Prorating

Accurate prorating involves the following four considerations:

- Nature of the item being prorated
- Whether the item is accrued and requires the determination of an earned amount
- Whether the item is prepaid and requires the determination of an unearned amount (i.e., a refund to the seller)
- What arithmetic processes must be used

The computation of a proration involves identifying a yearly charge for the item to be prorated, then dividing by 12 to determine a monthly charge for the item. Also, it is usually necessary to identify a daily charge for the item by dividing the monthly charge by the number of days in the month. These smaller portions are then multiplied by the number of months or days in the prorated period to determine the accrued or unearned amount that will be figured in the settlement.

Using this general principle, there are two methods of calculating prorations:

- The yearly charge is divided by a 360-day year (called a banking or statutory year), or 12 months of 30 days each.
- The yearly charge is divided by 365 (a calendar year) to determine the daily charge. Then the actual number of days in the proration period is determined, and this number is multiplied by the daily charge.

The final proration figure varies slightly, depending on which computation method is used. The final figure also varies according to the number of decimal places to which the division is carried. All the percentages in this chapter are computed by carrying the division to three decimal places. The third decimal place is rounded off to cents only after the final proration figure is determined.

Accrued Items

When the real estate tax is levied for the calendar year and is payable during that year or in the following year, the accrued portion is for the period from January 1 to the date of closing (or to the day before the closing in states where the sale date is excluded). If the current tax bill has not yet been issued, the parties must agree on an estimated amount based on the previous year's bill and any known changes in assessment or tax levy for the current year.

Sample proration calculation   Assume a sale is to be closed on September 17. Using a 360-day year, prorate the current real estate taxes of $3,600 for the accrued period of 8 months, 17 days. First determine the prorated cost of the real estate tax per month and day:

$3,600 ÷ 12 months = $300 per month
$300 ÷ 30 days = $10 per day

Next, multiply these figures by the accrued period and add the totals to determine the prorated real estate tax:

$300 × 8 months = $2,400
$10 × 17 days = $170
$2,400 + 170 = $2,570

Thus, the accrued real estate tax for 8 months and 17 days is $2,570. This amount represents the seller's accrued earned tax. It will be a credit to the buyer and a debit to the seller on the closing statement.

T A B L E 22.1

Credits and Debits

Item	Credit to Buyer	Debit to Buyer	Credit to Seller	Debit to Seller	Prorated
Principal amount of new mortgage	√				
Payoff of existing mortgage				√	
Unpaid principal balance if assumed mortgage	√			√	
Accrued interest on existing assumed mortgage	√			√	√
Tenants' security deposit	√			√	
Purchase-money mortgage	√			√	
Unpaid water and other utility bills	√			√	√
Buyer's earnest money	√				
Selling price of property		√	√		
Fuel oil on hand (valued at current market price)		√	√		√
Prepaid insurance and tax reserve for mortgage assumed by buyer		√	√		√
Refund to seller of prepaid water charges and similar utility expenses		√	√		√
Prepaid general real estate taxes		√	√		√

Note: This chart is based on generally applicable practices. Closing practices may be different in your state.

To compute this proration using the actual number of days in the accrued period, the following method is used:

The accrued period from January 1 to September 17 runs 260 days (January's 31 days plus February's 28 days and so on, plus the 17 days of September).

$3,600 ÷ 365 days = $9.863 per day
$9.863 × 260 days = $2,564.38

Although these examples show proration as of the date of settlement, the agreement of sale may indicate otherwise. For instance, if the buyer's possession date does not coincide with the settlement date, the parties could prorate according to the date of possession.

IN PRACTICE On state licensing examinations, tax prorations are usually based on a 30-day month (360-day year) unless specified otherwise. This may differ with local customs regarding tax prorations. Many title insurance companies provide proration charts that detail tax factors for each day in the year. To determine a tax proration using one of these charts, multiply the factor given for the closing date by the annual real estate tax.

Prepaid Items

A tax proration might be a prepaid item. Because real estate taxes may be paid in the early part of the year, a tax proration calculated for a closing that will take place later in the year must reflect the fact that the seller has already paid the tax. For example, in the preceding problem, suppose that all taxes had been paid. The buyer would then have to reimburse the seller; the proration would be credited to the seller and debited to the buyer.

In figuring the tax proration, the number of future days, months, and years for which taxes have been paid must be ascertained. The formula commonly used for this purpose is as follows:

	Years	Months	Days
Taxes paid to (Dec. 31, end of tax year)	201X	12	30
Date of closing (Sept. 17, 201X)	201X	−9	−17
Period for which tax must be paid		3	13

This formula will calculate the amount the buyer will reimburse the seller for the unearned portion of the real estate taxes. The prepaid period determined by the formula for prepaid items is three months and 13 days. Three months at $300 per month equals $900, and 13 days at $10 per day equals $130. Add these two figures to determine that the proration is $1,030 credited to the seller and debited to the buyer.

Sample prepaid item calculation One example of a prepaid item is a water bill. Assume that the unmetered water is billed in advance by the city. The six months' billing is $120 for the period ending October 31 ($120 ÷ 6 = $20 per month). The sale is to close on August 3. Because the water bill is paid through October 31, the prepaid time must be computed. Using a 30-day basis, the prepaid period is the 27 days left in August plus two full months. To compute one day's cost, divide $20 by 30, which equals $0.666 per day. The computation is as follows:

27 × $0.666 per day =	$17.982
2 months × $20 =	$40.000
	$57.982 or $57.98

This is a prepaid item; it is credited to the seller and debited to the buyer on the closing statement.

To figure this proration based on the actual days in the month of closing, the following process would be used:

$20 per month ÷ 31 days in August	=	$0.645 per day
August 4 through August 31	=	28 days
28 days × $0.645	=	$18.060
2 months × $20	=	$40.000
$18.06 + $40	=	$58.060

General Rules for Prorating

The rules or customs governing the computation of prorations for the closing of a real estate sale vary widely from state to state. The following are some general guidelines for preparing the closing statement:

- In most states, the seller owns the property on the day of closing, and prorations or apportionments are usually are made up to and including the day of closing. A few states specify that the buyer owns the property on the closing date. In that case, adjustments are made as of the day preceding the day on which title is closed.

- Mortgage interest, general real estate taxes, water taxes, insurance premiums, and similar expenses are usually computed by using 360 days in a year and 30 days in a month. However, the rules in some areas provide for computing prorations on the basis of the actual number of days in the calendar month of closing. The agreement of sale should specify which method will be used.

- Accrued or prepaid general real estate taxes are usually prorated at the closing. When the amount of the current real estate tax cannot be determined definitely, the proration is usually based on the last obtainable tax bill.

- Special assessments for municipal improvements such as sewers, water mains, or streets are usually paid in annual installments over several years, with annual interest charged on the outstanding balance of future payments. The seller normally makes the current payments, and the buyer assumes all future payments. The special assessment installment generally is not prorated at the closing. A buyer may insist that the seller allow the buyer a credit for the seller's share of the interest to the closing date. The agreement of sale may address the manner in which special assessments will be handled at closing.

- Rents are usually adjusted on the basis of the actual number of days in the month of closing. The seller customarily receives the rents for the day of closing and pays all expenses for that day. If any rents for the current month are uncollected when the sale is closed, the buyer often agrees by a separate letter to collect the rents, if possible, and remit the prorated rata share to the seller.

- Security deposits made by tenants to cover the last month's rent of the lease or to cover the cost of repairing damage caused by the tenant are generally transferred by the seller to the buyer.

Real estate taxes   Proration of real estate taxes varies widely depending on how the taxes are paid in the area where the real estate is located. In some states, real estate taxes are paid *in advance*—that is, if the tax year runs from January 1 to December 31, taxes for the coming year are due on January 1. In this case, the seller, who has prepaid a year's taxes, should be reimbursed for the portion of the year remaining after the buyer takes ownership of the property. In other areas, taxes are paid *in arrears*, on December 31 for the year just ended. In this case, the buyer should be credited by the seller for the time the seller occupied the property.

Sometimes, taxes are due during the tax year, partly in arrears and partly in advance; sometimes they are payable in installments. Tax payments can even be more complicated if city, state, school, and other property taxes start their tax years in different months. Whatever the case may be in a particular transaction, the licensee should understand how the taxes will be prorated.

Mortgage loan interest   On almost every mortgage loan, the interest is paid *in arrears*. The buyer and the seller must understand that a mortgage payment due on June 1, for example, includes interest due for May. Thus, the buyer who assumes a mortgage on May 31 and makes the June payment pays for the time the seller occupied the property and should be credited with a month's interest. On the other hand, the buyer who places a new mortgage loan on May 31 may be pleasantly surprised to learn that the first mortgage payment is not due for another month.

■ SAMPLE CLOSING STATEMENT

Settlement computations take many possible forms. A sample transaction follows, using the RESPA Uniform Settlement Statement (HUD-1) in Figure 22.3. Because customs differ in various parts of the country, the way certain expenses are charged in some locations may be different from the illustration.

Basic Information of Offer and Sale

A couple list their home at 3045 North Racine Avenue in Riverdale, East Dakota, with a real estate brokerage. The listing price is $237,000, and possession will take place within two weeks after all parties have signed the contract. Under the terms of the listing agreement, the sellers agree to pay the licensee a commission of 6 percent of the sales price.

The offer to purchase   On May 18, the real estate brokerage company submits a contract offer to the seller from the buyer, who resides at 22 King Court, Riverdale. The buyer offers $230,000, with earnest money and down payment of $46,000. The buyer expects to obtain a conventional 30-year fixed-rate mortgage for 80 percent of the purchase price and, therefore, will not need private mortgage insurance (PMI). The seller accepts the buyer's offer on May 29, with a closing date of June 15.

In this real estate transaction, taxes are paid in arrears. Taxes for this year, estimated at last year's figure of $3,450, have not been paid. According to the contract, prorations will be made on the basis of 30 days in a month.

FIGURE 22.3

Settlement Statement (HUD-1)

OMB Approval No. 2502-0265

A. Settlement Statement (HUD-1)

B. Type of Loan

1. ☐ FHA 2. ☐ RHS 3. ☐ Conv. Unins.	6. File Number:	7. Loan Number:	8. Mortgage Insurance Case Number:
4. ☐ VA 5. ☐ Conv. Ins.			

C. Note: This form is furnished to give you a statement of actual settlement costs. Amounts paid to and by the settlement agent are shown. Items marked "(p.o.c.)" were paid outside the closing; they are shown here for informational purposes and are not included in the totals.

D. Name & Address of Borrower:	E. Name & Address of Seller:	F. Name & Address of Lender:

G. Property Location:	H. Settlement Agent:	I. Settlement Date:
	Place of Settlement:	

J. Summary of Borrower's Transaction

100. Gross Amount Due from Borrower	
101. Contract sales price	
102. Personal property	
103. Settlement charges to borrower (line 1400)	
104.	
105.	
Adjustment for items paid by seller in advance	
106. City/town taxes to	
107. County taxes to	
108. Assessments to	
109.	
110.	
111.	
112.	
120. Gross Amount Due from Borrower	
200. Amount Paid by or in Behalf of Borrower	
201. Deposit or earnest money	
202. Principal amount of new loan(s)	
203. Existing loan(s) taken subject to	
204.	
205.	
206.	
207.	
208.	
209.	
Adjustments for items unpaid by seller	
210. City/town taxes to	
211. County taxes to	
212. Assessments to	
213.	
214.	
215.	
216.	
217.	
218.	
219.	
220. Total Paid by/for Borrower	
300. Cash at Settlement from/to Borrower	
301. Gross amount due from borrower (line 120)	
302. Less amounts paid by/for borrower (line 220)	( )
303. Cash ☐ From ☐ To Borrower	

K. Summary of Seller's Transaction

400. Gross Amount Due to Seller	
401. Contract sales price	
402. Personal property	
403.	
404.	
405.	
Adjustment for items paid by seller in advance	
406. City/town taxes to	
407. County taxes to	
408. Assessments to	
409.	
410.	
411.	
412.	
420. Gross Amount Due to Seller	
500. Reductions In Amount Due to seller	
501. Excess deposit (see instructions)	
502. Settlement charges to seller (line 1400)	
503. Existing loan(s) taken subject to	
504. Payoff of first mortgage loan	
505. Payoff of second mortgage loan	
506.	
507.	
508.	
509.	
Adjustments for items unpaid by seller	
510. City/town taxes to	
511. County taxes to	
512. Assessments to	
513.	
514.	
515.	
516.	
517.	
518.	
519.	
520. Total Reduction Amount Due Seller	
600. Cash at Settlement to/from Seller	
601. Gross amount due to seller (line 420)	
602. Less reductions in amounts due seller (line 520)	( )
603. Cash ☐ To ☐ From Seller	

The Public Reporting Burden for this collection of information is estimated at 35 minutes per response for collecting, reviewing, and reporting the data. This agency may not collect this information, and you are not required to complete this form, unless it displays a currently valid OMB control number. No confidentiality is assured; this disclosure is mandatory. This is designed to provide the parties to a RESPA covered transaction with information during the settlement process.

FIGURE 22.3

Settlement Statement (HUD-1) (Continued)

L. Settlement Charges			
700. Total Real Estate Broker Fees		**Paid From Borrower's Funds at Settlement**	**Paid From Seller's Funds at Settlement**
Division of commission (line 700) as follows :			
701. $ to			
702. $ to			
703. Commission paid at settlement			
704.			
800. Items Payable in Connection with Loan			
801. Our origination charge	$ (from GFE #1)		
802. Your credit or charge (points) for the specific interest rate chosen	$ (from GFE #2)		
803. Your adjusted origination charges	(from GFE #A)		
804. Appraisal fee to	(from GFE #3)		
805. Credit report to	(from GFE #3)		
806. Tax service to	(from GFE #3)		
807. Flood certification to	(from GFE #3)		
808.			
809.			
810.			
811.			
900. Items Required by Lender to be Paid in Advance			
901. Daily interest charges from to @ $ /day	(from GFE #10)		
902. Mortgage insurance premium for months to	(from GFE #3)		
903. Homeowner's insurance for years to	(from GFE #11)		
904.			
1000. Reserves Deposited with Lender			
1001. Initial deposit for your escrow account	(from GFE #9)		
1002. Homeowner's insurance months @ $ per month $			
1003. Mortgage insurance months @ $ per month $			
1004. Property Taxes months @ $ per month $			
1005. months @ $ per month $			
1006. months @ $ per month $			
1007. Aggregate Adjustment -$			
1100. Title Charges			
1101. Title services and lender's title insurance	(from GFE #4)		
1102. Settlement or closing fee	$		
1103. Owner's title insurance	(from GFE #5)		
1104. Lender's title insurance	$		
1105. Lender's title policy limit $			
1106. Owner's title policy limit $			
1107. Agent's portion of the total title insurance premium to	$		
1108. Underwriter's portion of the total title insurance premium to	$		
1109.			
1110.			
1111.			
1200. Government Recording and Transfer Charges			
1201. Government recording charges	(from GFE #7)		
1202. Deed $ Mortgage $ Release $			
1203. Transfer taxes	(from GFE #8)		
1204. City/County tax/stamps Deed $ Mortgage $			
1205. State tax/stamps Deed $ Mortgage $			
1206.			
1300. Additional Settlement Charges			
1301. Required services that you can shop for	(from GFE #6)		
1302. $			
1303. $			
1304.			
1305.			
1400. Total Settlement Charges (enter on lines 103, Section J and 502, Section K)			

FIGURE 22.3

Settlement Statement (HUD-1) (Continued)

Comparison of Good Faith Estimate (GFE) and HUD-1 Charrges		Good Faith Estimate	HUD-1
Charges That Cannot Increase	**HUD-1 Line Number**		
Our origination charge	# 801		
Your credit or charge (points) for the specific interest rate chosen	# 802		
Your adjusted origination charges	# 803		
Transfer taxes	# 1203		

Charges That In Total Cannot Increase More Than 10%		Good Faith Estimate	HUD-1
Government recording charges	# 1201		
	#		
	#		
	#		
	#		
	#		
	#		
	Total		
Increase between GFE and HUD-1 Charges		$ or	%

Charges That Can Change		Good Faith Estimate	HUD-1
Initial deposit for your escrow account	# 1001		
Daily interest charges $ /day	# 901		
Homeowner's insurance	# 903		
	#		
	#		
	#		

Loan Terms

Your initial loan amount is	$
Your loan term is	years
Your initial interest rate is	%
Your initial monthly amount owed for principal, interest, and any mortgage insurance is	$ includes ☐ Principal ☐ Interest ☐ Mortgage Insurance
Can your interest rate rise?	☐ No ☐ Yes, it can rise to a maximum of %. The first change will be on and can change again every after . Every change date, your interest rate can increase or decrease by %. Over the life of the loan, your interest rate is guaranteed to never be **lower** than % or **higher** than %.
Even if you make payments on time, can your loan balance rise?	☐ No ☐ Yes, it can rise to a maximum of $
Even if you make payments on time, can your monthly amount owed for principal, interest, and mortgage insurance rise?	☐ No ☐ Yes, the first increase can be on and the monthly amount owed can rise to $. The maximum it can ever rise to is $.
Does your loan have a prepayment penalty?	☐ No ☐ Yes, your maximum prepayment penalty is $
Does your loan have a balloon payment?	☐ No ☐ Yes, you have a balloon payment of $ due in years on .
Total monthly amount owed including escrow account payments	☐ You do not have a monthly escrow payment for items, such as property taxes and homeowner's insurance. You must pay these items directly yourself. ☐ You have an additional monthly escrow payment of $ that results in a total initial monthly amount owed of $. This includes principal, interest, any mortgage insurance and any items checked below: ☐ Property taxes ☐ Homeowner's insurance ☐ Flood insurance ☐ ☐ ☐

Note: If you have any questions about the Settlement Charges and Loan Terms listed on this form, please contact your lender.

The buyer's loan application   The buyer's new loan is for $184,000. The buyer is offered three interest rate options: 5 percent with ½ point, 6 percent with 1 point, or 4.5 percent with 2 points. These rate options would be listed on page 3 of the good-faith estimate (Figure 22.2). The buyer's locked-in rate of 6 percent is good until 4 PM June 20, 201X. The buyer will pay interest on the loan for the remainder of the month of closing: 15 days at $30.67 per day ($460.00). The first full payment, including July's interest, will be due on August 1. The loan origination fee is $1,840 and 1 discount point ($1,840). In connection with this loan, the buyer must provide a flood certification ($12), a survey ($395), and a pest inspection ($65).

In connection with this loan, the buyer will be charged $500 to have the property appraised. The buyer is only charged for the credit report at the time of loan application, but the appraisal fee must be paid upon loan approval and before closing. Both items are noted as POC on the settlement statement.

The cost of a one-year hazard insurance policy is $3 per $1,000 of appraised value ($230,000 ÷ 1,000 × 3 = $690) and will be paid at closing to the insurance company. The lender requires a reserve account for property taxes and insurance. The buyer's initial deposit is 7/12 of the anticipated county real estate tax of $3,450 ($2,012.50) and two months of the insurance policy ($115). The lender requires that 1/12 of the annual insurance premium ($57.50) and taxes ($287.50) be included in the monthly payment.

Closing costs   The unpaid balance of the seller's mortgage as of June 1, 201X, will be $115,500. Payments are $825 per month, with interest at 7 percent per year on the unpaid balance.

The seller submits evidence of title in the form of a title insurance binder at a cost of $30. The title insurance policy, to be paid by the buyer at the time of closing, costs an additional $540, which includes $395 for the lender's coverage and $145 for the owner's coverage. The seller must pay $20 for the recording of two instruments to clear defects in the seller's title. The seller must also pay an attorney's fee of $600 for preparing the deed and for legal representation, which will be paid from the closing proceeds.

The buyer has agreed to pay for the state transfer tax stamps in the amount of $115 ($0.50 per $500 of the sales price or fraction thereof). The buyer must pay an attorney's fee of $500 for examining the title evidence and for legal representation. The buyer must pay $20 to record the deed and $50 to record the mortgage.

Computing the prorations and charges   The following list illustrates the various steps in computing the prorations and other amounts to be included in the settlement to this point:

- Closing date: June 15
- Commission: 6% (0.06) × $230,000 sales price = $13,800
- Seller's mortgage interest: 7% (0.07) × $115,400 principal due after June 1 payment = $8,078 interest per year; $8,078 ÷ 360 days = $22.44 interest per day; 15 days of accrued interest to be paid by the seller × $22.44 = $336.60 interest owed by the seller; $115,400 + $336.60 = $115,736.60 payoff of seller's mortgage

- Real estate taxes (estimated at $3,450): $3,450 ÷ 12 months = $287.50 per month; $287.50 ÷ 30 days = $9.58 per day
- The earned period, from January 1 to and including June 15 (5 months, 15 days): $287.50 × 5 months = $1,437.50; $9.58 × 15 days = $143.70; $1437.50 + $143.70 = $1,581.20 seller owes buyer
- Transfer tax ($0.50 per $500 of consideration, or fraction thereof): $230,000 ÷ $500 = $460; $460 × $0.50 = $230 transfer tax owed by seller
- Buyer's tax reserve payment: $2,012.50 paid to separate account (7/12 of the anticipated county real estate taxes of $3,450)
- Buyer's one-year hazard insurance payment: $3 per $1,000 of appraised value ($230,000 ÷ 1,000 × 3 = $690 paid in advance to insurance company)
- Buyer's first full payment, including July's interest due (15 days × $25.56 = $383.40) on August 1

The seller's loan payoff is $115,736.60. The seller must pay an additional seller's fee of $25 to record the mortgage release, as well as $100 for a pest inspection and $200 for a survey, as negotiated between the parties.

The Uniform Settlement Statement

The **Uniform Settlement Statement (HUD-1)** used for most residential closings consists of three pages; Sections J and K on the first page are a summary of the borrower's and the seller's transactions. At the bottom of the first page, line 303 indicates the total amount of cash due from (or to) the borrower. Line 603 indicates the cash to (or from) the seller.

The second page itemizes the settlement charges to be paid from the borrower's funds or from the seller's funds at settlement. A number of the costs to the buyer must correlate to the GFE that the buyer received within three business days of loan application. All items in the borrower's column are added up and transferred to line 103 on the first page. All items in the seller's column are added up and transferred to line 502 on the first page.

■ KEY POINT REVIEW

Closing (settlement and transfer) is the point at which ownership of a property is transferred in exchange for the selling price.

To complete the transaction, the buyer requires the following:

- Title evidence—a current abstract of title with opinion of title from the buyer's attorney or title commitment from the title insurance company
- Seller's deed
- Affidavit of title by the seller and documents showing the removal of prior encumbrances
- Mortgage reduction certificate from the lender, if the buyer is assuming the loan
- Survey and the results of required inspections
- Leases, if tenants reside on the premises

- Successful final property inspection (walk-through)
- Closing statement showing the amount and distribution of funds

To complete the transaction, the seller requires the following:

- Payoff statement from the seller's lender noting the amount owed
- Evidence that the buyer has the necessary funds
- Closing statement showing the distribution of funds

Depending on state law and local custom, closing may be conducted through a

- **licensed escrow company**, in which case the parties may execute documents separately and never meet, or
- **face-to-face** meeting of the parties at the escrow company, title company, lender's office, or attorney's office.

An **escrow holder (escrow agent)** is a disinterested third party authorized to coordinate the closing activities.

The **Internal Revenue Service (IRS)** may require completion and submission of the Form 1099-S statement of income to the seller showing the seller's Social Security number. Form 1099-S is filed by a closing agent or the mortgage lender, with the brokers or the parties being ultimately liable for the filing.

The **Real Estate Settlement Procedures Act (RESPA)** is a federal law enacted to protect consumers in the settlement process as follows:

- Requires accurate and timely information about the actual costs of a transaction
- Eliminates **kickbacks** and other referral fees
- Prohibits lenders from requiring excessive escrow account deposits

RESPA does not apply to a transaction financed solely by a purchase-money mortgage taken back by a seller, installment contracts (contract for deed), or a buyer's assumption of a seller's existing loan.

RESPA requires that lenders and settlement agents provide a

- **special information booklet** produced by HUD to every person from whom they receive or for whom they prepare a loan application (except for refinancing),
- **good-faith estimate of settlement costs** to the borrower no later than three business days after receiving a loan application, and
- **Uniform Settlement Statement (HUD-1)** to the borrower and the seller that itemizes all charges to be paid in connection with closing.

A **closing (settlement) statement** involves an accounting of the amounts paid by or received by the parties, as follows:

- **Debit (give)** is a charge that must be paid by the buyer or the seller at closing.
- **Credit (receive)** is the amount entered in favor of the buyer or the seller.
- In most instances, a debit to one party is a credit to the other party.

- Certain charges are **prorated**, divided between the buyer and the seller, in one of two ways:
  - Yearly charge is divided by a **360-day year** (banking year), or 12 months of 30 days each.
  - Yearly charge is divided by a **365-day year** (366 days in leap year) to determine the daily charge, the actual number of days in the proration period is determined, and the number of days is multiplied by the daily charge.
- In most states, the charges are prorated as of the date of closing, with the seller being responsible for the date of closing.

■ RELATED WEB SITES

U.S. Department of Housing and Urban Development: RESPA:
www.hud.gov/offices/hsg/ramh/res/respa_hm.cfm

U.S. Department of Housing and Urban Development: RESPA FAQs:
www.hud.gov/offices/hsg/ramh/res/resparulefaqs.pdf

CHAPTER 22 QUIZ

1. Which statement is *TRUE* of real estate closings in most states?
   a. Closings are generally conducted by real estate salespersons.
   b. The buyer usually receives the rents for the day of closing.
   c. The buyer must reimburse the seller for any title evidence provided by the seller.
   d. The seller usually pays the expenses for the day of closing.

2. All encumbrances and liens shown on the report of title, other than those waived or agreed to by the purchaser and listed in the contract, must be removed so that the title can be delivered free and clear. The removal of such encumbrances is typically the duty of the
   a. buyer.
   b. seller.
   c. broker.
   d. title company.

3. Legal title *ALWAYS* passes from the seller to the buyer
   a. on the date of execution of the deed.
   b. when the closing statement has been signed.
   c. when the deed is placed in escrow.
   d. when the deed is delivered and accepted.

4. Which item would a lender generally require at the closing?
   a. Title insurance commitment
   b. Market value appraisal
   c. Application
   d. Credit report

5. A buyer purchases a home in an area where closings are traditionally conducted in escrow. Which item would a buyer deposit with the escrow agent before the closing date?
   a. Deed to the property
   b. Title evidence
   c. Estoppel certificate
   d. Cash needed to complete the purchase

6. The Uniform Settlement Statement must be used to illustrate all settlement charges for
   a. every real estate transaction.
   b. transactions financed by VA and FHA loans only.
   c. residential transactions financed by federally related mortgage loans.
   d. all transactions involving commercial property.

7. A mortgage reduction certificate is executed by a(n)
   a. abstract company.
   b. attorney.
   c. lending institution.
   d. grantor.

8. The principal amount of a purchaser's new mortgage loan is a
   a. credit to the seller.
   b. credit to the buyer.
   c. debit to the seller.
   d. debit to the buyer.

9. The earnest money left on deposit with the broker is a
   a. credit to the seller.
   b. credit to the buyer.
   c. balancing factor.
   d. debit to the buyer.

10. The annual real estate taxes on a property amount to $1,800. The seller has paid the taxes in advance for the calendar year. If the closing is set for June 15, which statement is *TRUE*?
    a. Credit the seller $825; debit the buyer $975.
    b. Credit the seller $1,800; debit the buyer $825.
    c. Credit the buyer $975; debit the seller $975.
    d. Credit the seller $975; debit the buyer $975.

11. If a seller collected rent of $900, payable in advance, on August 1, which statement is *TRUE* at the closing on August 15, if the closing date is an expense to the seller?

    a. The seller owes the buyer $900.
    b. The buyer owes the seller $900.
    c. The seller owes the buyer $450.
    d. The buyer owes the seller $450.

12. Security deposits should be listed on a closing statement as a credit to the

    a. buyer.
    b. seller.
    c. lender.
    d. broker.

13. A building was purchased for $85,000, with 10 percent down and a loan for the balance. If the lender charged the buyer two discount points, how much cash did the buyer need at closing if the buyer incurred no other costs?

    a. $1,700
    b. $8,500
    c. $10,030
    d. $10,200

14. Which charge noted on the Good Faith Estimate (GFE) must be the same or less than the charge noted on the HUD-1 form?

    a. Cost of settlement services when the lender selects the provider
    b. Lender charges for taking and underwriting the loan
    c. Cost of settlement services when the borrower selects the provider from the list provided by the lender
    d. Cost of homeowners' insurance

15. At closing, the listing broker's commission is usually shown as a

    a. credit to the seller.
    b. credit to the buyer.
    c. debit to the seller.
    d. debit to the buyer.

16. At the closing of a real estate transaction, the person performing the settlement gave the buyer a credit for certain accrued items. These items were

    a. bills relating to the property that had already been paid by the seller.
    b. bills relating to the property that the buyer needed to pay.
    c. all of the seller's real estate bills.
    d. all of the buyer's real estate bills.

17. A prepaid item by the seller is

    a. debited to the seller.
    b. evenly divided between the buyer and the seller.
    c. credited to the buyer.
    d. credited to the seller.

18. The purpose of the Real Estate Settlement Procedures Act (RESPA) is to

    a. make sure buyers do not borrow more than they can repay.
    b. make real estate brokers more responsive to buyers' needs.
    c. help buyers know how much money is required.
    d. ensure that buyers know all settlement costs that will be charged to them.

19. The document that provides borrowers with general information about settlement costs, RESPA provisions, and the Uniform Settlement Statement is the

    a. HUD-1 form.
    b. special information booklet.
    c. good-faith estimate of settlement costs.
    d. closing statement.

20. Under the new Mortgage Disclosure Improvement Act (MDIA), a lender must extend the closing how many days if the APR is increased prior to closing?

    a. Two days
    b. Three days
    c. Four days
    d. Five days

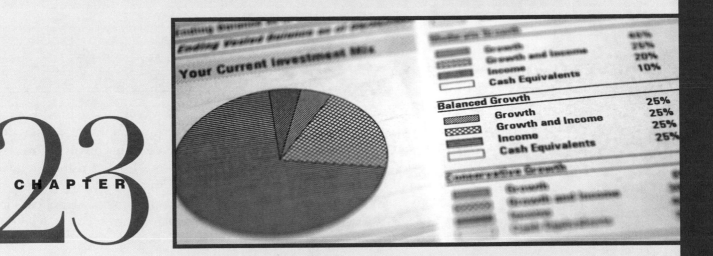

CHAPTER 23

Real Estate Investment

■ **LEARNING OBJECTIVES**   *When you have finished reading this chapter, you should be able to*

■ **identify** the advantages and disadvantages of property investing;

■ **describe** the difference between adjusted basis and capital gains;

■ **explain** the concepts of pyramiding;

■ **distinguish** between depreciation and appreciation; and

■ **define** the following *key terms*:

adjusted basis	equity buildup	real estate investment trust (REIT)
appreciation	exchange	
basis	income property	real estate mortgage investment conduit (REMIC)
boot	inflation	
capital gain	intrinsic value	syndicate
cash flow	leverage	
cost recovery	liquidity	
depreciation	pyramiding	

■ INVESTING IN REAL ESTATE

Real estate is a popular investment. Whichever way the overall market turns, the real estate investment market continues to initiate innovative and attractive investment strategies. These developments make it important for real estate licensees to have an elementary and up-to-date knowledge of real estate investment. Most homebuyers will also want assurance that a residential purchase is a good investment. A licensee should never act as an investment advisor but should instead refer investors to competent tax accountants, attorneys, or investment specialists.

Advantages of Real Estate

In recent years, real estate values nationwide have significantly changed. Some investments have failed to produce returns greater than the rate of inflation, but some real estate investments have shown above-average (or even high) *rates of return*. In theory, this means that an investor can use borrowed money to finance a real estate purchase and feel relatively sure that an asset, if held long enough, will return more money than the cost to finance the purchase.

Real estate offers investors a greater control over their investments than other options, such as stocks, bonds, or other securities. Real estate investors also receive certain tax benefits.

Disadvantages of Real Estate Investment

Unlike stocks and bonds, real estate is not highly liquid over the short term. **Liquidity** refers to how quickly an asset may be converted into cash. For instance, an investor who holds stocks can easily direct a stockbroker to sell stocks when funds are needed. The stockbroker sells the stock and the investor receives the cash. In contrast, a real estate investor may have to sell the property at a substantially lower price than desired to ensure a quick sale or to refinance the property.

Real estate investments are expensive. Large amounts of capital are usually required. Investing in real estate is difficult without expert advice. Investment decisions must be based on careful studies of all the facts, reinforced by a thorough knowledge of real estate and how it is affected by the marketplace.

Real estate requires active management. A real estate investor can rarely just sit and watch the money grow. Management decisions must be made. How much rent should be charged? How should repairs and tenant grievances be handled? The investor may choose to personally manage the property or hire a professional property manager.

Finally, despite its popularity, real estate investment does not guarantee profit. It involves a high degree of risk. The possibility that an investment property will decrease in value or not generate enough income to make it profitable is a fluctuating factor for the investor to consider.

The advantages and disadvantages of real estate investments are listed in Table 23.1.

T A B L E 23.1	Advantages	Disadvantages
Advantages and Disadvantages of Real Estate Investments	Generally, above-average rates of return Use leverage of borrowed money to purchase real estate Greater control over investment Tax benefits	Investment is expensive Real estate is not highly liquid Must actively manage investment High degree of risk

■ THE INVESTMENT

Real estate investors anticipate various investment objectives. Their goals can be reached more effectively depending on the type of property and ownership they choose. The most prevalent form of real estate investment is *direct ownership*. Both individuals and corporations may own real estate directly and manage it for appreciation or cash flow (income). This type of real estate is known as **income property**.

Real estate is an avenue of investment open to those interested in holding property primarily for increasing value, which is known as **appreciation**.

Two main factors affect appreciation: inflation and intrinsic value. **Inflation** is the increase in the amount of money in circulation. When more money is available, its value declines. When the value of money declines, wholesale and retail prices rise. This is essentially an operation of supply and demand, as discussed in Chapter 1. An **intrinsic value** of real estate is the result of a person's individual choices and preferences for a given geographic area. For example, property located in a pleasant neighborhood near attractive business and shopping areas has a greater intrinsic value to most people than similar property in a more isolated location. As a rule, the greater the intrinsic value, the more money a property commands on its sale.

Unimproved land   Often, investors speculate in purchases of either agricultural land or undeveloped land located in what they expect to be a major path of growth. In these cases, however, the property's intrinsic value and potential for appreciation are not easy to determine. This type of investment carries many inherent risks. How fast will the area develop? Will it grow sufficiently for the investor to make a good profit? Will the expected growth occur? More important, will the profits eventually realized from the property be great enough to offset the costs of holding it, such as property taxes? Because these questions often cannot be answered with any degree of certainty, lending institutions may be reluctant to lend money for the purchase of raw land.

Income tax laws do not allow for the depreciation of land. Land also might not be liquid (salable) at certain times under certain circumstances because few people will purchase raw or agricultural land on short notice. Despite all the risks, land has historically been a good inflation hedge if it is held for the long term.

Investment in land ultimately is best left to experts, and even they frequently make bad land investment decisions.

Income

A person who wishes to buy and personally manage real estate may find that rental income property is the best investment.

Cash flow   The objective of directing funds into income property is to generate spendable income, called **cash flow**. Cash flow is the total amount of money remaining after all expenditures have been paid. These expenses include taxes, operating costs, and maintenance. The cash flow produced by any given parcel of real estate is determined by at least three factors: amount of rent received, operating expenses, and method of debt repayment.

Generally, the amount of rent (income) that a property may command depends on a number of factors, including the property's location, physical appearance, and amenities. If the cash flow from rents is not enough to cover all expenses, negative cash flow may result. For example, Table 23.2 shows a negative cash flow.

To keep cash flow high, an investor should attempt to keep operating expenses reasonably low. Such operating expenses include general building maintenance, repairs, utilities, and tenant services.

An investor often stands to make more money by investing with borrowed money, usually obtained through a mortgage loan or deed of trust loan. Low mortgage payments spread over a long period result in a higher cash flow because they allow the investor to retain more income each month. In turn, high mortgage payments contribute to a lower cash flow.

The charts in Tables 23.2 and 23.3 compare the cash flows of taxable and tax-sheltered real estate investments.

Investment opportunities   Income-producing properties include apartment and office buildings, hotels, motels, shopping centers, and industrial properties, but some communities have experienced severe overbuilding of office space and shopping centers. The result has been higher-than-average vacancy rates.

TABLE 23.2

Cash Flow on Fully Taxed Property A

	Year 1	Year 2	Year 3
Beginning equity	$20,000	$20,000	$20,500
Rental income	+ 6,000	+ 6,300	+ 6,600
Mortgage payments	− 3,500	− 3,500	− 3,500
Operating expenses	− 1,000	− 1,000	− 1,000
Taxes	− 2,000	− 1,900	− 1,800
Cash flow	− 500	− 100	− 300
Equity + Cash flow	19,500	19,900	20,800
Debt retired	+ 500	+ 600	+ 700
Final equity	20,000	20,500	21,500
Straight-line depreciation (deduction on which taxes are based)	500	500	500

TABLE 23.3		Year 1	Year 2	Year 3
Cash Flow on Partially Tax-Sheltered Property A	Beginning equity	$20,000	$21,500	$23,400
	Rental income	+6,000	+ 6,300	+ 6,600
	Mortgage payments	– 3,500	– 3,500	– 3,500
	Operating expenses	– 1,000	– 1,000	– 1,000
	Taxes	– 500	– 500	– 500
	Cash flow	1,000	1,300	1,600
	Equity + Cash flow	21,000	22,800	25,000
	Debt retired	+ 500	+ 600	+ 700
	Final equity	21,500	23,400	25,700

■ LEVERAGE

Leverage is the use of borrowed money to finance an investment. As a rule, an investor can receive a maximum return from the initial investment by making a small down payment, paying a low interest rate, and spreading mortgage payments over as long a period as possible.

The effect of leveraging is to provide a return that reflects the result of market forces on the entire original purchase price but that is measured only against the actual cash invested. For example, if an investor spends $100,000 for rental property, makes a $20,000 down payment, and then sells the property five years later for $125,000, the return over five years is $25,000. Disregarding ownership expenses, the return is not 25 percent ($25,000 compared with $100,000), but 125 percent of the original amount invested ($25,000 compared with $20,000).

Risks *are directly proportionate to leverage.* A high degree of leverage translates into greater risk for the investor and the lender because of the high ratio of borrowed money to the value of the real estate. Lower leverage results in less risk. When property values drop in an area or vacancy rates rise, the highly leveraged investor may be unable to pay even the financing costs of the property.

Equity Buildup

Equity buildup is a result of a loan payment directed toward the principal rather than the interest, plus any gain in property value due to appreciation. In a sense, equity buildup is like money in the investor's bank account. This accumulated equity is not realized as cash unless the property is sold, refinanced, or exchanged.

Pyramiding

An effective method for real estate investors to increase their holdings without investing additional capital is through pyramiding. **Pyramiding** is the process of using one property to drive the acquisition of additional properties. Two methods of pyramiding can be used: pyramiding through sale and pyramiding through refinance.

In pyramiding through sale, an investor first acquires a property and then improves it for resale at a substantially higher price. The profit from the sale of the first property is used to purchase additional properties. The disadvantage is that the proceeds from each sale are subject to capital gains taxation.

■ **FOR EXAMPLE** A woman bought a house for $340,000. She put an addition on the house and a new roof. In three years, the woman sold the home for $420,000. After deducting commission and selling expenses, she used the $80,000 profit to buy another property.

The goal of pyramiding through refinancing is to use the value of the original property to drive the acquisition of additional properties while retaining all the properties acquired. The investor refinances the original property and uses the proceeds of the refinance to purchase additional properties. These properties are refinanced, enabling the investor to acquire further properties. By holding on to the properties, the investor may delay the capital gains taxes that would result from a sale.

■ TAX BENEFITS

Income tax laws change frequently, and some tax advantages of owning investment real estate are altered periodically by Congress. An investor can make a more educated and profitable real estate purchase with professional tax advice.

Capital Gains

Capital gain is defined as the difference between the adjusted basis of property and its net selling price. At various times, the tax law has excluded a portion of capital gains from income tax and taxed various types of gains differently.

Basis A property's cost basis determines the amount of gain to be taxed. The **basis** of the property is the investor's initial cost of the real estate. The investor adds to the basis the cost of any physical improvements subsequently made to the property. The amount of any depreciation claimed as a tax deduction is subtracted from the basis. The result is the property's **adjusted basis**. When the investor sells the property, the amount by which the sales price exceeds the property's adjusted basis is the capital gain.

■ **FOR EXAMPLE** Some time ago, an investor purchased a single-family home for use as a rental property. The purchase price was $95,000. The investor now sells the property for $200,000. Shortly before the sale date, the investor makes $5,000 worth of capital improvements to the home. Depreciation of $15,000 on the property improvements has been taken during the term of the investor's ownership.

The investor will pay a broker's commission of 7 percent of the sales price. The investor's closing costs will be $800. The capital gain is computed as follows:

Selling price		$200,000
Less:		
7% commission	$ 14,000	
Closing costs	+ 800	
	$ 14,800	– 14,800
Net sales price		$185,200
Basis:		
Original cost	$ 95,000	
Improvements	+ 5,000	
	$100,000	
Less:		
Depreciation	– 15,000	
Adjusted basis	$ 85,000	– 85,000
Total capital gain		$100,200

Depreciation (Cost Recovery)

Depreciation, or **cost recovery,** allows an investor to recover the cost of an income-producing asset through tax deductions over the asset's useful life. Though investors rarely purchase property without expecting it to appreciate over time, the tax laws maintain that all physical structures deteriorate (and lose value) over time. Cost recovery deductions may be taken only on personal property and improvements to land.

Depreciation taken periodically in equal amounts over an asset's useful life is called straight-line depreciation. For certain property purchased before 1987, it was also possible to use an accelerated cost recovery system (ACRS) to claim greater deductions in the early years of ownership, gradually reducing the amount deducted in each year of useful life. The Taxpayer Relief Act of 1997 established specific rules governing holding periods and taxability of depreciation for real property. Depreciation is set by statute. Currently, statutory depreciation is 27.5 years for residential real estate and 39 years for commercial real estate.

Exchanges

Real estate investors can defer taxation of capital gains by making property **exchanges.** Even property that has appreciated greatly since its initial purchase may be exchanged for other property. A property owner will incur tax liability on a sale only if additional capital or property is also received: the tax is *deferred*, not *eliminated*. Whenever the investor sells the property, the capital gain will be taxed. In many states, state income taxes can also be deferred by using the exchange form of property transfer.

To qualify as a tax-deferred exchange, the properties involved must be of *like kind* as defined under Section 1031 of the Internal Revenue Code. The exchanged property must be real estate of equal value and same use. Any additional capital or personal property included with the transaction to even out the value of the exchange is called **boot**. The IRS requires tax on the boot to be paid at the time of the exchange by the party who receives it. The value of the boot is added to the basis of the property for which it is given. Tax-deferred exchanges are governed by strict federal requirements, and competent guidance from a tax professional is essential.

■ **FOR EXAMPLE** A person owns an apartment building with an adjusted basis of $225,000 and a market value of $375,000. That person exchanges the building plus $75,000 in cash for another apartment building having a market value of $450,000. That building has an adjusted basis of $175,000. The owner's basis in the new building is $300,000 (the $225,000 basis of the building exchanged plus the $75,000 cash boot paid), and there is no tax liability on the exchange. The previous owner of the new building must pay tax on the $75,000 boot received and has a basis of $175,000 (the same as the previous building) in the building now owned.

Deductions

In addition to tax deductions for depreciation, investors may be able to deduct losses from their real estate investments. The tax laws are very complex. The amount of loss that may be deducted depends on whether an investor actively participates in the day-to-day management of the rental property or makes management decisions. Other factors are the amount of the loss and the source of the income from which the loss is to be deducted. Investors who do not actively participate in the management or operation of the real estate are considered passive investors. Passive investors may not use losses to offset active income derived from active participation in real estate management, wages, or income from stocks, bonds, and the like. The tax code cites specific rules for active and passive income and losses and may be subject to changes.

Certain tax credits are allowed for the renovation of older buildings, low-income housing projects, and historic property. A tax credit is a direct reduction in the tax due rather than a deduction from income before tax is computed. Tax credits encourage the revitalization of older properties and the creation of low-income housing.

Installment Sales

A taxpayer who sells real property and receives payment on an installment basis pays tax only on the profit portion of each payment received. Interest received is taxable as ordinary income.

REAL ESTATE INVESTMENT SYNDICATES

A real estate investment **syndicate** is a business venture in which people pool their resources to own or develop a particular piece of property. This structure permits people with only modest capital to invest in large-scale operations. Typical syndicate projects include highrise apartment buildings and shopping centers. Syndicate members realize some profit from rents collected on the investment. The main return usually comes when the syndicate sells the property.

Syndicate participation can take many legal forms. For instance, syndicate members may hold property as tenants in common or as joint tenants. Various kinds of partnership, corporate, and trust ownership options are possible.

Private syndication generally involves a small group of closely associated or experienced investors. Public syndication involves a much larger group of investors who may or may not be knowledgeable about real estate as an investment. Any pooling of individuals' funds raises questions of securities registration under federal and state securities laws, known as blue-sky laws.

REAL ESTATE INVESTMENT TRUSTS

By directing their funds into a **real estate investment trust (REIT)**, real estate investors take advantage of the same tax benefits as do mutual fund investors. A real estate investment trust does not have to pay corporate income tax as long as 95 percent of its income is distributed to its shareholders. Certain other conditions also must be met. To qualify as a REIT, at least 75 percent of the trust's income must come from real estate. Investors purchase certificates in the trust, which in turn invests in real estate or mortgages (or both). Profits are distributed to investors.

REAL ESTATE MORTGAGE INVESTMENT CONDUITS

A **real estate mortgage investment conduit (REMIC)** has complex qualification, transfer, and liquidation rules. For instance, the REMIC must satisfy the asset test. The asset test requires that after a start-up period, almost all assets must be qualified mortgages and permitted investments. Furthermore, investors' interests may consist of only one or more classes of regular interests and a single class of residual interests. Holders of regular interests receive interest or similar payments based on either a fixed rate or a variable rate. Holders of residual interests receive distributions (if any) on a pro rata basis.

■ KEY POINT REVIEW

Investment in real estate offers **advantages** of

- **leverage,** which is offered by the use of borrowed money;
- above-average rate of return, generally;
- greater control than ownership of securities;
- tax benefits in certain situations;
- **income (cash flow)** production; and
- possibility of property **appreciation** (increase in value over time).

Disadvantages of investment in real estate include

- lack of **liquidity** (ready conversion into cash),
- high cost to acquire,
- active management or cost of hiring a professional property manager, and
- high degree of **risk,** although an investor's ability to hold onto property long term tends to reduce risk.

Cash flow of income property, the amount remaining after all ownership expenses have been paid, tends to make it the safest form of real estate investment, but note the following:

- Rent paid by tenants is a major source of property income and depends on the property's location, physical appearance, and available amenities.
- When rent does not cover property expenses, negative cash flow results.

Pyramiding is a method of using the ownership of one property to drive the acquisition of more properties and usually consists of the following types:

- In pyramiding through selling, the investor acquires a property, improves it for resale at a substantially higher price, and then uses the profit from the sale to purchase another property.
- In pyramiding through refinance, the investor uses the refinance proceeds of one property to purchase new properties.

The tax benefits of owning investment real estate depend on current tax law.

- **Capital gain** is the difference between the adjusted cost basis of a property and its net selling price, and it may be taxed at a more favorable rate than a taxpayer's earned income.
- Adjusted cost basis is the investor's acquisition cost, plus the cost of any physical improvements made to the property, and less the amount of any **depreciation** claimed as a tax deduction.

- **Depreciation (cost recovery)** allows an investor to recover the cost of an income-producing asset through tax deductions over the asset's useful life:
  - Straight-line depreciation divides the cost attributable to the building by the number of years of projected useful life, currently set by federal law at 29.5 years for residential real estate and 39 years for commercial real estate.
  - Accelerated cost recovery system (ACRS) allows taxpayers to claim greater deductions in the early years of ownership, reducing the amount that may be deducted in each subsequent year of a property's defined useful life.
- Losses from the sale of a real estate investment may be deductible.
- Tax credits (direct reductions of tax owed) are available for the renovation of older buildings, low-income housing projects, and historic properties.

Exchanges offer investors the opportunity to defer the payment of taxes on profit indefinitely:

- Property may be **exchanged** for other like-kind property.
- Property owner is taxed only on additional capital or property received as part of the exchange (**boot**).
- Tax is **deferred** (not eliminated), with the capital gain taxed on the eventual sale.

A real estate investment syndicate is a business venture in which participants pool resources to own or develop property. Pooling of funds may involve securities registration under federal and state securities laws.

A **real estate investment trust (REIT)** does not pay corporate income tax as long as 95 percent of its income is distributed to its shareholders and other conditions are met. Restrictions and regulations on the formation and operation of REITs are complex.

A real estate mortgage investment conduit (REMIC) has complex qualification, transfer, and liquidation rules; it is notable because of the asset test requirement.

■ RELATED WEB SITES

American Investors in Real Estate Online: *www.aireo.com*
National Association of Real Estate Investment Trusts: *www.nariet.com*
National Real Estate Investors Association: *www.nationalreia.com*

CHAPTER 23 QUIZ

1. A small multifamily property generates $50,000 in rental income, $10,000 in expenses, and $35,000 in debt service. The property appreciates about $25,000 each year. What is the cash flow on this property?
   a. $5,000
   b. $15,000
   c. $25,000
   d. $30,000

2. Cash flow is
   a. equivalent to operating expense.
   b. the total amount of spendable income left after expenses.
   c. the use of borrowed money to finance an investment.
   d. selling costs plus depreciation.

3. The primary source of tax shelters in real estate investments comes from which accounting concept?
   a. Recapture
   b. Boot
   c. Net operating income
   d. Depreciation

4. A man made an initial real estate investment of $45,000. He subsequently made $20,000 worth of improvements to the property. If the man subtracts depreciation from the initial cost and adds the cost of improvements, what will be the result?
   a. Adjusted basis
   b. Capital gain
   c. Basis
   d. Salvage value

5. All of the following are associated with a Section 1031 exchange EXCEPT
   a. boot.
   b. qualified intermediary.
   c. like kind.
   d. the elimination of capital gains tax.

6. A woman refinanced her house and used the proceeds to purchase two rental properties. This method of increasing her holdings is called
   a. exchanging.
   b. pyramiding.
   c. syndicating.
   d. depreciating.

7. Which statement is TRUE about a syndicate?
   a. Members must hold title as joint tenants.
   b. Most profit on the investment is realized from rents.
   c. It is a private or public business venture to own property.
   d. Blue-sky laws do not apply.

8. A tax entity created by the Tax Reform Act of 1986 that issues securities backed by a pool of mortgages is a
   a. REIT.
   b. REMIC.
   c. limited partnership.
   d. pyramid.

9. A seller is selling an investment property. The original cost of the property was $80,000. The selling price is $125,000. The seller paid an 8 percent commission and $1,000 in closing costs. Two years ago, the seller made $10,000 worth of improvements to the property. Depreciation is $15,000. What is the seller's adjusted basis in the property?
   a. $65,000
   b. $75,000
   c. $80,000
   d. $90,000

10. Based on the information in Question 9, what is the seller's total capital gain?
    a. $39,000
    b. $45,000
    c. $80,000
    d. $90,000

11. Advantages of an investment in real estate include all of the following *EXCEPT*
    a. the possibility of a tax-deferred exchange.
    b. high liquidity.
    c. the use of leverage to increase rates of return.
    d. tax deductions.

12. The investor who sells property on an install-ment sale basis
    a. is taxed on all of the gain in the year the property is sold.
    b. is taxed on that part of the gain received in each year's installment payments.
    c. gives the buyer all the federal income tax liability.
    d. gives the buyer the privilege of deferring all the federal income tax liability.

13. One method a real estate investor may use to defer capital gains tax is to
    a. sell the property for cash only.
    b. obtain the maximum amount of leverage.
    c. exchange one property for a like-kind property.
    d. build a reserve account for items that are likely to wear out.

14. As part of a Section 1031 exchange, an investor had to give the other party $11,500 and a 1953 Chevrolet. The cash and car are
    a. equity.
    b. boot.
    c. collateral.
    d. like kind.

15. Which situation would result in the highest degree of leverage?
    a. Using your own funds entirely
    b. Using more of your own funds than those you borrow
    c. Using more of the funds you borrow than your own funds
    d. Using borrowed funds entirely

16. Someone looking for a tax-advantaged invest-ment similar to a mutual fund would probably invest in a
    a. real estate investment trust.
    b. general partnership.
    c. limited partnership.
    d. corporation.

17. When considering an investment in real estate, the prospective investor should consider all of the following *EXCEPT* the
    a. anticipated appreciation of the property.
    b. possible effects of inflation on the property.
    c. assessed valuation of the property.
    d. intrinsic value of the property.

18. *Cash flow* is a term that refers to the
    a. amount of money flowing into and out of a property.
    b. bookkeeping function that accounts for the cash each day.
    c. taxes, operating expenses, and loan pay-ments on the property.
    d. total amount of income left after all expenses have been paid.

19. Purchasing a property using leverage, refinanc-ing it after it has appreciated, and using the cash from the refinancing to purchase additional property is one form of
    a. plottage.
    b. pyramiding.
    c. consolidation.
    d. contribution.

20. The type of real estate investment that is required by federal law to distribute 95 percent of its income to its shareholders is the
    a. general partnership.
    b. limited partnership.
    c. real estate investment trust.
    d. time-share estate.

Web Links for State Statutes

Alabama: *www.legislature.state.al.us/CodeofAlabama/1975/coatoc.htm*
Alaska: *www.legis.state.ak.us/infolist.htm*
Arizona: *www.azleg.state.az.us/ArizonaRevisedStatutes.asp*
Arkansas: *www.arkleg.state.ar.us/bureau/Publications/Arkansas%20Code/
     ARCodeMainDoc.pdf*
California: *www.leginfo.ca.gov/calaw.html*
Colorado: *www.michie.com/colorado/*
Connecticut: *www.cga.ct.gov/asp/menu/statutes.asp*
District of Columbia:
     http://government.westlaw.com/linkedslice/default.asp?SP=DCC-1000
Florida: *www.leg.state.fl.us/statutes/*
Georgia: *www.lexis-nexis.com/hottopics/gacode/*
Hawaii: *www.capitol.hawaii.gov/session2010/*
Idaho: *www.legislature.idaho.gov/idstat/TOC/IDStatutesTOC.htm*
Illinois: *www.ilga.gov/legislation/ilcs/ilcs.asp*
Indiana: *www.in.gov/legislative/ic/code/*
Iowa: *www.legis.state.ia.us/IowaLaw.html*
Kansas: *www.kslegislature.org/legsrv-statutes/index.do*
Kentucky: *www.lrc.ky.gov/krs/titles.htm*
Louisiana: *www.legis.state.la.us/lss/tsrssearch.htm*
Maine: *www.mainelegislature.org/legis/statutes/*
Maryland: *www.sailor.lib.md.us/MD_topics/law/_cod.html*
Massachusetts: *www.mass.gov/legis/laws/mgl/*
Michigan: *www.legislature.mi.gov/doc.aspx?chapterindex*
Minnesota: *www.revisor.mn.gov/pubs/*
Mississippi: *www.michie.com/Mississippi/*
Missouri: *www.moga.mo.gov/statutesearch/*
Montana: *data.opi.state.mt.us/bills/mca_toc/index.htm*
Nebraska: *uniweb.legislature.ne.gov/laws/laws.php*
Nevada: *www.leg.state.nv.us/law1.cfm*
New Hampshire: *www.gencourt.state.nh.us/rsa/html/indexes/*
New Jersey: *www.njlawnet.com/njstatutes.html*
New Mexico:
     www.conwaygreene.com/nmsu/lpext.dll?f=templates&fn=main-h.htm&2.0
New York:
     http://public.leginfo.state.ny.us/menugetf.cgi?COMMONQUERY=LAWS
North Carolina: *www.ncga.state.nc.us/gascripts/Statutes/Statutes.asp*
North Dakota: *www.legis.nd.gov/information/statutes/cent-code.html*

Ohio: *http://codes.ohio.gov/orc/*
Oregon: *www.leg.state.or.us/ors/*
Pennsylvania: *www.pacode.com*
Rhode Island: *www.rilin.state.ri.us/statutes/*
South Carolina: *www.scstatehouse.net/code/statmast.htm*
South Dakota: *http://legis.state.sd.us/statutes/*
Tennessee: *www.tennesseeanytime.org/laws/laws.html*
Texas: *www.statutes.legis.state.tx.us*
Utah: *www.le.state.ut.us/~code/code.htm*
Vermont: *www.leg.state.vt.us/statutes/statutes2.htm*
Virginia: *legis.state.va.us/Laws/CodeofVa.htm*
Washington: *http://apps.leg.wa.gov/rcw/*
West Virginia: *www.legis.state.wv.us/WVCODE/Code.cfm*
Wisconsin: *www.legis.state.wi.us/rsb/statutes.html*
Wyoming: *http://legisweb.state.wy.us/titles/statutes.htm*

Web Links

■ CHAPTER 1

American Society of Home Inspectors: *www.ashi.org*
Appraisal Institute: *www.appraisalinstitute.org*
Building Owners and Managers Association International: *www.boma.org*
Commercial Investment Real Estate Institute: *www.ccim.com*
Counselors of Real Estate: *www.cre.org*
Fannie Mae: *www.fanniemae.com*
Federal Reserve Board: *www.federalreserve.gov*
Freddie Mac: *www.freddiemac.com*
Ginnie Mae: *www.ginniemae.gov*
Institute of Real Estate Management: *www.irem.org*
National Association of Exclusive Buyer Agents: *www.naeba.org*
National Association of Independent Fee Appraisers: *www.naifa.com*
National Association of Real Estate Brokers: *www.nareb.com*
National Association of REALTORS®: *www.realtor.org*
Real Estate Buyer's Agent Council: *www.rebac.net*
Real Estate Educators Association: *www.reea.org*
U.S. Department of Housing and Urban Development: *www.hud.gov*

■ CHAPTER 2

Manufactured Housing Institute: *www.manufacturedhousing.org*
Alabama Real Estate Commission: *www.arec.alabama.gov*
Alaska Real Estate Commission: *www.commerce.state.ak.us/occ/prec.htm*
Arizona Department of Real Estate: *www.re.state.az.us*
Arkansas Real Estate Commission: *www.state.ar.us/arec/frmain.htm*
California Department of Real Estate: *www.dre.ca.gov*
Colorado Department of Regulatory Agencies, Division of Real Estate:
    www.dora.state.co.us/real-estate/
Connecticut Department of Consumer Protection: *www.state.ct.us/dcp/*
District of Columbia Real Estate Commission: *app.dcra.dc.gov*
Florida Department of Business and Professional Regulation:
    www.myfloridalicense.com/dbpr/
Georgia Real Estate Commission: *www.grec.state.ga.us*

Hawaii Department of Commerce and Consumer Affairs, Real Estate
Branch: *www.hawaii.gov/dcca/real/*
Idaho Real Estate Commission: *www.idahorealestatecommission.com*
Illinois Division of Professional Regulation:
www.idfpr.com/DPR/RE/realmain.asp
Indiana Professional Licensing Agency: *www.ai.org/pla/real.htm*
Iowa Real Estate Commission:
www.state.ia.us/government/com/prof/sales/home.html
Kansas Real Estate Commission: *www.accesskansas.org/krec*
Kentucky Real Estate Commission: *www.krec.ky.gov*
Louisiana Real Estate Commission: *www.lrec.state.la.us*
Maine Real Estate Commission:
www.maine.gov/pfr/professionallicensing/professions/real_estate/
Maryland Real Estate Commission: *www.dllr.state.md.us/license/mrec/*
Massachusetts Division of Registration: *www.state.ma.us/reg/*
Michigan Department of Energy, Labor and Economic Growth:
www.michigan.gov/dleg/
Minnesota Department of Commerce: *www.commerce.state.mn.us*
Mississippi Real Estate Commission: *www.mrec.state.ms.us*
Missouri Real Estate Commission: *www.pr.mo.gov/realestate.asp*
Montana Department of Commerce: *www.commerce.mt.gov/*
Nebraska Real Estate Commission: *www.nrec.state.ne.us/*
Nevada Real Estate Division: *www.red.state.nv.us*
New Hampshire Real Estate Commission: *www.nh.gov/nhrec/*
New Jersey Real Estate Commission: *www.state.nj.us/dobi/division_rec/*
New Mexico Real Estate Commission:
www.rld.state.nm.us/realestatecommission/
New York Department of State, Division of Licensing Services:
www.dos.state.ny.us/lcns/
North Carolina Real Estate Commission: *www.ncrec.state.nc.us*
Ohio Division of Real Estate and Professional Licensing:
www.com.state.oh.us/real/
Oregon Real Estate Agency: *www.rea.state.or.us*
Pennsylvania Real Estate Commission: *www.dos.state.pa.us/bpoa*
South Carolina Real Estate Commission: *www.llr.state.sc.us/pol/rec/*
South Dakota Real Estate Commission: *www.state.sd.us/sdrec/*
Tennessee Real Estate Commission: *www.state.tn.us/commerce/boards/trec/*
Texas Real Estate Commission: *www.trec.state.tx.us*
Utah Division of Real Estate: *www.realestate.utah.gov*
Vermont Real Estate Commission: *www.vtprofessionals.org/opr1/real_estate*
Virginia Department of Professional and Occupational Regulation:
www.dpor.virginia.gov/dporweb/
Washington State Department of Licensing, Real Estate:
www.dol.wa.gov/business/realestate/
West Virginia Real Estate Commission: *www.wvrec.org*
Wisconsin Department of Regulation and Licensing: *www.drl.wi.gov*
Wyoming Real Estate Commission: *http://realestate.state.wy.us*

■ CHAPTER 3

Federal Emergency Management Agency: *www.fema.org*
U.S. Department of Housing and Urban Development: *www.hud.gov*
U.S. Department of Veterans Affairs: *www.va.gov*

■ CHAPTER 4

National Association of REALTORS®:   *www.realtor.org*

■ CHAPTER 5

Association of Real Estate License Law Officials: *www.arello.org*
Internet Listing Display Policy: *www.realtor.org/ild/*
National Do Not Call Registry: *www.donotcall.gov*
Uniform Electronic Transactions Act:
    www.law.upenn.edu/bll/archives/ulc/fnact99/1990s/ueta99.htm
U.S. Department of Justice, Antitrust Division: *www.justice.gov/atr/*
U.S. Internal Revenue Service: *www.irs.gov*

■ CHAPTER 7

Eminent Domain: *www.realtor.org/realtororg.nsf/pages/EminentDomain/*
Interests in Real Estate: *topics.law.cornell.edu/wex/Real_property/*

■ CHAPTER 8

Business Link to the U.S. Government: *www.business.gov*
Legal Information Institute, Uniform Condominium Act:
    www.law.cornell.edu/uniform/vol7.html#condo
U.S. Small Business Administration: *www.sba.gov*

■ CHAPTER 9

U.S. Geological Survey: *www.usgs.gov*

■ CHAPTER 10

U.S. Internal Revenue Service: *www.irs.gov*

■ CHAPTER 11

FindLaw: Contract Law: *www.findlaw.com/01topics/07contracts/*

■ CHAPTER 14

Legal Information Institute, Mortgages:
   http://topics.law.cornell.edu/wex/Mortgage/

■ CHAPTER 15

Fannie Mae: *www.fanniemae.com*
Farm Credit Network: *www.farmcreditnetwork.com*
Federal Reserve Board: *www.federalreserve.gov*
Freddie Mac: *www.freddiemac.com*
Ginnie Mae: *www.ginniemae.gov*
Mortgage Banker's Association: *www.mbaa.org*
National Association of Mortgage Bankers: *www.namb.org*
National Reverse Mortgage Lenders Association: *www.reversemortgage.org*
U.S. Department of Agriculture Rural Development Agency:
   www.rurdev.usda.gov
U.S. Department of Housing and Urban Development: *www.hud.gov*
U.S. Department of Veterans Affairs: *www.va.gov*
U.S. Farm Service Agency: *www.fsa.usda.gov*

■ CHAPTER 16

Legal Information Institute: Landlord-Tenant Law:
   http://topics.law.cornell.edu/wex/landlord tenant_law/

■ CHAPTER 17

American Management Association: *www.amanet.org*
Building Owners and Managers Association International: *www.boma.org*
Independent Institute for Property and Facility Management Education:
   www.bomi.org
Institute of Real Estate Management: *www.irem.org/home.cfm*
National Association of Home Builders: *www.nahb.com*
National Association of Residential Property Managers: *www.narpm.org*
U.S. Department of Justice, Civil Rights Division:
   www.justice.gov/crt/drs/drshome.php

■ CHAPTER 18

American Society of Appraisers: *www.appraisers.org*
American Society of Farm Managers and Rural Appraisers, Inc.:
   www.asfmra.org
Appraisal Foundation: *www.appraisalfoundation.org*
Appraisal Institute: *www.appraisalinstitute.org*
International Right of Way Association: *www.irwaonline.org*
National Association of Independent Fee Appraisers: *www.naifa.com*

■ CHAPTER 19

U.S. Department of Housing and Urban Development: Housing Discrimination:
   http://portal.hud.gov/portal/page/portal/HUD/topics/housing_discrimination/
U.S. Department of Housing and Urban Development: Office of Housing:
   http://portal.hud.gov/portal/page/portal/HUD/program_offices/housing/

■ CHAPTER 20

Legal Information Institute: *www.law.cornell.edu*
National Association of REALTORS®: Code of Ethics:
   www.realtor.org/mempolweb.nsf/pages/code/
National Fair Housing Advocate Online: *www.fairhousing.com*
U.S. Department of Housing and Urban Development: Fair Housing:
   http://portal.hud.gov/portal/page/portal/HUD/groups/fairhousing
U.S. Department of Housing and Urban Development: Fair Housing Laws and
   Presidential Executive Orders: *www.hud.gov/offices/fheo/FHLaws/index.cfm*
U.S. Department of Housing and Urban Development: Fair Housing Library:
   http://portal.hud.gov/portal/page/portal/HUD/library/bookshelf09/
U.S. Department of Housing and Urban Development: Fair Housing Logo:
   www.hud.gov/library/bookshelf15/hudgraphics/fheologo.cfm
U.S. Department of Housing and Urban Development: Housing Discrimination
   Complaints: *www.hud.gov/offices/fheo/complaint-process.cfm*
U.S. Department of Housing and Urban Development: Non-Discrimination and
   Accessibility for Persons with Disabilities:
   http://portal.hud.gov/portal/page/portal/HUD/program_offices/administration/
   hudclips/notices/pih/files/10-02pihn.doc
U.S. Department of Housing and Urban Development: People with Disabilities
   Frequently Asked Questions:
   www.hud.gov/offices/fheo/disabilities/sect504faq.cfm
U.S. Department of Housing and Urban Development: Public Service
   Announcements: *www.hud.gov/offices/fheo/adcampaign.cfm*

■ CHAPTER 21

Consumer Product Safety Commission: *www.cpsc.gov*
Legal Information Institute: Court Opinions: *www.law.cornell.edu/co.html*
National Safety Council Environmental Health Center: Lead:
 www.nsc.org/news_resources/Resources/Documents/Lead_Poisoning.pdf
U.S. Environmental Protection Agency: *www.epa.gov*
U.S. Environmental Protection Agency: Asbestos: *www.epa.gov/oppt/asbestos/*
U.S. Environmental Protection Agency: CERCLA/Superfund:
 www.epa.gov/superfund/policy/cercla.htm
U.S. Environmental Protection Agency: Compliance and Enforcement:
 www.epa.gov/compliance/
U.S. Environmental Protection Agency: Formaldehyde:
 www.epa.gov/iaq/formalde.html
U.S. Environmental Protection Agency: Indoor Air Quality: Mold:
 www.epa.gov/mold/
U.S. Environmental Protection Agency: Indoor Air Quality: Radon:
 www.epa.gov/radon/
U.S. Environmental Protection Agency: Lead: *www.epa.gov/lead/*
U.S. Environmental Protection Agency: Lead-Based Paint Disclosure
 Forms: *www.epa.gov/lead/pubs/leadbase.htm*
U.S. Environmental Protection Agency: Mold Remediation:
 www.epa.gov/mold/mold_remediation.html

■ CHAPTER 22

U.S. Department of Housing and Urban Development: RESPA:
 www.hud.gov/offices/hsg/ramh/res/respa_hm.cfm
U.S. Department of Housing and Urban Development: RESPA FAQs:
 www.hud.gov/offices/hsg/ramh/res/resparulefaqs.pdf

■ CHAPTER 23

American Investors in Real Estate Online: *www.aireo.com*
National Association of Real Estate Investment Trusts: *www.nariet.com*
National Real Estate Investors Association: *www.nationalreia.com*

■ WEB LINKS IN ALPHABETICAL ORDER

Alabama Real Estate Commission: *www.arec.alabama.gov*
Alaska Real Estate Commission: *www.commerce.state.ak.us/occ/prec.htm*
American Investors in Real Estate Online: *www.aireo.com*
American Management Association: *www.amanet.org*
American Society of Appraisers: *www.appraisers.org*
American Society of Farm Managers and Rural Appraisers, Inc.:
 www.asfmra.org
American Society of Home Inspectors: *www.ashi.org*

Appraisal Foundation: *www.appraisalfoundation.org*

Appraisal Institute: *www.appraisalinstitute.org*

Arizona Department of Real Estate: *www.re.state.az.us*

Arkansas Real Estate Commission: *www.state.ar.us/arec/frmain.htm*

Association of Real Estate License Law Officials: *www.arello.org*

Building Owners and Managers Association International: *www.boma.org*

Business Link to the U.S. Government: *www.business.gov*

California Department of Real Estate: *www.dre.ca.gov*

Colorado Department of Regulatory Agencies, Division of Real Estate: *www.dora.state.co.us/real-estate/*

Commercial Investment Real Estate Institute: *www.ccim.com*

Consumer Product Safety Commission: *www.cpsc.gov*

Connecticut Department of Consumer Protection: *www.state.ct.us/dcp/*

Counselors of Real Estate: *www.cre.org*

District of Columbia Real Estate Commission: *www.app.dcra.dc.gov*

Eminent Domain: *www.realtor.org/realtororg.nsf/pages/EminentDomain/*

Fannie Mae: *www.fanniemae.com*

Farm Credit Network: *www.farmcreditnetwork.com*

Federal Emergency Management Agency: *www.fema.gov*

Federal Reserve Board: *www.federalreserve.gov*

FindLaw: Contract Law: *www.findlaw.com/01topics/07contracts/*

Florida Department of Business and Professional Regulation: *www.myfloridalicense.com/dbpr/*

Freddie Mac: *www.freddiemac.com*

Georgia Real Estate Commission: *www.grec.state.ga.us*

Ginnie Mae: *www.ginniemae.gov*

Hawaii Department of Commerce and Consumer Affairs: Real Estate Branch: *www.hawaii.gov/dcca/real/*

Idaho Real Estate Commission: *www.idahorealestatecommission.com*

Illinois Division of Professional Regulation: *www.idfpr.com/DPR/RE/realmain.asp*

Independent Institute for Property and Facility Management Education: *www.bomi.org*

Indiana Professional Licensing Agency: *www.ai.org/pla/real.htm*

Institute of Real Estate Management: *www.irem.org/home.cfm*

Interests in Real Estate: *http://topics.law.cornell.edu/wex/Real_property/*

International Right of Way Association: *www.irwaonline.org*

Internet Listing Display Policy: *www.realtor.org/ild/*

Iowa Real Estate Commission: *www.state.ia.us/government/com/prof/sales/home.html*

Kansas Real Estate Commission: *www.accesskansas.org/krec*

Kentucky Real Estate Commission: *www.krec.ky.gov*

Legal Information Institute: *www.law.cornell.edu*

Legal Information Institute: Court Opinions: *www.law.cornell.edu/co.html*

Legal Information Institute: Landlord-Tenant Law: *http://topics.law.cornell.edu/wex/landlord-tenant_law/*

Legal Information Institute: Mortgages: *http://topics.law.cornell.edu/wex/Mortgage/*

Legal Information Institute: Uniform Condominium Act: *www.law.cornell.edu/uniform/vol7.html#condo*

Louisiana Real Estate Commission: *www.lrec.state.la.us*
Maine Real Estate Commission:
   www.maine.gov/pfr/professionallicensing/professions/real_estate/
Manufactured Housing Institute: *www.manufacturedhousing.org*
Maryland Real Estate Commission: *www.dllr.state.md.us/license/mrec/*
Massachusetts Division of Registration: *www.state.ma.us/reg*
Michigan Department of Energy, Labor and Economic Growth:
   www.michigan.gov/dleg/
Minnesota Department of Commerce: *www.commerce.state.mn.us*
Mississippi Real Estate Commission: *www.mrec.state.ms.us*
Missouri Real Estate Commission: *www.pr.mo.gov/realestate.asp*
Montana Department of Commerce: *www.commerce.mt.gov/*
Mortgage Banker's Association: *www.mbaa.org*
National Association of Exclusive Buyer Agents: *www.naeba.org*
National Association of Home Builders: *www.nahb.com*
National Association of Independent Fee Appraisers: *www.naifa.com*
National Association of Mortgage Bankers: *www.namb.org*
National Association of Real Estate Brokers: *www.nareb.com*
National Association of Real Estate Investment Trusts: *www.nariet.com*
National Real Estate Investors Association: *www.nationalreia.com*
National Association of REALTORS®: *www.realtor.org*
National Association of REALTORS®: Code of Ethics:
   www.realtor.org/mempolweb.nsf/pages/code/
National Association of Residential Property Managers: *www.narpm.org*
National Do Not Call Registry: *www.donotcall.gov*
National Fair Housing Advocate Online: *www.fairhousing.com*
National Reverse Mortgage Lenders Association: *www.reversemortgage.org*
National Safety Council Environmental Health Center: Lead:
   www.nsc.org/news_resources/Resources/Documents/Lead_Poisoning.pdf
Nebraska Real Estate Commission: *www.nrec.state.ne.us/*
Nevada Real Estate Division: *www.red.state.nv.us*
New Hampshire Real Estate Commission: *www.nh.gov/nhrec/*
New Jersey Real Estate Commission: *www.state.nj.us/dobi/division_rec/*
New Mexico Real Estate Commission:
   www.rld.state.nm.us/realestatecommission/
New York Department of State, Division of Licensing Services:
   www.dos.state.ny.us/lcns/
North Carolina Real Estate Commission: *www.ncrec.state.nc.us*
Ohio Division of Real Estate and Professional Licensing:
   www.com.state.oh.us/real/
Oregon Real Estate Agency: *www.rea.state.or.us*
Pennsylvania Real Estate Commission: *www.dos.state.pa.us/bpoa*
Real Estate Buyer's Agent Council: *www.rebac.net*
Real Estate Educators Association: *www.reea.org*
South Carolina Real Estate Commission: *www.llr.state.sc.us/pol/rec/*
South Dakota Real Estate Commission: *www.state.sd.us/sdrec/*
Tennessee Real Estate Commission: *www.state.tn.us/commerce/boards/trec/*
Texas Real Estate Commission: *www.trec.state.tx.us*
Uniform Electronic Transactions Act:
   www.law.upenn.edu/bll/archives/ulc/fnact99/1990s/ueta99.htm

U.S. Department of Agriculture Rural Development Agency:
www.rurdev.usda.gov

U.S. Department of Housing and Urban Development: *www.hud.gov*

U.S. Department of Housing and Urban Development: Fair Housing:
http://portal.hud.gov/portal/page/portal/HUD/groups/fairhousing

U.S. Department of Housing and Urban Development: Fair Housing Laws and
Presidential Executive Orders: *www.hud.gov/offices/fheo/FHLaws/index.cfm*

U.S. Department of Housing and Urban Development: Fair Housing Library:
http://portal.hud.gov/portal/page/portal/HUD/library/bookshelf09/

U.S. Department of Housing and Urban Development: Fair Housing Logo:
www.hud.gov/library/bookshelf15/hudgraphics/fheologo.cfm

U.S. Department of Housing and Urban Development: Housing Discrimination:
portal.hud.gov/portal/page/portal/HUD/topics/housing_discrimination/

U.S. Department of Housing and Urban Development: Housing Discrimination
Complaints: *www.hud.gov/offices/fheo/complaint-process.cfm*

U.S. Department of Housing and Urban Development: Non-Discrimination and
Accessibility for Persons with Disabilities:
http://portal.hud.gov/portal/page/portal/HUD/program_offices/administration/
hudclips/notices/pih/files/10-02pihn.doc

U.S. Department of Housing and Urban Development: Office of Housing:
http://portal.hud.gov/portal/page/portal/HUD/program_offices/housing/

U.S. Department of Housing and Urban Development: People with Disabilities
Frequently Asked Questions:
www.hud.gov/offices/fheo/disabilities/sect504faq.cfm

U.S. Department of Housing and Urban Development: Public Service
Announcements: *www.hud.gov/offices/fheo/adcampaign.cfm*

U.S. Department of Housing and Urban Development: RESPA:
www.hud.gov/offices/hsg/ramh/res/respa_hm.cfm

U.S. Department of Housing and Urban Development: RESPA FAQs:
www.hud.gov/offices/hsg/ramh/res/resparulefaqs.pdf

U.S. Department of Justice, Antitrust Division: *www.justice.gov/atr/*

U.S. Department of Justice, Civil Rights Division:
www.justice.gov/crt/drs/drshome.php

U.S. Department of Veterans Affairs: *www.va.gov*

U.S. Environmental Protection Agency: *www.epa.gov*

U.S. Environmental Protection Agency: Asbestos: *www.epa.gov/oppt/asbestos/*

U.S. Environmental Protection Agency: CERCLA/Superfund:
www.epa.gov/superfund/policy/cercla.htm

U.S. Environmental Protection Agency: Compliance and Enforcement:
www.epa.gov/compliance/

U.S. Environmental Protection Agency: Formaldehyde:
www.epa.gov/iaq/formalde.html

U.S. Environmental Protection Agency: Lead: *www.epa.gov/lead/*

U.S. Environmental Protection Agency: Lead-Based Paint Disclosure Forms:
www.epa.gov/lead/pubs/leadbase.htm

U.S. Environmental Protection Agency: Indoor Air Quality: Mold:
www.epa.gov/mold/

U.S. Environmental Protection Agency: Indoor Air Quality: Radon:
www.epa.gov/radon/

U.S. Environmental Protection Agency: Mold Remediation:
  www.epa.gov/mold/mold_remediation.html
U.S. Farm Service Agency: *www.fsa.usda.gov*
U.S. Geological Survey: *www.usgs.gov*
U.S. Internal Revenue Service: *www.irs.gov*
U.S. Small Business Administration: *www.sba.gov*
Utah Division of Real Estate: *www.realestate.utah.gov*
Vermont Real Estate Commission: *www.vtprofessionals.org/opr1/real_estate*
Virginia Department of Professional and Occupational Regulation:
  www.dpor.virginia.gov/dporweb/
Washington State Department of Licensing, Real Estate:
  www.dol.wa.gov/business/realestate/
West Virginia Real Estate Commission: *www.wvrec.org*
Wisconsin Department of Regulation and Licensing: *www.drl.wi.gov*
Wyoming Real Estate Commission: *http://realestate.state.wy.us*

MATH FAQs

Answers to Your Most Frequently
Asked Real Estate Math Questions

MATH FAQS CONTENTS

Math FAQS Introduction

Math is an integral part of the real estate profession. The amount and complexity of the math you encounter will vary, depending on your chosen area of real estate. Calculators and computers are great time-savers, but licensees still need a solid, basic knowledge of math. It is a matter of taking the math concepts and adapting them to the real estate profession.

People react differently to the word *math*. Some people like math. Some people are comfortable with math. Some people, though, are uncomfortable with math and become anxious and stressed when they encounter numbers. If you're that kind of person, you will find the approach taken here to be helpful. Even if you're someone who's comfortable working with numbers, this clear and simple review will reinforce what you know—and maybe teach you a few tricks and shortcuts, too.

This review covers the basics of real estate math to prepare you for the real-world situations you will encounter, as well as the math problems you will most likely find on your real estate licensing examination.

Study, review, and practice will help you overcome stress and anxiety so you can become comfortable with math. With practice and review, your confidence and ability in real estate math will grow.

■ USING THIS MATH REVIEW

This math review is designed to provide you with a quick check of your math knowledge and to help reinforce what you already know. It's organized in a way that makes it easy to look up just the information you need. The subject matter is presented in a straightforward manner with a minimum of wordy explanations and a maximum of quick tips, examples, formulas, memory aids, and shortcuts to help you become confident in real estate math.

Divided into sections, this review is organized into the following five general subject areas:

1. Calculators
2. Measurement
3. Fractions
4. Percentages
5. Proration

Within each general subject heading are a series of frequently asked questions (FAQs) and brief, clear explanations. If you read Math FAQs through from start to finish, you'll get a good, general review of real estate math principles. You also can use Math FAQs for a last-minute review of difficult issues or even as a reference in your daily real estate practice. Check the Math FAQs contents to see if your question is listed. If your question is more complicated or fact-specific, you may need to look at several different items to find your answer.

■ SPECIAL FEATURES

Throughout the text you will find **Math Tips** that offer insight into the trickier aspects of real estate math in general and the real estate exam's math content in particular. The **For Example** feature applies formulas and concepts to practical situations to show how the concept works in the real world. A generous collection of practice problems at the end of the review provides the opportunity to apply your understanding in an exam-style context. The **T-Bar method** is offered as a shortcut that's easy to understand and easy to apply.

1

Introduction to Calculators

Basic calculators are permitted when taking most state licensing examinations. The rules usually require that the calculator be silent, handheld, battery-operated, and nonprinting. Many states will not allow test takers to use a real estate or financial calculator while taking the real estate exam. Check with your state regarding the appropriate calculator for your exam.

■ WHAT KIND OF CALCULATOR DO I NEED?

A calculator that will add (+), subtract (−), multiply (×), and divide (÷) is all that is needed for licensing examinations. A calculator with a battery only or solar power with a battery backup is recommended over solar-powered only. Choose a calculator that is most comfortable for you; allow yourself time to learn to use it correctly and to become comfortable with it before you take the licensing examination.

■ WHAT ARE THE SPECIFIC REAL ESTATE FUNCTIONS I SHOULD LOOK FOR?

Many business or financial calculators have additional functions that are very beneficial to the real estate professional. Some of the keys you would want are "N" (number of interest compounding periods/number of payments), "I" (interest rate per period), "PV" (present value of money/loan), "PMT" (amount of payment), and "FV" (future value of money). Business or financial calculators vary according to brand and/or model; therefore, the user's manual should always be followed to use the calculator properly. For example, some have "TERM" instead of "N"; therefore, you enter the number of years of the term instead of the number of payments or compounding periods. Some have "LOAN" instead of "PV." Some instruct you to enter the interest rate as an annual rate instead of a monthly rate. You may wish to purchase a business or financial calculator that contains these extra functions. Check with your state real estate commission to see if you will be permitted to use them during the exam.

MATH TIP Be careful! Business or financial calculators are often set at the factory to round to two decimals. Follow the user's manual and set the decimal to float to a minimum of five decimals. This will enable you to arrive at an answer with enough decimals to match multiple-choice answers on exams. No matter which calculator you choose, *read the user's manual.*

■ HOW DO I USE THE PERCENT KEY?

If you use the "%" key on calculators to solve percentage problems, read the user's manual for the key's proper use. Some calculators require the use of the "%" key or the "=" key *but never both in the same calculation.* Other calculators require the use of *both* the "%" key and the "=" key to get a correct answer. No matter which calculator you choose, *read the user's manual.*

■ **FOR EXAMPLE** If a property sold for $100,000 and a 7 percent commission was paid to the broker, how much was the broker paid?

This question may be worked two ways, as illustrated below.

Convert 7 percent to the decimal 0.07. (How to convert percents to decimals is shown in Section 3.) Touch $100,000 into your calculator, then the × or multiplication key, then 0.07, then the = key to read $7,000.

Or, touch in $100,000, then the × or multiplication key, then 7, then the % key. If your calculator now reads $7,000, you've finished the question. If when you touch the % key, it reads 0.07, then you must touch the = key to complete the calculation.

The use of the % key allows the calculator to convert to the proper decimal place, and there's no question about the placement of the decimal. The choice is yours: you can convert the percent to a decimal or use the % key for the conversion.

FIGURE 1.1

Calculator Functions to Look For

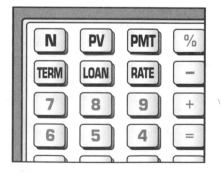

Measurement Problems

■ WHAT ARE LINEAR MEASUREMENTS?

Linear measures are used for length or distance (e.g., length of a wall). Linear measures include feet, yards, inches, and miles. Linear feet are sometimes called running feet and are used to measure frontage (front feet) on a road or lake. **Linear measurement** is line measurement. When the terms

- ■ *foot,*
- ■ *linear foot,*
- ■ *running foot,* or
- ■ *front foot*

are used, you are being asked to determine the *total length* of the object, whether measured in a straight line, crooked line, or curved line. The abbreviation for feet is '. Thus, 12 feet can be written as 12'. The abbreviation for inches is ". Thus, 12 inches can be written as 12".

■ WHAT DOES THE TERM *FRONT FOOT* REFER TO?

When the term *front foot* is used, you are dealing with the number of units on the **frontage** of a lot. The frontage is usually the street frontage, but it might be the water frontage if the lot is on a river, lake, or ocean. If two dimensions are given for a tract of land and they are not labeled, the first dimension is the frontage. The word *width* also means frontage; the length is called the *depth*.

■ HOW DO I CONVERT ONE KIND OF LINEAR MEASUREMENT TO ANOTHER?

12 inches = 1 foot
  Inches ÷ 12 = Feet (144 inches ÷ 12 = 12 feet)
  Feet × 12 = Inches (12 feet × 12 = 144 inches)

36 inches = 1 yard
  Inches ÷ 36 = Yards (144 inches ÷ 36 = 4 yards)
  Yards × 36 = Inches (4 yards × 36 = 144 inches)

3 feet = 1 yard
> Feet ÷ 3 = Yards (12 feet ÷ 3 = 4 yards)
> Yards × 3 = Feet (4 yards × 3 = 12 feet)

5,280 feet = 1 mile
> Feet ÷ 5,280 = Miles (10,560 feet ÷ 5,280 = 2 miles)
> Miles × 5,280 = Feet (2 miles × 5,280 = 10,560 feet)

16½ feet = 1 rod
> Feet ÷ 16.5 = Rods (82.5 feet ÷ 16.5 = 5 rods)
> Rods × 16.5 = Feet (5 rods × 16.5 = 82.5 feet)

320 rods = 1 mile
> Rods ÷ 320 = Miles (640 rods ÷ 320 = 2 miles)
> Miles × 320 = Rods (2 miles × 320 = 640 rods)

■ **FOR EXAMPLE** A rectangular lot is 50 feet by 150 feet. The cost to fence this lot is priced per linear/running foot. How many linear/running feet will be used to calculate the price of the fence?

50 feet + 150 feet + 50 feet + 150 feet = 400 linear/running feet

400 linear/running feet is the answer.

■ **FOR EXAMPLE** A parcel of land that fronts on Interstate 45 in Houston, Texas, is for sale at $5,000 per front foot. What will it cost to purchase this parcel of land if the dimensions are 150 feet by 100 feet?

150 is the frontage because it is the first dimension given.

150 front feet × $5,000 = $750,000 cost

$750,000 is the answer.

■ HOW DO I SOLVE FOR AREA MEASUREMENT?

Area is the two-dimensional surface of an object. Area is quoted in *square units* or in *acres*. A linear measure multiplied by another linear measure always equals a square measure: feet times feet equals square feet, miles times miles equals square miles, yards times yards equals square yards, and so on. We will look at calculating the area of squares, rectangles, and triangles. Squares and rectangles are four-sided objects. All four sides of a square are the same. Opposite sides of a rectangle are the same. A triangle is a three-sided object. The three sides of a triangle can be the same dimension or three different dimensions.

MATH TIP When two dimensions are given, assume it to be a rectangle unless told otherwise.

◼ HOW DO I CONVERT ONE KIND OF AREA MEASUREMENT TO ANOTHER?

144 square inches = 1 square foot
> Square inches ÷ 144 = Square feet (14,400 square inches ÷ 144 = 100 square feet)
> Square feet × 144 = Square inches ÷ (100 square feet × 144 = 14,400 square inches)

1,296 square inches = 1 square yard
> Square inches ÷ 1,296 = Square yards (12,960 ÷ 1,296 = 10 square yards)
> Square yards × 1,296 = Square inches (10 square yards × 1,296 = 12,960 square yards)

9 square feet = 1 square yard
> Square feet ÷ 9 = Square yards (90 square feet ÷ 9 = 10 square yards)
> Square yards × 9 = Square feet (10 square yards × 9 = 90 square feet)

43,560 square feet = 1 acre
> Square feet ÷ 43,560 = Acres (87,120 ÷ 43,560 = 2 acres)
> Acres × 43,560 = Square feet (2 acres × 43,560 = 87,120 square feet)

640 acres = 1 section = 1 square mile
> Acres ÷ 640 = Sections (square miles) (1,280 acres ÷ 640 = 2 sections)
> Sections (square miles) × 640 = Acres (2 sections × 640 = 1,280 acres)

◼ HOW DO I DETERMINE THE AREA OF A SQUARE OR RECTANGLE?

Length × Width = **Area of a square or rectangle**

◼ **FOR EXAMPLE** How many square feet are in a room 15'6" × 30'9"? Remember, we must use like dimensions, so the inches must be converted to foot.

6" ÷ 12 = 0.5' + 15' = 15.5' wide

9" ÷ 12 = 0.75' + 30' = 30.75' long

30.75' × 15.5' = 476.625 square feet

476.625 square feet is the answer.

◼ **FOR EXAMPLE** If carpet costs $63 per square yard to install, what would it cost to carpet the room in the previous example?

476.625 square feet ÷ 9 = 52.958333 square yards × $63 per square yard = $3,336.375, or $3,336.38 rounded

$3,336.38 is the answer.

■ **FOR EXAMPLE**   How many acres are there in a parcel of land that measures 450' × 484'?

484' × 450' = 217,800 square feet ÷ 43,560 = 5 acres of land

5 acres is the answer.

■ HOW DO I DETERMINE THE AREA OF A TRIANGLE?

½ Base × Height = **Area of a triangle**

or

Base × Height ÷ 2 = **Area of a triangle**

■ **FOR EXAMPLE**   How many square feet are contained in a triangular parcel of land that is 400 feet on the base and 200 feet high?

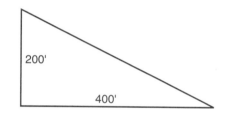

400' × 200' ÷ 2 = 40,000 square feet

40,000 square feet is the answer.

■ **FOR EXAMPLE**   How many acres are in a three-sided tract of land that is 300' on the base and 400' high?

300' × 400' ÷ 2 = 60,000 square feet ÷ 43,560 = 1.377 acres

1.377 acres is the answer.

■ HOW DO I SOLVE FOR VOLUME?

Volume is the space inside a three-dimensional object. Volume is measured in *cubic units*. We will look at calculating the volume of boxes and triangular prisms because there are three measures (length, width, and height). Multiplying three measures results in cubic units; for example, feet times feet times feet equals cubic feet.

■ HOW DO I CONVERT FROM ONE KIND OF VOLUME MEASUREMENT TO ANOTHER?

1,728 cubic inches = 1 cubic foot
   Cubic inches ÷ 1,728 = Cubic feet
   (17,280 cubic inches ÷ 1,728 = 10 cubic feet)

   Cubic feet × 1,728 = Cubic inches
   (10 cubic feet × 1,728 = 17,280 cubic inches)

46,656 cubic inches = 1 cubic yard
   Cubic inches ÷ 46,656 = Cubic yards
   (93,312 cubic inches ÷ 46,656 = 2 cubic yards)

   Cubic yards × 46,656 = Cubic inches
   (2 cubic yards × 46,656 = 93,312 cubic inches)

27 cubic feet = 1 cubic yard
   Cubic feet ÷ 27 = Cubic yards (270 cubic feet ÷ 27 = 10 cubic yards)
   Cubic yards × 27 = Cubic feet (10 cubic yards × 27 = 270 cubic feet)

■ HOW DO I DETERMINE THE VOLUME OF A ROOM?

For purposes of determining volume, think of a room as if it were a box.
   Length × Width × Height = **Volume of a box**

■ **F O R   E X A M P L E**   A building is 500 feet long, 400 feet wide, and 25 feet high. How many cubic feet of space are in this building?

   500' × 400' × 25' = 5,000,000 cubic feet

5,000,000 cubic feet is the answer.

■ **F O R   E X A M P L E**   How many cubic yards of concrete would it take to build a sidewalk measuring 120 feet long; 2 feet, 6 inches wide; and 3 inches thick?

   6" ÷ 12' = 0.5' + 2' = 2.5' wide

   3" ÷ 12' = 0.25' thick

   120' × 2.5' × 0.25' = 75 cubic feet ÷ 27 = 2.778 cubic yards (rounded)

2.778 cubic yards is the answer.

■ HOW DO I DETERMINE THE VOLUME OF A TRIANGULAR PRISM?

The terms *A-frame*, *A-shaped*, or *gable roof* on an exam describe a triangular prism.

½ Base × Height × Width = **Volume of a triangular prism**
or
Base × Height × Width ÷ 2 = **Volume of a triangular prism**

■ **FOR EXAMPLE**   An A-frame cabin in the mountains is 50 feet long and 30 feet wide. The cabin is 25 feet high from the base to the highest point. How many cubic feet of space does this A-frame cabin contain?

50' × 30' × 25' ÷ 2 = 18,750 cubic feet

18,750 cubic feet is the answer.

■ **FOR EXAMPLE**   A building is 40 feet by 25 feet with a 10-foot-high ceiling. The building has a gable roof that is 8 feet high at the tallest point. How many cubic feet are in this structure, including the roof?

40' × 25' × 10' = 10,000 cubic feet in the building

40' × 25' × 8' ÷ 2 = 4,000 cubic feet in the gable roof

10,000 cubic feet + 4,000 cubic feet = 14,000 cubic feet

14,000 cubic feet is the answer.

SECTION 3

Fractions, Decimals, and Percentages

■ WHAT ARE THE PARTS OF A FRACTION?

The **denominator** shows the number of equal parts in the whole or total. The **numerator** shows the number of those parts with which you are working. In the example below, the whole or total has been divided into eight equal parts, and you have seven of those equal parts.

$$\frac{7}{8} \qquad \frac{\text{Numerator}}{\text{Denominator}} \qquad \frac{\text{(Top number)}}{\text{(Bottom number)}}$$

■ WHAT IS MEANT BY A *PROPER* AND AN *IMPROPER* FRACTION?

The value of a proper fraction is always less than one whole. ⅞ is an example of a **proper fraction**. ⅞ represents 7 parts out of 8 parts needed to make one whole. All proper fractions have a numerator smaller than the denominator. For example, ⅝ < ¾ < 1.

$$\frac{11}{8} \qquad \frac{\text{Numerator}}{\text{Denominator}}$$

This is an example of an **improper fraction.** The value of an improper fraction is always equal to or greater than one whole. The improper fraction ¹¹⁄₈ states you have 11 parts but only need 8 parts to make one whole. All improper fractions have a numerator larger than the denominator. For example, ¹¹⁄₈ > ⁵⁄₄ > 1.

■ WHAT IS A MIXED NUMBER?

11½ is a **mixed number**. You have a whole number plus a fraction. A mixed number is greater than the whole or greater than 1.

■ HOW DO I MULTIPLY FRACTIONS?

When multiplying fractions, numerator is multiplied by numerator, and denominator by denominator. Let's start with an easy question. What is ½ × ¾?

First multiply the numerators (top numbers), $1 \times 3 = 3$; then the denominators (bottom numbers), $2 \times 4 = 8$. Thus, $\frac{1}{2} \times \frac{3}{4} = \frac{3}{8}$.

What is $4\frac{2}{3} \times 10\frac{5}{8}$? The first step is to convert the whole number 4 into thirds. This is done by multiplying $4 \times 3 = 12$. (Multiply the whole number 4 by the denominator of the fraction, 3.) Thus, the whole number 4 is equal to $\frac{12}{3}$.

$4\frac{2}{3}$ is equal to $\frac{12}{3} + \frac{2}{3} = \frac{14}{3}$.

The next step is to convert the whole number 10 into eighths. This is done by multiplying $10 \times 8 = 80$. (Multiply the whole number 10 by the denominator of the fraction, 8.) Thus, the whole number 10 is equal to $\frac{80}{8}$. $\frac{80}{8} + \frac{5}{8} = \frac{85}{8}$.

So, what is $\frac{14}{3} \times \frac{85}{8}$? First multiply $14 \times 85 = 1,190$. Then, $3 \times 8 = 24$. $\frac{1,190}{24} = 49.58$. (That is, $1,190 \div 24 = 49.58$.)

An easier way to work the question is to convert the fractions to decimals.

$\frac{2}{3}$ is equal to $2 \div 3$ or 0.67.

$\frac{5}{8}$ is equal to $5 \div 8$ or 0.625.

$4.67 \times 10.625 = 49.62$.

When working with fractions or decimal equivalents, you will find that the answers will be close but not exact.

■ HOW DO I DIVIDE BY FRACTIONS?

Dividing by fractions is a two-step process. What is $\frac{3}{4} \div \frac{1}{4}$?

First, invert the $\frac{1}{4}$ to $\frac{4}{1}$. Then, multiply $\frac{3}{4} \times \frac{4}{1} = \frac{12}{4}$. Finally, $12 \div 4 = 3$.

You may also convert $\frac{3}{4}$ to the decimal 0.75 and $\frac{1}{4}$ to the decimal 0.25.
   $0.75 \div 0.25 = 3$. (There are three 0.25 in 0.75.)

What is $100\frac{7}{8} \div \frac{3}{4}$?
   $100 \times 8 = 800$.
   $800 + 7 = 80\frac{7}{8}$.

$\frac{3}{4}$ is inverted to $\frac{4}{3}$.
   $80\frac{7}{8} \times \frac{4}{3} = 807 \times 4 = 3,228$; $8 \times 3 = 24$. $\frac{3,228}{24} = 3,228 \div 24 = 134.5$.
   Or, $7 \div 8 = 0.875$ and $3 \div 4 = 0.75$.
   $100.875 \div 0.75 = 134.50$.

■ HOW DO I CONVERT FRACTIONS TO DECIMALS?

Fractions will sometimes be used in real estate math problems. Because calculators may be used on most licensing examinations, it is best to convert fractions to decimals.

MATH TIP   To convert a fraction to a decimal, the top number, called the numerator, is divided by the bottom number, the denominator.

For example:

$$\frac{7}{8} = 7 \div 8 = \mathbf{0.875}$$
$$1\frac{1}{8} = 11 \div 8 = \mathbf{1.375}$$
$$11\frac{1}{2} = 1 \div 2 = 0.5 + 11 = \mathbf{11.5}$$

Once fractions have been converted to decimals, other calculations can be easily completed using the calculator. Note that many calculators automatically display the zero before the decimal point.

■ HOW DO I ADD OR SUBTRACT DECIMALS?

Line up the decimals, add or subtract, and bring the decimal down in the answer. You may add zeros if necessary as placeholders. For example, 0.5 is the same as 0.50, or .5.

$$\begin{array}{r} 0.50 \\ +3.25 \\ \hline = \mathbf{3.75} \end{array} \qquad \begin{array}{r} 8.20 \\ -0.75 \\ \hline = 7.45 \end{array}$$

MATH TIP   When you use a calculator, the decimal will be in the correct place in the answer (0.5 + 3.25 = 3.75, and 8.2 − 0.75 = 7.45).

■ HOW DO I MULTIPLY DECIMALS?

Multiply the numbers, then count the number of decimal places in each number. Next, start with the last number on the right and move the decimal the total number of decimal places to the left in the answer.

Multiply as you normally would to get the 1,500, then count the four decimal places in the numbers (.20 and .75). In the 1,500, start at the last zero on the right and count four decimal places to the left. The decimal is placed to the left of the 1.

$$\begin{array}{r} 0.20 \\ \times\, 0.75 \\ \hline 100 \\ 140 \\ \hline 0.1500 \text{ or } 0.15 \end{array}$$

MATH TIP   When you use a calculator, the decimal will be in the correct place in the answer (0.2 × 0.75 = 0.15).

■ HOW DO I DIVIDE DECIMALS?

Divide the **dividend** (the number being divided) by the **divisor** (the number you are dividing by) and bring the decimal in the dividend straight up in the **quotient** (answer). If the divisor has a decimal, move the decimal to the right of the divisor and move the decimal the same number of places to the right in the dividend. Now divide as stated above.

$$
\begin{array}{r}
= 0.75 \\
2\overline{)1.5} \\
\underline{1.4} \\
10 \\
\underline{10} \\
0
\end{array}
\qquad
\begin{array}{r}
1 = 31. \\
0.5\overline{)15.5} = 5\overline{)155.} \\
\underline{15} \\
05 \\
\underline{5} \\
0
\end{array}
$$

MATH TIP   When you use a calculator, you can have a decimal in the divisor and the decimal will be in the correct place in the answer (1.5 ÷ 2 = 0.75, and 15.5 ÷ 0.5 = 31).

■ WHAT IS A PERCENTAGE?

Percent (%) means *per hundred* or *per hundred parts*. The whole or total always represents 100 percent.

5%	= 5 parts of 100 parts, or 5 ÷ 100 = 0.05 or ¹⁄₂₀
75%	= 75 parts of 100 parts, or 75 ÷ 100 = 0.75 or ¾
120%	= 120 parts of 100 parts, or 120 ÷ 100 = 1.2 or 1⅕

■ HOW CAN I CONVERT A PERCENTAGE TO A DECIMAL?

Move the decimal *two places* to the *left* and *drop* the % sign.

20%	= 2 ÷ 100 = 0.20 or **0.2**
1%	= 1 ÷ 100 = **0.01**
12¼	= 12.25%, 12.25 ÷ 100 = **0.1225**

See Figure 3.1.

FIGURE 3.1

**Converting Decimal
to Percentage and
Percentage to Decimal**

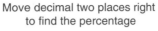

Decimal to Percentage	Percentage to Decimal
.10 ⟹ 10%	.10 ⟸ 10%
Move decimal two places right to find the percentage	Move percentage two places left to find the decimal

■ HOW CAN I CONVERT A DECIMAL TO A PERCENTAGE?

Move the decimal *two places* to the *right* and *add* the % sign.

$$0.25 \quad = 25\%$$
$$0.9 \quad = 90\%$$
$$0.0875 = 8.75\% \text{ or } 8\tfrac{3}{4}\%$$

See Figure 3.1.

■ HOW DO I MULTIPLY BY PERCENTAGES?

$$500 \times 25\% = 500 \times \tfrac{25}{100} = \tfrac{12,500}{100} = \mathbf{125}$$
or
$$500 \times 25\% = 125, \text{ or } 500 \times 0.25 = \mathbf{125}$$

■ HOW DO I DIVIDE BY PERCENTAGES?

$$100 \div 5\% = 100 \div \tfrac{5}{100} = 100 \times \tfrac{100}{5} = \tfrac{10,000}{5} = \mathbf{2,000}$$
or
$$100 \div 5\% = 2,000, \text{ or } 100 \div 0.05 = \mathbf{2,000}$$

■ IS THERE ANY EASY WAY TO REMEMBER HOW TO SOLVE PERCENTAGE PROBLEMS?

The following three formulas are important for solving all percentage problems:

Total	×	Rate	=	Part
Part	÷	Rate	=	Total
Part	÷	Total	=	Rate

There is a simple way to remember how to use these formulas:

- **Multiply** when **Part** is **unknown**.
- **Divide** when **Part** is **known**.
- When you divide, always enter **Part** into the calculator first.

■ WHAT IS THE T-BAR METHOD?

The T-Bar is another tool to use to solve percentage problems. For some people, the "three-formula method" is more difficult to remember than the visual image of a *T*.

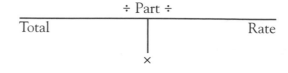

■ HOW DO I USE THE T-BAR?

The procedure for using the T-Bar is as follows:

1. Enter the two *known* items in the correct places.
2. If the line between the two items is *vertical*, you *multiply* to equal the missing item.
3. If the line between the two items is *horizontal*, you *divide* to equal the missing item. When you divide, the top (**Part**) always goes into the calculator first and is divided by the bottom (**Total** or **Rate**).

See Figure 3.2.

The following examples show how the T-Bar can be used to solve percentage problems. These examples deal with discounts because everyone can relate to buying an item that is on sale. Later, we will see how the T-Bar can be used for many types of real estate problems.

■ **FOR EXAMPLE** John purchased a new suit that was marked $500. How much did John save if it was on sale for 20 percent off?

	= ? ($100)	**$100 Saved**
$500		20%
total price		0.2
	×	

$500 × 20% (0.20) = $100

FIGURE 3.2

Using the T-Bar

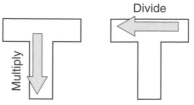

How much did John pay for the suit?

$500 total price – $100 discount = **$400 paid**

or

100% total price – 20% discount = 80% paid

= ? ($400)		**$400 paid**
$500	80%	
total price	0.8	
	×	

$500 × 80% (0.80) = $400

■ **FOR EXAMPLE** Susie paid $112.50 for a dress that was reduced 25 percent. How much was it originally marked?

100% original price – 25% discount = 75% paid

$112.50 ÷		
= ? ($150)	75%	$150 original price
	0.75	

$112.50 ÷ 75% (0.75) = $150

■ **FOR EXAMPLE** Chris paid $127.50 for a coat that was marked down from the original price of $150. What percent of discount did Chris receive?

$150 original price – $127.50 discount price = $22.50 discount

÷ 22.50 discount		
($150) = ?	**(0.15 = 15%) 15%**	**15% discount**
original price	0.85	

$22.50 ÷ $150 = 0.15, or 15%

or

÷ $127.50 paid		
$150	= (0.85 = 85%)	85% of original
original price	0.15	price paid

$127.50 ÷ $150 = 0.85, or 85%

85% was the percent paid; therefore

100% original price – 85% paid = **15% discount**

■ WORD PROBLEMS CAN BE TRICKY. HOW SHOULD I DEAL WITH THEM?

There are five important steps that must be taken to solve word problems.

1. **Read** the problem carefully and completely. Never touch the calculator until you have read the entire problem.
2. **Analyze** the problem to determine what is being asked, what facts are given that *will* be needed to solve for the answer, and what facts are given that *will not* be needed to solve for the answer. Eliminate any information and/or numbers given that are not needed to solve the problem. Take the remaining information and/or numbers and determine which will be needed first, second, and so on, depending on the number of steps it will take to solve the problem.
3. **Choose** the proper formula(s) and steps it will take to solve the problem.
4. **Insert** the known elements and calculate the answer.
5. **Check** your answer to be sure you keyed in the numbers and functions properly on your calculator. Be sure you finished the problem. For example, when the problem asks for the salesperson's share of the commission, do not stop at the broker's share of the commission and mark that answer just because it is one of the choices.

Percentage Problems

SECTION 4

■ HOW DO I WORK COMMISSION PROBLEMS?

The full **commission** is a percentage of the sales price, unless it is stated differently in the problem. Remember that full commission rates, commission splits between brokers, and commission splits between the broker and salespeople are always negotiable. Always read a problem carefully to determine the correct rate(s).

÷ Full commission ÷	
Sales price	Full commission rate

×

Sales price × Full commission rate = **Full commission**
Full commission ÷ Full commission rate = **Sales price**
Full commission ÷ Sales price = **Full commission rate**

÷ Broker's share of the commission ÷	
Full commission	% of full commission to the broker

×

Full commission	×	% of full commission to the broker	=	**Broker's share of the commission**
Broker's share of the commission	÷	% of full commission to the broker	=	Full commission
Broker's share of the commission	÷	Full commission	=	**% of full commission to the broker**

÷ Salesperson's share of the commission ÷	
Broker's share of the commission	Salesperson's % of the broker's share

×

Broker's share of the commission	×	Salesperson's % of the broker's share	=	**Salesperson's share of the commission**
Salesperson's share of the commission	×	Salesperson's % of the broker's share	=	**Broker's share of the commission**
Salesperson's share of the commission	×	Broker's share of the commission	=	**Salesperson's % of the broker's share**

■ **FOR EXAMPLE** A seller listed a home for $200,000 and agreed to pay a full commission rate of 5 percent. The home sold 4 weeks later for 90 percent of the list price. The listing broker agreed to give the selling broker 50 percent of the commission. The listing broker paid the listing salesperson 50 percent of her share of the commission, and the selling broker paid the selling salesperson 60 percent of his share of the commission. How much commission did the selling salesperson receive?

```
                = $180,000 sales price
─────────────────────────────────────────────
$200,000                              90%
list price                            or 0.9
              ×
```

$200,000 × 90% (0.90) = $180,000

```
                = $90,000 full commission
─────────────────────────────────────────────
$180,000                              5%
sales price                           or 0.05
              ×
```

$180,000 × 5% (0.05) = $9,000

```
         = $4,500 broker's share of the commission
─────────────────────────────────────────────
$9,000                                50%
full commission                       or 0.5
              ×
```

$9,000 × 50% (0.50) = $4,500

```
         = $2,700 salesperson's commission
─────────────────────────────────────────────
$4,500 broker's share                 60%
of commission                         or 0.6
              ×
```

$4,500 × 60% (0.60) = $2,700

$2,700 selling salesperson's commission is the answer.

◼ WHAT IS MEANT BY SELLER'S DOLLARS AFTER COMMISSION?

The first deduction from the sales price is the real estate commission. For example, if a house sold for $100,000 and a 7 percent commission was paid, that means $7,000 was paid in commissions. The seller still has 93 percent, or $93,000. The seller's dollars after commission will be used to pay the seller's other expenses and hopefully will leave some money for the seller.

÷ Seller's dollars after commission ÷	
Sales price	Percentage after commission
×	

Remember, the sales price is 100 percent. Thus, 100% – Commission % = Percent after commission.

Sales price	×	Percentage after commission	=	**Seller's dollars after commission**
Seller's dollars after commission	÷	Percentage after commission	=	**Sales price**
Seller's dollars after commission	÷	Sales price	=	**Percentage after commission**

◼ **FOR EXAMPLE**   After deducting $5,850 in closing costs and a 5 percent broker's commission, the sellers received their original cost of $175,000 plus a $4,400 profit. What was the sales price of the property?

$5,850 closing costs + $175,000 original cost + $4,400 profit = $185,250 seller's dollars after commission

100% sales price – 5% commission = 95% after commission

$185,250 seller's dollars after commission ÷	
= $195,000 sales price	95% or 0.95

$185,250 ÷ 95% (0.95) = $195,000

$195,000 sales price is the answer.

■ HOW DO I DETERMINE INTEREST?

Interest is the cost of using money. The amount of interest paid is determined by the agreed annual interest rate, the amount of money borrowed (loan amount) or the amount of money still owed (loan balance), and the period of time the money is held. When a lender grants a loan for real estate, the loan-to-value ratio (LTV) is the percentage of the sales price or appraised value, whichever is less, that the lender is willing to lend.

÷ Loan amount ÷

Sales price or appraised value (whichever is less)	Loan-to-value ratio (LTV)

×

Sales price or appraised value (whichever is less)	×	Loan-to-value ratio (LTV)	=	**Loan amount**
Loan amount	÷	Loan-to-value ratio (LTV)	=	**Sales price** or **appraised value** (whichever is less)
Loan amount	÷	Sales price or appraised value (whichever is less)	=	**Loan-to-value ratio** (LTV)

÷ Annual interest ÷

Loan amount (principal)	Annual interest rate

×

Loan amount	×	Annual interest rate	=	**Annual interest**
Annual interest	×	Annual interest rate	=	**Loan amount**
Annual interest	×	Loan amount	=	**Annual interest rate**

■ **FOR EXAMPLE**   A parcel of real estate sold for $335,200. The lender granted a 90 percent loan at 7.5 percent for 30 years. The appraised value on this parcel was $335,500. How much interest is paid to the lender in the first monthly payment?

= $301,680 loan amount ÷	
$335,200 sales price	90% or 0.9

×

$335,200 × 90% (0.90) = $301,680 Loan

= $22,626 annual interest	
$301,680 loan amount	7.5% or 0.075

×

$301,680 × 7.5% (0.075) = $22,626

$22,626 annual interest ÷ 12 months = $1,885.50 monthly interest

$1,885.50 interest in the first monthly payment is the answer.

■ HOW MUCH INTERIM INTEREST WILL BE DUE AT CLOSING?

Interim interest is charged by a lender when a borrower obtains a new loan. This interest is called *interim* because it is for the interim period of time from the day of closing through the end of the closing month. Most real estate loan interest is paid in arrears, but interim interest is an example of interest paid in advance.

If a borrower closes on a loan on June 12, then the borrower will owe interim interest for 19 days. The first full payment (PI) will be due August 1; this payment will include interest for July. If the closing is September 21, interim interest for 10 days will be paid at closing, and the first full payment will be due November 1 (paying interest for October).

■ **FOR EXAMPLE**   A borrower is closing on a $114,300 loan with an interest rate of 6.75 percent on November 18. How much interim interest will be due at closing? The first full payment is due January 1.

30 days in November − 18 (days until closing) = 12 days + 1 (day of closing) = 13 days

$114,300 × 6.75% = 7,715.25 annual interest

$7,715.25 ÷ 360 = $21.43125 interest per day

$21.43125 × 13 days = $278.61 (rounded) interim interest due at closing

$278.61 interim interest due at closing is the answer.

■ HOW DO I DETERMINE MONTHLY PRINCIPAL AND INTEREST PAYMENTS?

A **loan payment factor** can be used to calculate the monthly principal and interest payment on a loan. The factor represents the monthly principal and interest payment to amortize a $1,000 loan and is based on the annual interest rate and the term of the loan.

Loan amount ÷ $1,000 × Loan payment factor = **Monthly PI payment**
Monthly PI payment × Loan payment factor = **Loan amount**

■ **FOR EXAMPLE**   If the lender in the previous example uses a loan payment factor of $6.99 per $1,000 of loan amount, what will be the monthly PI (principal and interest) payment?

$301,680 loan amount ÷ $1,000 × $6.99 = $2,108.74 monthly PI payment

$2,108.74 monthly PI payment is the answer.

■ HOW DO I WORK PROBLEMS ABOUT POINTS?

The word *point* means percent. One **point** equals 1 percent of the loan amount.

Two points means 2 percent, or ½ point means ½ percent. A loan point is a percentage of the loan amount.

÷ Amount for points ÷	
Loan amount	Points converted to a percentage

×

Loan amount	×	Points converted to a percentage	=	**Amount for points**
Amount for points	÷	Points converted to a percentage	=	**Loan amount**
Amount for points	÷	Loan amount	=	**Points converted to a percentage**

■ **FOR EXAMPLE**   The lender will charge 3½ loan discount points on an $80,000 loan. What will be the total amount due?

÷ Amount for points ÷	
$80,000 loan amount	3.5% or 0.035

×

$80,000 × 3.5% (0.035) = $2,800

$2,800 for points is the answer.

■ HOW DO I DETERMINE PROFIT?

A **profit** is made when we sell something for more than we paid for it. If we sell something for less than we paid, we have suffered a **loss**.

Sales price – Cost = Profit

When setting the T-Bar, the whole is the original investment or cost (i.e., the amount paid years ago). The original cost must be the whole thing (the 100 percent) because percentages of profit or loss are percentages of the money invested. A 20 percent loss is 20 percent of the original investment.

÷ Profit ÷	
Cost	Percentage of profit
✕	

Cost	✕	Percentage of profit	=	**Profit**
Profit	÷	Percentage of profit	=	**Cost**
Profit	÷	Cost	=	**Percentage of profit**

The cost plus the profit equals the sales price. The cost minus the loss equals the sales price.

÷ Sales price ÷	
Cost	Percentage sold of cost
✕	

(100% Cost + % Profit = % Sales price)

Cost	✕	Percentage sold of cost	=	**Sales price**
Sales price	÷	Percentage sold of cost	=	**Cost**
Sales price	÷	Cost	=	**Percentage sold of cost**

■ **FOR EXAMPLE**   Your home listed for $285,000 and sold for $275,000, which gave you a 10 percent profit over the original cost. What was the original cost?

100% original cost + 10% profit = 110% sales price

÷ $275,000 sales price ÷	
Original cost	110% or 1.1
×	

$275,000 ÷ 110% (1.1) = $250,000

$250,000 original cost is the answer.

■ **FOR EXAMPLE**   You invested in a mountain cabin a few years ago. You just sold the cabin for $80,640 losing 16 percent of your investment. What was the original cost of the cabin? The $80,640 is today's value after suffering a 16 percent loss.

100% original investment − 16% loss = 84% today's value

÷ $80,640 sales price ÷	
Original investment	84% or 0.84
×	

$80,640 ÷ 0.84 = $96,000

$96,000 original investment is the answer.

■ WHAT IS THE DIFFERENCE BETWEEN APPRECIATION AND DEPRECIATION?

Appreciation is increase in value. **Depreciation** is decrease in value. Both are based on the original cost. We will only cover the **straight-line method**, which is what should be used in math problems, unless you are told differently. The straight-line method means that the value is increasing (appreciating) or decreasing (depreciating) the same amount each year. The amount of appreciation or depreciation is based on the original cost.

However, to calculate more than one year's worth of appreciation or depreciation while using an "average annual rate," lump them together. For example, 4 percent for 5 years = 20 percent. An "over previous year's value" means year by year. If depreciation is 2 percent for 3 years, then divide today's value by 98 percent three times. If the appreciation is 6 percent for two years, then divide today's value by 106 percent twice.

■ HOW DO I SOLVE APPRECIATION PROBLEMS?

÷ Annual appreciation ÷

Cost		Annual appreciation rate
	×	

Cost	×	Annual appreciation rate	=	**Annual appreciation**
Annual appreciation	×	Annual appreciation rate	=	**Cost**
Annual appreciation	×	Cost	=	**Annual appreciation rate**

Annual appreciation rate × Number of years = **Total appreciation rate**

100% Cost + Total appreciation rate = **Today's value as a percentage**

÷ Today's value (appreciated value) ÷

Cost		Today's value as a percentage
	×	

Cost	×	Today's value as a percentage	=	**Today's value (appreciated value)**
Today's value (appreciated value)	×	Today's value as a percentage	=	**Cost**
Today's value (appreciated value)	×	Cost	=	**Today's value as a percentage**

■ **FOR EXAMPLE**   Seven years ago you purchased a piece of real estate for $93,700, including the original cost of the land, which was $6,700. What is the total value of the land today using an appreciation rate of 8 percent per year?

8% appreciation per year × 7 years = 56% total appreciation rate

100% cost + 56% appreciation = 156% today's value

Today's value

$6,700		156%
original cost		or 1.56
	×	

$6,700 × 156% (1.56) = $10,452

$10,452 today's value is the answer.

▧ HOW DO I SOLVE DEPRECIATION PROBLEMS?

÷ Annual depreciation ÷

Cost		Annual depreciation rate
	×	

Cost	×	Annual depreciation rate	=	**Annual depreciation**

Annual depreciation	÷	Annual depreciation rate	=	**Cost**

Annual depreciation	÷	Cost	=	**Annual depreciation rate**

Annual depreciation rate × Number of years = **Total depreciation rate**
100% Cost − Total depreciation rate = **Today's value as a percentage**

÷ Today's value (depreciated value) ÷

Cost		Today's value as a percentage
	×	

Cost	×	Today's value as a percentage	=	**Today's value (depreciated value)**

Today's value (depreciated value)	÷	Today's value as a percentage	=	**Cost**

Today's value (depreciated value)	÷	Cost	=	**Today's value as a percentage**

■ **FOR EXAMPLE**   The value of a house without the lot at the end of four years is $132,300. What was the original cost of the house if the yearly rate of depreciation was 2.5 percent?

2.5% depreciation per year × 4 years = 10% total depreciation rate

100% cost – 10% depreciation = 90% today's value

$132,300 today's value ÷	
Original cost	90% or 0.9

×

$132,300 ÷ 90% (0.90) = $147,000

$147,000 original cost is the answer.

■ HOW DO I ESTIMATE VALUE FOR INCOME-PRODUCING PROPERTIES?

When appraising income-producing property, the value is estimated by using the annual net operating income (NOI) and the current market rate of return or capitalization rate. Annual scheduled gross income is adjusted for vacancies and credit losses to arrive at the annual effective gross income. The annual operating expenses are deducted from the annual effective gross income to arrive at the annual NOI.

Vacancy/credit loss is usually expressed as a percentage of the scheduled gross.

Scheduled gross income	–	Vacancies and credit losses	=	**Effective gross income**
Effective gross income	–	Annual operating expenses	=	**NOI**

÷ NOI ÷	
Value	Annual rate of return (capitalization rate)

×

NOI	÷	Rate of return	=	**Value**
Value	×	Rate of return	=	**NOI**
NOI	÷	Value	=	**Rate of return**

■ **FOR EXAMPLE**   An office building produces $132,600 annual gross income. If the annual expenses are $30,600 and the appraiser estimates the value using an 8.5 percent rate of return, what is the estimated value?

$132,600 annual gross income – $30,600 annual expenses = $102,000 NOI

$102,000 NOI	
Value	8.5% rate of return or 0.085
×	

$102,000 ÷ 8.5% = $1,200,000

$1,200,000 value is the answer.

The above formulas also can be used to calculate either the return on investment (ROI) for real estate investing or the monthly NOI. The total becomes *original cost* or *investment* instead of value.

■ **FOR EXAMPLE**   You invest $335,000 in a property that should produce a 9 percent rate of return. What monthly NOI will you receive?

NOI	
$335,000 investment	9% or 0.09
×	

$335,000 × 9% (0.09) = $30,150

$30,150 NOI ÷ 12 months = $2,512.50

$2,512.50 monthly NOI is the answer.

■ HOW DO I SOLVE PROBLEMS INVOLVING PERCENTAGE LEASES?

When establishing the rent to be charged in a lease for retail space, the lease may be a percentage lease instead of a lease based on dollars per square foot. In a **percentage lease**, there is normally a base or minimum monthly rent plus a percentage of the gross sales in excess of an amount set in the lease. The percentage lease also can be set up as a percentage of the total gross sales or of the base/minimum rent, whichever is larger. We will look at the minimum plus percentage lease only.

| Gross sales | – | Gross sales not subject to the percentage | = | **Gross sales subject to the percentage** |

$$\frac{\div\ \text{Percentage rent}\ \div}{\begin{array}{c|c} \text{Gross sales subject} & \text{\% in the lease} \\ \text{to the percentage} & \\ \times & \end{array}}$$

Gross sales subject to the percentage	$\times$	% in the lease	$=$	**Percentage rent**
Percentage rent	$\div$	% in the lease	$=$	**Gross sales subject to the percentage**
Percentage rent	$\div$	Gross sales subject to the percentage	$=$	**% in the lease**

Add the percentage rent and the base/minimum rent to find the total rent. Compute the total rent by combining the percentage rent and the base/minimum rent. Together they equal the total rent.

■ **FOR EXAMPLE**   A lease calls for monthly minimum rent of $900 plus 3 percent of annual gross sales in excess of $270,000. What was the annual rent in a year when the annual gross sales were $350,600?

$900 monthly minimum rent × 12 months = $10,800 annual minimum rent

$350,600 annual gross sales – $270,000 annual gross sales not subject to the percentage = $80,600 annual gross sales subject to the percentage

$$\frac{=\ \$2{,}418\ \text{annual percentage rent}}{\begin{array}{c|c} \$80{,}600\ \text{annual gross} & 3\% \\ \text{subject to the percentage} & \text{or } 0.03 \\ \times & \end{array}}$$

$80,600 × 3% = $2,418 annual percentage rent

$10,800 annual minimum rent + $2,418 annual percentage rent = $13,218 total annual rent

$13,218 total annual rent is the answer.

Proration Problems

Prorate means to divide proportionately. Some expenses and income may be prorated for the closing of a real estate transaction. We will look at prorating interest on a loan, ad valorem taxes on a property, homeowners' insurance on a property, and rent on income-producing property.

■ WHAT ARE THE DIFFERENT CALENDARS USED FOR PRORATING?

When we prorate, we calculate the number of days owed for the expense or the rental income. The days may be calculated using a *banker's year, statutory year,* or *calendar year.* The **banker's year** and **statutory year** are the same because they both contain 12 months with 30 days in each month. The total number of days in both a banker's year and a statutory year is 360 days. The **calendar year** contains 12 months with 28 to 31 days in each month. The total number of days in a calendar year is 365. The total number of days in a calendar *leap* year is 366. The following chart shows the days in each month.

	Banker's or Statutory Year	Calendar Year	Calendar Leap Year
January	30	31	31
February	30	28	29
March	30	31	31
April	30	30	30
May	30	31	31
June	30	30	30
July	30	31	31
August	30	31	31
September	30	30	30
October	30	31	31
November	30	30	30
December	30	31	31
Total days in a year	360	365	366

WHAT IS THE DIFFERENCE BETWEEN PRORATING *THROUGH* AND PRORATING *TO* THE DAY OF CLOSING?

In a proration problem, we will be told whether to prorate *through* the day of closing or *to* the day of closing. **This is very important when calculating the days owed**. When we prorate *through* the day of closing, the *seller* is responsible for the day of closing. When we prorate *to* the day of closing, the *buyer* is responsible for the day of closing.

HOW DO I CALCULATE PRORATION PROBLEMS?

Once we know the number of days owed, we then need to know the amount of the expense or income per day. We take either the annual amount divided by the total days in the year to get the daily amount or the monthly amount divided by the total days in the month to get the daily amount.

MATH TIP   Be sure you use the correct type of year (banker's or statutory year of 360 days, calendar year of 365 days, or calendar leap year of 366 days) when computing the daily amount.

The final step is to multiply the amount per day by the number of days owed to get the prorated amount.

WHAT IS THE DIFFERENCE BETWEEN DEBIT AND CREDIT IN A PRORATION PROBLEM?

To calculate a proration problem, you need to know how expenses and income are posted on the closing statement. **Debit** takes money from a person. **Credit** gives money to a person. (See Figure 5.1.) When the prorated amount involves both the buyer and the seller, there will always be a double entry (i.e., it appears twice, once as a debit to one party and once as a credit to the other party). If the seller owes the buyer, the prorated amount will be debited to the seller and credited to the buyer. If the buyer owes the seller, the prorated amount will be debited to the buyer and credited to the seller. When the prorated amount involves the buyer and someone other than the seller, there will be only a single entry. When the prorated amount involves the seller and someone other than the buyer, there will be only a single entry. We will discuss debits and credits as we learn to prorate each expense.

The five questions to ask when prorating are as follows:

1. What calendar do we use?
2. Is the expense paid in arrears or in advance?
3. Who has or will pay the expense?
4. Who has earned or received income?
5. When will the expense be paid?

FIGURE 5.1

The Debit/Credit Flow

		Buyer	Seller
	Sales Price	DEBIT	CREDIT
	Tenants' Security Deposits	CREDIT	DEBIT
	Fuel Oil (in tank)	DEBIT	CREDIT
	Prorated Accrued Water Bill	CREDIT	DEBIT
	Unearned Rents	CREDIT	DEBIT
	Tax Reserve Account	DEBIT	CREDIT

Different items are treated differently as credits or debits to the buyer or seller on a closing statement.

■ HOW DO I CALCULATE INTEREST IN A PRORATION PROBLEM?

When a loan is assumed or paid off, the accrued interest for the month of closing must be prorated. Interest is paid in arrears; therefore, the monthly payment made on the first day of the month pays interest for the entire previous month. The payment includes interest *up to but not including* the day of the payment unless specified otherwise. Not all payments are due on the first day of the month; therefore, pay attention when you are told what day the interest has been paid through. The sellers owe unpaid interest (also called accrued, earned, or current interest) from the date of the last payment to or through the closing date.

If the prorations are to be calculated *through* the day of closing, the seller will owe payments *including* the day of closing. If the prorations are to be calculated *to* the day of closing, the seller will *owe up to but not including* the day of closing. Remember to use the correct type of year. A banker's or statutory year has 360 days. A calendar year has 365 days. A calendar leap year has 366 days. When a loan is paid off, unpaid interest is calculated and added to the outstanding loan balance and is a **debit** *to the seller only*. Loan payoff is the sum of the principal balance and the accrued interest. On an assumption of the loan, the interest proration is a **debit** to the *seller* and a **credit** to the *buyer*.

■ **FOR EXAMPLE** A home was purchased on April 4, 2010, for $110,000, and the closing was set for May 8, 2010. The buyer assumed the balance of the seller's $93,600 loan with 11.5 percent interest and monthly payments of $990.29 due on the first day of each month. How much will the interest proration be, using a banker's year and prorating through the day of closing? Who will be debited and who will be credited?

Banker's Year/Statutory Year

Step 1. Find the exact number of days of earned or accrued interest.

Seller owes 8 days (May 1 *through* May 8).

Note: It would be 7 days (8 days minus 1 day) if the problem had said prorate *to* the day of closing.

Step 2. Find the daily interest charge. Outstanding loan balance ×
Annual interest rate = Annual interest ÷ 360 days per year =
Daily interest.

$93,600 × 11.5% (0.115) = $10,764 annual interest ÷ 360 days = $29.90 daily interest

Step 3. Compute the total amount of accrued interest. Daily interest × Days owed =
Interest proration.

$29.90 daily interest × 8 days = $239.20

$239.20 debit seller, credit buyer is the answer.

Calendar Year (if the problem had said to use a calendar year)

Step 1. Find the exact number of days of earned or accrued interest.

Seller owes 8 days (May 1 *through* May 8).

Note: It would be 7 days (8 days minus 1 day) if the problem had said prorate *to* the day of closing.

Step 2. Find the daily interest charge. Outstanding loan balance ×
Annual interest rate = Annual Interest ÷ 365 days per year =
Daily interest.

$93,600 × 11.5% (0.115) = $10,764 annual interest ÷ 365 days = $29.49041096 daily interest

Step 3. Compute the total amount of accrued interest. Daily interest × Days owed
= Interest proration.

$29.49041096 daily interest × 8 days = $235.92 rounded

$235.92 debit seller, credit buyer is the answer.

■ HOW DO I PRORATE TAXES?

Real estate taxes are normally assessed from January 1 through December 31. The tax rate is *always* applied *to the assessed value of the property* instead of the market value. Taxes are usually paid in arrears; therefore, the seller will owe the buyer for accrued taxes from January 1 *through* the day of closing or *to* the day of closing. The most recent tax bill is used to compute the proration, and this is usually the past year's tax bill. Remember to use the correct type of year. A banker's or statutory year has 360 days. A calendar year has 365 days. A calendar leap year has 366 days.

If the taxes are paid in arrears, the tax proration will be a **debit** to the *seller* and a **credit** to the *buyer*. If the taxes are paid in advance, the tax proration will be a **debit** to the *buyer* and a **credit** to the *seller*.

■ **FOR EXAMPLE**   The market value of a home is $115,000. For tax purposes, the home is assessed at 90 percent of the market value. The annual tax rate is $2.50 per $100 of assessed value. If the closing is on March 13, 2010, what is the prorated amount? Prorations are calculated through the day of closing and using a statutory year.

Banker's Year/Statutory Year

Step 1. Find the exact number of days of accrued taxes from the beginning of the tax period (January 1, 2010) up to and including the day of closing (March 13, 2010).

2 months (January and February) × 30 days per month = 60 days + 13 days in March = 73 days

Note: It would be 72 days (73 days minus 1 day) if the problem had said prorate *to* the day of closing.

Step 2. Calculate the annual taxes. Market value × Assessment ratio = Assessed value ÷ $100 × Tax rate per hundred = Annual taxes.

$115,000 × 90% = $103,500 ÷ $100 × $2.50 = $2,587.50 annual taxes

Step 3. Find the tax amount per day. Annual taxes ÷ 360 days per year = Daily taxes.

$2,587.50 ÷ 360 days = $7.1875 daily taxes

Step 4. Compute the prorated tax amount. Daily taxes × Days owed = Tax proration.

$7.1875 per day × 73 days = $524.69 rounded

$524.69 debit seller, credit buyer is the answer.

Calendar Year (if the problem had said to use a calendar year)

Step 1. Find the exact number of days of accrued taxes from the beginning of the tax period (January 1, 2010) up to and including the day of closing (March 13, 2010).

31 days in January + 28 days in February + 13 days in March = 72 days

Note: It would be 71 days (72 days minus 1 day) if the problem had said prorate *to* the day of closing.

Step 2. Calculate the annual taxes. Market value × Assessment ratio = Assessed value ÷ $100 × Tax rate per hundred = Annual taxes.

$115,000 × 90% = $103,500 ÷ $100 × $2.50 = $2,587.50 annual taxes

Step 3. Find the tax amount per day. Annual taxes ÷ 365 days per year = Daily taxes.

$2,587.50 ÷ 365 days = $7.089041096 daily taxes

Step 4. Compute the prorated tax amount. Daily taxes × Days owed = Tax proration.

$7.089041096 per day × 72 days = $510.41 rounded

$510.41 debit seller, credit buyer is the answer.

■ IS INSURANCE ALWAYS PRORATED?

When buying a home, insurance coverage must be provided by the owners if they have a loan. The buyers normally purchase their own insurance policy. There will *not* be a proration if the buyers purchase a new policy because the sellers will cancel their existing policy effective the day of closing and the buyer's new policy will become effective the day of closing.

■ IF INSURANCE IS PRORATED, HOW DO I CALCULATE IT?

If the insurance company will allow a policy to be assumed and the buyers choose to do so, an insurance proration is necessary. Today, insurance policies are written for one year. The premiums are payable in advance; therefore, the sellers have paid the entire yearly premium. If the policy is transferred to the buyers, the buyers owe the sellers for the unused portion of the policy. If you are to prorate *through* the day of closing, the buyers owe the sellers from the day after closing until the expiration of the policy. If you are to prorate *to* the day of closing, the buyers owe the sellers starting with the day of closing until the expiration of the policy. Insurance policies become effective at 12:01 AM and expire exactly one year later at 12:01 AM; therefore, no coverage is counted on the day of expiration of the insurance policy. Remember to use the correct type of year. A banker's or statutory year has 360 days. A calendar year has 365 days. A calendar leap year has 366 days. The insurance proration will be a **debit** to the *buyer* and a **credit** to the *seller*.

■ **F O R   E X A M P L E**   A one-year fire insurance policy expires on August 20, 2010. The total premium for this policy was $800 and was paid in full in 2009. The house was sold, and the closing date was set for January 25, 2010. The proration is to be calculated through the day of closing using a banker's year. What will be the total credit to the seller to transfer the insurance policy to the buyer?

Banker's Year/Statutory Year

Step 1. Compute the number of days of insurance coverage that the buyer assumed.

	30	days in January
–	25	day of closing
	5	days left in January
+	180	days (6 months × 30 days per month/February–July)
+	19	days coverage in August
	204	days left on the policy

Note: It would be 205 days (204 days plus 1 day) if the problem had said prorate *to* the day of closing.

Step 2. Compute the amount of the policy cost per day. Annual insurance premium ÷ 360 days per year = Daily insurance.

$800 insurance premium ÷ 360 days = $2.2222222 daily insurance

Step 3. Calculate what the buyer owes. Daily insurance × Days left on the policy = Insurance proration.

$2.2222222 daily insurance × 204 days = $453.33 rounded

$453.33 credit seller, debit buyer is the answer.

Calendar Year (if the problem had said to use a calendar year)

Step 1. Compute the number of days of insurance coverage that the buyer assumed.

	31	days in January
–	25	day of closing
	6	days left in January
+	28	days in February
+	31	days in March
+	30	days in April
+	31	days in May
+	30	days in June
+	31	days in July
+	19	days coverage in August
	206	days left on the policy

Note: It would be 207 days (206 days plus 1 day) if the problem had said prorate *to* the day of closing.

Step 2. Compute the amount of the policy cost per day. Annual insurance premium ÷ 365 days per year = Daily insurance.

$800 Insurance premium ÷ 365 days = $2.1917808 daily insurance

Step 3. Calculate what the buyer owes. Daily insurance × Days left on the policy = Insurance proration.

$2.1917808 daily insurance × 206 days = $451.51 rounded

$451.51 credit seller, debit buyer is the answer.

■ HOW DO I PRORATE RENT?

When prorating rents, the amount of rent collected for the month of closing is the only amount prorated. The seller owes the buyer for the unearned rent starting with the day after closing through the end of the month if you are prorating *through* the day of closing. The seller owes the buyer for the unearned rent starting with the day of closing through the end of the month if you are prorating *to* the day of closing. If security deposits are being held by the seller, they are not prorated; therefore, the entire amount of the security deposits are transferred to the buyer. Always use the actual number of days in the month of closing for rent prorations, unless you are told differently. Both the rent proration and the security deposit amount will be a **debit** to the *seller* and a **credit** to the *buyer*.

■ **FOR EXAMPLE**   A man is purchasing an apartment complex that contains 15 units that rent for $450 per month. A $450 security deposit is being held on each unit. The sale is to close on March 14, and the March rent has been received for all 15 units. Compute the rent proration by prorating through the day of closing. Compute the security deposit.

Calendar Days (remember to use actual days in the month unless specified differently)

Step 1. Compute the unearned days of rent for the month of closing.

```
   31   days in March
 - 14   day of closing
   17   days of unearned rent
```

Note: It would be 18 days (17 days plus 1 day) if the problem had said prorate *to* the day of closing.

Step 2. Compute the daily rent. Monthly rent × Number of units paid = Total rent collected ÷ Number of actual days in the month of closing = Daily rent.

$450 × 15 units = $6,750 monthly rent collected ÷ 31 days in March = $217.7419355 daily rent

Step 3. Compute the prorated rent amount. Daily rent × Days of unearned rent.

$217.7419355 daily rent × 17 days = $3,701.61 rounded

Step 4. Compute the security deposit.

$450 per unit × 15 units = $6,750

$3,701.61 rent proration and **$6,750 security deposit** are the answers. They are both **debit seller** and **credit buyer.**

Real Estate Math Practice Problems

1. The value of your house, not including the lot, is $91,000 today. What was the original cost if it has depreciated 5 percent per year for the past seven years?
   a. $67,407.41
   b. $95,789.47
   c. $122,850.00
   d. $140,000.00

2. What was the price per front foot for a 100' × 125' lot that sold for $125,000?
   a. $1,250
   b. $1,000
   c. $556
   d. $10

3. If the savings and loan gives you a 90 percent loan on a house valued at $88,500, how much additional cash must you produce as a down payment if you have already paid $4,500 in earnest money?
   a. $3,500
   b. $4,000
   c. $4,350
   d. $8,850

4. What did the owners originally pay for their home if they sold it for $98,672, which gave them a 12 percent profit over their original cost?
   a. $86,830
   b. $88,100
   c. $89,700
   d. $110,510

5. What would you pay for a building producing $11,250 annual net income and showing a minimum rate of return of 9 percent?
   a. $125,000
   b. $123,626
   c. $101,250
   d. $122,625

6. The sale of a home is to close on September 28. Included in the sale is a garage apartment that is rented to the tenant for $350 per month. The tenant has paid the September rent. What is the rent proration, using actual days and prorating through the day of closing?
   a. $325.67
   b. $23.33
   c. $350.00
   d. $175.00

7. What is the total cost of a driveway 15' wide, 40' long, and 4" thick if the concrete costs $60.00 per cubic yard and the labor costs $1.25 per square foot?
   a. $527.25
   b. $693.75
   c. $1,194.00
   d. $1,581.75

8. An owner agrees to list his property on the condition that he will receive at least $47,300 after paying a 5 percent broker's commission and paying $1,150 in closing costs. At what price must it sell?
   a. $48,450
   b. $50,815
   c. $50,875
   d. $51,000

9. A gift shop pays rent of $600 per month plus 2.5 percent of gross annual sales in excess of $50,000. What was the average monthly rent last year if gross annual sales were $75,000?
   a. $1,125.00
   b. $756.25
   c. $600.00
   d. $652.08

10. Your monthly rent is $525. What is your rent as a percentage of an annual income of $21,000?
    a. 25 percent
    b. 30 percent
    c. 33 percent
    d. 40 percent

11. Two brokers split the 6 percent commission on a $73,000 home. The selling salesperson was paid 70 percent of his broker's share. The listing salesperson was paid 30 of her broker's share. How much did the listing salesperson receive?

    a. $657
    b. $4,380
    c. $1,533
    d. $1,314

12. Find the number of square feet in a lot with a frontage of 75 feet 6 inches and a depth of 140 feet 9 inches.

    a. 10,626.63
    b. 10,652.04
    c. 216.25
    d. 25,510.81

13. You attempt to appraise a 28-unit apartment house, employing the income approach. You discover that each unit rents for $775 a month, an amount that seems consistent with like rental units in the vicinity. For the past five years, the annual expenses of operation have averaged $82,460. The complex has maintained a consistent vacancy rate of 5 percent. A potential investor is only interested if the return is 9.5 percent. What value would you arrive at using these variables?

    a. $2,741,100
    b. $868,000
    c. $1,736,000
    d. $1,873,100

14. How much interest will the seller owe the buyer for a closing date of August 10 if the outstanding loan balance is $43,580? The interest rate on this assumable loan is 10.5 percent, and the last payment was paid on August 1. Prorations are to be done through the day of closing, using a statutory year.

    a. $127.11
    b. $254.22
    c. $125.37
    d. $381.33

15. The buyer has agreed to pay $175,000 in sales price, 2.5 loan discount points, and a 1 percent origination fee. If the buyer receives a 90 percent loan-to-value ratio, how much will the buyer owe at closing for points and the origination fee?

    a. $1,575.00
    b. $3,937.50
    c. $5,512.50
    d. $6,125.00

16. Calculate eight months' interest on a $5,000 interest-only loan at 9.5 percent.

    a. $475.00
    b. $316.67
    c. $237.50
    d. $39.58

17. A 100-acre farm is divided into lots for homes. The streets require one-eighth of the whole farm, and there are 140 lots. How many square feet are in each lot?

    a. 43,560
    b. 35,004
    c. 31,114
    d. 27,225

18. The 2004 tax bill on a home was $1,282 and was paid in December 2009. The home sold and will close on April 23, 2010. How much will the tax proration be, using a calendar year and prorating to the day of closing?

    a. $393.38
    b. $402.41
    c. $396.89
    d. $427.33

19. What is the monthly net income on an investment of $115,000 if the rate of return is 12.5 percent?

    a. $1,150.00
    b. $1,197.92
    c. $7,666.67
    d. $14,375.00

20. A salesperson sells a property for $58,500. The contract he has with his broker is 40 percent of the full commission earned. The commission due the broker is 6 percent. What is the salesperson's share of the commission?

a. $2,106
b. $1,404
c. $3,510
d. $2,340

21. A woman buys 348,480 square feet of land at $0.75 per square foot. She divides the land into half-acre lots. If she keeps three lots for herself and sells the others for $24,125 each, what percentage of profit does she realize?

a. 47.4 percent
b. 32.2 percent
c. 20 percent
d. 16.7 percent

22. A homeowners' insurance premium of $437 was paid in full in 2009 for a one-year policy that expires June 6, 2010. The house is sold and scheduled to close on February 16, 2010. The buyers are assuming the sellers' insurance policy. What is the amount of the insurance proration if a banker's year is used and all prorations are done through the day of closing?

a. $132.31
b. $134.74
c. $302.26
d. $304.69

23. What is the interest rate on a $10,000 loan with semiannual interest of $450?

a. 7 percent
b. 9 percent
c. 11 percent
d. 13.5 percent

24. A warehouse is 80 feet wide and 120 feet long with ceilings 14 feet high. If 1,200 square feet of floor surface has been partitioned off, floor to ceiling, for an office, how many cubic feet of space will be left in the warehouse?

a. 151,200
b. 134,400
c. 133,200
d. 117,600

25. An office building produces $68,580 annual net operating income. What price would you pay for this property to show a minimum return of 12 percent on your investment?

a. $489,857
b. $571,500
c. $685,800
d. $768,096

26. A buyer is assuming the balance of a seller's loan. The interest rate is 8 percent and the last monthly payment of $578.16 was paid on April 1, leaving an outstanding balance of $18,450. Using a banker's year, compute the interest to be paid by the seller if the sale is to close on April 19. Prorate through the day of closing.

a. $110.83
b. $82.00
c. $77.90
d. $123.00

27. The lot you purchased five years ago for $15,000 has appreciated 3.5 percent per year. What is it worth today?

a. $12,375
b. $15,525
c. $17,250
d. $17,625

28. A lot has a frontage of 100 feet and a depth of 150 feet. If the building line regulations call for a setback of 25 feet at the front and 6 feet on the two sides, how many square feet of usable space are left for the building?

a. 10,350
b. 11,000
c. 11,750
d. 15,000

29. A lease calls for $1,000 per month minimum plus 2 percent of annual sales in excess of $100,000. What is the annual rent if the annual sales were $150,000?

a. $12,000
b. $13,000
c. $14,000
d. $15,000

30. In the year 2009, taxes on a home were paid in full and amounted to $1,468. The home was later sold, and the sale closed on August 29, 2010. What was the prorated tax amount using a calendar year if the proration was calculated to the day of closing?

    a. $965.26
    b. $502.74
    c. $970.51
    d. $497.49

31. A tract of land measures 1.25 acres. The lot is 150 feet deep. How much will the lot sell for at $65 per front foot?

    a. $9,750
    b. $8,125
    c. $23,595
    d. $25,420

32. If the broker received a 6.5 percent commission that was $5,200, what was the sales price of the house?

    a. $80,400
    b. $80,000
    c. $77,200
    d. $86,600

33. A man earns $20,000 per year and can qualify for a monthly PITI payment equal to 25 percent of his monthly salary. If the annual tax and insurance is $678.24, what loan amount will he will qualify for if the monthly PI payment factor is $10.29 per $1,000 of loan amount?

    a. $66,000
    b. $43,000
    c. $40,500
    d. $35,000

34. Find the cost of building a house 29' × 34' × 17' with a gable roof 8' high at the highest point. The cost of construction is $2.25 per cubic foot.

    a. $55,462.50
    b. $46,588.50
    c. $37,714.50
    d. $27,731.25

35. You invest $50,000 at a rate of return of 12 percent. What is the net operating income?

    a. $6,000
    b. $5,600
    c. $5,000
    d. $4,167

36. You pay $65.53 monthly interest on a loan bearing 9.25 percent annual interest. What is the loan amount rounded to the nearest hundred dollars?

    a. $1,400
    b. $2,800
    c. $6,300
    d. $8,500

37. What percentage of profit would you make if you paid $10,500 for a lot, built a home on the lot that cost $93,000, and then sold the lot and house together for $134,550?

    a. 13 percent
    b. 23 percent
    c. 30 percent
    d. 45 percent

38. You are purchasing a fourplex and closing on November 4. Each apartment rents for $575 per month. On November 1, one apartment is vacant and the other tenants paid their November rent. Compute the rent proration through the day of closing.

    a. $230.00
    b. $306.67
    c. $1,495.00
    d. $1,993.33

39. An income-producing property has $62,500 annual gross income and monthly expenses of $1,530. What is the appraised value if the appraiser uses a 10 percent capitalization rate?

    a. $441,400
    b. $625,000
    c. $183,600
    d. $609,700

40. A new house and lot cost the buyer $65,000. Of this total price, the lot was estimated to be worth $13,000. The buyer held the property for eight years. Using the straight-line method and assuming an annual depreciation of 1 percent on the house and an annual increase of 8 percent on the lot, what would be the total value of the property at the end of eight years?

    a. $47,840
    b. $69,160
    c. $81,120
    d. $101,400

41. The seller received a $121,600 check at closing after paying a 7 percent commission, $31,000 in other closing costs, and the $135,700 loan payoff. What was the total sales price?

    a. $288,300
    b. $306,300
    c. $308,500
    d. $310,000

42. A fence is being built to enclose a lot 125 feet by 350 feet. If there will be one 10-foot gate, how many running feet of fence will it take?

    a. 465
    b. 600
    c. 940
    d. 960

43. A buyer pays $2,500 each for four parcels of land. He subdivides them into six parcels and sells each of the six parcels for $1,950. What was the buyer's percentage of profit?

    a. 14.5 percent
    b. 17 percent
    c. 52 percent
    d. 78 percent

44. A property sells for $96,000. If it has appreciated 4 percent per year straight line for the past five years, what did the owner pay for the property five years ago?

    a. $76,800
    b. $80,000
    c. $92,300
    d. $115,200

45. A woman earns an annual income of $60,000, and her husband earns $2,400 per month. How much can the couple pay monthly for their mortgage payment if the lender uses a 28 percent qualifying ratio?

    a. $2,072
    b. $1,400
    c. $2,352
    d. $672

46. If a buyer borrows $4,400, agreeing to pay back principal and interest in 18 months, what annual interest rate is the buyer paying if the total payback is $5,588?

    a. 15 percent
    b. 18 percent
    c. 21.3 percent
    d. 27 percent

47. If you purchase a lot that is 125' × 150' for $6,468.75, what price did you pay per front foot?

    a. $23.52
    b. $43.13
    c. $51.75
    d. $64.69

48. A buyer is granted a 90 percent loan for $340,500. How much will her monthly principal and interest payment be, using a loan payment factor of $7.16 per $1,000 of loan?

    a. $2,194.18
    b. $4,755.59
    c. $2,437.98
    d. $3,064.50

49. Calculate the amount of commission earned by a broker on a property selling for $61,000 if 6 percent is paid on the first $50,000 and 3 percent on the remaining balance.

    a. $3,330
    b. $3,830
    c. $3,600
    d. $3,930

50. A 50' × 100' lot has a 2,400-square-foot house on it that contains four bedrooms and three bathrooms. What percentage of the lot is not taken up by the house?

a. 21 percent
b. 48 percent
c. 50 percent
d. 52 percent

Answer Key for Real Estate Math Practice Problems

1. **d** **$140,000.00 original cost**

   5% depreciation per year × 7 years = 35% total depreciation

   100% original cost − 35% total depreciation = 65% today's value

$91,000 today's value ÷	
= **$140,000** **original cost**	65% or 0.65

   $91,000 ÷ 65% (0.65) = **$140,000 original cost**

2. **a** **$1,250 per front foot**

   $125,000 sales price ÷ 100 front feet = **$1,250 per front foot**

3. **c** **$4,350 due at closing**

   100% value − 90% LTV = 10% down payment

= $8,850 down payment	
$88,500 value	10% or 0.1
×	

   $88,500 × 10% (0.10) = $8,850

   $8,850 down payment − $4,500 earnest money = **$4,350 due at closing**

4. **b** **$88,100 original cost**

   100% original cost + 12% profit = 112% sales price

$98,672 sales price ÷	
= **$88,100** **original cost**	112% or 1.12

   $98,672 ÷ 112% (1.12) = **$88,100 original cost**

5. **a** **$125,000 price**

$11,250 annual net income ÷	
= **$125,000** **price**	9% or 0.09

   $11,250 ÷ 9% (0.09) = **$125,000 price**

6. **b** **$23.33 rent proration**

   30 days in September − 28 day of closing = 2 days due

   $350 monthly rent ÷ 30 days = $11.666667 per day × 2 days = **$23.33 rent proration**

7. **c** **$1,194.00 total cost**

4" ÷ 12 = 0.333'

Concrete: 40' × 15' × 0.333' = 199.8 cubic feet ÷ 27 = 7.4 cubic yards × $60 per cubic yard = $444

Labor: 40' × 15' = 600 square feet × $1.25 per square foot = $750

$444 concrete + $750 labor = **$1,194.00 total cost**

8. **d** **$51,000 sales price**

$47,300 net to seller + $1,150 closing costs = $48,450 seller's dollars after commission

100% sales price − 5% commission = 95% seller's percentage after commission

$48,450 seller's dollars after commission ÷	
= $51,000 **sales price**	95% or 0.95

$48,450 ÷ 95% (0.95) = **$51,000 sales price**

9. **d** **$652.08 average monthly rent**

$75,000 gross annual sales − $50,000 = $25,000 gross annual sales subject to 2.5%

= $625 annual percentage rate	
$25,000 value gross annual sales ×	2.5% or 0.025

$25,000 × 2.5% (0.025) = $625

$625 annual percentage rent ÷ 12 months = $52.08 monthly percentage rent

$600 monthly minimum rent + $52.08 monthly percentage rent = **$652.08 average monthly rent**

10. **b** **30 percent**

$525 monthly rent × 12 months = $6,300 annual rent

÷ $6,300 annual rent	
$21,000 annual income	**= 0.3 or 30%**

$6,300 ÷ $21,000 = 0.30 or **30%**

11. **a** **$657**

$$\frac{= \$4{,}380 \text{ full commission}}{\begin{array}{c|c} \$73{,}000 & 6\% \\ \text{sales price} \quad \times & \text{or } 0.06 \end{array}}$$

$73,000 × 6% (0.06) = $4,380

$4,380 full commission ÷ 2 brokers = $2,190 broker's share of the commission

$$\frac{= \$657 \text{ listing salesperson's commission}}{\begin{array}{c|c} \$2{,}190 \text{ broker's share} & 30\% \\ \text{of the commission} \quad \times & 0.3 \end{array}}$$

$2,190 × 30% (0.30) = **$657 commission**

12. **a** **10,626.63 square feet**

6" ÷ 12 = 0.5' + 75' = 75.5' frontage

9" ÷ 12 = 0.75' + 140' = 140.75' depth

140.75' × 75.5' = **10,626.63 square feet**

13. **c** **$1,736,000 value**

$775 monthly rent × 28 units × 12 months = $260,400 annual scheduled gross income

$260,400 annual scheduled gross income − 5% vacancy rate = $247,380 annual effective gross income

$247,380 annual effective gross income − $82,460 annual expenses = $164,920 annual net operating income

$$\frac{\div \ \$164{,}920 \text{ annual net operating income } \div}{\begin{array}{c|c} = \$1{,}736{,}000 \text{ value} & 9.5\% \\ & \text{or } 0.095 \end{array}}$$

$164,920 ÷ 9.5% (0.095) = **$1,736,000 value**

14. **a** **$127.11 interest due**

Seller owes buyer 10 days (August 1 through August 10)

$$\frac{= \$4{,}575.90 \text{ annual interest}}{\begin{array}{c|c} \$43{,}580 \text{ loan balance} & 10.5\% \\ \times & 0.105 \end{array}}$$

$43,580 × 10.5% (0.105) = $4,575.90

$4,575.90 annual interest ÷ 360 days = $12.71083 per day × 10 days = **$127.11 interest due**

15. c $5,512.50 for points and origination fee

2.5 points loan discount + 1 point origination fee = 3.5 points

= $157,500 loan	
$175,000 sales price	90%
×	or 0.9

$175,000 × 90% or (0.90) = $157,500

= **$5,512.50 for points and origination fee**	
$157,500 loan	3.5%
×	or 0.035

$157,500 × 3.5% (0.035) = **$5,512.50 for points and origination fee**

16. b $316.67 interest

= $475 annual interest	
$5,000 loan	9.5%
×	or 0.095

$5,000 × 9.5% (0.095) = $475

$475 annual interest ÷ 12 months × 8 months = **$316.67 interest**

17. d   27,225 square feet per lot

1/8 = 1 ÷ 8 = 0.125 for streets

100 acres × 0.125 = 12.5 acres for streets

100 acres − 12.5 acres for streets = 87.5 acres for lots × 43,560 = 3,811,500 square feet ÷ 140 lots = **27,225 square feet per lot**

18. a $393.38 tax proration

Seller owes the buyer January 1 to April 23

   31 January

 + 28 February

 + 31 March

 + 22 April

 112 days due

$1,282 annual tax ÷ 365 days = $3.51233 per day × 112 days = **$393.38 tax proration**

19. b $1,197.92 monthly net operating income

= $14,375 annual net operating income	
$115,000 investment	12.5%
×	or 0.125

$115,000 × 12.5% (0.125) = $14,375

$14,375 annual net operating income ÷ 12 months = **$1,197.92 monthly net operating income**

20. b $1,404 salesperson's commission

$$\frac{= \$3,510 \text{ full commission}}{\$58,500 \text{ sales price} \quad | \quad \begin{array}{c} 6\% \\ \times \quad \text{or } 0.06 \end{array}}$$

$58,500 × 6% (0.06) = $3,510

$$\frac{= \mathbf{\$1,404 \text{ salesperson's commission}}}{\$3,510 \text{ full commission} \quad | \quad \begin{array}{c} 40\% \\ \times \quad \text{or } 0.4 \end{array}}$$

$3,510 × 40% (0.40) = **$1,404 salesperson's commission**

21. c 20 percent profit

348,480 square feet × $0.75 per square foot = $261,360 cost

348,480 square feet ÷ 43,560 = 8 acres × 2 lots per acre = 16 lots – 3 lots = 13 lots sold × $24,125 each = $313,625 total sales price

$313,625 sales price – $261,360 cost = $52,265 profit

$$\frac{\div \$52,265 \text{ profit}}{\$231,360 \text{ cost} \quad | \quad \begin{array}{c} = \mathbf{0.199973} \\ \text{or } \mathbf{20\% \text{ profit}} \end{array}}$$

$52,265 ÷ $261,360 = 0.199973 or **20% profit**

22. a $132.31 insurance proration

30	February
– 16	closing date
14	days left in February
+ 30	March
+ 30	April
+ 30	May
+ 5	June
109	days due

$437 annual premium ÷ 360 days = $1.21389 per day × 109 days due = **$132.31 insurance proration**

23. b 9 percent annual interest rate

$450 × 2 = $900 annual interest

$$\frac{\div \$900 \text{ annual interest}}{\$10,000 \text{ loan} \quad | \quad = \mathbf{0.09 \text{ or } 9\%}}$$

$900 ÷ $10,000 = **0.09 or 9% interest rate**

24. d 117,600 cubic feet

120' × 80' = 9,600 square feet in building – 1,200 square feet for office = 8,400 square feet left in warehouse × 14-foot ceiling = **117,600 cubic feet left in warehouse**

25. b $571,500 price

$68,580 annual net operating income ÷	
= $571,500 price	12% or 0.12

$68,580 ÷ 12% (0.12) = **$571,500 price**

26. c $77.90 interest proration

Seller owes buyer 19 days (April 1 *through* April 19)

= $1,476 annual interest	
$18,450 loan balance	8%
×	or 0.08

$18,450 × 8% (0.08) = $1,476

$1,476 annual interest ÷ 360 days = $4.10 per day × 19 days = **$77.90 interest proration**

27. d $17,625 today's value

3.5% appreciation per year × 5 years = 17.5% total appreciation

100% cost + 17.5% total appreciation = 117.5% today's value

= $17,625 today's value	
$15,000 original cost	117.5%
×	or 1.175

$15,000 × 117.5% (1.175) = **$17,625 today's value**

28. b 11,000 square feet left

150' depth – 25' setback = 125' left

100' frontage – 6' on one side – 6' on one side = 88' left

125' × 88' = **11,000 square feet left**

29. b $13,000 annual rent

$1,000 monthly minimum rent × 12 months = $12,000 annual minimum rent

$150,000 annual sales – $100,000 = $50,000 annual sales subject to 2%

= $1,000 annual percentage rent	
$50,000 annual sales	2%
×	or 0.02

$50,000 × 2% (0.02) = $1,000

$12,000 annual minimum rent + $1,000 annual percentage rent = **$13,000 annual rent**

30. **a**   **$965.26 tax proration**

Seller owes buyer January 1 to August 29

       31   January
    + 28   February
    + 31   March
    + 30   April
    + 31   May
    + 30   June
    + 31   July
    + 28   August
     240   days due

$1,468 annual tax ÷ 365 days = $4.02192 per day × 240 days = **$965.26 tax proration**

31. **c**   **$23,595 sales price**

1.25 acres × 43,560 = 54,450 square feet ÷ 150' deep = 363' frontage × $65 per front foot = **$23,595 sales price**

32. **b**   **$80,000 sales price**

$5,200 Full commission ÷	
= $80,000 sales price	6.5% or 0.065

$5,200 ÷ 6.5% (0.065) = **$80,000 sales price**

33. **d**   **$35,000 loan**

$20,000 annual salary ÷ 12 months = $1,666.67 monthly salary

= $416.67 monthly PTI payment	
$1,666.67 monthly salary	25% or 0.25
×	

$1,666.67 × 25% = $416.67

$678.24 annual taxes and insurance ÷ 12 months = $56.52 monthly taxes and insurance

$416.67 monthly PITI payment − $56.52 monthly TI = $360.15 monthly PI payment

$360.15 monthly PI payment ÷ $10.29 × $1,000 = **$35,000 loan**

34. **b**   **$46,588.50 cost**

29' × 34' × 17' = 16,762 cubic feet in house

29' × 34' × 8' ÷ 2 = 3,944 cubic feet in roof

16,762 cubic feet + 3,944 cubic feet = 20,706 cubic feet total × $2.25 per cubic foot = **$46,588.50 cost**

35. a $6,000 annual net operating income

$$\frac{= \$6,000 \text{ annual net operating income}}{\$50,000 \text{ investment} \quad \bigg| \quad \times \quad \begin{array}{c} 12\% \\ \text{or } 0.12 \end{array}}$$

$50,000 × 12% (0.12) = **$6,000 annual net operating income**

36. d $8,500 loan

$65.53 monthly interest × 12 months = $786.36 annual interest

$$\frac{\$786.36 \text{ annual interest} \div}{\begin{array}{c} = \$8,501.19 \\ \textbf{or } \$8,500 \text{ loan} \end{array} \quad \bigg| \quad \begin{array}{c} 9.25\% \\ \text{or } 0.0925 \end{array}}$$

$786.36 ÷ 9.25% (0.0925) = **$8501.19 loan**

37. c   30 percent

$10,500 cost of lot + $93,000 cost of home = $103,500 total cost

$134,550 sales price − $103,500 total cost = $31,050 profit

$$\frac{\div \$31,050 \text{ profit}}{\$103,500 \text{ total cost} \quad \bigg| \quad = 0.3 \text{ or } 30\%}$$

$31,050 ÷ $103,500 = **0.3 or 30%**

38. c $1,495.00 rent proration

  30 November

− 4 day of closing

  26 days due

$575 monthly rent × 3 units = $1,725 monthly rent ÷ 30 days = $57.50 per day × 26 days = **$1,495 rent proration**

39. a $441,400 value

$1,530 monthly expenses × 12 months = $18,360 annual expenses

$62,500 annual gross income − $18,360 annual expenses = $44,140 annual net operating income

$$\frac{\$44,140 \text{ annual net operating income} \div}{= \$441,400 \text{ value} \quad \bigg| \quad \begin{array}{c} 10\% \\ \text{or } 0.1 \end{array}}$$

$44,140 ÷ 10% (0.10) = **$441,400 value**

40. b $69,160 property value

$65,000 cost of house and lot – $13,000 cost of lot = $52,000 cost of house

Lot:

8% annual appreciation × 8 years = 64% total appreciation

100% cost + 64% total appreciation = 164% today's value

= $21,320 today's value of lot	
$13,000 cost of lot	164%
×	or 1.64

$13,000 × 164% (1.64) = $21,320

House:

1% annual depreciation × 8 years = 8% total depreciation

100% cost – 8% total depreciation = 92% today's value

= $47,840 today's value of house	
$52,000 cost of house	92%
×	or 0.92

$52,000 × 92% (0.92) = $47,840

$21,320 lot + $47,840 house = **$69,160 property value**

41. d $310,000 sales price

$121,600 seller's net + $31,000 closing costs + $135,700 loan payoff = $288,300 seller's dollars after commission

100% sales price – 7% commission = 93% seller's dollars after commission

$288,300 seller's dollars after commission ÷	
= **$310,000 sales price**	93%
	or 0.93

$288,300 ÷ 93% (0.93) = **$310,000 sales price**

42. c 940 running feet

125' + 350' + 125' + 350' – 10' gate = **940 running feet**

43. b 17 percent profit

$2,500 cost × 4 parcels = $10,000 total cost

$1,950 sales price × 6 parcels = $11,700 sales price

$11,700 sales price – $10,000 cost = $1,700 profit

÷ $1,700 profit	
$10,000 cost	= 0.17 or 17% profit

$1,700 ÷ $10,000 cost = 0.17 or **17% profit**

44. b $80,000 original cost

4% annual appreciation × 5 years = 20% total appreciation

100% cost + 20% total appreciation = 120% today's value

$$\frac{\$96,000 \text{ today's value} \div}{= \$80,000 \text{ original cost} \quad | \quad \substack{120\% \\ 1.2}}$$

$96,000 ÷ 120% (1.20) = **$80,000 original cost**

45. a $2,072 monthly payment

$60,000 annual salary ÷ 12 Months = $5,000 wife's monthly salary + $2,400 husband's monthly salary = $7,400 total monthly salary

$$\frac{= \$2,072 \text{ monthly payment}}{\substack{\$7,400 \text{ total} \\ \text{monthly salary}} \quad | \quad \substack{28\% \\ \times \quad \text{or } 0.28}}$$

$7,400 × 28% (0.28) = **$2,072 monthly payment**

46. b 18 percent annual interest rate

$5,588 payback (principal + interest) − $4,400 loan (principal) = $1,188 interest for 18 months ÷ 18 months = $66 monthly interest × 12 months = $792 annual interest

$$\frac{\div \$792 \text{ annual interest}}{\$4,400 \text{ loan} \quad | \quad \substack{= 0.18 \text{ or } 18\% \text{ annual} \\ \text{interest rate}}}$$

$792 ÷ $4,400 = 0.18 or **18% annual interest rate**

47. c $51.75 per front foot

$6,468.75 price ÷ 125 front feet = **$51.75 per front foot**

48. c $2,437.98 monthly principal and interest payment

$340,500 loan ÷ $1,000 × $7.16 =
$2,437.98 monthly principal and interest payment

49. a $3,330 total commission

$$\frac{- \$3,000 \text{ commission}}{\$50,000 \text{ sales price} \quad | \quad \substack{6\% \\ \times \quad \text{or } 0.06}}$$

$50,000 × 6% (0.06) = $3,000

$61,000 total sales price − $50,000 sales price at 6% = $11,000 sales price at 3%

$$\frac{= \$330 \text{ commission}}{\$11,000 \text{ sales price} \quad | \quad \substack{3\% \\ \times \quad \text{or } 0.03}}$$

$11,000 × 3% (0.03) = $330

$3,000 commission + $330 commission = **$3,330 total commission**

50. d 52 percent not taken up by house

50' × 100' = 5,000 square feet of lot − 2,400 square feet of house = 2,600 square feet not taken up by house

÷ 2,600 square feet	
5,000 square feet total	= 0.52 or 52% not taken up by house

2,600 ÷ 5,000 = **0.52 or 52% not taken up by house**

Sample Examinations

Several commercial organizations produce real estate licensing exams. Each state is free to choose its testing service. In some states, the real estate commission writes and administers the examination. In others, a commercial testing service prepares a two-part examination that includes both state-specific license law questions and questions on broader national issues and general principles. Most states use the examinations produced by Applied Measurement Professionals (AMP), PSI Examination Services (PSI), Promissor, and Thomson Prometric (formerly Experior). However, different states use many other testing services.

In this book, the chapter review questions and the following sample examinations are generally based on the format and focus of questions of two of the services MOST widely used: Promissor and PSI. Your state may use a different testing service. It's possible that the questions you encounter on your licensing examination may look slightly different from the practice questions you've been using here (i.e., an "a-b-c-d" format for answer choices rather than a "1-2-3-4" structure). Don't be flustered; just remember that there are still four choices, no matter how they are listed.

The sample examinations included here are not intended to be a review of *Modern Real Estate Practice* or your real estate course. Rather, they are designed to imitate real estate licensing exams, any one of which may emphasize some concepts and ignore others. The answer key for these sample examinations includes the relevant chapter from which each question was drawn. Questions that involve mathematical calculations in addition to one or more real estate concepts will refer you to the math skills review in "Math FAQs." If your answer is not correct, it is advisable to restudy the suggested material. *Note that proration calculations here are based on a 30-day month unless otherwise stated.*

Sample Exam 1

1. Which of the following is a lien on real estate?
   a. Recorded easement
   b. Recorded mortgage
   c. Encroachment
   d. Deed restriction

2. A sales contract was signed by a minor. Which of the following describes this contract?
   a. Voidable
   b. Breached
   c. Discharged
   d. Void

3. A broker receives a check for earnest money from a buyer and deposits the money in the broker's personal interest-bearing checking account over the weekend. This action exposes the broker to a charge of
   a. commingling.
   b. novation.
   c. subrogation.
   d. accretion.

4. A borrower takes out a mortgage loan that requires monthly payments of $875.70 for 20 years and a final payment of $24,095. This is what type of loan?
   a. Wraparound
   b. Accelerated
   c. Balloon
   d. Variable

5. If a borrower computed the interest charged for the previous month on a $260,000 loan balance as $1,300, what is the borrower's interest rate?
   a. 7 percent
   b. 7½ percent
   c. 6 percent
   d. 6½ percent

6. A broker signs a contract with a buyer. Under the contract, the broker agrees to help the buyer find a suitable property and to represent the buyer in negotiations with the seller. Although the buyer may not sign an agreement with any other broker, the buyer may look for and purchase a property without the broker's assistance. The broker is entitled to payment only if the broker locates the property that is ultimately purchased. What kind of agreement has this broker signed?
   a. Exclusive buyer agency agreement
   b. Exclusive-agency buyer agency agreement
   c. Open buyer agency agreement
   d. Option contract

7. A grantor conveys property by delivering a deed. The deed contains five covenants. This is MOST likely a
   a. general warranty deed.
   b. quitclaim deed.
   c. special warranty deed.
   d. deed in trust.

8. A real estate licensee does not show non-Asian clients any properties in several traditionally Asian neighborhoods. The licensee bases this practice on the need to preserve the valuable cultural integrity of Asian immigrant communities. Which statement is TRUE regarding the licensee's policy?
   a. The licensee's policy is steering and violates the fair housing laws regardless of motivation.
   b. Because the licensee is not attempting to restrict the rights of any single minority group, the practice does not constitute steering.
   c. The licensee's policy is steering, but it does not violate the fair housing laws because cultural preservation is the motive, not exclusion or discrimination.
   d. The licensee's policy has the effect, but not the intent, of steering.

9. A woman grants a life estate to her son-in-law and stipulates that upon his death, the title to the property will pass to her grandson. This second estate is known as a(n)

   a. remainder.
   b. reversion.
   c. estate at sufferance.
   d. estate for years.

10. A primary feature of property held in joint tenancy is that

   a. a maximum of two people can own the real estate.
   b. the fractional interests of the owners can be different.
   c. additional owners may be added later.
   d. there is always right of survivorship.

11. A licensee is a licensed real estate salesperson who has a written contract with his broker that specifies that he will not be treated as an employee. The licensee's entire income is from sales commissions rather than an hourly wage. Based on these facts, the licensee will be treated by the IRS as

   a. a real estate assistant.
   b. an employee.
   c. a subagent.
   d. self-employed.

12. The states in which the owner gives up legal title of mortgaged real estate are known as

   a. title theory states.
   b. lien theory states.
   c. statutory title states.
   d. strict title forfeiture states.

13. The form of tenancy that will expire on a specific date is a

   a. joint tenancy.
   b. tenancy for years.
   c. tenancy in common.
   d. tenancy by the entirety.

14. A suburban home that lacks sufficient indoor plumbing suffers from which condition?

   a. Functional obsolescence
   b. Curable physical deterioration
   c. Incurable physical deterioration
   d. External obsolescence

15. A developer built a structure that has six stories. Several years later, an ordinance was passed in that area banning any building six stories or higher. This building is a

   a. nonconforming use.
   b. situation in which the structure would have to be demolished.
   c. conditional use.
   d. violation of the zoning laws.

16. Assuming that the listing broker and the selling broker in a transaction split their commission equally, what was the sales price of the property if the commission rate was 6.5 percent and the listing broker received $12,593.50?

   a. $139,900
   b. $256,200
   c. $387,492
   d. $193,746

17. A real estate licensee specializes in helping both buyers and sellers with the necessary paperwork involved in transferring property. Although not an agent of either party, the licensee may not disclose either party's confidential information to the other. The licensee is BEST described as a(n)

   a. buyer's agent.
   b. independent contractor.
   c. dual agent.
   d. transactional broker.

18. Three women owned a house as joint tenants. In the year 2009, one died. Last month, another died. Based on these facts, which of the following correctly describes the remaining woman's ownership interest in the house?

   a. Joint tenancy with the deceased women's heirs
   b. Tenancy in common with the deceased women's heirs
   c. Severalty
   d. Partitioned tenancy by the entirety

19. The listing and selling brokers agree to split a 7 percent commission 50-50 on a $295,900 sale. The listing broker gives the listing salesperson 50 percent of the listing broker's share, and the selling broker gives the selling salesperson 65 percent. How much does the selling salesperson earn from the sale after deducting expenses of $1,300?

   a. $5,431.73
   b. $10,356.50
   c. $5,178.00
   d. $6,731.73

20. Police powers include all of the following EXCEPT

   a. zoning.
   b. deed restrictions.
   c. building codes.
   d. subdivision regulations.

21. A seller wants to net $165,000 from the sale of a house after paying the broker's fee of 6 percent. The seller's gross sales price will be

   a. $182,242.
   b. $174,900.
   c. $155,000.
   d. $175,532.

22. Three acres equals how many square feet?

   a. 43,560
   b. 130,680
   c. 156,840
   d. 27,878,400

23. A buyer is purchasing a condominium unit in a subdivision and obtains financing from a local savings and loan association. In this situation, which term BEST describes this buyer?

   a. Vendor
   b. Mortgagor
   c. Grantor
   d. Lessor

24. The current value of a property is $140,000. The property is assessed at 40 percent of its current value for real estate tax purposes, with an equalization factor of 1.5 applied to the assessed value. If the tax rate is $4 per $100 of assessed valuation, what is the amount of tax due on the property?

   a. $840
   b. $3,360
   c. $2,240
   d. $2,100

25. A building was sold for $260,000, with the purchaser putting 10 percent down and obtaining a loan for the balance. The lending institution charged a 1 percent loan origination fee. What was the total cash used for the purchase?

   a. $2,340
   b. $23,400
   c. $28,340
   d. $26,000

26. A parcel of vacant land has an assessed valuation of $274,550. If the assessment is 85 percent of market value, what is the market value?

   a. $315,732.50
   b. $320,000.00
   c. $323,000.00
   d. $830,333.33

27. Which of the following BEST describes a capitalization rate?

   a. Amount determined by the gross rent multiplier
   b. Rate of return an income property will produce
   c. Mathematical value determined by a sales price
   d. Rate at which the amount of depreciation in a property is measured

28. A parcel of land described as "the NW¼ and the SW¼ of Section 6, T4N, R8W of the Third Principal Meridian" was sold for $875 per acre. The listing broker will receive a 5 percent commission on the total sales price. How much will the broker receive?

    a. $1,750
    b. $5,040
    c. $14,000
    d. $15,040

29. If a house was sold for $180,000 and the buyer obtained an FHA-insured mortgage loan for $120,000, how much money would the buyer pay in discount points if the lender charged two points?

    a. $1,200
    b. $1,000
    c. $2,400
    d. $1,800

30. The commission rate is 7 percent on a sale of $250,000. What is the dollar amount of the commission?

    a. $35,000
    b. $17,500
    c. $1,750
    d. $3,571

31. A prospective buyer signs an offer to purchase a residential property. All of the following circumstances would automatically terminate the offer EXCEPT the

    a. buyer signed a written offer to buy a house and then died.
    b. buyer revoked the offer between the presentation and a possible acceptance.
    c. seller made a counteroffer.
    d. seller received a better offer from another buyer.

32. A buyer purchased a home under a land contract. Until the contract is paid in full, the buyer

    a. holds legal title to the premises.
    b. has no legal interest in the property.
    c. possesses a legal life estate in the premises.
    d. has equitable title in the property.

33. A buyer and a seller sign a contract for the sale of real property. A few days later, they decide to change many of the terms of the contract, while retaining the basic intent to buy and sell. The process by which the new contract replaces the old one is called

    a. assignment.
    b. novation.
    c. assemblage.
    d. rescission.

34. Using the services of a mortgage broker, a buyer borrowed $25,000 from a private lender. After the loan costs were deducted, the buyer received $24,255. What is the face amount of the note?

    a. $24,255
    b. $25,000
    c. $4,255
    d. $645

35. Whose signature is necessary for a signed offer to purchase real estate to become a contract?

    a. Buyer's only
    b. Buyer's and seller's
    c. Seller's only
    d. Seller's and seller's broker's

36. A borrower has just made the final payment on a mortgage loan. Regardless of this fact, the records will still show a lien on the mortgaged property until which event occurs?

    a. A mortgage satisfaction document is recorded.
    b. A reconveyance of the mortgage document is delivered to the mortgage holder.
    c. A novation of the mortgage document takes place.
    d. An estoppel of the mortgage document is filed with the clerk of the county in which the mortgagee is located.

37. If the annual net income from a commercial property is $75,000 and the capitalization rate is 8 percent, what is the property worth if the income approach is used?

    a. $694,000
    b. $600,000
    c. $810,000
    d. $937,500

38. A broker enters into a listing agreement with a seller in which the seller will receive $120,000 from the sale of a vacant lot and the broker will receive any sale proceeds exceeding that amount. This is what type of listing?

a. Exclusive-agency
b. Net
c. Exclusive-right-to-sell
d. Multiple

39. Under a cooperative form of ownership, an owner

a. is a shareholder in the corporation.
b. owns the unit outright and a share of the common areas.
c. will have to take out a new mortgage loan on a newly acquired unit.
d. receives a fixed-term lease for the unit.

40. A known defect or a cloud on title to property may be cured by

a. obtaining quitclaim deeds from all appropriate parties.
b. recording the title after closing.
c. paying cash for the property at the settlement.
d. purchasing a title insurance policy at closing.

41. A seller signed an exclusive-right-to-sell agreement with a licensee. If the seller finds a suitable buyer with no assistance, the licensee is entitled to

a. full compensation from the buyer.
b. no compensation from the seller.
c. partial compensation.
d. full compensation from the seller.

42. Under the terms of a net lease, a commercial tenant would usually be directly responsible for paying all the following property expenses EXCEPT

a. maintenance expenses.
b. mortgage debt service.
c. fire and extended-coverage insurance.
d. real estate taxes.

43. The Civil Rights Act of 1866 prohibits discrimination based on

a. sex.
b. religion.
c. race.
d. familial status.

44. What would it cost to put new carpeting in a room measuring 15 feet by 20 feet if the carpet costs $16.95 per square yard, plus a $250 installation charge?

a. $589
b. $815
c. $505
d. $5,335

45. What is the difference between a general lien and a specific lien?

a. A general lien cannot be enforced in court, while a specific lien can.
b. A specific lien is held by only one person, while a general lien must be held by two or more people.
c. A general lien is a lien against personal property, while a specific lien is a lien against real estate.
d. A specific lien is a lien against a certain parcel of real estate, while a general lien covers all of a debtor's property.

46. In an option to purchase real estate, which statement is TRUE of the optionee?

a. The optionee must purchase the property but may do so at any time within the option period.
b. The optionee is limited to a refund of the option consideration if the option is exercised.
c. The optionee cannot obtain third-party financing on the property until after the option has expired.
d. The optionee has no obligation to purchase the property during the option period.

47. A village board has decided that a parking lot would enhance the beauty, safety, and vitality of its community by keeping cars from parking on the streets. Unfortunately, a house is located on land needed for the new parking lot. Based on these facts, which statement is *TRUE*?

a. The homeowner's constitutional right to own property cannot be infringed by the village under any circumstances.

b. The village may tear down the house and build the parking lot without paying the homeowner any compensation, through the village's constitutional authority under the takings clause.

c. The village may tear down the house but must first pay the homeowner a fair amount for the home.

d. The village may not seize the house because it has insufficient reason to do so.

48. How many acres are there in the N½ of the SW¼ and the NE¼ of the SE¼ of a section?

a. 20
b. 40
c. 80
d. 120

49. A home is the smallest in a neighborhood of large, expensive houses. The effect of the other houses on the value of the small home is known as

a. regression.
b. progression.
c. substitution.
d. contribution.

50. A lien that arises as a result of a judgment, estate or inheritance taxes, a decedent's debts, or federal taxes is what type of lien?

a. Specific
b. General
c. Voluntary
d. Equitable

51. All of the following will terminate an offer to purchase real estate *EXCEPT*

a. failure to accept the offer within a prescribed period.

b. revocation by the offeror communicated to the offeree after acceptance.

c. a conditional acceptance of the offer by the offeree.

d. the death of the offeror or offeree.

52. Two men are joint tenants. One of the men sells his interest to another person. What is the remaining man's relationship to the new tenant regarding the property?

a. Joint tenants
b. Tenants in common
c. Tenants by the entirety
d. No relationship, because he cannot sell his joint tenancy interest

53. Two friends enter into a six-month oral lease. If one friend defaults, the other may

a. not bring a court action because leases must be in writing for a court to review them.

b. not bring a court action because the statute of frauds governs six-month leases.

c. bring a court action because six-month leases need not be in writing to be enforceable.

d. bring a court action because the statute of limitations does not apply to oral leases, regardless of their term.

54. On Monday, the buyer offers to purchase a vacant lot for $25,000. On Tuesday, the owner counteroffers to sell the lot for $29,000. On Friday, the owner withdraws the counteroffer and accepts the buyer's original offer of $25,000. Under these circumstances, which statement is *TRUE*?

a. A valid agreement exists because the seller accepted the buyer's offer exactly as it was made, regardless of the fact that it was not accepted immediately.

b. A valid agreement exists because the seller accepted before the buyer provided notice that the offer was withdrawn.

c. No valid agreement exists because the buyer's offer was not accepted within 72 hours of its having been made.

d. No valid agreement exists because the seller's counteroffer was a rejection of the buyer's offer, and once rejected, it cannot be accepted later.

55. A man's neighbors use his driveway to reach their garage, which is on their property. The man's attorney explains that the neighbors have the right to use the driveway. The man's property is the

a. dominant tenement.

b. servient tenement.

c. fee simple defeasible estate.

d. fee simple determinable estate.

56. If the quarterly interest at 7.5 percent is $562.50, what is the principal amount of the loan?

a. $7,500

b. $15,000

c. $30,000

d. $75,000

57. A deed conveys ownership to the grantee "as long as the existing building is not torn down." What type of estate does this deed create?

a. Fee simple determinable estate

b. Homestead estate

c. Fee simple absolute estate

d. Life estate pur autre vie, with the measuring life being the building's expected structural lifetime

58. If the mortgage loan is 80 percent of the appraised value of a house and the interest rate of 6 percent amounts to $460 for the first month, what is the appraised value of the house?

a. $92,000

b. $73,600

c. $115,000

d. $55,200

59. Local zoning ordinances may regulate all of the following *EXCEPT* the

a. height of buildings in an area.

b. density of population.

c. appropriate use of buildings in an area.

d. market value of a property.

60. A broker took a listing and later discovered that the client had been declared incompetent by a court. What is the current status of the listing?

a. The listing is unaffected because the broker acted in good faith as the owner's agent.

b. The listing is of no value to the broker because the contract is void.

c. The listing entitles the broker to collect a commission from the client's guardian or trustee if the broker produces a buyer.

d. The listing must be renegotiated between the broker and the client, based on the new information.

61. After a borrower's default on home mortgage loan payments, the lender obtained a court order to foreclose on the property. At the foreclosure sale, the property sold for $164,000; the unpaid balance on the loan at the time of foreclosure was $178,000. What must the lender do to recover the $14,000 that the borrower still owes?

a. Sue for specific performance

b. Sue for damages

c. Seek a deficiency judgment

d. Seek a judgment by default

62. Which activity is forbidden by the federal Fair Housing Act of 1968?

   a. Limitation by religion and nationality in the sale of a single-family home where the property is not advertised by the listing broker

   b. Limitation to members only in noncommercial lodgings of a private club

   c. Limitations against familial status and disability in the rental of a unit in an owner-occupied three-family dwelling when no discriminatory advertising is used

   d. Limitation by religion and sex in noncommercial housing in a convent or monastery

63. A buyer purchases a $137,000 property, depositing $3,000 as earnest money. The buyer obtains a 75 percent LTV loan on the property, with no additional items to be prorated and no closing costs to the buyer. How much more cash will the buyer need at the settlement?

   a. $34,250

   b. $33,500

   c. $10,275

   d. $31,250

64. A licensee arrives to present a purchase offer to a seller who is seriously ill and finds the seller's son and daughter-in-law also present. The son and daughter-in-law angrily urge the seller to accept the offer, even though it is much less than the asking price for the property. If the seller accepts the offer, she may not be bound by it because the

   a. licensee improperly presented an offer that was less than the asking price.

   b. licensee's failure to protect the seller from the son and daughter-in-law constituted a violation of the licensee's fiduciary duties.

   c. seller's rights under the ADA have been violated by the son and daughter-in-law.

   d. seller was under undue influence from the son and daughter-in-law, so the contract is voidable.

65. A property is sold. The deed of conveyance contained only the following guarantee: "This property was not encumbered during the time the seller owned it except as noted in this deed." What type of deed makes such a covenant?

   a. General warranty

   b. Special warranty

   c. Bargain and sale

   d. Quitclaim

66. An unmarried couple own a parcel of real estate. Each owns an undivided interest, with one owning one-third and the other owning two-thirds. The form of ownership under which the couple owns their property is

   a. severalty.

   b. joint tenancy.

   c. tenancy at will.

   d. tenancy in common.

67. A buyer agrees to purchase a house for $184,500. The buyer pays $2,000 as earnest money and obtains a new mortgage loan for $167,600. The purchase contract provides for a March 15 settlement. The buyer and the sellers prorate the previous year's real estate taxes of $1,880.96, which have been prepaid. The buyer has additional closing costs of $1,250, and the sellers have other closing costs of $850. How much cash must the buyer bring to the settlement?

   a. $16,389

   b. $17,639

   c. $17,839

   d. $19,639

68. A licensee listed a house for $247,900. A member of a racial minority group saw the house and was interested in it. When the prospective buyer asked the licensee the price of the house, the licensee said that it was listed for $253,000 and that the seller was very firm on the price. Under the federal Fair Housing Act of 1968, such a statement is

   a. legal because the law requires only that the buyer be given the opportunity to buy the house.
   b. legal because the representation was made by the licensee and not directly by the owner.
   c. illegal because the difference in the offering price and the quoted price was greater than 10 percent.
   d. illegal because the terms of the potential sale were changed for the prospective buyer.

69. A woman placed a property in a trust. When she died, her will directed the trustee to sell the property and distribute the proceeds of the sale to her heirs. The trustee sold the property in accordance with the will. What type of deed was delivered at settlement?

   a. Trustee's deed
   b. Trustor's deed
   c. Deed of trust
   d. Reconveyance deed

70. An appraiser has been hired to prepare an appraisal report of a property for loan purposes. The property is an elegant old mansion that is now used as a restaurant. Which approach to value should the appraiser probably give the greatest weight when making this appraisal?

   a. Income
   b. Sales comparison
   c. Replacement cost
   d. Reproduction cost

71. A borrower applies for a mortgage, and the loan officer suggests that the borrower consider a term mortgage loan. Which statement BEST explains what the loan officer means?

   a. All the interest is paid at the end of the term.
   b. The debt is partially amortized over the life of the loan.
   c. The length of the term is limited by state law.
   d. The entire principal amount is due at the end of the term.

72. A condominium community has a swimming pool, tennis courts, and a biking trail. These facilities are MOST likely owned by the

   a. condominium board.
   b. corporation in which the unit owners hold stock.
   c. unit owners in the form of proportional divided interests.
   d. unit owners in the form of percentage undivided interests.

In questions 73 and 74, identify how each item would be entered on a closing statement in a typical real estate transaction.

73. The buyer's earnest money deposit is a

   a. credit to the buyer only.
   b. credit to the seller, debit to the buyer.
   c. credit to the buyer and the seller.
   d. debit to the buyer only.

74. Prepaid insurance and tax reserves, where the buyer assumes the mortgage, is a

   a. credit to the buyer, debit to the seller.
   b. credit to the seller only.
   c. debit to the seller only.
   d. debit to the buyer, credit to the seller.

75. Real property can become personal property by the process known as

   a. annexation.
   b. severance.
   c. hypothecation.
   d. accretion.

76. A man and a woman are next-door neighbors. The man gives the woman permission to park a camper in his yard for a few weeks. He does not charge her rent for the use of the yard. The man has given the woman a(n)

   a. revocable trust.
   b. estate for years.
   c. license.
   d. permissive encroachment.

77. What is the cost of constructing a fence 6 feet 6 inches high around a lot measuring 90 feet by 175 feet, if the cost of erecting the fence is $1.25 per linear foot and the cost of materials is $0.825 per square foot of fence?

   a. $1,752
   b. $2,054
   c. $2,084
   d. $3,505

78. A seller signs a listing agreement with a licensee. A second licensee obtains a buyer for the house, and the first licensee does not receive a commission. The first licensee does not sue the seller, even though the seller compensated the second licensee. The listing agreement between the seller and the first licensee was probably which type?

   a. Exclusive-right-to-sell
   b. Open
   c. Exclusive-agency
   d. Dual-agency

79. Antitrust laws do NOT prohibit real estate

   a. companies agreeing on fees charged to sellers.
   b. brokers allocating markets based on the value of homes.
   c. companies allocating markets based on the location of commercial buildings.
   d. salespeople within the same office agreeing on a standard commission rate.

80. A tenant leased an apartment from a property owner. Because the owner failed to perform routine maintenance, the apartment building's central heating plant broke down in the fall. The owner neglected to have the heating system repaired, and the tenant had no heat for the first six weeks of winter. The tenant had reported this problem repeatedly to the owner. Although eight months remained on his lease, the tenant moved out of the apartment and refused to pay any rent. If the owner sues to recover the outstanding rent, what would be the tenant's BEST defense?

   a. Because the tenant lived in the apartment for more than 25 percent of the lease term, he was entitled to move out at any time without penalty.
   b. The tenant was entitled to vacate the premises because the landlord's failure to repair the heating system constituted abandonment.
   c. Because the apartment was made uninhabitable, the landlord's actions resulted in actual eviction.
   d. The landlord's actions resulted in constructive eviction.

Sample Exam 2

1. A tenant's landlord plans to sell the building in which the tenant lives to the state so that a freeway can be built. The tenant's lease has expired, but the landlord permits the tenant to stay in the apartment until the building is torn down. The tenant continues to pay the rent as prescribed in the lease. What kind of tenancy does this tenant have?
   a. Holdover tenancy
   b. Month-to-month tenancy
   c. Tenancy at sufferance
   d. Tenancy at will

2. The owner of a house wants to fence the yard for the family pet. When the fence is erected, the fencing materials become real estate through
   a. severance.
   b. subrogation.
   c. annexation.
   d. attachment.

3. A seller is interested in selling his house as quickly as possible and believes that the best way to do this is to have several brokers compete against each other for the commission. His listing agreements with four different brokers specifically promise that if one of them finds a buyer for his property, he will be obligated to pay a commission to that broker only. What type of agreement has the seller entered into?
   a. Executed
   b. Discharged
   c. Unilateral
   d. Bilateral

4. In some states, by paying the debt after a foreclosure sale, the delinquent borrower has the right to regain the property under which of the following?
   a. Novation
   b. Redemption
   c. Reversion
   d. Recovery

5. An owner of a ranch enters into a sale-and-leaseback agreement with a man. Which statement is *TRUE* of this arrangement?
   a. The owner retains title to the ranch.
   b. The man receives possession of the property.
   c. The man is the lessor.
   d. The owner is the lessor.

6. A licensee is employed by a buyer. When the licensee finds a property that the buyer might be interested in buying, she is careful to find out as much as possible about the property's owners and why their property is on the market. The licensee's efforts to keep the buyer informed of all facts that could affect a transaction is the duty of
   a. accounting.
   b. loyalty.
   c. confidentiality.
   d. disclosure.

7. A parcel of vacant land 80 feet wide and 200 feet deep was sold for $500 per front foot. How much money would a salesperson receive as a 60 percent share in the 10 percent commission?
   a. $1,600
   b. $2,400
   c. $6,000
   d. $4,000

8. Which situation does *NOT* violate the federal Fair Housing Act of 1968?
   a. The refusal of a property manager to rent an apartment to a Catholic couple who are otherwise qualified
   b. The general policy of a loan company to avoid granting home improvement loans to individuals living in transitional neighborhoods
   c. The intentional neglect of a broker to show an Asian family any property listings in all-white neighborhoods
   d. A widow's insistence on renting her spare bedroom only to another widowed woman

9. If a storage tank that measures 12 feet by 9 feet by 8 feet is designed to store gas that costs $1.82 per cubic foot, what does it cost to fill the tank to one-half of its capacity?

   a. $685
   b. $786
   c. $864
   d. $1,572

10. A buyer bought a house for $125,000. The house, which had originally sold for $118,250, appraised for $122,500. Based on these facts, if the buyer applies for an 80 percent mortgage, what will be the amount of the loan?

    a. $94,600
    b. $98,000
    c. $100,000
    d. $106,750

11. A purchaser offers to buy a seller's property by signing a purchase contract. The seller accepts the offer. What kind of title interest does the buyer have in the property at this point?

    a. Legal
    b. Equitable
    c. Defeasible
    d. No title interest

12. Which federal law requires that finance charges be stated as an annual percentage rate?

    a. Truth in Lending Act
    b. Real Estate Settlement Procedures Act (RESPA)
    c. Equal Credit Opportunity Act (ECOA)
    d. Fair Housing Act

13. A seller signed a 90-day listing agreement with a licensee. Two weeks later, the seller was killed in an accident. What is the present status of the listing?

    a. The listing agreement is binding on the seller's estate for the remainder of the 90 days.
    b. Because the seller's intention to sell was clearly defined, the listing agreement is still in effect and the licensee may proceed to market the property on behalf of the seller's estate.
    c. The listing agreement is binding on the seller's estate only if the licensee can produce an offer to purchase the property within the remainder of the listing period.
    d. The listing agreement was terminated automatically when the seller died.

14. A woman conveys the ownership of an office building to a nursing home. The nursing home agrees that the rental income will pay for the expenses of caring for the woman's parents. When her parents die, ownership of the office building will revert to the woman. The estate held by the nursing home is a

    a. remainder life estate.
    b. legal life estate.
    c. life estate pur autre vie.
    d. temporary leasehold estate.

15. A buyer signs a buyer's brokerage agreement under which the licensee will help this client find a three-bedroom house in the $185,000 to $200,000 price range. A seller comes into the licensee's office and signs a listing agreement to sell a two-bedroom condominium for $170,000. Based on these facts, which statement is *TRUE*?

    a. The buyer is the licensee's client; the seller is the licensee's customer.
    b. The buyer is the licensee's customer; the seller is the licensee's client.
    c. While both the buyer and the seller are clients, the licensee owes the fiduciary duties of an agent only to the seller.
    d. Because both the buyer and the seller are the licensee's clients, the licensee owes the fiduciary duties of an agent to both.

16. In a township of 36 sections, which statement is *TRUE*?

    a. Section 31 lies to the east of Section 32.

    b. Section 18 is by law set aside for school purposes.

    c. Section 6 lies in the northeast corner of the township.

    d. Section 16 lies to the north of Section 21.

17. A licensee representing a seller is asked by the client to make sure that the deed does not reveal the actual sales price. In this case, the licensee

    a. must inform the client that only the actual price of the real estate may appear on the deed.

    b. may ask that a deed be prepared that shows only nominal consideration of $10.

    c. should inform the seller that either the full price should be stated in the deed or all references to consideration should be removed from it.

    d. may show a price on the deed other than the actual price, provided that the variance is not greater than 10 percent of the purchase price.

18. A broker obtained a listing agreement to act as the agent in the sale of a house. A buyer has been found for the property, and all agreements have been signed. As an agent for the seller, the broker is responsible for which activity?

    a. Completing the buyer's loan application

    b. Making sure that the buyer receives copies of all documents the seller is required to deliver to the buyer

    c. Ensuring that the buyer is qualified for the new mortgage loan

    d. Scheduling the buyer's inspection of the property

19. A broker's office policy is that the salesperson's share of a commission is 65 percent. What is the salesperson's compensation if the sales price of a property is $195,000 and the broker is entitled to a 7½ percent commission?

    a. $950.63

    b. $8,872.50

    c. $9,506.25

    d. $95,062.50

20. Which component is among those an appraiser would use in preparing a cost-approach appraisal?

    a. Estimate the replacement cost of the improvements

    b. Deduct for the depreciation of the land and buildings

    c. Determine the original cost and adjust for depreciation

    d. Review the sales prices of comparable properties

21. When a mortgage lender provides the buyer with statements of all fees and charges the seller will incur, the lender is complying with which federal law?

    a. Equal Credit Opportunity Act (ECOA)

    b. Truth in Lending Act (Regulation Z)

    c. Real Estate Settlement Procedures Act (RESPA)

    d. Fair Housing Act

22. The landlord of an apartment building neglected to repair the building's plumbing system. As a result, the apartments did not receive water, as provided by the leases. If a tenant's unit becomes uninhabitable, what is the MOST likely result?

    a. Suit for possession

    b. Claim of constructive eviction

    c. Tenancy at sufferance

    d. Suit for negligence

23. A man conveys a life estate to his son. Under the terms of the man's conveyance, the property will pass to the man's nephew on his son's death. Which interest in the property BEST describes that of the nephew during the son's lifetime?

    a. Remainder

    b. Reversion

    c. Life estate pur autre vie

    d. Redemption

24. On a settlement statement, prorations for unpaid real estate taxes are shown as a

    a. credit to the seller and a debit to the buyer.

    b. debit to the seller and a credit to the buyer.

    c. credit to both the seller and the buyer.

    d. debit to both the seller and the buyer.

25. What type of lease establishes a rental payment and requires the lessor to pay for the taxes, insurance, and maintenance on the property?

   a. Percentage
   b. Net
   c. Expense-only
   d. Gross

26. A conventional loan closed on July 1 for $165,000 at 6.5 percent interest amortized over 25 years at $925.60 per month. Using a 360-day year, what would the principal amount be after the monthly payment was made August 1?

   a. $164,936.30
   b. $164,106.25
   c. $154,275.00
   d. $164,968.15

27. In the preceding question, what would the interest portion of the payment be?

   a. $925.60
   b. $31.85
   c. $893.75
   d. $800.00

28. A seller listed her home with a licensee for $220,000 but tells the licensee, who is acting as a seller's agent, "I've got to sell quickly because of a job transfer. If necessary, I can accept a price as low as $175,000." The licensee tells a prospective buyer to offer $180,000 "because the seller is desperate to sell." The seller accepts the buyer's offer. In this situation, which statement is *TRUE*?

   a. The licensee's action did not violate any agency relationship with the seller because the licensee did not actually reveal the seller's lowest acceptable price.
   b. The licensee violated an established agency relationship with the seller.
   c. The licensee acted properly to obtain a quick offer on the seller's property, in accordance with the seller's instructions.
   d. The licensee violated established fiduciary duties toward the buyer by failing to disclose that the seller would accept a lower price than the buyer offered.

29. Which of the following *BEST* describes the capitalization rate under the income approach to estimating the value of real estate?

   a. Rate at which a property increases in value
   b. Rate of return a property earns as an investment
   c. Rate of capital required to keep a property operating most efficiently
   d. Maximum rate of return allowed by law on an investment

30. On a settlement statement, the cost of the lender's title insurance policy required for a new loan is usually shown as which of the following?

   a. Credit to the seller
   b. Credit to the buyer
   c. Debit to the seller
   d. Debit to the buyer

31. An FHA-insured loan in the amount of $157,500 at 5½ percent for 30 years closed on July 17. The first monthly payment is due on September 1. Using a 360-day year and assuming that interest is being paid for the day of closing, what was the amount of the interest adjustment the buyer had to make at the settlement?

   a. $0
   b. $336.87
   c. $360.93
   d. $24.06

32. If a home that cost $142,500 three years ago is now valued at 127 percent of its original cost, what is its current market value?

   a. $164,025
   b. $172,205
   c. $174,310
   d. $180,975

33. A buyer makes an offer on a property and the seller accepts. Three weeks later, the buyer announces that "the deal's off" and refuses to go through with the sale. If the seller is entitled to keep the buyer's earnest money deposit, there MOST likely is what kind of clause in the sales contract?

   a. Liquidated damages clause
   b. Contingent damages clause
   c. Actual damages clause
   d. Revocation clause

34. A search of the public record regarding title to a property is MOST likely to provide information about which item?

   a. Encroachments
   b. Rights of parties in possession
   c. Inaccurate survey
   d. Mechanics' liens

35. A rectangular lot is worth $193,600. This value is the equivalent of $4.40 per square foot. If one lot dimension is 200 feet, what is the other dimension?

   a. 110 feet
   b. 220 feet
   c. 400 feet
   d. 880 feet

36. A broker listed a property at an 8 percent commission rate. After the property was sold and the settlement had taken place, the seller discovered that the broker had been listing similar properties at 6 percent commission rates. Based on this information, which statement is TRUE?

   a. The broker has done nothing wrong because a commission rate is always negotiable between the parties.
   b. If the broker inflated the usual commission rate for the area, the broker may be subject to discipline by the state real estate commission.
   c. The seller is entitled to rescind the transaction based on the principle of lack of reality of consent.
   d. The seller is entitled to a refund from the broker of 2 percent of the commission.

37. A renter has six months remaining on her apartment lease. The monthly rent is $875. The renter moves out of the apartment for four months, and a friend moves in. The friend pays the renter a monthly rental of $700, and the renter continues paying the full rental amount under her lease to the landlord. This is an example of

   a. subletting.
   b. assignment.
   c. rescission and renewal.
   d. surrender.

38. One broker asked another, "Will I have to prove that I was the procuring cause in order to collect a commission if my seller sells the property without my help?" The other broker answered, "No, not if you have an

   a. option listing."
   b. open listing."
   c. exclusive-agency listing."
   d. exclusive-right-to-sell listing."

39. The capitalization rate on a property reflects (among other things) which factor?

   a. Risk of the investment
   b. Replacement cost of the improvements
   c. Real estate taxes
   d. Debt service

40. An investment property now worth $180,000 was purchased seven years ago for $142,000. At the time of the purchase, the land was valued at $18,000. Assuming a 31½ year life for straight-line depreciation purposes, what is the present book value of the property?

   a. $95,071
   b. $113,071
   c. $114,444
   d. $126,000

41. After a buyer purchased a property from a seller, they both decided to rescind the recorded transfer. To do this, what must happen?

    a. The buyer must return the deed to the seller.

    b. The parties must record a notice of rescission.

    c. The parties must simply destroy the original deed in the presence of witnesses.

    d. The buyer must make a new deed to the seller.

42. A farmer owns the W½ of the NW¼ of the NW¼ of a section. The adjoining property can be purchased for $300 per acre. Owning all of the NW¼ of the section would cost the farmer

    a. $6,000.

    b. $12,000.

    c. $42,000.

    d. $48,000.

43. A broker received a deposit, along with a written offer from a buyer. The offer stated: "The offeror will leave this offer open for the seller's acceptance for a period of ten days." On the fifth day, and before acceptance by the seller, the offeror notified the broker that the offer was withdrawn and demanded the return of the deposit. Which statement is *TRUE* in this situation?

    a. The offeror cannot withdraw the offer; it must be held open for the full ten-day period, as promised.

    b. The offeror has the right to withdraw the offer and secure the return of the deposit any time before being notified of the seller's acceptance.

    c. The offeror can withdraw the offer, and the seller and the broker will each retain one-half of the forfeited deposit.

    d. While the offeror can withdraw the offer, the broker is legally entitled to declare the deposit forfeited and retain all of it in lieu of the lost commission.

44. For each new tenant that the property manager signs, a building's owner pays an 8½ percent commission based on the unit's annualized rent. Last year, the manager signed five new tenants. Three of the apartments rented for $795 per month, one rented for $1,200 per month, and one rented for $900 per month. What was the total amount of the manager's new-tenant commissions for that year?

    a. $381.23

    b. $2,952.90

    c. $3,685.47

    d. $4,574.70

45. The monthly rent on a warehouse is $1 per cubic yard. Assuming the warehouse is 36 feet by 200 feet by 12 feet high, what is the annual rent?

    a. $3,200

    b. $9,600

    c. $38,400

    d. $115,200

46. If a veteran wishes to refinance a home by changing to a VA-guaranteed loan and the lender insists on 3½ discount points, which option is available to the veteran?

    a. Refinance with a VA loan, provided the lender charges no discount points

    b. Refinance with a VA loan, provided the lender charges no more than two discount points

    c. Be required to pay a maximum of 1 percent of the loan as an origination fee

    d. Proceed with the refinance loan and pay the discount points

47. A woman owned property that she conveyed to a man "so long as no real estate broker or salesperson ever sets foot on the property." If a broker or a salesperson visits the property, ownership will revert to the woman. Based on these two conveyances, which statement is *TRUE*?

a. The man holds the property in fee simple determinable.

b. The man holds the property in fee simple defeasible, subject to a condition subsequent.

c. The man may not transfer ownership of the property without the woman's permission.

d. The woman has retained a right of re-entry with regard to the property.

48. A real estate transaction has a closing date of November 15. The seller, who is responsible for costs up to and including the date of settlement, has already paid the property taxes of $1,116 for the calendar year. On the closing statement, the buyer will be

a. debited $139.50.

b. debited $976.50.

c. credited $139.50.

d. credited $976.50.

49. After a storeowner's spouse died, he could no longer maintain the store. A woman who wished to open a store agreed to move into the entire space and pay for the remaining seven years on the lease. The landlord agreed to the arrangement. This is known as a lease

a. assumption.

b. assignment.

c. surrender.

d. breach.

50. A purchaser buys a house for $234,500 by making a $25,000 cash down payment and taking out a $209,500 mortgage for 30 years. The lot value is $80,000. If the purchaser wants to depreciate the property over a period of 31½ years, how much will be the annual depreciation amount using the straight-line method?

a. $3,818.18

b. $4,709.09

c. $4,904.76

d. $7,444.44

51. A property manager leased a store for three years. The first year, the store's rent was $1,000 per month, and the rent was to increase 10 percent per year thereafter. The manager received a 7 percent commission for the first year, 5 percent for the second year, and 3 percent for the balance of the lease. The total commission earned by the property manager was

a. $840.

b. $1,613.

c. $1,936.

d. $2,785.

52. Against a recorded deed from the owner of record, the party with the weakest position is a

a. person with a prior unrecorded deed and who is not in possession.

b. person in possession with a prior unrecorded deed.

c. tenant in possession with nine months remaining on the lease.

d. painter who is half-finished painting the house at the time of the sale and who has not yet been paid.

53. A married couple files their income taxes jointly. Last year they sold their home for $340,000. Seven years ago, when they were first married, they bought the house for $250,000 and have lived in it ever since. Based on these facts, which statement is *TRUE*?

a. Under current tax law, the couple will owe a capital gains tax this year on their $90,000 gain.

b. Current tax law permits the couple to exclude up to $250,000 in capital gain from their income tax.

c. Because their gain is less than $500,000, the couple will owe no capital gains tax this year.

d. Under current tax law, the couple will be entitled to a penalty-free withdrawal of up to $10,000 from a 401(k) retirement account to use as a down payment.

54. A squatter moved into an abandoned home and lived there for some years. Ultimately, the squatter was granted title to the property by a court. Which element is *NOT* basic to acquiring title in this manner?

    a. Permission of the true owner
    b. Open and notorious use
    c. Occupancy for a period of time prescribed by state law
    d. Occupancy hostile to the best interests of the true owner

55. Wilma, Frank, and Judy are joint tenants. Judy sells her interest to Laura, and then Frank dies. As a result, which statement is *TRUE*?

    a. Frank's heirs are joint tenants with Laura and Wilma.
    b. Frank's heirs and Wilma are joint tenants, but Laura is a tenant in common.
    c. Wilma is a tenant in common with Laura and Frank's heirs.
    d. Wilma and Laura are tenants in common.

56. In a settlement statement, the selling price is

    a. a debit to the buyer.
    b. a debit to the seller.
    c. a credit to the buyer.
    d. greater than the loan amount.

57. The state wants to acquire a strip of farmland to build a highway. Does the state have the right to acquire this land for public use?

    a. Yes, the state's right is called condemnation.
    b. Yes, the state's right is called eminent domain.
    c. Yes, the state's right is called escheat.
    d. No, under the U.S. Constitution, private property never may be taken by state governments or by the federal government.

58. A man died, and his estate was distributed according to his will as follows: 54 percent to his spouse, 18 percent to his children, 16 percent to his grandchildren, and the remainder to his college. The college received $79,000. How much did the man's children receive?

    a. $105,333
    b. $118,500
    c. $355,500
    d. $658,333

59. Which of the following is an example of external obsolescence?

    a. Numerous pillars supporting the ceiling in a store
    b. Leaks in the roof of a warehouse, making the premises unusable and, therefore, unrentable
    c. Coal cellar in a house with central heating
    d. Vacant, abandoned, and run-down buildings in an area

60. Which phrase, when placed in a print advertisement, would *MOST* nearly comply with the requirements of the Truth in Lending Act (Regulation Z)?

    a. "7½ percent interest"
    b. "7½ percent rate"
    c. "7½ percent annual interest"
    d. "7½ percent annual percentage rate"

61. Which statement is *FALSE* regarding a capitalization rate?

    a. The rate increases when the risk increases.
    b. An increase in rate, while other elements remain the same, means a decrease in value.
    c. The net income is divided by the rate to estimate value.
    d. A decrease in rate, while other elements remain the same, results in a decrease in value.

62. The Equal Credit Opportunity Act (ECOA) makes it illegal for lenders to refuse credit to or otherwise discriminate against which applicant?

    a. Parent of twins who receives public assistance and cannot afford the monthly mortgage payments
    b. New homebuyer who does not have a credit history
    c. Single person who receives public assistance
    d. Unemployed person with no job prospects and no identifiable source of income

63. When a woman died, a deed was found in her desk drawer. Although the deed had never been recorded, it was signed, dated, and acknowledged. The deed gave the woman's house to a local charity. The will, however, provided as follows: "I leave all of the real and personal property that I own to my beloved nephew." In this situation, the house MOST likely will go to the

   a. charity, because acknowledgment creates a presumption of delivery.
   b. charity, because the woman's intent was clear from the deed.
   c. nephew, because the deed was never delivered to or accepted by the charity.
   d. nephew, because the deed had not been recorded.

64. If a borrower takes out a $90,000 loan at 7½ percent interest to be repaid at the end of 15 years with interest paid annually, what is the total interest that the borrower will pay over the life of the loan?

   a. $10,125
   b. $80,000
   c. $101,250
   d. $180,000

65. After an offer is accepted, the seller finds that the broker was the undisclosed agent for the buyer as well as the agent for the seller. The seller may

   a. withdraw without obligation to the broker or the buyer.
   b. withdraw but be subject to liquidated damages.
   c. withdraw but only with the concurrence of the buyer.
   d. refuse to sell but be subject to a suit for specific performance.

66. To net the owner $90,000 after a 6 percent commission is paid, the list price would have to be

   a. $95,400.
   b. $95,745.
   c. $95,906.
   d. $96,000.

67. Which circumstance would MOST likely be legal under the provisions of the Civil Rights Act of 1968?

   a. A lender refuses to make loans in areas where more than 25 percent of the population is Hispanic.
   b. A private social club that discriminates against no protected group in granting membership refuses to rent a suite in its members-only vacation facility to a Nigerian family who are not members of the club.
   c. A church excludes African Americans from membership and rents its nonprofit housing to church members only.
   d. A licensee directs prospective buyers away from areas where they are likely to feel uncomfortable because of their race.

68. It is discovered after a sale that the land parcel is 10 percent smaller than the seller represented it to be. The licensee who passed this information on to the buyer is

   a. not liable as long as the licensee only repeated the seller's data.
   b. not liable if the misrepresentation was unintentional.
   c. not liable if the buyer actually inspected the parcel.
   d. liable if the licensee knew or should have known of the discrepancy.

69. An easement terminates

   a. automatically.
   b. when the owner of the dominant tenement wishes to do so.
   c. if the owners of the dominant and servient tenements become one and the same.
   d. when a property owner dies.

70. Which activity is *NOT* a violation of the Real Estate Settlement Procedures Act (RESPA)?
    a. Providing a HUD-1 Uniform Settlement Statement to a borrower one day before the closing
    b. Accepting a kickback on a loan subject to RESPA requirements
    c. Requiring the buyer to use a particular title insurance company
    d. Accepting a fee or charging for services that were not performed

71. The rescission provisions of the Truth in Lending Act (Regulation Z) apply to which transaction?
    a. Home purchase loans
    b. Construction lending
    c. Business financing
    d. Consumer credit

72. A property has a net income of $30,000. An appraiser decides to use a 12 percent capitalization rate rather than a 10 percent rate on this property. The use of the higher rate results in
    a. a 2 percent increase in the appraised value.
    b. a $50,000 increase in the appraised value.
    c. a $50,000 decrease in the appraised value.
    d. no change in the appraised value.

73. The section in a purchase contract that would provide for the buyer to forfeit any earnest money if the buyer fails to complete the purchase is known as a provision for
    a. liquidated damages.
    b. punitive damages.
    c. hypothecation.
    d. subordination.

74. In one commercial building, the tenant intends to start a small health food shop. An identical adjacent building houses a showroom leased to a major national retailing chain. Both tenants have long-term leases with identical rents. If the appraiser uses a capitalization rate for the store leased to the national retailing chain higher than the rate for the other building, which statement is *TRUE*?
    a. The indicated value of the chain's property will be lower than the indicated value of the food-shop property.
    b. The indicated value of the chain's property will be higher than the indicated value of the food-shop property.
    c. The appraiser would then be compelled to make use of the sales comparison approach to value.
    d. It would indicate the appraiser believes a building occupied by a chain-store tenant is more valuable than an identical one occupied by a health food shop.

75. An insurance company agreed to provide a developer with financing for a shopping center at 7 percent interest plus an equity position. What type of loan is this?
    a. Package
    b. Participation
    c. Open-end
    d. Blanket

76. A $100,000 loan at 6 percent could be amortized with monthly payments of $644 on a 15-year basis or payments of $600 on a 30-year basis. The 30-year loan results in total payments of what percentage of the 15-year total payments?
    a. 106 percent
    b. 158 percent
    c. 186 percent
    d. 154 percent

77. According to a broker's CMA, a property is worth $225,000. The homeowner bought the property for $190,000 and added $50,000 in improvements, for a total of $240,000. The property sold for $222,500. Which amount represents the property's market value?

    a. $190,000

    b. $222,500

    c. $225,000

    d. $240,000

78. What will be the amount of tax payable where the property's assessed value is $185,000 and the tax rate is 40 mills in a community in which an equalization factor of 110 percent is used?

    a. $4,625.00

    b. $5,087.50

    c. $7,400.40

    d. $8,140.00

79. In a settlement statement, how will a proration of prepaid water, gas, and electric charges be reflected?

    a. Debit to the seller, credit to the buyer

    b. Debit to the buyer, credit to the seller

    c. Debit to the buyer only

    d. Credit to the seller only

80. An apartment manager decides not to purchase flood insurance. Instead, the manager installs raised platforms in the basement storage areas and has the furnace placed on eight-inch legs. This form of risk management is known as

    a. avoiding the risk.

    b. controlling the risk.

    c. retaining the risk.

    d. transferring the risk.

Glossary

Note: Most of the entries in this glossary reference specific pages in *Modern Real Estate Practice*, 18th edition; however, page references are not provided for all terms. This is because we've included some terms that are used in everyday professional practice or are of purely historical interest. *Modern Real Estate Practice* emphasizes the vocabulary that is necessary both for passing your real estate exam and for a successful career in real estate.

abstract of title   The condensed history of a title to a particular parcel of real estate, consisting of a summary of the original grant and all subsequent conveyances and encumbrances affecting the property and a certification by the abstractor that the history is complete and accurate. **213**

acceleration clause   The clause in a mortgage or deed of trust that can be enforced to make the entire debt due immediately if the borrower defaults on an installment payment or other covenant. **228**

accession   Acquiring title to additions or improvements to real property as a result of the annexation of fixtures or the accretion of alluvial deposits along the banks of streams. **22**

accretion   The increase or addition of land by the deposit of sand or soil washed up naturally from a river, lake, or sea. **120**

accrued depreciation   Loss in value resulting from the property's physical deterioration, external depreciation (decrease in price), and functional obsolescence. **328**

accrued items   On a closing statement, items of expense that are incurred but not yet payable, such as interest on a mortgage loan or taxes on real property. **414**

acknowledgment   A formal declaration made before a duly authorized officer, usually a notary public, by a person who has signed a document. **197**

acre   A measure of land equal to 43,560 square feet, 4,840 square yards, 4,047 square meters, 160 square rods, or 0.4047 hectares. **156**

actual eviction   The legal process that results in the tenant's being physically removed from the leased premises. **281**

actual notice   Express information or fact; that which is known; direct knowledge. **212**

ad valorem tax   A tax levied according to value, generally used to refer to real estate tax. Also called the *general tax.* **163**

addendum   Any provision added to an existing contract without altering the content of the original. Must be signed by all parties. **187**

adjustable-rate mortgage (ARM)   A loan characterized by a fluctuating interest rate, usually one tied to a bank or savings and loan association cost-of-funds index. **244**

adjusted basis   *See* basis.

administrator/administratrix   A court-selected person who assists with the settlement of an estate of a person who died without leaving a will. **200**

adverse possession   The actual, open, notorious, hostile, and continuous possession of another's land under a claim of title. Possession for a statutory period may be a means of acquiring title. **202**

affidavit of title   A written statement, made under oath by a seller or grantor of real property and acknowledged by a notary public, in which the grantor (1) identifies himself or herself and indicates marital status, (2) certifies that since the examination of the title, on the date of the con-tract no defects have occurred in the title, and (3) certifies that he or she is in possession of the property (if applicable). **401**

agency   The relationship between a principal and an agent wherein the agent is authorized to represent the principal in certain transactions. **45**

Agency by ratification   An agency relationship created after the fact.

agent   One who acts or has the power to act for another. A fiduciary relationship is created under the *law of agency* when a property owner, as the principal, executes a listing agreement or management contract authorizing a licensed real estate broker to be his or her agent. **45**

air lots   Designated airspace over a piece of land. An air lot, like surface property, may be transferred. **153**

air rights   The right to use the open space above a property, usually allowing the surface to be used for another purpose. **18**

alienation The act of transferring property to another. Alienation may be voluntary, such as by gift or sale, or involuntary, as through eminent domain or adverse possession.

alienation clause The clause in a mortgage or deed of trust that states that the balance of the secured debt becomes immediately due and payable at the lender's option if the property is sold by the borrower. In effect, this clause prevents the borrower from assigning the debt without the lender's approval. **230**

allodial system A system of land ownership in which land is held free and clear of any rent or service due to the government; commonly contrasted to the feudal system. Land is held under the allodial system in the United States.

amendment A change to the existing content of a contract (i.e., if words or provisions are added to or deleted from the body of the contract). Must be initialed by all parties. **187**

American Land Title Association (ALTA) policy A title insurance policy that protects the interest in a collateral property of a mortgage lender who originates a new real estate loan. **215**

Americans with Disabilities Act (ADA) Act addresses rights of individuals with disabilities in employment and public accommodations. **360-61**

amortized loan A loan in which the principal as well as the interest is payable in monthly or other periodic installments over the term of the loan. **243-44**

annexation Process of converting personal property into real property. **20**

annual percentage rate (APR) The relationship of the total finance charges associated with a loan. This must be disclosed to borrowers by lenders under the Truth in Lending Act. **256**

anticipation The appraisal principle that holds that value can increase or decrease based on the expectation of some future benefit or detriment produced by the property. **325**

antitrust laws Laws designed to preserve the free enterprise of the open marketplace by making illegal certain private conspiracies and combinations formed to minimize competition. Most violations of antitrust laws in the real estate business involve either *price-fixing* (brokers conspiring to set fixed compensation rates) or *allocation of customers or markets* (brokers agreeing to limit their areas of trade or dealing to certain areas or properties). **76-79**

appraisal An estimate of the quantity, quality, or value of something. The process through which conclusions of property value are obtained; also refers to the report that sets forth the process of estimation and conclusion of value. **4**

appraiser An independent person trained to provide an unbiased estimate of value. **4**

appreciation An increase in the worth or value of a property due to economic or related causes, which may prove to be either temporary or permanent; opposite of depreciation. **431**

appurtenance A right, privilege, or improvement belonging to, and passing with, the land; "runs with the land." **18**

appurtenant easement An easement that is annexed to the ownership of one parcel and allows the owner the use of the neighbor's land. **116-17**

area A level surface or piece of ground; the size of a surface; the amount of a two-dimensional object. **464**

area preference People's desire for one area over another, based on a number of factors such as history, reputation, convenience, scenic beauty, and location. **23**

asbestos A mineral once used in insulation and other materials that can cause respiratory diseases. **375-77**

assemblage The combining of two or more adjoining lots into one larger tract to increase their total value. **326**

assessed value The value set on property for taxation purposes. **171**

assessment The imposition of a tax, charge, or levy, usually according to established rates. **164**

assignment The transfer in writing of interest in a bond, mortgage, lease, or other instrument. **180**

assume A buyer is personally obligated for the payment of the entire debt of a seller; that is, the buyer assumes the debt. The original seller is not liable for the debt if the property is foreclosed on. **230**

assumption of mortgage Acquiring title to property on which there is an existing mortgage and agreeing to be personally liable for the terms and conditions of the mortgage, including payments. **230**

attachment The act of taking a person's property into legal custody by writ or other judicial order to hold it available for application to that person's debt to a creditor. **25**

attorney's opinion of title An abstract of title that an attorney has examined and has certified to be, in his or her opinion, an accurate statement of the facts concerning the property's ownership. **215**

automated underwriting Computer systems that permit lenders to expedite the loan approval process and reduce lending costs. **259**

automatic extension   A listing agreement clause stating that the agreement will continue automatically for a certain period of time after its expiration date. In many states, use of this clause is discouraged or prohibited. **91**

avulsion   The sudden tearing away of land, as by earthquake, flood, volcanic action, or the sudden change in the course of a stream. **120**

balance   The appraisal principle that states that the greatest value in a property will occur when the type and size of the improvements are proportional to each other as well as the land.

balloon payment   A final payment of a mortgage loan that is considerably larger than the required periodic payments because the loan amount was not fully amortized. **243**

bargain and sale deed   A deed that carries with it no warranties against liens or other encumbrances but that does imply that the grantor has the right to convey title. The grantor may add warranties to the deed at his or her discretion. **199**

base line   The main imaginary line running east and west and crossing a principal meridian at a definite point; used by surveyors for reference in locating and describing land under the rectangular (government) survey system of legal description. **146**

basis   The financial interest that the Internal Revenue Service attributes to an owner of an investment property for the purpose of determining annual depreciation and gain or loss on the sale of the asset. If a property was acquired by purchase, the owner's basis is the cost of the property plus the value of any capital expenditures for improvements to the property, minus any depreciation allowable or actually taken. This new basis is called the *adjusted basis*. **434**

benchmarks   Permanent reference marks or points established for use by surveyors in measuring differences in elevation. **154**

beneficiary   (1) The person for whom a trust operates or in whose behalf the income from a trust estate is drawn. (2) A lender in a deed of trust loan transaction. **130**

bilateral contract   *See* contract.

binder   An agreement that may accompany an earnest money deposit for the purchase of real property as evidence of the purchaser's good faith and intent to complete the transaction. **184**

blanket loan   A mortgage covering more than one parcel of real estate, providing for each parcel's partial release from the mortgage lien upon repayment of a definite portion of the debt. **253-54**

blockbusting   The illegal practice of inducing homeowners to sell their properties by making representations regarding the entry or prospective entry of persons of a particular race or national origin into the neighborhood. **305**

blue-sky laws   Common name for those state and federal laws that regulate the registration and sale of investment securities. **437**

boot   Money or property given to make up any difference in value or equity between two properties in an *exchange*. **436**

branch office   A secondary place of business apart from the principal or main office from which real estate business is conducted. A branch office usually must be run by a licensed real estate broker working on behalf of the broker.

breach of contract   Violation of any terms or conditions in a contract without legal excuse; for example, failure to make a payment when it is due. **180-81**

broker   One who acts as an intermediary on behalf of others for a fee or commission. **4**

broker's price opinion (BPO)   An opinion of real estate value commissioned by a bank or attorney and provided by a broker. **316**

brokerage   The bringing together of parties interested in making a real estate transaction. **4**

brownfields   Defunct, derelict, or abandoned commercial or industrial sites; many have toxic wastes. **386-87**

budget comparison statement   Compares actual results with the original budget, often giving either percentages or a numerical variance of actual versus projected income and expenses. **298**

buffer zone   A strip of land, usually used as a park or designated for a similar use, separating land dedicated to one use from land dedicated to another use (e.g., residential from commercial). **341**

building code   An ordinance that specifies minimum standards of construction for buildings to protect public safety and health. **344**

building permit   Written governmental permission for the construction, alteration, or demolition of an improvement, showing compliance with building codes and zoning ordinances. **344**

building-related illness (BRI)   An illness due to air quality problems, typically toxic substances or pathogens; a clinically diagnosed condition. Symptoms include asthma, allergies, and hypersensitivity. **308**

bulk transfer   *See* Uniform Commercial Code.

bundle of legal rights   The concept of land ownership that includes ownership of all legal rights to the land—possession, control within the law, enjoyment, exclusion, and disposition. **17**

buydown   A financing technique used to reduce the monthly payments for the first few years of a loan. Funds in the form of discount points are given to the lender by the builder or seller to buy down or lower the effective interest rate paid by the buyer, thus reducing the monthly payments for a set time. **255**

buyer agency agreement   A principal-agent relationship in which the broker is the agent for the buyer, with fiduciary responsibilities to the buyer. The broker represents the buyer under the law of agency. **47**

buyer's agent   A residential real estate broker or salesperson who represents the prospective purchaser in a transaction. The buyer's agent owes the buyer-principal the common-law or statutory agency duties. **54**

buyer's broker   A residential real estate broker who represents prospective buyers exclusively. As the *buyer's agent*, the broker owes the buyer-principal the common-law or statutory agency duties. **89**

capital gain   Profit earned from the sale of an asset. **434-35**

capitalization   A mathematical process for estimating the value of a property using a proper rate of return on the investment and the annual net operating income expected to be produced by the property. The formula is expressed as follows: Income ÷ Rate = Value.

capitalization rate   The rate of return a property will produce on the owner's investment. **331**

capping   The process of laying two to four feet of soil over the top of a landfill site and then planting grass on it to enhance the aesthetic value and prevent erosion. **386**

carbon monoxide (CO)   A colorless, odorless gas that occurs as a by-product of fuel combustion that may result in death in poorly ventilated areas. **381**

cash flow   The net spendable income from an investment, determined by deducting all operating and fixed expenses from the gross income. When expenses exceed income, a *negative cash flow* results. **431**

cash flow report   A monthly statement that details the financial status of the property. **297**

caveat emptor   A Latin phrase meaning, *Let the buyer beware.* **68**

CC&Rs   *See* covenants, conditions, and restrictions.

certificate of occupancy   Permission by the municipal inspector to occupy a completed building structure after being inspected and having complied with building codes. **344**

certificate of reasonable value (CRV)   A form indicating the appraised value of a property being financed with a VA loan. **252**

certificate of sale   The document generally given to the purchaser at a tax foreclosure sale. A certificate of sale does not convey title; normally, it is an instrument certifying that the holder received title to the property after the redemption period passed and that the holder paid the property taxes for that interim period. **166**

certificate of title   A statement of opinion on the status of the title to a parcel of real property based on an examination of specified public records. **214-15**

chain of title   The succession of conveyances, from some accepted starting point, whereby the present holder of real property derives title. **213**

change   The appraisal principle that holds that no physical or economic condition remains constant. **325**

chattel   *See* personal property.

chlorofluorocarbons (CFCs)   Nontoxic, nonflammable chemicals containing atoms of carbon, chlorine, and fluorine, such as air conditioners and refrigerators. CFCs are safe in application but cause ozone depletion. **382**

Civil Rights Act of 1866   An act that prohibits racial discrimination in the sale and rental of housing. **354**

client   The principal. **46**

closing   An event where promises made in a sales contract are fulfilled and mortgage loan funds (if any) are distributed to the buyer. **398**

closing statement   A detailed cash accounting of a real estate transaction showing all cash received, all charges and credits made, and all cash paid out in the transaction. **412-14**

cloud on title   Any document, claim, unreleased lien, or encumbrance that may impair the title to real property or make the title doubtful; usually revealed by a title search and removed by either a quitclaim deed or suit to quiet title. **200**

code of ethics   A written system of standards for ethical conduct. **367**

codicil   A supplement or an addition to a will, executed with the same formalities as a will, which normally does not revoke the entire will. **204**

coinsurance clause   A clause in insurance policies covering real property that requires the policyholder to maintain fire insurance coverage generally equal to at least 80 percent of the property's actual replacement cost. **37**

collateral   Something having value that is given to secure repayment of a debt. **161**

commingling The illegal act by a real estate broker of placing client or customer funds with personal funds. By law, brokers are required to maintain a separate *trust* or *escrow account* for other parties' funds held temporarily by the broker. **184**

commission Payment to a broker for services rendered, such as in the sale or purchase of real property; usually a percentage of the selling price of the property. **71-72**

common elements Parts of a property that are necessary or convenient to the existence, maintenance, and safety of a condominium or are normally in common use by all of the condominium residents. Each condominium owner has an undivided ownership interest in the common elements. **32**

common law The body of law based on custom, usage, and court decisions. **45**

community association management Provides a team of property managers, accounting staff, office staff, and property consultants to manage property. **293**

community property A system of property ownership based on the theory that each spouse has an equal interest in the property acquired by the efforts of either spouse during marriage. A holdover of Spanish law found predominantly in the western U.S. states; the system was unknown under English common law. **129-30**

Community Reinvestment Act of 1977 (CRA) Under the act, financial institutions are expected to meet the deposit and credit needs of their communities; participate and invest in local community development and rehabilitation projects; and participate in loan programs for housing, small businesses, and small farms. **258**

comparables Properties used in an appraisal report that are substantially equivalent to the subject property. **327**

competent party A person who has the capacity to be engaged in a legal contract; being of sound mind and body.

competition The appraisal principle that states that excess profits generate competition. **325**

competitive market analysis (CMA) A comparison of the prices of recently sold homes that are similar to a listing seller's home in terms of location, style, and amenities. **315-16**

Comprehensive Environmental Response, Compensation, and Liability Act (CERCLA) A federal law administered by the Environmental Protection Agency that establishes a process for identifying parties responsible for creating hazardous waste sites, forcing liable parties to clean up toxic sites, bringing legal action against responsible parties, and funding the abatement of toxic sites. *See also* Superfund. **387-88**

Comprehensive Loss Underwriting Exchange (CLUE) A database of consumer claims history that allows insurance companies to access prior claims information in the underwriting and rating process. **38**

comprehensive plan *See* master plan.

computerized loan origination (CLO) An electronic network for handling loan applications through remote computer terminals linked to various lenders' computers. **258-59**

condemnation A judicial or administrative proceeding to exercise the power of eminent domain, through which a government agency takes private property for public use and compensates the owner. **110**

conditional-use permit Written governmental permission allowing a use inconsistent with zoning but necessary for the common good, such as locating an emergency medical facility in a predominantly residential area. **343**

condominium The absolute ownership of a unit in a multiunit building based on a legal description of the airspace the unit actually occupies, plus an undivided interest in the ownership of the common elements, which are owned jointly with the other condominium unit owners. **32**

confession of judgment clause Permits judgment to be entered against a debtor without the creditor's having to institute legal proceedings.

conformity The appraisal principle that holds that the greater the similarity among properties in an area, the better they will hold their value. **325**

consent Expressing or implying permission, approval, or agreement of an action or decision. **178-79**

consideration (1) That received by the grantor in exchange for his or her deed. (2) Something of value that induces a person to enter into a contract. **178**

construction loan *See* interim financing.

constructive eviction Actions of a landlord that so materially disturb or impair a tenant's enjoyment of the leased premises that the tenant is effectively forced to move out and terminate the lease without liability for any further rent. **282**

constructive notice Notice given to the world by recorded documents. All people are charged with knowledge of such documents and their contents, whether or not they have actually examined them. Possession of property is also considered constructive notice that the person in possession has an interest in the property. **212**

consumer An individual who purchases goods or services that are not for resale.

contingency A provision in a contract that requires a certain act to be done or a certain event to occur before the contract becomes binding. 186

contract A legally enforceable promise or set of promises that must be performed and for which, if a breach of the promise occurs, the law provides a remedy. A contract may be either *unilateral*, by which only one party is bound to act, or *bilateral*, by which all parties to the instrument are legally bound to act as prescribed. 176

contribution The appraisal principle that states that the value of any component of a property is what it gives to the value of the whole or what its absence detracts from that value. 325

controlled business arrangement (CBA) An arrangement where a package of services (e.g., a real estate firm, title insurance company, mortgage broker, and home inspection company) is offered to consumers. 406

conventional loan A loan that requires no insurance or guarantee. 247-48

conveyance A term used to refer to any document that transfers title to real property. The term is also used in describing the act of transferring. 194

cooperating broker *See* listing broker.

cooperative A residential multiunit building whose title is held by a trust or corporation that is owned by and operated for the benefit of people living within the building who are the beneficial owners of the trust or shareholders of the corporation, each possessing a proprietary lease. 33

co-ownership Title ownership held by two or more persons. 126

corporation An entity or organization, created by operation of law, whose rights of doing business are essentially the same as those of an individual. The entity has continuous existence until it is dissolved according to legal procedures. 132

corrective maintenance Corrects problems after they have occurred. 302

cost The total amount of money incurred for products or services.

cost approach The process of estimating the value of a property by adding to the estimated land value the appraiser's estimate of the reproduction or replacement cost of the building, less depreciation. 335

cost recovery An Internal Revenue Service term for *depreciation*. 435

counteroffer A new offer made in response to an offer received. It has the effect of rejecting the original offer, which cannot be accepted thereafter unless revived by the offeror. 183

covenant A written agreement between two or more parties in which a party or parties pledge to perform or not perform specified acts with regard to property; usually found in such real estate documents as deeds, mortgages, leases, and contracts for deed. 198

covenants, conditions, and restrictions (CC&Rs) Private agreements that affect the land use. They may be enforced by an owner of real estate and included in the seller's deed to the buyer. 116

covenant of quiet enjoyment The covenant implied by law by which a landlord guarantees that a tenant may take possession of leased premises and that the landlord will not interfere in the tenant's possession or use of the property. 198

credit On a closing statement, an amount entered in a person's favor—either an amount the party has paid or an amount for which the party must be reimbursed. 425

curtesy A life estate, usually a fractional interest, given by some states to the surviving husband in real estate owned by his deceased wife. Most states have abolished curtesy. 114-15

customer The third party or nonrepresented consumer for whom some level of service is provided. 46

datum A horizontal plane from which heights and depths are measured. 153

debit On a closing statement, an amount charged; that is, an amount that the debited party must pay. 425

decedent A person who has died. 202

dedication The voluntary transfer of private property by its owner to the public for some public use, such as for streets or schools.

deed A written instrument that, when executed and delivered, conveys title to or an interest in real estate. 17

deed in lieu of foreclosure A deed given by the mortgagor to the mortgagee when the mortgagor is in default under the terms of the mortgage. This is a way for the mortgagor to avoid foreclosure. 233

deed in trust An instrument that grants a trustee under a land trust full power to sell, mortgage, and subdivide a parcel of real estate. The beneficiary controls the trustee's use of these powers under the provisions of the trust agreement. 129

deed of reconveyance A document that transfers the title back to the borrower when the note is repaid. 229

deed of trust *See* trust deed.

deed of trust lien *See* trust deed lien.

deed restrictions Clauses in a deed limiting the future uses of the property. Deed restrictions may impose a vast variety of limitations and conditions—for example, they may limit the density of buildings, dictate the types of structures that can be erected, or prevent buildings from being used for specific purposes or even from being used at all. **116**

default The nonperformance of a duty, whether arising under a contract or otherwise; failure to meet an obligation when due. **228-29**

defeasance clause A clause used in leases and mortgages that cancels a specified right upon the occurrence of a certain condition, such as cancellation of a mortgage upon repayment of the mortgage loan. **229**

defeasible fee estate An estate in which the holder has a fee simple title that may be divested upon the occurrence or nonoccurrence of a specified event. There are two categories of defeasible fee estates: fee simple on condition precedent (fee simple determinable) and fee simple on condition subsequent. **112**

deficiency judgment A personal judgment levied against the borrower when a foreclosure sale does not produce sufficient funds to pay the mortgage debt in full. **234**

delinquent taxes Taxes that are unpaid and past due. **165-66**

delivery and acceptance When the title is delivered by the grantor and accepted by the grantee. **197**

demand The amount of goods people are willing and able to buy at a given price; often coupled with *supply*. **7-8**

denominator The number written below the line in a fraction. **469**

density zoning Zoning ordinances that restrict the maximum average number of houses per acre that may be built within a particular area, generally a subdivision. **346**

Department of Housing and Urban Development (HUD) Governmental department that has established rules and regulations that further interpret the practices affected by the law. In addition, HUD distributes an equal housing opportunity poster. **242**

depreciation (1) In appraisal, a loss of value in property due to any cause, including *physical deterioration*, *functional obsolescence*, and *external obsolescence*. (2) In real estate investment, an expense deduction for tax purposes taken over the period of ownership of income property. **329**

descent Acquisition of an estate by inheritance in which an heir succeeds to the property by operation of law. **209**

designated agency A process that accommodates an *in-house* sale in which two different agents are involved. The broker designates one agent to represent the seller and one agent to represent the buyer. **55**

designated agent A licensee authorized by a broker to act as the agent for a specific principal in a particular transaction. **53**

determinable fee estate A fee simple estate where the property returns to the original grantor or heirs when a specified condition occurs whereas the property is no longer being used for the purpose prescribed. **112**

developer One who attempts to put land to its most profitable use through the construction of improvements. **345**

devise A gift of real property by will. The donor is the devisor, and the recipient is the devisee. **203**

disclaimer A statement indicating no legal responsibility for information; no warranties or representations have been made. **77**

disclosure Relevant information or facts that are known or should have been known. **50-51**

discount point A unit of measurement used for various loan charges; one point equals 1 percent of the amount of the loan. **226**

discount rate The interest rate set by the Federal Reserve that member banks are charged when they borrow money through the Fed. **9**

divisor A number or quantity divided into another. **472**

dominant tenement A property that includes in its ownership the appurtenant right to use an easement over another person's property for a specific purpose. **116-17**

Do Not Call Registry A national registry, managed by the Federal Trade Commission, that lists the phone numbers of consumers who have indicated their preference to limit the telemarketing calls they receive. **79**

dower The legal right or interest, recognized in some states, that a wife acquires in the property her husband held or acquired during their marriage. During the husband's lifetime, the right is only a possibility of an interest; upon his death, it can become an interest in land. **114-15**

dual agency Representing both parties to a transaction. This is unethical unless both parties agree to it, and it is illegal in many states. **54-56**

due-on-sale clause A provision in the mortgage that states that the entire balance of the note is immediately due and payable if the mortgagor transfers (sells) the property. **230**

duress Unlawful constraint or action exercised upon a person whereby the person is forced to perform an act against his or her will. A contract entered into under duress is voidable. **179**

earnest money Money deposited by a buyer under the terms of a contract, to be forfeited if the buyer defaults but to be applied to the purchase price if the sale is closed. **184**

easement A right to use the land of another for a specific purpose, such as for a right-of-way or utilities; an incorporeal interest in land. **116**

easement appurtenant An easement that follows along with the land. **116**

easement by implication An easement that occurs when a party's actions reflect the intention of creating an easement.

easement by necessity An easement allowed by law as necessary for the full enjoyment of a parcel of real estate (e.g., a right of ingress and egress over a grantor's land). **118**

easement by prescription An easement acquired by continuous, open, and hostile use of the property for the period of time prescribed by state law. **118**

easement in gross An easement that is not created for the benefit of any land owned by the owner of the easement but that attaches *personally to the easement owner*. For example, a right granted by Eleanor Franks to Joe Fish to use a portion of her property for the rest of his life would be an easement in gross. **117**

economic life The number of years during which an improvement will add value to the land. **331**

electromagnetic fields (EMFs) Generated by the movement of electrical currents and may be related to a variety of health complaints. **384**

electronic contracting A process of integrating information electronically in a real estate transaction between clients, lender, and title and closing agents. **78**

Electronic Signatures in Global and National Commerce Act (E-Sign) An act that makes contracts (including signatures) and records legally enforceable regardless of the medium in which they are created. **78-79**

emblements Growing crops, such as corn, that are produced annually through labor and industry; also called *fructus industriales*. **20**

eminent domain The right of a government or municipal quasi-public body to acquire property for public use through a court action called *condemnation*, in which the court decides that the use is a public use and determines the compensation to be paid to the owner. **110-11**

employee Someone who works as a direct employee of an employer and has employee status. The employer is obligated to withhold income taxes and Social Security taxes from the compensation of employees. *See also* independent contractor. **75**

employment contract A document evidencing formal employment between employer and employee or between

principal and agent. In the real estate business, this generally takes the form of a listing agreement or management agreement. **104**

enabling acts State legislation that confers zoning powers on municipal governments. **339**

encapsulation A method of controlling environmental contamination by sealing off a dangerous substance. **376**

encroachment A building or some portion of it—a wall or fence, for instance—that extends beyond the land of the owner and illegally intrudes on some land of an adjoining owner or a street or alley. **119**

encumbrance Anything—such as a mortgage, tax, or judgment lien; an easement; a restriction on the use of the land; or an outstanding dower right—that may diminish the value or use and enjoyment of a property. **115**

environmental impact statement (EIS) A statement that details the impact a federally funded project will have on the environment. **390**

environmental site assessment (ESA) An evaluation of property to show that due care was exercised in the determination of environmental impairments. **390**

Equal Credit Opportunity Act (ECOA) The federal law that prohibits discrimination in the extension of credit because of race, color, religion, national origin, sex, age, or marital status. **257-58**

equalization The raising or lowering of assessed values for tax purposes in a particular county or taxing district to make them equal to assessments in other counties or districts. **164**

equalization factor A factor (number) by which the assessed value of a property is multiplied to arrive at a value for the property that is in line with statewide tax assessments. The *ad valorem tax* would be based on this adjusted value. **164**

equitable lien *See* statutory lien.

equitable right of redemption The right of a defaulted property owner to recover the property prior to its sale by paying the appropriate fees and charges. **233**

equitable title The interest held by a vendee under a contract for deed or an installment contract; the equitable right to obtain absolute ownership to property when legal title is held in another's name. **184-85**

equity The interest or value that an owner has in property over and above any indebtedness. **40**

equity buildup That portion of the loan payment directed toward the principal rather than the interest, plus any gain in property value due to appreciation. **433**

escheat The reversion of property to the state or county, as provided by state law, in cases where a decedent dies intestate without heirs capable of inheriting, or when the property is abandoned. 112

escrow The closing of a transaction through a third party called an *escrow agent*, or *escrowee*, who receives certain funds and documents to be delivered upon the performance of certain conditions outlined in the escrow instructions. 402

escrow account The trust account established by a broker under the provisions of the license law for the purpose of holding funds on behalf of the broker's principal or some other person until the consummation or termination of a transaction. 229-30

escrow closing A disinterested third party is authorized to act as escrow agent (escrow holder) and to coordinate the closing activities on behalf of the buyer and the seller. 402-3

escrow contract An agreement between a buyer, a seller, and an escrow holder setting forth rights and responsibilities of each. An escrow contract is entered into when earnest money is deposited in a broker's escrow account. 184

escrow instructions A document that sets forth the duties of the escrow agent, as well as the requirements and obligations of the parties, when a transaction is closed through an escrow. 401

estate (tenancy) at sufferance The tenancy of a lessee who lawfully comes into possession of a landlord's real estate but who continues to occupy the premises improperly after his or her lease rights have expired. 271

estate (tenancy) at will An estate that gives the lessee the right to possession until the estate is terminated by either party; the term of this estate is indefinite. 270

estate (tenancy) for years An interest for a certain, exact period of time in property leased for a specified consideration. 269

estate (tenancy) from period to period An interest in leased property that continues from period to period—week to week, month to month, or year to year. 269-70

estate in land The degree, quantity, nature, and extent of interest a person has in real property. 112

estate tax Federal tax on a decedent's real and personal property. 169

estoppel Method of creating an agency relationship in which someone states incorrectly that another person is his or her agent and a third person relies on that representation.

estoppel certificate A document in which a borrower certifies the amount owed on a mortgage loan and the rate of interest.

ethics The system of moral principles and rules that becomes standards for professional conduct. 367

eviction A legal process to oust a person from possession of real estate. 281

evidence of title Proof of ownership of property; commonly a certificate of title, an abstract of title with lawyer's opinion, title insurance, or a Torrens registration certificate. 402

exception The exclusion of a part of the property conveyed. 196

exchange A transaction in which all or part of the consideration is the transfer of *like-kind* property (e.g., real estate for real estate). 435-36

exclusive-agency listing A listing contract under which the owner appoints a real estate broker as his or her exclusive agent for a designated period of time to sell the property, on the owner's stated terms, for a commission. The owner reserves the right to sell without paying anyone a commission if the sale is to a prospect who has not been introduced or claimed by the broker. 89

exclusive-right-to-sell listing A listing contract under which the owner appoints a real estate broker as his or her exclusive agent for a designated period of time to sell the property on the owner's stated terms and agrees to pay the broker a commission when the property is sold, whether by the broker, the owner, or another broker. 88-89

executed contract A contract in which all parties have fulfilled their promises and thus performed the contract. 177

execution The signing and delivery of an instrument. Also, a legal order directing an official to enforce a judgment against the property of a debtor. 168

executor/executrix An appointed person who carries out the directions of a will. 205

executory contract A contract under which something remains to be done by one or more of the parties. 177

express agency An agency relationship based on a formal agreement between the parties. 47

express agreement An oral or written contract in which the parties state the contract's terms and express their intentions in words. 47

express contract *See* express agreement.

external depreciation Reduction in a property's value caused by outside factors (i.e., those that are off the property). 328

external obsolescence Incurable depreciation caused by factors not on the subject property, such as environmental, social, or economic factors. 330

facilitator *See* nonagent.

Fair Housing Act The federal law that prohibits discrimination in housing based on race, color, religion, sex, handicap, familial status, and national origin. **305**

Fair Housing Amendments Act of 1988 Expansion of the Fair Housing Act to include families with children and those with physical or mental disabilities. **282**

fair housing and civil rights laws Federal laws that prohibit discrimination in housing based on race, color, religion, sex, handicap, familial status, and national origin. **282**

Fannie Mae A government-sponsored enterprise established to purchase any kind of mortgage loans in the secondary mortgage market from the primary lenders. **248**

Federal Deposit Insurance Corporation (FDIC) An independent federal agency that insures the deposits in commercial banks. **240**

Federal Emergency Management Agency (FEMA) A federal agency that is responsible for assisting the nation in the event of a disaster providing response and recovery efforts. **38**

federal funds rate The rate recommended by the Federal Reserve for the member banks to charge each other on short-term loans. These rates form the basis on which the banks determine the percentage rate of interest they will charge their loan customers.

Federal Home Loan Mortgage Corporation *See* Freddie Mac.

Federal National Mortgage Association *See* Fannie Mae.

Federal Reserve System (Fed) The country's central banking system, which is responsible for the nation's monetary policy by regulating the sup-ply of money and interest rates. **239**

fee-for-service Arrangement where a consumer asks a licensee to perform specific real estate services for a set fee. **72**

fee simple The highest interest in real estate recognized by the law; the holder is entitled to all rights to the property. **121**

fee simple absolute The maximum possible estate or right of ownership of real property, continuing forever. **112**

fee simple defeasible *See* defeasible fee estate.

fee simple determinable A fee simple estate qualified by a special limitation. Language used to describe limitation includes the words *so long as*, *while*, or *during*. **112**

fee simple subject to a condition subsequent If an estate is no longer used for the purpose conveyed, it reverts to the original grantor by the right of reentry. **113**

feudal system A system of ownership usually associated with precolonial England, in which the king or other sovereign is the source of all rights. The right to possess real property was granted by the sovereign to an individual as a life estate only. Upon the death of the individual, title passed back to the sovereign, not to the decedent's heirs.

FHA loan A loan insured by the Federal Housing Administration and made by an approved lender in accordance with the FHA's regulations. **261**

fiduciary One in whom trust and confidence is placed; a reference to a broker employed under the terms of a listing contract or buyer agency agreement. **46**

fiduciary relationship A relationship of trust and confidence, as between trustee and beneficiary, attorney and client, or principal and agent. **48**

Financial Institutions Reform, Recovery, and Enforcement Act (FIRREA) This act restructured the savings and loan association regulatory system; enacted in response to the savings and loan crisis of the 1980s. **315**

first mortgage A mortgage that has priority over all other mortgages. **167**

fiscal policy The government's policy in regard to taxation and spending programs. The balance between these two areas determines the amount of money the government will withdraw from or feed into the economy, which can counter economic peaks and slumps.

fixture An item of personal property that has been converted to real property by being permanently affixed to the realty. **21**

forcible detainer Removal of a tenant from a rental property by the landlord if the tenant breached one of the terms of the lease agreement.

foreclosure A legal procedure whereby property used as security for a debt is sold to satisfy the debt in the event of default in payment of the mortgage note or default of other terms in the mortgage document. The foreclosure procedure brings the rights of all parties to a conclusion and passes the title in the mortgaged property to either the holder of the mortgage or a third party who may purchase the realty at the foreclosure sale, free of all encumbrances affecting the property subsequent to the mortgage. **232**

formal will/witnessed will A document having written instructions of property disbursements upon the death of the owner. The document must be signed and witnessed. **203**

formaldehyde An air pollutant that is a colorless chemical used to manufacture building materials and many household products, such as particleboard, hardwood plywood paneling, and urea-formaldehyde foam insulation. **391**

fraud Deception intended to cause a person to give up property or a lawful right. **59**

Freddie Mac A government-sponsored enterprise established to purchase primarily conventional mortgage loans in the secondary mortgage market. **260**

freehold estate An estate in land in which ownership is for an indeterminate length of time, in contrast to a *leasehold estate*. **117**

front footage The measurement of a parcel of land by the number of feet of street or road frontage.

frontage The length of property along the street or waterfront. **463**

fully amortized loan A loan consisting of equal, regular payments satisfying the total payment of principal and interest by the due date. **244**

functional obsolescence A loss of value to an improvement to real estate arising from functional problems, often caused by age or poor design. **330**

future interest A person's present right to an interest in real property that will not result in possession or enjoyment until some time in the future, such as a reversion or right of re-entry. **113**

gap A defect in the chain of title of a particular parcel of real estate; a missing document or conveyance that raises doubt as to the present ownership of the land. **213**

general agent One who is authorized by a principal to represent the principal in a specific range of matters. **52**

general lien The right of a creditor to have all of a debtor's property—both real and personal—sold to satisfy a debt. **162**

general partnership *See* partnership.

general real estate tax A tax that is made up of the taxes levied on the real estate by government agencies and municipalities. **163-64**

general warranty deed A deed in which the grantor fully warrants good, clear title to the premises. Used in most real estate deed transfers, a general warranty deed offers the greatest protection of any deed. **198**

Ginnie Mae A government agency that plays an important role in the secondary mortgage market. It guarantees mortgage-backed securities using FHA and VA loans as collateral. **260**

good and indefeasible title A title that cannot be annulled or rendered void.

Good Faith Estimate (GFE) A HUD form that estimates all closing fees that must be provided to a borrower within three days of the loan application as required by the Real Estate Settlement Procedures Act (RESPA). **407**

Government National Mortgage Association *See* Ginnie Mae.

government survey system *See* rectangular (government) survey system.

graduated-payment mortgage (GPM) A loan in which the monthly principal and interest payments increase by a certain percentage each year for a certain number of years and then level off for the remaining loan term.

grantee A person who receives a transfer of real property from a grantor. **194**

granting clause Words in a deed of conveyance that state the grantor's intention to convey the property at the present time. This clause is generally worded as "convey and warrant"; "grant"; "grant, bargain, and sell"; or the like. **196**

grantor The owner transferring title to or an interest in real property to a grantee. **194**

gross income multiplier (GIM) A figure used as a multiplier of the gross annual income of a property to produce an estimate of the property's value. **333**

gross lease A lease of property according to which a landlord pays all property charges regularly incurred through ownership, such as repairs, taxes, insurance, and operating expenses. Most residential leases are gross leases. **279**

gross rent multiplier (GRM) The figure used as a multiplier of the gross monthly income of a property to produce an estimate of the property's value. **333**

ground lease A lease of land only, on which the tenant usually owns a building or is required to build as specified in the lease. Such leases are usually long-term net leases; the tenant's rights and obligations continue until the lease expires or is terminated through default. **280**

groundwater Water that exists under the earth's surface within the tiny spaces or crevices in geological formations. **384**

groundwater rights Law that states that groundwater is the private property of the landowner.

growing-equity mortgage A loan in which the monthly payments increase annually, with the increased amount being used to reduce directly the principal balance outstanding and thus shorten the overall term of the loan. **245**

habendum clause That part of a deed beginning with the words "to have and to hold," following the granting clause and defining the extent of ownership the grantor is conveying. **196**

habitability A property that is suitable for living in or on.

heir One who might inherit or succeed to an interest in land under the state law of descent when the owner dies without leaving a valid will. 204

highest and best use The possible use of a property that would produce the greatest net income and, thereby, develop the highest value. 340

holdover tenancy A tenancy whereby a lessee retains possession of leased property after the lease has expired and the landlord, by continuing to accept rent, agrees to the tenant's continued occupancy as defined by state law. 270

holographic will A will that is written, dated, and signed in the testator's handwriting. 204

home equity loan A loan (sometimes called *a line of credit*) under which a property owner uses his or her residence as collateral and can then draw funds up to a prearranged amount against the property. 255-56

Home Mortgage Disclosure Act A federal law that requires lenders to annually disclose the number of loan applications and loans in certain areas, thus eliminating the practice of "redlining."

homeowners' insurance policy A standardized package insurance policy that covers a residential real estate owner against financial loss from fire, theft, public liability, and other common risks. 36-38

homestead Land that is owned and occupied as the family home. In many states, a portion of the area or value of this land is protected or exempt from judgments for debts. 115

HUD-1 A form that itemizes fees and services charged to a borrower and seller during a real estate transaction.

hypothecation To pledge property as security for an obligation or loan without giving up possession of it. 224

implied agency Based on the actions of the parties that imply that they have mutually consented to an agency relationship, an implied agency relationship is formed. 47

implied agreement A contract under which the agreement of the parties is demonstrated by their acts and conduct. 47

implied contract *See* implied agreement.

implied warranty of habitability A theory in landlord/tenant law in which the landlord renting residential property implies that the property is habitable and fit for its intended use.

impound account An account that most mortgage lenders require borrowers to have for funds to pay future real estate taxes and insurance premiums. 229-30

improvement (1) Any structure, usually privately owned, erected on a site to enhance the value of the property (e.g., building a fence or a driveway). (2) A publicly owned structure added to or benefiting land (e.g., a curb, sidewalk, street, or sewer). 17

income approach The process of estimating the value of an income-producing property through capitalization of the annual net income expected to be produced by the property during its remaining useful life. 331-33

income property Property held for current income as well as a potential profit upon its sale. 431

incorporeal right A nonpossessory right in real estate (e.g., an easement or a right-of-way).

independent contractor Someone who is retained to perform a certain act but who is subject to the control and direction of another only as to the end result and not as to the way in which the act is performed. Unlike an employee, an independent contractor pays for all expenses and Social Security and income taxes and receives no employee benefits. Most real estate salespeople are independent contractors. 75

index An objective economic indicator to which the interest rate for an adjustable-rate mortgage is tied. 244

inflation The gradual reduction of the purchasing power of the dollar, usually related directly to the increases in the money supply by the federal government. 431

inheritance taxes State-imposed taxes on a decedent's real and personal property. 162

installment sale A transaction in which the sales price is paid in two or more installments over two or more years. If the sale meets certain requirements, a taxpayer can postpone reporting such income until future years by paying tax each year only on the proceeds received that year. 436

interest A charge made by a lender for the use of money. 225

interest-only mortgage A mortgage that only requires the payment of interest for a stated period of time with the principal due at the end of the term. 242

interim financing A short-term loan usually made during the construction phase of a building project (often referred to as a *construction loan*). 255

Internal Revenue Service tax lien A lien charged by the Internal Revenue Service for nonpayment of income taxes. 170

Internet advertising A powerful computer tool for providing information about properties, relocation services, and particular communities; however, state laws do apply. 78

Internet Listing Display Policy A policy from the National Association of REALTORS® that allows all MLS members to have equal right to display MLS data, and respects the rights of property owners and their listing brokers to market a property as they wish. **77**

Interstate Land Sales Full Disclosure Act A federal law that regulates the sale of certain real estate in interstate commerce. **347-48**

intestate The condition of a property owner who dies without leaving a valid will. Title to the property will pass to the decedent's heirs as provided in the state law of descent. **202**

intrinsic value An appraisal term referring to the value created by a person's personal preferences for a particular type of property. **431**

inverse condemnation An action brought by a property owner seeking just compensation for land taken for public use when the taker of the property does not intend to bring eminent domain proceedings. Property is condemned because its use and value have been diminished due to an adjacent property's public use. **342**

investment Money directed toward the purchase, improvement, and development of an asset in expectation of income or profits. **23**

involuntary alienation *See* alienation.

involuntary lien A lien placed on property without the consent of the property owner. **161**

joint tenancy Ownership of real estate between two or more parties who have been named in one conveyance as joint tenants. Upon the death of a joint tenant, the decedent's interest passes to the surviving joint tenant or tenants by the *right of survivorship*. **127-28**

judgment The formal decision of a court upon the respective rights and claims of the parties to an action or suit. After a judgment has been entered and recorded with the county recorder, it usually becomes a general lien on the property of the defendant. **168-69**

judicial precedent In law, the requirements established by prior court decisions.

junior lien An obligation, such as a second mortgage, that is subordinate in right or lien priority to an existing lien on the same realty. **167**

laches An equitable doctrine used by courts to bar a legal claim or prevent the assertion of a right because of undue delay or failure to assert the claim or right. **347**

land The earth's surface, extending downward to the center of the earth and upward infinitely into space, including things permanently attached by nature, such as trees and water. **16-17**

land contract *See* installment sale.

latent defect A hidden structural defect that could not be discovered by ordinary inspection and that threatens the property's soundness or the safety of its inhabitants. Some states impose on sellers and licensees a duty to inspect for and disclose latent defects. **60**

law of agency *See* agency.

law of diminishing returns Law that applies when at the point where additional improvements do not increase income or value. **326**

law of increasing returns Law that applies as long as money being spent on improvements produces an increase in income or value. **326**

lead Used as a pigment and drying agent in alkyd oil-based paint in about 75 percent of housing built before 1978. An elevated level of lead in the body can cause serious damage to the brain, kidneys, nervous system, and red blood cells. Children under the age of six are most vulnerable. **277**

lease A written or oral contract between a landlord (the lessor) and a tenant (the lessee) that transfers the right to exclusive possession and use of the landlord's real property to the lessee for a specified period of time and for a stated consideration (rent). By state law, leases for longer than a certain period of time (generally one year) must be in writing to be enforceable. **268**

lease option A lease under which the tenant has the right to purchase the property either during the lease term or at its end. **278**

lease purchase The purchase of real property, the consummation of which is preceded by a lease, usually long-term, that is typically done for tax or financing purposes. **280**

leasehold estate A tenant's right to occupy real estate during the term of a lease, generally considered to be a personal property interest. **112**

legacy A disposition of money or personal property by will. **207**

legal description A description of a specific parcel of real estate complete enough for an independent surveyor to locate and identify it. **144**

legal life estate A form of life estate established by state law, rather than created voluntarily by an owner. It becomes effective when certain events occur. *See* dower, curtesy, and homestead for legal life estates used in some states. **114**

legally competent parties People who are recognized by law as being able to contract with others; those of legal age and sound mind. **179**

lessee *See* lease.

lessor *See* lease.

leverage   The use of borrowed money to finance an investment. 433-34

levy   To assess; to seize or collect. To levy a tax is to assess a property and set the rate of taxation. To levy an execution is to officially seize the property of a person in order to satisfy an obligation. 163

liability coverage   Insurance that covers injuries or losses sustained within the home. 37

license   (1) A privilege or right granted to a person by a state to operate as a real estate broker or salesperson. (2) The revocable permission for a temporary use of land—a personal right that cannot be sold. 69

licensee   A person who has the skills and knowledge to be licensed in real estate. 4

lien   A right given by law to certain creditors to have their debts paid out of the property of a defaulting debtor, usually by means of a court sale. 121

lien theory   Some states interpret a mortgage as being purely a lien on real property. The mortgagee thus has no right of possession but must foreclose the lien and sell the property if the mortgagor defaults. 223

life cycle costing   In property management, comparing one type of equipment with another based on both purchase cost and operating cost over its expected useful lifetime.

life estate   An interest in real or personal property that is limited in duration to the lifetime of its owner or some other designated person or persons. 112

life tenant   A person in possession of a life estate. 114

limited liability company (LLC)   A form of business organization that combines the most attractive features of limited partnerships and corporations. 133

limited partnership   *See* partnership.

linear measurement   Measurement in a straight line. 463

liquidated damages   An amount predetermined by the parties to a contract as the total compensation to an injured party should the other party breach the contract. 185

liquidity   The ability to sell an asset and convert it into cash, at a price close to its true value, in a short period of time. 430

lis pendens   A recorded legal document giving constructive notice that an action affecting a particular property has been filed in either a state or a federal court. 169

listing agreement   A contract between an owner (as principal) and a real estate broker (as agent) by which the broker is employed as agent to find a buyer for the owner's real estate on the owner's terms, for which service the owner agrees to pay a commission. 47

listing broker   The broker in a multiple-listing situation from whose office a listing agreement is initiated, as opposed to the *cooperating broker*, from whose office negotiations leading up to a sale are initiated. The listing broker and the cooperating broker may be the same person. 90

littoral rights   (1) A landowner's claim to use water in large navigable lakes and oceans adjacent to his or her property. (2) The ownership rights to land bordering these bodies of water up to the high-water mark. 119-20

living trust   A trust that is created during one's lifetime. 131

loan origination fee   A fee charged to the borrower by the lender for making a mortgage loan. The fee is usually computed as a percentage of the loan amount. 225-26

loan-to-value (LTV) ratio   The relationship between the amount of the mortgage loan and the value of the real estate being pledged as collateral. 247

lot-and-block (recorded plat) system   A method of describing real property that identifies a parcel of land by reference to lot and block numbers within a subdivision, as specified on a recorded subdivision plat. 151-52

management agreement   A contract between the owner of income property and a management firm or individual property manager that outlines the scope of the manager's authority. 10

management plan   A highly detailed plan that lays out the owner's objectives with the property, as well as what the property manager wants to accomplish and how, including all budgetary information. 295

manufactured housing   Dwellings that are built off-site and trucked to a building lot where they are installed or assembled. 19-20

margin   A premium added to the index rate representing the lender's cost of doing business. 244

market   A place where goods can be bought and sold and a price established. 7-10

marketable title   Good or clear title, reasonably free from the risk of litigation over possible defects. 214

market data approach   Also known as the *sales comparison approach*. An estimate of value obtained by comparing property being appraised with recently sold comparable properties. 327

market value   The most probable price property would bring in an arm's-length transaction under normal conditions on the open market. **324**

master plan   A comprehensive plan to guide the long-term physical development of a particular area. **339**

mechanic's lien   A statutory lien created in favor of contractors, laborers, and materialmen who have performed work or furnished materials in the erection or repair of a building. **167-68**

Megan's Law   Federal legislation that promotes the establishment of state registration systems to maintain residential information on every person who kidnaps children, commits sexual crimes against children, or commits sexually violent crimes. **60**

meridian   One of a set of imaginary lines running north and south and crossing a base line at a definite point, used in the rectangular (government) survey system of property description. **146**

metes-and-bounds description   A legal description of a parcel of land that begins at a well-marked point and follows the boundaries, using directions and distances around the tract, back to the place of beginning. **144-46**

mill   One-tenth of one cent. Some states use a mill rate to compute real estate taxes; for example, a rate of 52 mills would be $0.052 tax for each dollar of assessed valuation of a property. **165**

minimum level of service   Some states are requiring that licensees perform some minimum level of service to clients. **74-75**

minor   A person who has not reached the age of majority and, therefore, does not have legal capacity to transfer title to real property. **179**

mixed use   Property that accommodates more than one use, such as commercial use and residential use. **7**

Model Real Estate Time-Share Act   An act that governs the management, use, and termination of time-share units. **138**

mold   A form of fungus that can be found almost anywhere and can grow on almost any organic substance, so long as moisture, oxygen, and an organic food source are present. Mold growth can gradually destroy what it is growing on as well as cause serious health problems. **382-83**

monetary policy   Governmental regulation of the amount of money in circulation through such institutions as the Federal Reserve Board. **9**

month-to-month tenancy   A periodic tenancy under which the tenant rents for one month at a time. In the absence of a rental agreement (oral or written), a tenancy is generally considered to be month to month. **283**

monument   A fixed natural or artificial object used to establish real estate boundaries for a metes-and-bounds description. **145**

mortgage   A conditional transfer or pledge of real estate as security for the payment of a debt. Also, the document creating a mortgage lien. **223**

mortgage banker   Mortgage loan companies that originate, service, and sell loans to investors. **240-41**

mortgage broker   An agent of a lender who brings the lender and borrower together. The broker receives a fee for this service. **241**

Mortgage Disclosure Improvement Act (MDIA)   The timeliness of certain disclosures affects the date of closings. Lenders and licensees need to keep three numbers in mind: 3-7-3—three business days to provide a truth-in-lending statement (TIL) and good-faith estimate (GFE); seven business days before signing loan documents after the borrower receives final TIL and GFE; three business days for closing if the APR has changed more than 0.125 percent from the original or most recent TIL and GFE; and three business days before closing to provide consumer with copy of appraisal. **404-5**

mortgage insurance premium (MIP)   The FHA insurance that the borrower is charged with a percentage of the loan as a premium. **259**

mortgage lien   A lien or charge on the property of a mortgagor that secures the underlying debt obligations. **164**

mortgagee   A lender in a mortgage loan transaction. **223**

mortgagor   A borrower in a mortgage loan transaction. **223**

multiperil policies   Insurance policies that offer protection from a range of potential perils, such as those of a fire, hazard, public liability, and casualty. **307**

multiple-listing clause   A provision in an exclusive listing for the authority and obligation on the part of the listing broker to distribute the listing to other brokers in the multiple-listing organization. **89**

multiple listing service (MLS)   A marketing organization composed of member brokers who agree to share their listing agreements with one another in the hope of procuring ready, willing, and able buyers for their properties more quickly than they could on their own. Most multiple listing services accept exclusive-right-to-sell or exclusive-agency listings from their member brokers. **68**

National Association of REALTORS® (NAR)   The largest real estate organization in the world; NAR members subscribe to a strict code of ethics. Active brokers are allowed to use the trademarked designation, REALTOR®. **6**

National Do Not Call Registry *See* Do Not Call Registry.

negligent misrepresentation Occurs when the broker should have known that a statement about a material fact was false. **79**

negotiable instrument A written promise or order to pay a specific sum of money that may be transferred by endorsement or delivery. The transferee then has the original payee's right to payment. **225**

net lease A lease requiring the tenant to pay not only rent but also costs incurred in maintaining the property, including taxes, insurance, utilities, and repairs. **279**

net listing A listing based on the net price the seller will receive if the property is sold. Under a net listing, the broker can offer the property for sale at the highest price obtainable to increase the commission. This type of listing is illegal in many states. **90**

net operating income (NOI) The income projected for an income-producing property after deducting losses for vacancy and collection and operating expenses. **331**

nonagent An intermediary between a buyer and a seller, or a landlord and a tenant, who assists one or both parties with a transaction without representing either. Also known as a *facilitator, transaction broker, transaction coordinator,* and *contract broker.* **46**

nonconforming use A use of property that is permitted to continue after a zoning ordinance prohibiting it has been established for the area. **343**

nondisturbance clause A mortgage clause stating that the mortgagee agrees not to terminate the tenancies of the lessees in the event the mortgagee forecloses on the mortgagor-lessor's building. **278**

nonhomogeneity A lack of uniformity; dissimilarity. Because no two parcels of land are exactly alike, real estate is said to be nonhomogeneous. **23**

notarization To certify the validity of a signature on a document. **197**

note *See* promissory note.

novation Substituting a new obligation for an old one or substituting new parties to an existing obligation. **180**

numerator The number written above the line of a fraction representing the number to be divided by the denominator. **469**

nuncupative will An oral will declared by the testator in his or her final illness, made before witnesses and afterward reduced to writing. **204**

obsolescence The loss of value due to factors that are outmoded or less useful. Obsolescence may be functional or external. **330**

occupancy permit A permit issued by the appropriate local governing body to establish that the property is suitable for habitation by meeting certain safety and health standards. **344**

offer and acceptance Two essential components of a valid contract; a "meeting of the minds." **170**

offeror/offeree The person who makes the offer is the offeror. The person to whom the offer is made is the offeree. **177**

open-end loan A mortgage loan that is expandable by increments up to a maximum dollar amount, the full loan being secured by the same original mortgage. **254**

open listing A listing contract under which the broker's commission is contingent on the broker's producing a ready, willing, and able buyer before the property is sold by the seller or another broker. **89**

operating budget A guide of the property's financial performance in the present and future. It gives the owner a sense of expected profit. **297**

option An agreement to keep open for a set period an offer to sell or purchase property. **187**

ostensible agency A form of implied agency relationship created by the actions of the parties involved rather than by written agreement or document.

owelty lien A lien created by the order of the court to make an equitable partition of property when otherwise an agreeable partition is impossible or impractical (i.e., in a divorce).

owner financing The seller is the primary lender securing his or her interest with the use of a deed, note and mortgage, deed of trust, or contract for deed. The buyer takes possession of the property, but the seller retains legal title until paid in full. **231**

P&I Principal and interest.

package loan A real estate loan used to finance the purchase of both real property and personal property, such as in the purchase of a new home that includes carpeting, window coverings, and major appliances. **253**

panic peddling The illegal practice of soliciting people in a neighborhood to sell their homes because of fear or alarm; also referred to as blockbusting.

parol evidence Oral or verbal evidence.

parol evidence rule A rule of evidence providing that a written agreement is the final expression of the agreement of the parties, not to be varied or contradicted by prior or contemporaneous oral or written negotiations.

participation mortgage A mortgage loan wherein the lender has a partial equity interest in the property or receives a portion of the income from the property.

partition The division of cotenants' interests in real property when the parties do not all voluntarily agree to terminate the co-ownership; takes place through court procedures. **128-29**

partnership An association of two or more individuals who carry on a continuing business for profit as co-owners. Under the law, a partnership is regarded as a group of individuals rather than as a single entity. A *general partnership* is a typical form of joint venture in which each general partner shares in the administration, profits, and losses of the operation. A *limited partnership* is a business arrangement whereby the operation is administered by one or more general partners and funded, by and large, by limited or silent partners, who are by law responsible for losses only to the extent of their investments. **132**

patent A grant or franchise of land from the U.S. government.

payment cap The limit on the amount the monthly payment can be increased on an adjustable-rate mortgage when the interest rate is adjusted. **244**

payoff statement *See* reduction certificate.

percent One part in a hundred. **472**

percentage lease A lease, commonly used for commercial property, whose rental is based on the tenant's gross sales at the premises; it usually stipulates a base monthly rental plus a percentage of any gross sales above a certain amount. **284**

percolation test A test of the soil to determine if it will absorb and drain water adequately to use a septic system for sewage disposal.

periodic estate (tenancy) *See* estate from period to period. **269**

personal property Items, called *chattels*, that do not fit into the definition of real property; movable objects. **19**

personalty Personal property. **19**

physical deterioration A reduction in a property's value resulting from a decline in physical condition; can be caused by action of the elements or by ordinary wear and tear. **330**

PITI The basic costs of owning a home—mortgage Principal and Interest, real estate Taxes, and hazard Insurance. **35**

PITT Joint tenancy, where tenants enjoy the four unities: possession, interest, time, and title. **127**

planned unit development (PUD) A planned combination of diverse land uses, such as housing, recreation, and shopping, in one contained development or subdivision. **349**

plat A detailed map that illustrates the geographic boundaries of individual lots. **345**

plat map A map of a town, section, or subdivision indicating the location and boundaries of individual properties. **151**

plottage The increase in value or utility resulting from the consolidation (assemblage) of two or more adjacent lots into one larger lot. **326**

point A term used for a percentage of the principal loan amount charged by the lender. Each point is equal to 1 percent of the loan amount. **225**

point of beginning (POB) In a metes-and-bounds legal description, the starting point of the survey, situated in one corner of the parcel; all metes-and-bounds descriptions must follow the boundaries of the parcel to the point of ending, which is also the point of beginning. **145**

point of ending (POE) In a metes-and-bounds legal description, the ending point of the survey, which is also the point of beginning. **145**

police power The government's right to impose laws, statutes, and ordinances, including zoning ordinances and building codes, to protect the public health, safety, and welfare. **110**

polychlorinated biphenyls (PCBs) Used as an insulating material in dielectric oil. It can linger in the environment for long periods of time and can cause health problems. **382**

possession Owning or occupying a property. **276**

power of attorney A written instrument authorizing a person, the *attorney-in-fact*, to act as agent for another person to the extent indicated in the instrument. **197**

prepaid items On a closing statement, items that have been paid in advance by the seller, such as insurance premiums and some real estate taxes, for which the seller must be reimbursed by the buyer. **414**

prepayment penalty A charge imposed on a borrower who pays off the loan principal early. This penalty compensates the lender for interest and other charges that would otherwise be lost. **226-27**

preventive maintenance Small repairs that help prevent bigger problems and expenses. **302**

price The amount of money paid for an item or service. **7**

price-fixing *See* antitrust laws.

primary mortgage market The mortgage market in which loans are originated and consisting of lenders such as commercial banks, savings associations, and mutual savings banks. **239-41**

principal (1) A sum loaned or employed as a fund or an investment, as distinguished from its income or profits. (2) The original amount (as in a loan) of the total due and payable at a certain date. (3) A main party to a transaction—the person for whom the agent works. **46**

principal meridian The main imaginary line running north and south and crossing a base line at a definite point; used by surveyors for reference in locating and describing land under the rectangular (government) survey system of legal description. **146**

Principle of Conformity The belief of what a property will draw for a fair market price when located with similar properties of the same size, style, condition, and location. **325**

prior appropriation A concept of water ownership in which the landowner's right to use available water is based on a government-administered permit system. **122**

priority The order of position or time. The priority of liens is generally determined by the chronological order in which the lien documents are recorded; tax liens, however, have priority even over previously recorded liens. **212**

private mortgage insurance (PMI) Insurance provided by private carrier that protects a lender against a loss in the event of a foreclosure and deficiency. **261**

probate A legal process by which a court determines who will inherit a decedent's property and what the estate's assets are. **203**

procuring cause The effort that brings about the desired result. Under an open listing, the broker who is the procuring cause of the sale receives the commission. **71**

profit Making a gain from an investment after subtracting expenses. **483-84**

profit and loss statement A general financial picture based on the monthly cash flow reports; does not include itemized information. **298**

progression An appraisal principle that states that, between dissimilar properties, the value of the lesser-quality property is favorably affected by the presence of the better-quality property. **326**

promissory note A financing instrument that states the terms of the underlying obligation, is signed by its maker, and is negotiable (transferable to a third party). **224**

property manager Someone who manages real estate for another person for compensation. Duties include collecting rents, maintaining the property, and keeping up all accounting. **5**

property reports The mandatory federal and state documents compiled by subdividers and developers to provide potential purchasers with facts about a property prior to their purchase.

proprietary lease A lease given by the corporation that owns a cooperative apartment building to the shareholder for the shareholder's right as a tenant to an individual apartment. **33**

prorations Expenses, either prepaid or paid in arrears, that are divided or distributed between the buyer and the seller at the closing. **414**

protected class Any group of people designated as such by the Department of Housing and Urban Development (HUD) in consideration of federal and state civil rights legislation. Currently includes ethnic minorities, women, religious groups, the disabled, and others. **282**

public ownership Government-owned property.

puffing Exaggerated or superlative comments or opinions. **59**

pur autre vie "For the life of another." A life estate pur autre vie is a life estate that is measured by the life of a person other than the grantee. **114**

purchase-money mortgage (PMM) A note secured by a mortgage or deed of trust given by a buyer, as borrower, to a seller, as lender, as part of the purchase price of the real estate. **253**

purchase option Some leases grant the lessee the option to purchase the leased premises. This option normally gives the tenant the right to purchase the property at a predetermined price within a certain period, possibly the lease term. **278-79**

pyramiding The process of acquiring additional properties by refinancing properties already owned and investing the loan proceeds in additional properties. **438**

quiet title A court action to remove a cloud on the title. **213**

quitclaim deed A conveyance by which the grantor transfers whatever interest he or she has in the real estate, without warranties or obligations. **207**

quotient The number resulting from dividing one number by another. **472**

radon A naturally occurring gas that is suspected of causing lung cancer. **391**

range A strip of land six miles wide, extending north and south and numbered east and west according to its distance from the principal meridian in the rectangular (government) survey system of legal description. **146**

rate cap The limit on the amount the interest rate can be increased at each adjustment period in an adjustable-rate loan. The cap may also set the maximum interest rate that can be charged during the life of the loan. **244**

ratification Method of creating an agency relationship in which the principal accepts the conduct of someone who acted without prior authorization as the principal's agent.

ready, willing, and able buyer Person who is prepared to buy property on the seller's terms and is ready to take positive steps to consummate the transaction. **71**

real estate Land; a portion of the earth's surface extending downward to the center of the earth and upward infinitely into space, including all things permanently attached to it, whether naturally or artificially. **17**

real estate broker A person licensed to arrange the buying and selling of property for a fee. **4**

real estate investment syndicate *See* syndicate.

real estate investment trust (REIT) Trust ownership of real estate by a group of individuals who purchase certificates of ownership in the trust, which in turn invests the money in real property and distributes the profits back to the investors free of corporate income tax. **437**

real estate license law State law enacted to protect the public from fraud, dishonesty, and incompetence in the purchase and sale of real estate. **24**

real estate mortgage investment conduit (REMIC) A tax entity that issues multiple classes of investor interests (securities) backed by a pool of mortgages. **437**

real estate recovery fund A fund established in some states from real estate license revenues to cover claims of aggrieved parties who have suffered monetary damage through the actions of a real estate licensee.

Real Estate Settlement Procedures Act (RESPA) The federal law that requires certain disclosures to consumers about mortgage loan settlements. The law also prohibits the payment or receipt of kickbacks and certain kinds of referral fees. **405-6**

real property The interests, benefits, and rights inherent in real estate ownership. **25**

REALTOR® A registered trademarked term reserved for the sole use of active members of local REALTOR® boards affiliated with the National Association of REALTORS®. **6**

reconciliation The final step in the appraisal process, in which the appraiser combines the estimates of value received from the sales comparison, cost, and income approaches to arrive at a final estimate of market value for the subject property. **335**

reconveyance deed A deed used by a trustee under a deed of trust to return title to the trustor. **200**

recorded plat A map of a subdivision filed as a public record showing the location and boundaries of the individual parcels. **151-52**

recording The act of entering or recording documents affecting or conveying interests in real estate in the recorder's office established in each county. Until it is recorded, a deed or mortgage ordinarily is not effective against subsequent purchasers or mortgagees. **211-12**

rectangular survey system A system established in 1785 by the federal government, providing for surveying and describing land by reference to principal meridians and base lines. **155**

redemption The right of a defaulted property owner to recover his or her property by curing the default. **166**

redemption period A period of time established by state law during which a property owner has the right to redeem his or her real estate from a foreclosure or tax sale by paying the sales price, interest, and costs. Many states do not have mortgage redemption laws. **233**

redlining The illegal practice of a lending institution denying loans or restricting their number for certain areas of a community. **364**

reduction certificate (payoff statement) The document signed by a lender indicating the amount required to pay a loan balance in full and satisfy the debt; used in the settlement process to protect both the seller's and the buyer's interests. **400**

regression An appraisal principle that states that, between dissimilar properties, the value of the better-quality property is affected adversely by the presence of the lesser-quality property. **326**

Regulation Z Implements the Truth in Lending Act requiring credit institutions to inform borrowers of the true cost of obtaining credit. **262**

release deed A document, also known as a *deed of reconveyance*, that transfers all rights given a trustee under a deed of trust loan back to the grantor after the loan has been fully repaid. **229**

release of lien A lien on a property that is now free from a mortgage.

remainder interest The remnant of an estate that has been conveyed to take effect and be enjoyed after the termination of a prior estate, such as when an owner conveys a life estate to one party and the remainder to another. **114**

renewal option A clause in a lease that grants the lessee the privilege of renewing the lease. **278**

rent A fixed, periodic payment made by a tenant of a property to the owner for possession and use, usually by prior agreement of the parties. **309**

rent schedule A statement of proposed rental rates, determined by the owner or the property manager or both, based on a building's estimated expenses, market supply and demand, and the owner's long-range goals for the property.

replacement cost The construction cost at current prices of a property that is not necessarily an exact duplicate of the subject property but serves the same purpose or function as the original. 37

reproduction cost The construction cost at current prices of an exact duplicate of the subject property. 329

rescission The practice of one party canceling or terminating a contract, which has the effect of returning the parties to their original positions before the contract was made. 181

reservation Something that is retained by the seller (i.e., a life estate or an access easement). 181

Resolution Trust Corporation The organization created by the Financial Institutions Reform, Recovery, and Enforcement Act (FIRREA) to liquidate the assets of failed savings and loan associations.

restrictive covenants A clause in a deed that limits the way the real estate ownership may be used. 346

reverse mortgage A loan under which the homeowner receives monthly payments based on his or her accumulated equity rather than a lump sum. The loan must be repaid at a prearranged date, upon the death of the owner, or upon the sale of the property. 247

reversionary interest The remnant of an estate that the grantor holds after granting a life estate to another person. 114

reversionary right The return of the rights of possession and quiet enjoyment to the lessor at the expiration of a lease. 283

revocation Cancelling or annulling licensed privileges or rights. 69

right of first refusal A clause allowing the tenant the opportunity to buy the property before the owner accepts an offer from another party. 278

right of survivorship *See* joint tenancy.

right-of-way The right given by one landowner to another to pass over the land, construct a roadway, or use as a pathway, without actually transferring ownership. 116

riparian rights An owner's rights in land that borders on or includes a stream, river, or lake. These rights include access to and use of the water. 119

risk management Evaluation and selection of appropriate property and other insurance. 310

routine maintenance Day-to-day duties such as cleaning common areas, performing minor carpentry and plumbing adjustments, and providing regularly scheduled upkeep of heating, air-conditioning, and landscaping. 302

rules and regulations Real estate licensing authority orders that govern licensees' activities; they usually have the same force and effect as statutory law. 45

Safe Drinking Water Act An act to protect public health by authorizing the EPA to set national health-based standards for drinking water. 384

sale-and-leaseback A transaction in which an owner sells his or her improved property and, as part of the same transaction, signs a long-term lease to remain in possession of the premises. 280

sales comparison approach The process of estimating the value of a property by examining and comparing actual sales of comparable properties. 327

sales price The amount of money paid to a seller for a product bought. 327

salesperson A person who performs real estate activities while employed by or associated with a licensed real estate broker. 4

satisfaction Release or discharge of when a note has been fully paid. This document returns to the borrower all interest in the real estate originally conveyed to the lender. Entering this release in the public record shows that the debt has been removed from the property. 229

satisfaction of mortgage A document acknowledging the payment of a mortgage debt. 223

secondary mortgage market A market for the purchase and sale of existing mortgages, designed to provide greater liquidity for mortgages; also called the *secondary money market*. Mortgages are first originated in the *primary mortgage market*. 241

section A portion of township under the rectangular (government) survey system. A township is divided into 36 sections, numbered 1 through 36. A section is a square with mile-long sides and an area of one square mile, or 640 acres. 155

security agreement *See* Uniform Commercial Code.

security deposit A payment by a tenant, held by the landlord during the lease term, and kept (wholly or partially) on default, or on destruction of the premises by the tenant. 283

seller's broker The real estate broker who represents only the seller in transactions. 48

seller's disclosure notice Documents completed by the seller of a home listing any known issues of the property, including home improvements made. 60

separate property Under community property law, property owned solely by either spouse before the marriage, acquired by gift or inheritance after the marriage, or purchased with separate funds after the marriage. 139

servient tenement Land on which an easement exists in favor of an adjacent property (called a *dominant estate*); also called a *servient estate*. **116**

setback The amount of space local zoning regulations require between a lot line and a building line. **340**

severalty Ownership of real property by one person only; also called *sole ownership*. **138**

severance Changing an item of real estate to personal property by detaching it from the land (e.g., cutting down a tree). **20**

shared-appreciation mortgage (SAM) A mortgage loan in which the lender, in exchange for a loan with a favorable interest rate, participates in the profits (if any) the borrower receives when the property is eventually sold.

sick building syndrome (SBS) An illness caused by poor air quality, typically in office building settings. Symptoms include fatigue, nausea, headache, and sensitivity to odors. **308**

situs The personal preference of people for one area over another, not necessarily based on objective facts and knowledge. **23**

special agent One who is authorized by a principal to perform a single act or transaction; a real estate broker is usually a special agent authorized to find a ready, willing, and able buyer for a particular property. **52**

special assessment A tax or levy customarily imposed against only those specific parcels of real estate that will benefit from a proposed public improvement like a street or sewer. **166-67**

special warranty deed A deed in which the grantor warrants, or guarantees, the title only against defects arising during the period of his or her tenure and ownership of the property and not against defects existing before that time, generally using the language, "by, through, or under the grantor but not otherwise." **206**

specific lien A lien affecting or attaching only to a certain, specific parcel of land or piece of property. **170**

specific performance A legal action to compel a party to carry out the terms of a contract. **181**

spot zoning Granting a particular area a certain classification that differs from the classification of other land in the immediate area. This zoning is considered invalid.

statute of frauds That part of a state law that requires certain instruments, such as deeds, real estate sales contracts, and certain leases, to be in writing to be legally enforceable. **194**

statute of limitations That law pertaining to the period of time within which certain actions must be brought to court. **181**

statutory lien A lien imposed on property by statute—a tax lien, for example—in contrast to an *equitable lien*, which arises out of common law. **161**

statutory right of redemption The right of a defaulted property owner to recover the property after its sale by paying the appropriate fees and charges. **172**

statutory year A year composed of 12 months, with each month consisting of 30 days, for a total of 360 days in the year. Also referred to as a banker's year. **490**

steering The illegal practice of channeling home seekers to particular areas, either to maintain the homogeneity of an area or to change the character of an area, which limits their choices of where they can live. **305**

stigmatized property A property that has acquired an undesirable reputation due to an event that occurred on or near it, such as violent crime, gang-related activity, illness, or personal tragedy. Some states restrict the disclosure of information about stigmatized properties. **60-61**

straight (term) loan A loan in which only interest is paid during the term of the loan, with the entire principal amount due with the final interest payment. **242**

subdivider One who buys undeveloped land, divides it into smaller, usable lots and sells the lots to potential users. **345**

subdivision A tract of land divided by the owner, known as the *subdivider*, into blocks, building lots, and streets according to a recorded subdivision plat, which must comply with local ordinances and regulations. **5**

subdivision and development ordinances Municipal ordinances that establish requirements for subdivisions and development.

subdivision plat *See* plat map.

subject to Buyer takes title of property and makes payments on the existing loan but is not personally obligated to pay the debt in full. Original seller might continue to be liable for debt. **230**

"subject to" clause A clause in a contract specifying exceptions or contingencies of a purchase. **195**

subjective value The perceived value of an item based on the benefits given to the owner.

sublease *See* subletting.

subletting The leasing of premises by a lessee to a third party for part of the lessee's remaining term. *See also* assignment. **278**

subordination Relegation to a lesser position, usually in respect to a right or security. **48**

subordination agreement A written agreement between holders of liens on a property that changes the priority of mortgage, judgment, and other liens under certain circumstances. **163**

substitution An appraisal principle that states that the maximum value of a property tends to be set by the cost of purchasing an equally desirable and valuable substitute property, assuming that no costly delay is encountered in making the substitution. **326**

subsurface rights Ownership rights in a parcel of real estate to the water, minerals, gas, oil, and so forth that lie beneath the surface of the property. **18**

suit for possession A court suit initiated by a landlord to evict a tenant from leased premises after the tenant has breached one of the terms of the lease or has held possession of the property after the lease's expiration. **281**

suit for specific performance If the seller breaches a real estate sales contract, the buyer may sue, asking the court to force the seller to go through with the sale and convey the property as previously agreed. **181**

suit to quiet title A court action intended to establish or settle the title to a particular property, especially when there is a cloud on the title. **213**

Superfund Popular name of the hazardous-waste cleanup fund established by the Comprehensive Environmental Response, Compensation, and Liability Act (CERCLA). **388-89**

Superfund Amendments and Reauthorization Act (SARA) An amendatory statute that contains stronger cleanup standards for contaminated sites, increased funding for Superfund, and clarifications of lender liability and innocent landowner immunity. *See* Comprehensive Environmental Response, Compensation, and Liability Act (CERCLA). **387**

supply The amount of goods available in the market to be sold at a given price. The term is often coupled with *demand*. **7-8**

supply and demand The appraisal principle that follows the interrelationship of the supply of and demand for real estate. Because appraising is based on economic concepts, this principle recognizes that real property is subject to the influences of the marketplace as with any other commodity. **7-8**

surety bonds An agreement by an insurance or bonding company to be responsible for certain possible defaults, debts, or obligations contracted for by an insured party; in essence, a policy insuring one's personal and/or financial integrity. In the real estate business, a surety bond is generally used to ensure that a particular project will be completed at a certain date or that a contract will be performed as stated. **307**

surface rights Ownership rights in a parcel of real estate that are limited to the surface of the property and

do not include the air above it (*air rights*) or the minerals below the surface (*subsurface rights*). **18**

survey The process by which boundaries are measured and land areas are determined; the on-site measurement of lot lines, dimensions, and position of a house on a lot, including the determination of any existing encroachments or easements. **144**

syndicate A combination of people or firms formed to accomplish a business venture of mutual interest by pooling resources. In a *real estate investment syndicate*, the parties own and/or develop property, with the main profit generally arising from the sale of the property. **437**

T-bar method A math tool used to solve percentage problems. A common value X is on the top of the bar, with two different Y values under the bar. **474-75**

tax basis The point from which gains and losses are figured for tax purposes.

tax credit An amount by which tax owed is reduced directly. **436**

tax deed An instrument, similar to a certificate of sale, given to a purchaser at a tax sale. *See also* certificate of sale. **166**

tax lien A charge against property, created by operation of law. Tax liens and assessments take priority over all other liens. **163**

tax sale A court-ordered sale of real property to raise money to cover delinquent taxes. **165**

taxation The process by which a government or municipal quasi-public body raises monies to fund its operation. **111**

tenancy by the entirety The joint ownership, recognized in some states, of property acquired by husband and wife during marriage. Upon the death of one spouse, the survivor becomes the owner of the property. **129**

tenancy in common A form of co-ownership by which each owner holds an undivided interest in real property as if each were sole owner. Each individual owner has the right to partition. Unlike joint tenants, tenants in common have right of inheritance. **126-27**

tenant One who holds or possesses lands or tenements by any kind of right or title. **309**

tenant improvements Alterations to the interior of a building to meet the functional demands of the tenant. Also known as *build-outs*. **302-3**

tenant's insurance Insurance coverage that protects the personal belongings of tenants. **302**

testate Having made and left a valid will. **202**

testator A person who has made a valid will. A woman often is referred to as a *testatrix*, although *testator* can be used for either gender. **204**

tier (township strip) A strip of land six miles wide, extending east and west and numbered north and south according to its distance from the base line in the rectangular (government) survey system of legal description. **147**

time is of the essence A phrase in a contract that requires the performance of a certain act within a stated period of time. **180**

time-share A form of ownership interest that may include an estate interest in property and that allows use of the property for a fixed or variable time period. **34**

title (1) The right to ownership or the ownership of land. (2) The evidence of ownership of land. **17**

title insurance A policy insuring the owner or mortgagee against loss by reason of defects in the title to a parcel of real estate, other than encumbrances, defects, and matters specifically excluded by the policy. **215-16**

title search The examination of public records relating to real estate to determine the current state of the ownership. **213**

title theory Some states interpret a mortgage to mean that the lender is the owner of mortgaged land. Upon full payment of the mortgage debt, the borrower becomes the landowner. **223**

Title VIII of Civil Rights Act of 1968 (called the federal Fair Housing Act) Prohibits discrimination in housing based on race, color, religion, or national origin. **354**

Torrens system A method of evidencing title by registration with the proper public authority, generally called the *registrar*; named for its founder, Sir Robert Torrens. **216**

town house A type of residential dwelling with two floors that is connected to one or more dwellings by a common wall or walls. Title to the unit and lot vest in the owner who shares a fractional interest with other owners for the common areas. **136**

township The principal unit of the rectangular (government) survey system. A township is a square with 6-mile sides and an area of 36 square miles. **147**

township lines All the lines in a rectangular survey system that run east and west, parallel to the base line six miles apart. **147**

township strips *See* tier.

township tiers Township lines that form strips of land and are designated by consecutive numbers north or south of the base line. **147**

trade fixture An article installed by a tenant under the terms of a lease and removable by the tenant before the lease expires. **21-22**

transactional broker Helps both the buyer and the seller with paperwork and formalities in transferring ownership of real property, but who is not an agent of either party. **45**

transfer tax Tax stamps required to be affixed to a deed by state and/or local law. **201**

trigger terms Specific credit terms, such as down payment, monthly payment, and amount of finance charge or term of loan. **257**

trust A fiduciary arrangement whereby property is conveyed to a person or institution, called a *trustee*, to be held and administered on behalf of another person, called a *beneficiary*. The one who conveys the trust is called the *trustor*. **130-32**

trust deed An instrument used to create a mortgage lien by which the borrower conveys title to a trustee, who holds it as security for the benefit of the note holder (the lender); also called a *deed of trust*. **200**

trust deed lien A lien on the property of a trustor that secures a deed of trust loan. Also known as a mortgage lien. **162**

trustee One to whom something is entrusted and who holds legal title to property and administers the property for the benefit of a beneficiary. Or a member of a board entrusted with the administration of an institution or organization, such as a cooperative. **130**

trustee's deed A deed executed by a trustee conveying land held in a trust. **200**

trustor A borrower in a deed of trust loan transaction; one who places property in a trust. Also called a grantor or settler. **130**

Truth in Lending Act (TIL) Federal government regulates the lending practices of mortgage lenders through this act. **256-57**

unbundling services Offering real estate services in a piecemeal fashion. **73**

underground storage tanks (USTs) Commonly found on sites where petroleum products are used or where gas stations and auto repair shops are located. In residential areas, tanks are used to store heating oil. Over time, neglected tanks may leak hazardous substances into the environment. **385-86**

undivided interest *See* tenancy in common.

unenforceable contract A contract that has all the elements of a valid contract, yet neither party can sue the other to force performance of it. For example, an unsigned contract is generally unenforceable. **179**

Uniform Commercial Code (UCC) A codification of commercial law, adopted in most states, that attempts to make uniform all laws relating to commercial transactions, including chattel mortgages and bulk transfers. Security interests in chattels are created by an instrument known as a *security agreement*. To give notice of the security interest, a *financing statement* must be recorded. Article 6 of the code regulates *bulk transfers*—the sale of a business as a whole, including all fixtures, chattels, and merchandise.

Uniform Electronic Transactions Act (UETA) Sets forth rules for entering into an enforceable contract using electronic means. **7-8**

Uniform Settlement Statement (HUD-1) A special HUD form that itemizes all charges to be paid by a borrower and a seller in connection with the settlement. Also called the HUD-1 form. **424**

Uniform Standards of Professional Appraisal Practice (USPAP) A set of standards that details information required of an appraisal of residential property. The Uniform Residential Appraisal Report is required by many government agencies. **315**

unilateral contract A one-sided contract wherein one party makes a promise so as to induce a second party to do something. The second party is not legally bound to perform; however, if the second party does comply, the first party is obligated to keep the promise. **177**

unity of ownership The four unities that are traditionally needed to create a joint tenancy—unity of title, time, interest, and possession. **127-28**

universal agent A person empowered to do anything the principal could do personally. **52**

urea-formaldehyde foam insulation (UFFI) Insulating foam that can release harmful formaldehyde gases. Formaldehyde causes some individuals to suffer respiratory problems, as well as eye and skin irritations. **391**

usury Charging interest at a higher rate than the maximum rate established by state law. **225**

valid contract A contract that complies with all the essentials of a contract and is binding and enforceable on all parties to it. **179**

VA loan A mortgage loan on approved property made to a qualified veteran by an authorized lender and guaranteed by the Department of Veterans Affairs in order to limit the lender's possible loss. **261**

value The power of a good or service to command other goods in exchange for the present worth of future rights to its income or amenities. **324**

variable-rate mortgage A mortgage loan where the interest rate varies depending on market conditions. **257**

variance Permission obtained from zoning authorities to build a structure or conduct a use that is expressly prohibited by the current zoning laws; an exception from the zoning ordinances. **343-44**

vendee A buyer, usually under the terms of a land contract. **187**

vendor A seller, usually under the terms of a land contract. **187**

vendor's lien A lien that belongs to a vendor for the unpaid purchase price of land, where the vendor has not taken any other lien or security beyond the personal obligation of the purchaser. **162**

void contract A contract that has no legal force or effect because it does not meet the essential elements of a contract. **179**

voidable contract A contract that seems to be valid on the surface but may be rejected or disaffirmed by one or both of the parties. **179**

volume The amount of space of a three-dimensional object. **466**

voluntary alienation *See* alienation.

voluntary lien A lien placed on property with the knowledge and consent of the property owner. **161**

warranty clause A part of the deed where the seller warrants the title conveyed to the buyer.

waste An improper use or an abuse of a property by a possessor who holds less than fee ownership, such as a tenant, life tenant, mortgagor, or vendee. Such waste ordinarily impairs the value of the land or the interest of the person holding the title or the reversionary rights.

water rights Common law rights held by owners of land adjacent to rivers, lakes, or oceans; includes restrictions on those rights and land ownership. **19**

water table The natural level at which the ground is saturated. The water table may be several hundred feet underground or near the surface. **384**

will A written document, properly witnessed, providing for the transfer of title to property owned by the deceased, called the *testator*. **203-4**

workers' compensation acts Laws that require an employer to obtain insurance coverage to protect employees who are injured in the course of their employment. **307**

wraparound loan A method of refinancing in which the new mortgage is placed in a secondary, or subordinate, position; the new mortgage includes both the unpaid principal balance of the first mortgage and whatever additional sums are advanced by the lender. In essence, it is an additional mortgage in which another lender refinances a borrower by lending an amount over the existing first mortgage amount without disturbing the existence of the first mortgage. 254

writ of possession   A document ordered by the court to have a sheriff enter a leased property to give possession back to the owner. 126

zoning   A regulatory tool that helps communities regulate and control how land is used. 340

zoning board of appeals   A board that must be formed when the local legislature adopts a new zoning law. 343

zoning ordinance   An exercise of police power by a municipality to regulate and control the character and use of property. 340

Answer Key

Following are the correct answers to the review questions included in each Chapter of the text. In parentheses following the correct answers are references to the pages where the question topics are discussed or explained. The references for the Sample Examinations are to Chapter numbers. If you have answered a question incorrectly, be sure to go back to the page or pages noted and restudy the material until you understand the correct answer.

CHAPTER 1
Introduction to the Real Estate Business

1. b (4)
2. b (7)
3. d (9)
4. c (10)
5. b (4)
6. d (6)
7. b (9)
8. a (5)
9. d (6)
10. a (7)
11. b (8)
12. b (4)
13. a (8)
14. b (7)
15. d (9)
16. c (8)
17. d (5)
18. a (7)
19. c (5)
20. b (9)

CHAPTER 2
Real Property and the Law

1. c (17)
2. b (21)
3. c (23)
4. c (19)
5. d (17)
6. b (16)
7. a (19)
8. a (23)
9. a (20)
10. a (21)
11. c (18)
12. b (19)
13. c (21)
14. d (18)
15. a (19)
16. a (17)
17. b (17)
18. c (21)
19. b (23)
20. d (19)

CHAPTER 3
Concepts of Home Ownership

1. d (35)
2. d (36)
3. a (33)
4. b (33)
5. b (33)
6. c (35)
7. d (38)
8. b (35)
9. a (36)
10. b (35)
11. c (36)
12. c (36)
13. a (37)
14. b (33)
15. c (37)
16. c (34)
17. d (35)
18. d (37)
19. b (37)
20. d (35)

CHAPTER 4
Agency

1. d (46)
2. a (52)
3. a (50)
4. b (54)
5. c (54)
6. b (52)
7. d (55)
8. d (50)
9. b (50)
10. c (51)
11. c (56)
12. c (45)
13. c (56)
14. a (49)
15. d (59)
16. b (50)
17. a (54)
18. c (48)
19. a (49)
20. d (54)

CHAPTER 5
Real Estate Brokerage

1. b (71)
2. c (75)
3. b (75)
4. b (75)

5. a (71)
6. d (75)
7. d (77)
8. a (76)
9. c (69)
10. b (72)
11. d (70)
12. a (72)
13. c (72)
14. b (72)
15. c (69)
16. c (72)
17. c (76)
18. b (71)
19. b (75)
20. d (75)

CHAPTER 6
Listing Agreements and Buyer Representation

1. a (88)
2. c (88, 89)
3. c (90)
4. a (89)
5. b (93)
6. d (90)
7. a (89)
8. c (91)
9. a (88)
10. d (93)
11. c (89)
12. b (99)
13. c (100)
14. b (93)
15. c (88)
16. b (91)
17. b (90)
18. c (88)
19. b (89)
20. b (90)

CHAPTER 7
Interests in Real Estate

1. b (110)
2. a (112)
3. c (112)
4. c (116)
5. c (119)
6. d (116)
7. c (120)
8. a (110)
9. b (116)
10. c (115)
11. b (114)
12. b (119)

13. c (115)
14. d (119)
15. d (112)
16. b (115)
17. a (117)
18. c (119)
19. a (118)
20. d (118)

CHAPTER 8
Forms of Real Estate Ownership

1. d (127)
2. b (126)
3. a (128)
4. b (133)
5. c (130)
6. d (129)
7. b (126)
8. a (130)
9. d (135)
10. c (137)
11. c (132)
12. d (126)
13. d (129)
14. b (135)
15. b (127)
16. c (135)
17. b (137)
18. b (127, 129)
19. b (126)
20. a (127)

CHAPTER 9
Legal Descriptions

1. b (149)
2. d (146)
3. d (148)
4. b (145)
5. c (148)
6. c (148)
7. a (148)
8. a (148)
9. a (149)
10. b (154)
11. a (148)
12. d (154)
13. c (146)
14. b (154)
15. b (145)
16. b (Math FAQs)
17. b (Math FAQs)
18. b (148)
19. b (148)
20. c (144)

CHAPTER 10
Real Estate Taxes and Liens

1. d (162)
2. b (163)
3. b (166)
4. c (162)
5. b (163)
6. d (165)
7. c (163)
8. c (167)
9. d (165)
10. c (167)
11. d (168)
12. d (169)
13. c (163)
14. b (161)
15. b (161)
16. d (167)
17. d (166)
18. a (163)
19. b (163)
20. d (164)

CHAPTER 11
Real Estate Contracts

1. c (177)
2. b (179)
3. d (177)
4. b (177)
5. c (179)
6. d (181)
7. d (187)
8. a (184)
9. a (186)
10. d (184)
11. b (187)
12. d (187)
13. d (187)
14. c (176)
15. d (183)
16. b (184)
17. a (179)
18. b (183)
19. d (180)
20. b (187)

CHAPTER 12
Transfer of Title

1. a (194)
2. a (197)
3. d (195)
4. a (197)
5. b (198)
6. a (199)

7. d (198)
8. b (199)
9. c (197)
10. b (197)
11. c (202)
12. b (202)
13. d (202)
14. a (198)
15. a (198)
16. c (202)
17. d (203)
18. c (204)
19. c (205)
20. d (196)

CHAPTER 13
Title Records

1. a (211)
2. a (211)
3. c (211)
4. a (212)
5. a (212)
6. d (214)
7. d (214)
8. d (213)
9. c (214)
10. a (213)
11. c (211)
12. c (215)
13. b (215)
14. c (213)
15. c (215)
16. a (215)
17. c (211)
18. a (212)
19. b (215)
20. c (215)

CHAPTER 14
Real Estate Financing: Principles

1. b (226)
2. a (223)
3. c (223)
4. a (227)
5. c (231)
6. b (225)
7. d (233)
8. d (228)
9. a (229)
10. a (231)
11. c (231)
12. b (228)
13. b (232)
14. d (234)

15. b (226)
16. d (223)
17. a (223)
18. b (231)
19. b (231)
20. b (230)

CHAPTER 15
Real Estate Financing: Practice

1. d (253)
2. d (255)
3. c (241)
4. c (247)
5. b (240)
6. a (243)
7. c (243)
8. b (253)
9. c (249)
10. b (256)
11. b (244)
12. a (243)
13. b (242)
14. d (257)
15. b (246)
16. b (246)
17. c (247)
18. b (242)
19. c (244)
20. d (257)

CHAPTER 16
Leases

1. c (280)
2. c (279)
3. d (282)
4. c (281)
5. b (278)
6. d (270)
7. c (269)
8. b (271)
9. b (282)
10. b (269)
11. b (271)
12. a (281)
13. b (279)
14. d (271)
15. c (279)
16. a (279)
17. c (280)
18. d (280)
19. c (270)
20. c (282)

CHAPTE
Property M

1. b (307)
2. c (306)
3. b (302)
4. c (307)
5. c (295)
6. b (306)
7. d (308)
8. a (292)
9. c (297)
10. a (298)
11. c (307)
12. c (307)
13. c (298)
14. b (302)
15. b (295)
16. b (298)
17. b (307)
18. c (303)
19. c (303)
20. d (305)

CHAPTER 18
Real Estate Appraisal

1. c (331)
2. b (324)
3. b (326)
4. b (324)
5. d (326)
6. a (326)
7. d (330)
8. c (333)
9. a (331)
10. c (331)
11. c (331)
12. c (324)
13. b (331)
14. c (329)
15. d (327)
16. b (331, Math FAQs)
17. b (331, Math FAQs)
18. b (330)
19. b (325)
20. c (324)

CHAPTER 19
Land-Use Controls and Property Development

1. a (346)
2. a (343)
3. b (346)
4. c (339)
5. c (344)

7. (340)
8. a (343)
8. d (340)
9. b (346)
10. a (347)
11. a (345)
12. c (345)
13. b (346)
14. a (343)
15. b (339)
16. d (345)
17. a (345)
18. d (346)
19. a (347)
20. c (344)

CHAPTER 20
Fair Housing and Ethical Practices

1. c (355)
2. a (366)
3. d (358)
4. b (362)
5. c (362)
6. a (364)
7. b (359)
8. b (364)
9. c (360)
10. b (359)
11. a (358)
12. b (367)
13. d (365)
14. c (357)
15. d (363)
16. a (365)
17. d (355)
18. b (358)
19. d (358)
20. a (365)

CHAPTER 21
Environmental Issues and the Real Estate Transaction

1. b (377)
2. c (377)
3. c (377)
4. a (377)
5. a (382)
6. c (385)
7. b (386)
8. d (388)
9. c (380)
10. d (375, 377, 381)
11. b (377)
12. c (376)

13. d (377)
14. b (381)
15. c (378)
16. c (380)
17. b (385)
18. a (385)
19. d (387)
20. a (376)

CHAPTER 22
Closing the Real Estate Transaction

1. d (423)
2. b (402)
3. d (400)
4. a (400)
5. d (402)
6. c (405)
7. c (400)
8. b (416)
9. b (416)
10. d (417, Math FAQs)
11. c (418, Math FAQs)
12. a (416)
13. c (413, Math FAQs)
14. b (413)
15. c (416)
16. b (414)
17. d (414)
18. d (405)
19. b (407)
20. b (404)

CHAPTER 23
Real Estate Investment

1. a (432)
2. b (432)
3. d (435)
4. a (434)
5. d (435)
6. b (433)
7. c (437)
8. b (437)
9. b (434, Math FAQs)
10. a (434, Math FAQs)
11. b (430)
12. b (436)
13. c (435)
14. b (436)
15. d (433)
16. a (437)
17. c (431)
18. d (432)
19. b (433)
20. c (437)

1. b (10)
2. a (11)
3. a (11)
4. c (15)
5. c (15, Math FAQs)
6. b (6)
7. a (12)
8. a (20)
9. a (7)
10. d (8)
11. d (5)
12. a (14)
13. b (16)
14. a (18)
15. a (19)
16. c (5, Math FAQs)
17. d (4)
18. c (8)
19. a (5, Math FAQs)
20. b (7)
21. d (6, Math FAQs)
22. b (9, Math FAQs)
23. b (14)
24. b (10)
25. c (Math FAQs)
26. c (10)
27. b (18)
28. c (9, Math FAQs)
29. c (14, Math FAQs)
30. b (6, Math FAQs)
31. d (11)
32. d (11)
33. b (11)
34. b (14, 15)
35. b (11)
36. a (14)
37. d (18, Math FAQs)
38. b (6)
39. a (8)
40. a (12)
41. d (6)
42. b (16)
43. c (20)
44. b (Math FAQs)
45. d (10)
46. d (11)
47. c (7)
48. d (9)
49. b (18)
50. b (10)
51. b (11)
52. b (8)
53. c (16)
54. d (11)
55. b (7)

56. c (15, Math FAQs)
57. a (7)
58. c (Math FAQs)
59. d (19)
60. b (11)
61. c (14)
62. a (20)
63. d (22, Math FAQs)
64. d (11)
65. b (12)
66. d (8)
67. b (22, Math FAQs)
68. d (20)
69. a (12)
70. a (18)
71. d (15)
72. d (8)
73. a (22)
74. d (22)
75. b (2)
76. c (7)
77. d (Math FAQs)
78. b (6)
79. d (5)
80. d (16)

SAMPLE EXAM 2

1. d (16)
2. c (2)
3. c (11)
4. b (14)
5. c (16)
6. d (4)
7. b (5, Math FAQs)
8. d (20)
9. b (Math FAQs)
10. b (15)

11. b (11)
12. a (15)
13. d (6)
14. c (7)
15. d (4)
16. d (9)
17. b (12)
18. b (4)
19. c (5)
20. a (18)
21. c (22)
22. b (16)
23. a (7)
24. b (22)
25. d (16)
26. d (15, Math FAQs)
27. c (15, Math FAQs)
28. b (4)
29. b (18)
30. d (22)
31. b (22, Math FAQs)
32. d (18, Math FAQs)
33. a (11)
34. d (13)
35. b (Math FAQs)
36. a (5)
37. a (16)
38. d (6)
39. a (18)
40. c (18, Math FAQs)
41. d (12)
42. c (9)
43. b (11)
44. d (Math FAQs)
45. c (Math FAQs)
46. d (15)
47. a (7)

48. a (22, Math FAQs)
49. b (16)
50. c (18, Math FAQs)
51. c (17, Math FAQs)
52. a (13)
53. c (3)
54. a (12)
55. d (8)
56. a (22)
57. b (7)
58. b (12, Math FAQs)
59. d (18)
60. d (15)
61. d (18)
62. c (20)
63. c (12)
64. c (15, Math FAQs)
65. a (4)
66. b (6, Math FAQs)
67. b (20)
68. d (4)
69. c (7)
70. a (22)
71. d (15)
72. c (18, Math FAQs)
73. a (11)
74. a (18)
75. b (15)
76. c (15)
77. c (6)
78. d (10)
79. b (22)
80. b (17)

Index